CIMA'S Official
Learning System

Managerial Level

Financial Accounting and Tax Principles

Tom Rolfe

ELSEVIER

AMSTERDAM   BOSTON   HEIDELBERG   LONDON   NEW YORK   OXFORD
PARIS   SAN DIEGO   SAN FRANCISCO   SINGAPORE   SYDNEY   TOKYO

CIMA Publishing is an imprint of Elsevier
Linacre House, Jordan Hill, Oxford OX2 8DP, UK
30 Corporate Drive, Suite 400, Burlington, MA 01803, USA

First edition 2008

British Library Cataloguing in Publication Data
A catalogue record for this book is available from the British Library

978-0-7506-8700-3

For information on all CIMA publications
visit our website at www.elsevierdirect.com

Typeset by Charon Tec Ltd., A Macmillan Company. (www.macmillansolutions.com)

Printed and bound in Italy

08 09 10   10 9 8 7 6 5 4 3 2 1

Contents

CONTENTS

The CIMA Learning System

Acknowledgements

Every effort has been made to contact the holders of copyright material, but if any here have been inadvertently overlooked, the publishers will be pleased to make the necessary arrangements at the first opportunity.

We would also like to thank Luisa Robertson for her invaluable contribution as the reviewer and author of previous editions of this text.

How to use the CIMA *Learning System*

This *Financial Accounting and Tax Principles Learning System* has been devised as a resource for students attempting to pass their CIMA exams, and provides:

- a detailed explanation of all syllabus areas;
- extensive 'practical' materials, including readings from relevant journals;
- generous question practice, together with full solutions;
- an exam preparation section, complete with exam standard questions and solutions.

This Learning System has been designed with the needs of home-study and distance-learning candidates in mind. Such students require full coverage of the syllabus topics, and also the facility to undertake extensive question practice. However, the Learning System is also ideal for fully taught courses.

The main body of the text is divided into a number of chapters, each of which is organised in the following pattern:

- *Detailed learning outcomes.* These outcomes are expected after your studies of the chapters are complete. You should assimilate these before beginning detailed work on the chapter, so that you can appreciate where your studies are leading.
- *Step-by-step topic coverage.* This is the heart of each chapter, containing detailed explanatory text supported where appropriate by worked examples and exercises. You should work carefully through this section, ensuring that you understand the material being explained and can tackle the examples and exercises successfully. Remember that in many cases knowledge is cumulative: if you fail to digest the earlier material thoroughly, you may struggle to understand later chapters.

THE CIMA LEARNING SYSTEM

- *Readings and activities.* Most chapters are illustrated by more practical elements, such as relevant journal articles or other readings, together with comments and questions designed to stimulate discussion.
- *Question practice.* The test of how well you have learned the material is your ability to tackle exam-standard questions. Make a serious attempt at producing your own answers, but at this stage don't be too concerned about attempting the questions in exam conditions. In particular, it is more important to absorb the material thoroughly by completing a full solution than to observe the time limits that would apply in the actual exam.
- *Solutions.* Avoid the temptation to merely 'audit' the solutions provided. It is an illusion to think that this provides the same benefits as you would gain from a serious attempt of your own. However, if you are struggling to get started on a question, you should read the introductory guidance provided at the beginning of the solution, and then make your own attempt before referring back to the full solution.

Having worked through the chapters, you are ready to begin your final preparations for the examination. The final section of the CIMA *Learning System* provides you with the guidance you need. It includes the following features:

- A brief guide to revision technique.
- A note on the format of the examination. You should know what to expect when you tackle the real exam, and in particular the number of questions to attempt, which questions are compulsory and which optional, and so on.
- Guidance on how to tackle the examination itself.
- A table mapping revision questions to the syllabus learning outcomes allowing you to quickly identify questions by subject area.
- Revision questions. These are of exam standard and should be tackled in exam conditions, especially as regards the time allocation.
- Solutions to the revision questions. As before, these indicate the length and the quality of solution that would be expected of a well-prepared candidate.

If you work conscientiously through this CIMA *Learning System* according to the guidelines above, you will be giving yourself an excellent chance of exam success. Good luck with your studies!

Guide to the Icons used within this Text

 Key term or definition

 Equation to learn

 Exam tip to topic likely to appear in the exam

 Exercise

 Question

 Solution

 Comment or Note

Study technique

Passing exams is partly a matter of intellectual ability, but however accomplished you are in that respect, you can improve your chances significantly by the use of appropriate study and revision techniques. In this section we briefly outline some tips for effective study during the earlier stages of your approach to the exam. Later in the text we mention some techniques that you will find useful at the revision stage.

Planning

To begin with, formal planning is essential to get the best return from the time you spend studying. Estimate how much time you are going to need in total for each subject that you face. Remember that you need to allow time for revision as well as for initial study of the material. The amount of notional study time for any subject is the minimum estimated time that students will need to achieve the specified learning outcomes set out earlier in this chapter. This time includes all appropriate learning activities, for example, face-to-face tuition, private study, directed home study, learning at the workplace, revision time, etc. You may find it helpful to read *Better exam results* by Sam Malone, CIMA Publishing, ISBN: 075066357X. This book will provide you with proven study techniques. Chapter by chapter it covers the building blocks of successful learning and examination techniques.

The notional study time for *Managerial Level – Financial Accounting and Tax Principles* is 200 hours. Note that the standard amount of notional learning hours attributed to one full-time academic year of approximately 30 weeks is 1200 hours.

By way of example, the notional study time might be made up as follows:

	Hours
Face-to-face study: up to	60
Personal study: up to	100
'Other' study – e.g. learning at the workplace, revision, etc.: up to	40
	200

Note that all study and learning-time recommendations should be used only as a guideline and are intended as minimum amounts. The amount of time recommended for face-to-face tuition, personal study and/or additional learning will vary according to the type of course undertaken, prior learning of the student, and the pace at which different students learn.

Now split your total time requirement over the weeks between now and the examination. This will give you an idea of how much time you need to devote to study each week. Remember to allow for holidays or other periods during which you will not be able to study (e.g. because of seasonal workloads).

With your study material before you, decide which chapters you are going to study in each week, and which weeks you will devote to revision and final question practice.

Prepare a written schedule summarising the above – and stick to it!

The amount of space allocated to a topic in the study material is not a very good guide as to how long it will take you. For example, 'Summarising and Analysing Data' has a weight of 25 per cent in the syllabus and this is the best guide as to how long you should spend on it. It occupies 45 per cent of the main body of the text because it includes many tables and charts.

It is essential to know your syllabus. As your course progresses you will become more familiar with how long it takes to cover topics in sufficient depth. Your timetable may need to be adapted to allocate enough time for the whole syllabus.

Tips for effective studying

(1) Aim to find a quiet and undisturbed location for your study, and plan as far as possible to use the same period of time each day. Getting into a routine helps to avoid wasting time. Make sure that you have all the materials you need before you begin, so as to minimise interruptions.

(2) Store all your materials in one place, so that you don't waste time searching for items around the house. If you have to pack everything away after each study period, keep them in a box, or even a suitcase, which won't be disturbed until the next time.

(3) Limit distractions. To make the most effective use of your study periods, you should be able to apply total concentration, so turn off the TV, set your phones to message mode, and put up your 'do not disturb' sign.

(4) Your timetable will tell you which topic to study. However, before diving in and becoming engrossed in the finer points, make sure you have an overall picture of all the areas that need to be covered by the end of that session. After an hour, allow yourself a short break and move away from your books. With experience, you will learn to assess the pace you need to work at. You should also allow enough time to read relevant articles from newspapers and journals, which will supplement your knowledge and demonstrate a wider perspective.

(5) Work carefully through a chapter, making notes as you go. When you have covered a suitable amount of material, vary the pattern by attempting a practice question. Preparing an answer plan is a good habit to get into, while you are both studying and revising, and also in the examination room. It helps to impose a structure on your solutions, and avoids rambling. When you have finished your attempt, make notes of any mistakes you made, or any areas that you failed to cover or covered only skimpily.

(6) Make notes as you study, and discover the techniques that work best for you. Your notes may be in the form of lists, bullet points, diagrams, summaries, 'mind maps', or the written word, but remember that you will need to refer back to them at a later date, so they must be intelligible. If you are on a taught course, make sure you highlight any issues you would like to follow up with your lecturer.

(7) Organise your paperwork. There are now numerous paper storage systems available to ensure that all your notes, calculations and articles can be effectively filed and easily retrieved later.

Paper P7 – Financial Accounting and Tax Principles

First examined in May 2005

Syllabus outline

The syllabus comprises:

Topic	Study Weighting
A Principles of Business Taxation	20%
B Principles of Regulation of Financial Reporting	10%
C Single Entity Financial Accounts	45%
D Managing Short Term Finance	25%

Learning aims

Students should be able to:

- describe the types of business taxation rules and requirements likely to affect an enterprise (in respect of itself and its employees);
- describe and discuss how financial reporting can be regulated and the system of International Accounting Standards;
- prepare statutory accounts in appropriate form for a single enterprise;
- assess and control the short term financial requirements of a business entity.

Assessment strategy

There will be a written examination paper of 3 hours, with the following sections.

Section A – 40 marks

A variety of compulsory objective test questions, each worth between 2 and 4 marks. Mini-scenarios may be given, to which a group of questions relate.

Section B – 30 marks

Six compulsory short answer questions, each worth 5 marks. A short scenario may be given, to which some or all questions relate.

Section C – 30 marks

One compulsory question, worth 30 marks. A short scenario may be given, to which the questions relates.

Learning outcomes and syllabus content

A – Principles of Business Taxation – 20%

Learning outcomes

On completion of their studies students should be able to:

(i) identify the principal types of taxation likely to be of relevance to an incorporated business in a particular country, including direct tax on the enterprise's trading profits and capital gains, indirect taxes collected by the enterprise, employee taxation, withholding taxes on international payments;

(ii) describe the features of the principal types of taxation likely to be of relevance to an incorporated business in a particular country (e.g. in terms of who ultimately bears the tax cost, withholding responsibilities, principles of calculating the tax base);

(iii) describe the likely record-keeping, filing and tax payment requirements associated with the principal types of taxation likely to be of relevance to an incorporated business in a particular country;

(iv) describe the possible enquiry and investigation powers of taxing authorities;

(v) identify situations in which foreign tax obligations (reporting and liability) could arise and methods for relieving foreign tax;

(vi) explain the difference in principle between tax avoidance and tax evasion;

(vii) describe sources of tax rules and explain the importance of jurisdiction;

(viii) explain and apply the accounting rules contained in IAS 12 for current and deferred taxation.

Syllabus content

- Concepts of direct versus indirect taxes, taxable person and competent jurisdiction.
- Sources of tax rules (e.g. domestic primary legislation and court rulings, practice of the relevant taxing authority, supranational bodies, such as the EU in the case of value-added/sales tax, and international tax treaties).
- Direct taxes on enterprise profits and gains:
  - the principle of non-deductibility of dividends and systems of taxation defined according to the treatment of dividends in the hands of the shareholder (e.g. classical, partial imputation and imputation);
  - the distinction between accounting and taxable profits in absolute terms (e.g. disallowable expenditure on revenue account, such as entertaining, and on capital account, such as formation and acquisition costs) and in terms of timing (e.g. deduction on a paid basis, tax depreciation substituted for book depreciation);
  - the nature of rules recharacterising interest payments as dividends;
  - potential for variation in rules for calculating the tax base dependent on the nature or source of the income (schedular systems);
  - the need for rules dealing with the relief of losses;
  - the concept of tax consolidation (e.g. for relief of losses and deferral of capital gains on asset transfers within a group).
- Indirect taxes collected by the enterprise:
  - in the context of indirect taxes, the distinction between unit taxes (e.g. excise duties based on physical measures) and *ad valorem* taxes (e.g. sales tax based on value);
  - the mechanism of value-added/sales taxes, in which businesses are liable for tax on their outputs less credits for tax paid on their inputs, including the concepts of exemption and variation in tax rates depending on the type of output and disallowance of input credits for exempt outputs.
- Employee taxation:
  - the employee as a separate taxable person subject to a personal income tax regime;
  - use of employer reporting and withholding to ensure compliance and assist tax collection.
- The need for record-keeping and record retention that may be additional to that required for financial accounting purposes.
- The need for deadlines for reporting (filing returns) and tax payments.

- Types of powers of tax authorities to ensure compliance with tax rules:
  - power to review and query filed returns;
  - power to request special reports or returns;
  - power to examine records (generally extending back some years);
  - powers of entry and search;
  - exchange of information with tax authorities in other jurisdictions.
- International taxation:
  - the concept of corporate residence and the variation in rules for its determination across jurisdictions (e.g. place of incorporation versus place of management);
  - types of payments on which withholding tax may be required (especially interest, dividends, royalties and capital gains accruing to non-residents);
  - means of establishing a taxable presence in another country (local enterprise and branch);
  - the effect of double tax treaties (based on the OECD Model Convention) on the above (e.g. reduction of withholding tax rates, provisions for defining a permanent establishment);
  - principles of relief for foreign taxes by exemption, deduction and credit.
- The distinction between tax avoidance and tax evasion, and how these vary among jurisdictions (including the difference between the use of statutory general anti-avoidance provisions and case law based regimes).
- Accounting treatment of taxation and disclosure requirements under IAS 12.

Note: Examples of general principles should be drawn from a 'benchmark' tax regime (e.g. the UK, USA, etc.) or an appropriate local tax regime. Details of any specific tax regime will NOT be examined.

B – Principles of Regulation of Financial Reporting – 10%

Learning outcomes

On completion of their studies students should be able to:

 (i) explain the need for regulation of published accounts and the concept that regulatory regimes vary from country to country;
 (ii) explain potential elements that might be expected in a regulatory framework for published accounts;
(iii) describe the role and structure of the International Accounting Standards Board (IASB) and the International Organisation of Securities Commissions (IOSCO);
(iv) explain the IASB's Framework for the Presentation and Preparation of Financial Statements;
 (v) describe the process leading to the promulgation of an international accounting standard (IAS);
(vi) describe ways in which IAS's can interact with local regulatory frameworks;
(vii) explain in general terms, the role of the external auditor, the elements of the audit report and types of qualification of that report.

Syllabus content

- The need for regulation of accounts.
- Elements in a regulatory framework for published accounts (e.g. local law relating to enterprises, local GAAP, review of accounts by public bodies).

- GAAP based on prescriptive versus principles-based standards.
- The role and structure of the IASB and IOSCO.
- The IASB's *Framework for the Presentation and Preparation of Financial Statements.*
- The process leading to the promulgation of a standard practice.
- Ways in which IAS's are used: adoption as local GAAP, model for local GAAP, persuasive influence in formulating local GAAP.
- The powers and duties of the external auditors, the audit report and its qualification for accounting statements not in accordance with best practice.

C – Single Entity Financial Accounts – 45%

Learning outcomes

On completion of their studies students should be able to:

(i) prepare financial statements in a form suitable for publication, with appropriate notes;

(ii) prepare a cash flow statement in a form suitable for publication;

(iii) explain and apply the accounting rules contained in IAS's dealing with reporting performance, tangible non-current assets and inventories;

(iv) explain the accounting rules contained in IAS's governing share capital transactions;

(v) explain the principles of the accounting rules contained in IAS's dealing with disclosure of related parties to a business, construction contracts (and related financing costs), research and development expenditure, intangible non-current assets (other than goodwill on consolidation), impairment of assets, post-balance sheet events, contingencies and leases (lessee only).

Syllabus content

- Preparation of the financial statements of a single enterprise, including the statement of changes in equity (IAS 1).
- Preparation of cash flow statements (IAS 7).
- Reporting performance: recognition of revenue, measurement of profit or loss, extraordinary items, prior period items, discontinuing operations and segment reporting (IAS 1, 8, 14, 18 & IFRS 5).
- Property, Plant and Equipment (IAS 16): The calculation of depreciation and the effect of revaluations, changes to economic useful life, repairs, improvements and disposals.
- Inventories (IAS 2).
- Issue and redemption of shares, including treatment of share issue and redemption costs (IAS 32 and IAS 39), the share premium account, the accounting for maintenance of capital arising from the purchase by an enterprise of its own shares.
- The disclosure of related parties to a business (IAS 24).
- Construction contracts and related financing costs (IAS 11 & 23): determination of cost, net realisable value, the inclusion of overheads and the measurement of profit on uncompleted contracts.
- Research and development costs (IAS 38): criteria for capitalisation.
- Intangible Assets (IAS 38) and goodwill (excluding that arising on consolidation): recognition, valuation and amortisation.
- Impairment of Assets (IAS 36) and its effect on the above.
- Post-balance sheet events (IAS 10).

- Provisions and contingencies (IAS 37).
- Leases (IAS 17) – Operating and finance leases in the books of the lessee.

D – Managing Short-term Finance – 25%

Learning outcomes

On completion of their studies students should be able to:

(i) calculate and interpret working capital ratios for business sectors;
(ii) prepare and analyse cash flow forecasts over a 12-month period;
(iii) identify measures to improve a cash forecast situation;
(iv) compare and contrast the use and limitations of cash management models and identify when each model is most appropriate;
(v) analyse trade *receivable* information;
(vi) evaluate *receivable* and *payable* policies;
(vii) evaluate appropriate methods of inventory management;
(viii) identify alternatives for investment of short-term cash surpluses;
(ix) identify sources of short-term funding;
(x) identify appropriate methods of finance for trading internationally.

Syllabus content

- Working capital ratios (e.g. receivable days, inventory days, payable days, current ratio, quick ratio) and the working capital cycle.
- Working capital characteristics of different businesses (e.g. supermarkets being heavily funded by payables) and the importance of industry comparisons.
- Cash flow forecasts, use of spreadsheets to assist in this in terms of changing variables (e.g. interest rates, inflation) and in consolidating forecasts.
- Variables that are most easily changed, delayed or brought forward in a forecast.
- The link between cash, profit and the balance sheet.
- The Baumol and Miller–Orr cash management models.
- The credit cycle from receipt of customer order to cash receipt.
- Evaluation of payment terms and settlement discounts.
- Preparation and interpretation of age analyses of receivables and payables.
- Establishing collection targets on an appropriate basis (e.g. motivational issues in managing credit control).
- The payment cycle from agreeing the order to make payments.
- Centralised versus decentralised purchasing.
- The relationship between purchasing and inventory control.
- Principles of the economic order quantity (EOQ) model and criticisms thereof.
- Types and features of short-term finance: trade payables, overdrafts, short-term loans and debt factoring.
- Use and abuse of trade payables as a source of finance.
- The principles of investing short term (i.e. maturity, return, security, liquidity and diversification).
- Types of investments (e.g. interest-bearing bank accounts, negotiable instruments including certificates of deposit, short-term treasury bills, and securities).
- The difference between the coupon on debt and the yield to maturity.
- Export finance (e.g. documentary credits, bills of exchange, export factoring, forfeiting).

1

Principles of Business Taxation – Introduction

Principles of Business Taxation – Introduction

1

Learning aims

The learning aim of this part of the syllabus is that students should be able to 'describe the types of business taxation rules and requirements likely to affect an entity (in respect of itself and its employees)'.

The topics covered in this chapter are as follows:

- concepts of direct versus indirect taxes, taxable person and competent jurisdiction;
- sources of tax rules.

1.1 Introduction

Principles of business tax account for 20 per cent of the Financial accounting and tax principles syllabus and therefore 20 per cent of the examination paper. In the first six chapters of this text we will cover general principles of taxation. General principles should apply in most countries and are not specific to any one country. In your studies you can use examples of general principles drawn from a 'benchmark' tax regime (e.g. the UK, the USA, etc.) or an appropriate local tax regime. This text mainly refers to the UK tax system, but any system could be used to illustrate general principles.

> Knowledge of specific tax regimes is NOT REQUIRED and details of any specific tax regime will NOT be examined. If an examination question requires a tax computation, the question will be based on a fictitious country with fictitious tax rules and tax rates. The question will provide all the information, including tax rates, required to prepare the answer.

In the first part of this chapter, we will consider general principles of taxation, basic tax terminology and the classification of taxes. The chapter will then conclude with a consideration of the sources of tax rules in a country.

1.2 Taxation as a source of government revenue

It has been said that 'what the government gives it must first take away'. The economic resources available to society are limited, so an increase in a government's expenditure will mean a reduction in the spending capacity of the private sector. Taxation is the main means by which a government raises revenue to meet its expenditure. Taxation may also be used by a government as a means of influencing economic decisions or controlling the economy; in this way taxation will also reflect prevailing social values and priorities in a country. This characteristic helps explain why no two countries' tax systems will be identical in every respect and it also explains why governments continually change their tax systems.

Revenue raised from taxation is needed to finance government expenditure on items such as the health service, retirement pensions, unemployment benefit and other social benefits, education, financing government borrowing (interest on government stocks), etc.

1.3 Principles of taxation

No tax system is perfect, but an 'ideal' system should conform to certain principles if it is to achieve its objectives without producing negative effects.

1.3.1 Canons of taxation

In 1776 Adam Smith in his book *The Wealth of Nations* proposed that a 'good' tax should have the following characteristics:

- *Equity.* It should be fair to different individuals and should reflect a person's ability to pay.
- *Certainty.* It should not be arbitrary, it should be certain.
- *Convenience.* It should be convenient in terms of timing and payment.
- *Efficiency.* It should be administratively efficient with a relatively small cost of collection as a proportion of the revenue raised. It should not cause economic distortion by affecting the behaviour of taxpayers.

These principles still apply today; in a modern tax system the three major principles of taxation are:

1. *Efficiency.* A tax should be easy and cheap to collect. It is in pursuit of this objective that so much tax is collected 'at source', by deduction from income as it arises. The UK PAYE (pay-as-you-earn) tax on salaries and wages is an example.

2. *Equity.* It is important that tax should be fairly levied as between one taxpayer and another. For example, in the UK, tax legislation is often complex, both to reduce the opportunities to avoid the tax and to promote fairness, although this is not always achieved.
3. *Economic effects must be considered.* The ways in which tax is collected can have profound economic effects which must be taken into account when formulating a tax policy.

Tax reliefs can stimulate one sector, while the imposition of a heavy tax can stifle another. For example, special allowances for capital expenditure may encourage investment in industry, while imposing heavy taxes on cigarettes and alcoholic drink may operate to discourage sales.

1.3.2 The American Institute of Certified Public Accountants' (AICPA) statement – *Guiding Principles of Good Tax Policy: A Framework for Evaluating Tax Proposals*

The AICPA's Guiding Principles of Good Tax Policy: A Framework for Evaluating Tax Proposals lists ten principles for determining if an existing tax or a proposal to modify a tax rule follows good tax policy. The framework also recognises that it is not always possible to incorporate all ten principles into tax systems and that some balancing is needed.

The ten principles are:

1. equity and fairness,
2. transparency and visibility,
3. certainty,
4. convenience of payment,
5. economy in collection,
6. simplicity,
7. appropriate government revenues,
8. minimum tax gap,
9. neutrality,
10. economic growth and efficiency.

Most of these are included in Section 1.3.1; those that need additional explanation are:

- *Appropriate government revenues.* The tax system should enable the government to determine how much tax revenue is likely to be collected and when.
- *Minimum tax gap.* The tax gap is the difference between the amount of tax owed and the amount of tax collected. A tax should be structured to minimise non-compliance.

1.4 Basic tax terminology

> This section explains some basic taxation terms that are used in the following chapters and that you need to understand and possibly use to answer questions in the examination.

1.4.1 Direct taxes

A direct tax is one that falls directly on the person or entity who is expected to pay it. For example, the UK corporation tax is a direct tax. The formal incidence and effective incidence of a direct tax are usually the same, although in some situations if it is known in advance that tax will have to be paid, it may be possible to charge a higher rate for the work so that the tax due will be covered.

A direct tax is levied on an individual or entity, so it can be designed to take account of certain individual or entity circumstances, for example, family size, financial commitments, level of investment in non-current assets, etc.

1.4.2 Indirect taxes

An indirect tax is one that is levied on one part of the economy with the intention that it will be passed on to another. For example, in the UK, value-added tax (VAT) is levied on all businesses involved with the production and distribution of a good for a final customer. In most cases the VAT will be added to the final price paid by the customer.

As an indirect tax is not levied on the eventual payer of the tax, it cannot be related to the individual circumstances of that taxpayer.

1.4.3 Incidence

The incidence of tax refers to the distribution of the tax burden. The incidence of a tax is on the person who actually pays it. For example, the incidence of an income tax is on the taxpayer as it is the taxpayer who is assessed and pays the tax.

Incidence can be split into two elements:

1. *Formal incidence.* The person or entity who has direct contact with the tax authorities. For example, the formal incidence of a sales tax (or VAT) will be on the entity making the sale. It is the entity making the sale that must account for the transaction and pay the tax collected to the revenue collection authorities.
2. *Effective (or actual) incidence.* The person or entity who ends up bearing the cost of the tax as they cannot pass it on to someone else. If a sales tax is added to the selling price, it is passed on to the customer and it is actually the customer who ends up paying the tax. The effective incidence is on the customer.

1.4.4 Taxable person

A taxable person is the person accountable for the payment of a tax. Tax is levied on the taxable person who is responsible for its payment. For example, in the UK, traders have to register for VAT as a taxable person; they can then charge VAT to customers and recover the VAT paid to their suppliers (see Chapter 3 for more details on VAT).

1.4.5 Competent jurisdiction

Jurisdiction can be interpreted as meaning power. The tax authority must have the legal power to assess and collect taxes. Taxation is either the sole responsibility of the central government or the combined responsibility of the central government and local authorities within a country. The responsible authorities will pass one or more taxation laws. The primary characteristic of any law is that it is enforceable by sanction (i.e. fine, imprisonment, etc.). An unenforceable law will be ignored. Before a court can order enforcement, it must be competent to hear and determine the alleged non-compliance with the law.

For example, the UK legislation is applicable to UK subjects and non-UK subjects who by entering the UK, whether for a long or short time, have made themselves subject to the UK jurisdiction. UK statutes apply within the UK as jurisdiction is territorial.

For an entity to be subject to tax in a country, it must first be proved to be within that country's legal power to apply its tax rules to the entity. The competent jurisdiction is therefore the country whose tax laws apply to the entity.

The basis of jurisdiction can vary between countries, making it difficult to determine and collect taxes from multinational entities (see Chapter 5 for a discussion of the jurisdiction of multinational entities).

1.4.6 Hypothecation

Hypothecation means that the products of certain taxes are devoted to specific types of expenditures. For example, a tax on motor vehicles could be hypothecated (devoted entirely) to expenditure on building and maintaining roads. Earmarking is an informal hypothecation of taxes. Hypothecation is unpopular with Chancellors/Ministers of Finance as it considerably reduces their choices in public expenditure decisions.

1.4.7 Withholding responsibilities

Persons or entities paying various types of income to persons or entities abroad are usually required by the law of a country to deduct tax from the income before making a payment. The tax deducted is called withholding tax and it is the responsibility of the person or entity making the payment to correctly deduct it. The person or entity making the deduction is responsible for paying the tax deducted to the tax authorities and preparing the correct documents to properly account for it (see Section 5.5 for more detail on withholding taxes).

1.4.8 Tax rate structure

Direct taxes are assessed on individuals, so it is possible to set tax rates that cause marginal and average rates of tax to change according to the size of the individual's tax base. The government's political objectives and current social objectives determine the level of tax and the way rates vary with income. The three possibilities are:

1. progressive taxes, which take an increasing proportion of income as the income rises;
2. proportional taxes, which take the same proportion of income as income rises;
3. regressive taxes, which take a decreasing proportion of income as income rises.

Example of rate structures

A earns $95,000 profit for the year.
B earns $42,000 profit for the year.

In country 1 the tax on profits is 20 per cent on all earned profits.
In country 2 the tax on profits is 0 per cent on the first $20,000; 10 per cent on amounts between $20,001 and $50,000; and 30 per cent on amounts over $50,001.

How much tax would A and B be subject to in each of the countries?

		Total tax	Effective tax rate	Type
Country 1				
A	$95,000 × 20%	$19,000	20%	Proportional
B	$42,000 × 20%	$8,400	20%	Proportional
Country 2				
A	($30,000 × 10%) + ($45,000 × 30%)	$16,500	17.4%	Progressive
B	$22,000 × 10%	$2,200	5.2%	Progressive

Indirect taxes cannot normally be progressive on the individual as they are either assessed on:

- the number of goods (excise duty) or
- the value (VAT) of the goods.

These taxes can only be progressive or regressive on the individual if different rates of tax are charged on different goods. For example, if higher rates of tax are charged on goods that tend to be bought by those on higher incomes, the indirect tax could be said to be progressive.

1.4.9 The tax gap

The tax gap is the difference between actual tax revenue received and the amount that would have been received had 100 per cent of the amount due been collected. Tax authorities aim to minimise the tax gap by collecting as high a proportion of the tax due as possible.

1.5 Tax bases and classification of taxes

A tax base is something that is liable to tax. Taxes can be classified by tax base, that is, by what is being taxed. Taxes may be based on:

- *income* – for example, income taxes and taxes on an entity's profits;
- *capital or wealth* – for example, taxes on capital gains and taxes on inherited wealth;
- *consumption* – for example, excise duties and sales taxes/VAT.

For example, in the USA, the Federal government taxes income as its main source of revenue. State governments use taxes on income and consumption, while local governments rely almost entirely on taxing property and wealth.

A more detailed classification of taxes is that used by the Organisation for Economic Cooperation and Development (OECD 1976): taxes are grouped into categories similar to those above and then each group is sub-divided into more detailed headings.

The OECD classifications are used to assist when comparing one country with another. For example:

2000	*Taxes on income, profits and capital gains*
2100	Paid by households and institutions
2110	On income and profits
2120	On capital gains
2200	Paid by corporate enterprises
2210	On income and profits
2220	On capital gains

You can access the full OECD classification on the OECD website at http://www.oecd. org/dataoecd/20/39/35589632.pdf the full OECD classification is to be found at annexe 1 of the document.

 You do not need to learn the full OECD classification, but you must know the main categories of tax.

1.6 Sources of tax rules

The nature of tax rules vary considerably from one country to another; however, it is possible to categorise the sources and influences on those rules. Within any country the balance between each source will be different, but in most countries the same elements will be present to a greater or lesser extent. The main sources of tax rules in a country are usually as follows:

- All tax systems are based on domestic primary legislation either at the central government level or at the local authority level or both. In some countries the legislation is very detailed and specific, setting out every possible item of income and expense. In other countries the legislation is less detailed and is supplemented by court rulings or case law.
- The practice of the relevant taxing authority will create precedents which will be followed in the future. Tax authorities sometimes issue guidelines or interpretations which are aimed at clarifying the taxation legislation.
- Supranational bodies may issue directives which the government of a country has to include in the legislation, for example, European Union (EU) directives on VAT.
- International tax treaties signed with other states are also a source of tax rules as the agreements often vary from the country's own tax regulations.

1.7 Summary

This introductory chapter sets out general tax principles, basic terminology, classification models for taxation and sources of tax rules. You need to learn these definitions and be prepared to use them to answer questions in the examination.

Revision Questions

1

Question 1

Which of the following is NOT one of Adam Smith's characteristics of a good tax?

(A) Equity
(B) Certainty
(C) Simplicity
(D) Efficiency   **(2 marks)**

Question 2

In no more than 15 words define 'incidence of tax'.   **(2 marks)**

Question 3

An indirect tax is a tax that:

(A) is levied directly on an individual
(B) is based on earnings of an individual
(C) is paid indirectly to the tax authorities
(D) is levied on one person with the intention that it is passed on to another   **(2 marks)**

Question 4

List the three main tax bases used in developed countries.   **(2 marks)**

Question 5

Which of the following is not usually a source of tax rules in a country?

(A) Domestic primary legislation
(B) International tax treaties
(C) The practice of the tax authorities
(D) International law   **(2 marks)**

Question 6

With reference to an entity paying tax, which of the following is the best definition of 'competent jurisdiction':

(A) The country whose laws apply to the entity
(B) Any country where the entity has operations
(C) Any country where the entity has an office
(D) Any country where the entity has employees   **(2 marks)**

Question 7

The effective incidence of a tax is

(A) the date the tax is actually paid
(B) the person or entity who finally bears the cost of the tax
(C) the date the tax assessment is issued
(D) the person or entity receiving the tax assessment   **(2 marks)**

Question 8

An entity sells furniture and adds a sales tax to the selling price of all products sold.

A customer purchasing furniture from the entity has to pay the cost of the furniture plus the sales tax.

The customer therefore bears the cost of the sales tax.

This is referred to as

(A) formal incidence
(B) indirect incidence
(C) effective incidence
(D) direct incidence   **(2 marks)**

Question 9

BM has a taxable profit of $30,000 and receives a tax assessment of $3,000.

BV has a taxable profit of $60,000 and receives a tax assessment of $7,500.

BM and BV are resident in the same tax jurisdiction.

This tax could be said to be

(A) a progressive tax
(B) a regressive tax
(C) a direct tax
(D) a proportional tax   **(2 marks)**

Solutions to Revision Questions

 Solution 1

The correct answer is (C), see Section 1.3.1.

 Solution 2

The incidence of a tax is the person who actually pays it. See Section 1.4.3.

Solution 3

The correct answer is (D), see Section 1.6.

Solution 4

The tax bases are:

- Income
- Capital or wealth
- Consumption

See Section 1.5.

Solution 5

The correct answer is (D), see Section 1.6.

 Solution 6

The correct answer is (A), see Section 1.4.5.

 Solution 7

The correct answer is (B), see Section 1.4.3.

Solution 8

The correct answer is (C), see Section 1.4.3.

 Solution 9

The correct answer is (A), see Section 1.4.8.

2

Direct Taxes on an
Entity's Profits and
Gains

Direct Taxes on an Entity's Profits and Gains

2

LEARNING OUTCOME

After completing this chapter you should be able to:

▶ identify the principal types of taxation likely to be of relevance to an incorporated business in a particular country, including direct tax on the entity's trading profits and capital gains, indirect taxes collected by the entity, employee taxation, withholding taxes on international payments.

Note: To fully complete this learning outcome, Chapters 2 and 3 must be completed.

The topics covered in this chapter are as follows:

- Direct taxes on entity profits and gains:
  - the principle of non-deductibility of dividends and systems of taxation defined according to the treatment of dividends in the hands of the shareholder (e.g. classical, partial imputation and imputation);
  - the distinction between accounting and taxable profits in absolute terms (e.g. disallowable expenditure on revenue account, such as entertaining, and on capital account, such as formation and acquisition costs) and in terms of timing (e.g. deduction on a paid basis, tax depreciation substituted for book depreciation);
  - the nature of rules recharacterising interest payments as dividends;
  - potential for variation in rules for calculating the tax base dependent on the nature or source of the income (schedular systems);
  - the need for rules dealing with the relief of losses.

2.1 Introduction

In the first part of this chapter, we will consider the corporate tax base and some of the general principles applied to the determination of taxable profits. We will examine the concept of trading income and the adjustments to income and expenditure that are required to calculate taxable trading income. We will then discuss capital gains and relief available to entities for their capital gains. This chapter then examines different corporate income tax systems that can be used in a country and then looks at the treatment of losses and their application to groups of entities.

Direct taxation on entities can be referred to using a number of different terms, for example, corporate income tax, income tax and corporation tax are all used. In this chapter, for consistency, we will refer to all these direct taxes on entities as corporate income tax, except examples which directly refer to the UK corporation tax.

2.2 The corporate tax base

Income arising from all sources is usually included in an entity's tax base, whether:

- earnings from trading and other activities;
- gains from disposal of investments and assets;
- other non-business income.

Internationally, there are large differences in the definition of taxable income and therefore large differences in the tax base between countries. In some countries, such as Germany and France, taxable income is closely linked to the accounting profit shown in the income statement. Taxable profit therefore varies with the particular accounting rules used in the country. The accounting rules may also be driven to a large extent by the taxation laws. In countries such as the USA and the UK, there are substantial differences between accounting profits and taxable income, although the nature of the differences varies from country to country or even year to year.

In all countries, income is based on the accounting profit shown in an entity's financial statements, computed using generally accepted accounting practice in a particular country. In order to calculate taxable profit some adjustments are usually required by statute, although the type and number of adjustments will vary by country. These adjustments can give rise to deferred taxation (see Chapter 6 for a discussion on deferred taxation). The following sections cover the revenue and expenditure that can and cannot be included.

2.2.1 Schedular systems of corporate taxation

As stated above, it is common practice for countries to include all of an entity's earnings in their corporate income tax computations. An entity may receive income from several sources:

- trading profit,
- capital gains,
- interest received,
- rent received,
- patent royalties,
- other sources.

If all earnings are treated in the same way, there is little need to separate them when computing the tax charge for the year. However, some governments want more control over what is and is not taxed and at what rate. This is achieved by using a number of schedules for the tax calculations. Each schedule will relate to a specific type of income and will have specific rules that define how income should be measured and what expenditure will be allowed (if any). There may be a separate rate of tax applicable to each schedule.

In the UK corporation tax system, the main headings are referred to as 'Schedules', and some of the Schedules are divided into 'Cases'. Each schedule/case has its own specific rules for calculating the taxable income. After the taxable income for each schedule/case has been calculated, a total taxable income is prepared by adding all the schedule/case taxable incomes together. The entity's capital gains are then added on to give the total taxable profit for the period. The UK schedules and cases relevant for company taxation are:

UK Corporation tax schedules

Schedule A	Income from land and property
Schedule D	
Case I	Profits of a trade or business
Case III	Interest, etc., receivable
Case V	Dividends received from foreign companies
Case VI	Any income not chargeable under another Schedule or Case

Other items included in an entity's total profit for corporation tax purposes:

Capital gains
Surpluses on disposal of intangible assets

We will first consider income from a trade or business then capital gains.

2.2.2 Classification of income

In computing an entity's corporate income tax liability, the first step is to take the entity's income statement and compute taxable profits. If the tax system uses a schedular system, then separate figures for each category will need to be calculated by examining the entity's income statement and allocating incomes and expenditures to each tax category.

In arriving at the trading profit to be included in the entity's total taxable profit, certain expenses charged in the income statement have to be disallowed because they are not deductible for tax purposes. It is also necessary to remove any non-trading income that is taxable under other categories and capital gains. We need to calculate:

- What moneys received or receivable are taxable as trading income?
- What moneys expended or expendable can be deducted from those receipts?

As stated above, income is generally based on the profit shown in the entity financial statements, computed on generally accepted accounting practice. For example, in the UK, the requirement is that the profit of a trade, profession or vocation must be computed on an accounting basis which gives a true and fair view.

The income statement is then adjusted for tax purposes because not every item received is a taxable receipt of the trade, profession or vocation. Nor is every item of expenditure an allowable deduction for tax purposes. We will first consider receipts then deductions.

Income

Income could be either a profit or gain of the trade. A profit is income, whereas a gain is capital in nature. Most countries make a clear distinction between capital gains and revenue profits for tax purposes with, for example, capital gains tax and income tax. Any item credited to the income statement must be examined to determine if it is revenue or capital in nature. The questions that need to be asked are:

(a) Does the income arise directly from the trade?
(b) Is it a revenue or capital receipt?
(c) Is it a part of the profits of the year under review or of some other year?
(d) Is it taxable under any other category? For example, rents.
  - Non-trading receipts are usually treated separately for tax purposes.
  - Capital receipts will be dealt with under capital gains tax rules.
  - If the receipt relates to other years, it will probably be taxed in that year.
  - Receipts taxable under other categories are deducted from income and dealt with under the rules relating to the other categories.

2.2.3 Expenditure

The starting point for determining the profits or gains of a trade is the profit per financial statements. An item of expenditure or other debit to the income statement will be an allowable deduction in arriving at the trading profit, provided that either:

- it is revenue and not capital expenditure and is not prohibited by any provisions in the tax statute; or
- it is not specifically disallowed by the tax legislation.

We will consider expenditure under the following three sub-headings:

1. depreciation,
2. disallowable expenditure,
3. allowable expenditure.

Depreciation

Depreciation is by far the most common item of capital debited in the income statement. A deduction in respect of depreciation is a deduction that is related to the capital assets of the business and is therefore never allowable.

Depreciation provided in accounts is replaced by a standard deduction available for most, but generally not all, types of capital expenditure. The reason for this adjustment is that taxpayers can adopt a range of different depreciation rates and accounting policies. A standard deduction common to all taxpayers is fairer for tax purposes, and can also be used to provide investment incentives for businesses; generous allowances can be used to encourage capital expenditure on specific types of asset or in specific areas of the country. The standard deduction is usually referred to as tax depreciation or (as in the UK) capital allowances.

The main categories of expenditure qualifying for tax depreciation are usually:

- plant and machinery (broadly defined to include vehicles, computers, etc.);
- buildings.

Although buildings, plant and machinery are the main types of asset that all countries allow for tax depreciation, any non-current asset could be included, for example, research and development of a capital nature is allowable for capital allowances in the UK.

The way that depreciation is allowed for tax varies from country to country. All countries allow some form of charge to income for the use of assets. Most countries allow the declining balance method of calculating tax depreciation on plant and machinery and the majority use straight-line method for calculating tax depreciation on buildings (see Chapter 13 for an explanation of the methods of depreciation).

In some systems such as the UK, it is not necessary to calculate every asset separately, all assets of a similar type can be 'pooled' and treated as one large asset.

Incentives granted to encourage capital expenditure are usually in the form of accelerated tax depreciation, by allowing depreciation at a higher rate in the early years of the assets useful economic life. This practice is sometimes known as an initial allowance or first-year allowance. For example, in the UK, small companies can claim 100 per cent first-year allowances on some types of asset. Incentives can be used to encourage expenditure on assets generally or to help achieve a government objective, for example, in the UK, expenditure incurred by any business on the purchase of motor cars with low CO_2 emissions will qualify for a 100 per cent first-year allowance.

When an asset qualifying for tax depreciation is disposed of, a balancing charge or balancing allowance may arise. The total claimed for tax depreciation over the life of the asset must equal the original cost less sale proceeds. If there is a difference, a balancing adjustment will be made in the year of disposal.

> In your examination you will not be tested on any specific country's system of tax depreciation or depreciation rates. If computation questions are set, the details will be given along with all the tax rates needed to answer the question.

The following example illustrates the approach required in questions.

Example 2.A

HL commenced business on 1 June 2001, making up the first accounts for the year to 31 May 2002. The entity's purchases and sales of fixed assets were as follows:

Purchases			$
2001	1 June	Industrial building	260,000
	1 June	Plant	47,000
2004	1 June	Plant	58,000
Sales			
2004	31 May	Plant bought on 1 June 2001	9,500

HL qualifies for accelerated first-year allowance on the plant at the rate of 50% for the first year. The second and subsequent years will be at 25% on the reducing balance method. The industrial building qualifies for an annual tax depreciation allowance of 5% on the straight-line basis.

Calculate HL's tax depreciation for the years ended 31 May 2002, 2003 and 2004.

Solution

		Industrial building $	Plant $	Total tax depreciation for year $
01/06/2001	Purchase	260,000	47,000	
31/05/2002	First-year allowance		(23,500)	}
	Tax depreciation for the year	(13,000)		} 36,500
	Balance at 31/05/2002	247,000	23,500	
31/05/2003	Tax depreciation for the year	(13,000)	(5,875)	18,875
	Balance at 31/05/2003	234,000	17,625	
31/05/2004	Disposal		(9,500)	
	Balancing allowance		(8,125)	}
	Tax depreciation for the year	(13,000)		} 21,125
	Balance at 31/05/2004	221,000	0	
01/06/2004	Purchase		58,000	

This means that in the year to 31 May 2002, HL has a tax allowance for $36,500 tax depreciation. This will be deducted from HL's taxable profits before HL's tax liability is calculated.

In the year to 31 May 2003, HL receives an allowance for $18,875 tax depreciation and in the year to 31 May 2004, $21,125. This final amount includes a balancing allowance for the plant disposed of. The plant disposed of during the year cost $47,000 in 2001 and then received tax depreciation allowances of $23,500 and 5,875 leaving a tax written down balance of $17,625. When the plant was sold, $9,500 was received leaving a balance of $8,125 to be written off as a balancing allowance.

Disallowable expenditure

Disallowable expenditure is expenditure that has been incurred and charged to the income statement, but is not allowable for tax purposes. The expenditure therefore has to be added back on to the profit for the year to arrive at taxable profits.

Any expenditure that is deemed to be capital in nature will not usually be allowable expenditure when computing trading profits. For example:

- Losses on sale of non-current assets (also gains on sale).
- Legal, surveyors' and other fees related to capital matters; for example, new buildings, plant, etc.
- Repairs to assets purchased in a run-down condition, only the part attributable to use in the current trade is allowable.

Even if an item of expenditure is revenue expenditure, it may be specifically prohibited as a deduction by the tax legislation, for example, in the UK, expenses incurred in entertaining customers are specifically disallowed. Specifically disallowed items will vary from country to country, they also vary within a country from one year to another. The following items are often specifically disallowed:

- any disbursements or expenses of maintenance of the parties, their families or establishments, or any sums expended for any other domestic or private purposes distinct from the purposes of the trade, profession or vocation;
- any capital withdrawn from the business;
- any capital employed in improvements of the premises;
- any sum recoverable under an insurance;
- any expenditure on entertaining customers;
- any annuity or other annual payment (other than interest);

- donations to political parties;
- expenses that relate to an earlier year and arose in that earlier year.

Allowable expenditure

An item of expenditure or other debit to the income statement can usually be assumed to be an allowable deduction in arriving at the trading profit unless it is specifically disallowed by the tax legislation. Examination questions will specify which items of expenditure need to be disallowed.

2.2.4 Capital gains

Gains arising on the disposal of investments and other assets are not usually covered by income tax rules and are not included in the trading income. Capital gains tax attempts to tax those gains made on disposal of various types of investments and other assets. The assets included in the tax base vary from country to country. For example, in the UK, the most important type of transaction covered by capital gains tax is the sale of listed stocks and shares. The UK also has a large number of assets that are exempted from capital gains tax. The principle is usually that all assets are chargeable unless exempted, but the list of exemptions can be fairly long. In the UK, exemptions include:

- private motor vehicles;
- chattels (tangible movable property) sold for less than £6,000;
- chattels, which are wasting assets (i.e. those with a life of less than 50 years), for example, boats, caravans, animals;
- qualifying corporate bonds.

In addition to exempt *assets,* there can also be exemptions for certain types of *disposals* of assets, for example, in the UK, exempt disposals include:

- gifts to a non-profit-making body of land, buildings, works of art and the like, provided that the gift is for public benefit and public access is allowed;
- sale of works of art and the like to approved UK national or local institutions (e.g. art galleries or museums);
- gifts of any type of asset for charitable purposes to an approved charity.

In principle, the calculation of the gain or loss on a disposal is simply proceeds of sale less cost or value at a date specified in the tax legislation. Additional costs incurred to acquire the asset, improve it or dispose of it may be allowed to be deducted from the gain. When an entity disposes of a depreciable non-current asset, the capital gain or loss is normally calculated as the difference between the net disposal proceeds and the tax base of the asset at the time of disposal. The tax base is the original cost of the asset less accumulated tax depreciation to date.

In some countries the calculation is based on original cost but a few countries such as the UK allow the original cost to be indexed when calculating the gain. During periods of high inflation, a tax on capital gains would be unfair if based on the simple comparison of cost and sale proceeds. Some allowance for the effect of inflation over the period of ownership is needed. For example, in the UK, this is done by allowing the cost to be adjusted to current prices using an index published by the government, the retail price index. The movement in the index over the period of ownership is used to increase the original cost of the asset. Indexation cannot turn a capital gain into a loss, it merely reduces the gain to zero.

Example 2.B Indexation of the cost of an asset

An asset, which cost $10,000 in February 1988, was sold in April 2003 for $20,000. Retail price indices were:

February 1988	103.7
April 2003	180.0

The calculation of the chargeable gain will be:

	$	$
Proceeds of sale		20,000
Cost	10,000	
Indexation		
$10,000 × (180.0 − 103.7)/103.7		
i.e. $10,000 × 0.736	7,360	
Total allowable cost		17,360
Chargeable gain		2,640

Rollover relief

When an entity sells a business asset, it may give rise to a chargeable capital gain which, in most countries, will be included in the entity's corporate income tax calculation. In some countries, when an asset is replaced by another business asset, it is possible to defer the charge to tax until the replacement asset is sold. When the replacement asset is sold, any gain arising on that disposal may be deferred. There may be no limit to how often this deferral can take place. For example, in the UK, for an entity with a continuous existence, the deferral can be for an indefinite time, provided that the conditions are fulfilled. This relief from capital gains tax is sometimes known as rollover relief. Rollover relief allows a *deferral* of the payment of the corporate income tax on the gain till a later date, providing a cash flow advantage and allowing the corporate income tax to be paid in depreciated currency at a later date.

In a few countries rollover relief may also apply to intangible assets.

2.3 Nominal corporate tax rates

Corporate income tax rates vary considerably from one country to another. All countries have corporate income taxes at the central government level. Some countries have special lower rates for smaller entities while others have one rate for all entities. In some countries entities also have to pay taxes to other levels of government, for example, the USA and Canada. Any comparison of tax rates between countries is distorted by the range of treatments used for the calculation of tax base.

2.4 The interaction of the corporate tax system with the personal tax system

Dividends are appropriations of profit and are not usually allowed to be deducted from the income when calculating taxable profits. When dividends are paid to individual shareholders, the amount received has already been taxed. If it is then taxed in the hands of the shareholder, it is effectively being taxed twice.

The economic effect of corporate taxes depends on the system of corporate income tax used. The four main systems for taxing entity profits that are discussed below are:

1. classical system,
2. imputation system,
3. partial imputation system,
4. split rate systems.

2.4.1 Classical system

A classical system of corporate income tax does not differentiate between an entity's retained earnings and its distributed earnings and treats the shareholders as completely independent of the entity.

Under a classical system, the entity is liable for corporate income tax on all its taxable income and gains, whether they are distributed or not. The shareholder is liable to income tax on dividends received from the entity and capital gains tax on any taxable gains made on the disposal of their shares.

The classical system is relatively easy to understand and administer, but causes two main problems:

1. Double taxation of dividends, that is, distributed income is subject to corporate income tax and then to personal income tax.
2. A bias against distributing dividends, as distribution causes double taxation; non-distribution will avoid double taxation.

2.4.2 Imputation system

Under imputation systems of corporate income tax, all or a part of the underlying corporate income tax on distributions is imputed to the shareholders as a tax credit, therefore avoiding the problem of double taxation of dividends. With systems using the full imputation system, all of the underlying corporate income tax is passed to the shareholder as a tax credit. A full imputation system is economically neutral between debt and equity finance.

2.4.3 Partial imputation system

With systems using the partial imputation system, only a part of the underlying corporate income tax is passed to the shareholder as a tax credit.

2.4.4 Split rate systems

Split rate systems of corporate income tax distinguish between distributed profits and retained profits and charge a lower rate of corporate income tax on distributed profits so as to avoid the double taxation of dividends. Applying the lower rate for distributed dividends can operate under an imputation or classical system.

2.4.5 Examples to illustrate the difference between traditional and imputation systems

Example 2.C

Country X uses the classical system for corporate income tax. The entity's taxable profits are subject to 15% tax and shareholders are subject to income tax at 25% on all dividends received.

Country Y uses a full imputation system for corporate income tax. Entity taxable profits are subject to 30% tax. Shareholders receive a tax credit for the full amount of tax paid and are not subject to any further tax on dividends.

CT has taxable profits of $100,000 and decides to distribute 50% as dividends.

Calculate the total tax paid by CT and the shareholders, assuming that they are resident first in country X and then in Y.

Country X	$	$
Corporate income tax paid by CT	100,000 × 15%	15,000
Shareholders total income tax on dividends	50,000 × 25%	12,500
Total tax due if resident in country X		27,500
Country Y		
Corporate income tax paid by CT	100,000 × 30%	30,000
Shareholders total income tax on dividends	Nil	0
Total tax due if resident in country Y		30,000

Example 2.D

Country X and Country Y use the same rates of tax as in Example 2.C.

CD has taxable profits of $100,000 and decides to distribute 90% as dividends.

Calculate the total tax paid by CD and the shareholders, assuming again that they are resident in each country.

Country X	$	$
Corporate income tax paid by CD	100,000 × 15%	15,000
Shareholders total income tax on dividends	90,000 × 25%	22,500
Total tax due if resident in country X		37,500
Country Y		
Total tax due if resident in country Y (as Example 1)		30,000

In conclusion, in countries using the classical system, the total amount of tax paid depends on the amount of the profit that is paid as a dividend to shareholders. If less profit is distributed to shareholders, less tax is paid. In countries with a full imputation system, the corporate income tax is imputed to the shareholders receiving the dividend, so the total tax paid is not affected by the level of profits distributed as dividend.

2.5 Rules recharacterising interest as dividends

Interest on high-yield debt can cause otherwise profitable entities to have very low taxable incomes. This has caused some governments to consider limiting the amount of interest that can be charged to profits as an expense. For example, in the USA, certain types of high-yield debt are limited to the amount that can be set against the entity's taxable income. For certain types of debt instrument, where the yield is more than six points above the federal rate, the excess will be treated as a dividend. The result is that the issuing entity does not receive a tax deduction for the excess interest.

2.6 Treatment of losses

Trading and capital losses are usually dealt with separately under the legislation applicable to each.

2.6.1 Trading losses

Trading losses are calculated in the same way as trading profits. During the period when a trading loss occurs, the entity cannot claim a tax refund. The main ways of relieving the loss is by setting it off against profits during other periods or transferring it to another group entity (see Section 2.7 below).

All countries allow the loss to be set off against future profits, some countries limit the time that losses can be carried forward while others, such as the UK have no limit on the time allowed to recover the loss. The methods used to relieve losses can include:

(a) Carry forward of trading loss to offset against future trading income derived from the same trade.
(b) Offset against other income and chargeable gains of the same accounting period.
(c) Offset against other income and chargeable gains of one or more previous accounting periods.
(d) Group relief (see Section 2.7).

2.6.2 Capital losses

In principle, capital losses are calculated in the same way as capital gains. Capital losses are sometimes allowed to be deducted from trading income but most countries keep capital losses completely separate from trading activities. In most countries, capital losses are off-set against chargeable gains of the same accounting period. Any balance of loss is carried forward to be relieved against the first available chargeable gains. For example, in the UK, capital losses can be carried forward without time limit, they cannot be carried back to previous periods and cannot be set against any other income.

Example 2.E   To illustrate the treatment of losses

Country Z has the following tax regulations:

- Taxable profits are subject to tax at 25%.
- Capital gains are added to profits from trading to give taxable profits.
- Trading losses can be carried forward indefinitely but cannot be carried back to previous years.
- Capital gains/losses cannot be offset against trading gains/losses or vice versa.

LL started trading in 2002 and has the following profits/losses

	Trading profit/(loss) $'000	Capital profit/(loss) $'000
2002	(300)	400
2003	550	0
2004	700	(150)

Calculate the tax payable by LL in each year.

	Trading profit/(loss)	Capital profit/(loss)	Taxable profit	Tax due at 25%
2002		400	400	100
Loss carried forward	(300)			
2003	(550 – 300) = 250	0	250	62.50
Loss carried forward	0	0		
2004	700	(150)	700	175
Loss carried forward	0	(150)		

Note that in 2002 the trading loss cannot be offset against the capital gain and in 2004 the capital loss cannot be offset against the trading profit. This is a common situation that applies in many countries.

2.6.3 Cessation of business

If an entity makes a loss in its last 12 months of operation, its scope for relief under the rules we have considered so far is limited, since there can be no carry-forward. To remedy this most countries have special provisions in the legislation, for example, in the UK, a *terminal loss* relief exists, by which the loss may be carried back for up to 3 years to be set against total profits.

2.7 The concept of tax consolidation

The concept of tax consolidation is where for tax purposes a group is recognised so that entities within that group can transfer losses between themselves. If one entity in a group makes a loss while others are making profits, it is possible, subject to conditions, to transfer the benefit of the loss where it can most advantageously be relieved. If a loss is not transferred to another group entity, it could be carried forward for several years before it can be used to offset tax payable on future profits. If it is transferred to another group entity, they can use this year's loss to offset against this year's profits and therefore reduce the total group tax bill for the year.

The tax legislation that sets out the requirements for a group to be recognised varies considerably from country to country. Some countries only allow groups to consist of resident entities while others allow overseas entities to be included to the extent that they have profits/losses within the country. The requirements that need to be met for a tax group to be recognised will be set out in the tax legislation and will usually be different from that required to recognise a group for accounting purposes. For example, the UK requirement for a tax group is that there must be a direct or indirect holding of at least 75 per cent whereas for accounting purposes this will usually be 50 per cent.

Most countries have restrictions on the transfer, or surrender of losses between members of the group, which will limit the time or amount that can be surrendered. For example, in the UK, only losses of the current accounting period may be surrendered, and they may only be offset against the claimant entity's profits for the same period.

Non-trading losses may also be surrendered to other entities in the group.

2.7.1 Capital losses and tax groups

Different rules may apply to tax groups for capital gains. For example, the UK requirement for a capital gains tax group is different to a trading income tax group.

Capital losses are also different from trading and non-trading losses in that capital losses cannot usually be transferred from one entity to another. In the UK, all that is available is the right to transfer assets between members of the same capital gains tax group without triggering off a capital gain or loss. The asset is transferred on a 'no gain, no loss' basis. Where an asset, which will result in a capital loss, is about to be sold to a third party by a group member, and another group member is about to sell an asset to a third party, which would give rise to a chargeable gain, then this rule can be extremely helpful. The asset can be transferred at no loss to the entity making a sale at a profit. When the two assets are in the *same* entity, that entity could sell both assets to third parties and set the loss off against the gain.

2.8 Summary

In this chapter, we have discussed the two main methods of direct taxation that apply to entities, corporate income tax and capital gains tax. We have discussed the alternative systems of corporate income tax and their impact on the double taxation of dividends. We also considered the distinction between accounting and taxable profits, the treatment of losses and the concept of tax consolidation.

Revision Questions

2

? Question 1

A schedular system of corporate income tax means:

(A) A method used to calculate the corporate income tax payable
(B) A system that has a number of schedules which set out how different types of income should be taxed
(C) A system that has a number of schedules which set out when tax returns and tax payments should be made
(D) A system that has a number of schedules which set out the various tax rates **(2 marks)**

? Question 2

Accounting depreciation is replaced by tax depreciation:

(A) To reduce the amount of depreciation allowed for tax
(B) To increase the amount of depreciation allowed for tax
(C) To ensure that standard rates of depreciation are used by all organisations for tax purposes
(D) So that the government can more easily manipulate the amount of tax organisations pay
(2 marks)

? Question 3

KM commenced business on 1 June 2002, making up the first accounts for the year to 31 May 2003.

The entity's purchases and sales of fixed assets were as follows:

Purchases			$
2002	1 June	Industrial building	300,000
	1 June	Plant	40,000
2004	1 June	Plant	60,000
Sales			
2004	31 May	Plant bought on 1 June 2001	12,000

KM qualifies for accelerated first-year allowance on the plant at the rate of 50% for the first year. The second and subsequent years will be at 25% on the reducing balance method. No additional charge will result if the asset is disposed of early.

The industrial building qualifies for an annual tax depreciation allowance of 4% on the straight-line basis.

Calculate KM's tax depreciation for the year ended 31 May 2004. **(4 marks)**

? Question 4

The following is a list of payments which an organisation may incur during a year:

  (i) capital withdrawn from the business,
 (ii) interest paid,
(iii) legal expenses,
 (iv) payments for domestic expenses of the directors,
  (v) advertising.

Which two of the above items of expenditure will normally be disallowed for corporate income tax purposes?

(A) (i) and (iii)
(B) (i) and (iv)
(C) (ii) and (iv)
(D) (iii) and (v) **(2 marks)**

? Question 5

Rollover relief:

(A) allows deferral of the payment of corporate income tax on gains arising from the disposal of a business asset
(B) allows stock values to be rolled over, replacing cost of purchases with current values
(C) allows trading losses to be carried forward or rolled over to future periods
(D) allows capital losses to be carried forward or rolled over to future periods **(2 marks)**

? Question 6

An imputation system of corporate income tax means:

(A) All the underlying corporate income tax on the dividend distribution is passed as a credit to the shareholders
(B) The organisation pays corporate income tax on its profits and the shareholder pays income tax on the dividend received
(C) Withholding tax paid on dividends is passed as a credit to shareholders
(D) A percentage of the underlying tax is passed as a credit to shareholders **(2 marks)**

Question 7

Country W has the following tax regulations:

- Taxable profits are subject to tax at 25%
- Capital gains are added to profits from trading to give taxable profits
- Trading losses can be carried forward indefinitely, but cannot be carried back to previous years
- Capital gains/losses cannot be offset against trading gains/losses or vice versa

  LN started trading in 2002 and has the following profits/losses

	Trading profit/(loss) $'000	*Capital profit/(loss) $'000*
2002	(350)	0
2003	200	0
2004	700	(150)

Calculate the amount of tax due for 2004. **(3 marks)**

Question 8

A full imputation system of corporate income tax is one where an entity is taxable on

(A) all of its income and gains whether they are distributed or not. The shareholder is liable for taxation on all dividends received
(B) all of its income and gains whether they are distributed or not, but all the underlying corporation tax is passed to the shareholder as a tax credit
(C) all of its income and gains whether they are distributed or not, but only part of the underlying corporation tax is passed to the shareholder as a tax credit
(D) its retained profits at one rate and on its distributed profits at another (usually lower) rate of tax **(2 marks)**

Question 9

EG purchased a property for $630,000 on 1 September 2000. EG incurred additional costs for the purchase of $3,500 surveyors' fees and $6,500 legal fees. EG then spent $100,000 renovating the property prior to letting it. All of EG's expenditure was classified as capital expenditure according to the local tax regulations.

Indexation of the purchase and renovation costs is allowed on EE's property. The index increased by 50% between September 2000 and October 2007. Assume that acquisition and renovation costs were incurred in September 2000. EG sold the property on 1 October 2007 for $1,250,000, incurring tax allowable costs on disposal of $2,000.

Calculate EG's tax due on disposal assuming a tax rate of 30%. **(3 marks)**

Solutions to Revision Questions

2

 Solution 1

The correct answer is (B), see Section 2.2.1.

 Solution 2

The correct answer is (C), see Section 2.2.3.1.

 Solution 3

		Industrial building $	Plant $	Total tax depreciation for year $
01/06/2002	Purchase	300,000	40,000	
31/05/2003	First-year allowance		(20,000)	}
	Tax depreciation for the year	(12,000)		} 32,000
	Balance at 31/05/2004	288,000	20,000	
31/05/2004	Disposal		(12,000)	
	Balancing allowance		(8,000)	}
	Tax depreciation for the year	(12,000)		} 20,000
	Balance at 31/05/2004	276,000	0	
01/06/2004	Purchase		60,000	

The tax depreciation for the year to 31 May 2004 is $20,000.

 Solution 4

The correct answer is (B), see Sections 2.2.3.2 and 2.2.3.3.

 Solution 5

The correct answer is (A), see Section 2.2.4.1.

Solution 6

The correct answer is (A), see Section 2.5.2.

 Solution 7

	Trading profit/(loss) $'000	Capital profit/(loss) $'000	Taxable profit $'000	Tax due at 25% $'000
2002				
Loss carried forward	(350)			0
2003	(200 − 200) = 0	0	0	0
Loss carried forward	(350 − 200) = 150	0		
2004	(700 − 150) = 550	(150)	550	137.50
Loss carried forward	0	(150)		

The tax due in 2004 is $137,500.

 Solution 8

The correct answer is (B), see Section 2.4.2.

 Solution 9

Purchase price	$'000	$'000
Cost	630	
Fees	10	640
Renovation		100
		740
Indexation at 50%		370
		1,110
Selling price	1,250	
Less cost of disposal	2	1,248
Taxable amount		138

Tax at 30% = $41,400

Indirect Taxes and Employee Taxation

Indirect Taxes and Employee Taxation

3

LEARNING OUTCOME

After completing this chapter you should be able to identify the principal types of taxation likely to be of relevance to an incorporated business in a particular country, including direct tax on the entity's trading profits and capital gains, indirect taxes collected by the entity, employee taxation, withholding taxes on international payments.

The syllabus topics covered in this chapter are as follows:

- Indirect taxes collected by the entity:
  - In the context of indirect taxes, the distinction between unit taxes (e.g. excise duties based on physical measures) and *ad valorem* taxes (e.g. sales tax based on value).
  - The mechanism of value-added/sales taxes, in which businesses are liable for tax on their outputs less credits for tax paid on their inputs, including the concepts of exemption and variation in tax rates depending on the type of output and disallowance of input credits for exempt outputs.
- Employee taxation:
  - The employee as a separate taxable person subject to a personal income tax regime.
  - Use of employer reporting and withholding to ensure compliance and assist tax collection.

3.1 Introduction

In Chapter 1, we defined an indirect tax as one that is levied on one part of the economy with the intention that it will be passed on to another. In this chapter we are going to examine the types of indirect taxation that an entity may get involved with, either collecting the tax on behalf of government or paying the tax themselves.

In the first part of this chapter we will consider the main type of consumption tax, tax on sales, in its two main forms, sales tax and value-added tax. We then consider other consumption taxes that could effect an entity, including excise duties, property taxes and wealth taxes. In the final part of the chapter, we conclude with a discussion on employee taxation and pay-as-you-earn systems.

3.2 Indirect taxes collected by the entity

3.2.1 Unit taxes and *ad valorem* taxes

Taxes on consumption can be categorised in several ways.

1. Selective or general consumption taxes:
   (a) Selective consumption taxes – those levied on particular products, such as oil products, motor vehicles, alcohol and tobacco.
   (b) General consumption taxes – those levied on a wide range of goods and services, most of which are taxed on a percentage of value basis.
2. Specific or *ad valorem* taxes
   (a) Specific or unit taxes – taxes that are based on the weight or size of the tax base, for example, an excise duty of $5 per bottle of whiskey or $1 per 100 gram of tobacco.
   (b) *Ad valorem* taxes – based on values, these taxes are usually expressed as a percentage of the tax base, for example, a 5 per cent sales tax is calculated as 5 per cent of the selling price before tax.

3.3 Consumption taxes

In theory a general sales tax system could take one of many different forms, in practice there are two main types in use throughout the world, the single-level retail sales tax and value-added tax (VAT) systems. Sales taxes could be single- or multi-stage taxes.

3.3.1 Single-stage sales taxes

Single-stage sales taxes apply at one level of the production/distribution chain only; they can be applied to any one of the following levels:

- the manufacturing level;
- the wholesale level;
- the retail level.

There are very few countries using single-stage sales taxes, virtually no country uses a single-level sales tax at the manufacturing or wholesale level. The USA is the main example of a country using a retail sales tax, although the USA retail sales tax operates at the individual state government level rather than the federal government level.

3.3.2 Multi-stage sales taxes

A multi-stage sales tax charges tax each time a product or its components is sold in the chain from manufacturer, assembler, wholesaler to retailer. There are two types of multi-stage taxes:

1. A cumulative or cascade tax which does not allow credit for taxes paid on transfers between levels, this means that taxes paid at each stage are not refunded and are therefore treated as a business cost.
2. VAT and similar systems where credit is allowed for tax paid on purchases and traders are reimbursed all of the tax that they have paid. In these systems, the entire tax burden is usually passed on to the consumer.

Almost all countries have adopted VAT systems or are considering its adoption.

Example 3.A   Multi-stage cumulative tax

A manufacturer, M produces refrigerators. These are sold first to a wholesaler, W, who sells in turn to a retailer, R. Finally, R sells to the ultimate consumer, C. The prices at which these transactions take place (excluding sales tax) are as follows:

- M sells to W for $ 100
- W sells to R for $ 160
- R sells to C for $300

The country levies a multi-stage cumulative tax at the rate of 5% each time a sale is made.
   Calculate the sales tax due by each entity and in total.

		Tax due
M's sale to W	$100 × 5%	$5
W's sale to R	$160 × 5%	$8
R's sale to C	$300 × 5%	$15
Total tax due		$28

Each entity has to charge tax and then pay it to the tax authorities. The tax paid is not recoverable. The total tax due in this example is $28.

3.4   Value-added tax

VAT is not a tax on profits or gains, and is not even eventually borne by most businesses to a material extent. Nevertheless, it is important to businesses, because its charge and collection enter into many, even most business transactions. Ultimately, VAT falls mainly on the final consumer of goods or services. However, all those involved in the chain of transactions between the manufacturer and the retailer are first charged VAT and then pass it on to the next person in the chain. The standard rate of VAT varies from one country to another; even in Europe where all countries in the EU must have a VAT system, the rates are very varied. Most countries have more than one rate of VAT; sometimes many different rates are used. One rate often used is a 'zero' rate, we will see the significance of this later.

Example 3.B   VAT

Use the details in Example 3.A, but instead of a sales tax the country now has a VAT system, with VAT at 17.5%. Calculate the VAT finally due from C and the amount paid by M, W and R.
   The VAT finally due from C is:

$$\$300 \times 17.5\% = \$52.50$$

This is collected by R who pays it over to the tax authorities, along with the VAT due on other sales. But R first deducts all the VAT suffered on its *inputs*, its purchases. This will include the VAT charged by W on the supply of the refrigerator, and VAT suffered on items such as stationery, telephone and other overhead costs of goods and services. The overall effect on M, W and R is that most of the VAT paid by them on their *inputs* (purchases) is deducted when accounting for VAT on their *outputs* (sales).
   Input tax is VAT paid on purchases. Output tax is VAT charged on sales or services provided.

Considering only the VAT relating to the sale and purchase of one refrigerator, the accounting will be as follows:

Entity	Input tax $	Output tax $	VAT paid $
M			
Sale to W		17.50	17.50 paid by M
W			
Purchase from M	17.50		
Sale to R		28.00	10.50 paid by W
R			
Purchase from M	28.00		
Sale to C		52.50	24.50 paid by R
Total suffered by C			52.50

The overall effect on M, W and R is nil. Each has collected VAT on making a sale and paid this over to Customs and Excise, first deducting any VAT paid on purchases and other inputs. C, the ultimate consumer, pays $52.50 and has no-one to pass it on to. He or she thus bears the tax which has been collected by the tax authorities in the three stages shown. This is an oversimplification of the actual process as each registered trader has to submit a return, usually quarterly, showing VAT collected on outputs and VAT suffered on inputs. The difference must be paid to the tax authorities within a specified time after the period end.

3.4.1 Transactions liable to VAT

Most business transactions are within the scope of VAT, which has to be accounted for whenever there is a *taxable supply*. A taxable supply means the supply of goods or services in the course of business, other than supplies that are exempt for one reason or another.

A supply of goods or services in the course of business must be one of the following types of supply:

- *standard-rated* – within the scope of VAT and taxable at the standard rate;
- *subject to a higher or lower rate* – within the scope of VAT and taxable at the appropriate rate;
- *zero-rated* – within the scope of VAT and taxable at 0 per cent;
- *exempt* – an activity on which VAT is not charged.

A further possibility is that the transaction is outside the scope of VAT – examples in the UK include some forms of compensation and the transfer of a business as a going concern.

Exemption and zero-rating

At first sight there appears to be no practical difference between zero-rating and exemption, but there is an important difference. If a trade or business is concerned with transactions that are zero-rated (e.g. in the UK, the supply of most types of food), no VAT is charged on sales, but the supplier may obtain a refund of VAT suffered on input costs to the business.

If, on the other hand, the transaction is exempt, again no VAT is charged on sales but the VAT suffered on costs relating to exempt supplies will not usually be recovered.

The following are examples of UK zero-rated transactions:

- sale of most types of food (but not restaurant meals, etc.);
- printed matter including books, newspapers, etc.;
- children's clothing and footwear;
- transport (by bus, ships, aircraft, but not taxi fares and the like);

- exports;
- drugs and medicines supplied on prescription.

Although the exact list of zero-rated supplies will vary from one country to another, the general principle of zero-rated supplies is fairly universal.

Partially exempt trades

A business could conduct several activities, resulting in some of its sales being standard-rated, some zero-rated, and some 'exempt'.

Such businesses are *partially exempt*. This means that their right to offset input tax is restricted.

To calculate the proportion of input tax which is deductible, a method that is 'practical, accurate and fair' must be agreed. The standard method is to divide input tax into three, as shown in Table 3.1.

Table 3.1 VAT treatment for partially exempt businesses

Input tax category	VAT treatment
(a) Input tax on costs only incurred in making taxable supplies (whether standard-rated or zero-rated)	Reclaimable in full
(b) Input tax on costs only incurred in making exempt supplies or for any other activity (outside scope)	Not reclaimable at all
(c) Other input tax (partly for items used in making taxable supplies – 'unattributable VAT')	Reclaimable pro rata

The pro-rata calculation to establish the recoverable input VAT is made by apportioning the 'unattributable' input VAT (above) in the same ratio as the value of *all* taxable supplies bears to total supplies.

Entities are required to register for VAT when their *taxable* supplies *(including zero-rated supplies)* exceed the registration threshold. The registration threshold varies from country to country, but is designed to exempt small entities from the problems caused by having to keep VAT records. Exempt sales are generally *excluded* in determining whether a business has reached the registration threshold.

Entities can usually choose to register before their turnover reaches the level for compulsory registration. Only registered entities can charge VAT on sales or recover VAT paid on purchases.

3.5 Indirect taxes paid by the entity

3.5.1 Excise duties

Excise duties are specific taxes on certain commodities. As noted above, 'specific' or 'unit' taxes are based on the weight or size of the tax base.

From the revenue authority's point of view, the characteristics of commodities most suitable for excise duties are:

- few large producers;
- inelastic demand with no close substitutes;
- large sales volumes; and
- easy to define products covered by the tax.

The four main product groups, universally subject to excise duties – alcoholic drinks, tobacco and tobacco products, mineral oils and motor vehicles, all share these characteristics.

Special reasons cited for the existence of specific excise duties include:

- to discourage overconsumption of products which may harm the consumer or others, for example, duty on tobacco and alcohol;
- to alter the distribution of income by taxing 'luxuries', for example, in the USA, there are excise duties on heavy tyres, fishing equipment, firearms and airplane tickets;
- to seek to allow for externalities, so that the social and environmental cost of consuming the product is paid for by the consumer, for example, excise duty on tobacco to help pay for the increased cost of healthcare of smokers;
- to place the burden of paying the tax on the consumer of the product/service, for example, excise duty on petrol and diesel is used by some governments to build and maintain roads, bridges and mass transit systems.

Excise duties tend to have high yields and low cost of collection, so they are attractive to governments.

In recent years the number of products covered by specific excise duties has generally decreased in most countries, although the four product groups universally subject to excise duties, listed above, have not been affected.

VAT is usually payable on the goods as well as the excise duty. Excise duties have to be paid by entities and unlike VAT, the amount is not repayable. The duty must therefore be treated as a part of the cost of the item purchased.

3.5.2 Property taxes

Taxes on immovable property exist in many countries. The tax base is usually the capital value of the property although in some countries it is the annual rental value. The tax is usually on land and buildings, but a few countries and some states in the USA also tax other items of personal property such as cars, boats and livestock.

3.5.3 Wealth taxes

The tax base for a wealth tax is usually total wealth. The problem with total wealth is measuring and valuing all of the assets in the tax base. For example, total wealth may be deemed to include rights to a future pension, life insurance policies, etc. These assets are notoriously difficult to value. Problems also occur in areas such as antiques, collections and similar articles, for example, stamp collections.

Despite the difficulties, wealth taxes are levied in a number of countries. Wealth taxes can apply to:

- individuals only;
- entities only; or
- individuals and entities.

In countries where a wealth tax exists for entities, an entity's wealth, that is, a measure of their asset value, will be taxed each year.

3.6 Employee taxation

3.6.1 The employee as a separate taxable person subject to a personal income tax regime

Personal income tax paid by an employee varies from country to country as the result of the interaction of a number of different choices made by governments, for example:

- the way that the assessable earnings are measured, the basis of assessment;
- the way deductible expenses are calculated;
- the schedule of rates used to calculate tax payable.

Basis of assessment

Many countries such as the UK make a distinction between persons employed, earning a wage or salary and subject to tax under the employment income rules and self-employed person taxable under income tax rules. The normal basis of assessment for employed persons can vary from country to country; it could be based on any of the following:

- the amount actually received in the tax year, for example, in the UK;
- the amount earned in the previous year, for example, in France;
- the average of the previous 2 years earnings, for example, in Switzerland.

The assessment will cover basic salary or wage, commissions, fees, gratuities, profit-sharing payments, bonuses and benefits-in-kind. Pensions received after the cessation of employment are also usually taxable. Some expenses may be deductible.

Deductible expenses

There is wide variation of deductible expenses between different countries. In the UK, for expenses to be deductible from income, they must be 'incurred wholly, exclusively and necessarily in the performance of the duties'. Expenses that could meet this definition may include:

- professional subscriptions;
- donations to charity and through a payroll deduction scheme;
- retirement annuity premiums;
- contributions to personal pension plans;
- costs of security assets or services included in emoluments.

Benefits-in-kind

Benefits-in-kind are non-cash benefits given by the employer to an employee as part of a remuneration package, often in lieu of further cash payments. In the UK, senior employees and directors often have a remuneration package that includes a number of benefits-in-kind. The tax regulations provide for a number of these benefits to be included in the tax base. The range of benefits-in-kind given to employees varies enormously between countries and their tax treatment varies just as much.

3.6.2 Social security contributions

Social security contributions are not always regarded as taxes. However, they are assessed on individuals and deducted from earnings in the same way as employee taxation is deducted. Social security contributions constitute a significant tax burden on employees and employers, in some countries employee social security contributions may be more than their income tax each month.

Social security rates are progressive but usually less so than income tax, they are based on an employee's monthly earnings, without any adjustments for expenses or family circumstances. The employee pays a percentage of earnings, usually up to a maximum contribution per month.

The employer also has to make a payment; this usually has no maximum and is based on a percentage of the employees pay.

3.6.3 Other payroll taxes

In some countries, governments also impose other payroll taxes, for example, in the USA, in addition to social security contributions, there is a separate unemployment compensation tax.

3.7 Use of employer reporting and withholding to ensure compliance and assist tax collection

The bulk of income tax revenues in developed countries are provided by wage and salary earners. In most countries tax from employment income is collected by the employer using deduction at source; employers withhold tax along with social security contributions from the current earnings of employees.

The deductions are calculated using tables provided by the tax authorities and information about the total allowances to which each employee is entitled is given in the form of a code number. Employers deduct the tax from employees' pay each month and then pay the tax and social security contributions to the tax authorities on a monthly basis. For example, the UK system of tax deducted at source is known as the pay-as-you-earn (PAYE) system.

This arrangement has a number of advantages:

- the tax is collected earlier than systems that assess earnings at the end of the year, this improves the governments cash flow;
- it makes payment of taxes easier for individuals as there is not one large bill to pay, this reduces defaults and late payments;
- most of the administration costs are borne by the employers instead of government.

Other taxes are also withheld by employers or entities making the payment. For example, in the USA property taxes are collected by banks and other entities along with mortgage payments.

3.8 Summary

This chapter has considered indirect taxes and their impact on entities. We started with a consideration of sales taxes and VAT, then continued with other indirect taxes. The final section considered employee taxation and the operation of advance payment systems.

Revision Questions

3

? Question 1

Country IDT has a duty that is levied on vehicle fuel oils at 10% of their resale value before sales tax. This duty is a:

(A) *Ad valorem* tax
(B) Specific unit tax
(C) Direct tax
(D) VAT

(2 marks)

? Question 2

In no more than 25 words, define 'benefits-in-kind'.

(2 marks)

? Question 3

Country IDT has a duty that is levied on all drinks of an alcoholic nature where the alcohol is above 20% by volume. This levy is $2 per 1 litre bottle. This duty could be said to be:

(A) *Ad valorem* tax
(B) Specific unit tax
(C) Direct tax
(D) VAT

(2 marks)

? Question 4

List three advantages of requiring employers to deduct employee tax from employees' pay each month.

(3 marks)

? Question 5

Country V has a VAT system which allows organisations to reclaim input tax paid. VAT is at 15% of selling price.

B manufactures sports shoes and sells them to C, a wholesaler. C resells them to D, a retailer. D eventually sells them to E for $120. The prices at which transactions take place (excluding VAT) are as follows:

- B sells to C for $50
- C sells to D for $80

Calculate the VAT due from B, C and D. **(3 marks)**

? Question 6

An entity purchases products from a foreign entity. These products cost $21 each and on import are subject to an excise duty of $4 per item and VAT at 20%. If the entity imports 100 items, how much do they pay to the tax authorities?

(A) $400
(B) $420
(C) $500
(D) $900 **(2 marks)**

? Question 7

An entity purchases raw materials for $1,100 and pays VAT at a standard rate on them. The materials are used to produce two products X and Y. The entity sells 200 units of product X at $5 each and 400 units of product Y at $4 each. Product X is zero-rated for VAT purposes and product Y is standard-rated.

Assume that there are no other transactions affecting the VAT payments and that the standard rate of VAT is 20%.

At the end of the period the entity pays the net amount of VAT due to the tax authorities. How much VAT was paid:

(A) $100
(B) $300
(C) $320
(D) $520 **(2 marks)**

? Question 8

If a product is exempt for VAT purposes, it means that an entity:

(A) Can charge VAT on sales at standard rate and cannot reclaim input taxes paid
(B) Cannot charge VAT on sales and can reclaim input taxes paid
(C) Cannot charge VAT on sales and cannot reclaim input taxes paid
(D) Can charge VAT on sales and can reclaim input taxes paid **(2 marks)**

Question 9

Country OS has a VAT system, where VAT is charged on all goods and services. Registered VAT entities are allowed to recover input VAT paid on their purchases. VAT operates at different levels in OS:

Standard rate	10%
Luxury rate	20%
Zero rate	0%

During the last VAT period, an entity, BZ purchased materials and services costing $100,000, excluding VAT. All materials and services were at standard rate VAT.

BZ converted the materials into two products Z and L; product Z is zero-rated and product L is luxury-rated for VAT purposes.

During the VAT period, BZ made the following sales, excluding VAT:

	$
Z	60,000
L	120,000

At the end of the period, BZ paid the net VAT due to the tax authorities. Assuming BZ had no other VAT-related transactions, how much VAT did BZ pay?　　**(2 marks)**

Question 10

CU manufactures clothing and operates in a country that has a VAT system. This system allows entities to reclaim input tax that they have paid on taxable supplies. VAT is at 15% of the selling price at all stages of the manufacturing and distribution chain.

CU manufactures a batch of clothing and pays expenses (taxable inputs) of $100 plus VAT. CU sells the batch of clothing to a retailer CZ for $250 plus VAT. CZ unpacks the clothing and sells the items separately to various customers for a total of $600 plus VAT. How much VAT do CU and CZ each have to pay in respect of this one batch of clothing?

(2 marks)

Question 11

Country X uses a Pay-As-You-Earn (PAYE) system for collecting taxes from employees. Each employer is provided with information about each employee's tax position and tables showing the amount of tax to deduct each period. Employers are required to deduct tax from employees and pay it to the revenue authorities on a monthly basis.

From the perspective of the government, list THREE advantages of the PAYE system.

(3 marks)

Question 12

Excise duties are deemed to be most suitable for commodities that have certain specific characteristics.

List THREE characteristics of a commodity that, from a revenue authority's point of view, would make that commodity suitable for an excise duty to be imposed.　　**(3 marks)**

? Question 13

Country Y has a VAT system which allows entities to reclaim input tax paid.

In Country Y the VAT rates are:

Zero rated	0%
Standard rated	15%

DE runs a small retail store. DE's sales include items that are zero rated, standard rated and exempt.

DE's electronic cash register provides an analysis of sales. The figures for the three months to 30 April 2007 were:

	Sales value, excluding VAT
	$
Zero rated	11,000
Standard rated	15,000
Exempt	13,000
Total	39,000

DE's analysis of expenditure for the same period provided the following:

	Expenditure, excluding VAT
	$
Zero rated purchases	5,000
Standard rated purchases relating to standard rate outputs	9,000
Standard rated purchases relating to exempt outputs	7,000
Standard rated purchases relating to zero rated outputs	3,000
	24,000

Calculate the VAT due to/from DE for the three months ended 30 April 2007. (**2 marks**)

? Question 14

EF is an importer and imports perfumes and similar products in bulk. EF repackages the products and sells them to retailers. EF is registered for Value Added Tax (VAT).

EF imports a consignment of perfume priced at $10,000 (excluding excise duty and VAT) and pays excise duty of 20% and VAT on the total (including duty) at 15%.

EF pays $6,900 repackaging costs, including VAT at 15% and then sells all the perfume for $40,250 including VAT at 15%.

EF has not paid or received any VAT payments to/from the VAT authorities for this consignment.

Requirements

(i) Calculate EF's net profit on the perfume consignment.

(ii) Calculate the net VAT due to be paid by EF on the perfume consignment. (**5 marks**)

Solutions to Revision Questions

3

 Solution 1

The correct answer is (A), see Section 3.2.

 Solution 2

Benefits-in-kind are non-cash benefits given by the employer to an employee, often in lieu of further cash payments, see Section 3.6.1.3.

 Solution 3

The correct answer is (B), see Section 3.2.

 Solution 4

The advantages are:

- the tax is collected earlier than systems that assess earnings at the end of the year, this improves the governments cash flow;
- it makes payment of taxes easier for individuals as there is not one large bill to pay, this reduces defaults and late payments;
- most of the administration costs are borne by the employers instead of government, see Section 3.7.

 Solution 5

Entity	Input tax $	Output tax $	VAT paid $
B			
Sale to C		7.50	7.50 paid by B
C			
Purchase from B	7.50		
Sale to D		12.00	4.50 paid by C
D			
Purchase from C	12.00		
Sale to E		18.00	6.00 paid by D
Total suffered by E			18.00

See Section 3.4.

INDIRECT TAXES AND EMPLOYEE TAXATION

 Solution 6

Excise duty payable is usually added to the cost of the goods, the total being subject to VAT. The correct answer is (D), see Section 3.4.

 Solution 7

The entity can reclaim input tax paid and sets this off against VAT charged at the standard rate:

VAT charged at standard rate $(400 \times \$4) \times 20\%$ = $320
Input VAT paid $\quad\quad\quad\$1,100 \times 20\%\quad$ = $220
VAT paid to tax authorities $\quad\quad\quad\quad\quad\quad$ $100

The correct answer is (A), see Section 3.4.

 Solution 8

The correct answer is (C), see Section 3.4.1.1.

 Solution 9

Input VAT = $100 \times 10\%$ = 10
Output VAT = $(60 \times 0\%) + (120 \times 20\%)$ = 24
VAT due = $24 - 10$ = 14
VAT paid = $14,000

See Section 3.4.

 Solution 10

	Cost (Inputs) $	Sales $	Net $	VAT $
CU	100	250	150	22.5
CZ	250	600	350	52.5

See Section 3.4.

 Solution 11

Three advantages of PAYE are:

- The tax is collected earlier than systems that assess earnings at the end of the year; this improves the government's cash flow;
- It makes payment of taxes easier for individuals as there is not one large bill to pay; this reduces defaults and late payments;
- Most of the administration costs are borne by the employers, instead of government;
- Regular predictable receipts make government budgeting easier.

Note: Any other relevant point would have been acceptable in the exam.

Solution 12

From the revenue authority's point of view, the characteristics of commodities suitable for excise duties are:

- Few large producers/suppliers;
- Inelastic demand with no close substitutes;
- Large sales volumes; and
- Easy to define products covered by the tax.

Note: Any **three** of the above would have been acceptable in the exam.

 Solution 13

DE's outputs

$15,000 \times 15\% = 2,250$

Inputs

$[9,000 + 3,000] \times 15\% = 1,800$

Net payment due from DE $= 2,250 - 1,800 = 450$

VAT relatin g to exempt items cannot be reclaimed and is ignored.

 Solution 14

Perfume consignment income, expenditure and VAT are as follows:

	Total cost (incl VAT) $	VAT $	Net of VAT $
Expenditure			
Cost	10,000		10,000
Excise duty	2,000		2,000
	12,000		12,000
Input VAT @ 15%	1,800	1,800	0
	13,800		12,000
Repackaging costs	6,900	900	6,000
Total costs	20,700		18,000
Sales revenue	(40,250)	(5,250)	(35,000)
Net	19,550	2,550	17,000

(i) Net profit is $17,000

As EF is registered for VAT in its country VAT on expenses can be reclaimed and VAT must be charged on sales. VAT cannot be included in revenue or cost figures, so the revenue and cost must be calculated net of VAT.

(ii) Net VAT due to be paid is $2,550.

4

Administration of Taxation

Administration of Taxation

4

LEARNING OUTCOMES

After completing this chapter you should be able to:

▶ describe the likely record-keeping, filing and tax payment requirements associated with the principal types of taxation likely to be of relevance to an incorporated business in a particular country;

▶ describe the possible enquiry and investigation powers of taxing authorities;

▶ explain the difference in principle between tax avoidance and tax evasion.

The syllabus topics covered in this chapter are as follows:

- the need for record-keeping and record retention that may be additional to that required for financial accounting purposes;
- the need for deadlines for reporting (filing returns) and tax payments;
- types of powers of tax authorities to ensure compliance with tax rules:
  - power to review and query filed returns;
  - power to request special reports or returns;
  - power to examine records (generally extending back some years);
  - powers of entry and search;
  - exchange of information with tax authorities in other jurisdictions;
- the distinction between tax avoidance and tax evasion, and how these vary among jurisdictions (including the difference between the use of statutory general anti-avoidance provisions and case law based regimes).

4.1 Introduction

In the first part of this chapter, we will consider the need for entities to keep and retain records. Second, we consider the need for deadlines and the various types of powers that tax authorities may enjoy. We conclude the chapter with a discussion on tax avoidance and tax evasion.

4.2 The need for record-keeping and record retention

The requirement for entities to keep records is usually included in tax legislation, which will usually set out minimum time limits for the retention of records. Failure to maintain the correct records to support the tax return will usually render the entity liable to a financial penalty.

The range of records required to be kept for tax purposes will frequently be wider than those required to support financial statements as any type of document or record may be needed, for example, copies of contracts. Records need to be kept to support all types of tax that the entity has to pay to the tax authorities, whether the tax has been collected from others or is due from the entity in its own right. In other words, records will usually need to be kept for the following:

- corporate income tax, including capital gains;
- sales tax or VAT;
- excise duties, for example, in relation to sales of fuel oils;
- employee taxes, social security contributions and other payroll taxes deducted at source from employee salaries and wages.

4.2.1 Corporate income tax

All tax payers need to keep records to enable them to accurately prepare their financial statements in accordance with generally accepted accounting principles. Financial statements are the starting point of the calculation of taxable profits for the period. Entities therefore have to keep all of the records required to support their financial statements and also the additional documents required to support the adjustments made to those statements when completing their tax returns.

4.2.2 Sales tax or Vat

In countries where sales tax or VAT is used, appropriate records need to be kept. For example, in the UK, registered persons are required to keep adequate records and retain them for 6 years. Records must show details of all taxable goods and services received or supplied, and all exempt supplies made.

The records required to be kept include all business documents, such as:

- orders and delivery notes;
- relevant business correspondence;
- purchases and sales books;
- cashbooks and other account books;
- purchase invoices and sales invoices;
- records of daily takings such as till rolls;
- annual accounts, including income statements;
- import and export documents;
- bank statements and paying-in slips;
- VAT account;
- credit or debit notes issued or received.

Records may be computerised or maintained by a computer bureau, provided that they can be made available to the tax authorities when required.

The above list shows how much detail is usually required to be kept to justify tax returns when required to do so by the tax authorities.

4.2.3 Overseas subsidiaries

A further example of the detailed records required is where a resident entity has an overseas subsidiary. In some cases the tax authorities may be concerned about transfer pricing between the subsidiary and its parent. Tax authorities sometimes, for example, in the USA, have powers to require entities to provide them with detailed records providing evidence of the method used to calculate prices used in transactions between the subsidiary and its parent. Entities, therefore, have to keep detailed records of price calculations in case the tax authorities require them to be submitted (note you do not need to know any details about transfer pricing).

4.2.4 Employee taxes and social security

In countries where employee tax and social security contributions are deducted from employees' pay each week or month, the employer will need to keep detailed records of the employees' pay and also the amounts of tax and social security that have been deducted. At the year-end the employer will also need to complete a number of returns for the government that show the total deducted from each employee, the employer's contribution for each employee, and an analysis of the total amounts deducted. The employer will also have to provide details of amounts deducted, usually on standard government forms, to employees.

4.3 The need for deadlines for reporting (filing returns) and tax payments

Tax authorities set deadlines for taxpayers to submit tax returns and pay outstanding tax. There may be different deadlines for income tax and corporate income tax, sales tax and VAT.

There are generally three options available to tax authorities when collecting corporate income tax:

1. The tax authorities prepare an assessment, based on information provided by the entity and notify the entity of the amount of tax due.
2. The entity prepares a tax return and files this along with their computations of tax due.
3. The entity self assesses the tax due and pays the amount of tax it thinks is due.

In countries where an assessment is raised by the tax authorities, entities will be required to submit tax returns after their accounting year-end. The tax return will usually require a range of information to be provided in addition to the copy of the financial statements. Tax authorities may also require additional information from the entity before raising an assessment on the entity, which will have to be paid within a certain time limit.

Countries using a pay and file type of system, require the corporate income tax to be estimated by the entity and paid by a certain deadline. For example, in the UK, corporation tax

ADMINISTRATION OF TAXATION

for small and medium entities must be paid within 9 months of the end of the accounting period. The corporation tax return, with supporting calculations has to be submitted within 12 months of the end of the accounting period. Upon receipt of the corporation tax return, the tax authorities calculate the tax due and adjust the amount paid by issuing a demand for further payment or making a refund for any amounts overpaid.

In countries using self assessment, entities have to estimate the amount of corporation tax that they will be due to pay for the year and pay it, often in advance of the year-end. For example, in the UK, large entities have to estimate their corporation tax liability and then pay their corporation tax in four equal instalments, two within the period and two after the end of the tax period. They still have to submit a tax return which must include a self-assessment calculation and be supported by relevant financial accounts.

The deadline for filing returns and paying the tax will vary from country to country, but a deadline is required for the following reasons:

- without any deadline, entities would not know when payment was required;
- it enables the tax authorities to forecast their cash flows more accurately;
- without a deadline, there is no reference point for late payment, it would be difficult to enforce any penalties for entities not paying;
- if tax is deducted from employees at source and not paid to the tax authorities fairly quickly, there is more chance of an entity spending the amount deducted instead of paying it to the tax authorities.

4.4 Types of powers of tax authorities to ensure compliance with tax rules

Revenue authorities generally have powers to inflict penalties for various offences related to corporation tax and sales tax/VAT. For example, late filing of a tax return may attract a fixed penalty and unpaid tax may be subject to interest on the balance due.

4.4.1 Power to review and query filed returns

Tax authorities generally have the power to review and query corporation tax returns that have been filed. The tax legislation will usually specify deadlines limiting the time available for the tax authorities to decide to open an investigation. Tax authorities generally have the power to request any document, etc., relevant to their enquiry. The legislation will specify time limits allowed to comply with the request and will also provide for penalties for non-compliance.

Tax authorities usually have the power to check and query sales tax and VAT returns. There are usually a range of penalties in the legislation which apply to late submission of returns and misdeclaration of tax due.

4.4.2 Power to request special reports or returns

Tax authorities may have the power to request a special report to be made on an entity or to require an entity to complete special returns. They may take this type of action if they believe that the entity is not providing full or accurate information.

4.4.3 Power to examine records (generally extending back some years)

Tax authorities generally have the power to examine any records that support the corporate income tax. As the tax return is based on the financial accounts, this means that they also have the power to examine any documents or records that support the financial accounts.

If the tax authorities suspect fraud or serious understatement of the amount of corporate income tax due, they usually have the power to require the entity to allow them access to their records going back, in some cases as far as the tax authorities wish. For example, in the UK, in cases of fraud, the tax authorities can go back 20 years.

Sales tax and VAT legislation usually includes provisions for officers of the tax authority to visit the premises of registered entities from time to time to confirm that the regulations are being complied with.

4.4.4 Powers of entry and search

Tax authorities do not have the power of entry and search of an entity's premises in all countries. Some countries allow the tax authorities full and free access to an entity's business premises but other countries require a search warrant to be issued first. All countries allow access, with a search warrant if necessary, in fraud cases. In cases where fraud or some other contravention of the tax legislation is suspected, tax authorities also generally have the power to seize documents.

Sales tax and VAT legislation often give officers of the tax authority a statutory right to enter premises at any reasonable time and inspect goods and records to confirm that sales tax or VAT returns are complete and accurate.

4.4.5 Exchange of information with tax authorities in other jurisdictions

Tax authorities generally have the power to pass on information to foreign tax authorities as long as there is a tax treaty with the foreign country. The tax treaty will set out the terms and conditions that need to apply before information will be provided.

4.5 Tax avoidance and tax evasion

The causes of tax avoidance and evasion include high tax rates, imprecise laws, insufficient penalties and apparent inequity. When any of these situations apply, tax avoidance and evasion will tend to increase. For example:

- high tax rates make evasion or avoidance more rewarding and also make it worthwhile spending more on tax advice and using more complex schemes;
- imprecise laws mean that the letter of the law is not tight enough to stop avoidance and the spirit of the law may be unclear. In chapter 1, we saw that one of the canons of taxation was certainty, imprecise laws lead to uncertainty;
- insufficient penalties mean that it is more rewarding to evade tax and risk getting caught, even if caught the penalty will not be severe;
- apparent inequity can lead to an increased desire to evade tax and also make tax avoidance and evasion more socially acceptable.

4.5.1 Tax evasion

Tax evasion is the illegal manipulation of the tax system to avoid paying taxes. Tax evasion is the intentional disregard of the legislation in order to escape paying taxes; it can include falsifying tax returns and claiming fictitious expenses.

4.5.2 Tax avoidance

Tax avoidance is tax planning to the extent that the affairs of the entity are legally arranged in such a way as to minimise the corporation tax liability. Although tax avoidance is strictly legal and within the letter of the law, it is usually contrary to the spirit of the law. Many tax avoidance schemes exploit loopholes in the legislation, which the tax authorities try to close as soon as the loophole has been identified.

4.5.3 Statutory general anti-avoidance provisions and case law regimes

As mentioned above, one approach to tax avoidance schemes is to try and close loopholes in the tax system as soon as they are identified. This stops others exploiting the loophole, but does not usually apply retrospectively and so those already using the loophole will be able to continue using it. One problem with this approach is that closing loopholes means passing more legislations, thus making the tax system more and more complex; it may also create other (unintended) loopholes which can be exploited. Tax authorities therefore use other administrative methods of minimising both tax avoidance and tax evasion. The methods used can be summarised into four categories:

 (i) reducing opportunity;
 (ii) increasing the perceived risk;
(iii) reducing the overall gain;
(iv) changing social attitudes towards evasion and avoidance.

 (i) Reducing opportunity by:
   - deducting tax at source whenever possible, for example, interest payments and wages and salaries; if not possible, use third party reporting;
   - simplifying the tax structure to minimise opportunities for evasion and false returns. For example, minimising the number of reliefs, allowances, rebates and exemptions within the tax system will reduce the number of false deductions.
 (ii) Increasing the perceived risk by:
   - setting up an efficient system of auditing tax returns and payments to maximise revenue from given resources. This should be well publicised so that it increases the perceived risk of being found out;
   - developing good communications with other tax administrations.
(iii) Reducing the overall gain by:
   - carrying out regular reviews of the penalty structure, with appropriate publicity for increased penalties.
(iv) Changing social attitudes towards evasion and avoidance by:
   - encouraging, developing and maintaining an honest and customer-friendly tax administration;

- creating a tax system which is perceived as equitable to all parties;
- governments trying to encourage an increasing commitment of the population to obey the law.

The overall objective for tax authorities is to reduce the tax gap (see Section 1.4.9).

In countries using a system of common law, case law developed in the courts is important. Over time the cases decided by the courts will interpret and develop the tax legislation. Case law can evolve over time with decisions gradually developing and to some extent even reflecting changing social attitudes. For example, in the UK, anti-avoidance cases have been brought to the courts regularly over the years with the revenue authorities challenging avoidance schemes. The results of the court cases can then be relied upon in future court cases, although they may then be further refined by the court. In this way the case law is developed over time. The UK courts also look at the substance of the transaction instead of the legal form. For example, a UK court case (Ramsey Ltd v IRC) found that in a tax avoidance scheme, although each transaction was perfectly legal, they were in total self-cancelling; their only effect was to reduce tax and therefore should be disregarded for tax purposes. Another tax avoidance case (Furniss v Dawson) found that steps inserted in a series of transactions that had no commercial purpose other than to avoid tax, should be disregarded. A later tax avoidance case (Craven v White) limited this by finding that the series of transactions had to be set up with an intended result that was known at the time the transactions started.

 You do not need to remember any case names for your examination, these cases are here to illustrate the principle of case law, you only need to understand the principle.

4.6 Forum on tax administration

In January 2004, the OECD launched its new Forum on Tax Administration. The Forum is an initiative to promote the dialogue on strategic tax administration issues and to facilitate the exchange of best practices between tax authorities in different countries.

4.7 International tax dialogue

To better discharge their institutions' mandates, the staffs of the IMF, OECD and World Bank proposed to facilitate increased cooperation on tax matters among governments and international organisations through the establishment of a dialogue to share good practices and pursue common objectives in improving the functioning of national tax systems. The International Tax Dialogue (ITD) aims to facilitate such a process. The ITD will not however, at any stage have any power to make, enforce or mediate binding tax rules. The objectives of the ITD are:

- Promote effective international dialogue between governments on taxation, giving all countries a real input into the discussion of tax administration and policy issues;
- Identify and share good practices in taxation;
- Provide a clearer focus for technical assistance; and
- Avoid duplication of effort in respect of existing activities.

More information on the ITD can be found at http://www.itdweb.org

4.8 Summary

This chapter has reviewed some of the administrative aspects of taxation. We have looked at the need for records and their retention; the need for deadlines and the general powers that a tax authority would be expected to have. We have also considered the differences between tax avoidance and tax evasion.

Revision Questions

4

? Question 1

Which of the following taxes is an entity unlikely to need to keep additional detailed records for:

(A) Corporate income tax
(B) VAT
(C) Employee tax deducted from salaries
(D) Property tax   (2 marks)

? Question 2

In no more than 30 words, define the meaning of 'tax avoidance'.   (2 marks)

? Question 3

List four possible powers that a tax authority may have to help them enforce tax regulations.
(4 marks)

? Question 4

Which ONE of the following powers is a tax authority least likely to have granted to them?

(A) Power of arrest
(B) Power to examine records
(C) Power of entry and search
(D) Power to give information to other countries' tax authorities   (2 marks)

Question 5

Requirements

(i) Explain the difference between tax avoidance and tax evasion. **(2 marks)**

(ii) Briefly explain the methods that governments can use to reduce tax avoidance and tax evasion. **(3 marks)**

(Total marks = 5)

Question 6

List THREE possible reasons why governments set deadlines for filing returns and/or paying taxes **(3 marks)**

Solutions to Revision Questions

4

 Solution 1

The correct answer is (D), see Section 4.2.

 Solution 2

Tax avoidance is tax planning to the extent that the affairs of the entity are legally arranged in such a way as to minimise the corporate income tax liability.

　See Section 4.5.2.

 Solution 3

Any four of the following:

1. power to review and query filed returns;
2. power to request special reports or returns;
3. power to examine records (generally extending back some years);
4. powers of entry and search;
5. power to exchange of information with tax authorities in other jurisdictions.

See Section 4.4.

 Solution 4

The correct answer is (A), see Section 4.4.

 Solution 5

(i) **Tax avoidance** – Tax planning to the extent that the affairs of an entity are legally arranged in such a way as to minimise the tax liability. Although tax avoidance is strictly legal and within the letter of the law, it is usually contrary to the spirit of the law. Many tax avoidance schemes exploit loopholes in the legislation.

Tax evasion – The illegal manipulation of the tax system so as to avoid paying taxes. Tax evasion is the intentional disregard of the legislation in order to escape paying taxes; it can include falsifying tax returns and claiming fictitious expenses.

See Sections 4.5.1 and 4.5.2.

ADMINISTRATION OF TAXATION

(ii) A traditional response by governments is often to close loopholes by passing more legislations, but this can create additional opportunities for avoidance. More effective methods are:

Reducing opportunity by:

- deducting tax at source whenever possible;
- simplifying the tax structure to minimise opportunities for evasion and false returns.

Increasing the perceived risk by:

- setting up an efficient system of auditing tax returns and payments to maximize revenue from given resources;
- publicising a system of auditing so that it increases the perceived risk of being found out;
- developing good communications with other tax administrations.

Reducing the overall gain by:

- carrying out regular reviews of the penalty structure, with appropriate publicity for increased penalties.

Changing social attitudes towards evasion and avoidance by:

- encouraging, developing and maintaining an honest and customer-friendly tax administration;
- creating a tax system which is perceived as equitable to all parties;
- trying to encourage an increasing commitment of the population to obey the law.

See Section 4.5.3.

 Solution 6

Any three from the following:

1. So that entities know when payment is required;
2. It enables the tax authorities to forecast their cash flows more accurately;
3. Provides a reference point for late payment. It would otherwise be difficult to enforce any penalties for entities not paying;
4. To prevent entities spending tax money deducted from employees. If tax is deducted from employees at source and not paid to the tax authorities fairly quickly, there is more chance of an entity spending the amount deducted, instead of paying it to the tax authorities.

Note: Any other reasonable point would have been acceptable in the examination.

5

International
Taxation

International Taxation

5

LEARNING OUTCOME

After completing this chapter you should be able to:

▶ identify situations in which foreign tax obligations (reporting and liability) could arise and methods for relieving foreign tax.

The syllabus topics covered in this chapter are as follows:

- International taxation:
  - the concept of corporate residence and the variation in rules for its determination across jurisdictions (e.g. place of incorporation versus place of management);
  - types of payments on which withholding tax may be required (especially interest, dividends, royalties and capital gains accruing to non-residents);
  - means of establishing a taxable presence in another country (local entity and branch);
  - the effect of double tax treaties (based on the OECD Model Convention) on the above (e.g. reduction of withholding tax rates, provisions for defining a permanent establishment);
  - principles of relief for foreign taxes by exemption, deduction and credit.

5.1 Introduction

This chapter considers aspects of international taxation. We start with a consideration of the term residence; we then consider withholding taxes and different ways of an entity establishing a taxable presence. The chapter concludes with a discussion of double taxation treaties and the methods used to relieve foreign tax.

5.2 The Organisation for Economic Co-operation and Development (OECD) – Model tax convention

The OECD's taxation work covers a broad range of activities, including tax evasion, harmful tax practices, electronic commerce and environmental taxes. In relation to international taxation, the OECD has published a Model tax convention which is a model tax treaty that can be used by countries when drafting their double tax treaties. We will refer to the OECD model tax convention throughout this chapter.

5.3 The concept of corporate residence

Corporate income tax is usually a residence-based tax, whether corporate income tax will be charged depends on the residence, for tax purposes, of any particular entity.

The test for establishing residence of an entity varies from one country to another, the main types of test are discussed below.

5.3.1 Place of control and central management of an entity

Using this basis, the country from where control of the group is exercised is deemed to be the country of residence for tax purposes. The place where directors' meetings are held is usually an important criterion when examining the exercise of control.

5.3.2 Place of incorporation

The second method is a simple matter of fact as it will be absolutely clear which country an entity has been incorporated in. If a country uses the place of incorporation as a basis, any entity registered in that country will be deemed to be resident in that country for tax purposes, no matter where control is exercised.

5.3.3 Place of control and place of incorporation

Some countries, for example the UK, use both bases to establish whether an entity has residence for tax purposes. In these countries, an entity will be regarded as resident if it meets either of the above criteria. For example, an entity is regarded as resident in the UK:

- if it was incorporated in the UK; or
- if it was incorporated outside the UK, but control and central management is exercised within the UK.

This can lead to problems of double residence for taxation purposes. For instance, if an entity is registered in one country and its place of control and central management is in another country, it could be regarded as resident in both countries, if the first country bases their residence requirement on place of incorporation and the second country uses place of management. The OECD model tax convention sets out a basis for resolving this problem.

5.4 The OECD Articles of the model convention with respect to taxes on income and on capital

The OECD – *Articles of the model convention with respect to taxes on income and on capital* (hereafter referred to as the OECD model) defines the meaning of residence as follows:

'any person who, under the laws of that State, is liable to tax therein by reason of his domicile, residence, place of effective management or any other criterion of a similar nature.'

The OECD model defines person to include

'an individual, a company and any other body of persons.'

Under the OECD model an entity will have residence in the country of its effective management.

The OECD model provides that its status shall be determined as follows:

(a) it shall be deemed to be a resident only of the State in which its place of effective management is situated;

(b) if the State in which its place of effective management is situated cannot be determined or if its place of effective management is in neither State, it shall be deemed to be a resident only of the State with which its economic relations are closer;

(c) if the State with which its economic relations are closer cannot be determined, it shall be deemed to be a resident of the State from the laws of which it derives its legal status.

From this it should be clear that under an OECD model based tax treaty, residence due to place of incorporation will only apply if effective management and primary economic activity do not resolve the problem. The full text of the OECD model tax convention can be found at http://www.oecd.org/dataoecd/52/34/1914467.pdf

5.5 Withholding tax

In many countries, payments made abroad are subject to a 'withholding tax'. In Chapter 1, we defined a withholding tax as 'a tax deducted from a payment at source before it is made to the recipient abroad'. As countries cannot tax individuals in foreign countries, a withholding tax ensures that the government gains at least some revenue from such payments. The type of payments normally subject to withholding tax include:

- interest,
- royalties,
- rents,
- dividends,
- capital gains.

A Country will often have different rates of withholding tax for each of the above categories. Withholding tax is also deducted from payments between entities of the same group established in different countries, thus causing difficulties for business, including time consuming formalities, cashflow losses and sometimes double taxation.

Double taxation treaties between countries aim to reduce or eliminate withholding taxes and double taxation.

5.6 Underlying tax

If an entity receives a dividend from an overseas entity in which it holds at least a minimum percentage of the voting power, relief is also sometimes given for the tax on the profits out of which the dividend was paid. This tax is referred to as the underlying tax. The underlying tax is calculated as the gross amount of dividend received by the entity as a proportion of the after-tax profits of the foreign entity times the tax paid on those profits. This is the proportion of foreign tax paid on the profits that relates to the gross amount of the dividend paid to the entity.

Example 5.A

H owns 30% of the equity shares in S, an entity resident in a foreign country. H receives a dividend of $36,000 from S, the amount received is after deduction of withholding tax of 20%. S had before-tax profits for the year of $400,000 and paid corporate income tax of $100,000. Calculate the underlying tax that H can claim for double taxation relief.

Solution

H receives $36,000 net, this represents 80% of the gross amount, therefore the gross amount is $45,000 ($36,000/0.80).

The after-tax profits of S are $400,000 − $100,000 = $300,000.

The underlying tax is then $45,000/$300,000 × $100,000 = $15,000

5.7 Means of establishing a taxable presence in another country

A key decision that entities with trading interests abroad have to make is whether to run an overseas operation as a branch of the entity, which is merely an extension of the entity's business or to incorporate (in the overseas country) a newly formed subsidiary. There are many non-tax factors that influence this decision; however, taxation can also have an impact on the decision. The main taxation considerations in the decision between the two options are considered below.

5.7.1 Subsidiary

- An overseas subsidiary, set up in an overseas country and controlled from abroad may be able to escape tax on its profits, but the holding entity would be liable to tax on dividends received.
- Losses made by the non-resident subsidiary would not be available for a group loss relief. None of the advantages of being in a group can usually be enjoyed by a non-resident entity.
- A non-resident subsidiary cannot claim tax depreciation and any assets transferred to it by the parent may cause the parent to become subject to capital gains tax on the transfer.
- There might be a major problem in establishing that such a newly formed overseas subsidiary was not resident in the country of its parent. The subsidiary would probably be a fully owned subsidiary and would almost certainly be effectively managed by the parent.

- There could be transfer pricing problems. When the parent trades with an overseas subsidiary, the opportunity might be taken to effect the transactions at a price which effectively transfers profit from the home country to the overseas destination or visa-versa, depending on relative tax rates.

5.7.2 Branch

Where a resident entity runs an overseas operation as a branch of the entity, the following taxation implications usually arise:

- Corporate income tax will be payable by the resident entity on any profits earned by the branch. There will usually be relief for any foreign tax paid on these profits.
- Any capital gains made by the branch are also subject to the resident entity's tax whereas an overseas subsidiary will not generally cause the holding entity to be taxed on its capital gains.
- Assets can be transferred to the branch without triggering a capital gain.
- Tax depreciation can usually be claimed on any qualifying assets used in the trade of the branch.
- Losses sustained by the branch are usually immediately deductible against the resident entity's income.
- The specific tax law of the resident entity's country may apply to the specific character of a variety of overseas activities, some may qualify for favourable tax treatment on investment activities.
- Any money transferred from the overseas branch to the resident entity is not normally considered to be a dividend.

5.8 Double taxation treaties

There are two different approaches to taxing entities in a country:

1. the territorial approach to taxation: each country has the right to tax income earned inside its borders;
2. the worldwide approach: a country claims the right to tax income arising outside its border if that income is received by a corporation deemed resident within the country.

The worldwide approach leads to double taxation as income will usually be taxed in the country where it is earned and again in the country where the holding entity is resident. For example, an entity resident in the UK will generally be liable to UK corporate income tax on its income from all sources worldwide. It may also be liable to overseas tax to the extent that its overseas activities fall within the tax net of other countries. Double-tax relief, as its name implies, exists to reduce the heavy tax burden so arising. In essence, its effect is to ensure that the taxpayer finally suffers tax at no more than the higher of the two, home or overseas tax rate.

Most countries applying the worldwide approach grant some form of relief from double taxation. Double tax relief is given according to the terms of double-tax agreements that a country has entered into, for example, the UK has entered into tax treaties with most countries in the world. In this section we are going to consider the principles followed in most double taxation agreements.

5.8.1 The OECD model tax convention

Cross-border investment would be seriously impeded if there was a danger that the returns on such investments were taxed twice. The OECD model and the worldwide network of tax treaties based upon it help to avoid that danger by providing clear consensual rules for taxing income and capital.

The OECD model tax treaty says that business profits of an entity of a contracting state shall be taxable only in that state unless the entity carries on a business in the other contracting state through a permanent establishment in that state. If the entity carries on business in the other state, its business profits may be taxed in the other state to the extent that they are attributable to the permanent establishment.

Provisions for defining a permanent establishment

The OECD model in Article 5 paragraphs 1–3 contains the following definition:

1. For the purposes of this Convention, the term 'permanent establishment' means a fixed place of business through which the business of an entity is wholly or partly carried on.
2. The term 'permanent establishment' includes especially:
   (a) a place of management;
   (b) a branch;
   (c) an office;
   (d) a factory;
   (e) a workshop, and
   (f) a mine, an oil or gas well, a quarry or any other place of extraction of natural resources.
3. A building site or construction or installation project constitutes a permanent establishment only if it lasts more than 12 months.

If an entity has a permanent establishment in a country, it can be taxed in that country, causing a possible problem of double taxation.

5.8.2 Principles of relief for foreign taxes

Double taxation treaties can provide for the relief of foreign taxation by one of three possible methods:

1. *Exemption*: The parties to the agreement set out the categories of income that are partially or completely exempt from tax in one country or the other.
2. *Tax credit*: The treaty may allow the tax paid in one country to be allowed as a tax credit in the other country. Tax relief is therefore provided by deducting foreign tax suffered from tax due in the country of residence. This is by far the commonest form of relief. It will be given under a double-tax agreement or, if no such agreement exists some countries, will give it unilaterally. If the foreign tax rate is higher than the country of residence rate, the tax relief will be limited to the tax due using the lower rate. Some tax in high taxation countries may not therefore be fully relieved.
3. *Deduction*: It is almost always better for the taxpayer to claim the reliefs described above so that foreign tax suffered is deducted from tax due in the country of residence. There are a few instances when it will be preferable to make a claim to deduct the foreign tax

from the foreign income and bring the net sum into charge to tax in the home country. This could be beneficial if, for example, the entity has a loss in the home country.

5.9 Summary

In this chapter, we have discussed the meaning of residence and permanent establishment. We have considered problems of double taxation and double taxation treaties as well as ways of mitigating double taxation.

Revision Questions

? Question 1

Which of the following could NOT be used to indicate an organisation is resident in a country?

(A) Place of effective management
(B) Buying or selling goods in a country
(C) Place of incorporation
(D) Close economic relations with a country   **(2 marks)**

? Question 2

In no more than 15 words, define the meaning of a 'branch'.   **(2 marks)**

? Question 3

Which of the following would NOT normally be subject to a withholding tax?

(A) Rents
(B) Dividends
(C) Interest
(D) Profits   **(2 marks)**

? Question 4

A double taxation treaty between two countries usually allows relief of foreign tax through a number of methods. Which one of the following is NOT a method of relieving foreign tax?

(A) Refund
(B) Exemption
(C) Tax credits
(D) Deduction   **(2 marks)**

? Question 5

The OECD model tax convention defines a permanent establishment to include a number of different types of establishments:

  (i) A place of management
  (ii) A warehouse
  (iii) A workshop
  (iv) A quarry
  (v) A building site that was used for 9 months

Which of the above are included in the OECD's list of permanent establishments?

  (A) (i), (ii) and (iii) only
  (B) (i), (iii) and (iv) only
  (C) (ii), (iii) and (iv) only
  (D) (iii), (iv) and (v) only   **(2 marks)**

? Question 6

CW owns 40% of the equity shares in Z, an entity resident in a foreign country.

  CW receives a dividend of $45,000 from Z, the amount received is after deduction of withholding tax of 10%. Z had before tax profits for the year of $500,000 and paid corporate income tax of $100,000.

Requirements

  (i) Explain the meaning of 'withholding tax' and 'underlying tax.'   **(2 marks)**
  (ii) Calculate the amount of withholding tax paid by CW.   **(1 mark)**
  (iii) Calculate the amount of underlying tax that relates to CW's dividend.   **(2 marks)**
                                      (Total = 5 marks)

? Question 7

The following details relate to EA:

- Incorporated in Country A.
- Carries out its main business activities in Country B.
- Its senior management operate from Country C and effective control is exercised from Country C.

  Assume countries A, B and C have all signed double tax treaties with each other, based on the OECD model tax convention.

Which country will EA be deemed to be resident in for tax purposes?

  (A) Country A
  (B) Country B
  (C) Country C
  (D) Both Countries B and C   **(2 marks)**

? Question 8

EB has an investment of 25% of the equity shares in XY, an entity resident in a foreign country.

EB receives a dividend of $90,000 from XY, the amount being after the deduction of withholding tax of 10%.

XY had profits before tax for the year of $1,200,000 and paid corporate income tax of $200,000.

How much underlying tax can EB claim for double taxation relief?   **(3 marks)**

Solutions to Revision Questions

5

 Solution 1

The correct answer is (B), see Section 5.3.

 Solution 2

A branch of the entity is merely an extension of the entity's business, see Section 5.7.

 Solution 3

The correct answer is (D), see Section 5.5.

 Solution 4

The correct answer is (A), see Section 5.8.2.

 Solution 5

The correct answer is (B), see Section 5.8.1.1.

 Solution 6

(i) Withholding tax

A withholding tax is a tax deducted from a payment at source before it is made to the recipient. Withholding tax is most frequently used when payments are being made to recipients that are not resident within the same tax jurisdiction, but can also apply to some payments made to resident individuals.

Double taxation treaties between countries aim to reduce or eliminate withholding taxes and double taxation.

Underlying tax
Underlying tax is the tax on the profits out of which a dividend is paid. If an entity receives a dividend from an overseas entity, relief is sometimes given for the tax already deducted from the profits that were used to pay the dividend. This tax is referred to as the underlying tax.

INTERNATIONAL TAXATION

(ii) CW receives $45,000 net, this represents 90% of the gross amount, as withholding tax has been deducted. The gross amount is $50,000 ($45,000/9 × 10) and withholding tax is 5,000.

(iii) After-tax profits of Z are $500,000 − $100,000 = $400,000
Underlying tax is $50,000/$400,000 × $100,000 = $12,500
See Sections 5.5 and 5.6.

 Solution 7

The correct answer is (B), see Section 5.4.

 Solution 8

	$'000
Gross dividend = 90 × 100/90 =	100
After tax profits	1,000
Underlying tax = 100/1,000 × 200 =	20

See example 5a for method.

Taxation in Financial Statements

Taxation in Financial Statements

6

LEARNING OUTCOME

After completing this chapter you should be able to:

► explain and apply the accounting rules contained in IAS 12 for current and deferred taxation.

The syllabus topics covered in this chapter are as follows:

• Accounting treatment of taxation and disclosure requirements under IAS 12.

6.1 Introduction

In this chapter we will discuss the treatment of taxation in financial statements. The taxation system will vary from country to country, so this chapter focuses on the general principles of accounting for tax as prescribed in IAS 12 *Income Taxes*.

> Questions requiring the preparation of financial statements almost always require some calculation or adjustment to tax. The calculation of current tax or deferred tax may also feature as a five-mark question or as an objective test question.

Tax in financial statements may consist of three elements:

1. current tax expense;
2. adjustments to tax charges of prior periods (results of over/underprovisions);
3. transfers to or from deferred tax.

We will discuss each of these elements in turn.

> IAS 12 refers to *Income taxes,* this means any taxes on profits and gains payable by the entity, including corporate income taxes and capital gains tax.

TAXATION IN FINANCIAL STATEMENTS

6.2 Calculation of current tax

IAS 12 includes the following definitions:

- *Current tax.* The amount of income taxes payable (recoverable) in respect of the taxable profit (loss) for a period.
- *Taxable profit (loss).* Profit (loss) for a period, determined in accordance with the local tax authorities rules, upon which income taxes are payable (recoverable).
- *Tax expense.* The total of income tax for the period plus any charge in respect of deferred tax.

As we have seen in earlier chapters, the tax system will vary from country to country. In Chapter 2, we considered types of income and systems of corporate income tax. We also looked at different methods of calculating taxable profits. We will now use this knowledge to move on to discuss taxation in financial statements.

There is one further aspect to consider when calculating current tax, that is, different ways of treating the tax on dividend income received by an entity. IAS 12 does not specifically mention how entities should deal with dividend income, but the general principle is acknowledged.

There are two ways of treating dividends received in the financial statements:

1. The dividend received has already suffered tax and is not usually taxed again in the hands of the receiving entity, so the dividend is ignored when calculating taxable profits. To calculate the current tax, simply apply the income tax rate to the entity's taxable profits.
2. The dividend is grossed up and the recipient of the dividend shows the gross equivalent of the dividend received as a credit in the profit or loss and includes the tax on the dividend as a part of the tax charge for the year.

 Any examination question should specify how tax is to be calculated; if it does not, use the first method.

6.3 Accounting for current tax

Once calculated the income tax payable will be recorded as an expense in the profit or loss. The tax is normally recorded and paid at a later date, the amount which remains unpaid should be shown separately under current liabilities. The income tax charge is recorded as:

Debit	Income tax expense (profit or loss)
Credit	Income tax liability (statement of financial position)

Being the recording of the income tax expense for the year.

The tax calculated for the current year is estimated by the entity for the period. However, the actual amount that is paid sometime later may be slightly different than the estimate. In this case there will be an over- or underprovision of tax for prior periods. This difference will adjust the current tax charge that is included in the tax expense for the current period.

Example 6.A

The current tax charge for 20X1 is estimated at $36,000. This amount is recorded in the profit or loss for the year ended 31 December 20X1:

Debit	Income tax expense	$36,000
Credit	Income tax liability	$36,000

Being the recording of the income tax expense for the year.

The actual amount paid on 27 March 20X2 is $35,005. The payment is recorded as:

Debit	Income tax liability	$35,005
Credit	Bank	$35,005

Being the payment of the income tax expense for 20X1.

In 20X1, a liability of $36,000 was created and the following period $35,005 was debited against it. This leaves $995 included within the liability account.

This overprovision of income taxes will adjust the income tax expense that is recorded in the 20X2 profit or loss. Let us assume the tax charge for 20X2 is estimated at $40,000. The liability that must be included in the financial statements is $40,000 because that is what we are expecting to pay in early 20X3. However, there is already a liability amount existing of $995 and so the liability only requires to be increased by a further $39,005.

The current tax charge (including the expense for 20X2 and the adjustment for 20X1) can be recorded as one entry:

Debit	Income tax expense	$39,005
Credit	Income tax liability	$39,005

Being the recording of the income tax expense for 20X2.

Or as two entries:

Debit	Income tax expense	$40,000
Credit	Income tax liability	$40,000

Being the recording of the income tax expense for 20X2.

Debit	Income tax liability	$995
Credit	Income tax expense	$995

Being the reversal of the overprovision from 20X1.

6.4 Calculation of deferred tax

6.4.1 Introduction to deferred tax

Deferred taxation arises from differences between profit calculated for accounting purposes and profit for tax purposes. Differences may arise from temporary or permanent factors.

Permanent difference

Where an expense charged in the statement of comprehensive income is not allowed for income tax purposes, a permanent difference occurs. This difference will not reverse in future periods and need only be accounted for in the tax computation. In the case of a disallowable expense, the amount of the expense will be added back to profits in arriving at taxable profits within the computation (see disallowed expenses in Section 2.2).

Temporary difference

A temporary difference arises when an expense is allowed for both accounting and tax purposes, but there is a difference in the timing of the allowance. Consider the tax relief given for capital expenditure. In many countries, relief for tax purposes is given at a faster rate than most entities chose for accounting for depreciation in the financial statements. In Section 2.2.3.1, we looked at the need for tax depreciation to be used instead of accounting depreciation. The effect of using tax depreciation may be that in the first year the tax depreciation exceeds the accounting depreciation, giving a lower tax charge, since accounting depreciation is added back to accounting profit and tax depreciation is then deducted in arriving at taxable profits for taxation purposes. In subsequent periods, tax depreciation is likely to fall below the accounting depreciation charge and result in future increased taxes payable. It is the likelihood of a future tax liability that drives the need for some provision for this tax that is being deferred to future periods.

Example 6.B

An item of plant and machinery is purchased by U in 20X0 for $300,000. The asset's estimated useful life is 6 years, following which it will have no residual value. Plant and machinery is depreciated on a straight-line basis.
Tax depreciation for this item is given at 25% on the straight-line basis for the first 4 years.
Let us first calculate the figures that would appear in the *financial statements* over the six-year life of the asset:

	20X0 $'000	20X1 $'000	20X2 $'000	20X3 $'000	20X4 $'000	20X5 $'000
Financial statements						
Opening carrying value	300	250	200	150	100	50
Accounting depreciation charge	50	50	50	50	50	50
Carrying value (end of the reporting period)	250	200	150	100	50	0

Depreciation is charged at $50,000 per annum ($300,000/6 years).
Now let us look at how this asset would be treated for *tax purposes*:

	20X0 $'000	20X1 $'000	20X02 $'000	20X3 $'000	20X4 $'000	20X5 $'000
Tax computation						
Carrying value	300	225	150	75	0	0
Tax depreciation	75	75	75	75	0	0
(Tax written down value)	225	150	75	0	0	0

We can see from comparing the above two tables that the carrying value of the asset per accounts differs from the Tax written down value. The annual reduction in the carrying value applied by the entity (that is accounting depreciation) differs from the reduction applied in the tax computation. By the end of the asset's useful life, the two have caught up, as they both show the asset with a carrying value of 0, but the different treatment over 6 years creates the accounting problem that is known as deferred tax.

There are generally two ways to look at the need for deferred tax:

1. the timing difference approach;
2. the temporary difference approach.

6.4.2 Timing difference approach

The timing difference approach focuses on the impact to the statement of comprehensive income by calculating the amount of tax payable on income accounted for to date. Using the data from Example 6.B, we can see that tax depreciation is given in advance of accounting depreciation being charged. In arriving at taxable profit, we add back accounting depreciation and deduct tax depreciation. Let us look at the impact this has on the profit or loss.

Example 6.C

Assume that accounting profit for each of the years is $400,000 and the tax rate is 30%. We would expect to pay $120,000 in tax in each year. However, we have invested in plant and machinery and have been granted tax depreciation in respect of this item, so the calculation of taxable profits for 20X0 is as follows:

	20X0 $'000
Tax computation	
Accounting profit	400
Add back accounting depreciation charge	50
	450
Less tax depreciation	(75)
Taxable profits	375
Tax at 30%	112.5

We pay $112,500 in tax as opposed to $120,000 because we have capital investment which has earned tax depreciation in the early years. The situation reverses in future years; however, when tax depreciation falls to $0 and accounting depreciation is still being charged to the profit or loss.

Profits of $400,000 in 20X4 and a tax rate of 30%, would result in tax to pay of $120,000. However, the taxable profits would be calculated as:

	20X4 $'000
Tax computation	
Accounting profit	400
Add back accounting depreciation charge	50
Taxable profits	450
Tax at 30%	135

The tax payable has increased from $120,000 to $135,000 due to the add back of accounting depreciation.

The accounting treatment prudently requires that in the early years when tax depreciation exceeds accounting depreciation and the taxable profits are reduced, we provide for the future increased taxable profits by creating a provision for deferred tax and releasing this provision to cover the increased tax charge when tax depreciation falls below the accounting depreciation charge.

6.4.3 Temporary difference approach

The second approach to deferred tax focuses on the statement of financial position impact of the differences and calculates the tax that would have been paid if the net assets of the entity were realised at book value at the end of the reporting period. A temporary difference is the difference between the carrying amount of an asset or liability in the statement of financial position and its tax base (its value for tax purposes).

It is this approach that is adopted by IAS 12 for the recognition and measurement of deferred tax assets and liabilities and therefore we will concentrate on this approach for the remainder of the chapter.

Example 6.D

Let us use the information from Example 6.B:

An item of plant and machinery is purchased by U in 20X0 for $300,000. The asset's estimated useful life is 6 years, following which it will have no residual value. Plant and machinery is depreciated on a straight-line basis. Tax depreciation for this item is given at 25% on a straight-line basis for the first 4 years.

The figures for accounting and for taxation purposes would be as follows (from Example 6B):

	20X0 $'000	20X1 $'000	20X2 $'000	20X3 $'000	20X4 $'000	20X5 $'000
Financial statements						
Opening carrying value	300	250	200	150	100	50
Accounting depreciation charge	50	50	50	50	50	50
Carrying value (end of the reporting period)	250	200	150	100	50	0
Tax computation						
Carrying value	300	225	150	75	0	0
Tax depreciation	75	75	75	75	0	0
Tax written down value	225	150	75	0	0	0
Taxable temporary differences						
Carrying value (per accounts)	250	200	150	100	50	0
Tax written down value	225	150	75	0	0	0
Temporary difference	25	50	75	100	50	0

The provision for deferred tax under the temporary difference method is based on what tax would become payable if the assets were realised at book value at the end of the reporting period. We compare the carrying value of the item per accounts with the tax base, which is the value of the item for tax purposes (which in the case of fixed assets is usually the tax written down value).

Example 6.E

Using data in Example 6.D to illustrate the deferred tax impact.

The asset purchased above by U is sold at the end of 20X2 for $180,000 when the carrying value of the asset is $150,000 and the tax written down value is $75,000. The taxable profit and resulting tax charge are calculated as follows:

Accounting profit	$'000	Tax computation	$'000
Proceeds	180	Proceeds	180
Carrying value 20X2	150	Tax written down value 20X2	75
Accounting profit	30	Profit per tax computation	105
Tax on profit at 30%	9	Tax on profit at 30%	31.5

Based on the accounting records, we would expect to earn $30,000 profit on sale of the asset. However, due to accelerated tax depreciation, the tax written down value is considerably lower than the book value and so the gain on sale that would be recognised for tax purposes is $31,500. The additional $22,500 ($31,500 − $9,000) tax that would be payable if the asset was sold, must be provided for under the temporary differences method.

The table below shows the movement on the deferred tax liability account in the statement of financial position and the charge/(release) to the profit or loss in each of the 6 years of the asset's useful life.

	20X0 $'000	20X1 $'000	20X2 $'000	20X3 $'000	20X4 $'000	20X5 $'000
Temporary differences						
Carrying value (per accounts)	250	200	150	100	50	0
Tax written down value	225	150	75	0	0	0
Temporary difference	25	50	75	100	50	0
Deferred tax provision required (at a rate of 30%)	7.5	15	22.5	30	15	0

The provision for deferred tax increases in the first 4 years of the asset's life. This is the period that tax depreciation is applied which causes differences between the statement of financial position carrying value and the tax written down value. This taxable temporary difference then reduces in the last 2 years as the book value reduces to the asset's residual value of nil.

The deferred tax provision required is calculated at the tax rate (in this case 30%). This provision represents the additional tax the entity would pay on the gain if the asset was sold any time within its useful life, based on the tax written down value as opposed to the asset's book value.

Tax base

IAS 12 states that a temporary difference is the difference between the carrying value of an asset or liability and its tax base. The tax base is the amount attributed to that asset or liability for tax purposes. Consider the four scenarios below:

1. *Non-current assets.* The detailed illustration above dealt with a tax-deductible non-current asset. Its tax base was the tax written down value at the end of the reporting period. This is normally the case for non-current assets.
2. *Revalued non-current assets.* The temporary difference is defined as the difference between the carrying value of an asset and its tax base. As the tax base will remain the same, an upwards revaluation of a non-current asset will result in an increase in the deferred taxation provision.
3. *Accrued interest.* An entity has recorded accrued interest receivable of $5,000 in its accounts to 31 December 20X1. The interest receivable will only be taxed, however, when it is received. At 31 December 20X1, the asset has a tax base of nil and a carrying value (the value included in receivables in the statement of financial position) of $5,000. At 31 December 20X1, a temporary difference of $5,000 occurs. A deferred tax provision is required in respect of this difference of $1,500 ($5,000 at a rate of 30%).
4. *Pension costs.* In the year ended 30 June 20X3, an entity made provision for unfunded pension costs of $400,000. Tax relief on this item will be given when the retirement benefits are actually paid. The carrying value of the liability is $400,000 at 30 June 20X3; however, the tax base of the liability at that date is nil. It has no amount attributed to it for tax purposes until the liability is settled (when the benefits are actually paid). This creates a deductible temporary difference at 30 June 20X3 and a deferred tax asset must be recognised in the accounts. Assuming a rate of 30%, the deferred tax asset of $120,000 would be included in the statement of financial position.

6.4.4 Deferred tax assets

Deferred tax assets arising from deductible temporary differences should be recognised in the financial statements provided that it is probable that future taxable profits will be available for this asset to be utilised.

A deferred tax asset can arise from the following:

- deductible temporary difference,
- unused tax losses,
- unused tax credits.

A *deductible* temporary difference is a temporary difference that will result in a deduction from future taxable profits when sold or realised, for example, the pension costs referred to above that will be given tax relief when the benefits are paid. (This is in contrast to the *taxable* temporary difference that was created by the tax depreciation given on the purchase of the fixed asset – which if sold would create an additional tax charge on the increased gain on sale.)

6.4.5 Tax losses

Some tax authorities may permit the tax effect of losses to be carried forward and offset against future taxable profits. IAS 12 requires that these unused tax credits be recognised as assets, where it is probable that the entity will make future profits against which these losses can be offset.

Example 6.F

In 20X1, Delta made losses of $20,000. The associated tax credit on the losses (assuming a rate of 30%) is $6,000. This will be recorded in 20X1 as:

Dr	Income tax deferred asset (statement of financial position)	$6,000
Cr	Tax credit (statement of comprehensive income)	$6,000

Being the recording of the income tax credit for 20X1.

In 20X2, Delta made profits of $24,000. The tax charge for 20X2 is calculated as 30% × $24,000 = $7,200. Delta can offset the tax on the 20X1 losses against the tax on the 20X2 profits. This will be recorded as:

Dr	Income tax expense	$7,200
Cr	Income tax deferred credit	$6,000
Cr	Income tax liability	$1,200

Being the recording of the income tax expense for 20X2.

In summary, the calculation of deferred tax assets and liabilities is as follows:

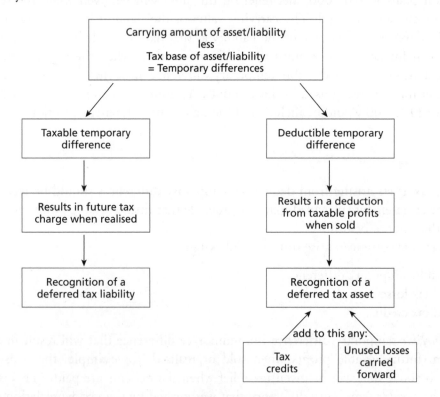

6.5 Accounting for deferred tax

Once the deferred tax position has been calculated, the accounting treatment is relatively straight forward. In the case of a deferred tax liability, the provision is created or increased by:

Dr	Income tax charge (statement of comprehensive income)
Cr	Deferred tax provision (statement of financial position)

Any reduction or release of the provision is recorded as:

| Dr | Deferred tax provision (statement of financial position) |
| Cr | Income tax charge (statement of comprehensive income) |

Consider the deferred tax position created in Example 6.D where temporary differences result from accelerated tax depreciation for the purchase of plant and machinery:

	20X0 $'000	20X1 $'000	20X2 $'000	20X3 $'000	20X4 $'000	20X5 $'000
Temporary difference						
Carrying value (per accounts)	250	200	150	100	50	0
Tax written down value	225	150	75	0	0	0
Temporary difference	25	50	75	100	50	0
Deferred tax provision required (at a rate of 30%)	7.5	15	22.5	30	15	0
Charge (credit) to profit or loss in respect of changes in the deferred tax provision	7.5	7.5	7.5	7.5	(15)	(15)

The deferred tax provision required in 20X0 is $7,500. This will be recorded as:

Dr	Income tax charge (profit or loss)	$7,500
Cr	Deferred tax provision (statement of financial position)	$7,500
	Being the deferred tax provision in respect of plant and machinery.	

From 20X1 to 20X3, the provision requires to be increased by $7,500 in each of these years and so the journal above will occur in 20X1, 20X2 and 20X3.

In 20X4, the required provision at 31 December is $15,000; however, the existing liability in the statement of financial position is $30,000. The reduction of the provision from $30,000 to $15,000 creates a release to the statement of comprehensive income of $15,000. It will be recorded as:

| Dr | Deferred tax provision (statement of financial position) | $15,000 |
| Cr | Income tax charge (statement of comprehensive income) | $15,000 |

The same journal entry will be required in 20X5 as the provision is reduced from $15,000 to nil.

6.6 Income tax charge

The income tax charge that appears in the profit or loss will include the following:

- the tax charge for the year (estimated based on profits);
- any under/overprovision of income tax from previous year;
- any increase in/release from the provision for deferred tax.

The 'other comprehensive income' section will include the tax implications of other comprehensive income items. The statement of financial position will include a current liability for income tax that will be paid in the following period. The liability will be for the estimated amount. When the tax is actually paid, this will lead to an over/underprovision of income tax, discussed earlier at Section 6.3.

The statement of financial position will also include any deferred tax liabilities or assets.

6.7 Disclosure

IAS 12 disclosure requirements include the following:

- the major components of tax expense should be disclosed separately (for example, current tax expense, adjustments for overprovision, amount for deferred tax expense or release, etc);
- tax expense relating to extraordinary items;
- tax expense relating to discontinuing operations;
- an explanation of the difference between accounting and taxable profits;
- details of temporary differences and the amount of deferred tax assets and liabilities that have been recognised in the financial statements as a result of those differences.

6.8 Summary

Having completed this chapter, we can now account for current tax, including adjustments for over/underprovisions.

We can explain the need for deferred tax, calculate the required provision or asset and account for it in financial statements. We can also explain the main disclosure requirements of IAS 12 in respect of current and deferred tax.

Revision Questions

? Question 1

The corporate income tax estimate for the current year is $420,000. The settlement of corporate income tax due for last year resulted in a credit balance of $10,000 outstanding on the income tax account. Deferred tax was estimated to require an increase of $18,000 in the statement of financial position provision. The corporate income tax charge for the year in the profit or loss and the current liability due in less than 1 year, corporate income tax on the statement of financial position should be:

	profit or loss	statement of financial position
(A)	$448,000	$430,000
(B)	$412,000	$410,000
(C)	$428,000	$420,000
(D)	$392,000	$420,000

(3 marks)

? Question 2

Timing differences arise because of:

(A) the timing of the entity's tax payments
(B) the time of year when a transaction occurs
(C) expenses are charged to the profit or loss in one period and to taxable profits in another period
(D) some items of expenditure are disallowed for tax purposes   **(2 marks)**

? Question 3

An asset cost $200,000 and had an estimated useful life of 10 years, with no residual value. Accounting depreciation was calculated on the straight-linebasis. Capital allowances were given at 25% on a reducing balance basis. Assume corporate income tax at 30%. At the end of the second year of operation, the deferred tax provision on the statement of financial position should be:

(A) $9,000
(B) $14,250

(C) $18,000

(D) $47,500 **(2 marks)**

? Question 4

List the three elements included in the heading 'Income tax expenses' in profit or loss.

(3 marks)

? Question 5

In no more than 30 words, define the meaning of 'permanent difference'. **(2 marks)**

? Question 6

WS prepares its financial statements to 30 June. The following profits were recorded from 20X1 to 20X3:

20X1	$100,000
20X2	$120,000
20X3	$110,000

The entity provides for tax at a rate of 30% and incorporates this figure in the year-end accounts. The actual amounts of tax paid in respect of 20X1 and 20X2 were $28,900 and $37,200.

Requirements

(a) Calculate the tax charge for each of the 3 years and prepare the accounting entries to record the tax charge and the subsequent payments of tax.

(b) Prepare extracts from the profit or loss and statement of financial position of WS for each of the 3 years, showing the tax charge and tax liability. **(5 marks)**

? Question 7

On 1 January 20X2, C had a credit balance brought forward on its deferred tax account of $1.5m. There was also an opening credit balance of $4,000 on its income taxation account, representing the remaining balance after settling the liability for the year ended 31 December 20X1. The entity has made profits in 20X2 of $3m that are subject to a tax rate of 30%. The deferred tax provision required is estimated at $1.7m at 31 December 20X2.

Requirements

(a) Calculate the income tax charge that will appear in the profit or loss for 20X2 and prepare the accounting entries to record the current income tax charge and any movement on the deferred tax account.

(b) Prepare the extracts from the statement of financial position for the year ended 31 December 20X2 in respect of income tax and deferred tax. **(5 marks)**

Question 8

S purchases an item of plant and machinery costing $400,000 in 20X0 which qualifies for 50% capital allowances in the first 2 years. S's policy in respect of plant and machinery is to charge depreciation on a straight-line basis over 4 years.

Requirement

Assuming there are no other capital transactions in the period and a tax rate of 30% over the 4 years, calculate the profit or loss and statement of financial position impact of deferred tax from 20X0 to 20X3.   **(4 marks)**

Question 9

HW buys an asset in 20X1 costing $80,000 that qualifies for an immediate 100% tax relief on cost. HW plans to depreciate the asset on a straight-line basis over 4 years. HW has accrued $30,000 for tax due for the year ended 31 December 20X1.

In 20X2, HW makes $120,000 profit that is subject to tax at 30%. During the year, $28,600 is paid in respect of tax on profits of 20X1. There were no additions to non-current assets in the year.

Requirements

Calculate the tax charge for 20X2 and any movement in deferred tax for the year.

Draft the extracts from the profit or loss and statement of financial position in respect of income tax and deferred tax.   **(5 marks)**

Question 10

RS has two accounting adjustments in 20X2 that create temporary differences for deferred tax purposes:

(i) At the year-end, $40,000 of accrued interest receivable has been included in the accounts. It is expected to be received in Spring 20X3 and it will be taxed only on receipt.

(ii) A provision of $80,000 has been made for unfunded pension costs. Tax relief on this will be given only when the retirement benefits are actually paid.

Requirement

Calculate the deferred tax impact of these adjustments for the year-end accounts of RS, assuming an effective tax rate of 30%.   **(3 marks)**

Question 11

AC made the following payments during the year ended 30 April 2005:

	$'000
Operating costs (excluding depreciation)	23
Finance costs	4
Capital repayment of loans	10
Payments for the purchase of new computer equipment for use in AC's business	20

AC's revenue for the period was $45,000 and the corporate income tax rate applicable to AC's profits was 25%. The computer equipment qualifies for tax allowances of 10% per year on a straight-line basis.

Calculate AC's tax payable for the year ended 30 April 2005. **(3 marks)**

Question 12

AB acquired non-current assets on 1 April 2003 costing $250,000. The assets qualified for accelerated first year tax allowance at the rate of 50% for the first year. The second and subsequent years were at a tax depreciation rate of 25% per year on the reducing balance method.

AB depreciates all non-current assets at 20% a year on a straight-line basis.

The rate of corporate income tax applying to AB for 2003/04 and 2004/05 was 30%. Assume AB has no other qualifying non-current assets.

Requirements

Apply IAS 12 *Income Taxes* and calculate:

(a) the deferred tax balance required at 31 March 2004;
(b) the deferred tax balance required at 31 March 2005;
(c) the charge to the profit or loss for the year ended 31 March 2005. **(5 marks)**

Question 13

BC, a small entity, purchased its only non-current tangible asset on 1 October 2003. The asset cost $900,000, all of which qualified for tax depreciation.

BC's asset qualified for an accelerated first year tax allowance of 50%. The second and subsequent years qualified for tax depreciation at 25% per year on the reducing balance method.

BC's accounting depreciation policy is to depreciate the asset over its useful economic life of 5 years, assuming a residual value of $50,000.

Assume that BC pays tax on its income at the rate of 30%.

Calculate BC's deferred tax balance required in the statement of financial position as at 30 September 2005 according to IAS 12 *Income taxes*. **(4 marks)**

Question 14

Country B has a corporate income tax system that treats capital gains/losses separately from trading profits/losses. Capital gains/losses cannot be offset against trading profits/losses. All losses can be carried forward indefinitely, but cannot be carried back to previous years. Trading profits and capital gains are both taxed at 20%.

BD had no brought forward losses on 1 October 2002. BD's results for 2003 to 2005 were as follows:

	Trading profit/(loss)	Capital gains/(loss)
	$'000	$'000
Year to September 2003	200	(100)
Year to September 2004	(120)	0
Year to September 2005	150	130

Calculate BD's corporate income tax due for each of the years ended 30 September 2003 to 2005. **(3 marks)**

? Question 15

CY had the following amounts for 2003 to 2005

Year ended 31 December:	2003	2004	2005
	$	$	$
Accounting depreciation for the year	1,630	1,590	1,530
Tax depreciation allowance for the year	2,120	1,860	1,320

At 31 December 2002, CY had the following balances brought forward:

	$
Cost of property, plant and equipment qualifying for tax depreciation	20,000
Accounting depreciation	5,000
Tax depreciation	12,500

CY had no non-current asset acquisitions or disposals during the period 2003 to 2005. Assume the corporate income tax rate is 25% for all years.

Calculate the deferred tax provision required by IAS 12 *Income Taxes* at 31 December 2005. **(3 marks)**

? Question 16

On 31 March 2006, CH had a credit balance brought forward on its deferred tax account of $642,000. There was also a credit balance on its corporate income tax account of $31,000, representing an over-estimate of the tax charge for the year ended 31 March 2005.

CH's taxable profit for the year ended 31 March 2006 was $946,000. CH's directors estimated the deferred tax provision required at 31 March 2006 to be $759,000 and the applicable income tax rate for the year to 31 March 2006 as 22%.

Calculate the income tax expense that CH will charge in its profit or loss for the year ended 31 March 2006, as required by IAS 12 *Income Taxes*. **(3 marks)**

? Question 17

DD purchased an item of plant and machinery costing $500,000 on 1 April 2004, which qualified for 50% capital allowances in the first year, and 20% each year thereafter, on the reducing balance basis.

DD's policy in respect of plant and machinery is to charge depreciation on a straight line basis over five years, with no residual value. On 1 April 2006, DD decides to revalue the item of plant and machinery upwards, from its net book value, by $120,000.

Assuming there are no other capital transactions in the three year period and a tax rate of 30% throughout, calculate the amount of deferred tax to be shown in DD's profit or loss for the year ended 31 March 2007, and the deferred tax provision to be included in its statement of financial position at 31 March 2007. **(4 marks)**

? Question 18

EE reported accounting profits of $822,000 for the period ended 30 November 2007. This was after deducting entertaining expenses of $32,000 and a donation to a political party of $50,000, both of which are disallowable for tax purposes.

EE's reported profit also included $103,000 government grant income that was exempt from taxation. EE paid dividends of $240,000 in the period.

Assume EE had no temporary differences between accounting profits and taxable profits.

Assume that a classical tax system applies to EE's profits and that the tax rate is 25%.

What would EE's tax payable be on its profits for the year to 30 November 2007?

(2 marks)

Question 19

A government wanted to encourage investment in new non-current assets by entities and decided to change tax allowances for non-current assets to give a 100% first year allowance on all new non-current assets purchased after 1 January 2005.

ED purchased new machinery for $400,000 on 1 October 2005 and claimed the 100% first year allowance. For accounting purposes ED depreciated the machinery on the reducing balance basis at 25% per year. The rate of corporate income tax to be applied to ED's taxable profits was 22%.

Assume ED had no other temporary differences.

Calculate the amount of deferred tax that ED would show in its statement of financial position at 30 September 2007.

(3 marks)

Question 20

Country Z has the following tax regulations in force for the years 2005 and 2006 (each year January to December):

- Corporate income is taxed at the following rates:
  - $1 to $10,000 at 0%;
  - $10,001 to $25,000 at 15%;
  - $25,001 and over at 25%.
- When calculating corporate income tax, Country Z does **not** allow the following types of expenses to be charged against taxable income:
  - Entertaining expenses;
  - Taxes paid to other public bodies;
  - Accounting depreciation of non-current assets.
- Tax relief on capital expenditure is available at the following rates:
  - Buildings at 4% per annum on straight line basis;
  - All other non-current tangible assets are allowed tax depreciation at 27% per annum on reducing balance basis.

DB commenced business on 1 January 2005 when all assets were purchased. No first year allowances were available for 2005.

Non-current assets cost at 1 January 2005

	$
Land	27,000
Buildings	70,000
Plant and equipment	80,000

On 1 January 2006, DB purchased another machine for $20,000. This machine qualified for a first year tax allowance of 50%.

DB's Income statement for the year to 31 December 2006

	$
Gross profit	160,000
Administrative expenses	81,000
Entertaining	600
Tax paid to local government	950
Depreciation on buildings	1,600
Depreciation on plant and equipment	20,000
Distribution costs	20,000
	35,850
Finance cost	1,900
Profit before tax	33,950

Requirement

Calculate DB's corporate income tax due for the year 2006.   **(5 marks)**

Solutions to Revision Questions

Solution 1

The correct answer is (C), see Section 6.3.

The credit balance on the corporate income tax account means that there was an over-provision last year. The overprovision of $10,000 can be deducted from the current year's estimate. The increase in deferred tax needs to be included under the tax charge for the year. The profit or loss would show the income tax expense as $428,000, the note to the profit or loss would show the $428,000 made up as follows:

	$
Estimate of current year's corporation tax charge	420,000
Over-provision previous year	(10,000)
Increase in deferred tax provision	18,000
	428,000

The statement of financial position current liability for corporation tax would be the estimate for the current years tax charge, $420,000.

Solution 2

The correct answer is (C), see Section 6.4.

Expenses are charged to the profit or loss in one period and to taxable profits in another period, giving rise to temporary timing differences. Income may also be credited to profit and loss in one period and be taxable in another period.

Solution 3

The correct answer is (B) see Section 6.4.3.

	$
Cost	200,000
Two years' accounting depreciation at 10% per year is	40,000
Carrying value in accounts	160,000
Cost	200,000
Two years' tax depreciation at 25% is	87,500
Tax written down value	112,500
Temporary difference (160,000 − 112,500)	47,500
Tax at 30%	14,250

Solution 4

The three elements that make up income tax expense (see Section 6.6) are:

1. current tax expense;
2. adjustments to tax charges of prior periods (results of over/underprovisions);
3. transfers to or from deferred tax.

 Solution 5

A permanent difference is where an expense charged in the profit or loss is not allowed for income tax purposes. A permanent difference will not reverse in future periods, see Section 6.4.1.1.

 Solution 6

(a) The tax charge for each of the 3 years can be calculated as follows:

Year	Profits	Tax charge based on profits @ 30%	Tax actually paid in respect of previous year	(Over)/ under provision	Income statement charge
20X1	$100,000	$30,000			$30,000
20X2	$120,000	$36,000	$28,900	($1,100)	$34,900
20X3	$110,000	$33,000	$37,200	$1,200	$34,200

The tax charge recorded in 20X1 is $30,000 and $28,900 is then actually paid resulting in an overprovision of $1,100.

The tax charge recorded in 20X2 is $36,000 and $37,200 is then actually paid resulting in an underprovision of $1,200.

The profit or loss charge is calculated as tax on profits plus any underprovision/less any overprovision.

The amounts will be recorded as follows:

In 20X1

Dr	Tax charge (profit or loss)	$30,000
Cr	Tax liability (statement of financial position)	$30,000

Being the recording of the estimated tax charge for 20X1.

In 20X2

Dr	Tax liability (statement of financial position)	$28,900
Cr	Bank	$28,900

Being the payment of tax in respect of the year ended 20X1.

Dr	Tax charge (profit or loss)	$34,900
Cr	Tax liability (statement of financial position)	$34,900

Being the recording of the estimated tax charge for 20X2 ($36,000 estimated tax less the overprovision in 20X1 of $1,100 – estimated $30,000 and paid $28,900).

In 20X3

Dr	Tax liability (statement of financial position)	$37,200
Cr	Bank	$37,200

Being the payment of tax in respect of the year ended 20X2.

Dr	Tax charge (profit or loss)	$34,200
Cr	Tax liability (statement of financial position)	$34,200

Being the recording of the estimated tax charge for 20X3 ($33,000 estimated tax plus the underprovision in 20X2 of $1,200 – estimated $36,000 and paid $37,200).

(b)

Income Statement extract	20X1	20X2	20X3
Tax charge on profits	$30,000	$36,000	$33,000
(Over)/under provision of tax		($1,100)	$1,200
Tax charge for the year	$30,000	$34,900	$34,200

Statement of financial position extract	20X1	20X2	20X3
Current liabilities			
Income tax liability	$30,000	$36,000	$33,000

See Section 6.5.

 ## Solution 7

(a) Income tax charge

	$'000	$'000
Tax on profits 30% × $3 m	900	
Less over-provision in 20X1	(4)	
Current tax charge		896
Deferred tax provision required	1,700	
Deferred tax provision b/f	1,500	
Increase in provision required		200
Total charge to profit or loss		1096

Accounting entries

Dr	Income tax charge (profit or loss)	896
Cr	Income tax liability (statement of financial position)	896

Being the current tax charge for 20X2.

Dr	Income tax charge (profit or loss)	200
Cr	Deferred tax provision (statement of financial position)	200

Being the increase required to the deferred tax provision for 20X2.

(b) Statement of financial position extract

Current liabilities	
Income tax ($4,000 + $896,000)	$900,000
Non-current liabilities	
Deferred tax	$1,700,000

See Section 6.5.

 ## Solution 8

	20X0	20X1	20X2	20X3
	$'000	$'000	$'000	$'000
Carrying value	400	300	200	100
Accounting depreciation	(100)	(100)	(100)	(100)
Closing carrying value	300	200	100	0
Opening balance for tax purposes	400	200	0	0
Tax depreciation	(200)	(200)	0	0
Tax written down value (tax base)	200	0	0	0
Temporary difference (carrying value − tax base)	100	200	100	0
Deferred tax provision required at 30%	30	60	30	0
Charge/(release) to profit or loss	30	30	(30)	(30)

Solution 9

Year ended 31 December 20X2

	$	$
Current tax charge $120,000 × 30%		36,000
Less over provision in 20X1 ($30,000 − $28,600)		(1,400)
		34,600

Deferred tax:		
Carrying value of asset ($80,000 − depreciation $40,000, 2 years)	40,000	
Tax base ($80,000 − capital allowances given $80,000)	0	
Temporary difference	40,000	
Deferred tax required @ 30%	12,000	
Release to profit or loss for reduction in deferred tax (18k − 12k)		(6,000)
Total charge to profit or loss		28,600

31 December 20X1	$
First-year allowance 100%	80,000
Less depreciation	20,000
Timing difference	60,000
Deferred tax @ 30%	18,000

Income statement extract 20X2

Income tax charge	
Tax change on profits	$36,000
Less overprovision in 20X1	($1,400)
Reduction in deferred tax	($6,000)
	$28,600

Statement of financial position extract 20X2

Current liabilities	
Income tax liability	$36,000
Non-current liabilities	
Deferred tax ($18,000 − $6,000)	$12,000

 Solution 10

	$	$
Deferred tax:		
Carrying value of asset	40,000	
Tax base (value for tax purposes at 31 December 20X2)	0	
Taxable temporary difference	40,000	
Deferred tax liability (at 30%)		12,000
Carrying value of liability − pension costs	80,000	
Tax base (value for tax purposes at 31 December 20X2)	0	
Deductible temporary difference	80,000	
Deferred tax asset (at 30%)		24,000

Solution 11

	$'000	$'000
Revenue		45
Operating costs	23	
Finance costs	4	
Tax allowances – computer	2	29
		16
Tax @ 25%		4

 Solution 12

Tax depreciation	$
Purchase cost at 1 April 2003	250,000
First-year allowance at 50%	125,000
	125,000
Tax depreciation second year at 25%	31,250
Tax written down value	93,750

Accounting depreciation	$
Purchase cost at 1 April 2003	250,000
Straight line depreciation at 20%	50,000
	200,000
Straight line depreciation at 20%	150,000
Accounting book value	150,000

Deferred tax provision	at 31 March 2004	at 31 March 2005
	$	$
Accounting book value	200,000	150,000
Tax written down value	125,000	93,750
	75,000	56,250
Tax at 30% on $56,250 =	22,500	16,875
Change in deferred tax = 22,500 − 16,875 =	5,625	
Statement of financial position at 31 March 2005		
Deferred tax	$16,875	

Income statement for the year ended 31 March 2005
Income tax expense − reduction in deferred tax $5,625 credit

 Solution 13

Accounting depreciation = cost − residual value = $900,000 − $50,000 = $850,000
$850,000/5 = $170,000 per year

2004/05

	$'000
Cost	900
Depreciation	(340)
Carrying value	560

	$'000
Tax base	
Cost	900
First year allowance 50% =	450
	450

| 30 September 25% | 112 |
| Tax base | 337 |

2004/05

	$'000
Carrying value	560.0
Tax base	337.5
	222.5

Tax at 30% 66.75
Required deferred tax provision $66,750

Solution 14

	Trading profit/(loss)		Taxable Capital gain/(loss)		Taxable tax
	$'000	$'000	$'000	$'000	$'000
2002/03	200	200	(100)	0	200 × 20% = 40
2003/04	(120)	0	0	0	0
2004/05	150	150 − 120 = 30	130	130 − 100 = 30	30 + 30 = 60 × 20% = 12

Solution 15

	2003	2004	2005
	$	$	$
Tax depreciation	2,120	1,860	1,320
Less: Accounting depreciation	1,630	1,590	1,530
	490	270	(210)

Cumulative difference at 31 December 2002	7,500
Add: Increase	490
Add: Increase	270
Less: Reduction	(210)
	8,050

Tax at 25% = 2,013
Required deferred tax provision $2,013

Solution 16

Income statement − Income Tax	$
Deferred tax increase (759,000 − 642,000)=	117,000
Charge for year (946,000 × 22%)=	208,120
Overprovision from previous year	(31,000)
	294,120

Solution 17

Tax base	$'000	Accounting book value	$'000
Cost	500	Cost	500
2004/05 First year allowance 50%	250	Depreciation 2004/05	100
	250		400
2005/06 20%	50	Depreciation 2005/06	100
	200		300
2006/07 20%	40	Revaluation	120
	160		420
		Depreciation 2006/07	140
			280

	2005/06	2006/07
	$'000	$'000
Accounting book value	300	280
Tax base	200	160
Temporary difference	100	120
Deferred tax at 30%	30	36

Profit or loss increase ($36,000 − $30,000) = $6,000

Statement of financial position − deferred tax provision 2007 $36,000

 Solution 18

	$'000
Profit	822
Add back entertaining expenses	32
Political party donation	50
	904
Less grant	(103)
	801

Tax due = $801,000 × 25% = $200,250

 Solution 19

Deferred tax balance:	$'000
Accounting depreciation:	
Cost	400
Depreciation to September 2006	100
	300
Depreciation to September 2007	75
	225
Tax allowances:	
Allowance to September 2006	400
Tax written down value	0

Temporary difference at September 2007 is book value less tax written down value
225 − 0 = 225

Deferred tax provision is 225 @ 22% = $49.5

Solution 20

DB – Corporate income tax		2006
		$
Profit before tax per Income statement		33,950
Add back:		
Entertaining		600
Local government tax		950
Depreciation on buidings		1,600
Depreciation on plant and equipment		20,000
		57,100
Less tax depreciation		
Building (70,000 × 4%)		2,800
Plant and equipment (W1)		25,768
Taxable profit		28,532

			Tax $
Taxable at 15%	(25,000 − 10,000) =	15,000	2,250
Taxable at 25%	(28,532 − 25,000) =	3,532	883
Corporate income tax 2006			3,133

(W1)

Plant and equipment	*Original purchase*	*New acquisition*	*Total tax depreciation*
	$	$	$
Cost	80,000		
2005 tax depreciation @ 27%	21,600		
	58,400		
Acquired		20,000	
2006 first year allowance @ 50%		10,000	10,000
2006 tax depreciation @ 27%	15,768		15,768
	42,632	10,000	25,768

The IASC and the Standard-Setting Process

The IASC and the Standard-Setting Process

7

Learning aims

The learning aim of this part of the syllabus is that students should be able to:
   'describe and discuss how financial reporting can be regulated and the system of *International Accounting Standards.*'
   The syllabus topics covered in this chapter are as follows:

- the need for regulation of accounts;
- elements in a regulatory framework for published accounts (e.g. company law, local GAAP, review of accounts by public bodies);
- GAAP based on prescriptive versus principles-based standards;
- the role and structure of the IASB and IOSCO;
- the process leading to the promulgation of a standard practice;
- ways in which IAS's are used: adoption as local GAAP, model for local GAAP, persuasive influence in formulating local GAAP.

7.1 The need for regulation of financial statements

Financial statements and reports for shareholders and other users are prepared using principles and rules that can be interpreted in different ways. To provide guidance and try and ensure that they are interpreted in the same way, each time some form of regulation is required.

In Section 2.2, we noted that taxable profits are based on accounting profit and that the number and type of adjustments required to compute taxable profits varies from country to country. Part of this variation was due to the differences in the tax regulations, but a part of it was due to the different approaches to the calculation of accounting profit. In Section 2.2, we noted that in some countries taxable income is closely linked to the accounting profit and that accounting rules are largely driven by taxation laws. These countries are usually known as code law countries, countries where the legal system originated in Roman law. These countries tend to have detailed laws relating to trading entities and accounting standards are usually embodied within the law. Accounting regulation in these countries is usually in the hands of the government and financial reporting is a matter of complying with a set of legal rules.

In other countries the common law system is used, common law is based on case law and tends to have less detailed regulations. In countries with common law systems, the accounting regulation within the legal system is usually kept to a minimum, with detailed accounting regulations produced by professional organisations or other private sector accounting standard setting bodies.

Whichever system is adopted, there is a need for every country to have a system for regulating the preparation of financial statements and reports.

7.2 Variation from country to country

Accounting and information disclosure practices around the world are influenced by a variety of economic, social and political factors. In addition to the legal system and tax legislation discussed in Section 7.1, a range of other factors that contribute to variations between the accounting regulations of countries are discussed below. The wide range of factors influencing the development of accounting regulations have resulted in a wide range of different systems, this has made it difficult and time consuming to try and harmonise accounting practices around the world. With the growth in international investing, there is a growing need for harmonisation of financial statements between countries.

7.2.1 Sources of finance and capital markets

There is more demand for financial information and disclosure where a higher proportion of capital is raised from external shareholders, rather than from banks or family members. Stock markets rely on published financial information by entities. Banks and family members are usually in a position to demand information directly from the entity, whereas shareholders have to rely on publicly available information.

7.2.2 The political system

The nature of regulation and control exerted on accounting will reflect political philosophies and objectives of the ruling party, for example, environmental concerns.

7.2.3 Entity ownership

The need for public accountability and disclosure will be greater where there is a broad ownership of shares as opposed to family ownership or government ownership.

7.2.4 Cultural differences

The culture within a country can influence societal and national values which can influence accounting regulations.

7.3 Harmonisation versus standardisation

Harmonisation tends to mean the process of increasing the compatibility of accounting practices by setting bounds to their degree of variation.

Standardisation tends to imply the imposition of a rigid and narrower set of rules. Standardisation also implies that one technically correct method can be identified for every aspect of accounting and then this can be imposed on all preparers of accounts.

Due to the variations between countries discussed above in Sections 7.1 and 7.2, full standardisation of accounting practices is unlikely. Harmonisation is more likely, as the agreement of a common conceptual framework of accounting may enable a closer harmonisation of accounting practices. See Section 7.9 for a discussion on some recent harmonisation developments.

7.3.1 The need for harmonisation of accounting standards

Each country has its own accounting regulation, financial statements and reports prepared for shareholders and other uses are based on principles and rules that can vary widely from country to country. Multinational entities may have to prepare reports on activities on several bases for use in different countries, and this can cause unnecessary financial costs. Furthermore, preparation of accounts based on different principles makes it difficult for investors and analysts to interpret financial information. This lack of comparability in financial reporting can affect the credibility of the entity's reporting and the analysts' reports and can have a detrimental effect on financial investment.

The increasing levels of cross-border financing transactions, securities trading and direct foreign investment has resulted in the need for a single set of rules by which assets, liabilities and income are recognised and measured.

The number of foreign listings on major exchanges around the world is continually increasing and many worldwide entities may find that they are preparing accounts using a number of different rules and regulations in order to be listed on various markets.

Exercise

Briefly explain possible benefits that could accrue from the development of a single set of accounting standards that could be applied in all countries.

Solution

Multinational entities could benefit from:

1. access to a wider range of international finance opportunities. If international standards were widely accepted, the international financial markets would be accessible by a wider range of entities. This could have the effect of reducing financing costs;
2. improved management control as all parts of the entity would be reporting using one consistent basis;
3. greater efficiency in accounting departments as they would not have to spend time converting data from one accounting basis to another;
4. easier consolidation of subsidiaries, preparation of group accounts would be simplified.

Investors should benefit by being able to compare the results of different entities more easily and make more informed investment decisions.

It would be easier for international economic groupings such as the EU to function, as the preparation of economic data would be easier.

7.4 Elements that might be expected in a regulatory framework for published accounts

There are several potential elements that might be expected in a regulatory framework within a particular country. The main ones are:

- local law that applies to entities;
- locally adopted accounting standards;
- local stock exchange requirements;
- international body requirements;
- international accounting standards;
- locally developed or international conceptual framework for accounting.

Every country is different, potentially every one of the above could be different if two countries are compared. Let us briefly consider each of these elements in turn.

7.4.1 Local law that applies to entities

Every country passes its own laws, some that relate to entities in that country. There are two main forms of law:

1. the roman law approach where *everything* is specified in the law directly;
2. the anglo-saxon common law approach where the legislation is more general and the courts interpret the legislation that becomes the case law.

Local legal requirements will have to be followed by entities. In some countries, the legal system embodies the accounting standards that entities are required to follow (see Section 7.1).

7.4.2 Locally adopted accounting standards

Each country will have their own local version of accounting standards. These local standards will be developed using local processes that reflect the social, economic and political factors of the country, or the country could choose to adopt international accounting standards, see Section 7.10.

7.4.3 Local stock exchange requirements

The local stock exchange may have further requirements for listed entities, which are additional to the other legal requirements that apply to all entities in the country.

7.4.4 International body requirements

International bodies can often have a significant influence on the regulatory requirements within a country. For example, EU directives apply to all countries within Europe; however, when they are embodied in local legislation they apply to entities. Another example of an international organisation influencing local regulations is the The International Organisation of Securities Commissions (IOSCO), see Section 7.7.

7.4.5 International accounting standards

International accounting standards are having an increasing influence on local accounting standards. This is discussed in detail in Section 7.11.

7.4.6 Locally developed or international conceptual framework for accounting

Some countries, such as the UK and USA have developed their own conceptual framework of accounting. Countries that have not developed their own conceptual framework may have adopted the IASB's Framework. See Chapter 8 for a discussion on the IASB's Framework.

Where a conceptual framework exists it will assist in the development of accounting standards and generally accepted accounting practice.

7.5 Generally accepted accounting practice (GAAP)

GAAP encompasses the conventions, rules and procedures necessary to define accepted accounting practice at a particular time. It includes not only broad guidelines of general application but also detailed practices and procedures. GAAP includes local legislation requirements, accounting standards and any other locally applicable regulations. GAAP is also dynamic and will change over time as new or different requirements become generally accepted.

GAAP will therefore vary from one country to another as different regulations apply in different countries. The IASB's convergence programme is aimed at reducing these differences over time.

GAAP can be based on legislation and accounting standards that are either:

- prescriptive in nature, setting out in detail every possible permutation that an accountant may come across; or
- principles-based accounting standards, which set out principles but are not specific and do not include many detailed requirements for their application.

Exercise

List the possible advantages of having GAAP based on prescriptive standards versus GAAP based on principles.

✓ Solution

You will probably have a number of points, the following is not intended to be an exhaustive list. Your answer could have included the following:

Advantages of GAAP based on prescriptive standards:

- precise, the requirements will be clear and well understood;
- there will be one 'correct' way of dealing with every item, it does not need professional judgement to be used when deciding how to treat an item;
- it should be more obvious when an entity does not follow GAAP;
- can be taught/learnt more easily;
- it should ensure that similar items are treated in the same way.

Advantages of GAAP on principles:

- It will be harder to construct ways of avoiding the requirements of individual standards, for example, a prescriptive standard may set out definitions or specify values that should be used when applying a standard. If an actual value is specified, it may be possible for some entities to construct various means of avoiding the application of that requirement. Whereas if the standard sets out general principles, it is much harder to avoid the standard's requirements as a principle will apply no matter what value is put on it.
- The requirements in certain situations will need to be applied using professional judgement, which can help ensure that the correct application is used. Whereas a prescriptive standard would require a certain treatment to be used, regardless of the situation, which could lead to similar items being treated the same way even if the circumstances are different.
- Principles-based GAAP should ensure that the spirit of the regulations are adhered to, whereas the prescriptive system is more likely to lead to the letter of the law being followed rather than the spirit.

IFRSs are principle-based standards.

7.6 The International Accounting Standards Committee Foundation (IASC Foundation)

In March 2001, the IASC Foundation was formed as a not-for-profit corporation. The IASC Foundation is the parent entity of the International Accounting Standards Board (IASB).

From 1 April 2001, the IASB assumed the accounting standard-setting responsibilities from its predecessor body, the International Accounting Standards Committee.

The restructuring of the IASC resulted from the recommendations made in the report, *Recommendations on Shaping IASC for the Future*. The overall objectives and principles remain consistent with the original set-up. However, the revised format brings a new committee structure and some changes to the standard-setting process.

7.6.1 Structure of the IASC foundation

The IASC Foundation is an independent organisation having two main bodies: the Trustees and the IASB. The structure also includes the Standards Advisory Council and the International Financial Reporting Interpretations Committee.

A graphical representation of the structure is given in Figure 7.1. The role of each committee will be discussed in turn.

7.6.2 IASC Foundation

The Trustees hold the responsibility for governance and fundraising, and for publishing an annual report on the IASC's activities, including audited financial statements and priorities for the coming year. They will review annually the strategy of the IASC and its effectiveness and approve the annual budget and determine the basis of funding.

The Trustees also appoint the members of the IASB, the Standards Advisory Council and the International Financial Reporting Interpretations Committee. Although the Trustees will decide on the operating procedures of the committees in the IASC family, they will be excluded from involvement in technical matters relating to accounting standards.

The Trustees must have sufficient financial knowledge and experience to allow them to fully appreciate the issues that are relevant to the IASC and the ability to meet the Committee's time commitment. Trustees will normally serve for a term of 3 years, renewable once.

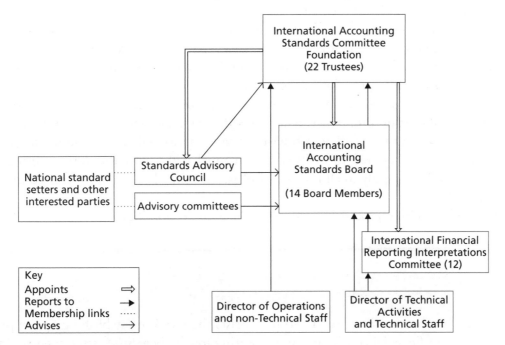

Figure 7.1 Structure of the IASC Foundation

*Source:*http://www.iasb.org/about/structure.asp

Reproduced with permission of the IASC Foundation.

The mix of trustees must be representative of the world's capital markets and therefore are appointed as follows:

- six from North America;
- six from Europe;
- six from the Asia/Oceania region;
- four from other areas giving overall geographic balance.

The IASC also defines the experience required for trustees to be appointed in order to ensure a balance of professional backgrounds. Two of the 22 will usually be senior partners from prominent international accounting firms. Preparers, users and academics should also be represented and the remaining 11 will be selected on the basis that they bring strong public interest backgrounds.

7.6.3 The International Accounting Standards Board (IASB)

The IASB has 14 members, 12 of whom are full-time employees. Appointment of members is primarily based on their having sufficient technical expertise to ensure the IASB has the experience to tackle the relevant business and economic issues.

The Trustees appoint one of the full-time members as chairman of the IASB, who is also the chief executive of the IASC. The current chairman is Sir David Tweedie, former chairman of the UK's Accounting Standards Board. Seven of the full-time members of staff are responsible for liaising with national standard-setters in order to promote the convergence of accounting standards.

IASB members are appointed for a term of 5 years, renewable once. The terms are staggered to ensure continuity of members.

The IASB has complete responsibility for all IASC technical matters, including the preparation and publication of international financial reporting standards (IFRS) and exposure drafts; withdrawal of IFRSs and final approval of interpretations by the International Financial Reporting Interpretations Committee.

IASB publishes its standards in a series of pronouncements called IFRSs. The IASB have also adopted all existing pronouncements issued by the IASC referred to as International Accounting Standards (IASs). The two have the same status and existing pronouncements will continue to be referred to as IASs. The manual will follow this format, using the generic term IFRS to apply to all IFRSs and IASs. The term IAS will only be used to refer to specific IASs only.

The standard-setting process is discussed in detail in Section 7.10.

7.6.4 The International Financial Reporting Interpretations Committee (IFRIC)

The IFRIC is a committee of the IASB that assists the IASB in establishing and improving standards of financial accounting and reporting for the benefit of users, preparers and auditors of financial statements.

The IASC Foundation Trustees established the IFRIC in March 2002 when it replaced the previous interpretations committee, the Standing Interpretations Committee (SIC).

The IFRIC provides timely guidance on the application and interpretation of IFRSs, normally dealing with complex accounting issues that could, in the absence of guidance, produce wide-ranging or unacceptable accounting treatments. In this way IFRIC promotes the rigorous and uniform application of IFRSs.

The IFRIC produces draft interpretations, which are open to public comment. If no more than three (of 12) of its voting members have voted against an interpretation, the IFRIC will ask the IASB to approve the final interpretation for issue. Published interpretations are numbered sequentially. Compliance with IFRSs requires compliance with the relevant IFRIC interpretations.

7.6.5 The Standards Advisory Council (SAC)

The Standards Advisory Council comprises 30 members or more, appointed by the trustees for renewable terms of 3 years. This committee is intended to provide a forum for wider participation for those with an interest in the standard-setting process, so its members have diverse geographical and professional backgrounds.

The Standards Advisory Council meets at least three times a year with the objectives of:

- giving advice to the board on agenda decisions and priorities for future work;
- informing the Board of public views on major standard-setting projects;
- giving other advice to the board or the Trustees.

7.7 Objectives of the IASC Foundation

The objectives of the IASC are as follows:

- to develop, in the public interest, a single set of high-quality, understandable and enforceable global accounting standards that require high-quality, transparent and comparable information in financial statements and other financial reporting to help participants in the world's capital markets and other users make economic decisions;
- to promote the use and rigorous application of those standards taking account of the needs of small- and medium-sized entities;
- to bring about convergence of national accounting standards and international accounting standards to high-quality solutions.

The IASC's financial support derives primarily from the professional accountancy bodies, the International Federation of Accountants (IFAC), and from contributions by entities, financial institutions and accounting firms. More than 150 professional accounting bodies in over 100 countries are members of IASC.

7.8 The International Organisation of Securities Commissions (IOSCO)

Securities commissions are the bodies responsible for the regulation of stock markets in their country. IOSCO encourages international investment by making stock market regulations more consistent between countries.

In 1995, IOSCO's Technical Committee agreed the core set of standards that IASC would develop. It was agreed that, should the core standards be acceptable to the IOSCO Technical Committee, IOSCO would recommend endorsement of IFRSs for cross-border capital raising and listing purposes in all global markets.

The process is now complete, and in May 2000 IOSCO recommended that its members permit incoming multinational issuers to use these standards to prepare their financial statements for cross-border offerings and listings.

7.9 Local regulatory bodies

Worldwide acceptance of IFRSs is to some extent dependent on the promotion by local regulatory bodies. The professional accountancy bodies are well represented on the membership of IASC. The G7 Finance Ministers and Central Bank Governors have also committed themselves to the promotion of IFRSs by ensuring that private sector institutions in their respective countries comply with internationally agreed principles, standards and codes of best practice. Furthermore, they called on all countries that participate in global capital markets similarly to commit to comply with IFRSs.

7.9.1 Convergence activities

IASB must meet with the Standards Advisory Council before it can confirm its technical agenda. Then it works with the chairs of the national accounting standard-setters to co-ordinate their agendas and priorities. The IASB then provides details of how it is co-operating with other key standard-setters and regulatory agencies worldwide towards achieving convergence of accounting standards.

7.9.2 International reaction

Europe

In June 2000, the European Commission issued a Communication proposing that all listed entities in the EU would be required to prepare their consolidated financial statements using IFRSs from 2005. EU Member States may extend this to permit non-publically traded entities to prepare their financial statements in accordance with IFRSs.

In late 2001, the EU published its Fair Value Directive. This formed a part of the process to change the EU's legal framework that allowed EU-listed entities to adopt IFRSs from 1 January 2005.

Many entities already state that their financial statements are prepared in accordance with IFRSs. In 2004 there were around 350 publically listed entities that complied with IFRSs, in 2005 this was approximately 7000 publically listed entities.

USA

The US Securities and Exchange Commission (SEC) is responsible for the regulation of the debt and equity securities markets in the US. In 1996, SEC expressed its support for the IASC's objective of developing accounting standards that could be used for preparing accounts used in cross-border offerings publicly, but the SEC still requires entities to use US GAAP or prepare a detailed reconciliation statement.

In 2002 a Memorandum of Understanding known as the 'Norwalk Agreement' was agreed between the FASB and the IASB. The agreement states that the respective parties agree to:

(a) Make their existing financial reporting standards fully compatible as soon as is practicable, and

(b) Co-ordinate their future work programs to ensure that once achieved, compatibility is maintained.

Since then the FASB and the IASB have been working to increase convergence between US GAAP and IFRSs.

In April 2005 the SEC staff published a 'Roadmap' that set out the steps required to be achieved before the reconciliation statement required from overseas entities could be eliminated. The full article and 'roadmap' can be found at http://www.SEC.gov/news/speech/spch040605dtn.htm

SEC staff have agreed a work plan with the Committee of European Securities Regulators, the main focus being the application by international entities of IFRS and US GAAP in the USA and EU respectively.

Other Countries

Many Countries already endorse IFRSs, and IFRSs are especially useful for developing countries that do not yet have a national standard-setting body.

7.10 The standard-setting process

The IASC Constitution permits the IASB to work in whatever way it considers most effective and cost efficient. The Board may form advisory committees or other specialist technical groups to advise on major projects. The Board may outsource detailed research or other work to national standard-setters.

7.10.1 Development of a standard

The process for the development of a standard involves the following steps:

- During the early stages of a project, IASB may establish an Advisory Committee to advise on the issues arising in the project. Consultation with this committee and the Standards Advisory Council occurs throughout the project.
- IASB may develop and publish *Discussion Documents* for public comment.
- Following receipt and review of comments, IASB develops and publishes an *Exposure Draft* for public comment.
- Following the receipt and review of comments, the IASB may hold a public hearing or carry out field tests. The IASB issues a final IFRS, along with any dissenting view expressed by an IASB member.

When the IASB publishes a standard, it also publishes a *Basis of Conclusions* to explain publicly how it reached its conclusions and to provide background information that may help users apply the standard in practice.

7.10.2 Other aspects of due process

Each IASB member has one vote on technical matters and the publication of a Standard, Exposure Draft, or final IFRIC Interpretation requires approval by eight of the Board's 14 members.

Other decisions, including agenda decisions and the issue of a Discussion Paper, require a simple majority of the Board members present at a meeting, provided the meeting is attended by at least 50 per cent of the members.

Meetings of the IASB, SAC and IFRIC are open to public observation. Where IASB issues Exposure Drafts, Discussion Documents and other documents for public comment, the usual comment period is 90 days. Draft IFRIC Interpretations are exposed for a 60-day comment period.

7.10.3 Co-ordination with national standard-setting

IASB is currently exploring ways in which it can integrate its standard-setting process more closely with those of national standard-setters. The Board is currently investigating the possibility that the procedure for projects that have international implications would include the following:

- IASB and national standard-setters co-ordinating their work plans, so that they can be reviewing an issue at the same time enabling each party to play a full part in developing international consensus.
- National standard-setters could consider this international consensus when voting on their own national standards, although they would not be required to vote for the IASB's preferred solution.
- IASB and national bodies would continue to issue their own exposure drafts, but may consider issuing them at the same time and invite comments on any significant differences in proposed accounting treatments.

7.10.4 Benchmark treatments and allowed alternatives

In some IFRSs, there are alternative treatments for a transaction or event. One is designated the 'benchmark' treatment. This is not necessarily to be taken as the preferred treatment. The term 'benchmark' reflects the Board's intention of identifying a point of reference when making its choice between alternatives.

7.11 Ways in which IFRS's are used by countries

A country chosing to adopt international standards can apply them in a number of ways:

- adoption as local GAAP;
- model for local GAAP;
- persuasive influence in formulating local GAAP.

Alternatively, local GAAP can be developed with little or no reference to IFRSs.

7.11.1 Adoption as local GAAP

Some countries, particularly countries where the accounting profession is not well developed, take international accounting standards and adopt them as their local standards with very little or no amendments. This approach has the advantage of being quick to implement after the decision is taken. The disadvantage is that it may not take into account any specific local traditions or variations. Examples include Honduras, Armenia, Bangladesh and Bahrain.

There have also been some examples where countries have changed their approach, for example, Malawi used 'IAS's adapted for use in Malawi', then in 2001 they changed to full adoption of IFRSs.

7.11.2 Model for local GAAP

Some countries use international accounting standards, but amend them to reflect local needs and conditions. These countries change some of the IASB standards to suit local needs and may also develop some local standards to cover topics for which there is no international standard. Examples include Tanzania, Egypt and Malaysia.

7.11.3 Persuasive influence in formulating local GAAP

Countries with a track record in setting accounting standards already had standards in place before the original IASC was formed. As these standards pre-dated IFRSs, they often did not conform with them. Many countries in this position have been working for many years to narrow the gap between their local standards and IFRSs. This usually takes the form of all new or revised standards being developed to take account of international standards and comply with them in all material respects. Although most of the standards now comply with IFRSs, they are often different in some way. Examples include Brazil, India, Japan and Australia.

7.11.4 Local GAAP developed with little or no reference to IFRS's

As mentioned in Section 7.11.3, some countries have accounting standards that pre-date IFRSs and whereas most have adjusted their standards in an attempt to converge with IFRSs, some have made no attempt. Others that may not pre-date IFRSs have decided to develop their own standards and make no real attempt to comply with IFRSs. Examples in this category include Jamaica, China and Colombia, although China has now decided to develop new accounting standards that are in harmony with IFRSs.

7.12 Summary

Having completed this chapter, you should be able to discuss briefly the need for the regulation of published accounts and identify the reasons why regulatory regimes vary. You should be able to explain the objectives, role and structure of the IASC Foundation and its various bodies and describe the relationship that IASC has with both IOSCO and the national regulatory bodies. In addition, you can now explain the IASBs standard-setting process and describe different ways that countries use IFRSs.

Revision Questions

? Question 1

A committee of the International Accounting Standards Board (IASB) is known as the IFRIC.

What does IFRIC stand for?

(A) International Financial Reporting Issues Committee
(B) International Financial Recommendations and Interpretations Committee
(C) International Financial Reporting Interpretations Committee
(D) International Financial Reporting Issues Council   **(2 marks)**

? Question 2

Which of the following is NOT a function of the International Accounting Standards Board?

(A) Issuing accounting standards
(B) Withdrawing accounting standards
(C) Developing accounting standards
(D) Enforcing accounting standards   **(2 marks)**

? Question 3

The international accounting standards committee foundation (IASC foundation) has two main bodies:

(i) International Accounting Standards Board
(ii) International financial reporting interpretations committee
(iii) Standards advisory council
(iv) Trustees

The two committees reporting to the IASC foundation are:

(A) (i) and (ii)
(B) (i) and (iv)
(C) (ii) and (iii)
(D) (iii)and (iv)   **(2 marks)**

? Question 4

Which of the following would not normally be expected to be included in the elements of a regulatory framework for published accounts:

(A) Local law that applies to entities
(B) Local taxation regulations
(C) Local stock exchange regulations
(D) A conceptual framework for accounting   **(2 marks)**

? Question 5

List three ways in which IFRSs can be implemented in a country.   **(3 marks)**

? Question 6

The existing procedures for setting international accounting standards are now well established.

Requirement

(a) Explain the roles of the following in relation to International Accounting Standards:
  (i) The International Accounting Standards Committee (IASC) Foundation;
  (ii) The International Accounting Standards Board (IASB);
  (iii) The International Financial Reporting Interpretations Committee (IFRIC).

                                                                           (5 marks)

? Question 7

Explain how the standard-setting authority approaches the task of producing a standard, with particular reference to the ways in which comment or feedback from interested parties is obtained.   **(5 marks)**

? Question 8

The Technical Committee of the International Organisation of Securities Commissions (IOSCO) and the IASC agree that there is a compelling need for high-quality, comprehensive international accounting standards.

Requirement

Discuss briefly why the development of international accounting standards is considered to be important.   **(5 marks)**

? Question 9

Explain the role that IOSCO has played in the development and promotion of international accounting standards.   **(5 marks)**

Question 10

The setting of International Accounting Standards is carried out by co-operation between a number of committees and boards, which include:

 (i) International Accounting Standards Committee Foundation (IASC Foundation)
 (ii) Standards Advisory Council (SAC)
(iii) International Financial Reporting Interpretations Committee (IFRIC)

Which of the above reports to, or advises, the International Accounting Standards Board (IASB)?

 Reports to Advises:

 (A) (i) and (iii) (ii)
 (B) (i) and (ii) (iii)
 (C) (iii) (ii)
 (D) (ii) (i)   **(2 marks)**

Question 11

C is a small developing country which passed a legislation to create a recognised professional accounting body 2 years ago. At the same time as the accounting body was created, new regulations governing financial reporting requirements of entities were passed. However, there are currently no accounting standards in C.

   C's government has asked the new professional accounting body to prepare a report setting out the country's options for developing and implementing a set of high quality local accounting standards. The government request also referred to the work of the IASB and its International Financial Reporting Standards.

Requirement

As an advisor to the professional accounting body, outline THREE options open to C for the development of a set of high quality local accounting standards. Identify ONE advantage and ONE disadvantage of each option.   **(5 marks)**

Solutions to Revision Questions

 Solution 1

The correct answer is (C), see Section 7.6.4.

 Solution 2

The correct answer is (D), see Section 7.6.3.

 Solution 3

The correct answer is (B), see Section 7.6.1.

 Solution 4

The correct answer is (B), see Section 7.4.

 Solution 5

Three ways in which IFRSs can be implemented are:

1. adoption as local GAAP
2. model for local GAAP
3. persuasive influence in formulating local GAAP

See Section 7.11.

 Solution 6

(i) The IASC Foundation

The IASC Foundation is an independent organisation having two main bodies: the Trustees and the IASB. The Trustees hold the responsibility for governance and fundraising and will publish an annual report on IASC's activities, including audited financial statements and priorities for the coming year. They will review annually the strategy of the IASC and its effectiveness and approve the annual budget and determine the basis of funding.

The Trustees also appoint the members of the IASB, the Standards Advisory Council and the International Financial Reporting Interpretations Committee. Although the Trustees will decide on the operating procedures of the committees in the IASC family, they will be excluded from involvement in technical matters relating to accounting standards.

(ii) The IASB

The Board has complete responsibility for all IASC technical matters, including the preparation and issuing of International Financial Reporting Standards and Exposure Drafts, and final approval of Interpretations by the International Financial Reporting Interpretations Committee. Some of the full-time members of staff are responsible for liaising with national standard-setters in order to promote the convergence of accounting standards.

IASB publishes its standards in a series of pronouncements called International Financial Reporting Standards (IFRSs). It has also adopted the standards issued by the board of the International Accounting Standards Committee.

The Board may form advisory committees or other specialist technical groups to advise on major projects and outsource detailed research or other work to national standard-setters.

(iii) The *International Financial Reporting* Interpretations Committee (IFRIC)

The IFRIC provides timely guidance on the application and interpretation of IFRSs, normally dealing with complex accounting issues that could, in the absence of guidance, produce wide-ranging or unacceptable accounting treatments, see Sections 7.6.2 to 7.6.4.

☑ Solution 7

The process for the development of a standard involves the following steps:

- During the early stages of a project, the IASB may establish an Advisory Committee to advise on the issues arising in the project. Consultation with this committee and the Standards Advisory Council occurs throughout the project.
- The IASB may develop and publish Discussion Documents for public comment.
- Following receipt and review of comments, the IASB develops and publishes an Exposure Draft for public comment.
- Following the receipt and review of comments, the IASB issues a final International Financial Reporting Standard.

When the IASB publishes a standard, it also publishes a Basis of Conclusions to explain publicly how it reached its conclusions and to provide background information that may help users apply the standard in practice.

Each IASB member has one vote on technical matters and the publication of a Standard, Exposure Draft, or final IFRIC Interpretation requires approval by eight of the Board's 14 members. Other decisions including agenda decisions and the issue of a Discussion Paper, require a simple majority of the Board members present at a meeting, provided that the meeting is attended by at least 50 per cent of the members.

Meetings of the IASB, SAC and IFRIC are open to public observation. Where the IASB issues Exposure Drafts, Discussion Documents and other documents for public comment, the usual comment period is 90 days. Draft IFRIC Interpretations are exposed for a 60-day comment period, see Section 7.10.

Solution 8

Investment decisions are largely based on financial information and analysis. Financial reports, which are prepared for shareholders, potential shareholders and other users are, however, based on principles and rules that vary from country to country. This makes comparability and transparency of financial information difficult. Some multinationals may have to prepare reports on activities on several bases for use in different countries and this can cause an unnecessary financial burden and damage the credibility of financial reports.

The increasing levels of cross-border financing transactions and securities trading have highlighted the need for financial information to be based on a single set of rules and principles.

An internationally accepted accounting framework is also beneficial to developing countries that cannot bear the cost of establishing a national standard-setting body, see Section 7.3.1.

 ## Solution 9

Worldwide acceptance of IFRSs will be dependent to some extent on other recognised bodies accepting and promoting their use. IOSCO is looking to the IASC to provide mutually acceptable international accounting standards for use in multinational securities markets.

In 1995, IASC agreed with IOSCO to develop a core set of standards. The standards were identified and, if completed to a satisfactory level, IOSCO would consider endorsing the core standards for cross-border capital-raising and listings in all global markets.

The IASC completed the core standards by 1999 and presented them for technical review by IOSCO. IOSCO had commented on the drafts as they progressed.

In May 2000, IOSCO recommended that its members permit incoming multinational users to use these standards to prepare their financial statements for cross-border trading and listings. There are a number of outstanding issues that are to be addressed by the IASC, but this was considered to be a significant development in gaining acceptance of IFRSs, see Section 7.8.

 ## Solution 10

The correct answer is C, see Section 7.6.3.

 ## Solution 11

The options available to a country developing accounting standards for the first time include:

1. Adopting International Financial Reporting Standards (IFRS) as its local standards with very little or no amendments. This approach is common in countries where the accounting profession is not well developed. The advantage of this approach is that it is quick to implement after the decision is taken. The disadvantage is that it may not take into account any specific local traditions or variations.
2. Modelling its local accounting standards on the IASB's IFRS's, amending them to reflect local needs and conditions. Some of the IASB Standards may be changed to suit local needs and C may also develop some additional local standards to cover topics for which there is no international standard. The advantage is that the standards should be more relevant to local needs, being tailor made to C's local requirements.

C's standards will be compliant with International Standards. The disadvantage is that it will take longer to implement and requires an adequate level of expertise to exist within the country. C may not yet have sufficient expertise.

3. C could develop its own accounting standards with little or no reference to IFRS's. The advantage is that any standards developed will be relevant to C, being tailor made to C's local requirements. The disadvantage is that as C does not yet have any accounting standards, it will be a long time before the project is completed as it is very slow process. Standards may not be compliant with International Standards. This approach requires expertise, which may not be available in C at present, see Section 7.11.

8

Regulatory
Framework

Regulatory Framework

8

LEARNING OUTCOME

After completing this chapter you should be able to:

► explain the IASB's Framework for the Presentation and Preparation of Financial Statements.

The syllabus topic covered in this chapter is as follows:

• IASBs Framework for the Presentation and Preparation of Financial Statements.

8.1 Introduction

One of the major challenges for those communicating financial information is the enormous range of potential users of that information. In addressing technical problems or developments, it is important to consider the context within which the problem has arisen and how the solution fits in with the objective of providing useful financial information.

The increasing complexity of financial transactions and the need for guidance on suitable and consistent treatment in financial reporting has created a vastly increased workload for standard-setters. As a result, they find themselves dealing with issues that vary in detail, but that have the same underlying technical issues: how should this be recorded? how should this be measured? how should this be presented to users?

As the number of accounting rules and standards increases, it is important that the standard-setters provide a set of rules that are based on principles that can be applied consistently to ensure that the overall objectives of financial reporting are met. Many, including the UK ASB and the US FASB, have developed conceptual Frameworks that establish a broad set of accounting principles on which their standards and accounting rules are based.

The IASB's conceptual Framework is the *Framework for the Preparation and Presentation of Financial Statements* (hereafter referred to as the IASB Framework or the Framework) published by the IASC in 1989. This chapter will discuss the purpose of the Framework, and explain the Framework in detail, including the definitions of assets and liabilities. The chapter concludes with a discussion of the usefulness of the Framework. This is an important chapter as the Framework's concepts underpin all of the IFRSs and will be referred to throughout the following sections.

8.2 The development of the Framework

8.2.1 Purpose of the Framework

According to the *Framework,* its purposes are to:

- assist the Board in the development of future IFRSs and its review of existing IFRSs;
- assist the Board in promoting harmonisation of regulations, accounting standards and procedures relating to the presentation of financial statements by providing a basis for reducing the number of alternative treatments permitted by IFRSs;
- assist national standard-setting bodies in developing national standards;
- assist preparers of financial statements in applying IFRSs and dealing with topics that have yet to be covered in an IFRS;
- assist auditors in forming an opinion as to whether financial statements conform with IFRSs;
- assist users of financial statements that are prepared using IFRSs;
- provide information about how the IASB has formulated its approach to the development of IFRSs.

8.2.2 Status of the Framework

The Framework does not have the status of an accounting standard and does not override any IFRS where conflicts arise. Generally, IFRSs are less prescriptive in nature than other national standards, and so the Framework is referred to more frequently by preparers of financial statements, and particularly where an accounting issue is not dealt with specifically by an IFRS.

Some IFRSs still permit alternative treatments of certain transactions. As the IASB continues to reduce the number of alternative treatments, it is expected that the number of conflicts between standards and the Framework will decrease. The required treatments within the IFRSs will then be consistent with the principles outlined in the Framework.

8.2.3 Scope of the Framework

The Framework applies to the general-purpose financial statements of both private and public entities. A full set of financial statements prepared using IFRSs will normally include a statement of financial position, a statement of comprehensive income, a statement of cash flows and any notes to the accounts which form an integral part of the accounts.

To ensure that the Framework helps to provide useful information, it is important to identify the users of the financial information.

The Framework identifies the following users of financial statements:

- investors,
- employees,
- lenders,
- suppliers,
- other trade creditors,
- customers,
- governments and their agencies,
- the public.

The Framework identifies that not all the needs of these users can be met and does not indicate that the needs of one set of users are more important than any other. The Framework does point out, however, that financial statements that meet the needs of investors will generally also meet the needs of other users.

8.3 The Framework

The Framework covers the following main topics:

- the objective of financial statements;
- underlying assumptions;
- the qualitative characteristics of financial information;
- the elements of financial statements;
- recognition of the elements of financial statements;
- measurement of the elements of financial statements;
- concepts of capital maintenance.

8.3.1 The objective of financial statements

The Framework states that 'the objective of financial statements is to provide information about the financial position, performance and changes in financial position of an entity that is useful to a wide range of users in making economic decisions'.

Information about the *financial position* is primarily provided in the *statement of financial position*. The resources the entity controls, its financial structure, liquidity and solvency all affect the financial position.

Information about *performance* is primarily found in the *statement of comprehensive income*. Performance measures, particularly profitability, are required to help assess the entity's ability to generate future cash flows from trading and other activities. It also helps users evaluate how effective the entity is at using its resources.

Information about *changes in financial position* is held primarily in a *statement of cash flows*. This is a useful illustration of the entity's investing, financing and operational activities and how these activities have affected the financial position over the reporting period.

The Framework goes on to say, 'financial statements prepared for this purpose meet the common needs of most users'. Financial statements do not provide all the information that users may need to make economic decisions as they illustrate the financial effects of past transactions. Users are expected to use this reliable historic information to help them evaluate future performance and make their economic decisions.

8.3.2 Underlying assumptions

There are two underlying assumptions outlined in the Framework.

1. *Going concern.* Financial statements are normally prepared on the assumption that an entity is a going concern and will continue in operation for the foreseeable future. Any intention to liquidate or significantly reduce the scale of its operations would require the accounts to be prepared on a different basis and this basis would have to be disclosed.

2. *Accruals basis of accounting.* Financial statements are prepared on the accrual basis of accounting where the effects of transactions are recognised when they occur and are recorded and reported in the accounting periods to which they relate, irrespective of cash flows arising from these transactions.

8.3.3 The qualitative characteristics of financial information

Qualitative characteristics are the attributes that make the information useful to users. The four principal characteristics are:

1. understandability,
2. relevance,
3. reliability,
4. comparability.

Understandability

An essential quality of financial information is that it is readily understandable by users. For this purpose, users are assumed to have a reasonable knowledge of business and economic activities and accounting and a willingness to study the information with reasonable diligence; information on complex issues should be included if relevant and should not be excluded on the grounds that it is too difficult for the average user to understand.

Relevance

To be useful, information must be relevant to the decision-making needs of users. Information is relevant when it influences the economic decisions of users by helping them to evaluate past, present or future economic events, or confirming correcting their past evaluations.

Financial statements do not normally contain information about future activities; however, historical information can be used as the basis for predicting future financial position and performance. The users will then use their predictions as the basis for their decision-making.

An example of this could be where the financial statements show the profitability of a division that has been sold during the year. The users then know to eliminate that division's resources and profitability in evaluating the performance of the total entity for the next year.

Information that helps users assess the future performance and financial position of an entity is likely to be relevant. An item is likely to be relevant by virtue of its nature and materiality. Information is material if its omission or misstatement could influence the decision-making of users.

Information can be relevant because of its nature irrespective of materiality. For example, if an entity has commenced operating activities in a country with an unstable economy, this could change the users' assessment of the overall risk that the entity is exposed to and as a result change the users' assessment of the entity's future results. Irrespective of the materiality of that segment's results, the information may be disclosed.

Information should be released on a timely basis to be relevant to users.

Reliability

To be useful, information must also be reliable. Information is reliable when it is free from material error and bias and can be considered by users to be a faithful representation of the underlying transactions and events.

Faithful representation	To be reliable, the information must faithfully represent the transactions it is intended to represent;
Substance over form	To show a faithful representation, the transactions must be accounted for and presented on the basis of their commercial reality rather than their legal form. Only by applying substance over form will users see the effects of the economic reality of the transactions;
Neutrality	To be reliable, information must be neutral, that is, free from bias;
Prudence	Many estimates are made in the preparation of financial statements, for example, stock valuation, estimated useful lives of assets, recoverability of debts. Being cautious when exercising judgement in arriving at these estimates is known as prudence. This is a generally accepted concept in accounts preparation. The concept does not, however, extend to including excess provisions, overstating liabilities or understating income or assets. This would bias the information and make it unreliable to users;
Completeness	To be reliable, the information must be complete. An omission can cause information to be false or misleading and therefore unreliable.

Comparability

Comparability of financial information is vital to users in their decision-making. The ability to identify trends in performance and financial position and compare those both from year to year and against other entities assists users in their assessments and decision-making.

It is important that users are able to understand the application of accounting policies in order to compare financial information. To achieve comparability, users must be able to identify where an entity has changed its policy from one year to the next and where other entities have used different accounting policies for similar transactions.

The requirement of IFRSs to disclose accounting policies adopted and the inclusion of prior periods' comparative figures helps promote comparability.

 You must learn the qualitative characteristics and be able to explain them as they are regularly examined.

8.3.4 The elements of financial statements

The Framework provides definitions of the elements of financial statements. These definitions, applied together with the recognition criteria, provide guidance as to how and when the financial effect of transactions or events should be recognised in the financial statements.

Asset	An asset is a resource controlled by the entity as a result of past events and from which future economic benefits are expected to flow to the entity;
Liability	A liability is a present obligation of the entity arising from past events, the settlement of which is expected to result in an outflow of resources from the entity;

Equity The residual interest in the assets of the entity after deducting all its liabilities;

Income Increases in economic benefits during the accounting period in the form of inflows or enhancements of assets or decreases of liabilities that result in increases in equity, other than those relating to contributions from equity participants;

Expenses Decreases in economic benefits during the accounting period in the form of outflows or depletions of assets that result in decreases in equity, other than those relating to distributions to equity participants.

> You must learn and be able to describe all of these definitions as they underpin the IFRSs. The most important from the examination viewpoint are the definitions of asset and liability.

8.3.5 Recognition of the elements of financial statements

To be recognised, the item must meet the definition of an element (given above). The Framework then has a further two criteria which must be met for an item to be recognised:

1. it is probable that any future economic benefit associated with the item will flow to or from the entity; and
2. the item has a cost or value that can be measured with reliability.

In the *first criterion*, the idea of *probability* is used regularly in the preparation of financial statements, for example, the probability that your credit customers will pay in order that you can reliably include receivables in the statement of financial position.

The assessment of the degree of uncertainty that an event will take place must be completed using the evidence available when the financial statements are prepared.

Where economic benefits are to arise over time, any related expenses should be systematically recognised over the same periods and matched with the income. Where no future benefits are anticipated, expenses should be recognised immediately.

The *second criterion* requires that a *monetary value* be attached to the item. For some transactions this is straightforward, but often the value we attach to items has to be estimated. This is acceptable, provided that it is a reasonable estimate and does not undermine reliability (a qualitative characteristic noted above).

Where information is relevant to users it should not be excluded from the financial statements because it fails to meet the recognition criteria. For example, where a contingent liability exists at the end of the reporting period but cannot be measured with any degree of certainty, it fails the second recognition criteria; however, due to its nature and existence it should be disclosed to users on the grounds that it is relevant.

8.3.6 Measurement of the elements of financial statements

Once it is decided that an item is to be recognised in the financial statements, it is then necessary to decide on what basis it is to be measured. To be included in the financial statements, the item must have a monetary value attached to it.

The Framework refers to four measurement bases that are often used in reporting, being historic cost, current cost, realisable value and present value. It highlights that historic cost is the most commonly adopted although often within a combination of bases, for example, valuing inventories using the lower of cost and net realisable value.

8.3.7 Concepts of capital and capital maintenance

Concepts of capital

The Framework refers to two concepts of capital: financial concept of capital and physical concept of capital.

Most entities adopt the financial concept of capital which deals with the net assets or equity of the entity. If, instead of being primarily concerned with the invested capital of the entity, the users are concerned with, for example, the operating capability of the entity, then the physical concept of capital should be used.

Determining profit

Under the financial concept of capital, a profit is earned if the financial amount of the net assets at the end of the period is greater than that at the beginning of the period, after deducting any distributions to and contributions from owners.

Under the physical concept of capital, a profit is earned if the physical productive capacity (or operating capacity) of the entity (or the resources or funds needed to achieve that capacity) at the end of the period is greater than that at the beginning of the period, after deducting any distributions to and contributions from owners.

Capital maintenance

In general terms, an entity has maintained its capital if it has as much capital at the end of the period as it had at the beginning of the period. The key in capital maintenance is deciding which concept is being adopted, because this then defines the basis on which profit is calculated.

Financial capital maintenance is measured in either nominal monetary units or units of constant purchasing power.

Physical capital maintenance requires the adoption of the current cost basis of measurement – an appreciation of what it would cost to replace assets at current prices.

The main difference between the two is how they treat the effects of increases in prices of assets and liabilities.

8.4   Usefulness of a conceptual Framework

As was mentioned earlier in this chapter, one of the major challenges for those communicating financial information is the *number and variety of users* of that information. It is difficult to assess its ultimate usefulness when you are unsure how the information is being used and by whom.

It would be almost impossible to address all technical issues in a business context that would meet the needs of every user. It is therefore important that all users appreciate the general principles of financial reporting – if you like, *the theory of how things should be treated.*

A conceptual Framework goes some way to providing this. It gives *guidance on the broad principles* on how items should be recorded, on how they should be measured and how they should be presented.

Where there are no standards specifically covering an issue, a conceptual Framework provides a *point of reference* for preparers of financial information. The Framework can provide guidance on how like items are treated and gives definitions and criteria that can be used in deciding the recognition and measurement of the item.

Where, in general, *accounting standards are less prescriptive,* a conceptual Framework can assist in this way also.

Accounting standards deal with a variety of specific technical issues. The existence of a conceptual Framework can *remove the need to address the underlying issues over and over* again. For example, the Framework gives definitions of assets and liabilities. These definitions must be met for items to be included in financial statements. This is an underlying principle, and as the accounting standards are based on the principles within the Framework, they need not be dealt with fully in each of the standards.

The increasing complexity of the business environment has resulted in a great number of specific accounting standards being developed. It is vital that each standard is developed within the broad Framework of principles. A conceptual Framework will assist standard-setters to develop specific accounting standards that follow a *consistent approach to recognition and measurement.*

The increased complexity of business provides a second challenge – the pace at which technical issues are raised and must be addressed. The process of creating a new accounting standard can be a long one, but where a conceptual Framework exists, the issue can be dealt with temporarily by *providing a short-term solution.* Providing the treatment is consistent with the principles within the Framework, then it will meet the criteria for useful information. This would be an acceptable solution until a specific standard was developed.

8.5 The IASB's Framework and the standard-setting process

We discussed above how a conceptual Framework can be useful in a regulatory environment. Many of the points raised above are true for the Framework and the IASB's standard-setting process. It will provide a reference point for those developing standards and help them provide consistent guidance. It does remove the need to address the underlying principles in each individual standard.

Where new technical issues and problems are raised and not covered specifically by an accounting standard, a short-term solution is provided by the IASB until it can be addressed fully. The International Financial Reporting Interpretations Committee (discussed in Chapter 7) issues such guidance and can use the Framework to ensure that the guidance it provides is consistent with the agreed underlying principles.

8.6 Summary

Having completed this chapter, we can now explain the purpose, status and scope of the Framework. We can identify the main topics included in the Framework and explain briefly what they cover. A number of points have been discussed, illustrating how useful a conceptual Framework can be. We can use these points together with the IASB's objectives of the Framework to evaluate its relationship to the standard-setting process.

Revision Questions

8

? Question 1

The IASB's *Framework* includes reliability as one of the characteristics that make financial information useful.

  (i) Complete,
 (ii) Predictive value,
(iii) Confirmatory value,
 (iv) Neutrality,
  (v) Faithful representation.

Which of the characteristics above are listed in the *Framework* as making financial information reliable?

(A) (i), (iv) and (v)
(B) (ii), (iii) and (iv)
(C) (ii) and (iii)
(D) (ii) and (v)   (2 marks)

? Question 2

The Framework for the Preparation and Presentation of Financial Statements has a number of purposes, including:

- assisting the Board in the development of future IFRSs and in its review of existing IFRSs;
- assisting the Board in promoting harmonisation of regulations, accounting standards and procedures relating to the presentation of financial statements by providing a basis for reducing the number of alternative treatments permitted by IFRSs;
- assisting preparers of financial statements in applying IFRSs and in dealing with topics that are yet to be covered in an IFRS.

Requirement

Discuss how a conceptual Framework could help IASB achieve these objectives.

(12 marks)

Question 3

The IASB's *Framework for the Preparation and Presentation of Financial Statements* (Framework) lists the qualitative characteristics of financial statements.

  (i) Comparability,
 (ii) Relevance,
(iii) Prudence,
 (iv) Reliability,
  (v) Understandability,
 (vi) Matching,
(vii) Consistency.

Which THREE of the above are NOT included in the principal qualitative characteristics listed by the Framework?

(A) (i), (iii) and (vii)
(B) (i), (ii) and (v)
(C) (iii), (vi) and (vii)
(D) (iii), (iv) and (vi)   **(2 marks)**

Question 4

Relevance and reliability are two of the four main qualitative characteristics of financial information, as set out in the Framework.

Requirements

(a) Briefly discuss what is meant by these terms.   **(5 marks)**
(b) Give an example of when these two attributes could come into conflict and what the outcome is likely to be.   **(5 marks)**
             (Total marks = 10)

Question 5

The *Framework* includes the following definition:

'an asset is a resource controlled by the entity as a result of past events and from which future economic benefits are expected to flow to the entity.'

Requirement

Explain this definition, using the example of a trade receivable.   **(5 marks)**

Question 6

The IASB *Framework for the Preparation and Presentation of Financial Statements* (Framework) provides definitions of the elements of financial statement. One of the elements defined by the framework is 'expenses'.

Requirement

In no more than 35 words, give the IASB Framework's definition of expenses.   **(2 marks)**

Question 7

The IASB's *Framework for the preparation and presentation of financial statements* (Framework) identifies four principal qualitative characteristics of financial information.

Requirement

Identify and explain EACH of the FOUR principal qualitative characteristics of financial information listed in the IASB's Framework. **(5 marks)**

Question 8

The International Accounting Standards Board's (IASB) Framework for the Preparation and Presentation of Financial Statements (Framework), sets out four qualitative characteristics of financial information.

Two of the characteristics are relevance and comparability. List the other TWO characteristics. **(2 marks)**

Question 9

According to the International Accounting Standards Board's Framework for the Preparation and Presentation of Financial Statements, what is the objective of financial statements?

Write your answer in no more than 35 words. **(2 marks)**

Question 10

The Framework for the Preparation and Presentation of Financial Statements (Framework) was first published in 1989 and was adopted by The International Accounting Standards Board (IASB).

Requirement

Explain the purposes of the Framework. **(5 marks)**

Solutions to Revision Questions

 Solution 1

The correct answer is (A).

Items (ii) and (iii) are included in the *Framework* as characteristics of relevance, see Section 8.3.3.

 Solution 2

A conceptual Framework provides guidance on the broad principles of financial reporting. It highlights how items should be recorded, on how they should be measured and presented. The setting of broad principles could assist in the development of accounting standards, ensuring that the principles are followed consistently as standards and rules are developed.

A conceptual Framework can provide guidance on how similar items are treated. By providing definitions and criteria that can be used in deciding the recognition and measurement of items, conceptual Frameworks can act as a point of reference for those setting standards, those preparing and those using financial information.

The existence of a conceptual Framework can remove the need to address the underlying issues over and over again. Where underlying principles have been established and the accounting standards are based on these principles, there is no need to deal with them fully in each of the standards. This will save the standard-setters time in developing standards and will again ensure consistent treatment of items.

Where a technical issue is raised but is not specifically addressed in an accounting standard, a conceptual Framework can help provide guidance on how such items should be treated. Where a short-term technical solution is provided by the standard-setters, the existence of a conceptual Framework will ensure that the treatment is consistent with the broad set of agreed principles, see Section 8.2.1.

 Solution 3

The correct answer is (C), see Section 8.3.3.

 Solution 4

(a) Information is *relevant* when it influences the economic decisions of users by helping them to evaluate past, present or future economic events, or confirming/correcting their past evaluations.

151

REGULATORY FRAMEWORK

Although financial statements do not normally contain information about future activities, any information that helps users assess the future performance and financial position of an entity is likely to be relevant. An item is likely to be relevant by virtue of its nature and materiality. Information is material if its omission or misstatement could influence the decision-making of users.

Information can also be relevant because of its unusual nature, irrespective of materiality. The directors would have to judge, in this case, if the nature of the information was such that its omission could influence the economic decision-making of users. Information should be released on a timely basis to be relevant to users.

Information is *reliable* when it is free from material error and bias and can be considered by users to be a faithful representation of the underlying transactions and events. To show a faithful representation, the transactions must be accounted for and presented on the basis of their commercial reality rather than their legal form.

In addition, the information must be neutral (free from bias) and complete. An omission can cause information to be false or misleading, as can the overstating of accounting estimates like provisions and valuations.

(b) An example of where relevance and reliability could come into conflict could be the existence of a contingent liability.

If the directors of an entity believe with reasonable certainty that a future liability has been identified they must first consider whether details on it should be included. If they consider that knowledge of it could affect the decision-making of users, then it should be included. However, given it is based on a future event, it cannot be measured with certainty and they may not have sufficient information to make a financial estimate with reasonable certainty. It may be questionable then if the information they could provide would be reliable.

In this case relevance and reliability must be traded off. It is likely that if omission of information on the potential liability would affect users' decision-making then, details should be included even if the financial amount cannot be stated with reasonable certainty. Relevance would override reliability in this case, see Sections 8.3.3.2 and 8.3.3.3.

 ## Solution 5

In the case of a trade receivable, the past event is the making of a credit sale. The goods are transferred and the amount receivable is included in the financial records of the entity making the sale. That entity now has a receivable that is expected to turn into cash on receipt of the payment. The entity can be reasonably certain of payment where the transaction is complete, there is no dispute with the debtor and the debtor is not considered to be a credit risk. In this case, the entity can be reasonably certain that the future economic benefit (cash) will flow to them at the end of the granted credit period and can recognise the receivable as an asset within the financial statements, see Section 8.3.4.

 ## Solution 6

Expenses are decreases in economic benefits during the accounting period in the form of outflows or depletions of assets that result in decreases in equity, other than those relating to distributions to equity participants, see Section 8.3.4.

Solution 7

Understandability

An essential quality of financial information is that it is readily understandable by users. For this purpose, users are assumed to have a reasonable knowledge of business and economic activities and accounting and a willingness to study the information with reasonable diligence. Information on complex issues should be included if relevant and should not be excluded on the ground that it is too difficult for the average user to understand.

Relevance

Information is relevant when it influences the economic decisions of users by helping them to evaluate past, present or future economic events, or confirming/correcting their past evaluations.

An item can be relevant by virtue of its nature or materiality. Information is material if its omission or misstatement could influence the decision making of users.

Information should be released on a timely basis to be relevant to users.

Reliability

Information is reliable when it is free from material error and bias and can be considered by users to be a faithful representation of the underlying transactions and events.

To be reliable the information must:

- faithfully represent the transactions it is intended to represent;
- be accounted for and presented on the basis of its commercial reality rather than its legal form – substance over form;
- be neutral, free from bias.

Comparability

The ability to identify trends in performance and financial position and compare those both from year to year and against other entities assists users in their assessments and decision-making. To achieve comparability, users must be able to identify where an entity has changed its policy from one year to the next, and where other entities have used different accounting policies for similar transactions, see Section 8.3.3.

 ## Solution 8

Reliability and understandability
See Section 8.3.3.

 ## Solution 9

The objective of financial statements is to provide information about the financial position, performance, and changes in that position, of an entity that is useful to a wide range of users in making economic decisions.

See Section 8.3.1.

Solution 10

According to the *Framework*, its purposes are to:

- assist the Board in the development of future IFRSs and in its review of existing IFRSs;
- assist the Board in promoting harmonisation of regulations, accounting standards and procedures relating to the presentation of financial statements by providing a basis for reducing the number of alternative treatments permitted by IFRSs;
- assist national standard-setting bodies in developing national standards;
- assist preparers of financial statements in applying IFRSs and in dealing with topics that have yet to be covered in an IFRS;
- assist auditors in forming an opinion as to whether financial statements conform with IFRSs;
- assist users of financial statements that are prepared using IFRSs;
- provide information about how the IASB has formulated its approach to the development of IFRSs.

See Section 8.2.1.

The Role of the External Auditor

The Role of the
External Auditor

The syllabus topics covered in this chapter are as follows:

• The powers and duties of the external auditors, the audit report and its qualification for accounting statements not in accordance with best practice.

9.1 External audit

Countries differ widely in their audit requirement. Small entities (variously defined) are often exempt. When an audit is required, the auditor's duty is to express an opinion on the truth and fairness of the entity's published financial statements. Exemptions are usually available for dormant entities (which – by definition – have not traded during the year and so have no transactions to report).

You may work for an entity which requires an external audit and may have encountered members of the audit team. It is, however, impossible to get any real idea of the scale of an audit unless you have actually participated in one. Most of the cost of an audit is staff time charged to the audit. Auditing is a time-consuming and costly activity. It is, therefore, worth spending some time thinking about the reasons why an audit might be carried out.

9.1.1 The purpose of an audit

Managers often feel under pressure to portray their entities in a favourable light when they report to any interested parties. This is one reason why we have a detailed set of accounting standards to regulate the presentation of contentious items in the financial statements. There is, however, an even more fundamental issue that must be addressed in the financial reporting process. It is not enough merely to *publish* rules and regulations governing the financial statements, there has to be some mechanism to *enforce* their implementation. Without enforcement, managers might distort the impression created by the statements in any number of ways. The nature of this distortion could vary from outright fabrication of the figures all the way through to the deliberate exploitation of a loophole in the system of rules.

Auditing is largely about providing the readers of the financial statements with confidence in the figures. This is highlighted by the accountancy profession's definition of an audit.

> Audit of financial statements: an exercise whose objective is to enable auditors to express an opinion as to whether the financial statements give a true and fair view ... of the affairs of the entity at the period end and of its profit or loss ... for the period then ended and have been properly prepared in accordance with the applicable reporting framework (e.g. relevant legislation and applicable accounting standards). *International Standard on Auditing (ISA) 2000 Objective and General Principles Governing an Audit of Financial Statements.*

The logic behind this definition is that the auditor's opinion will add some credibility to the financial statements. The auditor is an independent expert on financial reporting and will have conducted exhaustive checks before signing the audit report.

9.1.2 The auditor's duties

In most countries, the auditor has a statutory duty to make a report to the entity's members on the truth and fairness of the entity's annual accounts. As we have seen in the foregoing section, this report must state the auditor's opinion on whether the statements have been prepared in accordance with the relevant legislation and whether they give a true and fair view of the profit or loss for the year and state of affairs at the year-end. The duty to report on the truth and fairness of the financial statements is the primary duty associated with the external audit.

The auditor has a duty to form an opinion on certain other matters and to report any reservations. The auditor must consider whether:

1. the entity has kept proper accounting records;
2. the entity's statement of financial position and statement of comprehensive income agree with the underlying accounting records;
3. all the information and explanations that the auditor considers necessary for the purposes of the audit have been obtained and whether adequate returns for their audit have been received from branches not visited during the audit;
4. the entity has complied with the relevant legislation's requirements in respect of the necessary disclosures. If the entity has not made all the disclosures required, the audit report should, if possible, contain a statement of the required particulars.

We do not need to elaborate on the above, although it is worth noting that (3) above effectively gives the auditor the right of access to any information or material that seems relevant to checking the financial statements. The entity cannot refuse this request.

The auditor has a limited duty to review the other information issued alongside the audited financial statements. For example, the auditor must consider whether the information in any reports published with the financial statements are consistent with the information in the statement of comprehensive income and statement of financial position. Any inconsistency should be disclosed in the audit report.

The auditor must gather information and evidence in order to support an opinion on the truth and fairness of the financial statements. There is, however, no need to *guarantee* that the statements give a true and fair view. This is partly because the auditor is only required to form an opinion in order to discharge each of the duties described above. It is also because there will always be a limit to the amount of evidence that can be collected. The auditor is required to apply 'reasonable skill and care' in conducting the audit.

Contrary to popular opinion, the auditor does not have a specific duty to search for fraud. The auditor will, however, have to consider the possibility that the truth and fairness of the statements might have been distorted by any irregularity including the concealment of a fraud. In general, auditors rely on control systems within entities to ensure that there has not been any material distortion because of fraud. The auditor would, however, follow up on anything suspicious which came to light during the course of the audit.

Local legal requirements may impose additional duties on auditors.

9.1.3 The powers of auditors

Rights that are designed to ensure that the auditor is able to fulfil their statutory duties are usually given to them under local legislation relating to entities, for example, in the UK, the Companies Act 1985. To be able to carry out their duties, auditors must be independent of the entity that they are auditing. Independence is fundamental to the credibility of the audit process.

The powers granted to the auditor by legislation varies from country to country but typical powers found in many countries are:

- the right of access at all times to the books, records, documents and accounts of the entity;
- the right to be notified of, attend and speak at meetings of owners;
- the right to require officers of the entity to provide them with whatever information and explanations they think necessary for the performance of their duties;
- the right to present a counter-argument to any meeting of owners that is considering the removal of the auditors.

9.1.4 The audit process

The manner in which an audit is conducted is beyond the scope of the syllabus. You should, however, be aware of the broad outline of the manner in which an audit is conducted.

Figure 9.1 illustrates the main steps of an audit. The auditor is usually appointed by the shareholders during the entity's annual general meeting. This appointment is normally effective until the next annual general meeting. It is very common for the same firm to be

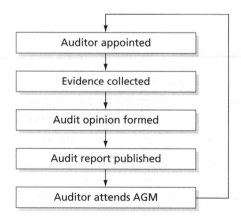

Figure 9.1 Steps in the audit cycle

reappointed annually for many years and so there is normally far more continuity than this annual cycle suggests.

The auditor sets about gathering evidence to support an opinion about the financial statements. There are two aspects to the preparation of the accounts and this means that there are two phases of the audit:

- *Bookkeeping phase.* The auditor must ensure that the transactions and balances recorded in the entity's books and ledgers are sufficiently complete and accurate to form the basis for an acceptable set of financial statements. This aspect of the audit work may be completed in stages, with most of the work undertaken during the year.
- *Accounting phase.* The auditor must review the accounting policies adopted by management in order to ensure that these are acceptable and that the statements give a true and fair view.

The gathering of audit evidence is not a part of our syllabus and so we will not discuss it further. The issues associated with the reporting stage of the audit are examinable. Basically, the auditor is responsible for forming an opinion on the truth and fairness of the financial statements and for reporting this opinion to the shareholders. We will discuss this duty in more detail below. Auditing is governed by a comprehensive set of international standards on auditing (ISAs) issued by the International Auditing and Assurance Standards Board (IAASB). The IAASB is a committee of the International Federation of Accountants (IFAC). Membership of IFAC is open to accountancy bodies worldwide.

9.2 The audit report

The provision of a clear expression of opinion on the financial statements lies at the heart of the external audit. The form and content of the audit report is governed by ISA 700 (Revised) *The Auditor's Report on Financial Statements*. ISA 700 was revised in December 2004, the new form of audit report is effective for auditor's reports dated on or after 31 December 2006. A typical audit report illustrated in ISA 700 is shown below.

Independent auditor's report

Appropriate addressee
We have audited the accompanying financial statements of ABC company, which comprise the statement of financial position as at 31 December 20X1, and the statement of comprehensive income, statement of changes in equity and statement of cash flows for the year then ended, and a summary of significant accounting policies and other explanatory notes.

Management's responsibility for the financial statements
Management is responsible for the preparation and fair presentation of these financial statements in accordance with International Financial Reporting Standards. This responsibility includes: designing, implementing and maintaining internal control relevant to the preparation and fair presentation of financial statements that are free from material misstatement, whether due to fraud or error; selecting and applying appropriate accounting policies; and making accounting estimates that are reasonable in the circumstances.

Auditor's responsibility

Our responsibility is to express an opinion on these financial statements based on our audit. We conducted our audit in accordance with International Standards on Auditing. Those standards require that we comply with ethical requirements and plan and perform the audit to obtain reasonable assurance whether the financial statements are free from material misstatement.

An audit involves performing procedures to obtain audit evidence about the amounts and disclosures in the financial statements. The procedures selected depend on the auditor's judgment, including the assessment of the risks of material misstatement of the financial statements, whether due to fraud or error. In making those risk assessments, the auditor considers internal control relevant to the entity's preparation and fair presentation of the financial statements in order to design audit procedures that are appropriate in the circumstances, but not for the purpose of expressing an opinion on the effectiveness of the entity's internal control. An audit also includes evaluating the appropriateness of accounting policies used and the reasonableness of accounting estimates made by management, as well as evaluating the overall presentation of the financial statements.

We believe that the audit evidence we have obtained is sufficient and appropriate to provide a basis for our audit opinion.

Opinion

In our opinion, the financial statements give a true and fair view of *(or present fairly, in all material respects,)* the financial position of ABC Company as of 31 December 20X1, and of its financial performance and its cash flows for the year then ended in accordance with International Financial Reporting Standards.

[Auditor's signature]
[Date of the auditor's report]
[Auditor's address]

You should look at this report carefully and then think about the following questions. They will help you to appreciate the extent of the auditor's duties.

- To what extent does this report state that the entity is well run?
- To what extent does it assure us that the board has been discharging its duties honestly?
- To what extent does it assure us that there has been no staff fraud?

The answer to each of the foregoing questions is 'not at all'. The audit report will never make any direct reference to the manner in which the entity is run. The financial statements could easily give a true and fair view even though the entity is not doing well. In that case, it would be up to the shareholders to infer that the entity had problems because it was making a loss or had a very poor return on capital employed. Similarly, the auditors do not provide any direct assurances about the stewardship of management or about the honesty of staff. We will return to this issue later, but the auditor's duties for the detection and reporting of fraud and other irregularities are quite severely restricted.

Thus, the only direct benefit to be had from the audit report is that it provides the shareholders with some assurance that the accounts give a true and fair view – in other words, it provides them with some assurance that the accounts provide a credible basis for making decisions.

9.2.1 A closer look at the report

A typical report is analysed in the following sections, to show what the various elements of it mean and why they are required:

Title

The auditor's report should have an appropriate title. It may be appropriate to use the term 'independent auditor' in the title to distinguish the auditor's report from reports that might be issued by others, such as by officers of the entity, the board of directors, or from the reports of other auditors who may not have to abide by the same ethical requirements as the independent auditor.

Addressee

The auditor's report should be appropriately addressed as required by the circumstances of the engagement and local regulations. The report is ordinarily addressed either to the shareholders or the board of directors of the entity whose financial statements are being audited.

Opening or introductory paragraph

The auditor's report should identify the entity whose financial statements have been audited and state that the financial statements have been audited. It should identify the title of each of the financial statements that comprise the complete set of financial statements. It should specify the date of and period covered by the financial statements.

Management's responsibility for the financial statements

The auditor's report should state that management is responsible for the preparation and the fair presentation of financial statements in accordance with the applicable financial reporting framework and that this responsibility includes:

(a) Designing, implementing and maintaining internal control relevant to the preparation and fair presentation of financial statements that are free from material misstatement, whether due to fraud or error;
(b) Selecting and applying appropriate accounting policies; and
(c) Making accounting estimates that are reasonable in the circumstances.

Financial statements are the representations of management. The preparation of such statements requires management to make significant accounting estimates and judgements, as well as to determine the appropriate accounting principles and methods used in preparation of the financial statements. In contrast, the auditor's responsibility is to audit these financial statements in order to express an opinion thereon.

Auditor's responsibility

The auditor's report should state that the responsibility of the auditor is to express an opinion on the financial statements based on the audit.

The auditor's report should state that the audit was conducted in accordance with International Standards on Auditing. The auditor's report should also explain that those standards require that the auditor comply with ethical requirements and that the auditor plan and perform the audit to obtain reasonable assurance whether the financial statements are free from material misstatement.

The auditor's report should describe an audit by stating that:

(a) An audit involves performing procedures to obtain audit evidence about the amounts and disclosures in the financial statements;

(b) The procedures selected depend on the auditor's judgement, including the assessment of the risks of material misstatement of the financial statements, whether due to fraud or error. In making those risk assessments, the auditor considers internal control relevant to the entity's preparation and fair presentation of the financial statements in order to design audit procedures that are appropriate in the circumstances, but not for the purpose of expressing an opinion on the effectiveness of the entity's internal control. In circumstances when the auditor also has a responsibility to express an opinion on the effectiveness of internal control in conjunction with the audit of the financial statements, the auditor should omit the phrase that the auditor's consideration of internal control is not for the purpose of expressing an opinion on the effectiveness of internal control; and

(c) An audit also includes evaluating the appropriateness of the accounting policies used, the reasonableness of accounting estimates made by management, as well as the overall presentation of the financial statements.

The auditor's report should state that the auditor believes that the audit evidence the auditor has obtained is sufficient and appropriate to provide a basis for the auditor's opinion.

Auditor's opinion

An unqualified opinion should be expressed when the auditor concludes that the financial statements give a true and fair view or are presented fairly, in all material respects, in accordance with the applicable financial reporting framework. When expressing an unqualified opinion, the opinion paragraph of the auditor's report should state the auditor's opinion that the financial statements give a true and fair view or present fairly, in all material respects, in accordance with the applicable financial reporting framework (unless the auditor is required by law or regulation to use different wording for the opinion, in which case the prescribed wording should be used).

The terms used to express the auditor's opinion are 'give a true and fair view' or 'present fairly, in all material respects,' and are equivalent. Both terms indicate, among other things, that the auditor considers only those matters that are material to the financial statements.

Date of report

The auditor should date the report as of the completion date of the audit. This informs the reader that the auditor has considered the effect on the financial statements and on the report of events and transactions of which the auditor became aware and that occurred up to that date.

Since the auditor's responsibility is to report on the financial statements as prepared and presented by management, the auditor should not date the report earlier than the date on which the financial statements are signed or approved by management.

Auditor's address

The report should name a specific location, which is ordinarily the city where the auditor maintains the office that has responsibility for the audit.

Auditor's signature

The report should be signed in the name of the audit firm, the personal name of the auditor, or both, as appropriate. The auditor's report is ordinarily signed in the name of the firm because the firm assumes responsibility for the audit.

An example of an audit report is given below.

Extract from the consolidated accounts of the Nestlé Group for the year ended 31 December 2005

Report of the group auditors

To: The General Meeting of Nestlé SA

As Group auditors we have audited the consolidated accounts (statement of financial position, a statement of comprehensive income, statement of cash flows, statement of changes in equity and annex) of the Nestlé Group for the year ended 31 December 2005.

These Consolidated Financial Statements are the responsibility of the Board of Directors. Our responsibility is to express an opinion on these Consolidated Financial Statements based on our audit. We confirm that we meet the legal requirements concerning professional qualification and independence.

Our audit was conducted in accordance with Swiss auditing standards and International Standards on Auditing, which require that an audit be planned and performed to obtain reasonable assurance about whether the Consolidated Financial Statements are free from material misstatement. We have examined on a test basis evidence supporting the amounts and disclosures in the Consolidated Financial Statements. We have also assessed the accounting principles used, significant estimates made and the overall Consolidated Financial Statements presentation. We believe that our audit provides a reasonable basis for our opinion.

In our opinion, the Consolidated Financial Statements give a true and fair view of the financial position, the net profit and cash flows in accordance with International Financial Reporting Standards (IFRS) and comply with Swiss law.

We recommend that the consolidated accounts submitted to you be approved.

KPMG Klynwed Peat Marwick Goerdeler SA

S. R. Cormack   Stéphane Gard

Auditor in charge

London and Zurich
23 February 2006

9.3 Modified audit reports

The auditor will almost always be able to conclude that the statements give a true and fair view, although it might be more difficult to do so in some cases. If an audit involves a particularly difficult problem, then the auditor might have to collect additional evidence before concluding that it has been accounted for correctly. Alternatively, the auditor might decide that the accounting policies chosen by management are unacceptable, in which case it will be necessary to negotiate a change of policy.

Occasionally, the auditor will be unable to conclude that the accounts give a true and fair view and is unable to persuade the directors to change their policy. In those cases, the auditor will have to express some reservation about the statements by giving a 'qualified' opinion. This means that the opinion paragraph of the report is modified to warn the readers that the auditor has some material reservation about the truth and fairness of the statements.

Modified reports are required where there has been a limitation on the scope of the auditor's examination or the auditor disagrees with the treatment or disclosure of a matter in the financial statements. Limitations of scope arise when the auditor is prevented from gathering all the evidence that is necessary in order to complete the audit.

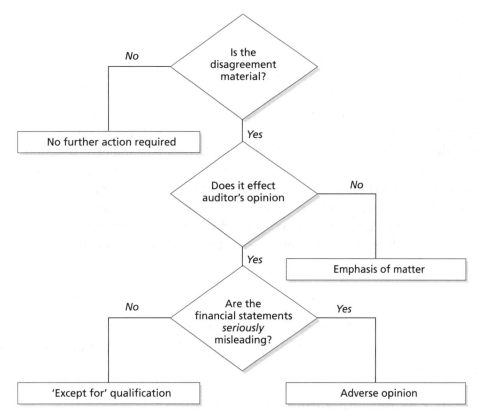

Figure 9.2 Classifying disagreements on the financial statements

While a limitation of scope is a serious problem for the auditor, it is specifically excluded from our syllabus and so we will not discuss it further. Qualifications arising from disagreement are, however, examinable.

The nature of accountancy means that there is always scope for disagreement over the facts, the application of an accounting standard or the amount of disclosure in the financial statements. The auditor would not necessarily treat a difference of opinion about the best possible treatment of a matter as disagreement. The matter would only become a problem if the auditor felt that the treatment adopted by management was unacceptable. Once such disagreement has been identified, the auditor must classify it as shown in Figure 9.2.

9.3.1 Materiality

By definition, a matter is material 'if its omission or misstatement could influence the economic decisions of users taken on the basis of the financial statements' (IASB *Framework*). This means that there is no real need to report on matters which are not material because they will not affect the behaviour of the readers. In other words, if something is immaterial then – by definition – it does not matter. Indeed, reporting on immaterial matters would be misleading because it would give them unnecessary prominence.

Materiality cannot be measured in terms of any objective criteria. Some audit firms use rules of thumb and treat anything which exceeds, say 5 or 10 per cent of profit or 1.2 or 1 per cent of turnover as material. These benchmarks are not sufficient in themselves because some matters are material by their very nature.

There should be very little doubt about the materiality or otherwise of an item in the exam. If materiality is to be determined by the amounts involved, then these will either be clearly material or immaterial, for example, well in excess of 10 per cent of profit or far less than 5 per cent.

Items which are to be judged in terms of their nature are rather more difficult. It is impossible to be categorical about whether such an item is material or not, but the issues ought either to be reasonably clear-cut or the marks awarded for the quality of arguments – either for or against the matter being material – rather than being for a correct distinction.

Figure 9.2 suggests that there is a second level of material disagreement, one which is so serious that the statements are rendered seriously misleading. The distinction between 'material' and more serious 'fundamental' qualifications is not clear-cut. A disagreement would have to be so serious as to guide readers in the wrong direction altogether before it would be regarded as more than merely material. Thus, this more extreme form of qualification might be reserved for circumstances in which, say the entity was reporting massive profits when the auditor was of the opinion that the entity was making massive losses.

9.3.2 The wording of a modified audit report

International Standard on Auditing 701(revised) *Modifications to the Independent Auditors Report* deals with modified audit reports. ISA 701 classifies modified audit reports into the following categories:

Matters that do not affect the auditor's opinion

(a) *Emphasis of matter* – In certain circumstances, an auditor's report may be modified by adding an emphasis of matter paragraph to highlight a matter affecting the financial statements which is included in a detailed note to the financial statements. The addition of such an emphasis of matter paragraph does not affect the auditor's opinion. The paragraph would usually be included after the paragraph containing the auditor's opinion and states that the auditor's opinion is not qualified in this respect.

An illustration of an emphasis of matter paragraph for a significant uncertainty in an auditor's report: *Without qualifying our opinion we draw attention to Note ... to the financial statements. The entity [brief explanation of circumstances explained in detail in the note].*

Matters that do affect the auditor's opinion

(a) *A qualified opinion* should be expressed when the auditor concludes that an unqualified opinion cannot be expressed but that the effect of any disagreement with management, or limitation on scope is not so material and pervasive as to require an adverse opinion or a disclaimer of opinion. A qualified opinion should be expressed as being 'except for' the effects of the matter to which the qualification relates.

(b) *A disclaimer of opinion* should be expressed when the possible effect of a limitation on scope is so material and pervasive that the auditor has not been able to obtain sufficient appropriate audit evidence and accordingly is unable to express an opinion on the financial statements.

(c) *An adverse opinion* should be expressed when the effect of a disagreement is so material and pervasive to the financial statements that the auditor concludes that a qualification of the report is not adequate to disclose the misleading or incomplete nature of the financial statements.

Whenever the auditor expresses an opinion that is other than unqualified, a clear description of all the substantive reasons should be included in the report and, unless impracticable, a quantification of the possible effect(s) on the financial statements.

9.3.3 Independent auditor's report showing qualified opinion

The most common form of qualified report is as follows. Read this report and compare it with the unqualified report shown above in 9.2.

Independent auditor's report

Appropriate addressee

Disagreement on Accounting Policies – Inappropriate Accounting Method – Qualified Opinion
We have audited the accompanying financial statements of ABC Company, which comprise the statement of financial position as at 31 December 20X1, and the a statement of comprehensive income, statement of changes in equity and statement of cash flows for the year then ended, and a summary of significant accounting policies and other explanatory notes.

Management's responsibility for the financial statements
Management is responsible for the preparation and fair presentation of these financial statements in accordance with International Financial Reporting Standards. This responsibility includes: designing, implementing and maintaining internal control relevant to the preparation and fair presentation of financial statements that are free from material misstatement, whether due to fraud or error; selecting and applying appropriate accounting policies; and making accounting estimates that are reasonable in the circumstances.

Auditor's responsibility
Our responsibility is to express an opinion on these financial statements based on our audit. We conducted our audit in accordance with International Standards on Auditing. Those standards require that we comply with ethical requirements and plan and perform the audit to obtain reasonable assurance whether the financial statements are free from material misstatement.

An audit involves performing procedures to obtain audit evidence about the amounts and disclosures in the financial statements. The procedures selected depend on the auditor's judgment, including the assessment of the risks of material misstatement of the financial statements, whether due to fraud or error. In making those risk assessments, the auditor considers internal control relevant to the entity's preparation and fair presentation of the financial statements in order to design audit procedures that are appropriate in the circumstances, but not for the purpose of expressing an opinion on the effectiveness of the entity's internal control. An audit also includes evaluating the appropriateness of accounting policies used and the reasonableness of accounting estimates made by management, as well as evaluating the overall presentation of financial statements.

We believe that the audit evidence we have obtained is sufficient and appropriate to provide a basis for our audit opinion.

Opinion
As discussed in Note X to the financial statements, no depreciation has been provided in the financial statements which practice, in our opinion, is not in accordance with International

THE ROLE OF THE EXTERNAL AUDITOR

Financial Reporting Standards. The provision for the year ended 31 December 20X1 should be xxx based on the straight-line method of depreciation using annual rates of 5% for the building and 20% for the equipment. Accordingly, the fixed assets should be reduced by accumulated depreciation of xxx and the loss for the year and accumulated deficit should be increased by xxx and xxx, respectively.

In our opinion, *except for the effect on the financial statements of the matter referred to in the preceding paragraph,* the financial statements give a true and fair view of (*or present fairly, in all material respects,*) the financial position of ABC Company as of 31 December 20X1, and of its financial performance and its cash flows for the year then ended in accordance with International Financial Reporting Standards.

[Auditor's signature]
[Date of the auditor's report]
[Auditor's address]

Much of the audit report is unchanged. The two main differences are that there is an additional paragraph which describes the specific area of disagreement between the auditor and the board and the opinion paragraph has been reworded.

The explanatory paragraph spells out the facts clearly and quantifies the matter. The readers of the report can now decide whether they agree with the auditor or the directors. If they support the auditor's opinion, then it is a simple matter to reduce both profit and current assets by the amount in question.

The opinion paragraph is also clear. The readers are left in no doubt that the auditor's only material reservation is in respect of the depreciation charge. This has been disclosed and the accounts otherwise give a true and fair view.

An extract from the more extreme form of qualification is shown below. Again, please read this and compare it with the examples shown above. *Note*: The wording of the first few paragraphs is not affected by the qualification, except that the report would be headed as shown.

9.3.4 Independant auditor's report-adverse opinion

Appropriate addressee
Disagreement on accounting policies – adverse opinion [...]

As more fully explained in note 7, no provision has been made for losses expected to arise on certain long-term contracts currently in progress, as the directors consider that such losses should be offset against amounts recoverable on other long-term contracts. In our opinion, provision should be made for foreseeable losses on individual contracts as required by IAS 11 *Construction Contracts*. If losses had been so recognised, the effect would have been to reduce the profit before and after tax for the year and the contract work in progress at 31 December 20X0 by $2.3 million.

In our opinion, in view of the effect of the failure to provide for the losses referred to above, the financial statements do not give a true and fair view of the financial position of ABC as at 31 December 20X0 and its financial performance and its cash flows for the year then ended in accordance with International Financial Reporting Standards and relevant statutes.

Auditor
Date
Address

The report is headed 'adverse opinion'. Again it contains a clear description of a difference of opinion between the directors and the auditor. This time, however, the auditor has concluded that the accounts do not give a true and fair view. Issuing such an opinion is an extreme step to take. Effectively, it suggests that the shareholders should not use the financial statements for decision-making purposes.

> You might be worried about distinguishing between the two types of qualified report. In general, you should decide whether the matter is material. If it is, then the 'except for' form will almost always be appropriate. You do have to be aware of the adverse opinion, but it is unlikely that you will ever use it in answering an examination question. You will not be asked to write out a full audit report in the examination. A question might ask you to decide which type of report is appropriate or to explain what the different types of audit report are, but you do not have to memorise the wording of the reports.

9.4 Summary

The auditor is responsible for forming an opinion on the truth and fairness of the financial statements and expressing this in a report addressed to the shareholders. This is necessary so that the readers of the financial statements can have some confidence that the directors have not manipulated the information in the accounts.

Having completed this chapter, we can now explain the purpose of an audit and the role and duties of the external auditor. We can describe the audit process and explain the contents of an audit report.

We can discuss the circumstances that could result in a qualified opinion being given and how that opinion would be reflected in the audit report.

Revision Questions

? Question 1

What is the objective of an audit?

(A) To check for fraud
(B) To check there are no errors in the accounts
(C) To enable the auditor to express an opinion as to whether the financial statements give a fair presentation of the company affairs
(D) To enable the auditor to approve the accounts   **(2 marks)**

? Question 2

Who is responsible for the preparation of the financial statements?

(A) The entity accountant
(B) The auditors
(C) The entity directors
(D) The shareholders   **(2 marks)**

? Question 3

What is the external auditor's statutory duty? *(max. 21 words)*.
   The auditor has a statutory duty to_____
                    (2 marks)

? Question 4

If an auditor disagrees with the treatment of a material item in the financial statements and the directors refuse to change their treatment, the auditor will in most situations:

(A) Issue a qualified audit report using the 'except for' qualification
(B) Issue an unqualified audit report
(C) Issue a qualified audit report using the 'adverse opinion' qualification
(D) Issue a qualified audit report using the 'disagreement of treatment' qualification
                    (2 marks)

? Question 5

If an external auditor does not agree with the directors' treatment of a material item in the accounts, the first action they should take is to

(A) give a qualified opinion of the financial statements
(B) give an unqualified opinion of the financial statements
(C) force the directors to change the treatment of the item in the accounts
(D) persuade the directors to change the treatment of the item in the accounts

(2 marks)

? Question 6

The external auditor has a duty to report on the truth and fairness of the financial statements and to report any reservations. The auditor is normally given a number of powers by statute to enable the statutory duties to be carried out.

List THREE powers that are usually granted to the auditor by statute.

(3 marks)

? Question 7

You are the partner in charge of the audit of G, a major quoted company. You are making a final review of the financial statements before finalising the audit report. The following matters have been marked for your attention:

(i) The draft financial statements indicate a turnover of $500 m and a profit of $50 m.
(ii) The directors have made no provision for the costs that are likely to be incurred as a result of a damages claim for $2.4 m, which is being pursued by one of the company's customers. G's legal department and its lawyers are quite sure that this claim will have to be met in full.
(iii) The directors have not provided for a sum of $2.3 m which ought to be written off in respect of debts that are almost certainly irrecoverable.

Requirements

(a) Explain the implications for your audit report of the matters described in (ii) and (iii) above.

Your answer should make a clear statement of the type of report which you consider appropriate, although a full audit report is *not* required. **(5 marks)**
(b) It has been suggested that the quality of audit reporting could be improved enormously if accounting standards were clearer and auditors had more explicit guidance on issues such as materiality.

Discuss this suggestion, making it clear how improved guidance on financial reporting might support the auditor. **(5 marks)**

(Total marks = 10)

❓ Question 8

You are the partner in charge of the audit of K. The following matter has been brought to your attention in the audit working papers.

The entity has refused to write the closing inventory down to the lower of cost and net realisable value, despite the requirements to do so in IAS 2. The audit senior estimates that closing inventory has been overstated by $500,000 because of this.

The draft financial statements show turnover of $40 million and profit of $4.5 million.

Requirements

(a) Explain what is meant by the term 'materiality'. Explain whether the matter highlighted above is material, giving reasons. **(5 marks)**

(b) Assuming that the directors refuse to amend the financial statements, explain what type of audit report would be appropriate to the above statements. **(5 marks)**

(Total marks = 10)

❓ Question 9

An external auditor gives a qualified audit report that is a "disclaimer of opinion".

This means that the auditor:

(A) has been unable to agree with an accounting treatment used by the directors in relation to a material item.

(B) has been prevented from obtaining sufficient appropriate audit evidence.

(C) has found extensive errors in the financial statements and concludes that they do not show a true and fair view.

(D) has discovered a few immaterial differences that do not affect the auditor's opinion.

(2 marks)

❓ Question 10

The International Standard on Auditing 701 Modifications to the Independent Auditor's Report, classifies modified audit reports into "matters that do not affect the auditor's opinion" and "matters that do affect the auditor's opinion". This latter category is further subdivided into three categories.

List these THREE categories. **(3 marks)**

Solutions to Revision Questions

In the real world, it is usually difficult to tell whether a problem is material or even if there is a serious disagreement. The nature of examination questions suggests that matters will always be more clear-cut.

Solution 1

The correct answer is (C).

The auditor does not check for fraud or errors specifically. The auditor does not 'approve' the accounts, see Section 9.1.1.

Solution 2

The correct answer is (C), see Section 9.1.2.

Solution 3

The auditor has a statutory duty to make a report to the company's members, expressing an opinion on the truth and fairness of the company's published financial statements, see Section 9.1.2

Solution 4

The correct answer is (A), see Section 9.3.

Solution 5

The correct answer is (D), see Section 9.1.2.

Solution 6

Powers of the auditor can include:

- Right of access at all times to the books, records, documents and accounts;
- Right to be notified, and attend meetings, of owners;

- Right to require officers of the entity to provide them with information and explanations;
- Right to speak at owners' meetings.

Note: Any three of the above would have gained the marks available.

 ## Solution 7

(a) The first question to be resolved is whether these amounts are material. If they are not then it would not matter whether the auditor disagreed or not.

Bear in mind that either item might be immaterial when taken on its own but the combined effect could be material. Both items tend to overstate profits and so we should consider whether their total value is misleading.

One half of 1 per cent of turnover = $2.5 million, as does 5 per cent of profit. This suggests that neither item is material in itself, but that the two taken together lead to a material overstatement of profits. If the directors refuse to alter their treatment of them, then the auditor will have to qualify the audit report.

IAS 37 requires that item (ii) should be accrued. This is on the grounds that the payment is probable and the amount can be estimated with reasonable accuracy. This accrual would reduce profits by $2.4 million and would create a current liability of the same amount.

The bad debt should be written off because of the need for prudence in the valuation of assets and recognition of losses. There is also a need to match the loss to the same period as the loss arose. This means that both profits and receivables should be decreased by $2.3 million.

In the absence of any change by the directors, we will need to qualify the financial statements on the grounds of disagreement. The extent of our disagreement is not so serious as to warrant an adverse opinion and so we will use the 'except for' form of words, see Section 9.3.

(b) The ambiguity of accounting standards is a major problem for the auditor. It is possible to create a slightly misleading impression without breaching any of the formal standards. It can be difficult for the auditor to justify a change to the financial statements if the directors argue that their treatment falls within the requirements of local company law and accounting standards. These same directors can, of course, seek out the loopholes and ambiguities in the standards in order to achieve the desired effect on the statements.

If accounting standards could be made clearer and less ambiguous, then the auditor could find it easier to demonstrate that a particular treatment was unacceptable. On the other hand, the statements might not be any more useful because the greater clarity might be arrived at by making the requirements more rigid – thereby reducing the scope for deciding on the most realistic treatment.

The other major problem facing the auditor is over the determination of materiality. It is never clear where the precise cut-off between material and immaterial actually lies. The danger is that the directors are aware of this and could bias the figures until just before the point at which the auditor would be forced to treat the matter as a material disagreement.

Greater clarity over materiality might help, but it could also provide management with a better idea of exactly how far they could push the figures. This suggests that it might not improve the overall quality of financial reporting and auditing.

Solution 8

(a) A matter is material if knowledge of it could influence users' decisions taken on the basis of the financial statements.

In strictly numerical terms, 0.5 per cent of turnover is $200,000 and 5 per cent of profit is $225,000.

The disagreement over inventory appears to be material because of its numerical significance. There is little point in considering the nature of the matter because it would be material by virtue of its effect on profit.

(b) This is a material disagreement and so the auditor must qualify the audit report in respect of the overstatement of stock.

The disagreement is material, but not fundamental and so the adverse opinion is not required.

The auditor would state that the accounts gave a true and fair view except for the overstatement of closing inventory and profits by $500,000, see Section 9.3.

 Solution 9

The correct answer is B, see Section 9.3.2.

 Solution 10

Qualified opinion
Adverse opinion
Disclaimer of opinion, see Section 9.3.2.

10

Published Financial
Statements

Published Financial Statements

10

Learning aims

The learning aims of this part of the syllabus are that students should be able to: 'prepare statutory accounts in appropriate form for a single company'.

With this chapter we commence the third section of the syllabus, section C. This section is a very important part of your studies and accounts for 45 per cent of your syllabus. Questions based on this section will appear in all three sections of the examination paper. The third section of the examination paper will comprise questions entirely from this section of the syllabus.

This text is based on IFRSs in force at January 2008. It includes all revisions made to IFRSs within the syllabus, during 2007.

The syllabus topics covered in this chapter are as follows:

- Preparation of the financial statements of a single company, including the statement of changes in equity (IAS 1).

10.1 Introduction

You will have prepared financial statements for sole traders and been introduced to the elements found in entity financial statements, either in the certificate level or in the examinations giving exemption from *Financial Accounting Fundamentals*. The work we will do at the Managerial level builds on that knowledge, so it would be advisable to refresh your knowledge of these areas before proceeding (The accounts of limited companies are covered in the CIMA study text for *Fundamentals of Financial Accounting*.)

The focus of the preparation of financial statements at this level is on entity financial statements that are prepared in a form suitable for publication. To ensure consistency and comparability of the information provided, the IASB prescribes the content for the main statements included in published financial statements.

IAS 1 was revised in 2007, the new version applies to financial statements beginning on or after 1 January 2009. The revised IAS 1 has made a number of changes to the terminology used in financial statements and changed the title of some of the statements and their content. The new terminology applies to all other IFRSs, these are changed by IAS 1 where appropriate.

Summary of the main changes made to terminology by IAS 1 revised 2007:

- 'On the face of' is amended to 'in'.
- 'Income statement' is amended to 'statement of comprehensive income'.
- 'Balance sheet' is amended to 'statement of financial position'.
- 'Cash flow statement' is amended to 'statement of cash flows'.
- 'Balance sheet date' is amended to 'end of the reporting period'.
- 'Equity holders' is amended to 'owners'.
- 'Removed from equity and recognized in profit or loss' and 'removed from equity and included in profit or loss' are amended to 'reclassified from equity to profit or loss as a reclassification adjustment'.
- 'Standard or Interpretation' is amended 'IFRS'.
- 'Standards and Interpretations' is amended to 'IFRSs'.
- References to the current version of IAS 7 Statement of Cash Flows.
- References to the current version of IAS 10 Events after the Balance Sheet Date are amended to IAS 10 Events after the Reporting Period.

This text has been written using the new IAS 1 terminology, the IFRSs are referred to by the new titles and the financial statements are referred to by the new titles through out the text, questions and answers.

This chapter will first discuss the general requirements for published financial statements and will then concentrate on the formats for the statement of financial position and the statement of comprehensive income, identifying the items to be presented in these statements and those to be included in the notes to the accounts.

The chapter focuses on the presentation aspects of the accounts, specifically addressed in IAS 1 (revised 2007) *Presentation of Financial Statements*. Accounting for and disclosing the effects of individual transactions will be covered in later chapters; however, the presentation requirements covered in this chapter will still apply.

Extracts from actual entity accounts cannot be included for the new formats as they are not mandatory until 2009 and entities have not published any financial statements using the new terminology and formats at the date of writing.

10.2 General requirements

10.2.1 Purpose of financial statements

IAS 1 states that financial statements are a structured financial representation of the financial position of an entity, showing the effect of the transactions it has undertaken.

We know from Chapter 8 that the objective of financial statements is to provide information about the financial position, performance and cash flows of an entity that is useful to a wide range of users in making economic decisions.

To meet this objective, financial statements provide information about an entity's

- assets;
- liabilities;
- equity;
- income and expenses, including gains and losses;
- contributions by and distributions to owners in their capacity as owners;
- cash flows.

This information, together with information contained in accompanying notes, assists users in evaluating the entity's future cash flows.

10.2.2 Responsibility for financial statements

The board of directors (and/or other governing body) of an entity is responsible for the preparation and presentation of its financial statements.

10.2.3 Components of financial statements

A complete set of financial statements normally includes:

- statement of financial position at the end of the period
- statement of comprehensive income for the period
- a statement of changes in equity for the period
- statement of cash flow for the period
- notes comprising a summary of significant accounting policies and other explanatory information.
- statement of financial position as at the start of the earliest comparative period, if the entity applies a change in accounting policy retrospectively or restates items in earlier periods or reclassifies items in its financial statements.

Entities are encouraged (but not required) to also present a financial review by management describing and explaining the main features of the entities' financial performance and financial position and the principle uncertainties it faces. This review may include:

- a description of the environment in which the entity operates;
- changes in the environment and how management has responded to them;
- resources not recognised in the balance sheet in accordance with IFRSs; and
- management policies on investment and dividends.

10.2.4 Fair presentation and compliance with IFRSs

Financial statements should present fairly the financial position, financial performance and cash flows of an entity. Fair presentation requires the faithful representation of the effects of transactions, other events and conditions in accordance with the definitions and recognition criteria for assets, liabilities, income and expenses set out in the Framework. The application of IFRSs, with additional disclosure when necessary, is presumed to result in financial statements that achieve a fair presentation. In virtually all circumstances, a fair presentation is achieved by compliance with applicable IFRSs. A fair presentation also requires an entity:

(a) to select and apply accounting policies in accordance with IAS 8 *Accounting Policies, Changes in Accounting Estimates and Errors.* IAS 8 sets out a hierarchy of authoritative guidance that management considers in the absence of a Standard or an Interpretation that specifically applies to an item;

(b) to present information, including accounting policies, in a manner that provides relevant, reliable, comparable and understandable information; and

(c) to provide additional disclosures when compliance with the specific requirements in IFRSs is insufficient to enable users to understand the impact of particular transactions, other events and conditions on the entity's financial position and financial performance.

Inappropriate accounting policies are not rectified either by disclosure of the accounting policies used or by notes or explanatory material.

Compliance with IFRSs requires that all relevant standards are complied with. IFRSs refer to international standards and IFRIC/SIC interpretations adopted by the IASB. When this text refers to IFRSs, it is referring to:

- IFRSs,
- IASs,
- IFRIC interpretations,
- SIC interpretations.

Entities should disclose the fact that they comply with IFRSs in the financial statements. This compliance statement is often included in the accounting policies and is usually the first stated policy.

Departure from requirements

In the unlikely event that the management decides that compliance with a particular requirement would result in misleading information, which would conflict with the objective of financial statements set out in the framework, they can *depart from that requirement in order to achieve fair presentation*. In this event, the entity should disclose:

- that management has concluded that the financial statements present fairly the entity's financial position, financial performance and cash flows;
- that it has complied with all relevant IFRSs except that it has departed from a standard to achieve fair presentation;
- the IFRS that it has departed from and details of the required treatment, why it was misleading and the treatment that has been adopted; and
- the financial impact of the departure for each period presented.

10.2.5 Other requirements affecting the preparation of financial statements

IAS 1 also outlines the following requirements for the preparation of financial statements. (Most of these you will be already familiar with, but are included for completeness.)

- *Accounting policies* should be selected so that financial statements will comply with IFRSs.
- Management should make an assessment of the entity's ability to continue as a going concern. Financial statements should then be prepared on a *going concern* basis, unless there are plans to liquidate or cease trading.

- The financial statements should be prepared under the *accruals basis* of accounting, with the exception of the cash flow information.
- The financial statements should retain a *consistent approach to presentation* and classification of items year-on-year.
- *Material amounts* should be *presented separately* in the financial statements. Immaterial amounts should be aggregated with other like items.
- *Assets and liabilities should not be offset,* except where required or permitted by another IFRS.
- *Income and expenses* should not be offset except where it is required or permitted by another IFRS.
- *Comparative information* should be disclosed for the previous period for all numerical information. Where presentation or classification of an item has changed, the comparative figures should be restated using the new treatment, if possible.
- Financial statements should be *presented at least annually* and should be issued on a timely basis (within 6 months of the end of the reporting period) to be useful to users.

IAS 1 does not specify the format of financial statements, but it does provide an appendix which sets out illustrative formats for the statements to be included in financial statements. In addition, it provides guidance on the items that should be disclosed in these statements and those that can be relegated to the notes that accompany the statements.

10.3 The statement of financial position

10.3.1 Specimen statement of financial position

A specimen statement of financial position (based on that provided in IAS 1) is set out below, this shows the minimum requirements for disclosure in the statement of financial position.

Take a moment to study the statement of financial position headings. The statement has two main sections – Assets and Equities and Liabilities. Most of the headings within the statement will be familiar to you, for example, property, plant and equipment, inventories, issued capital, reserves, trade and other payables. Most entities will have amounts that relate to these headings that are sufficiently material that they appear in the statement of financial position. Some of the other headings may not be so familiar, for example, goodwill. These amounts will only appear in the statement of financial position if the reporting entity has relevant amounts relating to these account categories.

IAS 1 (revised 2007) Specimen Format

Balance sheet as at 31 December 20X7

	$'000	$'000
Assets		
Non-current assets		
Property, plant and equipment	X	
Goodwill	X	
Other intangible assets	X	
Available for sale investments	X	
		X
Current assets		
Inventories	X	
Trade receivables	X	
Other current assets	X	
Cash and cash equivalents	X	
		X
Total assets		X
Equity and liabilities		
Equity		
Share capital	X	
Other components of equity	X	
Retained earnings	X	
Total equity		X
Non-current liabilities		
Long-term borrowings	X	
Deferred tax	X	
Long term provisions	X	
Total non-current liabilities		X
Current liabilities		
Trade and other payables	X	
Short-term borrowings	X	
Current portion of long-term borrowings	X	
Current tax payable	X	
Short term provisions	X	
Total current liabilities		X
Total liabilities		X
Total equity and liabilities		X

The format requires comparative figures for the previous year, these have been omitted as you will not need to prepare comparatives in questions.

10.3.2 Information to be presented in the statement of financial position

IAS 1 requires that, as a minimum, the following line items appear in the statement of financial position (where there are amounts to be classified within these categories):

(a) property, plant and equipment;
(b) investment property;
(c) intangible assets;
(d) financial assets (excluding amounts shown under (e), (h) and (i));
(e) investments accounted for using the equity method;**

(f) biological assets;

(g) inventories;

(h) trade and other receivables;

 (i) cash and cash equivalents;

 (j) the total of assets classified as held for sale in accordance with IFRS 5 *Non-current assets held for sale and discontinued operations*;

(k) trade and other payables;

 (l) provisions;

(m) financial liabilities (excluding amounts shown under (k) or (l));

(n) liabilities and assets for current tax as defined in IAS 12, *Income Taxes*;

(o) deferred tax liabilities and deferred tax assets, as defined in IAS 12, *Income Taxes*;

(p) liabilities included in disposal groups classified as held for sale in accordance with IFRS 5;

(q) minority interest, presented within equity;**

 (r) issued capital and reserves attributable to owners of the parent.

** These items relate to group accounts and are beyond the scope of this syllabus.

The above list includes items that the IASB believes are so different in nature or function that they should be separately disclosed, but *does not require them to appear in a fixed order or format.*

Additional line items, headings and subtotals should be shown in the statement of financial position if another IFRS requires it or where it is necessary to show a fair presentation of the financial position.

In deciding whether *additional items* should be separately presented, management should consider:

- the *nature and liquidity of assets* and their materiality (e.g. the separate disclosure of monetary and non-monetary amounts and current and non-current assets);
- their *function* within the entity (e.g. the separate disclosure of operating assets and financial assets, inventories and cash); and
- the *amounts, nature and timing of liabilities* (e.g. the separate disclosure of interest-bearing and non-interest-bearing liabilities and provisions and current and non-current liabilities).

Assets and liabilities that have a different nature or function within an entity are sometimes subject to different measurement bases, for example, plant and equipment may be carried at cost or held at a revalued amount (in accordance with IAS 16). The use of these different measurement bases for different classes of items suggests separate presentation is necessary for users to fully understand the accounts.

10.3.3 Information to be presented either in the statement of financial position or in the notes

Further subclassifications of the line items should be presented either in the statement of financial position or in the notes. The *size, nature and function* of the amounts involved, or the *requirements of another IFRS* will normally determine whether the disclosure is in the statement of financial position or in the notes.

The disclosures will vary for each item, but IAS 1 gives the following examples:

(a) *tangible assets* are analysed (IAS 16) by class: property, plant and equipment;
(b) *receivables* are analysed between:
  - amounts receivable from trade customers,
  - receivables from related parties,
  - prepayments,
  - other amounts;
(c) *inventories* are classified (IAS 2) into merchandise, production supplies, materials, work in progress and finished goods;
(d) *provisions* are analysed showing provisions for employee benefits separate from any other provisions;
(e) *equity capital and reserves* are analysed showing separately the various classes of paid-in capital, share premium and reserves.

10.3.4 Share capital and reserves disclosures

IAS 1 also requires that the following information on share capital and reserves be made *either in the statement of financial position or in the notes*:

(a) *for each class of share capital*:
  - the *number* of shares *authorised*,
  - the number of shares *issued and fully paid*, and issued but not fully paid,
  - *par value* per share, or that the shares have no par value,
  - *a reconciliation* of the number of shares outstanding at the beginning and at the end of the year,
  - the *rights, preferences and restrictions* attaching to that class, including restrictions on the distribution of dividends and the repayment of capital,
  - *shares* in the entity *held by the entity itself* or by subsidiaries or associates of the entity, and
  - shares reserved for issuance under *options and sales contracts*, including the terms and amounts;
(b) a description of the *nature and purpose of each reserve* within owners' equity;
  IAS 1 requires the following to be disclosed in the notes:
  - the amount of *dividends* that were proposed or declared after the reporting period but before the financial statements were authorised for issue;
  - the amount of any *cumulative preference dividends* not recognised.

Note: IAS 1 and IAS 10 do not allow proposed dividends to be included as a liability in the statement of financial position, unless the dividend was declared before the end of the reporting period.

10.3.5 The current/non-current distinction

An entity shall present current and non-current assets and current and non-current liabilities as separate classifications in the statement of financial position except when a presentation based on liquidity provides information that is reliable and more relevant.

Where an entity chooses not to classify by current and non-current, assets and liabilities should be presented broadly in order of their liquidity.

Whichever method of presentation is adopted, an entity should disclose, for each asset and liability, the amount that is expected to be recovered or settled *after more than 12 months.*

Most entities will show both current and non-current liabilities in the statement of financial position. However, say, for example, an entity does not normally have non-current trade liabilities but as a result of one particular transaction has a payable due 20 months from the end of the reporting period. The entity may, in this case, classify the entire amount as a trade payable under current liabilities and then show separately a one-off amount that is due in 20 months' time (i.e. in more than 12 months from the end of the reporting period).

In judging the most suitable presentation, management should consider the usefulness of the information they are providing. Information about the financial position of an entity is often used to predict the expected future cash flows and the timing of those cash flows. Information about the expected date of recovery and settlement of items is likely to be useful and therefore worth disclosing.

10.3.6 Current assets

An asset should be classified as a current asset when it is any of the following:

(a) is expected to be realised in, or is intended for sale or consumption in the entity's normal operating cycle;
(b) is held primarily for trading purposes;
(c) is expected to be realised within 12 months of the end of the reporting period; or
(d) is cash or cash equivalent.

All other assets should be classified as non-current assets.

10.3.7 Current liabilities

A liability should be classified as a current liability when it:

(a) is expected to be settled in the entity's normal operating cycle;
(b) is due to be settled within 12 months of the end of the reporting period;
(c) is held primarily for the purpose of being traded; or
(d) the entity does not have an unconditional right to defer settlement of the liability for at least 12 months after the end of the reporting period;

All other liabilities should be classified as non-current liabilities.

10.4 The statement of comprehensive income

IAS 1 (2007) requires an entity to present all items of income and expense recognised in the period, whether realised or unrealised, either:

(a) in a single statement of comprehensive income
(b) in two statements;
    (i) an income statement covering components of profit or loss;
    (ii) a statement comprehensive income that begins with profit or loss from the income statement and then adds/subtracts components of other comprehensive income.

10.4.1 Information to be presented in the statement of comprehensive income

IAS 1 requires that certain information (as a minimum) is presented in the statement of comprehensive income, including:

(a) revenue;
(b) finance costs;
(c) share of profits and losses of associates and joint ventures accounted for using the equity method (beyond the scope of this syllabus);
(d) tax expense;
(e) the total of the post tax profit or loss of discontinued operations and the post tax gain or loss recognised on the remeasurement to fair value less cost to sell, or on the disposal of the assets or disposal group constituting the discontinued operation;
(f) profit or loss;
(g) each component of other comprehensive income classified by nature (excluding amounts in (h));
(h) share of other comprehensive income of associates and joint ventures
(i) total comprehensive income.

Additional line items, headings and subtotals should be shown in the statement of comprehensive income if another IFRS requires it or where it is necessary to show a fair presentation of the financial position.

Materiality, the nature and function of the item are likely to be the main considerations when deciding whether to include an additional line item in the statement of comprehensive income.

10.4.2 Specimen statements of comprehensive income

Specimen statements of comprehensive income (based on those provided in IAS 1) are given below. Headings relating to items outside the scope of the syllabus have been omitted.

Statement of comprehensive income illustrating the presentation of comprehensive income in one statement

This first part illustrates the presentation of comprehensive income in one statement and the classification of expenses within profit by function.

Statement of comprehensive income for the year ended 31 December 20X7

	$'000
Revenue	X
Cost of sales	X
Gross profit	X
Other income	X
Distribution costs	(X)
Administrative expenses	(X)
Other expenses	(X)
Finance costs	(X)
Profit before tax	X
Income tax expense	(X)
Profit for the year from continuing operations	X
Loss for the year from discontinued operations	(X)
PROFIT FOR THE YEAR	X
Other comprehensive income:	
Available-for-sale financial assets	X
Gains on property revaluation	
Income tax relating to components of other comprehensive income	(X)
Other comprehensive income for the year, net of tax	X
TOTAL COMPREHENSIVE INCOME FOR THE YEAR	XX

Note that as an alternative the components of comprehensive income can be presented net of tax.

Statement of comprehensive income illustrating the presentation of comprehensive income in two statements

An entity may present two statements instead of one; a separate income statement and a statement of comprehensive income. In this case the statement of comprehensive income starts with the profit or loss from the income statement and includes components of other comprehensive income (items g to h above).

This second part illustrates the presentation of comprehensive income in two statements and classification of expenses within profit by function.

Income Statement for the year ended 31 December 20X7

	$'000
Revenue	X
Cost of sales	X
Gross profit	X
Other income	X
Distribution costs	(X)
Administrative expenses	(X)
Other expenses	(X)
Finance costs	(X)
Profit before tax	X
Income tax expense	(X)
Profit for the year from continuing operations	X
Loss for the year from discontinued operations	(X)
PROFIT FOR THE YEAR	X

XYZ Group – Statement of comprehensive income for the year ended 31 December 20X7

	$'000
Profit for the year	**XX**
Other comprehensive income:	
Available-for-sale financial assets	X
Gains on property revaluation	X
Income tax relating to components of other comprehensive income	X
Other comprehensive income for the year, net of tax	**X**
TOTAL COMPREHENSIVE INCOME FOR THE YEAR	**X**

Note that as an alternative the components of comprehensive income can be presented net of tax. This text will refer to the statement of comprehensive income where the full statement is used and will continue to refer to the income statement where either a two statement approach is used or where there are no entries to be disclosed in the 'other comprehensive income section'.

10.4.3 Information to be presented either in the statement of comprehensive income or in the notes

Certain items must be disclosed either in the statement of comprehensive income or in the notes, if material, including:
(a) write-downs of inventories or property, plant & equipment and reversals of write-downs;
(b) restructurings of the activities and reversals of any related provisions;
(c) disposals of property, plant and equipment;
(d) disposals of investments;
(e) discontinued operations;
(f) litigation settlements;
(g) other reversals of provisions.

An entity should present an *analysis of expenses* using a classification based on either the nature of expenses or their function within the entity.

This analysis can be in the statement of comprehensive income (which is encouraged) or in the notes.

Analysis of expenses – classification, nature of expenses

An analysis based on the *nature of expenses* would, for example, result in classifications for depreciation, purchases, wages and salaries, marketing costs, etc. The expenses would be presented in total for each type of expense. This format is normally adopted by manufacturing entities.

The analysis could look like this:

Revenue		X
Other income		X
Changes in inventories of finished goods and work in progress	X	
Raw materials and consumables used	X	
Employee benefits expense	X	
Depreciation and amortisation expense	X	
Impairment of property, plant and equipment	X	
Other expenses	X	
Total expenses		(X)
Finance costs		(X)
Profit before tax		X

The first item of expense in this format may be slightly confusing – changes in inventories of finished goods and work in progress. The change represents an adjustment to production expenses to reflect the fact that either:

- production has increased inventory levels, or
- sales exceeds production activity resulting in a reduction in inventory levels.

Note that changes in raw materials inventories are not included here. The change in raw materials inventories is in the next expense line and can be calculated as follows:

Opening inventory of raw materials	X
Plus: purchases of raw materials	X
	X
Less: closing inventory of raw materials	(X)
Raw materials and consumables used	X

Analysis of expenses – classification, function of expenses

An analysis based on the *function of the expense* (or cost of sales method) classifies expenses according to their function as part of cost of sales, distribution or administrative activities.

While this presentation can provide more relevant information to users, the allocation of costs to functions can often be arbitrary.

The analysis could look like this:

Revenue	X
Cost of sales	(X)
Gross profit	X
Other income	X
Distribution costs	(X)
Administrative expenses	(X)
Other expenses	(X)
Finance costs	(X)
Profit before tax	X

Entities choosing to classify expenses by function should disclose additional information on the nature of expenses, including depreciation and amortisation expense and employee benefits expense.

The entity should choose the analysis that is reliable and more relevant to the business activities.

 Most examination questions focus on the analysis by function, but occasional questions on analysis by nature of expense may occur.

Dividend Disclosures

An entity should disclose either in the statement of changes in equity or in the notes, the amount of dividends recognised as distributions to owners in the period, and the amount of *dividends per share*. An entity must disclose in the notes the amount of dividends proposed or declared but not recognised as a distribution to owners during the period.

10.5 Changes in equity

Changes in an entity's equity between two reporting period ends reflect the *increase or decrease in its net assets* or wealth during the period.

This information is useful to users as changes, excluding changes resulting from transactions with shareholders (e.g. capital injections and dividends) represents the total gains and losses generated by the entity in the period.

IAS 1 requires that certain information relating to equity be presented separately in a *statement of changes in equity.*

An entity must present, as a separate component of its financial statements, a statement showing:

(a) the *total comprehensive income* for the period, showing separately the total amounts attributable to owners of the parent and to minority interest;
(b) for each component of equity the effects of retrospective application or retrospective restatement recognised in accordance with IAS 8.
(c) transactions with owners in their capacity as owners, showing separately contributions by and distributions to owners;
(d) a *reconciliation* between the carrying amount of *each class of contributed equity and each reserve* at the beginning and end of the period, separately disclosing each movement.

The changes made by IAS 1 in 2007 mean that there is now only one format used for the statement of changes in equity. The specimen format provided by IAS 1 is given below.

10.5.1 Format for the statement of changes in equity

Specimen entity statement of changes in equity from IAS 1 (simplified by excluding items that are outside this syllabus)

Statement of changes in equity for the year ended 31 December 20X7

	Share capital $'000	Other reserves* $'000	Retained earnings $'000	Total $'000
Balance at 31 December 20X6	X	X	X	X
Changes in accounting policy			X	X
Restated balance	X	X	X	X
Changes in equity for 20X7				
Total comprehensive income for the period		X	X	X
Dividends			(X)	(X)
Transfer to retained earnings		(X)		X
issue of share capital	X			X
Balance at 31 December 20X7	X	X	X	X

* Other reserves are analysed into their components if materials

The above format provides a reconciliation between the opening and closing balances of each element within shareholders' equity.

Nestlé has adopted the following format in preparing its statement of changes in equity.

10.6 Notes to financial statements

Notes to the financial statements normally include narrative descriptions or more detailed analysis of items in the financial statements, as well as additional information such as contingent liabilities and commitments.

IAS 1 also provides guidance on the structure of the accompanying notes to financial statements, the accounting policies and other required disclosures.

10.6.1 Structure

> The Change in structure of paper 7 means that questions on the preparation of published financial statements will now be 30 marks. Questions requiring full disclosure of all the notes to a set of financial statements are unlikely. Questions are more likely to require either specific notes or no notes to be included in the answer. Disclosure requirements may also be tested in either of the other sections of the paper.

The notes to the financial statements of an entity should:

(a) present information about the *basis of preparation* of the financial statements and the specific *accounting policies* adopted for significant transactions;

(b) disclose the *information required by other IFRSs* that is not presented elsewhere in the financial statements;

(c) provide *additional information* which is not presented elsewhere in financial statements but is relevant to an understanding of any of them.

Notes to the financial statements should be presented in a systematic manner and any item in the financial statements should be *cross-referenced* to any related information in the notes.

Notes are normally provided in the following order, which assists users in understanding the financial statements and comparing them with those of other entities:

(a) statement of compliance with IFRSs;
(b) summary of the significant accounting policies applied;
(c) supporting information for items presented in each financial statement in the order in which each line item and each financial statement is presented;
(d) other disclosures, including:
- contingent liabilities, commitments and unrecognised contractual commitments other financial disclosures;
- non-financial disclosures.

10.6.2 Accounting policies

The summary of significant accounting policies in the notes to the financial statements should describe the following:

(a) the measurement basis (or bases) used in preparing the financial statements; and
(b) each specific accounting policy that is necessary for a proper understanding of the financial statements.

10.7 An illustrative question

Before completing the revision questions, please work through this illustrative question.

As you work through it, refer back to the relevant section of this chapter to see how the formats and disclosure requirements are adopted.

This illustrative question is a past CIMA examination question.

Scenario

The following information relates to V, a manufacturing entity.

Trial balance at 30 September 20X1

	Notes	$'000	$'000
Revenue			430
Inventory at 1 October 20X0		10	
Purchases		102	
Advertising		15	
Administration salaries		14	
Manufacturing wages		57	
Interest paid		14	
Dividends received	(e)		12
Audit fee		7	
Bad debts		10	
Taxation	(d) & (g)	10	
Dividends paid	(e)	120	
Premises (cost)	(b)	450	
Plant (cost)	(c)	280	
Premises (depreciation)			40
Plant (depreciation)			160
Investments (long term)		100	
Trade receivables		23	
Bank		157	
Payables			7
Deferred taxation	(f)		89
Loan notes			140
Share capital			100
Retained earnings at 1 October 20X0			391
		1,369	1,369

Notes

(a) Inventory was worth $13,000 on 30 September 20X1.

(b) Premises consist of land costing $250,000 and buildings costing $200,000. The buildings have an expected useful life of 50 years.

(c) Plant includes an item purchased during the year at a cost of $70,000. These were the only transactions involving non-current assets during the year.

 Depreciation of plant is to be charged at 10 per cent per annum on a straight-line basis.

(d) The balance on the tax account is an underprovision for tax brought forward from the year ended 30 September 20X0.

(e) The entity paid $48,000 on 27 November 20X0 as a final dividend for the year ended 30 September 20X0. A dividend of $12,000 was received on 13 January 20X1. The 20X1 interim dividend was paid on 15 April 20X1.

(f) The provision for deferred tax is to be reduced by $17,000.

(g) The directors have estimated that tax of $57,000 will be due on the profits of the year.

(h) The directors have proposed a final dividend for the year of $50,000.

Requirement

Prepare a single statement of comprehensive income (analysing expenses by income) for V for the year ended 30 September 20X1, a statement of changes in equity and a statement of financial position at that date. These should be in a form suitable for presentation to the shareholders in accordance with the requirements of IFRSs and be accompanied by notes to the accounts as far as is possible from the information given above.

 You are *not* required to prepare the note relating to accounting policies. **(25 marks)**

Discussion

This question carries 25 marks. You would therefore have 45 minutes to do it in an examination. You will only build up to that speed with a lot of practice. The question requires the expenses within profit to be disclosed by function, so we need to work out the totals for cost of sales, distribution costs and administrative expense.

Let us go through the question and pause to think about items needing attention. It is useful to begin with the additional information below the trial balance, deciding what to do with them and marking the related items in the trial balance where necessary.

Notes (a) and (b) and (c) are routine adjustments to inventory and non-current tangible assets.

Note (e) tells us about dividends received and paid. Both are shown net in profit or loss.

Note (f) gives us a straightforward movement on deferred tax.

Note (g) gives us the tax charge for the year and note (d) tells us about the underprovision of current tax in the previous year.

Note (h) gives us the proposed final dividend.

Now for the trial balance

- Revenue, put into the profit or loss section of the statement of comprehensive income
- *Inventory at 1 October 20X0*
- *Purchases*
- *Advertising*
- *Administration salaries*
- *Manufacturing wages.*

All these items go into a three-column working to arrive at the three disclosable totals – cost of sales, distribution costs and administrative expenses.

	Cost of sales $'000	Distribution costs $'000	Administrative expenses $'000
Inventory 1.10.X0	10		
Purchases	75		
Advertising		15	
Administrative salaries			14
Manufacturing wages, etc.	57		

For the rest of this working, see the answer below.

Returning to the trial balance, the items given here clearly direct us to the function of expense format for the profit or loss.

- *Interest paid.* There is no complication here. We simply include it as an expense at the correct place in the format. There is another point, not relevant for this question. Always check to confirm that the interest charge is for the full year, to find out whether an adjustment is needed. For example, if the trial balance includes 10 per cent loan notes $100,000 and interest paid is $5,000, clearly an accrual of $5,000 is required, unless the loan notes were issued halfway through the current year.
- *Audit fee.* Include in the expense working.
- *Bad debts.* Include in the expense working.
- *Taxation.* We shall need a working account for taxation (covered in detail in Chapter 6).
- *Dividend.* This is the interim dividend paid explained in note (e). The proposed dividend cannot be accrued, but must be disclosed as a note.

The remaining items are all routine statement of financial position headings.

V – Statement of comprehensive income for the year ended 30 September 20X1

Ref. To Notes		$'000	$'000
	Sales revenue		430
	Cost of sales		(188)
	Gross profit		242
1	Other income		12
	Distribution costs	(25)	
	Administrative expenses	(21)	(46)
			208
	Finance cost		(14)
	Profit before tax		194
2.	Income tax expense		(50)
	Net profit for the period		144
	Other comprehensive income		0
	Total comprehensive income for the year		144

V – Statement of financial position as at 30 September 20X1

Ref. To Notes		$'000	$'000
3.	Assets		
	Non-current assets		
	Property, plant and equipment		498
	Investments		100
			598
	Current assets		
	Inventory	13	
	Trade receivables	23	
	Cash and cash equivalents	157	
			193
			791
	Equity and Liabilities		
	Equity		
	Share capital	100	
	Retained earnings	415	
			515
	Non-current liabilities		
	Loan notes	140	
4.	Deferred tax	72	
			212
5.	*Current liabilities*		
	Trade and other payables	7	
	Current tax	57	
			64
			791

V – Statement of changes in equity for the year ended 30 September 20X1

	Share capital $'000	Retained earnings $'000	Total $'000
Balance at 30 September 20X0	100	391	491
Total comprehensive income for the period		144	144
Dividend paid		(120)	(120)
Balance at 30 September 20X1	100	415	515

Notes

1. *Profit from operations (required here as expenses are shown by function, see 10.4.3)*

   Profit from operations is arrived at after charging:

	$'000
Depreciation	32
Staff costs	74

2. *Taxation (profit or loss)*

	$'000
Taxation estimated for this year	57
Transfer from deferred tax	(17)
	40
Underprovision for previous year	10
Charge to profit or loss	50

3. *Dividends proposed*

   A final dividend of $50,000 is proposed for the year.

4. *Tangible non-current assets*

	Land and buildings $'000	Plant $'000	Total $'000
Cost 1 October 20X0	450	210	660
Additions	0	70	70
	450	280	730
Depreciation 1 October 20X0	(40)	(160)	(200)
Charge for year	(4)	(28)	(32)
	(44)	(188)	(232)
NBV 30 September 20X1	406	92	498
NBV 1 October 20X0	410	50	460

5. *Deferred taxation*

	$'000
Opening balance	89
Decrease in provision	(17)
Closing balance	72

Workings

Analysis of expenses

	Cost of sales $'000	Distribution costs $'000	Administrative expenses $'000
Opening inventory	10		
Purchases	102		
Advertising		15	
Administration salaries			14
Manufacturing wages	57		
Audit fee			7
Bad debts		10	
Depreciation:			
building	4		
plant	28		
Closing inventory	(13)		
	188	25	21

10.8 Summary

Having Completed this chapter, we can now explain the general requirements for the preparation of published financial statements as set out by IAS 1.

We are familiar with the recommended layouts of the main components of financial statements being statement of financial position, statement of comprehensive income and statement of changes in equity (statement of cash flows is covered in Chapter 12) and can adopt these formats in the preparation of financial statements.

Revision Questions

In the exam you may have to produce financial statements in a form suitable for publication. Use these examples to build your knowledge of the formats provided by IAS 1. You need to learn them.

Data for Questions 1 and 2

Trade receivables as at 31 December 20X1 were $18,000.

The bad debt provision as at 1 January 20X1 was $900.

During the year, bad debts of $12,000 have been written off to administrative expenses.

After the year-end, but before the accounts had been completed, the entity discovered that a major customer had gone into liquidation and that their outstanding balance of $2,000 was unlikely to be paid.

Furthermore, as a result of the recent bad debt experience, the directors have decided to increase the bad debt provision at 31 December 20X1 to 10 per cent of outstanding trade receivables.

❓ Question 1

What is the correct balance for trade receivables, net of bad debt provision, as at 31 December 20X1?

(A) $3,600
(B) $5,400
(C) $14,400
(D) $16,200   **(2 marks)**

❓ Question 2

What is the correct charge to profit or loss for bad debts and bad debt provisions for the year to 31 December 20X1?

(A) $14,000
(B) $14,400
(C) $14,700
(D) $15,600   **(2 marks)**

Question 3

IAS 1 *Presentation of financial statements* requires some of the items to be disclosed in the financial statements and others to be disclosed in the notes.

 (i) Depreciation
 (ii) Revenue
(iii) Closing inventory
(iv) Finance cost
 (v) Dividends

Which TWO of the above have to be shown in profit or loss, rather than in the notes:

(A) (i) and (iv)
(B) (iii) and (v)
(C) (ii) and (iii)
(D) (ii) and (iv)   **(2 marks)**

Question 4

IAS 1 *Presentation of Financial Statements* encourages an analysis of expenses to be presented in profit or loss. The analysis of expenses must use a classification based on either the nature of expense, or its function, within the entity such as:

 (i) Raw materials and consumables used;
 (ii) Distribution costs;
(iii) Employee benefit costs;
(iv) Cost of sales;
 (v) Depreciation and amortisation expense.

Which of the above would be disclosed in profit or loss if a manufacturing entity uses analysis based on function?

(A) (i), (iii) and (iv)
(B) (ii) and (iv)
(C) (i) and (v)
(D) (ii), (iii) and (v)   **(2 marks)**

Question 5

The following is an extract from the trial balance of CE at 31 March 2006:

	$'000	$'000
Administration expenses	260	
Cost of sales	480	
Interest paid	190	
Interest bearing borrowings		2,200
Inventory at 31 March 2006	220	
Property, plant and equipment at cost	1,500	
Property, plant and equipment, depreciation to 31 March 2005		540
Distribution costs	200	
Revenue		2,000

Notes:

(i) Included in the closing inventory at the end of the reporting period was inventory at a cost of $35,000, which was sold during April 2006 for $19,000.

(ii) Depreciation is provided for on property, plant and equipment at 20 per cent per year using the reducing balance method. Depreciation is regarded as cost of sales.

(iii) A member of the public was seriously injured while using one of CE's products on 4 October 2005. Professional legal advice is that CE will probably have to pay $500,000 compensation.

Requirement

Prepare CE's Income Statement for the year ended 31 March 2006 down to the line 'profit before tax'. **(5 marks)**

? Question 6

The following information has been extracted from the accounting reports of P:

P – trial balance at 31 March 20X1

	$'000	$'000
Sales revenue		5,300
Cost of sales	1,350	
Dividends received		210
Administrative expenses	490	
Distribution costs	370	
Interest payable	190	
Income tax	25	
Dividends paid	390	
Property, plant and equipment	4,250	
Short-term investments	2,700	
Inventory	114	
Trade receivables	418	
Bank	12	
Trade payables		136
Long-term loans (repayable 20X9)		1,200
Share capital		1,500
Share premium		800
Accumulated profits		1,163
	10,309	10,309

(a) During the year, P paid a final dividend of $240,000 in respect of the year ended 31 March 20X0. This was in addition to the interim dividend paid on 1 September 20X0 in respect of the year ended 31 March 20X1.

(b) The balance on the taxation account comprises the balance remaining from the settlement of the estimated tax charge for the year ended 31 March 20X0. The tax charge for this year has been estimated at $470,000.

(c) The directors have proposed a final dividend of $270,000.

Requirement

Prepare a statement of comprehensive income and a statement of changes in equity for the year ended 31 March 20X1, and a statement of financial position at that date. These should be in a form suitable for publication.

Your answer should include any notes intended for publication and these should be distinguished from workings.

You are *not* required to provide a note on accounting policies.   **(30 marks)**

 ## Question 7

Z imports electronic goods and resells these to large retail organisations. It specialises in luxury products such as electronic games and portable audio equipment. Almost half of Z's sales occur during the months of October and November.

Z faces intense competition and attempts to compete by anticipating consumer trends and offering products which are new to the market.

Z's trial balance at 30 September 20X2 is as follows:

	$'000	$'000
Sales revenue		9,800
Purchases	1,300	
Inventory at 30 September 20X1	480	
Warehouse and delivery wages	350	
Sales commissions	180	
Sundry distribution costs	310	
Sundry administrative expenses	85	
Administrative staff salaries	220	
Legal fees and damages	270	
Tax	45	
Dividends paid	1,775	
Warehouse premises – cost	8,500	
Warehouse premises – depreciation		800
Computer network – cost	900	
Computer network – depreciation		200
Delivery vehicles – cost	700	
Delivery vehicles – depreciation		280
Trade receivables	535	
Trade payables		470
Bank	90	
Loan – repayable 20X7		500
Loan interest	25	
Share capital		1,000
Accumulated profits		2,715
	15,765	15,765

Notes:

 (i) The closing inventory was counted on 30 September 20X2 and was valued at $520,000.

 (ii) The legal fees and damages were paid in settlement of a claim against Z for a faulty product that had caused injury to a customer. Z has introduced safety checks on new products which will help to prevent any recurrence of this type of accident.

(iii) Depreciation has still to be charged for the year on the following bases:

Warehouse premises	2% of cost
Computer network	25% of book value
Vehicles	25% of book value

(iv) The tax expense for the year has been estimated at $1,900,000.

(v) Z paid a final dividend of $800,000 for the year ended 30 September 20X1 and an interim dividend of $975,000 during the year. The directors propose a final dividend of $1 m.

Requirement

Prepare a statement of comprehensive income and a statement of changes in equity for the year ended 30 September 20X2, and a statement of financial position at that date, together with notes to the financial statements for Z. These should be in a form suitable for publication in so far as is possible given the information provided. You are not required to provide a statement of accounting policies. **(30 marks)**

Solutions to Revision Questions

 Solution 1

The correct answer is (C). The bad debts already written off have already been deducted from the receivables balance. As the $2,000 is unlikely to be paid, it should be provided for as a bad debt. Deduct this specific bad debt provision first then calculate the 10% provision.

	$
Trade receiveables	18,000
Less bad debt	2,000
	16,000
Less 10% provision	1,600
	14,400

 Solution 2

The correct answer is (C).

The total charge to profit or loss will include the amount already written off plus the new bad debt provision plus the increase in the general bad debt provision.

	$	$
Bad debts already written off		12,000
Bad debt at year-end		2,000
		14,000
Increase in provision		
Bad debt provision b/f	900	
Bad debt provision c/f	1,600	
Increase		700
Total		14,700

 Solution 3

The correct answer is D, see Section 10.4.3.

 Solution 4

The correct answer is B, see Section 10.4.3.

Solution 5

CE – Income statement for the year ended 31 March 2006

	$'000
Revenue	2,000
Cost of sales	(688)
Gross profit	1,312
Distribution costs	(200)
Administrative expenses	(760)
Profit	352
Finance costs	(190)
Profit before tax	162

Workings:
Cost of sales = 480 + 192 + 16 = 688
Administration = 260 + 500 = 760

 Solution 6

P – statement of comprehensive income for the year ended 31 March 20X1

	Notes	$'000
Revenue		5,300
Cost of sales		(1,350)
Gross profit		3,950
Other income		210
Distribution costs		(370)
Administrative expenses		(490)
Profit		3,300
Finance cost		(190)
Profit before tax		3,110
Income tax expense	1	(495)
Profit for the year		2,615
Other comprehensive income		0
Total comprehensive income for the year		2,615

P – statement of financial position at 31 March 20X1

	Notes	$'000	$'000
Assets			
Non-current assets			
Property, plant and equipment			4,250
Current assets			
Inventory		114	
Trade receivables		418	
Investments		2,700	
Cash and cash equivalents		12	
			3,244
Total assets			7,494

Equity and Liabilities
Capital and reserves

Issued capital	1,500	
Share premium	800	
Retained earnings	3,388	
		5,688
Non-current liabilities		
Long-term loans		1,200
Current liabilities		
Trade payables	136	
Taxation	470	
		606
Total equity and liabilities		7,494

P – statement of changes in equity for the year ended 31 March 20X1

	Share capital $'000	Share premium $'000	Retained earnings $'000	Total $'000
Balance at 31 March 20X0	1,500	800	1,163	3,463
Total comprehensive income for the period			2,615	2,615
Dividends paid			(390)	(390)
Balance at 31 March 20X1	1,500	800	3,388	5,688

Notes to the accounts
1. *Taxation*

	$'000
Tax for the year	470
20X0 underprovision	25
	495

2. *Dividends*

	$'000
Dividends paid:	
Final, year ended 31 March 20X0	240
Interim, year ended 31 March 20X1	150
	390

The directors propose a final dividend of $270,000 for the year ended 31 March 20X1.

Solution 7

Z – statement of comprehensive income for the year ended 30 September 20X2

	Note	$'000
Revenue		9,800
Cost of sales		(1,430)
Gross profit		8,370
Distribution costs		(945)
Administrative expenses		(750)
Profit	1	6,675
Finance costs		(25)
Profit before tax		6,650
Tax expense	2	(1,945)
Profit for the period		4,705

Z – statement of financial position at 30 September 20X2

	Note	$'000	$'000
Assets			
Non-current assets			
Property, plant and equipment	4		8,370
Current assets			
Inventory		520	
Receivables		535	
Cash and cash equivalents		90	
			1,145
			9,515
Equity and Liabilities			
Capital and reserves			
Issued capital		1,000	
Retained earnings		5,645	
			6,645
Non-current liabilities			
Long-term loan	5		500
Current liabilities	6		
Trade payables		470	
Tax		1,900	
			2,370
			9,515

Z – statement of changes in equity, year ended 30 September 20X2

	Share capital $'000	Retained earnings $'000	Total $'000
Balance at 30 September 20X1	1,000	2,715	3,715
Total comprehensive income for the period		4,705	4,705
Dividends paid:			
Final, year ended 30 September 20X1		(800)	(800)
Interim, year ended 30 September 20X2		(975)	(975)
Balance at 30 September 20X2	1,000	5,645	6,645

Z – notes to the financial statements

1. *Operating profit*
   Operating profit is stated after charging:

	$'000
Depreciation	450
Exceptional item – non-recurring legal fees and damages (see Chapter 11 for treatment)	270
	720

2. *Taxation*

	$'000
Tax charge for the year	1,900
Underprovision from previous years	45
	1,945

3. *Dividends*
   The directors propose a final dividend of $1,000,000 for the year.

4. *Tangible non-current assets*

	Premises $'000	Computer $'000	Delivery vehicles $'000	Total $'000
Cost at 30 September 20X1 and 20X2	8,500	900	700	10,100
Depreciation at 30 September 20X1	800	200	280	1,280
Charge for the year	170	175	105	450
Depreciation at 30 September 20X2	970	375	385	1,730
Net book value at 30 September 20X2	7,530	525	315	8,370
Net book value at 30 September 20X1	7,700	700	420	8,820

5. *Long-term loan*
   This loan is due to be repaid in 5 years.

6. *Current liabilities*

	$'000
Trade payables	470
Tax	1,900
	2,370

Workings

	$'000
Cost of sales	
Opening inventory	480
Purchases	1,300
Closing inventory	(520)
	1,260
Depreciation on premises (2% × 8,500)	170
	1,430
Distribution costs	

Warehouse and delivery wages	350
Sales commissions	180
Sundry distribution costs	310
Depreciation on vehicles (25% × 700 − 280)	105
	945

Administrative expenses	
Sundry administrative expenses	85
Administrative staff salaries	220
Legal fees and damages	270
Depreciation on computer (25% × 900 − 200)	175
	750

11

Reporting Financial Performance

Reporting Financial Performance

11

LEARNING OUTCOME

After completing this chapter, you should be able to:

► explain and apply the accounting rules contained in IAS's dealing with reporting performance.

The syllabus topics covered in this chapter are as follows:

- Reporting performance: recognition of revenue, measurement of profit or loss, extraordinary items, prior period items, discontinuing operations and segment reporting (IAS 1, 8, 14, 18 and 35).

11.1 Introduction

In the previous chapter, we studied the requirements (primarily of IAS 1 *Presentation of Financial Statements*) for the presentation of financial statements. This chapter builds on the knowledge gained in Chapter 10, but focuses on the statement of comprehensive income and separate income statement if one is presented.

In this chapter, we are going to consider the recognition of revenue, the measurement of profit, presentation issues regarding unusual items in the statement of comprehensive income or separate income statement and presentation and disclosure requirements regarding segmental information.

The five accounting standards covered in this chapter are all concerned with specific items, transactions and adjustments that appear either in profit or loss or in the accompanying notes. Note that since the syllabus was published, IAS 35 has been replaced by IFRS 5 and IAS 14 has been superseded by IFRS 8.

Some of the standards give illustrative formats and where these are helpful in understanding the presentation aspects of these items, they will be included in the chapter.

Remember that although we are now looking in more detail at items within the statement of comprehensive income or income statement, if a separate one is presented, the recommended format outlined in Chapter 10 will still apply, if the accounts are to be in a form suitable for publication.

11.2 IAS 18 *Revenue Recognition*

11.2.1 Introduction

IAS 18 defines when revenue may be recognised on the sale of goods, the rendering of services and the receipt of interest, royalties and dividends.

11.2.2 Sale of goods

Revenue from the sale of goods should be recognised when the following five conditions have been met:

1. the significant risks and rewards of ownership of the goods have been transferred to the buyer;
2. the entity selling does not retain any continuing influence or control over the goods;
3. revenue can be measured reliably;
4. it is reasonably certain that the buyer will pay for the goods;
5. the costs to the selling entity can be measured reliably.

11.2.3 Rendering of services

The conditions to be met for services are similar to those for the supply of goods.
   Revenue from services should be recognised when:

(a) the amount of revenue can be measured reliably;
(b) it is reasonably certain that the client will pay for the services;
(c) the stage of completion of the transaction can be measured reliably;
(d) the costs to the entity supplying the service can be measured reliably.

Revenue is recognised acccording to the degree of completion.

11.2.4 Interest, royalties and dividends

The prime conditions for interest, royalties and dividends are that the amount of revenue can be measured reliably and their receipt is reasonably certain.
   Once those conditions are met, interest and royalties should be recognised on an accruals basis and dividends recognised when the right to receive them is established.

11.2.5 Disclosure requirements

(a) The accounting policies adopted for the recognition of revenue;
(b) The amount of each significant category of revenue recognised (i.e. figures for sale of goods, rendering of services, interest, royalties and dividends, if material).

   IAS 18 states that when the selling price includes an amount for subsequent servicing or support, for example, free support and updates for software for a period after purchase, some revenue should not be recognised immediately. Instead, a proportion of the revenue should be deferred and recognised as revenue in the period when the service is provided. The amount deferred should cover expected costs plus a proportion for profit.

11.3 Profit or loss for the period

The objective of *IAS 8 Accounting Policies, Changes in Accounting Estimates and Errors* (2003) is to prescribe the criteria for selecting and changing accounting policies, together with the accounting treatment and disclosure changes in accounting policies, changes in accounting estimates and corrections of errors. The standard is intended to enhance the relevance and reliability of an entity's financial statements, and the comparability of those statements over time and with the financial statements of other entities. The financial information provided by the statement of comprehensive income about the financial performance of an entity is historical; however, users often use this statement as a basis to evaluate the entity's future performance and any information that can assist in this process is relevant.

11.3.1 Extraordinary items

IAS 8 *Accounting Policies, Changes in Accounting Estimates and Errors* replaces IAS 8 *Net Profit or Loss for the Period, Fundamental Errors and Changes in Accounting Policies (revised in 1993). The 1993 version of IAS 8* required that profit or loss for the period, shown in the income statement, be separated into two components:

1. profit or loss from ordinary activities;
2. extraordinary items.

The original standard defined *extraordinary items* and included extensive disclosure requirements if extraordinary items were present in the income statement. The new IAS 8 eliminates extraordinary items and as a result you will not be examined on them even although they are referred to in the syllabus. There is no reference in IAS 8 now, it was transferred to IAS 1 *Presentation of Financial Statements.* The revised IAS 1 says that an entity should not present any items of income and expense as extraordinary items, either in the statement of comprehensive income or the separate income statement (if presented) or in the notes.

11.3.2 Profit or loss from ordinary activities

The term 'from ordinary activities' is now redundant as IAS 1 has removed extraordinary items; there is now only one category of profit, which is referred to simply as profit or loss.

There may be items of income or expense that occur within the normal course of business but, because of their size or unusual nature, should be separately disclosed.

Providing information about *large or unusual items* reported within profit will again help users to evaluate the profit or loss that the entity is likely to generate in future periods (from trading activities).

The standard gives some examples of circumstances that may result in the separate disclosure of items. They include:

(a) the write-down of inventories to net realisable value;
(b) the write-down of property, plant and equipment to recoverable amount and reversals of previous write-downs;
(c) restructuring of the activities of an entity and the reversal of any provisions made for the costs of restructuring;
(d) disposals of items of property, plant and equipment;
(e) disposals of long-term investments;

(f) discontinuing operations;
(g) litigation settlements;
(h) other reversals of provisions.

11.4 Definitions – Accounting policies, accounting estimates and errors

- Accounting policies are the specific principles, bases, conventions and practices applied by an entity in preparing their financial statements.
- A change in accounting estimates is an adjustment of the carrying amount of an asset or liability or the periodic charge to the profit or loss arising from the use of an asset that results from a change to the expected future benefits or future obligations associated with the asset or liability. Changes in accounting estimates arise from new information or developments and are not corrections of errors.
- Errors are material omissions or misstatements in the financial statements. Ideally errors should be found and corrected within the same accounting period, but if they are not discovered until a later period they are treated as prior period adjustments.

11.5 Changes in accounting policies

The need for comparability means that, where possible, an entity will adopt the same accounting policies year after year. However, changes are sometimes needed. Possible reasons being:

- a new statutory requirement;
- a new accounting standard;
- the change will result in a more appropriate presentation of events or transactions in the financial statements

According to IAS 8, when an accounting standard is applied to conditions that differ in substance from the previous situation, it is not to be treated as a change in accounting policy. If an accounting policy is applied to transactions or events that had not previously occurred or was previously immaterial, then it is not a change in accounting policies as there would not be an existing policy to change.

11.5.1 Treatment and disclosure

The required treatment in IAS 8 for changes in accounting policy is for the change to be applied retrospectively. This means that the effect of the change should be reported as an adjustment to the opening balance of retained earnings, with comparative information being restated unless impracticable.

When a change in accounting policy has a material effect on the current period or any prior period presented, or may have a material effect in subsequent periods, an entity should disclose the following:

- the reason for the change;
- the nature of the change;

- a description of transitional provisions, including those that might have an effect on future periods;
- the amount of the adjustment for the current period and for comparative figures for each financial statement line affected; and
- the amount of the adjustment relating to periods prior to those included in the comparative information;
- the fact that comparative information has been restated or that it is impracticable to do so.

Where entities choose to change an accounting policy, as opposed to a change caused by a new standard or interpretation, they should also disclose the reasons why applying the new accounting policy provides reliable and more relevant information.

The following example is amended from the example given in the appendix of IAS 8.

Example 11.A

During 20X2, Gamma changes its accounting policy with respect to the treatment of borrowing costs that are directly attributable to the acquisition of a hydroelectric power station, which is in course of construction (borrowing costs are specifically covered in Chapter 13). In previous periods, Gamma had capitalised such costs (the allowed alternative treatment in IAS 23). Gamma has now decided to treat these costs as an expense, rather than capitalise them (the benchmark treatment).

Gamma capitalised borrowing costs incurred of $2,600 during 20X1 and $5,200 in periods prior to 20X1 . All borrowing costs incurred in previous years were capitalised.

In 20X1, Gamma reported:

Profit before interest and income taxes	$18,000
Interest expense	–
Profit before income taxes	$18,000
Income taxes	($5,400)
Profit	$12,600

20X1 opening retained earnings was $20,000 and closing retained earnings totalled $32,600 ($20,000 plus profit of $12,600). Gamma's tax rate was 30% for 20X2 and 20X1.

The extract from the income statement for 20X2 for Gamma, prepared under the benchmark treatment, will be as follows:

	20X2 $	20X1 $ (restated)
Profit before interest and income taxes	30,000	18,000
Interest expense	(3,000)	(2,600)
Profit before income taxes	27,000	15,400
Income taxes	(8,100)	(4,620)
Profit	18,900	10,780

The Statement of changes in equity for Gamma, prepared under the benchmark treatment, will be as follows:

	20X2 $	20X1 $ (restated)
Opening retained earnings as previously reported	32,600	20,000
Change in accounting policy with respect to the capitalisation of interest (net of income taxes of $2,340 for 20X2 and $1,560 for 20X1) (Note 1)	(5,460)	(3,640)
Opening retained earnings as restated	27,140	16,360
Profit	18,900	10,780
Closing retained earnings	46,040	27,140

Extract from notes to the financial statements
Note 1

During 20X2, Gamma changed its accounting policy with respect to the treatment of borrowing costs that are directly attributable to the acquisition of a hydroelectric power station which is in course of construction. In order to conform with the benchmark treatment in IAS 23, *Borrowing Costs,* the entity now expense rather than capitalise such costs. This change in accounting policy has been accounted for retrospectively. The comparative statements for 20X1 have been restated to conform to the changed policy.

The effect of the change is an increase in interest expense of $3,000 (20X2) and $2,600 (20X1).

Opening retained earnings for 20X1 have been reduced by $3,640, ($5,200 less tax $1,560) which is the amount of the adjustment relating to periods prior to 20X1.

Opening retained earnings for 20X2 are adjusted for $5,460 ($3,640 plus ($2,600 less tax of $780)).

11.6 Changes in accounting estimates

The process of accounting requires estimation in many areas, for example, allowances for doubtful debts, inventory obsolescence or the estimated useful lives of non-current assets. The estimation process involves judgements based on the latest information available, and by their nature accounting estimates can rarely be measured with precision.

Where circumstances change or new information becomes available, the accounting estimate may need to be revised. The effect of the change of an accounting estimate should be reported as a part of the profit or loss for the period in which the change occurs.

It can be difficult to distinguish between a change in accounting policy and a change in an accounting estimate. Where this is the case, the change is treated as a change in an accounting estimate.

> Remember, a change in accounting policy will usually need a prior period adjustment, but a change in accounting estimate must be adjusted in profit or loss for the period and is not allowed to be treated as a prior period adjustment.

11.7 Errors

The 1993 version of IAS 8 referred to fundamental errors. The revised version of IAS 8 refers to material omissions and misstatements and prior period material omissions and misstatements, there is no mention of fundamental errors.

An omission or misstatement is material if individually or collectively they influence economic decisions of users taken on the basis of the financial statements. Materiality depends on the size and nature of the omission or misstatement judged according to its circumstances. An item could therefore be material because of its relative size or because of the nature of the error.

A prior period error is one where the material omissions and misstatements occurred in a previous period as a result of the failure to use or the misuse of reliable information that was available at the time and could reasonably be expected to have been obtained and taken into account when preparing the financial statements.

Such errors could be the result of:

- mathematical mistakes;
- mistakes in applying accounting policies;
- misinterpretation of facts;

- fraud;
- oversights.

Financial statements do not comply with IFRSs if they contain either material errors or immaterial errors made intentionally to achieve a particular presentation of the entities financial position, financial performance or cash flows.

11.7.1 Treatment and disclosure

The treatment for the correction of prior period errors is that the opening balance of retained earnings, in the first set of financial statements after the error is discovered, be adjusted by restating the comparative information, unless this is impracticable.

This means that the financial statements for the current period are presented as if the error had been corrected in the period in which the error was made. The financial statements for the current period must, however, disclose:

- the nature of the prior period error;
- the amount of the correction for the current period and for comparative figures presented for each line item affected;
- the amount of the correction relating to periods prior to those included in the comparative information;
- the fact that comparative information has been restated or that it is impracticable to do so.

The following example is amended from the example given in the appendix of IAS 8.

Example 11.B

During 20X2, Beta Co. discovered that certain products that had been sold during 20X1 were incorrectly included in inventory at 31 December 19X1 at $6,500.

Beta's accounting records for 20X2 show sales of $104,000, cost of goods sold of $86,500 (including $6,500 for error in opening inventory), and income taxes of $5,250.

In 20X1, Beta reported:

Sales	73,500
Cost of goods sold	(53,500)
Profit before income taxes	20,000
Income taxes	(6,000)
Profit	14,000

20X1 opening retained earnings was $20,000 and closing retained earnings totalled $34,000 ($20,000 plus profit for 20X1 of $14,000). Beta's income tax rate was 30 per cent for 20X2 and 20X1.

The extract from the income statement for 20X2 for Beta, will be as follows:

	20X2 $	20X1 $ (restated)
Sales	104,000	73,500
Cost of goods sold	(80,000)	(60,000)
Profit before income taxes	24,000	13,500
Income taxes	(7,200)	(4,050)
Profit	16,800	9,450

Note: 20X1 closing stock is overstated and therefore 20X1 cost of goods sold is understated by $6,500. Correction of this increases cost of goods sold from $53,500 to $60,000. Income taxes are calculated at 30% of $ 13,500, which is the revised profit.

20X2 cost of goods sold is correctly recorded at $80,000 ($86,500 less the $6,500 overstatement of opening stock charged to cost sales).

The retained earnings for Beta part of the Statement of changes in equity will be as follows:

	20X2 $	20X1 $ (restated)
Opening retained earnings as previously reported	34,000	20,000
Correction of prior year error (net of taxes of $ 1,950) (Note 1)	(4,550)	
Opening retained earnings as restated	29,450	20,000
Profit	16,800	9,450
Closing retained earnings	46,250	29,450

Extract from notes to the financial statements
Note 1

Certain products that had been sold in 20X1 were incorrectly included in inventory at 31 December 20X1 at $6,500. The financial statements of 20X1 have been restated to correct this error. The effect of the restatement on those financial statements is summarised below. There is no effect in 20X2.

		Effect on 20X1 $
Income statement	(Increase) in cost of goods sold	(6,500)
	Decrease in income tax expense	1,950
	(Decrease) in profit	(4,550)
Statement of financial position	(Decrease) in inventory	(6,500)
	Decrease in income tax payable	1,950
	(Decrease) in equity	(4,550)

11.8 Discontinuing operations

International Financial Reporting Standard 5 *Non-current Assets Held for Sale* and *Discontinued Operations* (IFRS 5) sets out requirements for the classification, measurement and presentation of non-current assets held for sale and the presentation and disclosure of discontinued operations. IFRS 5 replaces IAS 35 *Discontinuing Operations*. IFRS 5 applies to accounting periods commencing on or after 1 January 2005.

11.8.1 Objective

The objective of IFRS 5 is to specify the accounting for assets held for sale, and the presentation and disclosure of discontinued operations.

IFRS 5 sets principles for reporting information about discontinued operations, to enable users of financial statements to more easily evaluate an entity's future performance and cash flows.

Separate disclosure of results relating to discontinued operations will allow them to evaluate more accurately the likely performance of the operations that will be generating income in future periods.

11.8.2 Definition of a discontinued operation

IFRS 5 defines a discontinued operation as a component of an entity that has been disposed of, or is classified as held for sale and:

(a) is part of a single plan to dispose of a separate major line of business or geographical area of operations; or
(b) that represents a separate major line of business or geographical area of operations; or
(c) is a subsidiary acquired exclusively with a view to resale.

A component of an entity is defined as operations and cash flows that can be clearly distinguished, operationally and for financial reporting purposes, from the rest of the entity.

IFRS 5 introduces the concept of a disposal group, being a group of assets and liabilities directly associated with those assets, to be disposed of, by sale or otherwise, together as a group in a single transaction.

A disposal group may be a group of *cash-generating units,* a single cash-generating unit, or part of a cash-generating unit.

Classification of non-current assets (or disposal groups) as held for sale
Non-current asset (or disposal group) already held by the entity:

1. Classified as held for sale if its carrying amount will be recovered principally through a sale transaction rather than through continuing use. This occurs where:
   (a) The asset (or disposal group) is available for immediate sale in its present condition subject only to terms that are usual and customary for sales of such assets (or disposal groups) and its sale must be highly probable.
   (b) To be highly probable, the appropriate level of management must be committed to a plan to sell the asset (or disposal group), and an active programme to locate a buyer and complete the plan must have been initiated. The asset (or disposal group) must be actively marketed for sale at a price that is reasonable in relation to its current fair value and the sale should be expected to qualify for recognition as a completed sale within 1 year from the date of classification.

Non-current asset (or disposal group) acquired exclusively with a view to its subsequent disposal:

1. Classified as held for sale at the acquisition date only if the one-year requirement is met.

If either categories criteria are met after the reporting period, an entity shall not classify a non-current asset (or disposal group) as held for sale in those financial statements when issued. If the criteria are met after the reporting period but before the authorisation of the financial statements for issue, the entity shall disclose the information in the notes.

Assets classified as non-current in accordance with IAS 1 *Presentation of Financial Statements* (as revised in 2003) cannot be reclassified as current assets until they meet the IFRS 5 criteria to be classified as held for sale.

Assets of a class that an entity would normally regard as non-current that are acquired exclusively with a view to resale cannot be classified as current unless they meet the IFRS 5 criteria to be classified as held for sale.

For example, if a retail entity, Markies, which provides food, clothing and homewear, decides to withdraw from the food sector, then the related costs of that withdrawal would be recorded within discontinued operations, as long as it was discontinued before the end of the reporting period. The direct costs of abandoning the food division such as redundancy of staff and gain or loss on the sale of assets would be classified under discontinued operations. The costs of restructuring the remaining divisions, even if that restructuring is required as a result of the decision to close the food division, would however be classified as restructuring costs within continuing activities, as the costs relate to clothing and homewear and these are continuing trading activities.

A decision to withdraw from supplying dairy products would not constitute a discontinued operation as the entity is still operating in the food sector. It is not a withdrawal of a separate major line of business and so the related costs would be shown within continuing operations, probably as restructuring costs.

For the results of the discontinued operation to be separately disclosed, it follows that the related profits, losses, gains, assets and liabilities must be separately identifiable to be included in the financial statements.

11.8.3 Measurement of a non-current asset (or disposal group) held for sale

Non-current assets (or disposal group) classified as held for sale are valued at the lower of:

- The assets carrying amount as measured in accordance with applicable IFRSs.
- Fair value less costs to sell.

Recognition of impairment losses and reversals

When the non-current assets (or disposal group) are measured at fair value on initial recognition as held for sale, an impairment is recognised (in accordance with IAS 36) if the fair value less costs to sell are less than the assets carrying amount.

An entity can recognise a gain for any subsequent increase in fair value less costs to sell of an asset, but not in excess of the cumulative impairment loss that has been recognised either in accordance with this IFRS or previously in accordance with IAS 36 *Impairment of Assets*.

Depreciation

A non-current asset that is classified as held for sale or is part of a disposal group classified as held for sale *must not* be depreciated or amortised.

Interest and other expenses attributable to the liabilities of a disposal group classified as held for sale shall continue to be recognised.

11.8.4 Presentation and disclosure

An entity shall present and disclose information that enables users of the financial statements to evaluate the financial effects of discontinued operations and disposals of non-current assets (or disposal groups).

Presenting discontinued operations

(a) An entity shall disclose in the statement of comprehensive income or the separate income statement:
   - a single amount comprising the total of:
     - (i) the post-tax profit or loss of discontinued operations; and
     - (ii) the post-tax gain or loss recognised on the measurement to fair value less costs to sell;
     - (iii) the post-tax gain or loss on disposal of the assets or disposal group(s).

(b) An entity shall disclose in the notes or in the statement of comprehensive income or the separate income statement:
   - an analysis of the single amount in (a) above into:
     - (i) the revenue, expenses and pre-tax profit or loss of discontinued operations;
     - (ii) the related income tax expense (as required by IAS 12);
     - (iii) the gain or loss recognised on the measurement to fair value less costs to sell and the related income tax expense;
     - (iv) the gain or loss on the disposal of the assets or disposal group(s) and the related income tax expense.
   - If presented in the statement of comprehensive income or the separate income statement, it must be presented in a section identified as relating to discontinued operations, and be kept separate from continuing operations.

An entity shall disclose on the statement of cash flows or in the notes, net cash flows attributable to the operating, investing and financing activities of discontinued operations.

Comparative information for prior periods should be restated based on the classifications established in the current reporting period. For example, if the retail division is classified as a discontinued operation in 20X2 and its results are disclosed as such separately in the financial statements, then the comparative information for 20X1 should be restated (from continuing operations where it was included last year) and included as a direct comparison within discontinued operations.

Example 11.C

Let us consider the retail entity mentioned above. The results of Markies were as follows:

	20X2 $m	20X1 $m
Revenue	140	140
Operating expenses	(120)	(92)
Impairment loss	(10)	(20)
	10	28
Interest expense	(25)	(15)
Profit (loss) before tax	(15)	13
Income tax expense	4	(6)
Profit (loss) after tax	(11)	7

Note: The impairment losses both in 20X1 and 20X2 relate to the food division.

The decision was taken to withdraw from the food sector and a formal plan to abandon food related activities was formulated and implemented during the 20X2 financial year. The food division generated the following revenues and costs during 20X1 and 20X2.

	20X2	20X1
	$m	$m
Revenue	40	50
Operating expenses	(60)	(27)
Impairment loss	(10)	(20)
	(30)	3
Interest expense	(5)	(5)
Profit (loss) before tax	(35)	(2)
Income tax expense	10	1
Profit (loss) after tax	(25)	(1)

The 20X2 operating expenses for the food division includes a $30 million provision for employee terminations as a result of the closure.

When the final accounts are prepared, the 20X2 revenues and costs of the food division are shown separately within discontinued operations.

It was noted above that IFRS 5 requires comparative information for prior periods be restated based on the classifications of this reporting period. This means that the revenues and costs generated by the food division in 20X1 must be removed from the continuing operations total in 20X1 and restated as a direct comparison for the discontinued operations. In effect we can now see what revenues and costs were generated by the food division in 20X2 and what that same division generated the previous year.

IFRS 5 Format illustrating the discontinued information shown in the notes:

	20X2	20X1
Continuing operations	$m	$m
Revenue	100	90
Operating expenses	(60)	(65)
	40	25
Finance costs	(20)	(10)
Profit before tax	20	15
Income tax expense	(6)	(7)
Profit for the period from continuing operations	14	8
Discontinued operations		
Loss for the period from discontinued operations*	(25)	(1)
Profit for the period	(11)	7

* The required analysis would be given in the notes

Notes:
Discontinued operations

	20X2	20X1
	$m	$m
Revenue	40	50
Operating expenses	(30)	(27)
Impairment loss	(10)	(20)
Provision for employee termination	(30)	–
	(30)	3
Interest expense	(5)	(5)
Loss before tax	(35)	(2)
Income tax expense	10	1
Loss after tax	(25)	(1)

From the income statement above, we can now clearly see the figures generated by the food division in the last 2 years. The amounts generated by continuing operations are now separately disclosed and can be used to evaluate future income streams. (This is one of the aims of IFRS 5 – that relevant information about the components of profit be disclosed in order that users can evaluate future profits, which helps them make investment decisions based on this historic information.)

Note: The provision for employee redundancies of $30 million is likely to be reversed in the following period and offset against the actual expense incurred — remember this is the accruals concept being applied; you provide for an expense and you recognise it in the period when it was incurred; when the operation is discontinued, a provision is made for items that are still outstanding at the end of the reporting period. For example, the actual cost of redundancies within the food division may amount to $36 million in 20X3 less the amount previously provided (in 20X2) of $30 million, which results in an additional charge in 20X3 of $6 million, this will be disclosed separately under discontinued operations in 20X3.

Presentation of a non-current asset or disposal group classified as held for sale

Non-current assets classified as held for sale and the assets of a disposal group classified as held for sale are shown separately from other assets in the statement of financial position, under current assets.

The liabilities of a disposal group classified as held for sale shall be presented separately from other liabilities in the statement of financial position, under current liabilities. Assets and liabilities shall not be offset and presented as a single amount.

The major classes of assets and liabilities classified as held for sale must be separately disclosed either in the statement of financial position or in the notes.

Any cumulative income or expense recognised directly in equity relating to a non-current asset (or disposal group) classified as held for sale must be shown separately under equity.

Prior year balances for non-current assets are not adjusted to take account of the reclassification in the statement of financial position for the latest period.

Example 11.D

At the end of 20X5, an entity decides to dispose of part of its assets (and directly associated liabilities). The disposal, which meets the criteria in IFRS 5 to be classified as held for sale, takes the form of two disposal groups, as follows:

	Carrying amount after classification as held for sale	
	Disposal group I: $'000	Disposal group II: $'000
Property, plant and equipment	4,900	1,700
Financial asset	1,400*	–
Liabilities	(2,400)	(900)
Net carrying amount of disposal group	3,900	800

* An amount of $400,000 relating to these assets has been recognised directly in equity.

The presentation in the entity's statement of financial position of the disposal groups classified as held for sale can be shown as follows:

Statement of financial position	20X5	20X4
ASSETS		
Non-current assets		
Tangible	X	X
Intangible	X	X
	X	X
Current assets		
Inventory	X	X
Receivables	X	X
Cash	X	X
	X	X
Non-current assets classified as held for sale	8,000	–
	X	X
Total assets	X	X

	20X5	20X4
EQUITY AND LIABILITIES		
Equity		
Equity shares	X	X
Reserves	X	X
Amounts recognised directly in equity relating to non-current assets held for sale	400	–
	X	X
Total equity	X	X
Non-current liabilities		
Loans	X	X
Current liabilities		
Payables	X	X
Liabilities directly associated with non-current assets classified as held for sale	3,300	–
	X	X
Total liabilities	X	X
Total equity and liabilities	X	X

The presentation requirements for assets (or disposal groups) classified as held for sale at the end of the reporting period do not apply retrospectively. The comparative statement of financial position for any previous periods are therefore not represented.

Additional disclosures

An entity must disclose the following information in the notes in the period in which a non-current asset (or disposal group) has been either classified as held for sale or sold:

(a) a description of the non-current asset or disposal group;
(b) a description of the facts and circumstances of the sale;
(c) in respect of held for sale items, the facts and circumstances leading to the expected disposal, and the expected timing of that disposal.

11.9 International financial reporting standard 8 *Operating Segments* (IFRS 8)

IFRS 8 *Operating Segments* was issued on October 2006 and replaces IAS 14 *Segment Reporting* which it supersedes. IFRS 8 is mandatory for annual periods beginning on or after 1 January 2009.

11.9.1 IFRS 8 *Operating Segments* – core principle

IFRS 8 *Operating Segments* does not specify an objective as previous IAS's have, instead IFRS 8 has a 'core principle'. The core principle of IFRS 8 is: 'An entity shall disclose information to enable users of its financial statements to evaluate the nature and financial effects of the business activities in which it engages and the economic environments in which it operates.' IFRS 8 sets out requirements for disclosure of information about an entity's operating segments and also about the entity's products and services, the geographical areas in which it operates, and its major customers.

11.9.2 Definition of operating segment

The only definition given in IFRS 8 is that of an operating segment. An operating segment is a component of an entity:

(a) that engages in business activities from which it may earn revenues and incur expenses (including revenues and expenses relating to transactions with other components of the same entity);

(b) whose operating results are regularly reviewed by the entity's chief operating decision maker to make decisions about resources to be allocated to the segment and assess its performance; and

(c) for which discrete financial information is available.

Operating segments can be aggregated where they have similar economic characteristics and are similar in each of the following:

- the nature of the products or services;
- the nature of the production process;
- the type of customer for the products or services;
- the methods used to distribute the products or services;
- the nature of the regulatory environment (banking, insurance, etc.).

11.9.3 Reportable segments

An operating segment is a reportable segment if the operation contributes at least 10 per cent of:

- total sales revenue, including sales to other segments; or
- total profits of all profit-making segments; or
- total losses of all loss-making segments; or
- total assets.

An operating segment that falls below all of the 10 per cent thresholds listed above may still be shown as a reportable segment despite its size, should the management believe that it is necessary for users to fully understand the financial statements.

If it is not included as a separately identified reportable segment, it should be included in an 'all other segments' category.

If the total external revenue attributable to reportable segments amounts to less than 75 per cent of the total revenue, additional segments should be identified as reportable segments, even if they do not meet the 10 per cent thresholds, until at least 75 per cent of the revenue is allocated to reportable segments.

11.9.4 Segment accounting policies

IFRS 8 requires the amount reported for each operating segment to be the measure reported to the chief operating decision maker for the purpose of allocating resources to the segment and assessing its performance.

IFRS 8 also requires an explanation to be given of how segment profit or loss, assets and liabilities are measured.

11.9.5 Disclosure

An entity shall disclose information to enable users of its financial statements to evaluate the nature and financial effects of the business activities in which it engages and the economic environments in which it operates.

An entity shall report a measure of profit or loss and total assets for each reportable segment. An entity shall report a measure of liabilities for each reportable segment if such an amount is regularly provided to the chief operating decision maker. An entity shall also disclose the following about each reportable segment if the specified amounts are included in the measure of segment profit or loss reviewed by the chief operating decision maker, or are otherwise regularly provided to the chief operating deicision maker, even if not included in that measure of segment profit or loss:

(a) revenues from external customers;
(b) revenues from transactions with other operating segments of the same entity;
(c) interest revenue;
(d) interest expense;
(e) depreciation and amortisation;
(f) material items of income and expense separately disclosed in the statement of comprehensive income;
(g) the entity's interest in the profit or loss of associates and joint ventures accounted for by the equity method;
(h) income tax expense or income; and
(i) material non-cash items other than depreciation and amortisation.

Extracts from IFRS 8 implementation guidance are given below as illustrations of the likely formats of segmental information

CU = currency units

	Car parts CU	Motor vessels CU	Software CU	Electronics CU	Finance CU	All other CU	Totals CU
Revenues from external customers	3,000	5,000	9,500	12,000	5,000	1,000[a]	35,500
Intersegment revenues	–	–	3,000	1,500	–	–	4,500
Interest revenue	450	800	1,000	1,500	–	–	3,750
Interest expense	350	600	700	1,100	–	–	2,750
Net interest revenue[b]	–	–	–	–	1,000	–	1,000
Depreciation and amortization	200	100	50	1,500	1,100	–	2,950
Reportable segment profit	200	70	900	2,300	500	100	4,070
Other material non-cash items:							
Impairment of assets	–	200	–	–	–	–	200
Reportable segment assets	2,000	5,000	3,000	12,000	57,000	2,000	81,000
Expenditures for reportable segment non-current assets	300	700	500	800	600	–	2,900
Reportable segment liabilities	1,050	3,000	1,800	8,000	30,000	–	43,850

11.9.6 Reconciliations

An entity shall provide reconciliations of all of the following:

(a) the total of the reportable segments' revenues to the entity's revenue.
(b) the total of the reportable segments' measures of profit or loss to the entity's profit or loss before tax expense (tax income) and discontinued operations. However, if an entity allocates to reportable segments items such as tax expense (tax income), the entity may reconcile the total of the segments' measures of profit or loss to the entity's profit or loss after those items.
(c) the total of the reportable segments' assets to the entity's assets.
(d) the total of the reportable segments' liabilities to the entity's liabilities if segment liabilities are reported
(e) the total of the reportable segments' amounts for every other material item of information disclosed to the corresponding amount for the entity.

Although the IFRS does not require assets to be identified by segment the requirement to reconcile reportable segments assets and liabilities to total assets and total liabilities effectively means that assets and liabilities have to be disclosed by segment.

Extracts from IFRS 8 showing reconciliations of reportable segment revenues, profit or loss, assets and liabilities

Revenues	**CU**
Total revenues for reportable segments	39,000
Other revenues	1,000
Elimination of intersegment revenues	(4,500)
Entity's revenues	35,500

Profit or loss	**CU**
Total profit or loss for reportable segments	3,970
Other profit or loss	100
Elimination of intersegment profits	(500)
Unallocated amounts:	
Litigation settlement received	500
Other corporate expenses	(750)
Adjustment to pension expense in consolidation	(250)
Income before income tax expense	3,070

Assets	**CU**
Total assets for reportable segments	79,000
Other assets	2,000
Elimination of receivable from corporate headquarters	(1,000)
Other unallocated amounts	1,500
Entity's assets	81,500

Liabilities	**CU**
Total liabilities for reportable segments	43,850
Unallocated defined benefit pension liabilities	30,000
Entity's liabilities	73,850

Other material items	Reportable segment totals CU	Adjustments CU	Entity totals CU
Interest revenue	3,750	75	3,825
Interest expense	2,750	(50)	2,700
Net interest revenue (finance segment only)	1,000	–	1,000
Expenditures for assets	2,900	1,000	3,900
Depreciation and amortization	2,950	–	2,950
Impairment of assets	200	–	200

Geographical information	Revenues[a] CU	Non-current assets CU
United States	19,000	11,000
Canada	4,200	–
China	3,400	6,500
Japan	2,900	3,500
Other countries	6,000	3,000
Total	35,500	24,000

11.9.7 Information about geographical areas

Although IFRS 8 does not require a full geographical analysis it does require an entity to report the following geographical information, unless the necessary information is not available and the cost to develop it would be excessive:

(a) revenues from external customers:
   (i) attributed to the entity's country of domicile and
   (ii) attributed to all foreign countries in total from which the entity derives revenues. If revenues from external customers attributed to an individual foreign country are material, those revenues shall be disclosed separately.

An entity shall disclose the basis for attributing revenues from external customers to individual countries.

(b) non-current assets other than financial instruments, deferred tax assets, post-employment benefit assets, and rights arising under insurance contracts:
   (i) located in the entity's country of domicile and
   (ii) located in all foreign countries in total in which the entity holds assets. If assets in an individual foreign country are material, those assets shall be disclosed separately.

If the necessary information is not available and the cost to develop it would be excessive, that fact shall be disclosed.

11.9.8 Information about major customers

IFRS 8 requires an entity to provide information about the extent of its reliance on its major customers. If revenues from transactions with a single external customer amount to 10 per cent or more of an entity's revenues, the entity shall disclose:

(a) the percentage of revenue for each such customer
(b) the total amount of revenues from each such customer,
(c) the identity of the segment or segments reporting the revenues.

The entity need not disclose the identity of a major customer or the amount of revenues that each segment reports from that customer. IFRS 8 regards a group of entities known to a reporting entity to be under common control as a single customer, and a government (national, state, provincial, territorial, local or foreign) and entities known to the reporting entity to be under the control of that government as a single customer.

11.10 Main differences between IAS 14 *segment reporting* and IFRS 8 *operating segments*

The main differences between IAS 14 and IFRS 8 are:

- IAS 14 requires identification of two sets of segments – one based on related products and services, and the other on geographical areas. IAS 14 regards one set as primary segments and the other as secondary segments. The requirements of IFRS 8 are based on the information about the components of the entity that management uses to make decisions about operating matters. IFRS 8 requires identification of operating segments on the basis of internal reports that are regularly reviewed by the entity's chief operating decision maker in order to allocate resources to the segment and assess its performance.
- IAS 14 limits reportable segments to those that earn a majority of their revenue from sales to external customers. IFRS 8's definition of an operating segment includes a component of an entity that sells primarily or exclusively to other operating segments of the entity, if the entity is managed in that way.
- IAS 14 requires segment information to be prepared in conformity with the accounting policies adopted for preparing and presenting the financial statements of the consolidated group or entity. IFRS 8 requires the amount reported for each operating segment item to be the measure reported to the chief operating decision maker for the purposes of allocating resources to the segment and assessing its performance.
- IAS 14 defines segment revenue, segment expense, segment result, segment assets and segment liabilities. The IFRS 8 does not define these terms, but requires an explanation of how segment profit or loss, segment assets and segment liabilities are measured for each reportable segment.
- IAS 14 requires the entity to disclose specified items of information about its primary segments. IFRS 8 requires an entity to disclose specified amounts about each reportable segment, if the specified amounts are included in the measure of segment profit or loss and are reviewed by or regularly provided to the chief operating decision maker.
- IAS 14 does not require interest income and expense to be split between segments. IFRS 8 requires an entity to report interest revenue separately from interest expense for each reportable segment unless a majority of the segment's revenues are from interest and the chief operating decision maker relies primarily on net interest revenue to assess the performance of the segment and make decisions about resources to be allocated to the segment.
- IAS 14 requires the disclosure of secondary segment information for either industry or geographical segments, to supplement the information given for the primary segments. IFRS 8 requires an entity, including an entity with a single reportable segment, to disclose information for the entity as a whole about its products and services, geographical areas and major customers. This requirement applies, regardless of the entity's organisation, if the information is not included as a part of the disclosures about segments.

11.11 Summary

Having completed this chapter, we can now explain the recognition criteria for revenue and can apply the correct accounting treatment for large or unusual items in arriving at profit for the period. We can also apply the appropriate treatment for changes in accounting policies, accounting estimates, and prior period errors.

We can define non-current assets held for sale and a discontinued operation and explain the disclosures required for non-current assets held for sale and discontinued operations.

We can identify reportable segments and describe the disclosures required in respect of segment reporting.

Revision Questions

Question 1

IFRS 8 Operating Segments

  (i) Revenue; from external sources
 (ii) Cost of sales;
(iii) Interest expense
(iv) Segment profit/loss;
 (v) Depreciation
(vi) Capital employed.

Which of the following are required by IFRS 8 Operating Segments to be analysed by segment and disclosed in an entity's financial statements:

(A) (i), (ii), and (iv)
(B) (i), (iv) and (vi)
(C) (i), (iii), and (v)
(D) (i), (iv), and (vi).   **(2 marks)**

Question 2

Revenue from the sale of goods should be recognised when certain conditions are met.

  (i) the entity selling does not retain any continuing influence or control over the goods;
 (ii) when the goods are dispatched to the buyer;
(iii) revenue can be measured reliably;
(iv) the supplier is paid for the goods;
 (v) it is reasonably certain that the buyer will pay for the goods;
(vi) the buyer has paid for the goods.

Which of the above are included in IAS 18 *Revenue recognition's* conditions for recognition:

(A) (i), (ii) and (v)
(B) (ii), (iii) and (iv)
(C) (i), (iii) and (v)
(D) (i), (iv) and (vi)   **(2 marks)**

Question 3

In no more than 15 words, define the IAS 8 meaning of an 'error'. **(2 marks)**

Question 4

Which ONE of the following would be regarded as a change of accounting policy under IAS 8 *Accounting Policies, Changes in Accounting Estimates and Errors?*

(A) An entity changes its method of depreciation of machinery from straight line to reducing balance

(B) An entity has started capitalising borrowing costs for assets under the alternative treatment allowed by IAS 23 *Borrowing Costs.* The borrowing costs previously had been charged to profit or loss

(C) An entity changes its method of calculating the provision for warranty claims on its products sold

(D) An entity disclosed a contingent liability for a legal claim in the previous year's accounts. In the current year, a provision has been made for the same legal claim

(2 marks)

Question 5

IAS 18 *Revenue Recognition* defines when revenue may be recognised on the sale of goods.

List FOUR of the five conditions that IAS 18 requires to be met for income to be recognised. **(2 marks)**

Question 6

On 31 March 2007, DT received an order from a new customer, XX, for products with a sales value of $900,000. XX enclosed a deposit with the order of $90,000.

On 31 March 2007, DT had not completed credit referencing of XX and had not despatched any goods. DT is considering the following possible entries for this transaction in its financial statements for the year ended 31 March 2007:

 (i) include $900,000 in profit or loss revenue for the year;
 (ii) include $90,000 in profit or loss revenue for the year;
(iii) do not include anything in profit or loss revenue for the year;
(iv) create a trade receivable for $810,000;
 (v) create a trade payable for $90,000.

According to IAS 18 *Revenue Recognition*, how should DT record this transaction in its financial statements for the year ended 31 March 2007?

(A) (i) and (iv)
(B) (ii) and (v)
(C) (iii) and (iv)
(D) (iii) and (v) **(2 marks)**

? Question 7

While Presario was preparing its financial statements for the year to 30 June 20X2, they discovered that goods with a cost of $70,000, which had been sold during 20X1, had been incorrectly included in inventory at 30 June 20X1.

The draft figures for 20X2 and the actual reported figures for 20X1 are given below:

	20X2 (draft)	20X1
	$'000	$'000
Sales	460	400
Cost of sales	(250)	(220)
Gross profit	210	180
Administrative expenses	(50)	(40)
Distribution costs	(40)	(30)
Profit before tax	120	110
Income tax (at 30%)	(36)	(33)
Profit	84	77

The opening retained earnings at 1 July 20X0 was $120,000 and closing retained earnings at 30 June 20X1 totalled $197,000.

The directors have decided that this amounts to a material misstatement in the reported financial statements and wish this to be corrected immediately.

Requirements

(a) Redraft the 20X2 income statement and restate the 20X1 figures where necessary to take account of this prior period error. **(6 marks)**

(b) Prepare the statement of retained earnings for inclusion in the published financial statements of Presario for the year ended 30 June 20X2. **(4 marks)**

(Total = 10 marks)

? Question 8

D is a diversified entity that has operated in four main areas for many years. Each of these activities has usually contributed approximately one-quarter of the entity's annual operating profit. During the year ended 31 December 20X3, the entity disposed of its glass-making division.

The entity's chief accountant has prepared the following summary of revenues and expenses:

D – analysis of costs and revenues, year ended 31 December 20X3

	Glass-making	Other division
	$'000	$'000
Sales revenue	150	820
Operating expenses	(98)	(470)
Losses on disposal of non-current assets	(205)	(61)

The entity also incurred interest charges of $37,000 during the year, all of which relates to continuing activities. The income tax charge for the year has been estimated at $24,000, made up of a $50,000 charge on the continuing activities and a $26,000 refund for discontinued activities. A dividend of $30,000 was paid during the year.

The entity made an issue of 100,000 $1 shares at a premium of 80¢ per share during the year. Shareholders' funds at the beginning of the year were made up as follows:

	$'000
Share capital	250
Share premium account	150
Revaluation reserve	160
Retained earnings	670
	1,230

The balance on the revaluation reserve arose when the entity valued the land occupied by the properties used in its retail division. In view of recent developments, it has been S: decided that this reserve should be reduced to $90,000 to reflect the reduced value of the properties.

Requirements

(a) Explain how the analysis required by IFRS 5 *Non-current Assets Held for Sale and Discontinued Operations* assists in assessing a business's future results and cash flows.

(6 marks)

(b) Prepare an statement of comprehensive income (showing the detail in notes to the statement of comprehensive income) for the year ended 31 December 20X3 for D in a form suitable for publication, complying with the requirements of IAS 1 and IFRS 5.

(8 marks)

(c) Prepare a statement of changes in equity for D in accordance with the requirements of IAS 1.

(5 marks)

(Total marks = 19)

? Question 9

Topaz makes up its accounts regularly to 31 December each year. The entity has operated for some years with four divisions, A, B, C and D, but on 30 July 20X2, Division B was sold for $8 million, realising a profit of $2.5 million.

The trial balance of the entity at 31 December 20X2 included the following balances.

	Division B		Divisions A, C and D combined	
	Dr	Cr	Dr	Cr
	$m	$m	$m	$m
Sales revenue		13		68
Costs of sales	8		41	
Distribution costs (including a bad debt of $1.9 m – Division D)	1		6	
Administrative expenses	2		4	
Profit on sale of Division B		2.5		
Cost of fundamental reorganisation			1.8	
Interest on $10 m 10% loan notes issued 20X2			1	
Income tax			4.8	
Interim dividend paid			6	
Revaluation reserve				10
Retained earnings 31 December 20X1				50

The balance on the revaluation reserve relates to the entity's property and arose as follows.

	$m
Balance at 1 January 20X2	6
Revaluation during 20X2	4
Balance at 31 December 20X2 per trial balance	10

The share capital of $100 million has remained unchanged throughout the year. The whole of the interest paid relates to continuing operations. The income tax should be divided as $3.6 million for continuing operations and $1.2 million for discontinued operations.

The costs of fundamental reorganisation of $1.8 million relate to the restructuring of Divisions A, C and D following the sale of Division B.

Requirements

(a) (i) Prepare the statement of comprehensive income of Topaz for the year ended 31 December 20X2, complying as far as possible with the provisions of IAS 1 and IFRS 5, (IFRS 5 requirements should be shown in the statement of comprehensive income)

   (ii) Prepare the statement of changes in equity for the year as required by IAS 1.

(16 marks)

(b) Explain why the changes to the statement of comprehensive income introduced by IFRS 5 improve the quality of information available to users of the financial statements.

(4 marks)
(Total marks = 20)

Question 10

On 1 September 2007, the Directors of EK decided to sell EK's retailing division and concentrate activities entirely on its manufacturing division.

The retailing division was available for immediate sale, but EK had not succeeded in disposing of the operation by 31 October 2007. EK identified a potential buyer for the retailing division, but negotiations were at an early stage. The Directors of EK are certain that the sale will be completed by 31 August 2008.

The retailing division's carrying value at 31 August 2007 was:

	$'000
Non-current tangible assets – property, plant and equipment	300
Non-current tangible assets – goodwill	100
Net current assets	43
Total carrying value	443

The retailing division has been valued at $423,000, comprising:

	$000
Non-current tangible assets – property, plant and equipment	320
Non-current tangible assets – goodwill	60
Net current assets	43
Total carrying value	423

EK's directors have estimated that EK will incur consultancy and legal fees for the disposal of $25,000.

Requirments

(i) Explain whether EK can treat the sale of its retailing division as a 'discontinued operation', as defined by IFRS 5 *Non-current Assets held for Sale and Discontinued Operations*, in its financial statements for the year ended 31 October 2007.

(3 marks)

(ii) Explain how EK should treat the retailing division in its financial statements for the year ended 31 October 2007, assuming the sale of its retailing division meets the classification requirements for a disposal group (IFRS 5). **(2 marks)**

(5 marks)

Solutions to Revision Questions

 Solution 1

The correct answer is (C), see Section 11.9.5.

 Solution 2

The correct answer is (C), see Section 11.2.2.

 Solution 3

Errors are defined by IAS 8 as 'material omissions or misstatements in the financial statements', see Section 11.4.

 Solution 4

The correct answer is B, see Section 11.5.

 Solution 5

Any FOUR of the following five conditions would gain the marks available.

1. the significant risks and rewards of ownership of the goods have been transferred to the buyer;
2. the entity selling does not retain any continuing influence or control over the goods;
3. revenue can be measured reliably;
4. it is reasonably certain that the buyer will pay for the goods;
5. the costs to the selling entity can be measured reliably, see Section 11.9.2.

 Solution 6

The correct answer is D, see Section 11.2.2.

REPORTING FINANCIAL PERFORMANCE

 Solution 7

(a) Extract from the income statement for Presario for the year ended 30 June 20X2.

	20X2	20X1 (restated)
	$'000	$'000
Sales	460	400
Cost of sales	(180)	(290)
Gross profit	280	110
Administrative expenses	(50)	(40)
Distribution costs	(40)	(30)
Profit before tax	190	40
Income tax (at 30%)	(57)	(12)
Profit	133	28

Workings

20X1 closing inventory was overstated by $70,000. This resulted in cost of sales being overstated and 20X1 profit and retained earnings being understated. Following the correction, 20X1 cost of sales is restated at $290,000 ($220,000 + $70,000). Profit before tax is now restated at $40,000 and income tax (at 30%) recalculated at $12,000.

The 20X2 cost of sales is correctly recorded at $180,000 ($250,000 less $70,000 overstatement of opening inventory charged to cost of sales in the draft accounts).

(b) The statement of retained earnings for Presario for the year ended 30 June 20X2

	20X2	20X1 (restated)
	$'000	$'000
Opening retained earnings as previously reported	197	120
Correction of error (net of taxes of $70 K × 30% = $21 K)	(49)	—
Opening retained earnings as restated	148	120
Profit	133	28
Closing retained earnings	281	148

Note X

Products with a cost of $70,000, which were sold during 20X1, were incorrectly included in inventory as at 30 June 20X1. The financial statements of 20X1 have been restated to correct this error.

 Solution 8

(a) The information provided in financial statements, while historic, is often used by readers of accounts to evaluate future performance. Any additional information about what makes up profits and cash flows can help in the assessment of what is likely to be generated in future periods.

IFRS 5 requires that the financial information be analysed between results from continuing operations and those from discontinued operations. Discontinued operations can be an entire part of the business operations being sold or terminated. It follows then that a discontinued operation will not generate results in future periods and so should not be included in the users' assessment of future performance. The results of continuing operations are likely to recur in future periods and users can then focus on these results when evaluating what the entity is likely to generate in the future.

The analysis of continuing operations and discontinued operations is required for financial performance, assets and liabilities and cash flows.

(b) D – statement of comprehensive income for the year ended 31 December 20X3

Continuing operations	$'000
Sales revenue	820
Operating expenses	(470)
Operating profit	350
Loss on disposal of fixed assets	(61)
Profit before interest	289
Finance costs	(37)
Profit before tax	252
Income tax expense	(50)
Profit for the period from continuing operations	202
Loss for the period from discontinued operations (Note 1)	(127)
Profit for the period	75
Other comprehensive income:	
Net reduction in value of property	(70)
Total comprehensive income for the period	5

Note 1

Discontinued operations	$'000
Sales revenue	150
Operating expenses	(98)
Operating profit	52
Loss on disposal of fixed assets	(205)
Profit before interest	(153)
Finance costs	—
Profit before tax	(153)
Income tax expense	26
Loss for the period from discontinued operations	(127)

(c) Statement of changes in equity, year ended 31 December 20X3

	Share capital $'000	Share premium $'000	Revaluation reserve $'000	Retained earnings $'000	Total $'000
Balance at 31 December 20X2	250	150	160	670	1,230
Total comprehensive income for the period	(70)	75	5		
Dividends paid				(30)	(30)
Issue of share capital	(ii) 100	(ii) 80			180
Balance at 31 December 20X3	350	230	90	715	1,385

Workings

(i) Revaluation reserve to be reduced from $160,000 to $90,000.

(ii) Share issue, 100,000 shares @ 80¢ premium; per value 100,000 × $1 included in share capital and the (100,000 × 80¢) $80,000 premium included in share premium.

REPORTING FINANCIAL PERFORMANCE

 Solution 9

(a) (i) Topaz – statement of comprehensive income for the year ended 31 December 20X2

	Continuing operations $m
Sales revenue	68.0
Cost of sales	(41.0)
Gross profit	27.0
Distribution costs (Note 1)	(6.0)
Administrative expenses	(4.0)
Profit from operations	17.0
Profit on sale of discontinued operations (Note 2)	
Costs of fundamental reorganisation (Note 3)	(1.8)
Profit before interest	15.2
Finance cost	(1.0)
Profit before tax	14.2
Income tax expense	(3.6)
Profit for the period from continuing operations	10.6
Profit for the period from discontinued operations (Note 1)	3.3
Profit for the period	13.9
Other comprehensive income:	
Net gain on revaluation of property	4.0
Total comprehensive income for the period	17.9

Note

1.

Discontinued operations	$m
Sales revenue	13.0
Cost of sales	(8.0)
Gross profit	5.0
Distribution costs (Note 1)	(1.0)
Administrative expenses	(2.0)
Profit from operations	2.0
Profit on sale of discontinued operation (Note 2)	2.5
Profit before tax	4.5
Income tax expense	(1.2)
Profit after tax	3.3

2. *Distribution costs.* Distribution costs include a bad debt of $1.9 million which arose on the continuing operations.

3. *Discontinued operations.* Division B was sold on 30 July 20X2 for $8 million, realis ing a profit on sale of $2.5 million. The results of Division B for the period to 31 December 20X2 are classified as discontinued operations.

4. *Fundamental reorganisation.* Following the sale of Division B in July 20X2 the entity undertook the restructuring of the remaining divisions at a cost of $1.8 million. (Note, this amount is required to be disclosed separately in the statement of comprehensive income because it is material. The restructuring is as a result of the discontinued operation but the costs are incurred reorganising the remaining divisions and so the amount is included in continuing operations.)

(ii) Topaz – statement of changes in equity, year ended 31 December 20X2

	Share capital $'000	Revaluation reserve $'000	Retained earnings $'000	Total $'000
Balance at 31 December 20X1	100	6	50	156
Total comprehensive income for the period		4	13.9	17.9
Dividends paid			(6)	(6)
Balance at 31 December 20X2	100	10	57.9	167.9

(b) The information provided in financial statements, while historic, is often used by readers of accounts to evaluate future performance. Any additional information about what makes up profits can help in the assessment of what is likely to be generated in future periods.

IFRS 5 requires that revenue, expenses and pre-tax profit be analysed between results from continuing operations and those from discontinued operations. Discontinued operations can be an entire part of the business operations being sold or terminated. It follows then that a discontinued operation will not generate results in future periods and so should not be included in the users' assessment of future performance. The results of continuing operations are likely to recur in future periods and users can then focus on these results when evaluating what the entity is likely to generate in the future.

IFRS 5 also requires that any gain or loss on the disposal of the discontinued operation be disclosed in the financial statements. This enables users to identify one-off profits or losses outwith the trading activities.

The additional information required by IFRS 5 is relevant and useful to users when making their investment decisions and therefore improves the quality of the information provided.

✅ Solution 10

(i) EK can treat the disposal of its retailing division as discontinued if it is a component of EK that has been disposed of, or is classified as held for sale. It must also be the disposal of a major line of business or a geographical area of operations. EK's disposal has not been completed by the balance sheet date, so does not meet that requirement.

IFRS 5 says that non-current assets or a disposal group can be classified as held for sale, where the carrying value will be recovered through a sale transaction, rather than their continuing use. The assets must be available for immediate sale in their present condition and the sale must be 'highly probable'. Highly probable means that the directors are committed to the sale and there is an active programme to locate a buyer and the assets are being actively marketed at a reasonable price. The sale must be expected to be completed within a year.

These terms appear to be met in EK's case and the retail division will be designated as held for sale. This means that they will be treated as discontinued operations in the year to 31 October 2007.

(ii) A disposal group is valued at fair value less cost to sell. If this gives rise to a lower value than the current book value, the assets have become impaired and must be written down. The reduction in value is charged to the income statement.

EK has valued the retail division at $423,000 and cost to sell is estimated at $25,000; this will give a net value of $398,000.

The assets in the disposal group will be recognised at the lower of their book value or fair value less cost to sell as follows:

	$000
Non-current assets, property, plant and equipment	300
Non-current assets, goodwill	55
Net current assets	43
	398

The reduction of $45,000 will be charged to the income statement.

Assets and disposal groups designated as held for sale are shown separately on the balance sheet and are not depreciated.

12

Statement of
Cash Flows

Statement of
Cash Flows

12

LEARNING OUTCOME

After completing this chapter you should be able to:

► prepare a cash flow statement in a form suitable for publication.

The syllabus topic covered in this chapter is as follows:

• Preparation of cash flow statements (IAS 7).

12.1 Introduction

> The statement of cash flows is an important primary statement. The preparation of statement of cash flows is not difficult, provided that you keep a clear head and adopt a systematic approach to the presentation of the statement itself and also the preparation of workings. 'T'-accounts are often the most efficient means of drawing conclusions from the information provided in examination questions. It is not sufficient to be able to prepare a statement of cash flows; it is also necessary to be able to interpret it. Essentially, this involves thinking about the extent to which the business in question actually needs cash.

The fundamental purpose of being in business is to generate profit. Ultimately, it is profit that increases the owners' wealth. Profitability is, however, a long-term objective. In the short term, the business' viability is determined by its ability to generate cash. Even profitable entities will collapse if they do not have access to sufficient cash resources when it becomes necessary to settle a bill. Very few businesses could survive a prolonged outflow of cash.

The profit figure for the year is unlikely to bear any resemblance to the increase or decrease in the entity's bank balance over that period. Several of the entries in the statement of comprehensive income, such as depreciation, do not involve receipts or payments of cash. There are also many types of receipt or payment, such as the proceeds of a share issue or a loan repayment, which have no immediate impact on profit. This means that it would be possible for an entity to be trading at a profit and still run into liquidity problems.

The bank balance can, of course, be obtained from the statement of financial position. Comparing statements of financial position at the beginning and end of the year will even show whether cash has increased or decreased. It is, however, difficult to identify the major causes of changes in the balance from doing so. Shareholders and other readers require a more structured presentation of the cash flows.

The statement of cash flows, therefore, is intended to answer questions such as:

- Why has the bank overdraft increased, despite the entity having had a profitable year?
- Is the entity capable of generating funds, as opposed to profit, from its trading activities?
- What was done with the loan that was taken out during the year?

Note: IAS 7 Cash flow statements was renamed by IAS 1 in 2007. IAS is now Statement of cash flows.

12.2 Objective of IAS 7 *Statement of Cash Flows*

The objective of IAS 7 *Statement of Cash Flows* is to ensure that entities provide information about the historical changes in cash and cash equivalents in a standard format by means of a statement of cash flows.

Information about the cash flows of an entity is useful in providing users of financial statements with a basis to assess the ability of the entity to generate and utilise cash and cash equivalents.

IAS 7 defines cash and cash equivalents as follows:

- cash comprises cash on hand and demand deposits.
- cash equivalents are short-term, highly liquid investments that are readily convertible to known amounts of cash and which are subject to an insignificant risk of changes in value.

12.3 Statement of cash flows format

The statement of cash flows should report cash flows during the period classified by operating, investing and financing activities. The detailed format used by an entity should be the one that is most appropriate to its business. IAS 7 contains a standard format that should always be used in answering examination questions. The format is as follows (note, headings that relate to items excluded from the syllabus have been left out):

Indirect Method statement of cash flows

	$	$
Cash flows from operating activities		
Profit before taxation	X	
Adjustments for:		
Depreciation	X	
Investment income	X	
Interest expense	X̲	
	X	
Increase/Decrease in trade and other receivables	X	
Increase/Decrease in inventories	X	
Increase/Decrease in trade payables	X̲	
Cash generated from operations	X	
Interest paid	X	
Income taxes paid	X̲	
Net cash from operating activities		X

Cash flows from investing activities

Purchase of property, plant and equipment	X	
Proceeds from sale of equipment	X	
Interest received	X	
Dividends received	X̲	
Net cash used in investing activities		X
Cash flows from financing activities		
Proceeds from issue of share capital	X	
Proceeds from long-term borrowings	X	
Payment of finance lease liabilities	X	
Dividends paid*	X̲	
Net cash used in financing activities		X̲
Net increase in cash and cash equivalents		X
Cash and cash equivalents at beginning of period		X̲
Cash and cash equivalents at end of period		X̲

*This could also be shown as an operating cash flow.

Each of the main headings shown above is discussed in detail below.

12.3.1 Cash flows from operating activities

Cash flows from operating activities are normally those arising from transactions relating to trading activities. It is intended to give an indication of the cash generated from operations.

Cash flows from operating activities can be calculated in two ways, using the direct method or the indirect method.

The direct method

The direct method shows operating cash receipts and payments, for example, cash paid to suppliers and employees and cash received from customers. This is useful to users as it shows the actual sources and uses of cash. However, many entities will not generate this information as a matter of course and so it may prove expensive to produce.

The indirect method

The indirect method instead starts with profit before taxation, adding back items shown elsewhere on the statement of cash flows (e.g. finance cost) and adjusting for non-cash items included in arriving at the operating profit figure. Non-cash items would include the following:

- *Depreciation* This is a book adjustment to reflect the wearing out of an asset; the cash impact of non-current assets is the buying of the asset.
- *Profits/losses on disposal of non-current assets* Profit is not cash – the cash impact of the disposal is the disposal proceeds.
- *Changes in inventories* As operating profit is calculated after charging cost of sales, which has been adjusted for opening and closing inventory we need the figure for total cash spent on materials in the year, not the cost of the goods used in the year.
- *Changes in receivables* The figure included in the profit or loss is the sales revenue – we need the cash received from customers and so we must take account of opening and closing receivables for the year.
- *Changes in payables* For the same reason as above – we need to get to the figure for actual cash paid to suppliers, but the direct method will occasionally be examined.

Entities are required to disclose the calculation using the indirect method as it provides the reconciliation of operating profit to cash flows from operating activities, which is an integral part of the statement of cash flows (it is therefore more likely to be the indirect method that is requested in examinations, but the direct method will occasionally be examined).

For illustration purposes, we now look at the calculations using both of these methods in arriving at cash flow from operations.

Example 12.A

The following financial information relates to Weir for the year ended 30 September 20X1.

Income statement for the year ended 30 September 20X1

	$'000
Revenue	222
Operating expenses	(156)
Operating profit	66
Finance costs	(9)
Profit before tax	57
Income tax expense	(21)
Profit	36

The following operating expenses were incurred in the year:

	$'000
Wages	(36)
Auditor's remuneration	(6)
Depreciation	(42)
Cost of materials used	(111)
Gain on sale of non-current assets	30
Rental income	9
	(156)

The following information is also available:

	30.9.X1 $'000	30.9.X0 $'000
Inventories	21	12
Trade receivables	24	21
Trade payables	(15)	(9)

Solution

(i) Direct method

	Workings	$,000
Receipts from customers	1	219
Rental income		9
Payments to suppliers	2	(114)
Wages		(36)
Auditor's remuneration		(6)
Net cash inflow from operations		72

Workings

1. Receipts from customers

	$'000
Sales revenue for the year	222
Plus opening receivables (would have paid in the year)	21
Less closing receivables (cash is outstanding at the year-end)	(24)
Cash received from customers in the year	219

2. Payments to suppliers

	$'000
Cost of materials used	111
Plus closing inventories	21
Less opening inventories	(12)
Materials purchased in the year	120
Plus opening payables	9
Less closing payables	(15)
Payments made to suppliers in the year	114

(ii) Indirect method

	Note	$'000
Profit before tax		57
Add back finance cost		9
Depreciation	1	42
Gain on disposal of non-current assets	2	(30)
Increase in receivables	3	(3)
Increase in inventories	4	(9)
Increase in payables	5	6
Net cash inflow from operations		72

Notes
1. Depreciation has been deducted in arriving at operating profit. However, it is not a cash item and so must be added back in calculating cash inflow from operating activities.
2. Similarly the gain on disposal has been included in operating profit but does not represent the cash flow associated with the disposal and so must be removed. (The cash flow for the disposal is the disposal proceeds total which will be included in 'cash flows from investing activities' further down the statement of cash flows.)
3. An increase in the balance of year-end receivables means that more cash is outstanding, less has been received than is represented in revenue. This is a net cash outflow and is therefore deducted.
4. Increase in inventories is a utilisation of cash resources and so is also deducted.
5. Increase in payables means that cash has been held back rather than paid to suppliers. This is a cash inflow and is therefore added.

12.3.2 Cash flows from investing activities

Cash payments to purchase property, plant and equipment and receipts from the sale of these items, along with cash payments to acquire equity of other entities, will be included under this heading.

12.3.3 Cash flows from financing activities

Proceeds of issuance of shares or loan notes, or cash paid for their redemption, appear here, along with dividends paid. (Dividends paid may be shown as operating cash flows instead.) The repayment of the principal amount of a finance lease in included here.

12.3.4 Increase (or decrease) in cash and cash equivalents during period

This is a net movement from all the cash flows in the period. The opening and closing balances of cash and cash equivalents complete the statement.

12.4   A worked example

The following example is intended to demonstrate some of the techniques that might be used in preparing a statement of cash flows. The intention is that you work through it line by line and think about the method. Do not expect every cash flow question to follow exactly the same pattern – you might have to adapt your approach in the exam.

12.4.1   Worked example

Requirements

Prepare Charlie's statement of cash flows for the year ended 31 March 20X1 from the following:

Charlie – income statement for the year ended 31 March 20X1

	$'000
Sales revenue	1,700
Cost of sales	(900)
Gross profit	800
Distribution costs	(50)
Administrative expenses	(120)
Operating profit	630
Interest received	80
Interest paid	(65)
Profit before tax	645
Income tax expense	(28)
Profit for the financial year	617

Charlie – Statement of financial position as at 31 March

	20X1		20X0	
	$m	$m	$m	$m
Non-current assets				
Tangible assets		1,580		1,000
Current assets				
Inventor		250		130
Receivables		450		360
Prepaid distribution costs		4		2
Cash at bank and in hand		220		144
		2,504		1,636
Capital and reserves				
Issued share capital		120		100
Share premium account		88		49
Revaluation reserve		203		130
Accumulated profits		877		315
		1,288		594
Non-current liabilities				
Loans	800		700	
Deferred tax	10		7	
		810		707
Current liabilities				
Trade payables	374		310	
Accrued administrative expenses	6		3	
Income tax	26		22	
		406		335
		2,504		1,636

Additional information

(a) The entity sold some tangible non-current assets, which had a net book value of $200 million. The cost of sales figure includes a loss of $10 million on this disposal.

(b) Cost of sales is arrived at after charging depreciation on the tangible non-current assets of $42 million.

(c) Dividends paid during the year were $55,000.

> ✎ *A word about balancing figures.* The trick to answering this type of question is to make the greatest possible use of the information that has been provided in order to determine the figures that have not been provided directly. For example, the question does not tell us how much has been paid for new tangible non-current assets. The secret is to use working schedules or open a 'T'-account and to insert all of the relevant information related to the book value of these assets. We can infer the cost of new assets purchased during the year by calculating a balancing figure in this account.

For example, we could use a working schedule as follows:

Non-current assets	$m
Balance at 1 April 20X0	1,000
Add revaluation	73
Less disposals	(200)
Less depreciation	(42)
	831
Balance at 31 March 20X1	1,580
Purchases	749

Or we could open a 'T' account as follows:

		Non-current assets			
	–	$m			$m
1 Apr. X0	Balance b/d	1,000		Disposals	200
	Revaluation	73		Depreciation	42
Bal. figure	Additions	749	31 Mar. X1	Balance c/d	1,580
		1,822			1,822
1 Apr. X1	Balance b/d	1,580			

The question does not actually tell us that the entity spent $749 m on new non-current assets, but we can derive this figure simply by using a consistent method of working/account to draw together the various pieces of information that we do have.

> ✎ In the exam, there is no guarantee that the information in respect of non-current assets will follow this particular pattern. You might, for example, find yourself drawing up a disposal account in order to derive the proceeds of the sale. Try the working schedule method and the 'T' account method, decide which one you prefer and then always use that method.

12.4.2 Cash flow from operations

For the sake of illustration, we will calculate this figure using both the direct and indirect methods. There is, however, no need to provide the information in both formats when the reconciliation using the indirect method is stated.

Direct method

The question does not state the cash received from customers. We can derive this easily though by preparing our workings. Workings can be prepared using either 'T' accounts or working schedules. First we will consider drawing up a 'T' account:

Receivables

		$m			$m
1 Apr. X0	Balance b/d	360	*Bal. figure*	Cash received	1,610
	Sales	1,700	31 Mar. X1	Balance c/d	450
		2,060			2,060
1 Apr. X1	Balance b/d	450			

We would include all information given in the question in this account, including any details of bad debts written off.

It would not matter if the entity made some sales for cash. Provided that we include the cash sales in the debit to receivables, the balancing figure in respect of cash received will include all receipts, whether from cash sales or credit customers.

Payments to suppliers are slightly more complicated. Cost of sales has two non-cash stages: the goods are purchased on credit and they also spend some time sitting in inventory. This means that we have to determine the figure for purchases and then derive the figure for cash paid to suppliers:

Cost of sales

		$m			$m
1 Apr. X0	Opening inventory	130	31 Mar. X1	Profit or loss (see note)	848
Bal. figure	Purchases	968	31 Mar. X1	Balance c/d	250
		1,098			1,098

Payables

		$m			$m
Bal. figure	Cash paid	904	1 Apr. X0	Balance b/d	310
31 Mar. X1	Balance c/d	374		Purchases	968
		1,278			1,278

Distribution costs

		$m			$m
1 Apr. X0	Prepayments b/d	2	31 Mar. X1	Profit or loss	50
Bal. figure	Cash paid	52	31 Mar. X1	Prepayments c/d	4
		54			54

Administrative expenses

		$m			$m
Bal. figure	Cash paid	117	1 Apr. X0	Accruals b/d	3
31 Max. X1	Accruals c/d	6	31 Mar. X1	Profit or loss	120
		123			123

Note: The figure inserted in the cost of sales account excludes the non-cash items of loss on disposal and depreciation (i.e. $900 - 10 - 42 = 848$).

Now we have sufficient information to determine the cash inflow from operating activities:

Charlie: cash inflow from operating activities (direct method)

	$m
Cash received from customers	1,610
Cash paid to suppliers	(904)
Other operating expenses (52 + 117)	(169)
Cash generated from operations	537
Interest paid (see Note 1)	(65)
Income taxes paid (see Note 2)	(21)
Net cash from operating activities	451

Note 1

Interest had been removed in arriving at cash generated from operations. To arrive at 'net cash from operating activities', which is the heading required for the statement of cash flows, we must now deduct interest paid, which is likely to have been incurred as a result of funding general trading activity and so remains within this first heading. The interest element of a finance lease repayment is included here.

Note that interest received is likely to have been earned as a result of a deliberate investing activity and so is reclassified within 'cash flows from investing activities'.

Note 2

The calculation for tax paid must adjust the income statement charge for opening and closing balances on the tax accounts held in the statement of financial position.

	$m
Income tax expense as per income statement	28
Opening creditor (paid during the year)	22
Closing creditor (outstanding at the year-end)	(26)
	24
Increase in deferred tax provision (a non-cash item that has been included in the income tax expense in the Profit or loss)	(3)
Tax paid in the year	(21)

Alternatively, you could set up a 'T'-account to arrive at the balance paid in the year, as shown below:

Taxation

		$m			$m
Bal. fig.	Cash paid	21	1 Apr. X0	Balance b/d	22
31 Mar. X1	Balance c/d	26	1 Apr. X0	Balance b/d	7
31 Mar. X1	Balance c/d	10	31 Mar. X1	Profit or loss	28
		57			57

Now we will use working schedules to prepare the same figures:

Receivables

Balance 1 April 20X0	360
Add sales	1,700
	2,060
Less balance at 31 March 20X1	450
Cash received	1,610

Cost of sales	
Opening inventory 1 April 20X0	130
Closing inventory 31 March 20X1	250
Increase in inventory	120
Charged to Profit or loss	848
Purchases	968
Payables	
Balance 1 April 20X0	310
Add purchases	968
	1,278
Less balance at 31 March 20X1	374
Cash paid	904
Distribution costs	
Balance 1 April 20X0 – prepayment	2
Balance at 31 March 20X1 – prepayment	4
Increase in prepayments	2
Charged to Profit or loss	50
Cash paid	52
Administrative expenses	
Balance 1 April 20X0 – accruals	3
Balance at 31 March 20X1 – accruals	6
Increase in accruals	(3)
Profit or loss	120
Cash paid	117

Indirect method

The indirect method is required to be disclosed as it provides the reconciliation of operating profit (from the profit or loss) to the net cash flow from operating activities that appears in the statement of cash flows. This calculation should, of course, give the same result as the direct method.

The indirect method reconciliation starts with 'profit before tax'.

Charlie: cash inflow from operating activities (indirect method)

	Note	$'000
Profit before taxation		645
Depreciation	1	42
Loss on disposal of non-current assets	2	10
Interest received	3	(80)
Interest paid	3	65
Operating profit before working capital changes		682
Increase in inventories	4	(120)
Increase in receivables	4	(90)
Increase in payables	4	64
Increase in prepaid expenses	5	(2)
Increase in accrued expenses	5	3
Cash generated from operations		537
Interest paid		(65)
Income taxes paid		(21)
Net cash inflow from operating activities		451

(agrees to the total calculated using the direct method)

Notes

1. Depreciation has been deducted in arriving at operating profit. However, it is not a cash item and so must be added back in calculating cash inflow from operating activities.

2. Similarly, the gain on disposal has been included in operating profit but does not represent the cash flow associated with the disposal and so must be removed. (The cash flow for the disposal is the disposal proceeds total which will be included in 'cash flows from investing activities' further down the statement of cash flows.)
3. Interest received and paid have been included in arriving at profit before tax in the profit or loss. They are removed to arrive at cash generated from operating activities.
4. The changes in working capital elements are discussed in detail in Section 12.3.1.
5. The adjustments made for prepayments and accruals are made for similar reasons to the changes in working capital – some expenses included in the profit or loss are those that relate to the year but are not necessarily paid in the year. Adjusting for prepayments and accruals will ensure that the actual cash flows associated with the expenses are included.

> The simplest way to proceed through any question involving the preparation of an accounting statement is to have a sheet of paper for the statement itself and another for the workings. This makes it easier to work through the statement in a methodical manner, with plenty of space set aside for the workings.

12.4.3 Cash flows from investing activities

Purchase of tangible assets

This figure will be calculated as a balancing figure (discussed in Section 12.4.1). We will use all of the information we are given about tangible assets and conclude that the difference is the additions in the year.

		Tangible non-current assets			
		$m			$m
1 Apr. X0	Balance b/d	1,000		Disposals	200
	Revaluation	73		Depreciation	42
Bal. fig.	Additions	749	31 Mar. X1	Balance c/d	1,580
		1,822			1,822
1 Apr. X1	Balance b/d	1,580			

The opening balance of $1,000 m and the closing balance (balance carried down at 31 March 20X1) are taken from the statement of financial position information.

The net book value of disposals and the depreciation charge for the year are given in the additional information.

There is a movement on the revaluation reserve of $73 m, this is also included as we attempt to reconcile the opening and closing balances for the net book value of tangible assets with the balancing figure being taken as additions in the year.

Proceeds of sale of plant

We are told in the additional information that cost of sales includes a loss of $10 million in respect of a disposal of tangible non-current assets (we removed this figure in arriving at cash flow from operating activities in Section 12.4.2). We are also told that the net book value of the disposed assets totalled $200 million.

We know that the gain or loss on disposal is calculated by comparing the proceeds with the net book value and so can calculate the proceeds as:

	$m
Net book value	200
Loss on disposal	(10)
Proceeds from disposal	190

Interest received

As noted above, this income is likely to have been earned as a result of a specific investing activity and so is included within this category.

12.4.4 Cash flows from financing activities

Proceeds of share issue

The cash inflow resulting from the share issue is calculated by looking at the movements on the share capital and share premium accounts combined.

	$m
Increase in issued share capital (120 − 100)	20
Increase in share premium (88 − 49)	39
Total proceeds from share issue in the year	59

Proceeds from long-term borrowings

The $100 million cash inflow is arrived at by simply comparing the opening and closing balances on the loans account. It moves from $700 million last year to $800 million this year, resulting in a net cash inflow from loans of $100 million.

12.4.5 The statement of cash flows

Now we put together all of the above elements, using the standard IAS 7 format, the complete answer is as follows:

Charlie – Statement of cash flows for the year 31 March 20X1

	$m	$m
Cash flows from operating activities		
Profit before taxation	645	
Adjustments for		
Depreciation	42	
Loss on sale of plant	10	
Interest received	(80)	
Interest paid	65	

Operating profit before working capital changes	682	
Inventory – increase	(120)	
Receivables – increase	(90)	
Payables – increase	64	
Prepayments – increase	(2)	
Accruals – increase	3	
Cash generated from operations	537	
Interest paid	(65)	
Income taxes paid	(21)	
Net cash from operating activities		451
Cash flows from investing activities		
Purchase of tangible non-current assets	(749)	
Proceeds of sale of plant	190	
Interest received	80	
Net cash used in investing activities		(479)
Cash flows from financing activities		
Proceeds of issue of shares	59	
Proceeds from long-term borrowings	100	
Dividends paid	(55)	
Net cash from financing activities		104
Net increase in cash and cash equivalents		76
Cash and cash equivalents at 1 April 20X0		144
Cash and cash equivalents at 31 March 20X1		220

12.5 Interpreting a statement of cash flows

We can see that Charlie managed to generate a net increase in cash during the period in question. Normally that would be desirable, but one can never be too categorical about such matters.

While very few entities can survive a prolonged outflow of cash, some businesses have too much tied up in liquid assets. The shareholders of such businesses would probably benefit from a deliberate disbursement of cash. For example, excess funds could be invested in non-current assets or inventories, or even returned to the shareholders by way of a dividend.

It is also worth bearing in mind that it is not difficult to distort cash balances in the short term. If the finance director delayed the payment of suppliers by a few days just before the year-end, then that could increase bank balances by a month's worth of payments to suppliers. Similarly, delaying the replenishment of inventories or encouraging prompt payment from receivables by means of a discount could artificially increase the bank balance.

The statement of cash flows does not give enough information on its own to enable a reader to tell whether a entity's funds have been well managed. The effects of any net movement can only be measured by looking at the closing statement of financial position and considering whether the relationships between the various components of working capital and long-term finance are acceptable.

Even if a net inflow was necessary, the statement cannot show whether the most appropriate type of finance has been raised or whether it has been obtained from the cheapest source.

12.6 Summary

Having completed this chapter, we can now follow the provisions of IAS 7 *Statement of Cash Flows* in arriving at cash flows from operating activities, using both the direct and indirect methods. We can calculate cash flows from investing and financing activities and prepare a statement of cash flows in a form suitable for publication.

Revision Questions

12

The preparation and interpretation of statement of cash flows has been a common source of examination questions in the past. This is likely to continue to be the case.

Question 1

How much interest was paid during the year?

	$'000
Interest accrued b/f	600
Interest charged to income statement	700
Interest accrued c/f	500

(A) $600,000
(B) $700,000
(C) $800,000
(D) $1,300,000   **(2 marks)**

Data for Questions 2–7

For each cash flow listed below, identify the IAS 7 *Statement of Cash Flows* heading where the cash flow would be included. The headings to use are:

(A) cash flows from investing activities;
(B) cash flows from financing activities;
(C) cash and cash equivalents;
(D) cash flow from operating activities.

Question 2

Profit on disposal of a fixed asset.
(A) (B) (C) (D)   **(2 marks)**

Question 3

Dividends paid on preferred shares.
(A) (B) (C) (D)   **(2 marks)**

? Question 4

Cash paid on redemption of debenture maturing during the year.
(A) (B) (C) (D)   (2 marks)

? Question 5

Surplus cash used to purchase own shares on the stock exchange.
(A) (B) (C) (D)   (2 marks)

? Question 6

A 60 day, 5% government bond purchased 1 month before the year-end.
(A) (B) (C) (D)   (2 marks)

? Question 7

Depreciation of property, plant and equipment.
(A) (B) (C) (D)   (2 marks)

? Question 8

At 30 September 2005, BY had the following balances, with comparatives:

Statement of financial position extracts: As at 30 September

	2005 $'000	2004 $'000
Non-current tangible assets		
Property, plant and equipment	260	180
Equity and reserves		
Property plant and equipment revaluation reserve	30	10

The profit or loss for the year ended 30 September 2005 included:
Gain on disposal of an item of equipment $10,000
Depreciation charge for the year $40,000

Notes to the accounts:
Equipment disposed of had cost $90,000. The proceeds received on disposal were $15,000.

Calculate the property, plant and equipment purchases that BY would show in its statement of cash flows for the year ended 30 September 2005, as required by IAS 7 *Statement of Cash Flows*.   (4 marks)

? Question 9

At 1 October 2004, BK had the following balance:
Accrued interest payable $12,000 credit

During the year ended 30 September 2005, BK charged interest payable of $41,000 to its profit or loss. The closing balance on accrued interest payable account at 30 September 2005 was $15,000 credit.

How much interest paid should BK show on its statement of cash flows for the year ended 30 September 2005?

(A) $38,000
(B) $41,000
(C) $44,000
(D) $53,000 **(2 marks)**

? Question 10

Accrued income tax payable, balance at 31 March 2002 $920,000.

Accrued income tax payable, balance at 31 March 2003 $890,000.
Taxation charge to the profit or loss for the year to 31 March 2003 $850,000.
Deferred tax balance at 31 March 2002 $200,000.
Deferred tax balance at 31 March 2003 $250,000.
How much should be included in the statement of cash flows for income tax paid in the year?

(A) $800,000
(B) $830,000
(C) $850,000
(D) $880,000 **(4 marks)**

? Question 11

Y's income statement for the year ended 31 December 20X3 and statements of financial position at 31 December 20X2 and 31 December 20X3 were as follows:

Y – income statement for the year ended 31 December 20X3

	$'000	$'000
Sales revenue		360
Raw materials consumed	(35)	
Staff costs	(47)	
Depreciation	(59)	
Loss on disposal	(9)	
		(150)
Operating profit		210
Interest payable		(14)
Profit before tax		196
Income tax expense		(62)
Profit after tax		134

Y – Statements of financial position as at 31 December

| | 20X3 | | 20X2 | |
	$'000	$'000	$'000	$'000
Non-current assets				
Cost		798		780
Depreciation		(159)		(112)
		639		668
Current assets				
Inventory	12		10	
Trade receivables	33		25	
Bank	24		28	
		69		63
		708		731
Capital and reserves				
Share capital	180		170	
Share premium	18		12	
Retained earnings	358		257	
		556		439
Non-current Liabilities				
Long-term loans		100		250
Current liabilities				
Trade payables	6		3	
Income tax	46		39	
		52		42
		708		731

During the year, the entity paid $45,000 for a new piece of machinery.
A dividend of $33,000 was paid during the year.

Requirement

Prepare a statement of cash flows for Y for the year ended 31 December 20X3 in accordance with the requirements of IAS 7. **(15 marks)**

? Question 12

It has been suggested that 'cash is king' and that readers of an entity's accounts should pay more attention to information concerning its cash flows and balances than to its profits and other assets. It is argued that cash is more difficult to manipulate than profit and that cash flows are more important.

Requirements

(a) Explain whether you agree with the suggestion that cash flows and balances are more difficult to manipulate than profit and non-cash assets. **(8 marks)**
(b) Explain why it might be dangerous to concentrate on cash to the exclusion of profit when analysing a set of financial statements. **(7 marks)**

(Total marks = 15)

? Question 13

The following information relates to Neave for the year ended 31 December 20X3.

Income statement for the year ended 31 December 20X3

	$'000
Sales revenue	16,200
Raw materials consumed	(13,000)
	3,200
Depreciation	(200)
Other operating costs	(2,880)
Investment income	60
Operating profit	180
Gain on sale of investment	600
Interest payable	(40)
Profit before tax	740
Income tax expense	(320)
Profit after tax	420

Statements of financial position as at 31 December 20X3

	20X3 $'000	20X3 $'000	20X2 $'000	20X2 $'000
Non-current assets				
Tangible (NBV)		5,400		5,000
Investments		1,200		1,400
		6,600		6,400
Current assets				
Inventories	1,240		1,020	
Trade receivables	1,000		1,040	
Bank	400		140	
		2,640		2,200
		9,240		8,600
Capital and reserves				
Share capital		2,800		2,600
Share premium		1,600		1,400
Revaluation reserve		800		720
Retained earnings		2,400		2,260
		7,600		6,980
Non-current liabilities				
Long-term loans		400		300
Deferred tax		200		120
Current liabilities				
Trade payables	800		1,000	
Income tax	240		200	
		1,040		1,200
		9,240		8,600

Additional information

1. 200,000 $1 ordinary shares were issued during the year for $2.00 per share for cash.
2. $150,000 was raised by a new long-term loan being arranged during the year. Repayments under the existing loan totalled $50,000 in the year.

3. No investments were acquired in the year.

4. The taxation charge in the income statement is made up of:

	$'000
Income tax	240
Deferred tax	80
	320

5. No tangible non-current assets were sold in the year. However, land was revalued upwards by $80,000.

6. Interim dividends paid in the year amounted to $280,000.

Requirement

Prepare the statement of cash flows for the year ended 31 December 20X3 for Neave.

(20 marks)

? Question 14

The financial statements of CJ for the year to 31 March 2006 were as follows:

Statement of Financial Position at	31 March 2006		31 March 2005	
	$'000	$'000	$'000	$'000
Non-current tangible assets				
Property	19,160		18,000	
Plant and equipment	8,500		10,000	
Available for sale investments	1,500		2,100	
		29,160		30,100
Current assets				
Inventory	2,714		2,500	
Trade receivables	2,106		1,800	
Cash at bank	6,553		0	
Cash in hand	409		320	
		11,782		4,620
Total assets		40,942		34,720
Equity and liabilities				
Ordinary shares $0.50 each	12,000			7,000
Share premium	10,000			5,000
Revaluation reserve	4,200			2,700
Retained profit	3,009			1,510
		29,209		16,210
Non-current liabilities				
Interest bearing borrowings	7,000		13,000	
Provision for deferred tax	999	7,999	800	13,800
Current liabilities				
Bank overdraft	0		1,200	
Trade and other payables	1,820		1,700	
Corporate income tax payable	914		1,810	
		3,734		4,710
		40,942		34,720

Income Statement for the Year to 31 March 2006

	$'000
Revenue	31,000
Cost of sales	(19,000)
Gross profit	12,000
Other income	200
Administrative expenses	(3,900)
Distribution costs	(2,600)
	5,700
Finance cost	(1,302)
Profit before tax	4,398
Income tax expense	(2,099)
Profit for the period	2,299

Additional information

1. On 1 April 2005, CJ issued 10,000,000 $0.50 ordinary shares at a premium of 100%.
2. No additional available for sale investments were acquired during the year.
3. On 1 July 2005, CJ repaid $6,000,000 of its interest bearing borrowings.
4. Properties were revalued by $1,500,000 during the year.
5. Plant disposed of in the year had a net book value of $95,000; cash received on disposal was $118,000.
6. Depreciation charged for the year was properties $2,070,000 and plant and equipment $1,985,000.
7. The trade and other payables balance includes interest payable of $650,000 at 31 March 2005 and $350,000 at 31 March 2006.
8. Dividends paid during the year, $800,000 comprised last year's final dividend plus the current year's interim dividend. CJ's accounting policy is not to accrue proposed dividends.
9. Other income comprises:

	$
Dividends received	180,000
Gain on disposal of available for sale investments	20,000
	200,000

Dividends receivable are not accrued.

10. Income tax expense comprises:

	$
Corporate income tax	1,900,000
Deferred tax for sale investments	199,000
	2,099,000

Dividends receivable are not accrued.

Requirement

Prepare CJ's Statement of cash flows for the year ended 31 March 2006, in accordance with IAS 7 Statement of Cash Flows. **(20 marks)**

Solutions to Revision Questions

12

 Solution 1

The correct answer is (C), see Section 12.4.2.

 Solution 2

The correct answer is (A), see Section 12.4.3.
    The profit is adjusted in the reconciliation.

 Solution 3

The correct answer is (B), see Section 12.4.4.

 Solution 4

The correct answer is (B), see Section 12.4.4.

 Solution 5

The correct answer is (B), see Section 12.4.4.

 Solution 6

The correct answer is (C), see Section 12.2.

 Solution 7

The correct answer is (D), see Section 12.4.2.

Solution 8

	$'000
Balance b/fwd	180
Revaluation (30 − 10)	20
Disposal (15 − 10)	(5)
Depreciation	(40)
	155
Balance c/fwd	(260)
Purchases	105

 # Solution 9

	$'000
Income statement	41
Add balance b/fwd	12
	53
Less balance c/fwd	15
	38

 # Solution 10

The correct answer is (B).

	$
Deferred tax 31 March 02	200,000
Deferred tax 31 March 03	250,000
Increase	50,000
Total tax charged to profit or loss	(850,000)
Income tax for year	800,000
Tax balance 31 March 2002	920,000
Income tax charge for the year	800,000
	1,720,000
Outstanding at 31 March 2003	890,000
Corporation tax paid in the year	830,000

 # Solution 11

Y – Statement of cash flows for the year ended 31 December 20X3

	$'000	$'000
Cash flows from operating activities		
Profit before taxation	196	
Adjustments for		
Depreciation	59	
Loss on sale of plant	9	
Interest payable	14	
Operating profit before working capital changes	278	
Inventory – increase	(2)	
Receivables – increase	(8)	
Payables – increase	3	
Cash generated from operations	271	
Interest paid	(14)	
Income taxes paid	(55)	

Net cash from operating activities		202
Cash flows from investing activities		
Purchase of non-current assets	(45)	
Proceeds of sale of plant	6	
Net cash used in investing activities		(39)
Cash flows from financing activities		
Proceeds of issue of shares	16	
Repayments of loans	(150)	
Dividends paid	(33)	
Net cash used in financing activities		(167)
Net increase/decrease in cash and cash equivalents		(4)
Cash and cash equivalents at 1 January 20X3		28
Cash and cash equivalents at 31 December 20X3		24

Working notes

Taxation

	$'000
Balance due at 31 December 20X2	39
Add: tax charge for the year to 31 December 20X3	62
	101
Less: tax liability at 31 December 20X3	(46)
Tax paid during year	55

Non-current assets – cost

	$'000
Balance at 31 December 20X2	780
Add: machinery purchased	45
	825
Less: balance at 31 December 20X3	(798)
Disposal in the year	27

Non-current assets – depreciation

	$'000
Balance at 31 December 20X2	112
Add: charge for the year	59
	171
Less: balance at 31 December 20X3	(159)
Depreciation on disposal	12

Receipts from sales of non-current tangible assets

	$'000
Cost (calculated above)	27
Depreciation (calculated above)	(12)
Written-down value	15
Loss on sale	(9)
Proceeds from sale	6

✓ Solution 12

(a) Cash is the most liquid of assets, and it is also the most tangible. A banknote with a face value of $10 can be held in the hand, and there can be no dispute that maybe it is really $11 or $9. Profits, however, are not tangible or liquid, and it is possible to argue that profit should be restated at a higher (or lower) amount.

STATEMENT OF CASH FLOWS

With simple income and expenditure accounts, the excess corresponds to an amount of cash, and is therefore difficult to manipulate. But, with accruals accounting, problems of estimation arise (e.g. how much to provide for depreciation and bad debts). In the case of modern, multinational groups of entities, the potential for manipulation of profit is much greater still.

It is possible, however, to manipulate cash flows and balances as well as profits. Cash balances can be boosted at the year-end by withholding payment to suppliers; customers can be given incentives to pay any large balances; loans can be taken out (and repaid immediately after the year-end); and assets can be sold for cash.

The International Accounting Standards Committee has been developing and issuing financial reporting standards which attempt to minimise the opportunities for manipulation of profits, cash flows and balances.

(b) Positive cash flows are extremely important for entities to ensure their survival. Many profitable entities have gone into liquidation simply because of their inability to generate sufficient cash. But in the longer term, entities that are unable to make profits will cease to generate cash, and will also fold. Of the two, the ability to generate profits is the most important for the long-term security of the entity. By focusing purely on increasing cash balances, the managers of an entity might neglect their main task, which is to make a profit for shareholders.

It is also not in the best interests of an entity to habitually hold large cash deposits (unless interest rates are running at an abnormally high rate). It makes more sense for the directors to reinvest available funds in non-current assets, which should increase the entity's profitability. The entity's working capital management policy should ensure that enough cash is held to meet its day-to-day requirements, but no more. In the same way, as an entity gains nothing from carrying large amounts of excess inventory, it is likely that better returns can be found for excess cash by alternative investments.

☑ Solution 13

Neave – Statement of cash flows for the year ended 31 December 20X3

	Notes	$'000	$'000
Cash flows from operating activities			
Profit before taxation			740
Adjustments for:			
Depreciation	1	200	
Gain on sale of Investments	2	(600)	
Interest paid	3	40	
Investment income Received	4	(60)	
			(420)
Operating profit before working capital changes			320
Inventory – increase	5	(220)	
Receivables – decrease	5	40	
Payables – decrease	5	(200)	
			(380)
			(60)
Cash generated from operations			
Interest paid		(40)	
Income taxes paid	6	(200)	
			(240)

Net Cash from operating activities			(300)
Cash flows from investing activities			
Purchase of non-current assets	7	(520)	
Proceeds from sale of investments	8	800	
Investment income		60	
Net cash generated from investing activities			340
Cash flows from financing activities			
Proceeds of share issue	9	400	
Increase in long-term loans		150	
Repayments of loan		(50)	
Dividends paid		(280)	
Net cash from financing activities			220
Net increase in cash and cash equivalents			260
Cash and cash equivalents at 1 January 20X3	10		140
Cash and cash equivalents at 31 December 20X3	10		400

Notes

1. Depreciation is a non-cash item that has been deducted in arriving at profit before tax, and so is added back in the calculation for cash flow from operations.

2. The gain on sale is calculated by comparing the proceeds and the book value of investments, it is not a cash item and so is deducted. The proceeds of the sale will appear later in the cash flow within investing activities.

3. Interest paid has been deducted in arriving at profit before tax. It is added back to arrive at actual cash generated from operations and then appears later as a deduction in arriving at net cash from operating activities as it is likely to have been incurred in the financing of the business's general trading activities (for format purposes).

4. Investment income is removed in arriving at cash flow from operations as it likely to have been earned as a result of deliberate investment activities. It is included further down the statement of cash flows under 'Cash flows from investing activities'.

5. Changes in working capital must be accounted for as turnover and cost of materials used are not cash items – they do not take account of credit extended to customers and by suppliers. Increase in inventory means more inventory has been purchased and is an outflow of cash. Payables decreasing means that payments are being made, which again is an outflow of cash. Receivables decreasing means that cash is being received faster from customers, and so is a source of cash.

6. Income tax paid is then deducted in arriving at net cash from operating activities as this has been incurred by trading. The actual tax paid must be calculated, as there are two statements of financial position balances and a statement of comprehensive income charge all relating to tax. It is calculated as follows:

	$'000
Opening liability – income tax	200
Opening deferred tax balance	120
Charge for the year	320
Closing liability – income tax	(240)
Closing deferred tax balance	(200)
Cash paid in respect of tax	200

7. The purchase of non-current assets appears under investing activities. We are not told the figure for purchases and so must derive it using all the information relating to the non-current assets given in the question. The additions in the year will be the balancing

figure. We want to track all the movements in the year in order to reconcile the opening and closing net book value that are in the statement of financial position.

	$'000
Opening net book value (B/S)	5,000
Depreciation charge (decreases book value)	(200)
Revaluation in the year (increases book value)	80
Balancing figure – additions in the year	520
Closing net book value	5,400

This calculation could also be performed with the use of a 'T'-account (you should use whatever you feel most confident with):

Tangible non-current assets

		$'000			$'000
1 Jan. X1	Balance b/d	5,000		Depreciation	200
	Revaluation	80			
Bal. fig.	Additions	520	31 Dec. X1	Balance c/d	5,400
		5,600			5,600
1 Jan. X2	Balance b/d	5,400			

8. The cash proceeds from the sale of investments is also included within investing activities although this is a source of cash. We are not told the proceeds but can easily work them out. We know the gain on disposal (from profit or loss) and we know the book value of the investments (from the statement of financial position). We know that the gain is calculated as proceeds less book value and so gain plus book value must equal proceeds:

	$'000
Gain on sale	600
Decrease in book value of investments in the year (1,400 − 1,200)	200
Proceeds from disposal	800

9. The additional information in the question tells us that the share issue was for cash and so the proceeds of share issue are 200,000 × $2 per share = $400,000 cash inflow. This is a method of financing the business and so is included in the cash flows from financing activities.

The opening and closing bank balances are found in the statement of financial position and the net cash flow in the year should reconcile the opening and closing balances for bank and cash.

 Solution 14

CJ – Statement of cash flows for the year ended 31 March 2006

	$'000	$'000
Cash flows from operating activities		
Profit before taxation	4,398	
Adjustments for:		
Other income	(200)	
Depreciation	4,055	
Finance cost	1,302	
Gain on disposal of plant (W2)	(23)	

	9,532	
Increase in inventory	(214)	
Increase in trade receivables	(306)	
Increase in trade and other payables (W6)	420	
Cash generated from operations	9,432	
Interest paid (W3)	(1,602)	
Income taxes paid (W4)	(1,796)	
Net cash from operating activities		6,034
Cash flows from investing activities		
Purchase of property, plant and equipment (W1)	(2,310)	
Investment income received	180	
Proceeds from sale of equipment	118	
Proceeds from disposal of available for sale investments (W5)	620	
Net cash used in investing activities		(1,392)
Cash flows from financing activities		
Proceeds from issue of share capital (W7)	10,000	
Repayment of interest bearing borrowings	(6,000)	
Equity dividends paid*	(800)	
Net cash from financing activities		3,200
Net increase in cash and cash equivalents		7,842
Cash and cash equivalents at 1 April 2005		1(880)
Cash and cash equivalents at 31 March 2006		6,962

*this could also be shown as an operating cash flow

Workings

(W1)

Net book values	Property $'000	Plant $'000	Available for sale investments $'000
Balance b/fwd	18,000	10,000	2,100
Revaluation	1,500	0	0
	19,500	10,000	2,100
Disposal	0	(95)	(600)
Depreciation for year	(2,070)	(1,985)	0
	17,430	7,920	1,500
Acquired in year (to balance)	1,730	580	0
Balance c/fwd	19,160	8,500	1,500

(W2)
Gain on disposal of plant

Net book value	95
Cash received	118
	23

(W3)
Interest paid

Balance b/fwd	650
Finance cost in profit or loss	1,302
	1,952
Balance c/fwd	(350)
Interest paid in year	1,602

(W4)

Tax paid

Balance b/fwd – Current tax	1,810	
Deferred tax	800	2,610
Profit or loss charge		2,099
		4,709
Balance c/fwd – Current tax	1,914	
Deferred tax	999	2,913
Paid in year		1,796

(W5)

Proceeds from disposal of available for sale investments

Disposal per (W1)	600
Add gain on disposal	20
	620

(W6)

Increase in trade payables

Trade and other payables balance b/fwd		1,700
Less: Interest b/fwd		(650)
		1,050
Trade and other payables balance c/fwd	1,820	
Less: Interest c/fwd	350	1,470
Increase in trade payables		420

(W7)

Proceeds from issue of equity share capital

Equity shares	5,000
Share premium	5,000
	10,000

13

Non-current
Tangible Asset
Standards

Non-current Tangible Asset Standards

13

The syllabus topics covered in this chapter are as follows:

- Property, plant and equipment (IAS 16): the calculation of depreciation and the effect of revaluations, changes to economic useful life, repairs, improvements and disposals.
- Related financing costs (IAS 23).

You will have studied the basic accounting for tangible non-current assets in Financial Accounting Fundamentals or the course giving you exemption from it. If required, refresh your knowledge by revisiting your previous text.

13.1 IAS 16 *Property, Plant and Equipment*

13.1.1 Objective

The objective of IAS 16 is to prescribe the accounting treatment for property, plant and equipment so that users of the financial statements have information about the entity's investment in its property, plant and equipment and changes in that investment. The main issues being the recognition of the assets, determining their carrying amounts and associated depreciation charges.

13.2 Revision of some definitions in IAS 16

 You should know these definitions from your earlier studies. You need to ensure that you know all of the following definitions for your examination.

13.2.1 Property, plant and equipment

Property, plant and equipment are tangible items that are held for use in the production or supply of goods or services, for rental to others, or for administrative purposes.

13.2.2 Carrying amount

The amount at which an asset is recognized, after deducting any accumulated depreciation and impairment losses. Also referred to as book value.

13.2.3 Cost

The amount paid and the fair value of other consideration given to acquire an asset at the time of its acquisition or construction. See Section 13.3.1.

13.2.4 Depreciable amount

The cost or valuation of an asset less its residual value.

13.2.5 Depreciation

The systematic allocation of the depreciable amount of an asset over its useful life.

13.2.6 Fair value

The amount for which an asset can be exchanged between knowledgeable, willing parties in an arm's length transaction.

13.2.7 Impairment loss

The amount by which the carrying amount exceeds its recoverable amount.

13.2.8 Recoverable amount

The higher of an asset's net realisable value and its value in use.

13.2.9 Residual value

The residual value of an asset is the amount that the entity would currently obtain from disposal of the asset, after deducting the estimated costs of disposal, assuming that the asset was already at the point where it would be disposed of (using the age and condition that would be assumed to apply at the time of disposal).

13.2.10 Useful life

IAS 16 defines useful life as the period over which the asset is expected to be available for use by the entity or the volume of output expected from the asset.

13.3   Recognition

IAS 16 requires that an item of property, plant or equipment should be recognised as an asset when:

- it is probable that future economic benefits associated with the asset will flow to the entity;
- the cost of the item can be measured reliably.

The first point is based on the principle that the item should only be recognised as an asset and included in the financial statements when it reaches its location and condition necessary for it to be capable of operating in the manner intended by management.

The second point deals with cost. If the asset has been purchased, then the asset is initially recognised at its original cost.

13.3.1   Elements of cost

The cost of an item of property, plant or equipment can include any of the following:

- Invoice price, including any import duties and non-refundable purchase taxes;
- Any costs directly attributable to bringing the asset to the location and condition necessary for it to be capable of operating in the manner intended. Directly attributable costs can include:
  - site preparation,
  - initial delivery and handling costs,
  - installation and assembly costs,
  - testing and initial set up costs,
  - professional fees.
  Note: Administration expenses and general overhead costs cannot be included.
- The initial estimate of dismantling and removing the item and restoring the site on which it is located. This will involve creating a provision which is dealt with in Chapter 18.

13.3.2   Self-constructed assets

Where the entity constructs the asset itself for its own use, then the cost is determined using the same principles as for an acquired asset. Attributable costs are likely to include the cost of materials and labour and other inputs used in the construction and will exclude any profit element.

13.3.3   Recognising parts of an asset as separate assets

IAS 16 allows significant parts of an asset to be recorded separately if each part has a different useful economic life. For example, a furnace may require relining after a specified number of hours of use, or aircraft interiors such as seats and galleys may require replacement several times during the life of the airframe.

13.4   Measurement

IAS 16 requires that an entity must choose between the cost model or the revaluation model as its accounting policy and apply that policy to an entire class of property, plant and equipment.

13.4.1 Cost model

Once recognised as an asset, the item should be carried at its cost less any accumulated depreciation and any accumulated impairment losses.

13.4.2 Revaluation model

Once recognised as an asset, an asset whose fair value can be measured reliably, can be held at a revalued amount less any subsequent accumulated depreciation and impairment losses. The revalued amount being its fair value at the date of revaluation. Revaluation should be undertaken regularly to ensure that value of the asset does not vary significantly from its fair value. The fair value of land and buildings will usually be market value determined by a professional valuer. The fair value of plant and equipment is usually current market value. If the asset is of a specialised type that is rarely sold, an entity may have to estimate fair value using depreciated replacement cost.

13.5 Subsequent expenditure

IAS 16 requires the recognition principle to be applied to the subsequent expenditure, in other words:

- it is probable that future economic benefits associated with the asset (that is the additional expenditure) will flow to the entity;
- the cost of the item (additional expenditure) can be measured reliably.

If the recognition criteria are met, an entity recognises in the carrying amount of an item of property, plant and equipment the cost of replacing part of such an item when that cost is incurred. The carrying amount of those parts that are replaced is derecognised in accordance with the derecognition provisions. If a part of an item of property, plant and equipment is depreciated separately, when it is replaced, it will be treated as a disposal. The part replaced will be derecognised and the new part treated as an acquisition.

A condition of continuing to operate an item of property, plant and equipment (for example, an aircraft) may be performing regular major inspections for faults regardless of whether parts of the item are replaced. When each major inspection is performed, its cost is recognised in the carrying amount of the item of property, plant and equipment as a replacement if the recognition criteria are satisfied. Any remaining carrying amount of the cost of the previous inspection (as distinct from physical parts) is derecognised. This occurs regardless of whether the cost of the previous inspection was identified in the transaction in which the item was acquired or constructed.

13.6 Accounting for depreciation

All assets with a limited useful life must be depreciated. Land has an unlimited useful life (unless it is a mine, quarry, etc.) and is not depreciated. Depreciation should be allocated on a systematic basis over the asset's economic useful life and charged as an expense to profit or loss, unless it is included in the carrying amount of another asset. For example, depreciation of assets used in development work may be included in the carrying amount of intangible assets recognised under IAS 38 *Intangible Assets* (see Chapter 16 for details).

IAS 16 requires that each part of an item of property, plant and equipment with a cost that is significant in relation to the total cost of the item shall be depreciated separately. The initial cost of the asset will need to be allocated to its significant parts, for example, the airframe and engines of an aircraft would need to be treated separately as they have different useful lives. If the significant parts have the same useful lives, they can be grouped together for depreciation purposes.

IAS 16 also requires the assets residual value and useful life to be reviewed at every year-end. If changes are made to either, it will count as a change in accounting estimate and be dealt with using IAS 8, as previously discussed in Chapter 11.

IAS 16 specifically states that repair and maintenance of an asset does not remove the need to provide for depreciation. The residual value of an asset may increase to an amount equal to or greater than its carrying value, if this happens depreciation will be zero.

Depreciation commences when the asset reaches the location and condition necessary for it to be capable of operating in the manner intended by management and only ceases when it is fully depreciated or when it is derecognised.

Example 13.A

A machine was purchased on 1 January 2003 for $50,000. The asset is used from the date of acquisition and its estimated economic useful life is 5 years. The following entry will be recorded in respect of depreciation in the year ended 31 December 2003:

		$	$
Debit	Depreciation expense	10,000	
Credit	Accumulated depreciation		10,000
Being the depreciation expense for the year			

The machine will be included in the statement of financial position as at 31 December 2003 at $40,000 (cost $50,000 less accumulated depreciation of $10,000).

13.6.1 Review of useful life

The useful life of the asset and its residual value should be reviewed periodically (at least at each financial year-end), and if there are significant changes then future depreciation charges should be adjusted. The useful life of an asset to an entity may be less than its total economic life as an entity may have a policy to replace each type of asset after a fixed period of time or after a fixed amount of usage.

Example 13.B

A machine was purchased on 1 January 2000 for $50,000. The asset is used from the date of acquisition and its estimated economic useful life is 10 years. After 3 years of use, the asset's useful life is reviewed. The machine is expected to last only a further 5 years from the date of review.

The depreciation charge will now be calculated based on the carrying value of $35,000 (cost less 3 years' depreciation) and a remaining useful life of 5 years. The charge for the next 5 years will be $7,000.

The higher charge to profit or loss will ensure the original cost of the asset is expensed to the profit or loss over its total revised life of 8 years – 3 years of $5,000 and 5 years of $7,000.

13.6.2 Depreciation method

IAS 16 requires that the depreciation method used should reflect the actual pattern in which the assets' future economic benefits are expected to be consumed by the entity. The depreciation method should also be reviewed at the end of each year and if there is a change in the pattern of usage, the method should be changed to reflect the new consumption of economic benefits. Any change in depreciation method will be treated as a change in accounting estimate under IAS 8.

> A variety of depreciation methods can be used to allocate the depreciable amount of an asset over its useful life. The most common in examinations are the straight-line method and the reducing balance method. You should have covered depreciation methods in your foundation studies, you may find it useful to revise the different methods of depreciation.

Example 13.C

Depreciation methods revision

A machine is purchased on 1 January 2000 for $100,000. It has a useful economic life of 5 years and at the end of that time it is expected to have a residual value of $10,000.
Calculate depreciation for each year using:

(a) straight-line depreciation
(b) reducing balance depreciation at 35%

Straight-line depreciation

The depreciable amount is $100,000 − $10,000 = $90,000. This will be depreciated over 5 years, therefore each years depreciation is $90,000/5 = $18,000.

Reducing balance depreciation

When calculating reducing balance depreciation, ignore the residual value and apply the depreciation rate to the carrying amount. In year 1, the carrying amount is the cost $100,000 × 35% = $35,000.

In year 2, deduct the first years depreciation from the cost to give the carrying amount, $100,000 − $35,000 = $65,000. This is then multiplied by the depreciation rate to give the annual depreciation charge, $65,000 × 35% = $22,750.

In year 3, deduct the second years depreciation, $65,000 − $22,750 = $42,250. The third years' depreciation is then $42,250 × 35% = $14,788.

And so on:

Year 4 = $42,250 − $14,788 = $27,462 × 35% = $9,612
Year 5 = $27,462 − $9,612 = $17,850 × 35% = $6,248

Carrying value at end of year 5 is $17,850 − $6,248 = $11,602, a little over the $10,000 estimated.

13.7 Retirements and disposals

The carrying amount of an asset should be derecognised on disposal of that asset or when there is no future economic benefit expected from its continued use or disposal. Derecognition means removing the asset from the statement of financial position. **Gains or losses on disposal** are calculated by comparing the net disposal proceeds and the carrying value of the asset at the date of disposal. Gains or losses should be recognised in profit or loss as income or expense, but IAS 16 specifies that they cannot be included as revenue.

Example 13.D

A machine was purchased on 1 January 2001 for $50,000. The asset is used from the date of acquisition and its estimated economic useful life is 5 years. The asset is sold on 1 March 2004 for $24,000. The entity policy is to charge a full year's depreciation in the year of acquisition and none in the year of disposal.

The gain on disposal is the difference between the proceeds of $24,000 and the carrying value of the asset, $20,000 (cost of $50,000 less 3 years' depreciation).

The disposal will be recorded as:

		$	$
Debit	Bank	24,000	
Debit	Accumulated depreciation	30,000	
Credit	Cost of asset		50,000
Credit	Gain on disposal profit or loss		4,000

Being the disposal of the asset and recognition of the gain.

13.8 Revaluation of assets

Property is often revalued as it better reflects the fair value of the asset, due to changes in property valuations. The valuations are usually performed by professional valuers and if valuation fluctuations are frequent, it may be necessary to revalue annually; if not, every 3 or 5 years is sufficient.

If an item of property, plant or equipment is revalued, that entire class of property, plant or equipment must be revalued. A class is a grouping of assets of a similar nature, for example:

- land,
- buildings,
- machinery,
- motor vehicles,
- office equipment,
- furniture and fittings.

13.8.1 Revaluation surplus

When an asset is revalued, the asset's carrying value is increased and the increase recognised in other comprehensive income and accumulated in equity under the heading *revaluation reserve*.

Example 13.E

An asset was purchased on 1 January 2001 for $500,000. The asset is used from the date of acquisition and its estimated economic useful life is 50 years. After 3 years of use, the asset is revalued on 1 January 2004 at $540,000. The revaluation surplus is the difference between the revalued amount and the carrying value of the asset which is $70,000, $540,000 less $470,000. The revaluation is recorded as follows:

		$	$
Debit	Accumulated depreciation	30,000	
Debit	Cost of asset	40,000	
Credit	Revaluation reserve		70,000

Being the revaluation of the asset at 1 January 2004.

Accumulated depreciation on the asset is **eliminated** and the balance of the surplus is debited to the cost of the asset. The asset will now be **held at valuation less any subsequent accumulated depreciation**, calculated on the revalued amount over the asset's remaining useful life.

13.8.2 Revaluation deficits

If future revaluations result in a fair value that is less than the carrying value, then the decrease is recognised in other comprehensive income to the extent that there is a credit balance in the revaluation reserve for that asset. The decrease recognised in other comprehensive income reduces the amount accumulated in equity under revaluation reserve. If there is an insufficient amount in the revaluation reserve in respect of the asset, then the balance of the deficit will be charged to profit or loss.

The effect of taxes on income resulting from revaluations must be recognized and disclosed in accordance with IAS 12, this will usually mean an increase in asset value will give rise to an increase in deferred tax. Tax effects are shown in the same section of the statement of comprehensive income as the item giving rise to them, so an increase in deferred tax arising from an asset revaluation will be shown under other comprehensive income.

Example 13.F

If the asset in Example 13.E was revalued again 5 years after purchase at $500,000, the calculations would be as follows:

	$	$
Original cost	500,000	
3 years depreciation (3/50)	(30,000)	
Net book value	470,000	
Revaluation to	540,000	
Gain on revaluation		70,000
2 years depreciation (2/47 × 540,000)	22,978	
Net book value	517,022	
Revalued to	500,000	
Loss on revaluation, charged to revaluation reserve		17,022
Balance on revaluation reserve		52,978

Example 13.G

If the asset in Example 13.E was revalued to $440,000 after 3 years, a deficit of $30,000 would arise. This would be calculated as follows:

	$
Original cost	500,000
3 years depreciation (3/50)	(30,000)
Net book value	470,000
Revaluation to	440,000
Loss on revaluation	30,000

In this example, the asset has not previously been revalued, the loss must be charged to profit or loss.

13.8.3 Disposal of a revalued asset

When a previously revalued asset is disposed of, the gain on disposal is measured as the difference between the carrying value at the date of disposal and the proceeds received.

Example 13.H

Continue with Example 13.E, an asset was purchased on 1 January 2001 for $500,000. The asset is used from the date of acquisition and its estimated economic useful life is 50 years. After 3 years of use, the asset is revalued on 1 January 2004 at $540,000. Depreciation is charged on a monthly basis.

If the asset is sold on 30 June 2004 for $550,000, how much profit should be recognized in the profit or loss.

	$	$
Original cost	500,000	
3 years depreciation (3/50)	(30,000)	
Net book value	470,000	
Revaluation to	540,000	
Gain on revaluation		70,000
Depreciation (6/12 × 540,000/47)	5,745	
Net book value at date of disposal	534,255	
Proceeds	550,000	
Gain on disposal, recognized in the profit or loss		15,745

When this asset is disposed of, the revaluation surplus included in equity in respect of an item of property, plant and equipment may be transferred directly to retained earnings. This may involve transferring the whole of the surplus when the asset is retired or disposed of. IAS 16 specifically says that transfers from revaluation surplus to retained earnings are not made through profit or loss. The transfer will be shown in the statement of changes in equity.

IAS 16 also allows some of the revaluation surplus to be transferred as the asset is used by an entity. In such a case, the amount of the surplus transferred would be the difference between depreciation based on the revalued carrying amount of the asset and depreciation based on the asset's original cost. This amount can be transferred to retained earnings each year.

Example 13.I

In Example 13.H, the disposal takes place within the following period, so the whole of the revaluation surplus can be transferred to retained earnings. The amount transferred is $70,000.

Example 13.J

Using the data and answer to Example 13.F:

	$	$	$
Original cost	500,000		
3 years depreciation (3/50)	(30,000)		
Net book value	470,000		
Revaluation to	540,000		
Gain on revaluation			70,000
2 years depreciation (2/47 × 540,000)	22,978	22,978	
2 years depreciation based on cost is		20,000	
Transfer to retained earnings from revaluation reserve (1,489 each year)			(2,978)
Net book value	517,022		
Revalued to	500,000		
Loss on revaluation, charged to revaluation reserve			(17,022)
Balance on revaluation reserve			50,000
Depreciation (500,000/45)		11,111	
Depreciation based on cost		10,000	
Transfer to retained earnings from revaluation reserve			(1,111)
Balance on revaluation reserve			48,889

13.9 Disclosure requirements

IAS 16 has extensive disclosure requirements:

(a) measurement bases used (e.g. cost or valuation);
(b) depreciation methods used;
(c) useful lives or depreciation rates used;
(d) gross carrying amount and accumulated depreciation at the beginning and end of the period;
(e) reconciliation of opening and closing figures with details of additions, disposals, revaluations, impairments and depreciation;
(f) details of any pledging of items of property, plant and equipment as security for liabilities;
(g) commitments for future capital expenditure;
(h) if the asset has been revalued:
   (i) basis of valuation;
   (ii) date of valuation;
   (iii) whether an independent valuer was used;
   (iv) the carrying value of the asset if no revaluation had taken place;
   (v) the revaluation surplus.

13.10 IAS 23 *Borrowing Costs* (revised 2007)

13.10.1 Introduction

IAS 23 deals with the accounting treatment of interest, etc., including the extent to which it may be capitalised as a part of the cost of a non-current asset.

13.10.2 Borrowing costs – accounting treatment

IAS 23 was revised in 2007. The new IAS 23 requires that borrowing costs are capitalised if they are directly attributable to the acquisition, construction or production of a qualifying asset (one that takes a long time to get ready for use or sale). The borrowing costs that are directly attributable to the acquisition, construction or production of a qualifying asset are those borrowing costs that would have been avoided if the expenditure on the qualifying asset had not been made.

Debit	Asset
Credit	Bank

13.10.3 Interest rate

For specific borrowings, the actual interest cost will be used. For general borrowings, the weighted average cost will be used.

13.10.4 Period of capitalisation

Capitalisation will commence when expenditure on the asset and borrowing costs are being incurred, and must cease when substantially all the activities necessary to prepare the asset for sale or use are complete. If development work is interrupted for any extended period, capitalisation of borrowing costs should be suspended for that period.

13.10.5 Disclosure

The financial statements must disclose:

(a) borrowing costs capitalised in the period;
(b) the capitalisation rate used.

13.11   Available for sale financial assets

You do not need to know the detail of IAS 32 – *Financial Instruments: Disclosure and Presentation* or IAS 39 – *Financial Instruments: Recognition and Measurement* as the only part of these standards in the syllabus relates to share capital which is dealt with in Chapter 17. However, the asset headings defined in IAS 32 and IAS 39 have to be used in the statement of financial position, so you need to understand what the headings mean.

IAS 32 defines financial assets, the definition includes equity instruments in other entities.

IAS 39 categorises financial assets into four categories, the only category effecting this syllabus is 'available for sale investments'. These are investments in equity and other types of shares in other entities. They appear on the statement of financial position under the non-current asset heading as financial assets. They are measured at fair value and revalued to fair value on each end of the reporting period.

Note that being classified as available for sale does not mean that there is any intention to sell them.

13.12   Summary

Having completed this chapter, we can now account for and disclose the amounts relating to property, plant and equipment, including depreciation, changes in useful life, disposal and the effects of revaluation.

Finally, we can explain how to treat and disclose amounts relating to borrowing costs.

Revision Questions

13

? Question 1

A building contractor decides to build an office building, to be occupied by his own staff. Tangible non-current assets are initially measured at cost. Which of the following expenses incurred by the building contractor cannot be included as a part of the cost of the office building?

(A) Interest incurred on a specific loan taken out to pay for the construction of the new offices;
(B) Direct building labour costs;
(C) A proportion of the contractor's general administration costs;
(D) Hire of plant and machinery for use on the office building site. **(2 marks)**

? Question 2

The purpose of depreciation is to:

(A) Allocate the cost less residual value on a systematic basis over the asset's useful economic life;
(B) Write the asset down to its market value each period;
(C) Charge profits for the use of the asset;
(D) Recognise that assets lose value over time. **(2 marks)**

? Question 3

Which of the following tangible non-current assets are NOT usually depreciated:

(A) Machinery purchased through a finance lease;
(B) Land;
(C) Buildings with a life in excess of 30 years;
(D) Vehicles. **(2 marks)**

? Question 4

IAS 16 *Property, Plant and Equipment* requires an asset to be measured at cost on its original recognition in the financial statements.

EW used its own staff, assisted by contractors when required, to construct a new warehouse for its own use.

Which ONE of the following costs would NOT be included in attributable costs of the non-current asset?

(A) Clearance of the site prior to work commencing.
(B) Professional surveyors' fees for managing the construction work.
(C) EW's own staff wages for time spent working on the construction.
(D) An allocation of EW's administration costs, based on EW staff time spent on the construction as a percentage of the total staff time. **(2 marks)**

⁇ Question 5

AB purchased a specialized machine for $20,000 on 1 April 2000. The machine had an expected useful life of 10 years and was depreciated using the straight-line method. Residual value was assumed to be zero.

Due to a worldwide shortage of specialized parts for manufacturing new machines of this type, the price of new machines of a similar type more than doubled by 31 March 2003. AB decided to revalue their machine on 31 March 2003 to market value. The market value of a two-year old machine was $35,000.

AB ceased the production of a product line and no longer required the machine. They sold the machine for $32,000 on 31 March 2004.

On disposal of the machine AB should:

 (i) Transfer $21,000 from revaluation reserve to retained earnings;
 (ii) Credit a gain on disposal of $2,000 to the profit or loss;
(iii) Debit loss on disposal of $1,000 to profit or loss;
(iv) Transfer $15,000 from revaluation reserve to retained earnings;
 (v) Credit gain on disposal of $23,000 to profit or loss.

Which of the following are the correct entries to record the gain/loss on disposal?

(A) (i) and (iv)
(B) (iii) and (iv)
(C) (v) only
(D) (i) and (ii) **(4 marks)**

⁇ Question 6

Plant and machinery, costing $50,000, was purchased on 1 April 20X0. This was depreciated for 2 years at 20 per cent using the reducing balance method. On 1 April 20X2, the machinery (original cost $25,000) was sold for $12,000. Replacement machines were acquired on the same date for $34,000. What was the net book value of plant and machinery at 1 April 20X3?

(A) $39,800
(B) $43,200
(C) $40,800
(D) $40,000 **(4 marks)**

Question 7

Roming purchased property costing $440,000 on 1 January 2000. The property is being depreciated over 50 years on a straight-line basis.

The property was revalued on 1 January 2004 at $520,000. The useful life was also reviewed at that date and is estimated to be a further 40 years.

Requirement

Prepare the accounting entries to record the revaluation and calculate the depreciation charge that will apply from 1 January 2004. **(5 marks)**

Question 8

The financial statements are being prepared for Diska and the accountant has asked you how the borrowing costs of $30 million should be treated in the accounts. Of the $30 million, $7 million relates specifically to the construction of the entity's new manufacturing plant (at a total cost of $60 million).

Requirement

Discuss the appropriate accounting treatment for the above costs, explaining what options are available and the disclosures that would be required. **(4 marks)**

Question 9

CI purchased equipment on 1 April 2002 for $100,000. The equipment was depreciated using the reducing balance method at 25% per year. CI's period end is 31 March.

Depreciation was charged up to and including 31 March 2006. At that date, the recoverable amount was $28,000.

Calculate the impairment loss on the equipment according to IAS 36 *Impairment of Assets*. **(3 marks)**

Question 10

Which ONE of the following items would CM recognise as subsequent expenditure on a non-current asset and capitalise it as required by IAS 16 *Property, Plant and Equipment?*

(A) CM purchased a furnace five years ago, when the furnace lining was separately identified in the accounting records. The furnace now requires relining at a cost of $200,000. When the furnace is relined, it will be used in CM's business for a further 5 years

(B) CM's office building has been badly damaged by a fire. CM intends to restore the building to its original condition at a cost of $250,000

(C) CM's delivery vehicle broke down. When it was inspected by the repairers, it was discovered that it needed a new engine. The engine and associated labour costs are estimated to be $5,000

(D) CM closes its factory for 2 weeks every year. During this time, all plant and equipment has its routine annual maintenance check and any necessary repairs are carried out. The cost of the current year's maintenance check and repairs was $75,000

(2 marks)

Question 11

A property was purchased on 1 January 1998 for $800,000. The asset is used from the date of acquisition and its estimated economic useful life is 50 years. After 5 years of use, the asset is revalued on 1 January 2003 at $830,000.

A subsequent valuation was completed 1 year later, as the property valuations in that area were experiencing significant fluctuations, and the property valuation was $750,000.

Requirements

(a) Explain the treatment and prepare the accounting entries to record the revaluation on 1 January 2003. **(4 marks)**

(b) Explain the treatment and prepare the accounting entries to record the revaluation on 1 January 2004. **(6 marks)**

(Total marks = 10)

Question 12

AD owns three hotels. The entity has employed C and J, a firm of chartered surveyors, to revalue its properties during the past year. The directors have decided that the valuations should be incorporated into the entity's financial statements.

This is the first time that such a revaluation has taken place and the clerk responsible for the preparation of the non-current asset note in the statement of financial position is unsure of the correct treatment of the amounts involved. The entity's year-end is 30 September 20X3.

The clerk has extracted the following table from the report prepared by C and J:

	Original cost	Depreciation to 30.9.X2	Market value at 1.1.X3	Estimated useful life 1.1.X3
	$'000	$'000	$'000	Years
Hotel G	400	96	650	50
Hotel H	350	56	420	30
Hotel K	250	35	160	40

Depreciation for the first 3 months of the year is to be based on the entity's original depreciation policy of writing off 2 per cent of cost per annum. Depreciation for the remainder of the year is to be based on the estimated asset lives stated in the surveyors' report.

Requirements

(a) Prepare the non-current asset note, which would appear as a part of A's published accounts, assuming that A owns no non-current assets apart from the three hotels listed above.

(You are *not* required to prepare the description of accounting policies which would appear in respect of non-current assets.) **(8 marks)**

(b) Answer the following queries posed by the accounts clerk:

  (i) The book value of Hotel K has fallen as a result of the revaluation. How should this decrease be reflected in the financial statements? **(4 marks)**

  (ii) Does all of the depreciation based on the revalued amounts for Hotels G and H have to be charged to profit or loss or can a proportion be offset against the revaluation reserve instead? **(2 marks)**

(Total marks = 14)

Solutions to Revision Questions

 Solution 1

The correct answer is (C), see Section 13.3.1.

Only specific costs incurred directly on the asset can be included. Finance costs can be included. Direct labour costs are also specific, as are the hire costs.

 Solution 2

The correct answer is (A), see Section 13.5.

 Solution 3

The correct answer is (B), see Section 13.5.

All tangible fixed assets, with finite useful lives are usually depreciated.

 Solution 4

The correct answer is (D), see Section 13.3.

 Solution 5

The correct answer is (D), see Sections 13.6 and 13.7.

	$
Original cost	20,000
3 years depreciation	(6,000)
	14,000
Revaluation, transfer to reserve	21,000
	35,000
Depreciation (1/7)	(5,000)
	30,000
Less cash on disposal	32,000
Gain on disposal	2,000
Reversal of revaluation gain to retained earnings	21,000

Solution 6

The answer is (D), see Section 13.5.

	$	$
Cost		50,000
20% depreciation		(10,000)
		40,000
20% depreciation		(8,000)
		32,000
Less disposal, net book value		
Cost	25,000	
Depreciation, 2 years	9,000	
		(16,000)
		16,000
Add acquisition		34,000
NBV 1 April 20X2		50,000
Less 20% depreciation		10,000
NBV 1 April 20X3		40,000

 Solution 7

The annual charge for depreciation was $440,000/50 years = $8,800.

The asset had been used and depreciated for 4 years (2000 to 2003).

The carrying value of the asset at the date of valuation was therefore $404,800 (cost of $440,000 – accumulated depreciation of $35,200).

The revaluation surplus is calculated as the valuation amount of $520,000 less the carrying value of the asset of $404,800. The surplus is therefore $115,200.

The revaluation at 1 January 2004 will be recorded as:

		$	$
Debit	Accumulated depreciation	35,200	
Debit	Cost of asset	80,000	
Credit	Revaluation surplus		115,200

Being the revaluation of the asset at 1 January 2004.

The depreciation charge for 2004 and beyond will be based on the asset's valuation over the remaining useful life of the property. The useful life has also been revised to 40 years, so the depreciation will now be $13,000, being value of $520,000 over 40 years, see Section 13.8.

 Solution 8

IAS 23 *Borrowing Costs* requires that borrowing costs be capitalised if they are directly attributable to the acquisition, construction or production of a qualifying asset.

Diska should charge $23m to the profit or loss and $7 million would be capitalised and included in the cost of constructing the plant.

The financial statements would disclose:

- the accounting policy adopted;
- the amount of borrowing costs capitalised in the period, see Section 13.10.

 Solution 9

	$
Cost	100,000
Depreciation 2002/03	(25,000)
	75,000
Depreciation 2003/04	(18,750)
	56,250
Depreciation 2004/05	(14,063)
	42,187
Depreciation 2005/06	(10,547)
	31,640
Impaired value	(28,000)
Reduction	3,640

See Section 13.8.2.

 Solution 10

The correct answer is A, see Section 13.5.

 Solution 11

At 1 January 2003

The annual charge for depreciation was $800,000/50 years = $16,000.

The asset had been used and depreciated for 5 years (1998–2002).

The carrying value of the asset at the date of valuation was therefore $720,000 (cost of $800,000 – accumulated depreciation of $80,000).

The revaluation surplus is calculated as the valuation amount of $830,000 less the carrying value of the asset of $720,000. The surplus is therefore $110,000.

The revaluation at 1 January 2003 will be recorded as:

		$	$
Debit	Accumulated depreciation	80,000	
Debit	Cost of asset	30,000	
Credit	Revaluation surplus		110,000

Being the revaluation of the asset at 1 January 2003.

At 1 January 2004

The annual charge for depreciation is now $830,000/45 years (the remaining useful life of the asset) = $18,444.

The asset had been used and depreciated one further year: 2003.

The carrying value of the asset at the date of the second valuation was therefore $811,556 (valuation of $830,000 – accumulated depreciation of $18,444).

The revaluation effect is calculated as the new valuation amount of $750,000 less the carrying value of the asset of $811,556. This results in a deficit on revaluation of $61,556.

The deficit will first be charged against any surplus relating to this asset's previous revaluations, with any balance of the deficit being charged in profit or loss.

There are sufficient amounts in the revaluation reserve, in this case to absorb the deficit at 1 January 2004, and so the revaluation at 1 January 2004 will be recorded as:

		$	$
Debit	Revaluation surplus	61,556	
Credit	Carrying value of the asset		61,556

Being the revaluation of the asset at 1 January 2004, resulting in an impairment deficit.

See Section 13.8.

 Solution 12

(a) Tangible non-current assets

	$'000
Land and buildings at cost or valuation	
At 1 October 20X2 (400 + 350 + 250)	1,000
Revaluation gain (To Balance)	230
At 30 September 20X3 (650 + 420 + 160)	1,230
Depreciation	
At 1 October 20X2 (96 + 56 + 35)	187
Revaluation adjustment (187 + 5)	(192)
Charge for year (workings)	28
At 30 September 20X3 (for 9 months)	23
Net book value	
At 1 October 20X2	813
At 30 September 20X3	1,207

Land and buildings (hotels) were revalued at 1 January 20X3 on an open-market basis.

Depreciation	$'000
Charge for first 3 months (400 + 350 + 250) × 2% × 3/12	5
Charge for the last 9 months	
((650/50) + (420/30) + (160/40)) × 9/12	23
	28

(b) IAS 16 requires that any revaluation loss which is caused by a clear consumption of economic benefit should be recognised as an expense in profit or loss. It is unlikely that this would apply to a hotel, where increased occupancy is unlikely to have any real effect on wear and tear on the fabric of the building.

If the building has previously been revalued, then the loss would be shown in other comprehensive income and decrease revaluation surplus to the extent that any credit balance existed in the revaluation reserve for that asset. When all the previous revaluation gain has been eliminated, the balance will be written off to profit or loss.

14

Accounting for
Leases

Accounting for Leases

14

LEARNING OUTCOME

After completing this chapter, you should be able to:

► explain the principles of the accounting rues contained in IAS's dealing with leases (lessee only).

The syllabus topics covered in this chapter are as follows:

- Leases (IAS 17) – Operating and finance leases in the books of the lessee.

14.1 Introduction

The IASB defines an asset as '... a resource controlled by the entity as a result of past events and from which economic benefits are expected to flow to the entity'.

In general terms, we normally consider assets to be items that we own. The definition above, however, is based on an entity having 'control' over an asset and determining how that asset will be used in order to generate revenues. The accounting treatment for leasing transactions is based on the essence of this definition.

The recognition of assets and liabilities should reflect the commercial reality of business transactions.

Most entities want to have a strong statement of financial position and, historically, many abused the accounting rules in order to enhance their financial position. One of the most common ways was to sell the assets that were necessary to the business and then lease them back. The assets, and more importantly, any associated liability for the financing of the assets, were removed and replaced with a simple annual leasing charge.

The commercial reality was, of course, that the entity still determined how the assets were to be used; in substance, they retained control over the assets. The fact that legal title had transferred was irrelevant in accounting terms. The accounting treatment for leases now ensures that the entity controlling the assets, irrespective of ownership, recognises the assets and associated liability in order to show a true and fair view of their financial position.

Note: The paper 7 syllabus only requires a knowledge of the treatment of leases in the lessee's financial statements. Accounting by the lessor is outside the syllabus.

14.2 Key definitions

The following definitions are given in the standard and help to explain terms used later in this chapter.

 A *lease* is an agreement whereby the lessor conveys to the lessee in return for a payment or series of payments the right to use an asset for an agreed period of time. (This definition includes hire purchase agreements.)

A *finance lease* is a lease that transfers substantially all the risks and rewards incidental to ownership of an asset. Title may or may not be eventually transferred.

An *operating lease* is a lease other than a finance lease.

The *lease term* is the non-cancellable period for which the lessee has contracted to lease the asset. Where the lessee has the option to continue to lease the asset for further terms, with or without further payment, and it is reasonably certain at the inception of the lease that this right will be exercised, then the lease term can be taken to include this further period.

14.3 Characteristics of leases

14.3.1 Finance leases

The classification of leases is based on the definitions of operating and finance leases given above; however, in practice, deciding on the classification can be extremely complex. IAS 17 does not provide a quantifiable test for deciding the classification; instead, we should consider all the features within the lease agreement, focusing on which party has the significant rights and rewards normally associated with ownership.

For the purposes of this syllabus, you will be expected to identify and discuss the main characteristics of leases and arrive at a decision as to how the lease should be classified and then accounted for. When asked to decide on or evaluate the classification of a lease, refer to the list given below.

A lease is classified as a finance lease if it transfers substantially all the risks and rewards incidental to ownership from the lessor to lessee. The classification is based on the substance of the transaction rather than the legal form, so greater weight should be given to those features that have a commercial effect in practice. The standard gives some situations that could indicate that transfer of ownership has taken place:

- legal title is transferred to the lessee at the end of the lease;
- the lease term is for the majority of the asset's economic useful life, irrespective of title transfer;
- at the inception of the lease, the present value of the minimum lease payment amounts to at least substantially all of the fair value of the leased asset;
- the lessee has the option to purchase the asset for a price sufficiently below the fair value of the asset at the date this option can be exercised;
- the leased assets are of a specialised nature and as such can only be used by the lessee unless modifications are made;

- where the lessee can cancel the lease but has to bear any losses associated with the cancellation;
- the lessee has the ability to continue the lease for a secondary period at a rate substantially below the market rent;
- gains or losses from the fluctuation in the fair value of the residual value of the asset fall to the lessee.

In answering a question, these *badges of ownership* should always form the basis of your justification for the classification of a lease.

Example 14.A

On 1 January 2003, Dixon Doors leased a new machine from EK Finance. The capital cost of the machine is $25,000. Six half-yearly payments of $5,000 are payable in advance, the first instalment being due on 1 January 2003. A secondary term of 3 years is being offered by EK Finance for $100 per annum. Dixon Doors have not yet decided if they will use the secondary term.

The estimated economic useful life of the asset is 5 years with a nil residual value. After 3 years (primary lease term), the asset is expected to have a residual value of $5,000. Under the lease agreement, Dixon Doors is entitled to 95 per cent of the proceeds should the asset be sold.

Explain, with justifications, how this lease should be classified.

Solution

From the information given, we can calculate that the minimum lease payments (six payments of $5,000 × $30,000) are greater than the fair value of the asset (capital cost $25,000). The difference is the finance cost associated with the lease.

The primary lease term is in this case 3 years (Dixon Doors has not yet decided on taking a secondary term), which is for the majority of the assets economic useful life.

The lessee has the option to lease the asset for a secondary term at a substantially reduced rate ($100 p.a. for an asset worth $5,000 at the inception of the secondary term).

And finally the fact that Dixon Doors are entitled to 95 per cent of the proceeds should the asset be sold at the end of the primary lease term.

These are all badges of ownership which indicate that the risks and rewards normally associated with owning an asset are transferred to the lessee, Dixon Doors. This lease would therefore be classified as a finance lease.

14.3.2 Operating leases

If the information given does not point to the lease being a finance lease, that is, there are no clear indicators that ownership has transferred to the lessee, then the lease should be classified as an operating lease.

14.3.3 Leases of land and buildings

The land and buildings elements of a lease of property should be considered separately, unless the land element is immaterial. To achieve this, the minimum lease payments need to be allocated between the land and buildings element in proportion to the relative fair values of the leasehold interests in the land element and the buildings element. The land is normally classified as an operating lease, unless title is expected to pass to the lessee at the end of the lease term, then it will be a finance lease. The buildings element will need to be classified as either an operating lease or a finance lease based on the criteria in 14.3.1. If it is not possible to allocate the minimum lease payments reliably between the land element and the building element, the entire lease should be classified as a finance lease, unless it is clear that both elements are operating leases.

Where the amount of land to be separately recognised is immaterial, the lease of land and buildings can be treated as a single unit in determining the classification of the lease.

14.4 Accounting for operating leases

Operating lease rentals are viewed as an annual expense of the business and should be charged to the profit or loss on a systematic basis (normally straight-line basis) over the term of the lease.

The accounting policies will normally state this.

Rentals payable under operating leases are charged to profit or loss as incurred.

Example 14.B

Buyer Products has a non-cancellable five-year operating lease costing $2,000 per annum for 5 years. The machine has an estimated useful life of 20 years. The annual charge in respect of this operating lease will be recorded as follows:

		$	$
Debit	Operating lease charges	2,000	
Credit	Bank		2,000
Being the payment of the operating lease charge.			

Property leases often give incentives to lessees to encourage uptake of leases, such as rent-free periods and reverse premiums. Although no specific reference is made to these in the standard, the principle to be applied is straightforward, and that is to charge the profit or loss on a straight-line basis over the term of the lease. This ensures that the expense is charged and matched against the income that the asset generates while leased. Consider the two basic examples below.

14.4.1 Rent-free period

Example 14.C

Buyer Products enters into a second non-cancellable five-year operating lease. Under the terms of the lease, $5,000 is payable for 4 years commencing in year 2. The machine has an estimated useful life of 20 years.

Buyer Products will use the asset to help generate income for the next 5 years and so should charge the profit or loss with an expense in respect of leasing this asset. The annual charge should be $4,000 ($5,000 × 4 years = $20,000. $20,000 over 5 years = $4,000 per annum.)

The charge in respect of this operating lease in year 1 will be recorded as follows:

		$	$
Debit	Operating lease charges	4,000	
Credit	Accrued lease charges		4,000
Being the recording of the operating lease charge in year 1.			

The charge in respect of this operating lease in years 2–5 will be recorded as follows:

		$	$
Debit	Operating lease charges	4,000	
Debit	Accrued lease charges	1,000	
Credit	Bank		5,000
Being the recording of the operating lease charge in years 2–5.			

14.4.2 Cashback incentives

The recording of the operating lease charge where a cashback incentive has been granted, relies on the matching principle and requires that the total payable under the operating lease be allocated over the full term of the lease.

Example 14.D

Buyer Products enters into a third non-cancellable five-year operating lease. Under the terms of the lease, $4,000 is payable for 5 years; however, there is a cashback incentive of $2,500 paid at the start of the lease. The machine has an estimated useful life of 20 years.

Buyer Products will use the asset to help generate income for the next 5 years and so should charge the profit or loss with an expense in respect of leasing this asset. The annual charge should be $3,500 ($4,000 × 5 years = $20,000. $20,000 − $2,500 = $17,500 over 5 years = $3,500 per annum).

The recording of the cashback in year 1 will be recorded as follows:

		$	$
Debit	Bank	2,500	
Credit	Deferred income		2,500

Being the recording of the cashback in year 1.

The charge in respect of this operating lease in years 1–5 will be recorded as follows:

		$	$
Debit	Operating lease charges	3,500	
Debit	Deferred income ($2,500/5 years)	500	
Credit	Bank		4,000

Being the recording of the operating lease charge in years 2–5.

Note: The cashback of $2,500 is released to the profit or loss over the lease term at $500 per annum.

14.5 Disclosures for operating leases

A note to the financial statements should show:

- Lease payments recognised as an expense in the period;
- A general description of the entity's significant lease arrangements;
- The total of future minimum lease payments under non-cancellable operating leases for each of the following periods:
  - not later than 1 year;
  - later than 1 year and not later than 5 years;
  - later than 5 years.

An example will help us understand this disclosure requirement.

Example 14.E

Snowyday Boots have three non-cancellable operating leases as at 31 December 2002. The details for the leases are as follows:

Lease 1	$10,000 per annum	Expires 31 December 2003
Lease 2	$20,000 per annum	Expires 31 December 2005
Lease 3	$30,000 per annum	Expires 31 December 2009

This disclosure is intended to show the cash commitment that the business has underoperating leases in future periods. Remember that operating leases are an expense item, there is no asset or liability on the statement of financial position of the lessee. The leases are, however, non-cancellable and so the business must disclose this commitment somewhere in the financial statements to provide a true and fair view. The note will be as follows:

Snowyday Boots – extract from the notes to the accounts

Lease commitments
  Operating leases
  The following charges arise from non-cancellable operating leases:

	$
Minimum lease payments	
Not later than 1 year	60,000
Later than 1 year and not later than 5 years	160,000
Later than 5 years	60,000
	280,000

Workings

The total of the minimum lease payments is $280,000 calculated from the annual lease payment multiplied by the remaining lease term as at 31 December 2002:

	Years remaining	Due less than 1 year $	Due in 2–5 years $	Due in more than 5 years $
Lease 1	1	10,000	0	0
Lease 2	3	20,000	40,000 (20K × 2 yrs)	0
Lease 3	7	30,000	120,000 (30K × 4 yrs)	60,000 (30K × 2 yrs)
Total		60,000	160,000	60,000

14.6 Accounting for finance leases

Before we consider the treatment of finance leases, let us remind ourselves of the business reasons for entering into such an arrangement.

There are a number of ways that a business can acquire an asset:

- it can purchase the asset outright

Debit	Fixed asset
Credit	Bank

Being the purchase of a fixed asset for cash.

- it can take a loan and then purchase the asset

Debit	Bank
Credit	Bank loan

Being the receipt of the loan.

Debit	Fixed asset
Credit	Bank

Being the purchase of a fixed asset using the loaned cash.

- it can lease the asset

Debit	Fixed asset
Credit	Finance lease creditor

Being the leasing of the asset and the recognition of the associated liability.

A finance lease allows the lessee the use of the asset as if it were his/her own and creates a liability to the lessor for the capital amount to be repaid. This is effectively like a loan from the lessor – it just cuts out the bank as a middle man.

Similarly to the bank, the lessor will charge the lessee finance costs or interest for financing the acquisition of the fixed asset, and just as we do with a bank loan we have to allocate the repayments between those amounts that relate to interest and those that reduce the liability. (The difference with an asset acquired using a finance lease is that legal title is not transferred.)

The accounting for these transactions is straightforward:

Debit	Fixed asset
Credit	Finance lease creditor

Being the acquisition of the asset and the recognition of the associated liability.

Debit	Finance lease creditor
Debit	Interest expense
Credit	Bank

Being the repayments made to the lessor allocated between interest and capital.

Debit	Depreciation expense
Credit	Accumulated depreciation

Being the depreciation of the leased asset by the lessee.

These entries result in the asset being held at book value in the accounts of the lessee and the asset is depreciated by the lessee, ensuring that the expense associated with the asset, depreciation, is matched against the income that the asset is helping to generate.

This treatment ensures that the business reality of the transaction and not its legal form prevails. The leased asset is included in the total assets of the business and the liability associated with funding the acquisition of the leased asset is disclosed on the statement of financial position. Business ratios, for example, gearing and return on capital employed, are more meaningful with the leased assets included.

Do not lose sight of the basic accounting entries. The recording of finance lease transactions is straightforward and must not be overshadowed by the calculation of implied interest, which is what we are about to look at.

With many loan agreements the bank will simply calculate the interest due based on the interest rate to be applied and the outstanding liability at that date. Under finance lease agreements, it is generally the total rentals payable that is stated. We then must compare this with the fair value (usually the cost) of the fixed asset to establish the total amount of interest that is to be paid over the term of the lease. The main calculation then is how best to allocate the interest expense to profit or loss.

14.7 Calculating the implied interest on finance leases

The standard requires that finance lease interest allocated to periods should be calculated so as to produce a constant periodic rate of interest on the outstanding balance of the liability for each period. This is then charged as a finance expense.

There are three methods of allocating the finance charges in a finance lease:

1. the straight-line method;
2. the sum-of-digits method;
3. the actuarial method.

The method which gives the constant periodic rate of interest on the outstanding liability is the actuarial rate. This rate can be computer generated. The standard, however, permits the use of some approximation to the rate in order to simplify the calculation.

The sum of digits (also known as the 'rule of 78') gives a suitable approximation to the actuarial method. The straight-line method is the easiest to calculate but does not provide us with a constant rate of interest.

You will be expected to apply all three methods within this syllabus. Remember that this calculation is just for calculating the interest. Once this calculation is completed we can then record the lease repayments, allocating the payment between interest and reduction of capital.

Let us work through an example of a finance lease in the books of a lessee. We will use one set of information and calculate the interest allocation using all three methods. We will then select one of these methods and record the accounting entries and draft the relevant extracts and disclosures.

Example 14.F Shanks and Ward – lease information

- The accounting year-end is 31 December.
- The cost of the leased asset is $280,000.
- The estimated economic useful life is eight years.
- The asset has a nil residual value.
- The lease commences 1 January 2003.
- The primary lease term is 7 years.
- The lease repayments are $50,000 per annum in advance.
- Residual value at the end of the primary lease term is $35,000.
- Lessee is entitled to 95 per cent of the residual value at the end of the primary term.

Step 1. Confirm that the lease is to be treated as a finance lease. This lease is a finance lease. The total rentals exceed the fair value of the asset at the inception of the lease. The lease term is for the majority of the asset's economic useful life. The lessee is entitled to the majority of the proceeds should the asset be sold at the end of the primary lease term. These are clear indicators that the benefits of ownership of the asset has transferred to the lessee.

Step 2. Calculate the total finance charge. The total finance charge is calculated by comparing the total rentals payable and the fair value (cost) of the asset. In this case the total finance charge is $70,000, being total rentals of $350,000 ($50,000 for 7 years) less the cost of the asset $280,000.

Step 3. Establish the basis for allocating the total finance charge. Decide (or follow requirement in any exam question) on the method of allocation from one of the three methods. Establish the total number of periods being financed.

It is vitally important for your calculations that you correctly identify the number of periods over which you want to charge interest. The clue is in the repayment details.

If the repayments are to be made in advance, then your first payment will reduce your capital immediately before you start receiving funding, and when you make the final instalment, your final period of use of the asset will be with no outstanding liability. To calculate the finance periods for repayments in advance, take the total number of repayments and deduct 1.

If the repayments are in arrears, then you will not have extinguished the lease liability until the end of the primary lease term. The finance periods will equal the number of repayments.

Let us look at a quick illustration of this calculation before we continue.

The date of the inception of the lease is 1 January 2001. If the lease term is 3 years and the repayments are half-yearly in arrears, then the total finance periods over which you will allocate any interest is six (twice a year for 3 years).

The first instalment is made on 30 June 2001 and the last instalment you make under this lease will be on 31 December 2003. A lease liability exists until the end of the lease term and is not extinguished until 31 December 2003 when the final instalment is made. It follows then that if the lessor was providing you with funding for the full six periods then you will allocate interest over the six periods.

However, if the repayments are in advance then the first instalment will be made on 1 January 2001, at the inception of the lease. The final instalment will be made on 1 July 2003. For the period from 1 July 2003 to 31 December 2003, you will use the asset; however, you have extinguished the lease liability at the start of the period.

You are not receiving funding for the final six months and therefore should not be allocating interest for this final period. The total finance periods are then five (half-yearly for 3 years less one) which results in us allocating interest from 1 January 2001 until 30 June 2003.

Step 4. Calculate the interest to be charged to each period. Use one of the three methods mentioned above. We will use all three in this example for illustration purposes.

Step 5. Record the relevant accounting entries for the year. Capitalise and depreciate the leased assets, create the lease creditor and record the repayments allocating the payments between interest and capital based on the calculations in step 4.

Let us now calculate the interest using the three methods based on the lease information for Shanks and Ward. The first three steps are the same for each of the three methods.

- Step 1. Confirm the lease is a finance lease – justification is given above in Section 14.7.1 Step 1.
- Step 2. Calculate the total interest to be allocated – completed above – $70,000.
- Step 3. Establish the basis for allocation – the number of finance periods. The repayments are annual in advance and the lease term is 7 years. Total finance periods = $(7 - 1) = 6$.
- Step 4. Calculate the interest to be allocated to each period.

Straight-line method

$$\frac{\text{Total finance cost to be allocated}}{\text{Number of finance periods}} = \frac{\$70,000}{6} = 11,667 \text{ per period}$$

This is the most straightforward method to use as it simply allocates the same amount of interest to each finance period. It may not reflect the commercial reality of the transaction as the liability is reducing each period and therefore the interest incurred is also reducing.

Step 5. Record the relevant accounting entries for the year.

		$	$
Debit	Fixed asset	280,000	
Credit	Finance lease creditor		280,000

Being the capitalisation of the leased asset on 1 January 2003.

		$	$
Debit	Finance lease creditor	38,333	
Debit	Finance lease interest	11,667	
Credit	Bank		50,000

Being the repayment made on 1 January 2003.

(The total repaid is $50,000. We calculated implied interest of $11,667 using the straight-line method. The difference is the amount of the repayment that reduces the liability.)

		$	$
Debit	Depreciation charge for the year	35,250	
Credit	Accumulated depreciation		35,250

Being the depreciation of the leased asset for the year to 31 December 2003.

(Total cost of asset $280,000, less the residual value that Shanks and Ward is entitled to at the end of the primary lease term: 95% × $35,000 = $33,250.)

$$\frac{\$280,000 - 33,250}{7 \text{ years}} = 35,250 \text{ per annum}$$

Remember, the amount you want to depreciate is the net cost of the asset to the lessee. There is no indication that a secondary lease term will be used and so we depreciate over the primary lease term of 7 years.

ACCOUNTING FOR LEASES

Let us look at how the liability would be extinguished over the period of the lease using this method.

Period	Liability at start of period $	Rental paid $	Liability during period $	Allocated interest $	Liability at end of period $
1 Jan. 2003	280,000	(50,000)	230,000	11,667	241,667
1 Jan. 2004	241,667	(50,000)	191,667	11,667	203,334
1 Jan. 2005	203,334	(50,000)	153,334	11,667	165,001
1 Jan. 2006	165,001	(50,000)	115,001	11,667	126,668
1 Jan. 2007	126,668	(50,000)	76,668	11,666	88,334
1 Jan. 2008	88,334	(50,000)	38,334	11,666	50,000
1 Jan. 2009	50,000	(50,000)	–	–	–
Totals		(350,000)		70,000	

Let us have a look at the information this table provides:

- compare the opening and closing liabilities each year – it reduces by the amount of the repayment which represents capital $38,333 ($50,000 – $11,667);
- the total rentals paid is $350,000;
- the total interest allocated is $70,000 – which is what we calculated above;
- the interest has been allocated over six finance periods;
- the final instalments made on 1 January 2009 extinguishes the lease liability – remember, the repayments were in advance.

Let us now complete steps 4 and 5 using the sum-of-digits method of allocating interest.

Sum-of-digits method

The sum of digits can be calculated using a simple formula:

$$\frac{n(n + 1)}{2}$$

where n is the number of finance periods.

In this example, the sum of digits is 21, being $(6 \times 7)/2$. We calculated the number of finance periods in step 3 above.

The total interest of $70,000 (calculated in step 2 above) is allocated by multiplying it by the 'relevant digit' divided by the sum of digits. The relevant digit will be the number of finance periods remaining at the date the repayment is made. In this example, the first instalment made on 1 January 2003 will be digit 6, as there are six finance periods remaining when this repayment is made. The relevant digit then reduces by one each period as the number of funding periods remaining decreases.

Let us recreate our table to see the whole repayment plan using the sum-of-digits method.

Period	Liability at start of period $	Rental paid $	Liability during the period $	Interest calculation	Allocated interest $	Liability at end of period $
1 Jan. 2003	280,000	(50,000)	230,000	6/21 × $70,000	20,000	250,000
1 Jan. 2004	250,000	(50,000)	200,000	5/21 × $70,000	16,667	216,667
1 Jan. 2005	216,667	(50,000)	166,667	4/21 × $70,000	13,333	180,000
1 Jan. 2006	180,000	(50,000)	130,000	3/21 × $70,000	10,000	140,000
1 Jan. 2007	140,000	(50,000)	90,000	2/21 × $70,000	6,667	96,667
1 Jan. 2008	96,667	(50,000)	46,667	1/21 × $70,000	3,333	50,000
1 Jan. 2009	50,000	(50,000)	–		–	–
Totals		(350,000)			70,000	

Let us have a look at the information this table provides:

- compare the opening and closing liabilities each year – it reduces by the amount of the repayment which represents capital
  - $30,000 ($50,000 – $20,000) in year 1
  - $33,333 ($50,000 – 16,667) in year 2 and so on;
- the total rentals paid is $350,000;
- the total interest allocated is still $70,000 – it is just allocated on a different basis;

- the interest has again been allocated over six finance periods;
- the final instalment made on 1 January 2009 extinguishes the lease liability – remember, the repayments were in advance.

Step 5. Record the entries for the year-end 31 December 2003

		$	$
Debit	Fixed asset	280,000	
Credit	Finance lease creditor		280,000

Being the capitalisation of the leased asset at 1 January 2003.

		$	$
Debit	Finance lease creditor	30,000	
Debit	Finance lease interest	20,000	
Credit	Bank		50,000

Being the repayment made on 1 January 2003.

(The total repaid is $50,000. We calculated implied interest of $20,000 using the sum-of-digits method. The difference is the amount paid towards reducing the liability.)

		$	$
Debit	Depreciation charge for the year	35,250	
Credit	Accumulated depreciation		35,250

Being the depreciation of the leased asset for the year to 31 December 2003 (as calculated earlier during the straight-line method)

Note that the accounting entries are the same as those for the straight-line method – the only difference is the amount of the repayment that has been allocated to interest and capital, respectively.

Actuarial method

The constant rate of interest can only be computer-generated or by a long process of trial 2and error.

> If you are asked to use this method in an examination, an interest rate will be provided. If an interest rate is provided, then the examiner wants you to use the actuarial method of allocation. If an interest rate is not given, use the sum-of-digits method.

For the Shanks and Ward example, the approximate rate of interest (rounded to two decimal places) is 8.16 per cent. This rate is applied to the outstanding liability at the start of the period to give the interest expense to be charged for the period.

We will recreate our table to see the full effect:

Period	Liability at start of period $	Rental paid $	Liability during period $	Interest at 8.16% applied to liability during period $	Liability at end of period $
1 Jan. 2003	280,000	(50,000)	230,000	18,768	248,768
1 Jan. 2004	248,768	(50,000)	198,768	16,219	214,987
1 Jan. 2005	214,987	(50,000)	164,987	13,463	178,450
1 Jan. 2006	178,450	(50,000)	128,450	10,482	138,932
1 Jan. 2007	138,932	(50,000)	88,932	7,257	96,189
1 Jan. 2008	96,189	(50,000)	46,189	3,811*	50,000
1 Jan. 2009	50,000	(50,000)	–	–	–
Totals		(350,000)		70,000	

* This amount includes $42 rounding as the rate used is the closest approximation rounded to two decimal places.

Let us have a look at the information this table provides:

- compare the opening and closing liabilities each year – it reduces by the amount of the repayment which represents capital:
  - $31,232 ($50,000 − $18,768) in year 1
  - $33,781 ($50,000 − $16,219) in year 2 and so on;
- the total rental paid is $350,000;
- the total interest allocated is still $70,000 – it is just allocated on a different basis;
- the interest has again been allocated over six finance periods;
- the final instalment made on 1 January 2006 extinguishes the lease liability – remember, the repayments were in advance.

Step 5. Record the entries for the year to 31 December 2000.

The accounting entries for step 5 are once again those for the other methods, the only difference being the amount of the repayment allocated to interest and capital.

We have now calculated the allocated interest using the three permitted methods. The results can be summarised as follows:

Year ended 31 December	Interest calculated using straight line $	Interest calculated using sum of digits $	Interest calculated using actuarial $
2003	11,667	20,000	18,768
2004	11,667	16,667	16,219
2005	11,667	13,333	13,463
2006	11,667	10,000	10,482
2007	11,666	6,667	7,257
2008	11,666	3,333	3,811
2009	–	–	–
Totals	70,000	70,000	70,000

The sum-of-digits method gives a close approximation to the actuarial method. The straight-line method, while being the simplest to calculate, provides a somewhat arbitrary allocation.

14.7.1 In advance/in arrears

The tables and calculations we have performed in this example are based on a lease agreement with repayments in advance. Note that if the repayments were to be in arrears, then the total finance periods would be seven and not six. The lease liability would not be extinguished until the final instalment was made on 31 December 2009 and as a result there would be interest charged in this period. For completeness, let us consider the same lease as above but with repayments in arrears, the interest being apportioned using the sum-of-digits basis.

Example 14.G

We will use the example in 14.F above.

The sum of digits is calculated as:

$$\frac{n(n+1)}{2}$$

where *n* is the number of finance periods.

In this example, the sum of digits is 28, being (7 × 8)/2. The finance periods now total seven as the repayments are in arrears and the lessee is receiving funding until the end of the lease term.

The total interest of $70,000 (calculated in step 2 above) is allocated by multiplying it by the 'relevant digit' divided by the sum of digits. The relevant digit will be the number of finance periods remaining at the date the repayment is made.

In this example, the first instalment made on 31 December 2003 will be digit 7, as there are seven finance periods remaining when this repayment is made. The relevant digit then reduces by one each period as the number of funding periods remaining decreases.

Let us recreate our table to see the whole repayment plan, using sum of digits for *repayments in arrears*.

Period	Liability at start of period $	Interest calculation	Allocated interest $	Rental paid $	Liability of end of period $
1 Jan. 2003	280,000	7/28 × $70,000	17,500	(50,000)	247,500
1 Jan. 2004	247,500	6/28 × $70,000	15,000	(50,000)	212,500
1 Jan. 2005	212,500	5/28 × $70,000	12,500	(50,000)	175,000
1 Jan. 2006	175,000	4/28 × $70,000	10,000	(50,000)	135,000
1 Jan. 2007	135,000	3/28 × $70,000	7,500	(50,000)	92,500
1 Jan. 2008	92,500	2/28 × $70,000	5,000	(50,000)	47,500
1 Jan. 2009	47,500	1/28 × $70,000	2,500	(50,000)	–
Totals			70,000	350,000	

Let us have a look at the information this table provides:

- compare the opening and closing liabilities each year – it reduces by the amount of the repayment which represents capital ($50,000 − $17,500 = $32,500 in year 1);
- there is no column for 'capital during the period' as the repayment is made at the end of the period and therefore the entire amount is outstanding for the period;
- the total rentals paid is $350,000;
- the total interest allocated is still $70,000 – it is just allocated on a different basis;
- the interest has been allocated over seven finance periods;
- the final instalment made on 31 December 2009 extinguishes the lease liability – remember, the repayments were in arrears.

14.8 Disclosures for finance leases

From the accounting entries we processed in the above examples, we can draft any relevant extracts from the financial statements, using the sum-of-digits figures from Example 14.F above:

Shanks and Ward – extracts from the financial statements for the year ended 31 December 2003.

Income statement

	$
Operating expenses	
Depreciation charge for the year	35,250
Finance lease interest (sum of digits)	20,000

Statement of financial position

Non-current assets	
Property, plant and equipment	
(cost $280,000 less $35,250)	244,750
Current liabilities	
Finance lease creditor	33,333
Non-current liabilities	
Finance lease creditor	216,667

To understand how the creditor figures are calculated, refer back to Example 14.F. The creditor within current liabilities will represent the amount of next year's repayment that will be allocated to capital, that is $50,000 less interest of $16,667.

The non-current liability creditor is the outstanding balance at the end of the following year or it can be calculated by taking the closing liability at the end of the reporting period

($250,000) and deducting the amount that is due within 1 year (just calculated above) of $33,333.

It is not necessary to complete the full schedule of repayments, unless it is asked for. In order to calculate the creditor due within 1 year and greater than 1 year, however, you will have to calculate the interest to be allocated for the following period – remember that next year's repayment less interest allocated to next year leaves the amount which is due to be repaid to capital next year.

Lessees are required to make the following disclosures in respect of finance leases:

- for each class of asset, the net carrying amount at the end of the reporting period;
- a reconciliation between the total of future minimum lease payments at the end of the reporting period and their present value analysed between:
  - not later than 1 year;
  - later than 1 year and not later than 5 years;
  - later than 5 years.

The disclosure note for the Shanks and Ward example would be as follows:
Obligations under finance leases as at 31 December 2003
The minimum lease payments payable under finance leases are as follows:

	$
Not later than 1 year	50,000
Later than one year and not later than 5 years	250,000
Later than 5 years	–
	300,000
Less finance charges allocated to future periods (70,000 − 20,000, see Example 14.F)	(50,000)
Present value of lease payments	250,000

You can check this present value calculation – it should equal the total of the creditors due within and greater than 1 year that is recorded in the statement of financial position (see extracts above). $33,333 + $216,667 which equals $250,000.

14.9 Summary

Having completed this chapter, we can now correctly classify operating and finance leases, using the badges of ownership to justify our treatment. We can prepare the accounting entries to record an operating lease and draft the relevant extracts and additional disclosures for incorporation into the financial statements.

In accounting for finance leases, we can use the three acceptable methods of calculating the implied rate of interest on the lease, namely straight line, sum of digits and actuarial. Once the finance costs are calculated, we can prepare the accounting entries that correctly allocate revenue and capital elements of lease repayments. The relevant extracts and notes to the accounts can also be drafted.

Revision Questions

14

? Question 1

A finance lease runs for 5 years, with annual payments in arrears of $25,000. The fair value of the asset was $90,000. Using the sum-of-digits method, what would the outstanding lease creditor be at the end of year 2?

(A) $47,000
(B) $61,000
(C) $64,500
(D) $40,000   (2 marks)

? Question 2

An operating lease is:

(A) a lease that is not a finance lease;
(B) a lease that transfers substantially all risks and rewards to the lessor;
(C) a lease that is for virtually all the estimated useful life of the asset;
(D) a lease where the lessee is responsible for repairs, insurance and other running costs.

                                                                 (2 marks)

? Question 3

L leases a delivery vehicle to D on an operating lease. The terms of the lease are:

- term 3 years,
- special introductory discount in year one, rental reduced to $2,000,
- annual rentals of $5,000 per year for years two and three.

How much should D recognize as an expense in its profit or loss for the first year of the lease?

(A) $2,000
(B) $4,000
(C) $5,000
(D) $12,000   (2 marks)

Question 4

Logan's Locks are preparing financial statements for the year ended 31 December 2003. During the year, Logan's entered into two operating lease agreements which are detailed below.

(a) On 1 August 2003, the entity entered into an operating lease for plant and machinery. The lease term is 3 years and quarterly rentals of $9,000 are payable in arrears.
(b) The entity entered into a second agreement on 1 October 2003 for the lease of motor vehicles. This agreement was again for 3 years. Under the terms of the contract, Logan has paid an initial rental of $75,000, this will be followed by quarterly rentals of $4,000. The rentals are payable in advance and commence on 1 April 2004.

Requirement

Prepare the accounting entries to account for the operating leases above in the financial statements for Logan's Locks for the year ended 31 December 2003 and draft the relevant extracts and disclosure notes. **(5 marks)**

 # Question 5

An item of machinery leased under a five-year finance lease on 1 October 2003 had a fair value of $51,900 at date of purchase.

The lease payments were $12,000 per year, payable in arrears.

If the sum-of-digits method is used to apportion interest to accounting periods, calculate the finance cost for the year ended 30 September 2005. **(3 marks)**

Data for questions 6–7

CS acquired a machine, using a finance lease, on 1 January 2004. The machine had an expected useful life of 12,000 operating hours, after which it would have no residual value.

The finance lease was for a five-year term with rentals of $20,000 per year payable in arrears. The cost price of the machine was $80,000 and the implied interest rate is $7 \times 93\%$ per year. CS used the machine for 2,600 hours in 2004 and 2,350 hours in 2005.

 # Question 6

Using the actuarial method, calculate the non-current liability and current liability figures required by IAS 17 *Leases* to be shown in CS's Statement of financial position at 31 December 2005. **(3 marks)**

 # Question 7

Calculate the non-current asset – property, plant and equipment net book value that would be shown in CS's Statement of financial position at 31 December 2005. Calculate the depreciation charge using the machine hours method. **(2 marks)**

Question 8

On 1 April 2005, DX acquired plant and machinery with a fair value of $900,000 on a finance lease. The lease is for five years with the annual lease payments of $228,000 being paid in advance on 1 April each year. The interest rate implicit in the lease is 13.44%. The first payment was made on 1 April 2005.

Requiredments

(i) Calculate the finance charge in respect of the lease that will be shown in DX's income statement for the year ended 31 March 2007.
(ii) Calculate the amount to be shown as a current liability and a non-current liability in DX's balance sheet at 31 March 2007.

(All workings should be to the nearest $'000.) **(5 marks)**

Question 9

On 1 January 2003, Caps leased a new machine from ITC Finance. The cost of the machine is $100,000. The asset has an estimated useful life of 5 years and has a nil residual value.

Under the terms of the three-year lease, six half-yearly payments of $20,000 each are payable in advance, commencing 1 January 2003. There is a secondary two-year term available to Caps for $200 per annum. Caps have not yet decided whether or not they will take advantage of this offer.

At the end of the primary term of the lease, the asset has an estimated residual value of $20,000. Caps are entitled to 95 per cent of this should the asset be sold.

Requirements

(a) Explain, with reasons, why the above lease should be classified as an operating or finance lease. **(4 marks)**
(b) Using the sum-of-digits method of calculating implied finance charges on the lease, prepare all the relevant accounting entries to record this transaction in the financial statements of Caps Incorporated for the year ended 31 December 2003. **(10 marks)**
(c) Draft extracts from the accounts for the following account categories:
  • non-current assets,
  • current liabilities,
  • non-current liabilities. **(6 marks)**
(Total marks = 20)

Question 10

Campbells Framing leased a new machine from Greenan Finance on 1 October 2002. The capital cost of the machine is $180,000. Under the terms of the finance lease agreement, six annual payments of $40,000 are payable in arrears with the first payment due on 30 September 2003.

There is an indefinite secondary term to the lease for a nominal fee and Campbells are anticipating taking advantage of this term. The asset has an estimated useful life of 10 years with an estimated residual value at the end of its life of nil. The residual value at the end of six years is $40,000 and Campbells have a 90 per cent interest in this value.

Requirements

(a) Using the sum-of-digits method of allocating interest, calculate the finance charge to be included in the profit or loss for the year ended 30 September 2003 and draft all relevant accounting entries for this period for incorporation into the accounts.

(10 marks)

(b) Draft the relevant extracts from profit or loss and the statement of financial position for the year ended 30 September 2003. **(6 marks)**

(Total marks = 16)

Solutions to Revision Questions

☑ Solution 1

The correct answer is (B) see Example 14.F $61,000 calculated as follows:

	$
Payments (5 × $25,000) =	125,000
Fair value	90,000
Finance charge	35,000
no. of finance periods =	5
N(n + 1)/2 = (5 × 6)/2 =	15
Interest charges	
Year 1–5/15 * 35K =	11,667
Year 2–4/15 * 35K =	9,333
Lease creditor	
Initial balance	90,000
Interest	11,667
Payment 1	(25,000)
Interest	9,333
Payment 2	(25,000)
Balance	61,000

☑ Solution 2

The correct answer is (A), see Section 14.2.

☑ Solution 3

The correct answer is (B), see Section 14.4.

IAS 17 requires interest expense to be recognized evenly over the life of the lease.
Total expense $2,000 + $5,000 + $5,000 = $12,000 divided by 3 years is $4,000 a year.

☑ Solution 4

(a) The lease agreement commences 1 August 2003 and the reporting year-end is 31 December 2003. The lease payments are made quarterly in arrears and so the first payment made is on 31 October 2003, recorded as:

ACCOUNTING FOR LEASES

		$	$
Debit	Operating lease charges	9,000	
Credit	Bank		9,000

Being the payment and recording of the lease repayment on 31 October.

We must also account for the operating lease charges for November and December, although the payment will not be made until January. It will therefore be accrued by recording:

		$	$
Debit	Operating lease charges	6,000	
Credit	Accrued charges		6,000

Being the accrued operating lease charges for November and December.

(b) The total amount payable under this lease should be allocated to match against the period of use irrespective of the cash flow.

The total payable can be calculated as follows:

	$
Initial payment	75,000
Ten payments of $4,000	40,000
Total payable over 3 years	115,000

$$\left(\frac{\$115,000}{36 \text{ months}}\right) \times \text{months} = \$9,583$$

The accounting entries for the year-end 31 December 2003 will be:

		$	$
Debit	Deferred lease charges	75,000	
Credit	Bank		75,000

Being the initial payment of $75,000 paid on 1 October 2003.

		$	$
Debit	Operating lease charges	9,583	
Credit	Deferred lease charges		9,583

Being the lease charges recognised for the 3 months to 31 December 2003.

Logan's Locks – financial statement extracts for the year ended 31 December 2003.

Income statement

	$
Operating expenses	
Operating lease charges ($9,000 + $6,000 + $9,583)	24,583

Notes to the accounts

Commitments under non-cancellable operating leases
At 31 December 2003, the entity were committed to making the following payments in respect of non-cancellable operating leases:

	$
Not later than 1 year	48,000
Later than 1 and not later than 5 years	91,000
Later than 5 years	–

Workings for the note

	Contract (a)	Contract (b)	Total
Payable in 2004	4 × $9,000 = $36,000 (first payment: 1 April)	3 × $4,000 = $12,000	$48,000
Payable beyond 2004	12 payments in total, one made in 2003 and four in 2004. The remainder will be paid beyond 2004: $9,000 × 7 = $63,000.	10 repayments of $4,000 will be made, three in 2004 and the remainder in the periods beyond 2004. 7 × $4,000 = $28,000.	$91,000

See Section 14.4

 Solution 5

	$
Lease payments (5 × 12)	60,000
Fair value	51,900
Finance cost	8,100
Sum of digits (5 × 6)/2 =	15
Year 2 digit =	4
Finance charge = 8,100 × 4/15 = 2,160	

See Section 14.7.

 Solution 6

Interest rate 7 × 93%

	Bal b/fwd	Interest	Payment	Balance c/fwd
2004	80,000	6,344	−20,000	66,344
2005	66,344	5,261	−20,000	51,605
2006	51,605	4,092	−20,000	35,697
2007	35,697	2,831	−20,000	18,528
2008	18,528	1,472	−20,000	0

Note: Only the first three rows needed to be calculated to answer the question.

Answer – Non-current liability	$35,697
Current liability (51,605 − 35,697) =	$15,908

See Section 14.7.

 Solution 7

	$
Cost	80,000
Depreciation	33,000
	47,000

See Section 14.7.

ACCOUNTING FOR LEASES

 Solution 8

Finance lease – finance cost

Interest Year ended 31 March	13.44% Bal b/fwd	Payment	Subtotal	Interest	Bal c/fwd
	$'000	$'000	$'000	$'000	$'000
2006	900	−228	672	90	762
2007	762	−228	534	72	606
2008	606	−228	378	51	429
2009	429	−228	201	27	228
2010	228	−228	0	0	0

(i) Finance charge for year ended 31 March 2007 = $72,000

(ii)

		$'000
Current liability	(606 − 378) =	228
Non-current liability		378

 Solution 9

(a) This lease should be classified as a finance lease. There are clear indicators that the rights normally associated with ownership have been transferred from the lessor to the lessee:

- The minimum lease payments ($20,000 × 6) totalling $120,000 exceed the capital cost of the asset ($100,000).
- The lease term is 3 years and the useful life is estimated at 5 years, so the lease agreement is for the majority of the asset's useful life.
- Should the asset be sold, 95 per cent of the proceeds would accrue to the lessee.
- A secondary term has been offered at a nominal rate below the market rate for leasing the asset.

Remind yourself of the steps we used when dealing with a finance lease question. Refer back to the chapter text if necessary.

(b) *Step 1:* Confirm classification as a finance lease – done in part (a).

Step 2: Calculate the total finance charge:

	$
Total repayments (6 × $20,000)	120,000
Capital cost of the asset	100,000
Total interest to be allocated	20,000

Step 3: Establish the number of finance periods over which to allocate interest. There are six repayments but they are payable in advance, so the last finance period has no outstanding liability as the final instalment payable on 1 July 2005 extinguishes the creditor balance. The lease term then continues to 31 December 2005. The finance periods total 6 − 1 = 5.

Step 4: Calculate the interest to be charged to the periods. The question requires the use of the sum-of-digits method of allocating interest.

Sum of digits = $n(n + 1)/2$, where n is the number of finance periods

Sum of digits = $(5 \times 6)/2 = 15$

Period	Capital at start	Payment	Outstanding during period	Interest to be allocated	Capital at end
	$	$	$	$	$
1/1/03	100,000	(20,000)	80,000	20,000 × 5/15 = 6,667	86,667
1/7/03	86,667	(20,000)	66,667	20,000 × 4/15 = 5,333	72,000
1/1/04	72,000	(20,000)	52,000	20,000 × 3/15 = 4,000	56,000
1/7/04	56,000	(20,000)	36,000	20,000 × 2/15 = 2,667	38,667
1/1/05	38,667	(20,000)	18,667	20,000 × 1/15 = 1,333	20,000
1/7/05	20,000	(20,000)	–		–
		(120,000)		(20,000)	

Note: The full allocation is given above for illustration purposes only. In order to answer this question, the calculation need only go as far as 1/7/04 – that is, to calculate the entries for 2003 and the creditor due within 1 year (i.e. payable in 2004) for part (c).

The accounting entries for the year to 31 December 2003 are as follows:

		$	$
Debit	Asset	100,000	
Credit	Lease creditor		100,000

Being the acquisition of the asset under finance lease on 1 January.

		$	$
Debit	Finance lease creditor	28,000	
Debit	Finance lease interest	12,000	
Credit	Bank		40,000

Being the lease repayments on 1 January and 1 July allocated between interest and capital.

		$	$
Debit	Depreciation	27,000	
Credit	Accumulated depreciation		27,000

Being the depreciation charge for the asset for the year ($100,000 – residual value $19,000 ($20,000 × 95%) = $81,000; $81,000/3 years = $27,000.)

(c) Extracts from accounts: Caps Statement of financial position at 31 December 2003

	$
Non-current assets	
Plant and machinery ($100,000 − $27,000)	73,000
Current liabilities	
Finance lease creditor ($40,000 − $6,667)	33,333
Non-current liabilities	
Finance lease creditor ($72,000 − $33,333)	38,667

✅ Solution 10

(a) *Step 1:* Confirm classification as a finance lease – given in question.

Step 2: Calculate the total finance charge:

	$
Total repayments 6 × $40,000	240,000
Capital cost of the asset	180,000
Total interest to be allocated	60,000

Step 3: Establish the number of finance periods over which to allocate interest.

There are six repayments and they are payable in arrears. The final payment is due on 30 September 2008, which is the end of the lease term. The lessee is therefore getting funding for the entire lease term and so the interest should be allocated over all six periods. Finance periods total six.

Step 4: Calculate the interest to be charged to the periods.

The question requires the use of the sum-of-digits method of allocating interest.

Sum of digits = $n(n + 1)/2 = (6 \times 7)/2 = 21$

Period	Capital at start	Interest to be allocated	Payment	Capital at end
	$	$	$	$
30/09/03	180,000	$60,000 × 6/21 =17,143	(40,000)	157,143
30/09/04	157,143	$60,000 × 5/21 =14,286	(40,000)	131,429
30/09/05	131,429	$60,000 × 4/21 =11,429	(40,000)	102,858
30/09/06	102,858	$60,000 × 3/21 = 8,571	(40,000)	71,429
30/09/07	1,429	$60,000 × 2/21 = 5,714	(40,000)	37,143
30/09/08	37,143	$60,000 × 1/21 = 2,857	(40,000)	–
		60,000	240,000	

Note: The full allocation is given above for illustration purposes only. In order to answer this question, the calculation need only go as far as 30/09/04, that is, to calculate the entries for the year ended 30 September 2003 and the creditor due within 1 year which can only be calculated by calculating the interest allocated to 2004.

The accounting entries for the year to 30 September 2003 are as follows:

		$	$
Debit	Asset	180,000	
Credit	Lease creditor		180,000

Being the acquisition of the asset under finance lease on 1 October 2002.

		$	$
Debit	Finance lease creditor	22,857	
Debit	Finance lease interest	17,143	
Credit	Bank		40,000

Being the lease repayment on 30 September 2003 allocated between interest and capital.

		$	$
Debit	Depreciation	18,000	
Credit	Accumulated depreciation		18,000

Being the depreciation charge for the asset for the year ($180,000/10 years – Campbells expect to use the asset for its entire useful life by exercising the secondary lease term.)

(b) Campbells: financial statements for the year ended 30 September 2003 (extracts)

Income statement

	$
Operating expenses	
Depreciation charge	18,000
Finance lease interest	17,143

Statement of financial position

	$
Non-current assets	
Plant and machinery ($180,000 − $18,000)	162,000
Current liabilities	
Finance lease creditor ($40,000 − $14,286)	25,714
Non-current liabilities	
Finance lease creditor ($157,143 − $25,714)	131,429

15

Inventories and Construction Contracts

Inventories and Construction Contracts

15

The syllabus topics covered in this chapter are as follows:

- Inventories (IAS 2);
- Construction contracts and related financing costs (IAS 11 and 23): determination of cost, net realisable value, the inclusion of overheads and the measurement of profit on uncompleted contracts.

15.1 Introduction

This chapter will cover two specific areas: inventories and construction costs. They are dealt with in separate accounting standards.

We will look first at IAS 2 *Inventories*, which prescribes the accounting treatment for inventories. The standard provides guidance on the amount of cost to be recognised as an asset and carried forward until the related revenues are generated. The standard also gives guidance on what constitutes cost and how to write down the asset to net realisable value. Chapter 22 discusses inventory management.

IAS 11 *Construction Contracts* prescribes the accounting treatment of revenue and costs associated with construction contracts. The standard gives guidance on how to recognise contract revenues and associated costs and how these amounts should be recorded and disclosed.

15.2 IAS 2 *Inventories*

15.2.1 Definition of inventories

The standard defines inventories as assets:

- held *for sale* in the ordinary course of business (like items of clothing in a retail clothing business);

- in the *process of production* for such sale (like cloth in a clothing manufacturing business); or
- in the form of materials or *supplies to be consumed* in the production process or in the rendering of services (like thread and buttons in a clothing manufacturing business).

15.2.2 Measurement

The underlying principle of IAS 2 is that inventories should be measured at the lower of cost and net realisable value.

- *Net realisable value* is the estimated selling price (in the normal course of business) less the estimated costs of completion and the estimated costs of making the sale.

  Inventories are usually written down to net realisable value, item by item or groups of similar items where it is not practical to evaluate separate items.
- *Cost* should comprise all costs of purchase, costs of conversion (if manufacturing) and other costs incurred in bringing the inventories to their present location and condition.

15.2.3 Determining cost

- *Costs of purchase* include the purchase price, import duties and other taxes (to the extent that they are not recoverable from the tax authority), handling costs and other costs directly attributable to the acquisition.
- *Costs of conversion* include costs directly related to the units being produced, for example, direct labour costs. The costs also include an allocation of fixed and variable overhead that are incurred, in converting materials into finished goods.
- *Variable production overheads* are those indirect costs of production that vary directly with the volume being produced, for example indirect materials and indirect labour.
- *Fixed production overheads* are those indirect costs of production that remain constant irrespective of the numbers of units produced, for example, depreciation of factory buildings and equipment and the cost of factory management and administration.
- *Financing costs*, if the requirements of IAS 23 are satisfied, financing costs can be included (see Section 13.10).

15.2.4 Costs not included in cost of inventory

Examples of costs excluded from the cost of inventories and recognised as expenses in the period in which they are incurred are:

(a) abnormal amounts of wasted materials, labour or other production costs;
(b) storage costs, unless those costs are necessary in the production process before a further production stage;
(c) administrative overheads that do not contribute to bringing inventories to their present location and condition;
(d) selling and distribution costs.

15.2.5 Allocation of overheads

The allocation of fixed production overheads to the cost of production is based on the normal capacity of the business. Any abnormal production problems that occur during the period should be charged to that period's profit or loss.

Example 15.A

The following costs have been included in the month of July:

	$
Cost of raw materials	20,000
Cost of related consumables	10,000
Direct wages	4,000
Indirect production costs	6,000
Power	1,000
Administration – production	1,200
Administration – general	1,100
Selling and marketing costs	2,300
Depreciation	3,950

Additional information

1. All administration and 40 per cent of indirect production costs are fixed.
2. Depreciation figure above includes $1,850, which relates to the production equipment.
3. 95 per cent of the power relates to the production of goods.
4. There was a breakdown during the month and 10 per cent of the month's production was lost.
5. During July, 250,000 units were produced.

Calculate the unit cost of the goods.

Solution

The costs that can be charged to the cost of the goods are as follows:

	$
Raw material costs	20,000
Cost of related consumables	10,000
Direct wages	4,000
Variable indirect production costs (60% – remaining 40% is a fixed cost)	3,600
Power (95%)	950
Depreciation	1,850
	40,400
Fixed indirect production costs (normal activity of 90% × 40% fixed element × 6,000)	2,160
Fixed production administration (90% × $1,200)	1,080
Total cost	43,640
Cost per unit	17.5¢

Note that fixed costs are allocated based on the normal level of activity – the question tells us that 10 per cent of production is lost due to a breakdown. The costs associated with this are not included in the cost of inventory but instead charged to profit or loss in the period in which the loss occurred.

Other costs can be included in the cost of inventories if they have been incurred to bring the goods to their present location or condition, for example, the design costs of specific goods.

15.2.6 Calculation of costs

Inventory should be valued at either cost itself or reasonably close approximations to actual cost, the most common methods of valuation are:

(a) Actual unit cost.
(b) *First in first out (FIFO).* The inventory is assumed to consist of the latest purchases made which cover the quantity in inventory and is priced accordingly.

(c) *Average cost.* The weighted average cost at which an inventory item has been purchased during the period is taken.

(d) *Standard cost.* This is acceptable, provided that the standard costs are reviewed frequently to ensure that they bear a reasonable relationship to actual costs during the period.

(e) *Selling price less gross profit margin.* This method is acceptable only if it can be demonstrated that it gives a reasonable approximation of the actual cost.

The same basis must be used for all inventories that are similar in nature or use. Inventories of a different nature or use can be valued on a different basis.

15.2.7 Allowed alternative method

When IAS 2 was revised in 2003, the allowed alternative method of last in first out was removed. IAS 2 now has no allowed alternative treatment.

15.2.8 Disclosures for inventories

The financial statements should disclose:

(a) the accounting policies adopted in measuring inventories including the cost formula used;
(b) the total amount of inventories in classifications appropriate to the business;
(c) the carrying amount of inventories carried at net realisable value.

15.3 IAS 11 *Construction Contracts*

15.3.1 General principle

A construction contract is a contract for the construction of a single asset or a combination of assets that are related. Contracts can often span more than one accounting period and this creates additional accounting problems:

- how much revenue should be included in profit or loss
- how much should be charged for related costs?
- how much profit should be recognised in the period in respect of this contract?

Normally revenues and profits are only recognised in profit or loss once they are realised. However, the nature of construction contracts can mean that the contract is only invoiced and revenues realised on completion of the contract. The statement of comprehensive income must show a fair representation of the activities of the entity for the period. Here the prudence concept and the matching concept are head to head.

The matching concept wins, and for the sake of the financial statements showing a fair presentation of the activities of the entity and providing useful and relevant information to users, we include an appropriate part of revenue and profits of the contract in the period in which the activity has taken place.

Each contract must be accounted for separately and then the totals aggregated and included in the financial statements.

15.3.2 Accounting treatment

When the outcome of a contract can be assessed with reasonable certainty, IAS 11 provides that contract revenues and costs can be recognised according to the stage of completion of the contract. The stage of completion is usually assessed and then certified by a professional surveyor.

The treatment required by IAS 11 results in our accounting entries being based, to a great extent, on judgement rather than on actual transactions.

The economic reality with a construction contract is that it may span more than one accounting period and the related invoice may not be raised until the contract is completed. However, the contractor will not wish to bear the full cost of financing the project throughout its duration, so the customer will often pay for stages of work completed on the contract. These interim payments are known as *progress payments* and are usually paid once a piece of work completed has been certified by a surveyor or other professional.

As progress payments are not for the completed project, they are not credited directly to sales or turnover, as would happen with a completed sale, but are recorded for each invoice raised during the course of the contract.

The recording for invoices raised for construction contracts is:

- We raise an invoice

Debit	Receivables
Credit	Progress payments

- We receive payment

Debit	Bank
Credit	Receivables

This is fine for the invoice-raising, but when is the sales revenue recorded?

Well, as we noted above, we must include an appropriate part of total revenue and profits of the contract in the accounting period where there is activity on the contract. However, since no final transaction has taken place, it is the preparer who must decide how much should be included for revenue, related costs and profit.

The standard gives guidance as to how these figures should be arrived at (discussed below). However, the recording is as follows:

- We record sales revenue

Debit	Progress payments
Credit	Sales revenue

- We match related costs

Debit	Cost of sales
Credit	Contract costs

Note

- When revenue is recorded, the debit entry is to progress payments – this could be considered to be like a contract account, recording all customer monies received during the contract and recording any revenues recognised. Remember that the trade receivables account is only affected by the raising of an invoice – in the entry seen above.
- Any contract costs not yet transferred to cost of sales (may have purchased all the materials for the contract at the start of the contract to secure discount) will be included within

assets in the statement of financial position. As the costs are incurred, however, they are held within a contract cost account, there is one for each contract (because each contract must be accounted for separately) and then the balances are aggregated in the financial statements.

Accounting for construction costs affects a number of headings in the statement of comprehensive income and statement of financial position:

1. Sales value of work completed is included in 'revenue' in profit or loss. Related costs of the work completed are included in 'cost of sales' in profit or loss.
2. If the contract is expected to be profitable overall, then an appropriate part of that profit is recognised within profit or loss by the above entries.
3. If the contract is expected to make a loss overall, then all of the loss must be recognised as soon as it is anticipated, by adding the expected loss for future periods on to the cost of sales.
4. If the outcome of the contract cannot be measured with reasonable certainty (e.g. if the contract is at an early stage of completion), then revenue recognised must be made to equal contract costs in order to create no profit or loss in the period.
5. Any contract costs incurred but not yet transferred to cost of sales should be included within contract costs under the heading 'gross amounts due from customers for contract work' in the statement of financial position.
6. Where sales revenue recognised exceeds the progress payments received, the balance should be included in 'gross amounts due from customers for contract work' within assets.
7. Where sales revenue recognised is less than the progress payments received, the balance should be included as a separate item within 'payables', as 'gross amounts due to customers for contract work'.

For the last two points, remember that the preparer decides the level of revenue to be included in profit or loss at the end of the accounting period based on the stage of completion. However, this may not be the same as the work that has been completed and certified, so the figures for revenue and progress payments received are unlikely to match unless a certification takes place at the end of the reporting period.

We are now going to look at the detailed accounting for construction contracts using examples wherever possible to reinforce a practical understanding of the procedure.

15.3.3 Sales revenue

In order to estimate an appropriate part of contract revenue to be included in profit or loss, we must first establish the stage of completion of each contract. There is no set rule on how to determine turnover, but the two main methods used in practice are:

- *By reference to the proportion of work done.* Established either by certification of work by the surveyor, or by comparing the costs incurred to date to the total contract costs anticipated to give an estimate of work completed so far.
- *By identifying specific points in the contract where the work completed has separately ascertainable sales values.* For example, a contract for residential property development could have a sales value for the building of a house, and separate values for the construction of a garage, swimming pool, stables, etc.

Sales revenue should be recognised based on the activity on the contract in the period, regardless of the profit that is likely.

Remember that items included in profit or loss are recorded only once, so for a contract that spans, say, 4 years, we must deduct any contract revenues previously recognised. The calculations will be:

Year 1   (Total contract revenue × % stage of completion) = sales revenue for year 1

Year 2   (Total contract revenue × % stage of completion) − revenue recognised in year 1 = sales revenue for year 2

Year 3   (Total contract revenue × % stage of completion) − revenue recognised in year 1 and 2 = sales revenue for year 3

Example 15.B

Moby has the following contract details for a contract that started in 20X2:

	20X2	20X3	20X4
Total contract sales value	$10m	$11m	$11.5m
Estimated % completion	40%	75%	100%

Note that the total contract value has changed over the duration of the contract – this can only be included in the revenue calculations if these amendments have been agreed with the customer. This is a common occurrence as the costs associated with labour and materials during the course of the contract may change, an unforeseen obstacle may occur which is beyond the control of the contractor, or the customer specifications may change.

The revenue to be recognised is as follows:

	20X2 $m	20X3 $m	20X4 $m
Revenues recognisable to date:			
20X2: 40% × $10m	4.00		
20X3: 75% × $11m		8.25	
20X4: 100% × $11.5m			11.50
Less revenues recognised in prior periods		(4.00)	(8.25)
Revenue for the period	4.00	4.25	3.25

15.3.4   Recognisable contract profits

The recognition of contract profit is usually based on the percentage of work completed on the contract.

The amount of revenue and profit to be included are both calculated (based on work done) and the cost of sales figure is the balancing figure.

Example 15.C

Plusman contract A commenced in 20X2 and has the following details for the year ended 31 December 20X3:

Total contract value	$80m
Costs incurred to date	$50m
Estimated costs to complete	$7m
Completion	80%
Profit recognised in 20X2	$11m

The first step to calculate the total estimated profit on the contract:

	$m	$m
Total sales value of the contract		80
Less: contract costs incurred to date	(50)	
estimated costs to completion	(7)	
Total estimated contract costs		(57)
Total estimated contract profit		23

The second step is to establish the stage of completion of the contract and calculate the profit recognisable to date:

Total estimated contract profit × % completion of the contract
= recognisable profit to date $23m × 80% completion = $18.4m

The third step is to calculate the profit reportable for this accounting period:

	$m
Recognisable profit to date	18.4
Less cumulative profit recognised in prior periods	(11.0)
Profit recognisable in this period	7.4

In this case, turnover and cost of sales will be recognised to give the $7.4m profit in profit or loss for the period.

15.3.5 Expected contract losses

Whenever an overall contract loss is expected, the loss must be recognised as soon as it is anticipated.

The first step, calculating the overall profit or loss on the contract, would still be performed. However, if the overall contract is loss-making, the full amount of the loss will be recognised immediately.

Example 15.D

Plusman's contract B commenced during 20X3 and will complete in 20X4. It has the following details for the year ended 31 December 20X3:

Total contract value	$70m
Costs incurred to date	$40m
Estimated costs to complete	$39m
Completion	50%

The first step is to calculate the overall outcome for this contract:

	$m	$m
Total sales value of the contract		70
Less contract costs incurred to date	(40)	
estimated costs to completion	(39)	
Total estimated contract costs		(79)
Total estimated contract loss		(9)

Contact B is 50 per cent complete and revenue recognised must reflect this activity in the period, so the fact that the contract is loss-making does not remove the need to recognise sales revenue.

If we follow the previous example, the revenues and costs will occur as follows (50 per cent of revenue and 50 per cent of costs, resulting in 50 per cent of loss in the period. This would leave the same again to be recognised next year).

Income statement (extract)

	2003	2004
	$m	$m
Sales revenue (50% in each of the 2 years)	35.0	35.0
Cost of sales	(39.5)	(39.5)
Loss on contract	(4.5)	(4.5)

IAS 11 and prudence require that we recognise the whole of the loss as soon as it is anticipated and so the $4.5 million loss expected to occur in 20X4 is pulled back and charged to 20X3's profit or loss through cost of sales. What it does mean is that cost of sales must be charged with an amount that results in the full contract loss of $9 million being recognised immediately. The income statement extract now shows:

Income statement (extract)

	2003	2004
	$m	$m
Sales revenue (50% in each of the two years)	35	35
Cost of sales (39.5 + 4.5)	(44)	(35)
Profit/(loss) on contract	(9)	–

We know that cost of sales must be charged with $44 million to ensure that the full contact loss of $9 million is recognised in the first year (i.e. as soon as it is anticipated).

In this case the cost of sales charge is made up of two elements:

1. 50 per cent of total contract costs of $79m = $39.5 million;
2. the remaining amount of the loss that is expected to occur next year, which is $4.5 million.

15.3.6 Uncertain outcome

If the outcome of the contract cannot be estimated with reasonable certainty, then no profit should be recognised. However, profit or loss must still reflect the activity in the period and so an appropriate part of revenue and cost of sales must be recognised.

Example 15.E

Plusman's contract C commenced in 20X3 and has the following details for the year ended 31 December 20X3:

Total contract value	$40m
Costs incurred to date	$3m
Estimated costs to complete	$30m
Completion	10%

Plusman has only just commenced work on this contract and cannot be certain of its outcome at the year-end date. The overall contract is expected to be profit-making. However, the contract has only just started (10 per cent complete) and so the outcome cannot be measured with reasonable certainty. In this case, prudence dictates that no profit should be recognised in the year ended December 20X3.

Revenue would normally include 10 per cent of revenue and cost of sales would be made to match the revenue to create a nil profit:

Income statement (extract)

	$m
Sales revenue (10% × $40m)	4
Cost of sales	(4)
Profit/loss on contract	–

However, in this case we cannot transfer $4 million to cost of sales as we have only incurred costs of $3 million to date. Where costs to date are less than the required cost of sales charge, we instead restrict the revenue figure to the level of costs incurred to date. The income statement for 20X3 would therefore include the following for contract C:

Income statement (extract)

	$m
Sales revenue	3
Cost of sales	(3)
Profit/loss on contract	–

15.3.7 Inventories

Any contract costs incurred but not yet transferred to cost of sales should be included within contract costs under the heading 'gross amounts due from customers for contract work' in the statement of financial performance.

Remember that each contract is accounted for separately, so some contracts may have inventories, some may not. Each contract is calculated and then the total from each contract is aggregated in the statement of financial performance.

Example 15.F

Let us look at Plusman's contract A again.

Plusman's contract A commenced in 20X2 and has the following details for the year ended 31 December 20X3:

Total contract value	$80m
Costs incurred to date	$50m
Estimated costs to complete	$7m
Completion	80%
Profit recognised in 20X2	$11m

Solution

Costs incurred to date total $50m:

		$m	$m
Debit	Contract costs	50	
Credit	Bank/payables		50

The amount we will have charged to cost of sales to date (20X2 and 20X3) is based on the percentage completion × the total contract costs (80% × $57 million) × $45.6 million. Over the 2 years of the contract we will have recorded:

Transfer to cost of sales:

		$m	$m
Debit	Cost of sales	45.6	
Credit	Contract costs		45.6

There is therefore a balance remaining on contract costs at 31 December 20X3 of $4.4m ($50m − $45.6m). This amount represents contract costs incurred that relate to a future activity and is therefore recognised as an asset and will be included in 'gross amounts due from customers'.

15.3.8 Receivables

Let us stay with this example and look at the impact on receivables in the balance sheet. Where sales revenue recognised to date exceeds the progress payments received, the balance should be included in the statement of financial position as an asset and referred to as 'unbilled contract revenue' within the heading 'gross amounts due from customers for contract work'.

The progress payments received to date at 31 December 20X3 for Contract A totalled $60 million:

		$m	$m
Debit	Bank	60	
Credit	Progress payments		60

The total sales revenue recognised to date at 31 December 20X3 is $64 million (80% × $80 million).

		$m	$m
Debit	Progress payments	64	
Credit	Sales revenue		64

This results in a $4 million receivable in respect of this contract. We have calculated (based on percentage completion) that sales and therefore amounts due from customers to date totals $64 million and the customer has paid $60 million to date. The remaining $4 million is therefore a receivable and is referred to as 'unbilled contract revenue' within 'gross amounts due from customers for contract work'.

IAS 11 specifies that an entity should present the gross amount due from customers for contract work as an asset. Note that it does not specify where the asset should be recorded.

 In an examination question, gross amounts due from customers should be treated as a current asset.

15.3.9 Payables

Where sales revenue recognised to date is less than the progress payments received, the balance should be included as a separate item within payables, and referred to as 'gross amounts due to customers for contract work'

Let us assume that for Contract A the progress payments received at 31 December 2003 totalled $70 million.

		$m	$m
Debit	Bank	70	
Credit	Progress payments		70

The total sales revenue recognised to date at 31 December 20X3 is $64 million (80% × $80m).

		$m	$m
Debit	Progress payments	64	
Credit	Sales revenue		64

In this case, we have calculated that $64 million is due on this contract and the customer has already paid $70 million. We have received customer monies that have not yet been earned and so the balance of $6 million is included within payables as 'gross amounts due to customers for contract work' (included as a liability until the money has been earned through next year's activity on the contract).

IAS 11 specifies that an entity should present the gross amount due to customers for contract work as a liability. It does not state how the liability should be included.

 In an examination question, gross amounts due to customers should be included as a current liability.

15.3.10 Provisions for foreseeable losses

Whenever a loss is provided for, it is charged to profit or loss and the corresponding credit entry is made in the statement of financial position. IAS 11 permits foreseeable losses to be deducted from 'gross amounts due from customers for contract work' on a contract-by-contract basis, in some cases this will turn an amount due from the customer into an amount due to the customer, see Section 15.3.13. Forseeable losses charged to cost of sales are therefore recorded as:

Debit	Cost of sales
Credit	Contract costs/unbilled contract revenue

15.3.11 Disclosure requirements

An entity should disclose the following for construction contracts:

(a) contract revenue recognised;
(b) methods used to determine contract revenue recognised;
(c) methods used to determine stage of completion of contracts;
(d) for work-in-progress:
    (i) costs incurred and profits less losses to date;
    (ii) advances received (i.e. payments from customers before the related work is performed);
    (iii) retentions (i.e. progress billings not paid until satisfaction of conditions in contract or until defects are rectified).

15.3.12 Illustrations from IAS 11

IAS 11 also contains illustrations showing the procedure. They are given below and you should work through them once you have fully understood the procedure described above.

Illustration 1

A contractor has a fixed-price contract for $9,000 to build a bridge. The initial amount of revenue agreed in the contract is $9,000. The contractor's initial estimate of contract costs is $8,000. It will take 3 years to build the bridge.

By the end of year 1, the contractor's estimate of contract costs has increased to $8,050.

In year 2, the customer approves a variation resulting in an increase in contract revenue of $200 and estimated additional contract costs of $150. At the end of year 2, costs incurred include $100 for standard materials stored at the site to be used in year 3 to complete the project.

The contractor determines the stage of completion of the contract by comparing the proportion of contract costs incurred for work performed to date with the latest estimated total contract costs. A summary of the financial data during the construction period is as follows:

	Year 1 $	Year 2 $	Year 3 $
Initial amount of revenue agreed in contract	9,000	9,000	9,000
Variation	–	200	200
Total contract revenue	9,000	9,200	9,200
Contract costs incurred to date	2,093	6,168	8,200
Contract costs to complete	5,957	2,032	–
Total estimated contract costs	8,050	8,200	8,200
Estimated profit	950	1,000	1,000
Stage of completion	26%	74%	100%

The stage of completion for year 2 (74 per cent) is determined by excluding from contract costs incurred for work performed to date the $100 of standard materials stored at the site for use in year 3.

The amounts of revenue, expenses and profit recognised in profit or loss in the 3 years are as follows:

		To date $	Recognised in prior year $	Recognised in current year $
Year 1	Revenue (9,000 × .26)	2,340		2,340
	Expenses (8,050 × .26)	2,093		2,093
	Profit	247		247
Year 2	Revenue (9,200 × .74)	6,808	2,340	4,468
	Expenses (8,200 × .74)	6,068	2,093	3,975
	Profit	740	247	493
Year 3	Revenue (9,200 × 1.00)	9,200	6,808	2,392
	Expenses	8,200	6,068	2,132
	Profit	1,000	740	260

Illustration 2

A contractor has reached the end of its first year of operation. All its contract costs incurred have been paid for in cash and all its progress billings and advances have been received in cash. Contract costs incurred for contracts B, C and E include the costs of materials that have been purchased for the contract but which have not been used in contract performance to date. For contracts B, C and E, the customers have made advances to the contractor for work not yet performed.

The status of its five contracts in progress at the end of year 1 is as follows:

			Contract			
	A	B	C	D	E	Total
	$'000	$'000	$'000	$'000	$'000	$'000
Contract revenue recognised	145	520	380	200	55	1,300
Contract expenses recognised	110	450	350	250	55	1,215
Expected losses recognised	–	–	–	40	30	70
Recognised profits less recognised losses	35	70	30	(90)	(30)	15
Contract costs incurred in the period	110	510	450	250	100	1,420
Contract costs incurred recognised as contract expenses	110	450	350	250	55	1,215
Contract costs that relate to future activity recognised as an asset	–	60	100	–	45	205
Contract revenue (see above)	145	520	380	200	55	1,300
Progress billings	100	520	380	180	55	1,235
Unbilled contract revenue	45	–	–	20	–	65
Advances	–	80	20	–	25	125

Let us examine this information step by step.

The first section shows us the information required for profit or loss:

			Contract			
	A	B	C	D	E	Total
	$'000	$'000	$'000	$'000	$'000	$'000
Contract revenue recognised	145	520	380	200	55	1,300
Contract expenses recognised	110	450	350	250	55	1,215
Expected losses recognised	–	–	–	40	30	70
Recognised profits less recognised losses	35	70	30	(90)	(30)	15

The totals provide us with the detail we need to complete profit or loss:

Income statement (extract)	$'000	$'000
Contract revenue		1,300
Contract expenses	1,215	
Expected losses	70	1,285
Profit		15

The middle section provides information on the contract costs incurred and those recognised as contract expenses in the period and transferred to cost of sales:

			Contract			
	A	B	C	D	E	Total
	$'000	$'000	$'000	$'000	$'000	$'000
Contract costs incurred in the period	110	510	450	250	100	1,420
Contract costs incurred recognised as contract expenses	110	450	350	250	55	1,215
Contract costs that relate to future activity recognised as an asset	–	60	100	–	45	205

The third section provides information on the revenue recognised in the period and the progress billings:

			Contract			
	A	B	C	D	E	Total
	$'000	$'000	$'000	$'000	$'000	$'000
Contract revenue (see above)	145	520	380	200	55	1,300
Progress billings	100	520	380	180	55	1,235
Unbilled contract revenue	45	–	–	20	–	65

From the above we can now calculate the 'gross amounts due from/to customers for contract work'. This is calculated as the contract costs that relate to future activities plus the unbilled contract revenue less provisions for losses.

			Contract			
	A	B	C	D	E	Total
	$'000	$'000	$'000	$'000	$'000	$'000
Contract costs that relate to future activity recognised as an asset	0	60	100	0	45	205
Unbilled contract revenue	45	0	0	20	0	65
Expected losses recognised	0	0	0	(40)	(30)	(70)
'gross amounts due from customers for contract work'	45	60	100	0	15	220
'gross amounts due to customers for contract work'	0	0	0	(20)	0	(20)

Note that contract D has unbilled contract revenue of $20,000, but with the expected loss this is turned in to an amount due to the customer and is treated as a liability in the statement of financial position.

Payments received in advance from customers are shown separately as liabilities:

			Contract			
	A	B	C	D	E	Total
	$'000	$'000	$'000	$'000	$'000	$'000
Payments in advance shown as a liability	–	80	20	–	25	125

In summary, the statement of financial position entries for the five contracts would be:

	$'000
Payments due from customers for contract work, shown as an asset	220
Payments due to customers for contract work, shown as a liability	(20)
Payments in advance, shown as a current liability	(125)

IAS 11 also requires the following amounts to be disclosed:

	$'000
Contract revenue recognised as revenue in the period	1,300
Contract costs incurred and recognised profits (less recognised losses) to date	1,435
Advances received, presented as a current liability	(125)
Gross amount due from customers for contract work – presented as an asset	220
Gross amount due to customers for contract work – presented as a liability	(20)

The above figures can also be arrived at as follows:

				Contract			
	A	B	C	D	E	Total
	$'000	$'000	$'000	$'000	$'000	$'000
Contract costs incurred	110	510	450	250	100	1,420
Recognised profits less recognised losses	35	70	30	(90)	(30)	15
	145	580	480	160	70	1,435
Progress billings	(100)	(520)	(380)	(180)	(55)	(1,235)
Due from customers	45	60	100		15	220
Due to customers				(20)		(20)

15.3.13 A comprehensive example

This worked example includes all of the headings discussed above.

Example 15.G

Crave has three contracts in progress during the year and the following details are available for the year ended 31 December 2003:

Contract	Alpha	Beta	Gamma
Commenced	June 20X2	Jan 20X3	Nov 20X3
Total contract value	$90m	$60m	$100m
Costs incurred to date	$70m	$45m	$15m
Estimated costs to complete	$10m	$23m	$70m
Completion	80%	60%	10%
Progress payments received	$65m	$32m	$20m

Additional information

- Contract Alpha commenced during 20X2 and at 31 December 20X2 was 50 per cent complete; accordingly appropriate amounts for revenue and profit were included in the 20X2 profit or loss.
- Crave has a policy of recognising profit on contracts once the contracts have reached a minimum of 30 per cent completion, to ensure that their outcome can be assessed with reasonable certainty.

Solution

	Sales revenue		
	Alpha $m	Beta $m	Gamma $m
Revenues recognisable to date			
Alpha (80% × $90m)	72		
Beta (60% × $60m)		36	
Gamma (10% × $100m)			10
Revenues previously recognised			
Alpha (50% × $90m)	(45)		
Revenues recognisable in the period	27	36	10

Total sales revenue that is recognisable and will be included in profit or loss for the year ended 31 December 20X3 is $73 million (27 + 36 + 10).

Contract profits and losses

	Alpha $m	Beta $m	Gamma $m
Overall contract position			
Total contract value	90	60	100
Total contract costs (incurred to date plus costs to complete)	(80)	(68)	(85)
Contract profit/(loss)	10	(8)	15
Profits/losses recognisable to date			
Alpha (80% × $10m)	(8)		
Beta (100% × (loss of $8m))		(8)	
Gamma (Nil − only 10% complete)			–
Amounts previously recognised			
Alpha (50% × $10m)	(5)		
Profits/(losses) in the period	3	(8)	–

Using the revenues and profits calculated above, we can now draft profit or loss extract for Crave for December 20X3:

Income statement (extract)

	Alpha $m	Beta $m	Gamma $m	Total $m
Sales revenue	27	36	10	73
Cost of sales	(24)	(44)	(10)	78
Contract profits/(losses)	3	(8)	–	(5)

Note

- Alpha − we must remember to deduct the revenues and profits previously recognised.
- Beta − the overall contract is expected to make a loss of $8 million and the entire loss must be recognised immediately. The cost of sales figure therefore includes cost of sales for 20X3 of $40.8 million (60% × total contract costs of $68m) plus anticipated loss for 20X4 of $3.2 million (40% X $8m); rounded to $41 million and $3 million.
- Gamma − the contract is only 10 per cent complete and so 10 per cent of revenue can be recognised but no profit must be recognised as the contract outcome cannot be assessed with reasonable certainty. Cost of sales is therefore charged with an amount to match revenue (provided that there is sufficient in contract costs from this contract to transfer to cost of sales).

Inventories

	Alpha $m	Beta $m	Gamma $m	Total $m
Contract costs incurred to date	70	45	15	
Transferred to cost of sales to date	(64)	(41)	(10)	
Balance contract costs that relate to future activities	6	4	5	15

Note: Alpha is 80 per cent complete to date and has therefore transferred 80 per cent of total contract costs to cost of sales over 20X2 and 20X3.

Receivables and payables

	Alpha $m	Beta $m	Gamma $m	Total $m
Progress payments received	65	32	20	
Sales revenue recognised to date	72	36	10	
Receivables − unbilled contract revenue	7	4		11
Payables − progress payments received			(10)	(10)

Summary

	Alpha $m	Beta $m	Gamma $m	Total $m
Inventories, contract costs that relate to future activities	6	4	5	15
Receivables – unbilled contract revenue	7	4	0	11
Expected loss recognised	0	(3)	0	(3)
Payments due from customers for contract work	13	5	5	23
Payments due to customers for contract work	0	0	(10)	(10)

15.4 Summary

Having completed this chapter, we can now define and account for inventories, including the determination of cost and net realisable value. We can also explain the disclosures required by IAS 2 *Inventories*.

In addition, we can explain the principle of revenue recognition with regard to construction contracts. We can correctly account for construction contracts, including the treatment of losses, and explain the required disclosures required by IAS 11 *Construction Contracts*.

Revision Questions

15

? Question 1

Item code ZYX321 had 320 items in inventory at 31 March, the entity year-end. The original cost of the inventory, according to the inventory control system, was $5,000. Alternative valuations were obtained at 31 March for this inventory item. Which value should be used in the accounts at 31 March?

(A) Net realisable value $4,750
(B) Original cost $5,000
(C) Replacement cost $5,500
(D) Selling price $6,000

(2 marks)

Data for Questions 2–4

Details of contract AB1375 are:

	$'000	$'000
Certified work completed		300
Costs incurred to date:		
Attributable to work completed	345	
Further costs attributable to partly completed work	50	
		395
Progress payments received		320
Expected further loss on completion		40

Using the above data, identify the correct entries for contract AB1375 items in Questions 2–4.

? Question 2

The revenue and cost of sales figure should be:

	Revenue $'000	Cost of sales $'000
(A)	340	395
(B)	320	395
(C)	300	385
(D)	300	435

(2 marks)

Question 3

The liability shown in the statement of financial position for 'progress payments received in advance' should be:

(A) $5,000
(B) $10,000
(C) $20,000
(D) $30,000

(2 marks)

Question 4

The asset shown in the statement of financial position for 'gross amounts due from customers for contract work' should be:

(A) $0
(B) $10,000
(C) $50,000
(D) $395,000

(2 marks)

Question 5

	$'000
Total contract value	370
Certified work completed	320
Costs to date – attributable to work completed	360
Progress payments received	300
Expected further costs to completion	50

The amounts shown in the profit or loss for Revenue and Cost of Sales should be:

	Revenue $'000	Cost of Sales $'000
(A)	320	360
(B)	320	400
(C)	370	360
(D)	370	410

(2 marks)

Question 6

BL started a contract on 1 November 2004. The contract was scheduled to run for 2 years and has a sales value of $40 million. At 31 October 2005, the following details were obtained from BL's records:

	$m
Costs incurred to date	16
Estimated costs to completion	18
Percentage complete at 31 October 2005	45%

Applying IAS 11 *Construction Contracts*, how much revenue and profit should BL recognise in profit or loss for the year ended 31 October 2005. **(2 marks)**

? Question 7

Details from DV's long-term contract, which commenced on 1 May 2006, at 30 April 2007 were:

	$'000
Invoiced to client for work done	2,000
Costs incurred to date:	
Attributable to work completed	1,500
Inventory purchased, but not yet used	250
Progress payment received from client	900
Expected further costs to complete project	400
Total contract value	3,000

DV uses the percentage of costs incurred to total costs to calculate attributable profit.

Calculate the amount that DV should recognise in its income statement for the year ended 30 April 2007 for revenue, cost of sales and attributable profits on this contract according to IAS 11 *Construction Contracts*. **(4 marks)**

? Question 8

(a) IAS 2 *Inventories* requires inventories of raw materials and finished goods to be valued in financial statements at lower cost and net realisable value.

Requirements

(i) Describe the three methods of arriving at the cost of inventory which are benchmark treatments in IAS 2. **(4 marks)**

(ii) Explain how the cost of an inventory of finished goods held by a manufacturer would normally be arrived at when obtaining the figure for the financial statements. **(3 marks)**

(b) Sampi is a manufacturer of garden furniture. The entity has consistently used FIFO (first in first out) in valuing inventory, but it is interested to know the effect on its inventory valuation of using weighted average cost instead of FIFO.

At 28 February 20X8, the entity had a inventory of 4,000 standard plastic tables, and has computed its value on each of the two bases as:

Basis	Unit cost	Total value
	$	$
FIFO	16	64,000
Weighted average	13	52,000

During March 20X8, the movements on the inventory of tables were as follows:

Received from factory

Date	Number of units	Production cost per unit
		$
8 March	3,800	15
22 March	6,000	18

Sales

Date	Number of units
12 March	5,000
18 March	2,000
24 March	3,000
28 March	2,000

On a FIFO basis, the inventory at 31 March 20X8 was $32,400.

Requirements

Compute what the value of the inventory at 31 March 20X8 would be using weighted average cost. **(5 marks)**

In arriving at the total inventory values you should make calculations to two decimal places (where necessary) and deal with each inventory movement in date order.

(Total marks = 12)

Data for Questions 9 and 10

CN started a three-year contract to build a new university campus on 1 April 2004. The contract had a fixed price of $90 million.

CN incurred costs to 31 March 2006 of $77 million and estimated that a further $33 million would need to be spent to complete the contract.

CN uses the percentage of cost incurred to date to total cost method to calculate stage of completion of the contract.

Question 9

Calculate revenue earned on the contract to 31 March 2006, according to IAS 11 *Construction Contracts*. **(2 marks)**

Question 10

State how much gross profit/loss CN should recognise in its profit or loss for the year ended 31 March 2006, according to IAS 11 *Construction Contracts*. **(2 marks)**

Question 11

Basset, a construction entity, prepares its accounts to 31 December 2001. During the year, the entity undertook five contracts all of which commenced in the period and will require more than 12 months to complete.

The position of each contract at 31 December 2001 is as follows:

Contract	1001	1002	1003	1004	1005
	$'000	$'000	$'000	$'000	$'000
Contract value	1,800	390	260	4,800	2,000
Certified work to date	1,010	240	200	1,500	1,700
Progress payments received	1,300	200	200	1,900	1,400
Costs to be transferred to cost of sales	1,010	240	200	1,200	1,300
Costs incurred to date	1,310	240	200	1,450	1,400

In addition to the amounts transferred to cost of sales, foreseeable losses are anticipated on two contracts: contract 1001 a loss of $50,000 and contract 1002 a loss of $80,000.

Basset recognises turnover based on the value of work certified at the end of the reporting period.

Requirement

Prepare a summary statement showing profits and losses on all five contracts and the related statement of financial position totals for each. **(20 marks)**

Solutions to Revision Questions

15

✅ Solution 1

The correct answer is (A), see Section 15.2.2.

IAS 2 requires inventory to be valued at cost or net realisable value whichever is the lower.

✅ Solution 2

The correct answer is (C), see Section 15.3.5.

The cost of sales must include the full provision for expected future losses:
345 + 40 = 385.

✅ Solution 3

The correct answer is (C), see Section 15.3.9.

The excess payments received in advance from customers is 320 − 300 = 20.

✅ Solution 4

The correct answer is (B), see Section 15.3.7.

The provision for future losses is subtracted from further costs attributable to partly completed work, 50 − 40 = 10.

✅ Solution 5

The correct answer is (A), see Section 15.3.5.

	$'000
Total contract:	
Contract price	370
Costs (360 + 50)	410
Loss	(40)
To date:	
Revenue	320
Cost of sales	360
Loss	(40)

$40,000 loss is recognised, there is no need for a provision.

Solution 6

	$m
Total revenue	40
Total cost 16 + 18 =	34
Profit	6

Recognise — Revenue 40 × 45% = £18 million
— Profit 6 × 45% = £2 × 7 million

See Section 15.3.3 and 15.3.4.

 Solution 7

	$'000
Total cost	
Cost incurred on attributable work	1,500
Inventory not yet used	250
Expected further costs	400
	2,150

Cost incurred on attributable work 1,500
% complete 1,500/2, 150 = 69.76% (round to 70%)

Total contract revenue	3,000
Total cost	2,150
Total profit	850

Income statement figures for contract	
Revenue (3,000 × 70%)	2,100
Cost of sales	1,500
Profit	600

 Solution 8

(a) (i) 1. *First in first out.* Under FIFO, inventory is valued at the price of the most recent purchases, whether or not it is composed of these particular items.

2. *Unit cost.* Inventory is valued at the price paid for each inventory item held.

3. *Average cost.* Inventory is priced at the weighted average price at which each item has been purchased during the year.

All these methods represent actual cost (method 2) or a reasonably close approximation to actual cost (methods 1 and 3).

(ii) The cost of an inventory of finished goods would be arrived at by taking the cost of the labour and materials used in their manufacture plus an allocation of overheads. In allocating overheads, a normal level of production must be assumed, and selling and general administrative overheads excluded.

(b) Closing inventory is therefore:

Value of inventory using weighted average

	Units	Weighted average cost $	Value of closing inventory $
Opening inventory	4,000	13.00	
8 March	3,800	15.00	
Balance	7,800	13.97	
12 March	(5,000)		
	2,800	13.97	
18 March	(2,000)		
	800	13.97	
22 March	6,000	18.00	
	6,800	17.53	
24 March	(3,000)		
	3,800	17.53	
28 March	(2,000)		
	1,800	17.53	31,554

Summary

		$
Inventory value:	FIFO	32,400
	Weighted average	31,554

See Section 15.2.6.

 ## Solution 9

	$m
Revenue earned	63

See Section 15.3.3.

 ## Solution 10

Income statement for year ended 31 March 2006

	$m
Gross loss	(20)

See Section 15.3.4.

 ## Solution 11

Income statement figures for 2001

Contract	1001 $'000	1002 $'000	1003 $'000	1004 $'000	1005 $'000	Total $'000
Certified work to date	1,010	240	200	1,500	1,700	4,650
Costs to be transferred to cost of sales	(1,010)	(240)	(200)	(1,200)	(1,300)	(3,950)
Less foreseeable losses on contracts	50	80	–	–	–	(130)
Profit/(loss) on contracts	(50)	(80)	–	300	400	570

Inventories

Inventories are calculated by comparing the costs incurred to date with amounts transferred to cost of sales. Any balance remaining is included in 'gross amounts due from customers for contract work'.

Contract	1001	1002	1003	1004	1005	Total
	$'000	$'000	$'000	$'000	$'000	$'000
Costs incurred to date	1,310	240	200	1,450	1,400	4,600
Costs to be transferred to cost of sales	(1,010)	(240)	(200)	(1,200)	(1,300)	3,950
Contract costs that relate to future activity	300	–	–	250	100	650

Receivable/payables

To establish amounts to be included in either receivables or payables we compare the sales revenue recognised to date with the progress payments received to date.

Contract	1001	1002	1003	1004	1005	Total
	$'000	$'000	$'000	$'000	$'000	$'000
Costs work to date	1,010	240	200	1,500	1,700	4,650
Progress payments received	(1,300)	(200)	(200)	(1,900)	(1,400)	5,000
Receivables – unbilled contract revenue		40	–	–	300	340
Excess progress payments received	(290)			(400)		(690)

Contract	1001	1002	1003	1004	1005	Total
	$'000	$'000	$'000	$'000	$'000	$'000
Contract costs that relate to future activity	300	–	–	250	100	650
Unbilled contract revenue	–	40	–		300	340
Foreseeable losses on contracts	(50)	(80)	–	–	–	(130)
Gross amounts due from customers for contract work	250		0	250	400	860
Gross amounts due to customers for contract work		(40)				(40)

Statement of financial position extract	$'000
Gross amounts due from customers for contract work, treated as an asset	860
Gross amounts due to customers for contract work, treat as a liability	(40)
Progress payments received in advance, treated as a current liability	(690)

See Section 15.3.13.

16

Non-current
Intangible Assets

Non-current
Intangible Assets

16

LEARNING OUTCOME

After completing this chapter, you should be able to:

▶ explain the principles of the accounting rules contained in IAS's dealing with disclosure of research and development expenditure, intangible fixed assets (other than goodwill on consolidation), impairment of assets.

The syllabus topics covered in this chapter are as follows:

- research and development costs (IAS 38): criteria for capitalisation;
- intangible assets (IAS 38) and goodwill (excluding that arising on consolidation): recognition, valuation and amortisation;
- impairment of assets (IAS 36) and its effect on the above.

16.1   Introduction

In Chapter 13, we examined non-current tangible assets. In this chapter, we will consider non-current intangible assets and goodwill and then the impairment of non-current assets (tangible and intangible). Goodwill will be discussed in relation to individual entities as groups are outside the scope of the syllabus. Non-current intangible assets are covered by IAS 38 *Intangible Assets*, goodwill is dealt with by IFRS 3 *Business Combinations* and impairment of assets is IAS 36 *Impairment of Assets*.

16.1.1   Objective of IAS 38 *Intangible Assets*

An intangible asset is an identifiable non-monetary asset without physical substance held for use in the business. Entities often use resources to acquire or develop intangibles such as scientific or technical knowledge, design and implementation of a new process or system, licences, trademarks and intellectual property. If it is probable that this investment in the intangible will result in future economic benefits flowing to the entity, then the cost can be recognised as an asset instead of an expense.

16.1.2 Recognition and initial measurement

The recognition of a purchased intangible asset requires an entity to demonstrate that the item meets the definition and recognition criteria set out in IAS 38: an intangible asset should be recognised if and only if:

- it is probable that the future economic benefits from the asset will flow to the entity;
- the cost of the asset can be measured reliably.

An intangible asset purchased separately from a business should be capitalised at cost.

Where an intangible asset is acquired when a business is bought, it should be capitalised separately from purchased goodwill, provided that it can be measured reliably on initial recognition. Cost being the fair value of the asset.

If the fair value of an intangible asset purchased as a part of the acquisition of a business cannot be measured reliably, it should not be recognised and will be included within goodwill.

The cost of an intangible asset is measured in the same way as a tangible non-current asset. The cost of an intangible asset comprises:

(a) its purchase price, including import duties and non-refundable purchase taxes, after deducting trade discounts and rebates;
(b) any directly attributable cost of preparing the asset for its intended use.

Examples of directly attributable costs are:

(a) costs of employee benefits arising directly from bringing the asset to its working condition;
(b) professional fees.

Examples of costs that are not a cost of an intangible asset are:

(a) costs of introducing a new product or service (including costs of advertising and promotional activities);
(b) costs of conducting business in a new location or with a new class of customer (including costs of staff training);
(c) administration and other general overhead costs.

In Section 8.3.4, we considered the 'Framework' and its definition of an asset: 'an asset is a resource controlled by the entity as a result of past events and from which future economic benefits are expected to flow to the entity'. To be recognised as an intangible asset, expenditure must give access to future economic benefits.

The management of the entity must consider the economic conditions that exist and are likely to exist over the useful life of the asset, and then assess the probability of future economic benefits. The assessment should be management's best estimate using all the evidence available, giving greater weight to external evidence. The asset should be measured initially at cost and amortised over its useful life.

16.1.3 Internally generated goodwill

Some expenditure may be incurred with the aim of generating future revenues but does not result in an intangible asset being recognised in the accounts. For example, money spent on developing customer relationships may help generate future revenues but won't result in an identifiable asset that could be sold separately from the business activities. This expenditure is often referred to as contributing to internally generated goodwill.

Internally generated goodwill is not recognised as an asset, as it is not an identifiable resource that can be measured reliably. Where the market value of an entity exceeds the carrying value of the net assets, this could be an indication that internally generated goodwill exists but it is not reliable enough to allow an intangible asset to be included in the accounts. This expenditure is written off to profit or loss as it is incurred.

16.1.4 Internally generated intangible asset

For an internally generated intangible asset to be recognised in the financial statements, the item must first meet the detailed criteria set out in IAS 38. The creation of the asset must be separated into:

- a research phase;
- a development phase.

If the entity is unable to distinguish between the research and development phases, then the entire expenditure must be recorded as research phase expense.

The accounting treatment for internally generated intangibles is determined first by how research and development activities are defined:

- *Research.* Original and planned investigation undertaken with the prospect of gaining new scientific or technical knowledge and understanding.
- *Development.* The application of research findings or other knowledge to a plan or design for the production of new or substantially improved materials, devices, products, processes, systems or services prior to the commencement of commercial production or use.

Research phase

Expenditure on research should be recognised in profit or loss as an expense when it is incurred. It is unlikely that entities could be certain that research expenditure would ultimately create an asset that would generate revenues, capitalisation of research expenditure is not allowed. Only when expenditure creates an asset that can directly be sold or used to make goods that will be sold will recognition be allowable.

Development phase

In the development phase of a project, an entity may be able to identify an intangible asset and demonstrate that it will generate probable future economic benefits. Development activities could include:

- the design and construction of tools involving new technology;
- the design, construction and testing of a chosen alternative for new or improved materials, products, processes or services;
- the design, construction and operation of a pilot plant that is not big enough for commercial production.

An intangible asset should be recognised if, and only if, an entity can demonstrate *all* of the following:

(a) the technical feasibility of completing the intangible asset so that it can be used or sold;
(b) the intention to complete the asset to use it or sell it;
(c) the ability to use or sell the asset;

(d) that the asset will in fact generate probable future economic benefit – does a market exist for the asset if it is to be sold, or can the asset's usefulness be proven if the asset is to be used internally;

(e) that it has the technical, financial and other resources to complete the project to make and use or sell the asset;

(f) that it can measure the expenditure on the development of the asset reliably in order to incorporate the amount in the financial statements.

A detailed business or project plan could be used to illustrate the availability of the entity's resources (point (e) above).

The *cost* of an internally generated intangible asset (point (f) above) can include expenditure such as:

- materials and services used or consumed in generating the intangible asset;
- cost of employee benefits arising from the generation of the intangible asset (wages and salaries);
- other direct costs like patents and licences;
- overheads that were incurred to generate the asset like depreciation on plant, property and equipment used in the process;
- interest charges, as specified in IAS 23 *Borrowing Costs* (see Chapter 13).

Selling and administrative expenses and costs of staff training to use the new product or process are not to be included in establishing the cost of the intangible. Costs can include expenditure incurred from the date that the asset meets all of the above criteria, but cannot include expenditure previously included as an expense in prior years' accounts.

Internally generated brands, mastheads, publishing titles, customer lists and items similar in nature *should not be recognised* as intangibles, as it is unlikely that expenditure on developing such items can be distinguished from expenditure on developing the business as a whole.

Entities may incur other items of expenditure designed to provide future benefits, such as start-up costs (legal costs and product launches), training activities, advertising and promotions; however, no separable item is created and no asset would be recognised. The expenditure would be charged to profit or loss as it was incurred.

16.1.5 Subsequent expenditure

The nature of intangible assets is such that, in many cases, there are no additions to an asset or replacements of part of an asset. Accordingly, most subsequent expenditures are likely to maintain the future economic benefits embodied in an existing intangible asset rather than meet the definition of an intangible asset and the recognition criteria set out in IAS 38. In addition, it is often difficult to attribute subsequent expenditure directly to a particular intangible asset rather than to the business as a whole. Therefore, only rarely will subsequent expenditure – expenditure incurred after the initial recognition of a purchased intangible asset or after completion of an internally generated intangible asset – be recognised in the carrying amount of an asset.

After initial recognition at cost, intangible assets should be carried at cost less any accumulated amortisation or impairment losses.

16.1.6 Subsequent measurement

IAS 38 allows intangible non-current assets to be carried at amortised cost or at revalued amount, being its fair value at the date of the revaluation less any subsequent accumulated amortisation and any subsequent accumulated impairment losses. For the purpose of revaluations under IAS 38, fair value should be determined by reference to an active market. IAS 38 suggests that there will not usually be an active market in an intangible asset, therefore the revaluation model will not be used. Revaluations should be made with sufficient regularity such that the carrying amount does not differ materially from that which would be determined using fair value at the end of the reporting period.

If an intangible asset is revalued, all the other assets in its class should also be revalued, unless there is no active market for those assets. If an intangible asset in a class of revalued intangible assets cannot be revalued because there is no active market for this asset, the asset should be carried at its cost less any accumulated amortisation and impairment losses.

If the fair value of a revalued intangible asset can no longer be determined by reference to an active market, the carrying amount of the asset should be its revalued amount at the date of the last revaluation by reference to the active market less any subsequent accumulated amortisation and any subsequent accumulated impairment losses.

If an intangible asset's carrying amount is increased as a result of a revaluation, the increase shall be recognised in other comprehensive income and accumulated in equity under the heading of revaluation surplus. However, the increase shall be recognised in profit or loss to the extent that it reverses a revaluation decrease of the same asset previously recognised in profit or loss.

If an intangible asset's carrying amount is decreased as a result of a revaluation, the decrease is recognised in profit or loss unless the intangible asset has previously been revalued. If an intangible non-current asset has previously been revalued upwards, any decrease in value can be recognised in other comprehensive income and deducted from the heading of revaluation surplus in equity, to the extent of any credit balance existing in the revaluation surplus in respect of that asset. The decrease recognised in comprehensive income reduces the amount accumulated in equity under the heading of revaluation surplus.

The cumulative revaluation surplus included in equity may be transferred directly to retained earnings when the surplus is realised. The whole surplus may be realised on the retirement or disposal of the asset. However, some of the surplus may be realised as the asset is used by the entity; each year, the amount of the surplus realised is the difference between amortisation based on the revalued carrying amount of the asset and amortisation that would have been recognised based on the asset's historical cost. The transfer from revaluation surplus to retained earnings is made through the statement of changes in equity.

16.1.7 Amortisation

The depreciable amount of an intangible asset should be allocated on a systematic basis over the best estimate of its useful life. Amortisation should start from the date the asset is available for use.

As with tangible assets, the most difficult decision for management is determining the useful life of the asset. The useful life of an intangible asset should take account of such things as:

- the expected usage of the asset;
- possible obsolescence and expected actions by competitors;
- the stability of the industry;
- market demand for the products and services that the asset is generating.

The method of amortising the asset should reflect the pattern in which the assets' economic benefits are expected to be consumed by the entity. If that proves difficult to determine, then the straight-line method is acceptable. The residual value of the intangible should be assumed to be zero unless there is a commitment from a third party to purchase the asset or the entity intends to sell the asset and a readily available active market exists. The annual amortisation amount will be charged to profit or loss as an expense.

The useful life and method of amortisation should be reviewed at least at each financial year-end. Changes to useful life or method of amortisation should be effective as soon as they are identified and should be accounted for as changes in accounting estimates (IAS 8), by adjusting the amortisation charge for the current and future periods.

16.1.8 Impairment losses

The treatment for impairment of assets is dealt with by IAS 36, *Impairment of Assets*. In addition to the requirements of IAS 36 (discussed in Section 16.3), an entity should estimate the recoverable amount of intangibles at least at every year-end, including assets that are not yet available for use.

16.1.9 Retirements and disposals

An intangible asset should be removed from the statement of financial position on disposal or when no future economic benefits are expected from its use or future disposal. Any gains or losses from disposal (the difference between the net proceeds and the carrying value of the asset) should be recognised as income or expense in profit or loss. Amortisation ceases when the asset is derecognised or is designated as 'held for sale' in accordance with IFRS 5.

16.1.10 Disclosure

The financial statements should disclose the following for each class of intangible assets, distinguishing between internally generated intangible assets and other intangible assets:

(a) the useful lives or amortisation rates used;
(b) the amortisation methods used;
(c) the gross carrying amount and the accumulated amortisation (together with accumulated impairment losses) at the beginning and end of the period;
(d) the amount of amortisation charged to profit or loss;
(e) a reconciliation of the carrying amount at the beginning and the end of the period showing:
  - additions (internally developed assets and acquisitions);
  - retirements and disposals;
  - changes to the intangible assets due to revaluations, impairment losses and other changes;
  - impairment losses recognised and reversed in profit or loss;
  - amortisation recognised during the period.

In addition, an entity must disclose details of any intangible given an indefinite useful life and any individual intangible that is material to the financial statements as a whole.

If intangible assets are carried at revalued amounts, the following should be disclosed:

(a) by class of intangible assets:
  (i) the effective date of the revaluation;
  (ii) the carrying amount of revalued intangible assets;

(b) the amount of the revaluation surplus that relates to intangible assets at the beginning and end of the period, indicating the changes during the period and any restrictions on the distribution of the balance to shareholders;

(c) the methods and significant assumptions applied in estimating the assets' fair values.

16.2 Purchased goodwill

IFRS 3 Business combinations regulates the treatment of purchased goodwill. Although business combinations and group accounting is outside of your syllabus, non-group aspects of goodwill are in the syllabus. The basic issues involved with the treatment of goodwill do not involve principles of consolidation, so they can be dealt with in this syllabus.

Goodwill arises on the acquisition of an entity or an entity's assets or assets and liabilities. IFRS 3 defines purchased goodwill as *'future economic benefits arising from assets that are not capable of being individually and separately recognised.'* Purchased goodwill is calculated as *'excess of the cost of acquisition over the acquirer's interest in the fair value of the identifiable net assets and liabilities acquired as at the date of the transaction.'* The excess payment is made in anticipation of future economic benefits arising from the acquisition.

The IFRS 3 definition can give rise to 'positive goodwill' where the purchase consideration exceeds the fair value of the net assets, or negative goodwill where the fair value of the net assets exceeds the purchase consideration.

IFRS 3 requires positive goodwill to be recognised as an asset and recorded on the statement of financial position as an asset.

16.2.1 Purchased goodwill – recognition and measurement

Positive goodwill should be recognised as an asset and carried at cost less any accumulated impairment losses (IFRS 3).

IFRS 3 requires that the entity carrys out annual assessments of the recoverable amount of the goodwill to identify any impairment losses arising each year. These impairment losses are recognised instead of amortisation.

16.2.2 Negative purchased goodwill

Negative purchased goodwill is conceptually the equivalent of a discount on the purchase price. When negative goodwill arises, IFRS 3 emphasises the need to check that the correct fair values of the assets and liabilities acquired have been used in the calculation of the goodwill figure.

Negative goodwill is credited to profit or loss in the year of acquisition.

16.3 IAS 36 *Impairment of Assets*

16.3.1 Introduction

Your syllabus requires only knowledge of the principles of IAS 36.

The object of IAS 36 is to ensure that an entity does not carry its assets at a value above their recoverable amount. (Recoverable amount means the higher of an asset's net selling price and its value in use.)

16.3.2 Procedures to check for impairment

At the end of each reporting period an entity should assess whether there are internal or external indications that the value of any asset is impaired.

In assessing whether there is any indication that an asset may be impaired, an entity shall consider, as a minimum, the following indications:

External sources of information:
(a) during the period, an asset's market value has declined significantly more than would be expected as a result of the passage of time or normal use;
(b) significant changes with an adverse effect on the entity have taken place during the period, or will take place in the near future, in the technological, market, economic or legal environment in which the entity operates or in the market to which an asset is dedicated;
(c) market interest rates or other market rates of return on investments have increased during the period, and those increases are likely to affect the discount rate used in calculating an asset's value in use and decrease the asset's recoverable amount materially;
(d) the carrying amount of the net assets of the reporting entity is more than its market capitalisation.

Internal sources of information:
(a) evidence is available of obsolescence or physical damage of an asset;
(b) significant changes with an adverse effect on the entity have taken place during the period, or are expected to take place in the near future, in the extent to which, or manner in which, an asset is used or is expected to be used. These changes include the asset becoming idle, plans to discontinue or restructure the operation to which an asset belongs, and plans to dispose of an asset before the previously expected date;
(c) evidence is available from internal reporting that indicates that the economic performance of an asset is, or will be, worse than expected.

16.3.3 Recognition and measurement of an impairment loss

An impairment review follows the long-established principle that an asset's statement of financial position carrying value should not exceed its recoverable amount, which is measured by reference to the future cash flows that can be generated from its continued use or disposal. An asset is impaired when the carrying amount of the asset exceeds its recoverable amount. If any of the indications listed in Section 16.3.2 are present, an entity is required to make a formal estimate of recoverable amount. If no indication of a potential impairment loss is present, there is no requirement to make a formal estimate of recoverable amount.

If the carrying value of an asset is in fact less than the recoverable amount, the shortfall (an impairment loss) must be recognised in profit or loss as an expense. The only exception to this is that an impairment loss on an asset that has previously been revalued may be recognised in other comprehensive income, up to the amount of the surplus relating to that asset, any additional impairment is then recognised in profit or loss.

An asset's recoverable amount is defined in IAS 36 as the higher of an asset's net selling price and value in use. Net selling price is the asset's market price less the costs of disposal. Calculating the asset's value in use involves the following steps:

(a) estimating the future cash inflows and outflows to be derived from continuing use of the asset and from its ultimate disposal;

(b) applying the appropriate discount rate to these future cash flows.

It is not always necessary to determine both an asset's net selling price and its value in use. For example, if either of these amounts exceeds the asset's carrying amount, the asset is not impaired and it is not necessary to estimate the other amount. It may be possible to determine net selling price, even if an asset is not traded in an active market. However, sometimes it will not be possible to determine net selling price because there is no basis for making a reliable estimate of the amount obtainable from the sale of the asset in an arm's length transaction between knowledgeable and willing parties. In this case, the recoverable amount of the asset may be taken to be its value in use.

If there is no reason to believe that an asset's value in use materially exceeds its net selling price, the asset's recoverable amount may be taken to be its net selling price.

Recoverable amount is determined for an individual asset, unless the asset does not generate cash inflows from continuing use that are largely independent of those from other assets or groups of assets. If this is the case, recoverable amount is determined for the cash-generating unit to which the asset belongs.

The carrying amount of a cash-generating unit:

(a) includes the carrying amount of only those assets that can be attributed directly, or allocated on a reasonable and consistent basis, to the cash-generating unit and that will generate the future cash inflows estimated in determining the cash-generating unit's value in use. It is important to include in the cash-generating unit all assets that generate the relevant stream of cash inflows from continuing use. In some cases, certain assets contribute to the estimated future cash flows of a cash-generating unit, need to be allocated to the cash-generating unit on a reasonable and consistent basis. This might be the case for goodwill or corporate assets such as head office assets;

(b) does not include the carrying amount of any recognised liability, unless the recoverable amount of the cash-generating unit cannot be determined without consideration of this liability.

In outline, the stages of an impairment review are:

- identifying separate cash-generating units;
- establishing a statement of financial position for each cash-generating unit, comprising the net tangible and intangible assets plus allocated purchased goodwill for each cash-generating unit;
- forecasting the future cash flows of the cash-generating unit and discounting them to present value using the rate of return the market would expect for an equally risky investment;
- comparing the present value of the cash flows with the net assets of each cash-generating unit and recognising any shortfall as an impairment loss;
- allocating any impairment loss to write down the assets of the cash-generating unit. Any impairment is allocated first, to goodwill allocated to the cash-generating unit (if any); and then, to the other assets of the unit on a pro-rata basis based on the carrying amount of each asset in the unit.

In allocating an impairment loss, the carrying amount of an asset should not be reduced below the highest of:

(a) its net selling price (if determinable);
(b) its value in use (if determinable);
(c) zero.

Example 16.A

An asset costing $100,000 when purchased on 1 January 2001 has an estimated useful life of 10 years. On 1 January 2004, the asset is estimated to have a recoverable amount of $50,000.

The assets carrying value on 1 January 2004 is cost $100,000 less accumulated depreciation of $30,000 ($10,000 × 3 years).

The $20,000 impairment in value will be charged as an expense to profit or loss.

		$	$
Debit	Profit or loss – impairment loss	20,000	
Credit	Net book value of asset		20,000

Being impairment loss reducing asset value from $70,000 to $50,000.

Future depreciation expense will be based on the new value of $50,000 – note, however, the estimated useful life of the asset has not changed, so the depreciation will be calculated as $50,000 over the remaining seven years = $7,143.

Example 16.B

Using the same asset as in Example 16.A, let us assume the asset was revalued to $110,000 on 1 January 2003. This created a revaluation surplus of $30,000, being $110,000 less the carrying value of the asset ($100,000 − $20,000).

If on 1 January 2004 the asset is estimated to have a recoverable amount of $90,000, then the impairment loss of $9,000 (recoverable amount ($110,000 − $11,000 = $99,000 − $90,000 = $9,000)) will be recognised in other comprehensive income and deducted from the revaluation reserve, reducing the amount in respect of this asset.

		$	$
Debit	Revaluation reserve	9,000	
Credit	Net book value of asset		9,000

Being the recording of the impairment loss.

If the revaluation surplus did not have sufficient amounts relating to this specific asset, then the balance of the impairment loss would be charged to profit or loss.

16.4 Disclosure of impairments

For each class of assets, the financial statements should disclose:

(a) the amount of impairment losses recognised in profit or loss during the period and the line item(s) of the statement of comprehensive income in which those impairment losses are included;
(b) the amount of reversals of impairment losses recognised in the statement of comprehensive income during the period and the line item(s) of the statement of comprehensive income in which those impairment losses are reversed;
(c) the amount of impairment losses recognised in other comprehensive income during the period;
(d) the amount of reversals of impairment losses recognised in other comprehensive income during the period.

16.5 Summary

Having completed this chapter, we can discuss the recognition and valuation of intangible assets, including purchased goodwill, internally generated goodwill and research and development costs. We can explain the requirement to amortise goodwill and can discuss the criteria for the capitalisation of development costs. We can also explain the main disclosure requirements in respect of intangible assets.

We can explain the principle of impairment of assets and can record the effect of impairment losses on assets.

Revision Questions

16

? Question 1

When can internally developed intangible assets be capitalised? (*max. 35 words*) **(2 marks)**

? Question 2

When should a full impairment review be carried out?

(A) When circumstances indicate that an impairment may have occurred
(B) When the directors want to reduce the value of their assets
(C) When the book value of assets seems too high
(D) Every 5 years   **(2 marks)**

? Question 3

Purchased goodwill is defined by IAS 38 as:

(A) The amount paid for intangible assets
(B) The difference between the statement of financial position value and the amount paid for the business
(C) The difference between the fair value of the tangible non-current assets acquired and the amount paid
(D) The difference between the cost of the acquisition and the fair values of the net assets acquired   **(2 marks)**

? Question 4

Which of the following can be capitalised and carried forward in the statement of financial position as an asset:

(A) a payment of $10,000 to XY University for original research
(B) $50,000 spent on applied research to develop a new discovery into a possible new product
(C) $22,000 being the cost of developing a new product for final launch on the market. The product is expected to be profitable
(D) $17,000 the cost of developing a product that was then found to be non-viable
                                                    (2 marks)

? Question 5

IAS 38 specifies criteria that must be met before development expenditure can be deferred:

1. the technical feasibility of completing the project so that the asset can be used;
2. the project has a useful economic life of more than 1 year;
3. the ability to use the asset;
4. total deferred expenditure is less than 10% of turnover;
5. financial resources are sufficient to complete the project and use the asset;
6. adequate resources exist to complete the project and make use of the asset.

Which of the above criteria are included in IAS 36 requirements to defer development expenditure?

(A) 1, 2, 3 and 4
(B) 1, 2, 4 and 5
(C) 1, 3, 5 and 6
(D) 2, 3, 4 and 6   **(2 marks)**

? Question 6

The following measures relate to a non-current asset:

(i) Net book value $20,000
(ii) Net realisable value $18,000
(iii) Value in use $22,000
(iv) Replacement cost $50,000

The recoverable amount of the asset is

(A) $18,000
(B) $20,000
(C) $22,000
(D) $50,000   **(2 marks)**

? Question 7

BI owns a building which it uses as its offices, warehouse and garage. The land is carried as a separate non-current tangible asset in the statement of financial position.

BI has a policy of regularly revaluing its non-current tangible assets. The original cost of the building in October 2002 was $1,000,000; it was assumed to have a remaining useful life of 20 years at that date, with no residual value. The building was revalued on 30 September 2004 by a professional valuer at $1,800,000.

BI also owns a brand name which it acquired 1 October 2000 for $500,000. The brand name is being amortised over 10 years.

The economic climate had deteriorated during 2005, causing BI to carry out an impairment review of its assets at 30 September 2005. BI's building was valued at a market value of $1,500,000 on 30 September 2005 by an independent valuer. A brand specialist valued BI's brand name at market value of $200,000 on the same date.

BI's management accountant calculated that the brand name's value in use at 30 September 2005 was $150,000.

Requirement

Explain how BI should report the events described above and quantify any amounts required to be included in its financial statements for the year ended 30 September 2005.

(5 marks)

? Question 8

CD is a manufacturing entity that runs a number of operations including a bottling plant that bottles carbonated soft drinks. CD has been developing a new bottling process that will allow the bottles to be filled and sealed more efficiently.

The new process took a year to develop. At the start of development, CD estimated that the new process would increase output by 15% with no additional cost (other than the extra bottles and their contents). Development work commenced on 1 May 2005 and was completed on 20 April 2006. Testing at the end of the development confirmed CD's original estimates.

CD incurred an expenditure of $180,000 on the above development in 2005/06.

CD plans to install the new process in its bottling plant and start operating the new process from 1 May 2006.

The end of CD's reporting period is 30 April.

Requirements

(i) Explain the requirements of IAS 38 *Intangible Assets* for the treatment of development costs

(ii) Explain how CD should treat its development costs in its financial statements for the year ended 30 April 2006. **(2 marks)**

(5 marks)

Scenario for Questions 9 and 10

T manufactures radar equipment for military and civil aircraft. The entity's latest trial balance as at 31 December 20X1 is as follows:

	$'000	$'000
Administrative costs	800	
Bank overdraft		700
Receivables	2,000	
Factory – cost	18,000	
Factory – depreciation		1,800
Factory running costs	1,200	
Loan interest	1,680	
Long-term loans		12,000
Machinery – cost	13,000	
Machinery – depreciation		8,000
Manufacturing wages	1,300	
Opening inventory – parts and materials	400	
Opening inventory – work in progress	900	
Retained earnings		380
Purchases – parts and materials	2,300	
Research and development	5,300	

Sales revenue		10,000
Sales salaries	600	
Share capital		15,000
Trade payables		600
Trade fair costs	1,000	
	48,480	48,480

(i) The inventory was counted at 31 December 20X1. Closing inventories of parts and materials were valued at $520,000 and closing inventories of work in progress were valued at $710,000. There are no inventories of finished goods because all production is for specific customer orders and goods are usually shipped as soon as they are completed.

(ii) No depreciation has been charged for the year ended 31 December 20X1. The entity depreciates the factory at 2 per cent of cost per annum and all machinery at 25 per cent per annum on the reducing balance basis.

(iii) The balance on the research and development account is made up as follows:

	$
Opening balance (development costs brought forward)	2,100,000
Calibrating equipment purchased for laboratory	600,000
Long-range radar project	900,000
Wide-angle microwave project	1,700,000
	5,300,000

The opening balance comprises expenditure on new products which have just been introduced to the market. The entity has decided that these costs should be written off over 10 years, starting with the year ended 31 December 20X1. T has a policy of capitalising all development costs which meet the criteria laid down by IAS 38.

The new calibrating equipment is used in the entity's research laboratory. It is used to ensure that the measurement devices used during experiments are properly adjusted.

The long-range radar project is intended to adapt existing military radar technology for civilian air traffic control purposes. The entity has built a successful prototype and has had strong expressions of interest from a number of potential customers. It is almost certain that the entity will start to sell this product early in the year 20X3 and that it will make a profit.

The wide-angle microwave project is an attempt to apply some theoretical concepts to create a new radar system for use in fighter aircraft. Initial experiments have been promising, but there is little immediate prospect of a saleable product because the transmitter is far too large and heavy to install in an aeroplane.

(iv) During the year the entity spent $1,000,000 in order to exhibit its product range at a major trade fair. This was the first time that T had attended such an event. No orders have been received as a direct result of this fair, although the sales director has argued that contacts were made, which will generate sales over the next few years.

(v) T has made losses for tax purposes for several years. It does not expect to pay any tax for the year ended 31 December 20X1.

The directors do not plan to pay any dividends for the year ended 31 December 20X1.

? Question 9

(a) Prepare T's statement of comprehensive income for the year ended 31 December 20X1 and its statement of financial position at that date. These should be in a form suitable for publication.

    Do *not* prepare notes to the accounts except for those required in part (b).

    Do *not* prepare a statement of accounting policies or a statement of changes in equity.

(b) Prepare the following notes to T's accounts:
- (i) Intangible non-current assets
- (ii) Tangible non-current assets

(20 marks)

? Question 10

(a) Explain how each of the following items should be treated in T's financial statements:

Research and development

(i) New calibrating equipment purchased for laboratory	**(3 marks)**
(ii) Long-range radar project	**(4 marks)**
(iii) Wide-angle microwave project	**(4 marks)**

(b) Explain how the costs associated with the trade fair should be treated in T's financial statements. **(4 marks)**

(c) The directors of T have read that the calculation of an entity's profit figure involves a great deal of subjective judgement and that some entities increase or decrease their profits by biasing the subjective decisions which are associated with accounting. Explain how T's chief accountant should respond if the directors ask for the financial statements to be restated in a manner which makes the entity appear to be more profitable than it actually is. **(5 marks)**

(Total marks = 20)

? Question 11

Z acquired the business and assets of Q, a sole trader, on 31 October 2002.

    The fair value of the assets acquired from Q were:

	$'000
Non-current intangible assets	
Brand X – brand name	220
Non-current tangible assets	
Plant and equipment	268
Inventory	5
	493
Cash paid to Q	523

Z spent the following amounts creating and promoting the Brand Z brand name:

Year to 31 October 2000	$100,000
Year to 31 October 2001	$90,000
Year to 31 October 2002	$80,000

Z's accounting policy on recognised non-current intangible assets is that brand names are amortised over 10 years.

On 31 October 2003, Z's brand names were valued by an independent valuer as follows:

Brand X at $250,000
Brand Z at $300,000

The directors of Z have been very impressed with the increase in profits from Q's former business. They are certain that the goodwill has increased since they acquired Q's business. Z's directors have estimated that the goodwill is worth $45,000 at 31 October 2003.

Requirements

Explain how Z should treat:

(i) the brand names; **(9 marks)**

(ii) goodwill; **(6 marks)**

in its financial statements for the years ended 31 October 2002 and 2003. Your explanation should include reference to relevant International Accounting Standards.

(Total marks = 15)

Solutions to Revision Questions

☑ Solution 1

Internally developed intangible assets can be capitalised if during the development the entity is able to identify that the development expenditure will enable the generation of probable future economic benefits.

☑ Solution 2

The correct answer is (A), see Section 16.3.2.

☑ Solution 3

The correct answer is (D), see Section 16.2.

☑ Solution 4

The correct answer is (C), see Section 16.1.4.

This specification could meet the requirements of IAS 38 to enable development expenditure to be carried forward to future periods.

☑ Solution 5

The correct answer is (C), see Section 16.1.4.

☑ Solution 6

The correct answer is (C), see Section 16.3.3.

Solution 7

Workings

	$
October 2002 Original cost 1,000,000	
Depreciation 2002/03 (1,000,000/20)	(50,000)
	950,000
Depreciation 2003/04	(50,000)
	900,000
Revalued 30 September 2004, gain	900,000
	1,800,000
Depreciation 2004/05 (1,800,000/18)	(100,000)
	1,700,000
Revalued 30 September 2005	1,500,000
Loss on revaluation	200,000

IAS 16 *Property, Plant and Equipment* requires the $200,000 loss on revaluation shown in the statement of comprehensive income and deducted from the revaluation reserve. It does not go to profit or loss as the building has been previously revalued and the gain is more than the current loss. The buildings will be shown in the statement of financial position at $1,500,000 and be depreciated over the remaining 17 years.

The brand name acquired for $500,000 5 years ago. Net book value at 30 September 2005 is $500,000 × 5/10 = $250,000. The brand name's market value is $200,000 and its value in use is $150,000.

A non-current asset is valued at the higher of its market value or value in use (IAS 36 *Impairment of Assets*). Therefore, the brand names carrying amount should be adjusted to $200,000 and $50,000 written off to profit or loss for the year to 30 September 2005, see Section 16.3.3.

 Solution 8

(i) Development expenditure could be regarded as an intangible asset. IAS 38 only allows an intangible asset to be recognised if, and only if, an entity can demonstrate all of the following:

- the technical feasibility of completing the intangible asset so that it can be used or sold;
- the intention to complete the asset to use it or sell it;
- the ability to use or sell the asset;
- that the asset will in fact generate probable future economic benefit – does a market exist for the asset if it is to be sold, or can the asset's usefulness be proven if the asset is to be used internally;
- that it has the technical, financial and other resources to complete the project to make and use or sell the asset;
- that it can measure the expenditure on the development of the asset reliably in order to incorporate the amount in the financial statements.

(ii) All of the above criteria seem to have been met by CD's new process:

- it is technically feasible, it has been tested and is about to be implemented;
- it has been completed and CD intends to use it;

- the new process is estimated to increase output by 15% with no additional costs other than direct material costs;
- the expenditure can be measured as the figures have been given.

CD will treat the $180,000 development cost as an intangible non-current asset in its statement of financial position at 30 April 2006. Amortisation will start from 1 May 2006 when the new process starts operation, see Section 16.1.4.2.

 Solution 9

(a)   T – statement of comprehensive income for the year ended 31 December 20X1

	Notes	$'000
Sales revenue		10,000
Cost of sales		(8,540)
Gross profit		1,460
Selling and distribution costs		(1,600)
Administrative expenses		(800)
Loss from operations	1	(940)
Finance cost		(1,680)
Retained Loss for the year		(2,620)
Other comprehensive income		0
Total comprehensive income for the year		(2,620)

T – statement of financial position at 31 December 20X1

	Notes	$'000	$'000
Non-current assets			
Intangible non-current assets	2		2,790
Tangible non-current assets	3		20,040
			22,830
Current assets			
Inventory	4	1,230	
Receivables		2,000	
			3,230
			26,060
Share Capital and reserves			
Issued capital			15,000
Retained earnings			(2,240)
			12,760
Non-current liabilities			
Long-term loans			12,000
Current liabilities			
Bank overdraft		700	
Trade payables		600	
			1,300
			26,060

NON-CURRENT INTANGIBLE ASSETS

(b) *T – notes to the financial statements*

Intangible non-current assets

	Cost $'000	Amortisation $'000	Net book value $'000
Development expenditure			
At 1 January 20X1	2,100	–	2,100
Additions	900	–	900
Amortised in the year	–	(210)	(210)
At 31 December 20X1	3,000	(210)	2,790

T has capitalised these development costs in order to match them with anticipated revenue. Development costs of $2,100,000 are being written off over 10 years. The balance of costs are not yet being amortised, as commercial production has not yet commenced.

Tangible non-current assets

	Land and buildings $'000	Plant and machinery $'000	Total $'000
Cost at 1.1.20X1	18,000	13,000	31,000
Additions	–	600	600
Cost at 31.12.20X1	18,000	13,600	31,600
Depreciation at 1.1.20X1	1,800	8,000	9,800
Charge for the year	360	1,400	1,760
Depreciation at 31.12.20X1	2,160	9,400	11,560
Net book value at 31.12.20X1	15,840	4,200	20,040
Net book value at 1.1.20X1	16,200	5,000	21,200

Workings

	$'000
Cost of sales	
Opening inventory – parts and materials	400
Opening inventory – work in progress	900
Purchases	2,300
	3,600
Closing inventory – parts and materials	(520)
Closing inventory – work in progress	(710)
	2,370
Depreciation – factory (18,000 × 2%)	360
Depreciation – machinery ((13,000 + 600 − 8,000) × 25%)	1,400
Factory running costs	1,200
Manufacturing wages	1,300
Research costs written off	1,700
Amortisation of development costs (2,100 × 10%)	210
	8,540

	$'000
Selling and distribution costs	
Sales salaries	600
Trade fair costs	1,000
	1,600

Solution 10

(a) (i) The cost of assets acquired to provide facilities for research and development (R&D) should be capitalised and depreciated over their useful lives, and included as part of the R&D expense. Where an asset is used in development activities, the depreciation can be included as development costs and capitalised. The new calibrating equipment purchased for the laboratory is an asset which will be used on various projects, not solely R&D projects. Because the various projects on which it will be used cannot be identified, the machine should be classed as a tangible non-current asset. It should be depreciated in the same way as T's existing machinery.

(ii) The long-range radar project satisfies the criteria stated in IAS 38, which requires R&D expenditure to be deferred to future periods. The project is clearly defined, and its related expenditure is separately identifiable. The outcome of the project has been assessed as technically feasible and commercially viable, and is expected to make a profit. The costs should therefore be included in the statement of financial position as an intangible non-current asset, and amortised when commercial production commences.

(iii) The outcome of the wide-angle microwave project is much less certain. The project may be commercially successful, but it is too early to be sure. IAS 38 does not allow expenditure of this kind to be deferred to future periods. The costs must be written off in profit or loss as they are incurred. This is because certain expenditure can be regarded as part of the continuing operation required to maintain a entity's business and competitive position. It is also in accordance with the fundamental accounting concept of prudence.

(b) Given that there are no specific accounting standards governing the accounting treatment of the trade fair, T should turn to the IASB Framework. If the costs are carried forward, they need to meet the definition of an asset set out in the Framework. An asset must have future economic benefit to the entity. Since there is no indication of any increase in future sales revenue, the trade fair cost does not seem to have any future economic benefit. It should therefore be treated as an expense not an asset.

Because the cost is significant, and not a normal part of selling and distribution, it should be disclosed separately in a note to the statement of comprehensive income.

(c) Financial statements must be prepared in accordance with accounting standards. It is sometimes possible for an entity to adhere to the *letter* of the law while failing to comply with the *spirit* of the law. The most important requirement is that the accounts show a true and fair view. Thus, even if the directors of T have come up with a creative accounting scheme which does not appear to break any accounting rules or legislation, the chief accountant should explain to the directors that the financial statements must be adjusted to show a true and fair view of the entity's profitability.

The accountant could perhaps ask for the support of T's external auditor, who could explain that any material distortion of the accounts would inevitably lead to a qualified audit report.

NON-CURRENT INTANGIBLE ASSETS

 Solution 11

(i) Brand names

Purchase of Brand X brand name

A brand name is an intangible non-current asset. Intangible non-current assets are covered by IAS 38 *Intangible Assets.*

IAS 38 allows purchased intangible non-current assets to be recognised in the financial statements, if it is probable that future economic benefits will flow from the assets and if their value can be measured reliably at the date of purchase. As a value has been given for the brand X, it is reasonable to assume that its value can be measured reliably. The brand name 'Brand X' should be recognised in the statement of financial position at $220,000 at 31 October 2002 and amortised over its useful economic life of 10 years. $22,000 per year will be charged to profit or loss.

The entity must carry out an impairment review at the end of the first financial year after the acquisition, and consider whether the performance of the entity, after the acquisition of the brand, has improved in line with expectations.

Internally generated brand names. Brand Z is an internally generated brand name. Some types of internally generated intangible non-current assets can be recognised in the statement of financial position if they meet specific criteria; however, IAS 38 specifically states that internally generated brand names should not be recognised as assets under any circumstances.

All expenditure will be charged to profit or loss in the year it was incurred.

(ii) *Goodwill*

Purchased goodwill from Q. Purchased goodwill is the price paid over and above the fair value of the assets acquired.

	$'000
Assets acquired (including brand)	493
Cash paid	523
Goodwill	30

Positive purchased goodwill of $30,000 will be recognised in the statement of financial position at cost at 31 October 2002. Annual impairment reviews will be carried out as required by IFRS 3 *Business Combinations* but no amortisation will be provided.

Increase in value of purchased goodwill. IFRS 3 does not allow goodwill to be revalued upwards, so no action should be taken on the directors' valuation. Purchased goodwill will gradually be replaced by self-generated goodwill, so the increase in the valuation is due to internally generated goodwill arising since the acquisition. IFRS 3 specifically forbids the capitalisation of internally generated goodwill.

17

Share Capital
Transactions

Share Capital Transactions

17

The syllabus topics covered in this chapter are as follows:

● Issue and redemption of shares, including treatment of share issue and redemption costs (IAS 32 and IAS 39), the share premium account, the accounting for maintenance of capital arising from the purchase by a entity of its own shares.

17.1 Introduction

This chapter deals with the accounting entries in respect of the issue and redemption of shares. You could view this as a series of journal entries which have to be learned by rote. This would, however, make the topic much more difficult and certainly far less interesting than it can be. Try to understand the principles involved, you will then be able to work out the journals required, rather than try to memorise them.

This topic is usually governed by local legal requirements that relate to the entity together with IFRS requirements. Countries differ in their legislation governing the issue and redemption of shares. From an international standpoint, it is thus possible only to consider the general principles and the requirements of international accounting standards. IAS 32 *Financial Instruments: Disclosure and Presentation* and IAS 39 *Financial Instruments: Recognition and Measurement* both deal with share and debt classification, presentation, measurement and treatment in the financial statements. These two standards are very long and complex standards that cover a wide range of possibilities relating to financial instruments. As part of your syllabus, you are only required to have a knowledge of the accounting rules governing share capital transactions, the rules relating to debt are outside the syllabus.

17.2 IAS 1 requirements

17.2.1 Interests of shareholders

The notes to an entity's financial statements contain a detailed note about the entity's share capital. This is hardly surprising given that the shareholders are regarded as the primary audience for the published accounts. They are the owners of the entity and need to be able to see how their ownership interests are reflected in the statement of financial position. They need to know how their interests might be affected by the issue of new shares.

A new issue will raise funds which will increase the value of their existing shares if the proceeds are invested wisely. This will, however, dilute their control. They also need to know about the interests of the other shareholders. In particular, they need to know how the existence of different classes of shares might affect their interests.

17.2.2 Disclosures

We studied the requirements of IAS 1 *Presentation of Financial Statements* in detail in Chapter 7. The following disclosures are required by the standard in respect of share capital.

IAS 1 requires that, issued capital and reserves attributable to owners must be shown in the statement of financial position. In addition, IAS 1 requires that, in the statement of financial position or in the notes, equity capital and reserves are analysed showing separately the various classes of paid-in capital, share premium and reserves.

IAS 1 also requires that the following information on share capital and reserves be made available either in the statement of financial position or in the notes:

(a) for each class of share capital:
- the number of shares authorised;
- the number of shares issued and fully paid, and issued but not fully paid;
- par value per share, or that the shares have no par value;
- a reconciliation of the number of shares outstanding at the beginning and at the end of the year;
- the rights, preferences and restrictions attaching to that class including restrictions on the distribution of dividends and the repayment of capital;
- shares in the entity held by the entity itself; and
- shares reserved for issuance under options and sales contracts, including the terms and amounts.

(b) a description of the nature and purpose of each reserve within equity.

IAS 1 requires the following to be disclosed in the notes:

(a) the amount of dividends proposed or declared before the financial statements were authorised for issue, but not recognised as a distribution to owners during the period, and the related amount per share;

(b) the amount of any cumulative preference dividends not recognised.

Example 17.A

Some extracts from the annual report of an imaginary entity quoted on the local stock exchange are shown below.

You are required to read through the extracts and answer the following questions.

1. How many additional shares of each class can the entity's directors issue?
2. What was the selling price of the new shares issued by the entity?
3. What differences are there likely to be between the preference and ordinary shares?

Statement of financial position

	Notes	20X7 $m	20X6 $m
Issued share capital*	23	1,353.7	1,345.2
Share premium account		320.0	310.0
Reserves		2,200.0	2,050.0
		3,873.7	3,705.2

Notes
* Issued share capital

	20X7 $m	20X6 $m
Authorised		
6,000,000,000 ordinary shares of 25¢ each	1,500.0	1,500.0
700,000 7.0% cumulative preference shares of $1 each	0.7	0.7
2,000,000 4.9% cumulative preference shares of $1 each	2.0	2.0
	1,502.7	1,502.7
Issued and fully paid		
5,400,000,000 ordinary shares of 25¢ each	1,350.0	1,342.5
700,000 7.0% cumulative preference shares of $1 each	0.7	0.7
2,000,000 4.9% cumulative preference shares of $1 each	2.0	2.0
	1,353.7	1,345.2

Solution

During the year, the entity issued 30,000,000 ordinary shares with a nominal value of $7,500,000. The aggregate consideration raised was $17,500,000.

The entity has three classes of shares. The directors are authorised to issue up to 6 billion ordinary shares, 700,000 7.0 per cent preference shares and 2 million 4.9 per cent preference shares. They can, therefore, issue a further 0.6 billion ordinary shares without seeking the permission of the shareholders. They can ask the shareholders to increase this limit by changing the internal regulations. The two types of preference shares are at their authorised limits and so the internal regulations would have to be changed before any further issues could be made.

The entity raised $17.5 million from a sale of 30 million shares. The shares must have been sold for 58.3 cents each. The shares have a nominal value of 25 cents each, although their value on the stock market is determined by the market's expectations of the entity's future profitability. In this case, the directors have been able to sell the shares at a premium of 58.3 − 25 = 33.3¢.

17.3 Different classes of shares

There are several different dimensions that can be used to describe and classify share capital. These include:

- authorised versus issued;
- nominal value versus issue price;
- specific classes of shares, as described in the entity's internal regulations;
- equity versus non-equity.

The precise rights attached to each class of shares is a matter for the entity's internal regulations. The usual differences can be summed up as follows:

	Ordinary shares	Preference shares
Voting rights	Ordinary shareholders almost always have the right to vote at general meetings, although some entities issue both voting and non-voting ordinary shares	Preference shareholders would not normally have any voting rights
Rewards	The ordinary dividend is decided by the directors. The ordinary shareholders are entitled to all of the profits after all other claims have been met. Any profits which are not distributed as a dividend will increase the ordinary shareholders' equity	The preference dividend is usually fixed (e.g. 7.0 per cent of nominal value). The directors may, however, be able to suspend the preference dividend if the entity could not afford to pay it. In this case, the directors will probably be required to suspend the ordinary dividend. If the preference shares are 'cumulative', then any unpaid preference dividend will be paid once the entity's circumstances permit, before the ordinary shareholders can receive any dividend
Risks	The ordinary shareholders are the last to be paid if the entity fails. In practice, this means that they may lose everything they have invested	The preference shareholders will not be paid until after all of the entity's debts have been repaid

Preference shares have become unpopular. From the shareholder's point of view, they carry a higher risk than making a loan and they do not have the potential for unlimited dividends offered by ordinary shares. This means that they have to carry a high rate of dividend to make them attractive.

From the entity's point of view, preference dividends cannot be charged as expenses for tax purposes and so they are a very expensive source of finance. There was, however, a brief period when unusual types of preference and other shares became popular as a result of a surge of interest in 'new financial instruments'. These were a means of raising finance which could be treated as share capital in the statement of financial position (thereby reducing the gearing ratio) but which gave the buyer the same rights as debt (thereby making them a cheap source of funds). Now IAS 32 and IAS 39 require these types of shares to be treated as debt in the financial statements (see below).

The disclosure requirements in respect of shares are illustrated quite fully in Exercise 17.A. Entities are required to disclose the authorised share capital and the numbers and nominal value of each class of share which has been allotted. The effects of any allotment which took place during the year should be stated. The entity also has to disclose any options which have been granted to subscribers, stating the numbers of shares involved, the period during which this right can be exercised and the price to be paid. Details also have to be given of any redeemable shares, including the terms on which redemption will take place and the dates when this may occur.

17.4 IAS 32 *Financial Instruments – Presentation*

IAS 32 was introduced to ensure that 'financial instruments' (briefly shares and loan notes) were shown in the financial statements according to their true nature. This means that there must be a clear distinction between equity (e.g. ordinary shares) and liabilities (e.g. loan notes).

The distinction must be made according to the true substance of the financial instrument. In most cases this is not too difficult. To help sort things out, IAS 32 contains several definitions:

Financial instrument: Any contract that gives rise to both a financial asset of one entity and a financial liability or equity instrument of another entity.

Equity instrument: Defined in IAS 32 as any contract that evidences a residual interest in the assets of an entity after deducting all of its liabilities, e.g. ordinary shares.

Financial liability: Any liability that is a contractual obligation to make one or more payments in the future, e.g. bonds and bank loans.

If we apply these definitions to the main elements of the long-term capital in a statement of financial position, we arrive at these conclusions:

(a) *ordinary shares* are clearly equity instruments and will always be classified as such;

(b) *loan notes and bonds* are financial liabilities and will appear as such on the statement of financial position;

(c) *preference shares* are not so easily classified. IAS 32 requires the particular rights attaching to a preference share to be analysed to determine whether it exhibits the fundamental characteristic of a financial liability. For example, if the terms of issue provide for mandatory redemption for cash, they qualify as liabilities as there is an obligation to transfer financial asssets to the holder of the share. If the preference shares are non-redeemable, the appropriate classification is based on an assessment of the substance of the contractual arrangements and the definitions of a financial liability and equity instrument. For example, if the payment of a dividend is at the discretion of the issuer they are equity shares. The classification as equity is not affected by the previous history of making dividend payments or the intention of the entity to make payments in the future. If the substance of a preference share is determined to be a liability, the preference share will be treated as debt in the statement of financial position and will be shown under non-current liabilities. The dividend paid on preference shares treated as debt must be treated as finance cost in statement of comprehensive income.

17.5 Issue of shares

17.5.1 Process

The bookkeeping entries in respect of the issue of shares are not complicated. The exact legal requirements may vary from one country to another and there may be additional requirements specified for entities quoted on the local stock exchange. In general, the procedures required to issue a share will follow a similar sequence of events. The accounting entries will follow the chronology of the share issue itself, for example:

1. The entity announces the availability of the shares and their selling price, usually in a formal document.

2. Applicants for shares submit formal requests for part of the issue. These applications will be accompanied by a proportion of the asking price, as requested by the entity in its announcement.

3. If the issue is oversubscribed, then the entity has to decide how the shares should be allocated to the applicants. Any unsuccessful applicants will have their application money returned.
4. The entity will 'allot' or formally issue the shares. The new shareholders will be asked to pay for a further proportion of the total asking price or the full balance outstanding.
5. The entity will make further 'calls' of cash until the shares have been paid for in full. The timing of these calls will be determined by the entity's needs for long-term finance.

The selling price of the shares will be set so as to make the offer attractive to potential investors, but not so attractive that the shares are significantly underpriced. If the shares are sold too cheaply, then the existing shareholders will have their investment diluted. The price is, therefore, likely to be set just below the current market price. If this exceeds the nominal value of the shares, then the difference is called the 'share premium'.

Entities usually take precautions to ensure that the issue is fully sold. If there is a risk that some shares will be left over, then the entity can pay a financial institution to underwrite the offer. In return for a premium, the underwriter will agree to buy any unpaid shares left at the closing date of the offer.

If a shareholder does not pay the amounts due on the allotment or calls, then there will usually be provisions included in the issue documents that specify that the shares will be forfeited if payment is not made when due. The entity will be entitled to sell the forfeited shares for any amount that it can get, provided the total amount paid by the original shareholder and the new owner exceeds the nominal value of the shares.

17.5.2 Accounting for the issue of shares

The simplest way to organise the bookkeeping in respect of share capital is to have one account for the nominal value of the shares which have been issued and another for the premium, if any, created when those shares were issued. The balance on these accounts increases as soon as any allotment is made or any call is requested.

The cash received on application is recorded in an 'application and allotment' account. This is like a suspense account with the balance representing the amount paid to the entity in anticipation of either the receipt of some shares or the return of the payment. Once the shares have been allotted, the cash paid on application becomes the property of the entity and the shares transferred to the new shareholders discharge the entity's commitment to them. The entries on application are:

1. Debit   Bank
    Credit   Application and allotment account
    Being recording of monies received on applications for new shares.

2. Debit   Application and allotment account
    Credit   Bank
    Being return of monies to unsuccessful applicants.

3. Debit   Application and allotment account
    Credit   Share capital
    Credit   Share premium
    Being transfer of application monies to share capital and share premium (if shares issued at a premium) on allotment of shares.

Application and allotment	
1. Cash received with applications	2. Cash returns to unsuccessful applicants
	3. Balance transferred to share capital

The allotment account is then clear and can be used to record the amount due from shareholders in respect of the entity's request for any further payments. This is recorded by crediting share capital and share premium with the amount requested and debiting the allotment account. Cash received is debited to bank and credited to allotment. The entries on allotment are:

4. Debit Application and allotment account
  Credit Share capital
  Credit Share premium
  Being amounts due on allotment.

5. Debit Bank
  Credit Application and allotment account
  Being allotment monies received.

6. Debit Investment in own shares
  Credit Application and allotment account
  Being transfer of balance of allotment monies due but not received.

Application and allotment	
4. Amount requested on allotment	5. Cash received
	6. Balance transferred to Investment – own shares

If further calls are required, a similar set of entries will be made. The amount requested will be debited to a call account and credited to share capital. Cash will be credited to the call account as it is received. If there is any balance left on the allotment or call accounts once the final deadline for receipt of payments has passed, then the shares will be forfeited. The balance on the account will be transferred to an 'investment in own shares' account. These shares will normally be reissued. Any amount received in excess of the original shareholder's default will be credited to share premium. The entries are:

10. Debit Bank
  Credit Investment in own shares
  Being amounts received on reissue of forfeited shares.

11. Debit Investment in own shares
  Credit Share premium
  Being transfer of balance to share premium.

Investment own shares	
6. Balance transferred from application and allotment	9. Balance transferred from call
10. Cash received from new shareholder	11. Balance transferred to share premium

Example 17.B

Randall had a balance on its share capital account of $2 million and a balance on share premium of $600,000. The directors decided to issue a further 500,000 $1 shares for $1.40 each.

The issue was announced and all applicants were asked to send a cheque for 10¢ for every share applied for. A total of 1,100,000 shares were applied for on the due date.

The directors decided to reject the smaller applications and returned application monies for a total of 100,000 shares. The remaining applicants were allotted one share for every two applied for, and were deemed to have paid 20¢ per share.

Applicants were asked to pay a further 90¢ per share, this being deemed to include the share premium associated with the issue. All allotment monies were received by the due date.

A final call of 30¢ per share was made. Payments were received in respect of 495,000 shares. The holder of 5,000 shares defaulted on this call and his shares were forfeited.

The forfeited shares were reissued for 50¢ each.

You are required to prepare the following accounts and enter the transactions described above.

- share capital;
- share premium;
- application and allotment;
- call;
- investment in own shares.

Solution

The entries required to record this series of transactions are as follows:

			$	$
1.	Debit	Bank	110,000	
	Credit	Application and allotment account	110,000	
	Being application monies received.			
2.	Debit	Application and allotment account	10,000	
	Credit	Bank	10,000	
	Being return of application monies.			
3.	Debit	Application and allotment account	100,000	
	Credit	Share capital		100,000
	Being allocation of shares (500,000 shares × 20¢ per share).			
4.	Debit	Bank	450,000	
	Credit	Application and allotment		450,000
	Being further monies received (500,000 shares × 90¢ per share).			
5.	Debit	Application and allotment	450,000	
	Credit	Share capital		250,000
	Credit	Share premium		200,000
	Being allocation of shares including premium of 40¢ per share.			
6.	Debit	Call account	150,000	
	Credit	Share capital	150,000	
	Being amounts due on call (500,000 shares × 30¢).			
7.	Debit	Bank	148,500	
	Credit	Call account		148,500
	Being amounts received on call (495,000 shares × 30¢).			
8.	Debit	Investment in own shares	1,500	
	Credit	Call account		1,500
	Being transfer of call monies due but not received.			

9. Debit   Bank   2,500
  Credit   Investment in own shares   2,500
  Being amounts received on reissue of shares (5,000 shares × 50¢ per share).

10. Debit   Investment in own shares   1,000
  Credit   Share premium   1,000
  Being transfer of balance to share premium account (5,000 shares reissued at further premium of 20¢, i.e. 50¢ − 30¢).

Share capital

	$		$
		Balance b/d	2,000,000
		3. Application and allotment	100,000
		5. Application and allotment	250,000
Balance c/d	2,500,000	6. Call	150,000
	2,500,000		2,500,000
		Balance b/d	2,500,000

Share premium

	$		$
		Balance b/d	600,000
		5. Application and allotment	200,000
Balance c/d	801,000	10. Investment − own share	1,000
	801,000		801,000
		Balance b/d	801,000

Application and allotment

	$		$
2. Bank	10,000	1. Bank	110,000
3. Share capital	100,000		
	110,000		110,000
5. Share capital	250,000	4. Bank	450,000
5. Share premium	200,000		
	450,000		450,000

Call

	$		$
6. Share capital	150,000	7. Bank	148,500
		8. Investment − own share	1,500
	150,000		150,000

Investment in own shares

	$		$
8. Call	1,500	9. Bank	2,500
10. Share premium	1,000		
	2,500		2,500

Bank			
	$		$
1. Application and allotment	110,000	2. Application and allotment	10,000
4. Application and allotment	450,000		
7. Call account	148,500		
8. Investment in own shares		Balance c/d	
	2,500		701,000
	711,000		711,000

Randall has raised a net total of $701,000 from the issue of shares (495,000 issued at $1.40 and 5,000 issued at $1.60).

17.5.3 Share issue costs, redemption costs and dividends

IAS 39 requires:

(i) interest, dividends, gains and losses relating to a financial liability to be recognised as an expense in the statement of comprehensive income or separate profit or loss (if presented).

This means that:

- dividends on preference shares classified as debt will be treated as an expense in the statement of comprehensive income or separate profit or loss (if presented) and included under finance cost.
- any gains/losses on redemption of a preference share classified as debt will be taken to the statement of comprehensive income or separate profit and loss (if presented) and

(ii) transaction costs of any equity transaction must be recognised in other comprehensive income.

This means that cost of issuing equity shares must be deducted from a reserve and not recognised in profit or loss. Issue costs are usually deducted from share premium, if one exists, or any other reserve. Equity dividends paid are shown in the statement of changes in equity.

IAS 1 requires that equity dividends must be declared before the end of the reporting period if they are to be recognised in the financial statements. Dividends declared after the end of the reporting period cannot be recognised in the financial statements.

17.5.4 Redeemable shares

Any shares that are redeemable for cash are defined as a financial liability. Financial liabilities finance costs are charged to profit or loss on an annual basis. IAS 32 and IAS 39 require that the total finance cost of a financial liability (from issue to redemption) be charged to profit or loss over the life of the shares in such a way as to give a constant annual rate of interest on the outstanding balance of the liability.

The total cost will include:

  (i) Any issue costs less any premiums payable on issue;
 (ii) Annual dividends;
(iii) Any redemption costs plus any premium payable on redemption.

The initial amount used to calculate the constant rate of interest is the amount of cash raised, that is, the issue price less any costs. Each year the amount of dividend paid is debited to the reserve and the finance charge (debited to profit or loss) is credited.

See Section 17.9 for a discussion on the treatment of a redemption of shares.

Example 17.C

An entity issued 1,000,000 $1 redeemable 4% preference shares at par on 1 April 2002, which was redeemable on 31 March 2006 at a 10% premium. The issue costs were $100,000.
    The constant annual rate of interest is approximately 9.283%. Ignore all tax implications.
    Calculate the total finance cost, and the annual finance charge to profit or loss.

Solution

The total finance cost is:

Issue costs	$100,000
Redemption costs ($1,000,000 × 10%)	$100,000
Annual dividends at 4% ($40,000 × 4 years)	$1,600,000
	$1,800,000

Year	Opening balance	Interest at 9.283%	Dividend at 4%	Closing balance
2002/3	900,000	83,547	40,000	943,547
2003/4	943,547	87,589	40,000	991,136
2004/5	991,136	92,007	40,000	1,043,144
2005/6	1,043,144	96,856	40,000	1,100,000

The annual finance cost is that shown under the column headed 'interest at 9.283%'

17.5.5 Convertible debt

A convertible debt must be examined to establish if it is a debt instrument, an equity instrument or both (a compound instrument).

Compound instruments must be split into its two elements, debt and equity. Each element is then accounted for separately. The value of the debt is calculated as the fair value of a similar debt instrument without the equity element. The value of the equity element is the difference between the fair value of the total instrument and the fair value of the debt element. For example, the debt element of a 10 per cent bond convertible into equity shares on a two-for-one basis after 5 years would be valued by calculating the value of a similar 10 per cent bond without the conversion. This would be deducted from the value of the bond to give the value of the equity element.

17.6 Bonus issues

17.6.1 Process

An entity can convert part of its reserves into shares. These shares can then be given to the existing shareholders in proportion to their holdings at the time of the issue. These 'free shares' are often called bonus shares but may be given other names in some countries.

For example, X might give its shareholders one fully paid $1 ordinary share for every two that they had previously held. If the entity had 1,000,000 ordinary shares outstanding before the issue, then share capital would increase to 1,500,000 shares of $1, or $1,500,000. This credit to share capital would have a corresponding debit of $500,000 to reserves.

Example 17.D

How would a bonus issue affect:

- the market price of shares? (up or down);
- distributable profits? (up or down).

Common sense suggests that the share price would fall in proportion to the size of the issue. Thus a market price of $2.40 before a two-for-one issue would fall to $1.60 immediately after. Two shares before the issue would have been worth $4.80, the same as three shares held afterwards. It is, however, *possible* that the stock market will react positively to the announcement of the bonus because there is a tendency for entities to increase dividend payments after making these issues. Of course, this price change would be because of the expected increase in dividends rather than the increase in the number of shares.

If the reserve account which was debited with the value of the bonus is part of distributable profits, then this will reduce the maximum dividend. This might, therefore, provide lenders with a measure of protection because a greater proportion of the entity's equity is being locked in'. The buffer effect referred to earlier will, therefore, be enhanced. Of course, it is highly unlikely that the entity would make a bonus issue if doing so would severely limit its ability to pay dividends. Thus, the size of a bonus issue is likely to be small in relation to total reserves.

17.6.2 Accounting for a bonus issue

Example 17.E

The directors of A have decided to make a bonus issue of one share for every three previously held. The entity's statement of financial position just before the issue was as follows:

A – statement of financial position as at 31 December 20X2

	$m
Non-current assets	14
Current assets	4
	18
Share capital	9
Retained earnings	4
	13
Liabilities	5
	18

You are required to redraft A's statement of financial position to take the bonus issue into account. Show the journal entry required to bring about your change.

Solution

The share capital will increase by one-third. This means that share capital will increase and the retained earnings decrease by $3 million. This can be shown as a journal entry:

		$m	$m
Debit	Retained earnings	3	
Credit	Share capital		3

The statement of financial position would, therefore, become:

A – statement of financial position as at 31 December 20X2

	$m
Non-current assets	14
Working capital	4
	18
Share capital	12
Accumulated profits	1
	13
Liabilities	5
	18

17.7 Accounting for a rights issue

If an entity issues new shares for cash, it is often required to first offer them to its existing ordinary shareholders in proportion to their shareholdings. This is called a rights issue.

Example 17.F

Using the information provided above in Example 17.E and assuming that the share capital consists of 9 million $1 shares, let us assume the directors of A decide to make a rights issue instead of a bonus issue. The terms of the rights issue are one for every three shares held at $1.20.

Assuming that all the shareholders take up the rights, the transaction would be recorded as follows:

		$m	$m
Debit	Cash	3.6	
Credit	Share capital		3.0
Credit	Share premium		0.6

The rights issue would generate new funds. At a one-for-three rights issue, 3 million new shares would be issued and the balance raised would be credited to share premium.

The new statement of financial position would be:

A – statement of financial position as at 31 December 20X2

	$m
Non-current assets	14.0
Working capital	7.6
	21.6
Share capital	12.0
Share premium	0.6
Accumulated profits	4.0
	16.6
Liabilities	5.0
	21.6

17.8 Accounting for treasury shares

Where an entity acquires its own equity shares, and at the end of the reporting period has not cancelled them, they are referred to as treasury shares.

IAS 32 states that any change in equity resulting from the purchase, sale, issue and cancellation of the entity's own shares should not result in any gain or loss being recognised in profit or loss. Where an entity reacquires its own shares, it should be recorded as a change in equity and the reacquired shares should be reclassified as treasury shares and shown as a deduction from equity. This should be shown in the statement of financial position or in the notes to the financial statements. The transaction would then be included within the statement of changes in equity.

Example 17.G

Murray has 1 million $1 ordinary shares in issue at 31 December 20 × 1. The equity and reserves included the following:

Equity and reserves	$'000
Share capital, $1 shares, fully paid	1,000
Share premium	600
Retained earnings	500
	2,100

In the year to 31 December 20X2, the entity reacquired 300,000 of its shares for $1.30 each. Retained profit for 20X2 was $60,000.

IAS 32 requires that no gain or loss be recorded on the reacquisition of an entity's own shares. Instead, the full amount of issued capital will remain on the statement of financial position and the shares reacquired and held by the entity (and reclassified as treasury shares) will be shown as a deduction from equity. The presentation of this is reasonably flexible. The simplest presentation is to show the total cost of redemption as a deduction from total equity. This could be presented as follows:

Equity and reserves	$'000
Share capital, $1 shares, fully paid	1,000
Share premium	600
	1,600
Treasury shares	(390)
	1,210
Retained earnings	560
Total equity and reserves	1,770

Alternative presentations include showing the deduction for the nominal value of treasury shares against share capital and the premium paid on redemption against share premium.

17.9   The purchase and redemption of shares

One of the basic principles followed in most countries is that the equity capital invested by the shareholders cannot normally be repaid or distributed to the shareholders unless the entity is wound up.

Dividends payments are normally restricted to being paid out of 'distributable' reserves which are, at least essentially, equivalent to retained earnings. This protects the lenders and creditors from the possibility that the entity could use an excessive dividend to reduce the equity base and leave the liabilities uncovered by assets.

While these regulations have a very clear purpose, they may prove unduly restrictive. If an entity is not quoted on a stock market, then it would be difficult for shareholders to sell their investments. It might be preferable for a small entity to be able to buy out individual shareholders rather than have them sell their shares to an outsider. There is, therefore, often some scope in the local legal regulations for the reduction of share capital, subject to some stringent safeguards.

The basic principle almost universally applied is that the equity capital has a 'permanent' component which can never be repaid unless the entity is wound up. Entities can either purchase or redeem their shares, but must normally do so in such a way that this 'permanent' capital is preserved. There are few exceptions to this general rule.

17.9.1 Purchases out of distributable profits

In the simplest possible case an entity can buy back its shares. It is usually required to ensure that equity capital is maintained. This can be achieved by making a transfer from distributable reserves to a reserve that is usually legally classified as non-distributable. This reserve could be called a 'capital redemption reserve' or a capital reserve. This is best illustrated by an example:

Example 17.H

Peters: statement of financial position as at 30 September 20X5

	$'000
Net assets	4,000
Share capital – $1 shares, fully paid	2,000
Share premium	500
Permanent capital	2,500
Distributable profit	1,500
	4,000

The entity is owned by the Peters family, one of whose members wants to sell her shares and retire. The other shareholders are keen to keep all of the entity's shares in the family, but none can afford to buy the retiring shareholder's equity. It has, therefore, been decided that the entity will purchase 100,000 shares for $180,000. This requires two journal entries:

	$	$
Debit Share capital	100,000	
Premium on purchase	80,000	
Credit Bank		180,000
Debit Distributable profits	180,000	
Credit Premium on purchase		80,000
Capital redemption reserve		100,000

The first journal reduces both bank and share capital by the appropriate amounts. The premium on purchase account is used to maintain double entry. The balance on this account will be cancelled by the next step.

The second journal is required to make a transfer from distributable profits which is equal to the amount paid for the purchase of the shares. The corresponding credits go to premium on purchase and capital redemption reserve. These transactions and adjustments would have the following effect on Peters's statement of financial position.

Peters: statement of financial position as at 30 September 20X5

	$'000
Net assets	3,820
Share capital $1 shares, fully paid	1,900
Share premium	500
Capital redemption reserve	100
Permanent capital	2,500
Distributable profit	1,320
	3,820

 Exercise

Look back at the above example. How has the transfer to the capital redemption reserve protected Peters's creditors?

Solution

Clearly, both the entity's capital and net assets have been reduced by $180,000. The transfer to capital redemption reserve has, however, used part of the entity's distributable profits to replace the permanent capital which was used to make the repurchase. The lenders' security will have been affected by the outflow of cash and the reduction of equity. This could, however, have happened anyway if the directors had decided to pay a dividend of $180,000.

It is never going to be in the lenders' interests for the entity to return equity to the shareholders, whether this is accomplished by either dividend or the repurchase of shares. There is, however, some protection from the fact that distributable profits place an upper limit on such payments. Entities can also purchase their own shares from the proceeds of a new share issue. This could be done to repay redeemable shares when they are due for repayment; to 'tidy' up the statement of financial position, that is, redeem separate classes of shares and issue one new class, or to reduce the amount of committed dividends that are required to be paid by redeeming high dividend preference shares and replacing them with lower dividend preference shares or equity. For example:

Example 17.1

ABC: statement of financial position as at 30 September 20X5

	$'000
Net assets	4,000
Share capital $1 equity shares, fully paid	1,500
10% Preference shares (redeemable)	1,000
Permanent capital	2,500
Retained earnings	1,500
	4,000

ABC need to redeem their redeemable preference shares. The preference shares are redeemable for $1.50 per share.

ABC are raising the cash required for the purchase by an issue of 750 $1 equity shares at $2.00 per share.

Prepare ABC's statement of financial position after the redemption of the preference shares.

Solution

Cost of redemption is 1,000 shares at $1.50 equals $1,500. $1,000 is debited to preference share capital and the balance, $500, will be debited to retained earnings.

The issue will raise 750 times $2, $1,500 in cash. This will be allocated to equity: share capital $750 and share premium $750.

The cash raised will be used to redeem the preference shares: debit bank $1,500 and credit bank $1,500.

The statement of financial position after the transactions have taken place will be:

ABC: statement of financial position as at 30 September 20X5

	$'000
Net assets	4,000
Share capital – $1 equity shares, fully paid (1,500 + 750)	2,250
10% Preference shares (redeemable)	0
Share premium	750
Permanent capital	3,000
Retained earnings (1,500 – 500)	1,000
	4,000

Note that in this case the permanent capital is maintained and there is no requirement to make a transfer from retained earnings to a capital reserve. There are often quite complex regulations regarding share redemptions and how much must be transferred to a capital reserve. There are also variations in the treatment of cash raised by a new issue. In some cases, the full amount of the issue proceeds are counted and in others only the equity element is counted.

> If you are not told otherwise in the question, in exam questions you should assume that the nominal amount of the share capital will be maintained and if it is not covered by a new issue it must be appropriated from retained earnings.

17.10 Summary

Having completed this chapter, we can now explain the disclosure requirements of both IAS 1 and IAS 32, and we can discuss the main characteristics of equity and non-equity share capital.

We can account for the issue of shares, including a bonus issue and a rights issue, and can account for the purchase and redemption of shares.

Revision Questions

Question 1

ZZ redeemed their redeemable preference shares with a cash payment, paying a premium of 20 per cent.

Nominal value of shares redeemed	$70,000
Cash paid on redemption	$84,000

How much should be transferred to the capital redemption reserve (CRR) and how much should be charged to distributable reserves?

	CRR	Distributable reserves
(A)	$70,000	$14,000
(B)	$84,000	$84,000
(C)	$70,000	$84,000
(D)	$84,000	$70,000

(2 marks)

Question 2

Ordinary shares are usually classified as:

(A) Equity shares
(B) Non-equity shares
(C) Loans
(D) Deferred shares   **(2 marks)**

Question 3

Which type of financial instrument has the following characteristics?
– they do not normally have any voting rights;
– they usually have a fixed rate of return;
– they are ranked after unsecured creditors;
– the return can be suspended by directors, but will have to be paid in later years.

(A) Convertible stock
(B) Ordinary shares
(C) Preference shares
(D) Cumulative preference shares   **(2 marks)**

Question 4

BN is a listed entity and has the following balances included on its opening statement of financial position:

	$'000
Equity and reserves:	
Equity shares, $1 shares, fully paid	750
Share premium	250
Retained earnings	500
	1,500

BN reacquired 100,000 of its shares and classified them as 'treasury shares'. BN still held the treasury shares at the year end.

How should BN classify the treasury shares on its closing statement of financial position in accordance with IAS 32 *Financial instruments – disclosure and presentation?*

(A) As a non-current asset investment.
(B) As a deduction from equity.
(C) As a current asset investment.
(D) As a non-current liability.   **(2 marks)**

Question 5

Treasury shares are defined as

(A) equity shares sold by an entity in the period.
(B) equity shares repurchased by the issuing entity, not cancelled before the period end.
(C) non-equity shares sold by an entity in the period.
(D) equity shares repurchased by the issuing entity and cancelled before the period end.

                                                                       (2 marks)

Question 6

The directors of Alpha have decided to make a bonus issue of one for every five shares held by existing shareholders. The statement of financial position of Alpha immediately before the issue was as follows:

Alpha: statement of financial position as at 31 December 20X9

	$'000
Non-current assets	10,500
Working capital	4,800
	15,300
Share capital	10,000
Retained earnings	2,300
	12,300
Liabilities	3,000
	15,300

Share capital consists of 20 million 50¢ ordinary shares.

Requirement

Prepare the accounting entry that records the bonus issue and redraft the statement of financial position immediately after the bonus issue takes place.   **(5 marks)**

? Question 7

The directors of Beta have decided to make a rights issue of two for every five shares held by existing shareholders at $1.15. All the existing shareholders have chosen to take up this offer. The statement of financial position of Beta immediately before the issue was as follows:

Beta: statement of financial position as at 31 December 20X9

	$'000
Non-current assets	15,500
Current assets	8,800
	24,300
Share capital	15,000
Retained earnings	4,300
	19,300
Liabilities	5,000
	24,300

Share capital consists of 15 million $1 ordinary shares.

Requirement

Prepare the accounting entry that records the rights issue and redraft the statement of financial position immediately after the rights issue takes place.   **(5 marks)**

? Question 8

CR issued 200,000 $10 redeemable 5% preference shares at par on 1 April 2005. The shares were redeemable on 31 March 2010 at a premium of 15%. Issue costs amounted to $192,800.

Requirements

(a) Calculate the total finance cost over the life of the preference share.   **(2 marks)**
(b) Calculate the annual charge to profit or loss for finance expense, as required by IAS 39 *Financial Instruments: Recognition and Measurement*, for each of the five years 2006 to 2010. Assume the constant annual rate of interest as 10%.   **(3 marks)**

(Total marks = 5)

Question 9

Optima issued 500,000 $1 ordinary shares for $1.30 on 1 August 20X2. At the end of the reporting period, 31 December 20X2 all the shares issued were fully paid. Costs related to this issue totalled $60,000 and the financial accountant has charged this amount to finance costs in profit or loss. The retained profit for the year as per the draft accounts is $210,000. The equity and reserves of Optima at 31 December 20X1 was as follows:

	$'000
Equity and reserves	
Share capital, $1 shares, fully paid	3,500
Share premium	600
Revaluation reserves	400
Retained earnings	940
	5,440

Requirement

Prepare the accounting adjustments required to ensure that the costs of this share issue are recorded correctly and draft the equity and reserves section of the statement of financial position for inclusion in the financial statements for the year ended 31 December 20X2.

(10 marks)

Solutions to Revision Questions

 Solution 1

The correct answer is (C), see Section 17.9.

Nominal share capital has reduced by $70,000, therefore CRR is credited with $70,000. The cash paid, including the premium, is $84,000, and this needs to be charged to distributable reserves.

 Solution 2

The correct answer is (A), see Section 17.3.

 Solution 3

The correct answer is (D), see Section 17.3.

 Solution 4

The correct answer is (B), see Section 17.8.

 Solution 5

The correct answer is (B), see Section 17.8.

 Solution 6

Share capital will increase by one-fifth. Share capital will increase by $2 million and accumulated profits will reduce by $2 million. The transaction would be recorded as follows:

		$m	$m
Debit	Accumulated profits	2m	
Credit	Share capital		2m

The new statement of financial position would be as follows:

Alpha: statement of financial position as at 31 December 20X9

	$'000
Non-current assets	10,500
Working capital	4,800
	15,300
Share capital	12,000
Accumulated profits	300
	12,300
Liabilities	3,000
	15,300

See Section 17.6.2.

 ## Solution 7

Assuming that all the shareholders take up the rights, then 6 million new shares are created. The transaction would be recorded as follows:

		$m	$m
Debit	Cash	6.9	
Credit	Share capital		6.0
Credit	Share premium		0.9

The rights issue would generate new funds. At a two-for-five rights issue, 6 million new shares would be issued and the balance raised would be credited to share premium.

The new statement of financial position would be as follows:

Beta: statement of financial position as at 31 December 20X9

	$'000
Non-current assets	15,500
Working capital	15,700
	31,200
Share capital	21,000
Share premium	900
Retained earnings	4,300
	26,200
Liabilities	5,000
	31,200

See Section 17.7.

 ## Solution 8

(a) The total finance cost is:

	$
Issue costs	192,800
Annual dividend (200,000 × $10 × 5%) × 5	500,000
Redemption cost (200,000 × $10 × 15%)	300,000
	992,800

(b)

	Balance b/fwd	Finance cost 10%	Dividend paid	Redemption	Balance c/fwd
	$	$	$	$	$
2005/06	1,807,200	180,720	−100,000		1,887,920
2006/07	1,887,920	188,792	−100,000		1,976,712
2007/08	1,976,712	197,671	−100,000		2,074,383
2008/09	2,074,383	207,438	−100,000		2,181,821
2009/10	2,181,821	218,179	−100,000		2,300,000
31/10/2010	2,300,000			−2,300,000	0

Note: Finance cost in 2009/10 includes a rounding adjustment of −$3, See Section 17.5.4.

 Solution 9

The financial accountant has recorded the issue costs as:

Dr	Finance costs	$60,000
Cr	Bank	$60,000

Being the recording of the share issue costs.

The standard requires that costs relating to a new issue of equity should be offset against share premium rather than being charged to profit or loss. The entry that should have been recorded by the accountant was:

Dr	Share premium	$60,000
Cr	Bank	$60,000

Being the recording of the share issue costs.

The bank entry that has been posted is correct. The charge to finance costs, however, should be reversed and the costs debited against share premium in accordance with the standard. The correcting entry is:

Dr	Share premium	$60,000
Cr	Finance costs	$60,000

Being the correcting entry to record the share issue costs.

Extract from the statement of financial position of Optima as at 31 December 20X2

Equity and reserves	$'000
Share capital, $1 shares, fully paid	4,000
Share premium (see workings)	690
Revaluation reserves	400
Retained earnings (see workings)	1,210
	6,300

SHARE CAPITAL TRANSACTIONS

Workings

Share premium	$'000
As at 31/12/X1	600
Premium on issue in 20X1	150
(500K shares × 30 cents)	
Less issue costs	(60)
As at 31/12/X2	690

Retained earnings	$'000
As at 31/12/X1	940
Profit per draft accounts	210
Plus the add back of the issue costs incorrectly charged within finance costs in arriving at profit	60
As at 31/12/X2	1,210

18

Recognition and Disclosure of Other Significant Accounting Transactions

Recognition and Disclosure of Other Significant Accounting Transactions

18

The syllabus topics covered in this chapter are as follows:

- post-balance sheet events (IAS 10),
- provisions and contingencies (IAS 37),
- the disclosure of related parties to a business (IAS 24).

18.1 Introduction

In this chapter, we cover three IASs which deal with various aspects of recognition and disclosure of other significant transactions. They are:

- IAS 10 *Events After the Reporting Period*,
- IAS 37 *Provisions, Contingent Liabilities and Contingent Assets*,
- IAS 24 *Related Party Disclosures*.

18.2 IAS 10 *Events After the Reporting Period*

18.2.1 Introduction

It is a fundamental principle of accounting that regard must be had to all available information when preparing financial statements. This must include relevant events occurring after the reporting period, up to the date on which the financial statements are authorised for issue. The objective of IAS 10 is to:

- define the extent to which different types of events after the reporting period are to be reflected in financial statements;
- define when an entity should adjust its financial statements for events after the reporting period;
- set out the disclosures that the entity should provide about the date the statement of financial position was authorised;
- specify disclosures required about events arising after the end of the reporting period.

18.2.2 Definitions

IAS 10 defines an event after the end of the reporting period as 'events after the end of the reporting period are those events, favourable and unfavourable, that occur between the end of the reporting period and the date when the financial statements are authorised for issue.'

IAS 10 identifies two main types of events after the reporting period: adjusting events and non-adjusting events.

18.2.3 Adjusting events

These are 'events which provide evidence of conditions that existed at the end of the reporting period'. They require changes in amounts to be included in financial statements, because financial statements should reflect all available evidence as to conditions existing at the end of the reporting period.

Examples of *adjusting events* are:

1. *Non-current assets.* The subsequent determination of the purchase price or of the proceeds of sale of assets purchased or sold before the year-end.
2. *Property.* A valuation which provides evidence of a permanent diminution in value.
3. *Investments.* The receipt of a copy of the financial statements or other information in respect of an unlisted entity which provides evidence of a permanent diminution in the value of a long-term investment.
4. *Inventories and work in progress.*
   - The receipt of proceeds of sales after the end of the reporting period or other evidence concerning the net realisable value of inventories.
   - The receipt of evidence that the previous estimate of accrued profit on a long-term construction contract was materially inaccurate.
5. *Receivables.* The renegotiation of amounts owing by customers, or the insolvency of a customer.
6. *Taxation.* The receipt of information regarding rates of taxation.
7. *Claims.* Amounts received or receivable in respect of insurance claims, which were in the course of negotiation at the end of the reporting period.
8. *Obligations.* The settlement after the end of the reporting period of a court case that confirms that the entity had a present obligation at the end of the reporting period.
9. *Discoveries.* The discovery of errors or frauds which show that the financial statements were incorrect.

18.2.4 Non-adjusting events

Non-adjusting events are events that are indicative of conditions that arose after the end of the reporting period. Consequently, they do not result in changes in amounts in financial statements.

Although non-adjusting events do not lead to changes in amounts in financial statements, they should still be disclosed by note, if material.

Examples of *non-adjusting events* are:

1. issues of shares and loan notes;
2. purchases and sales of non-current assets and investments;
3. losses of fixed assets or inventories as a result of a catastrophe, such as fire or flood;
4. opening new trading activities or extending existing trading activities;
5. closing a significant part of the trading activities if this was not anticipated at the year end;
6. decline in the value of property and investments held as non-current assets, if it can be demonstrated that the decline occurred after the year-end;
7. government action, such as nationalisation;
8. strikes and other labour disputes.

18.3 Proposed dividends

IAS 10 was revised in 1999 and 2003, an important change made in 1999 and reinforced in 2003 was to prevent proposed equity dividends being recognised as liabilities unless they are declared before the end of the reporting period. Declared means that the dividend is appropriately authorised, and is no longer at the discretion of the entity.

> IAS 1 requires the disclosure by note to the financial statements of the amounts of dividends proposed or declared before the financial statements were authorised for issue but not recognised as a distribution to owners during the period. It is, of course, unusual for entities to propose or declare a final dividend before the end of the reporting period.

18.4 Going concern

If management determines after the end of the reporting period that it is necessary to liquidate the entity or cease trading, or that it has no realistic alternative but to do so, the financial statements should not be prepared on a going-concern basis.

18.5 Disclosure requirements of IAS 10

(a) *Events after the end of the reporting period requiring changes to the financial statements.* A material adjusting event after the end of the reporting period requires changes to the financial statements.

(b) *Events after the end of the reporting period requiring disclosure by note.* A material event after the end of the reporting period should be disclosed [by note] where it is a non-adjusting event of such importance that its non-disclosure would affect the ability of users of financial statements to reach a proper understanding of the financial position.

The note should disclose the nature of the event and an estimate of the financial effect, or a statement that it is not practicable to make such an estimate. The estimate should be made before taking account of taxation, with an explanation of the taxation implications where necessary for a proper understanding of the financial position.

(c) *Date directors approve financial statements.* The date on which the financial statements are authorised for issue should be disclosed.

18.6 IAS 37 Provisions, Contingent Liabilities and Contingent Assets

18.6.1 Introduction

IAS 37 *Provisions, Contingent Liabilities and Contingent Assets* regulates the recognition and disclosure of provisions and contingencies. For your examination, you need to understand the principles relating to provisions, contingent liabilities and contingent assets and be able to apply those principles.

18.6.2 Provisions

The term 'provision' is defined in IAS 37 as 'a liability of uncertain timing or amount'. The main objectives of IAS 37 in this area are to ensure that entities make provisions for all such liabilities and do not make excessive provisions.

A provision should be recognised when, and only when:

(a) an entity has a present obligation (legal or constructive) as a result of a past event;
(b) it is probable (i.e. more likely than not) that an outflow of resources embodying economic benefits will be required to settle the obligation; and
(c) a reliable estimate can be made of the amount of the obligation.

(a) *An entity has a present obligation (legal or constructive) arising from a past event:*
- There is a present obligation if it is more likely than not that an obligation exists at the end of the reporting period.
- A legal obligation could arise from a contract, legislation or other legal requirement.
- A constructive obligation derives from the entity's actions:
  ○ by an established pattern of past practice, published policies or a sufficiently specific current statement, the entity has indicated to current parties that it will accept certain responsibilities; and
  ○ as a result, the entity has created a valid expectation on the part of those other parties that it will discharge those responsibilities.

(b) *It is probable (i.e. more likely than not) that an outflow of resources embodying economic benefits will be required to settle the obligation:*
- A transfer of economic benefits is regarded as probable if it is more likely than not to occur.
- Where there are a number of similar obligations the probability that a transfer will be required is determined by considering the class of obligations as a whole, for example, warranties.

(c) *A reliable estimate can be made of the amount:*
  • If it is not possible to make a reliable estimate, a provision cannot be made. The item must be disclosed as a contingent liability. IAS 37 notes that it is only in extremely rare cases that a reliable estimate will not be possible.

A reimbursement from a third party, to pay for part or all of the expenditure provided as a provision should only be recognised if it is reasonably certain that it will be received. If it is recognised, it should be treated as a separate asset, rather than set off against the provision.

18.6.3 Measurement of provisions

The amount recognised should be the best estimate of expenditure required to settle the obligation at the end of the reporting period.

– if the obligation is one item, the most likely outcome is the best estimate
– if the provision involves a large number of items, the estimate should be made using expected values, see 18.6.5.

18.6.4 Provision for decommissioning costs

When a facility such as an oil well or a mine is authorised by the government, the licence normally includes a legal obligation for the entity to decommission the facility at the end of its useful life. IAS 37 requires a provision for decommissioning costs to be recognised immediately after the facility commences operation. The provision will be debited to the cost of the asset and credited to provisions. Where the decommissioning cost occurs several years in the future and is material, the amount should be discounted to present value and the discounted amount provided for. The discount must be recalculated each year. The unwinding of the discount is charged to profit or loss under the heading of finance cost and credited to the provision.

18.6.5 Provision for warranties

If an entity sells goods and provides a warranty against faults occurring after sale, a provision needs to be created for the future warranty claims. The process is known as *expected values* and uses estimates of the likely cost and the probability of it occurring.

Example 18.1

An entity provides a one-year warranty on its goods. The entity estimates that at the year-end if all goods needed minor repairs, the cost would be $4 million and if all goods needed major repairs, the cost would be $15 million. The probability of goods needing no repair 90% minor repair 8% and major repair 2%.

Calculate the provision for warranty claims.

Solution

The amount, using expected values is ($4m × 0.08) + ($15m × 0.02) = $620,000

For each class of provision, the financial statements should disclose, if material:

(a) the opening and closing balance;
(b) additional provisions made in the period;
(c) amounts used (i.e. incurred and charged against the provision);
(d) details of the nature of the obligation provided for, including expected timing and any uncertainties relating to the obligation.

A provision once created, can only be used for expenditures for which the provision was originally recognised. Any unused provision is credited to profit or loss when it is no longer required.

18.7 Contingent liabilities and contingent assets

A contingent liability is:

(i) a possible obligation that arises from past events and whose existence will be confirmed only by the occurrence of one or more uncertain future events not wholly within the control of the entity; or
(ii) a present obligation that arises from past events but is not recognised because it is not probable that a transfer of economic benefits will be required to settle the obligation; or the amount of the obligation cannot be measured with sufficient reliability.

A contingent asset is:

A possible asset that arises from past events and whose existence will be confirmed only by the occurrence or non-occurrence of one or more uncertain future events not wholly within the control of the entity.

The accounting treatment of contingent liabilities and contingent assets depends upon the degree of probability. The following table shows the requirements.

Likelihood of occurrence	Material contingent asset	Material contingent liability
Remote	No disclosure allowed*	No disclosure
Possible	No disclosure allowed*	Disclose by note
Probable	Disclose by note	In these two categories the contingent
Virtually certain	Accrual	liability requires a provision

* Note that disclosure is not allowed for 'remote' or 'possible' contingent gains. The prudence concept dictates that contingent gains are treated with more caution than contigent losses.

When a contingency is disclosed by note, the following information should be given:

(i) the nature of the contingency;
(ii) an estimate of the financial effect.

The following extract illustrates these disclosure requirements, as it describes the nature of the contingency and the financial effect of it.

Extract from the consolidated accounts of the Nestlé Group for the year ended 31 December 2005

Notes to the accounts
35. Contingent assets and liabilities
The Group is exposed to contingent liabilities amounting to CHF 870 million (2004: CHF 690 million) representing various potential litigations (CHF 784 million) and other items (CHF 86 million). Contingent assets for litigation claims in favour of the Group amount to CHF 258 million (2004: CHF 170 million).

18.8 Problems with IAS 37 as regards contingencies

(a) *Determining level of probability.* It must be a matter of judgement in many cases to determine the appropriate level of probability of an event, and hence the appropriate accounting treatment of it. Opinion is bound to differ both as to the percentage probability of an event and as to the category a given percentage should be placed into. *UK GAAP,* an authoritative work on accounting standards and practice in the UK, suggests an answer to the second of these uncertainties by proposing the following:

Likelihood of outcome	Level of probability
Remote	0–5%
Possible	5–50%
Probable	50–95%
Virtually certain	95–100%

(b) *Disclosure of information* about a claim which may prejudice the settlement of that claim. Entities will typically attempt to limit damage to their cause by including in the disclosure note a statement declaring that the claims will be strenuously resisted.

(c) *Counterclaims.* An entity may have a contingent liability for a claim against it which is matched by a counterclaim or a claim by the entity against a third party. The likelihood of success, and the probable amounts of the claim and the counterclaim, should be separately assessed and disclosed where appropriate. For example, an entity might have an action brought against it which it could in turn bring against a subcontractor. If the subcontractor had no material assets, the claim would, if successful, fall upon the entity, with no practical recourse to the subcontractor.

18.9 Related party disclosures

IAS 24 *Related Party Disclosures* was issued in March 1984, reformatted in 1994 and updated in 2003. The objective of the standard is to ensure that financial statements disclose to shareholders the effect of the existence of related parties, any material transactions with them and any outstanding balances.

In the absence of information to the contrary, we assume that an organisation has independent discretionary power over its transactions and resources, and pursues its activities independently of the interests of its owners, managers and others. We presume that transactions have been undertaken 'at arm's length'.

These assumptions may not be justified when related party relationships exist, because the requisite conditions for competitive, free-market dealings may not be present. The parties themselves may endeavour to trade at arm's length, but the very nature of the relationship may preclude this. Even when trading does take place at arm's length, it is still useful to report on the nature of the relationship.

18.10 Definitions

IAS 24 includes the following definitions:

Related party: A party is related to an entity if:

(a) directly, or indirectly through one or more intermediaries, the party:
  (i) controls, is controlled by, or is under common control with the entity (this includes parents, subsidiaries and fellow subsidiaries);
  (ii) has an interest in the entity that gives it significant influence over the entity; or
  (iii) has joint control over the entity;
(b) the party is an associate (as defined in IAS 28 Investments in Associates) of the entity;
(c) the party is a joint venture in which the entity is a venturer (see IAS 31 *Interests in Joint Ventures*);
(d) the party is a member of the key management personnel of the entity or its parent;
(e) the party is a close member of the family of any individual referred to in (a) or (d);
(f) the party is an entity that is controlled, jointly controlled or significantly influenced by, or for which significant voting power in such entity resides with, directly or indirectly, any individual referred to in (d) or (e); or
(g) the party is a post-employment benefit plan for the benefit of employees of the entity, or of any entity that is a related party of the entity.

Note: Parents, subsidiaries, associates, joint ventures and post-retirement benefits are all outside the scope of your syllabus.

Related party transaction: A transfer of resources or obligations between related parties, regardless of whether a price is charged.

You can see from the above definition that 'related parties' include entities in the same group as the reporting entity, associated entities, directors and their close families, and pension funds for the benefit of employees of the reporting entity. In addition, key managers and those controlling 20 per cent or more of the voting rights are presumed to be related parties unless it can be demonstrated that neither party has influenced the financial and operating policies of the other in such a way as to inhibit the pursuit of separate interests.

18.10.1 Exclusions

In the context of this standard, the following are not necessarily related parties:

(a) two entities simply because they have a director or other member of key management personnel in common, notwithstanding (d) and (f) in the definition of 'related party'.
(b) two venturers simply because they share joint control over a joint venture.
(c) (i) providers of finance;
  (ii) trade unions;
  (iii) public utilities; and
  (iv) government departments and agencies.
    Simply by virtue of their normal dealings with an entity (even though they may affect the freedom of action of an entity or participate in its decision-making process); and
(d) a customer, supplier, franchisor, distributor or general agent with whom an entity transacts a significant volume of business, merely by virtue of the resulting economic dependence.

18.11 Disclosure

The standard concerns the disclosure of related party transactions in order to make readers of financial statements aware of the position and to ensure that the financial statements show a true and fair view.

18.11.1 Disclosure of control

Related party relationships where control exists should be disclosed irrespective of whether any transactions took place.

18.11.2 Disclosure of transactions and balances

If there have been transactions between related parties, an entity shall disclose the nature of the related party relationship as well as information about the transactions and outstanding balances necessary for an understanding of the potential effect of the relationship on the financial statements.

Disclosures that related party transactions were made on terms equivalent to those that prevail in arm's length transactions are made only if such terms can be substantiated.

At a minimum, disclosures shall include:

(a) the amount of the transactions;
(b) the amount of outstanding balances:
   (i) their terms and conditions, including whether they are secured, and the nature of the consideration to be provided in settlement;
   (ii) details of any guarantees given or received;
(c) provisions for doubtful debts related to the amount of outstanding balances;
(d) the expense recognised during the period in respect of bad or doubtful debts due from related parties.

In addition, IAS 24 requires an entity to disclose key management personnel compensation in total and for each of the following categories:

(a) short-term employee benefits;
(b) post-employment benefits;
(c) other long-term benefits;
(d) termination benefits;
(e) equity compensation benefits.

18.11.3 Examples of related party transactions

- purchases or sales of goods;
- purchases or sales of property and other assets;
- rendering or receipt of services;
- agency arrangements;
- leasing arrangements;
- management contracts;
- any of these or similar transactions would require to be disclosed if material;

- transfers of research and development;
- transfers under licence agreements;
- transfers under finance arrangements (including loans and equity contributions in cash or in kind);
- provision of guarantees or collateral;
- settlement of liabilities on behalf of the entity or by the entity on behalf of another party.

18.12 Summary

Having completed this chapter, we can now account for adjusting and non-adjusting events occurring after the end of the reporting period and can discuss the principles of recognising provisions and can define and account for contingencies.

We can define related parties and related party transactions and can explain the disclosures required by IAS 24 *Related Party Disclosures*.

Revision Questions

18

? Question 1

Which of the following could be classified as an adjusting event occurring after the end of the reporting period:

(A) A serious fire, occurring 1 month after the year-end, that damaged the sole production facility, causing production to cease for 3 months.

(B) One month after the year-end, a notification was received advising that the large balance on a receivable would not be paid as the customer was being wound up. No payments are expected from the customer.

(C) A large quantity of parts for a discontinued production line was discovered at the back of the warehouse during the year-end inventory count. The parts have no value except a nominal scrap value and need to be written off.

(D) The entity took delivery of a new machine from the USA in the last week of the financial year. It was discovered almost immediately afterwards that the entity supplying the machine had filed for bankruptcy and would not be able to honour the warranties and repair contract on the new machine. Because the machine was so advanced, it was unlikely that any local entity could provide maintenance cover. **(2 marks)**

? Question 2

X is currently defending two legal actions:

(i) An employee, who suffered severe acid burns as a result of an accident in X's factory, is suing for $20,000, claiming that the directors failed to provide adequate safety equipment. X's lawyers are contesting the claim, but have advised the directors that they will probably lose.

(ii) A customer is suing for $50,000, claiming that X's hair-care products damaged her hair. X's lawyers are contesting this claim, and have advised that the claim is unlikely to succeed.

How much should X provide for these legal claims in its financial statements?

(A) $0
(B) $20,000
(C) $50,000
(D) $70,000 **(2 marks)**

? Question 3

Which of the following could be regarded as a related party of X:

(A) P is X's main customer, taking 50 per cent of their turnover.
(B) S is X's main supplier, supplying approximately 40 per cent of X's purchases.
(C) A is the managing director of X and is the largest single shareholder, holding 35 per cent of the equity.
(D) B is X's banker and has provided X with an overdraft facility and a short-term loan.

(2 marks)

? Question 4

Which ONE of the following would be regarded as a related party of BS:

(A) BX, a customer of BS.
(B) The president of the BS Board, who is also the chief executive officer of another entity, BU, that supplies goods to BS.
(C) BQ, a supplier of BS.
(D) BY, BS's main banker.

(2 marks)

? Question 5

Which ONE of the following would require a provision to be created by BW at the end of it's reporting period, 31 October 2005:

(A) The government introduced new laws on data protection which come into force on 1 January 2006. BW's directors have agreed that this will require a large number of staff to be retrained. At 31 October 2005, the directors were waiting on a report they had commissioned that would identify the actual training requirements.
(B) At the end of the reporting period, BW is negotiating with its insurance provider about the amount of an insurance claim that it had filed. On 20 November 2005, the insurance provider agreed to pay $200,000.
(C) BW makes refunds to customers for any goods returned within 30 days of sale, and has done so for many years.
(D) A customer is suing BW for damages alleged to have been caused by BW's product. BW is contesting the claim and, at 31 October 2005, the directors have been advised by BW's legal advisers it is unlikely to lose the case. **(2 marks)**

? Question 6

DH has the following two legal claims outstanding:

- A legal action against DH claiming compensation of $700,000, filed in February 2007. DH has been advised that it is probable that the liability will materialise.
- A legal action taken by DH against another entity, claiming damages of $300,000, started in March 2004. DH has been advised that it is probable that it will win the case.

How should DH report these legal actions in its financial statements for the year ended 30 April 2007?

	Legal action against DH	*Legal action taken by DH*
(A)	Disclose by a note to the accounts	No disclosure
(B)	Make a provision	No disclosure
(C)	Make a provision	Disclose as a note
(D)	Make a provision	Accrue the income

(2 marks)

? Question 7

EP sells refrigerators and freezers and provides a 1 year warranty against faults occurring after sale.

EP estimates that if all goods with an outstanding warranty at the balance sheet date need minor repairs the total cost would be $3 million. If all the products under warranty needed major repairs the total cost would be $12 million.

Based on previous years' experience, EP estimates that 85% of the products will require no repairs; 14% will require minor repairs and 1% will require major repairs.

Calculate the expected value of the cost of the repair of goods with an outstanding warranty at the balance sheet date. **(3 marks)**

? Question 8

The objective of IAS 24 *Related Party Disclosures* is to ensure that financial statements disclose the effect of the existence of related parties.

Requirement

With reference to *IAS 24*, explain the meaning of the terms 'related party' and 'related party transaction'. **(5 marks)**

? Question 9

BJ is an entity that provides a range of facilities for holidaymakers and travellers.
At 1 October 2004 these included:

- a short haul airline operating within Europe; and
- a travel agency specialising in arranging holidays to more exotic destinations, such as Hawaii and Fiji.

BJ's airline operation has made significant losses for the last 2 years. On 31 January 2005, the directors of BJ decided that, due to a significant increase in competition on short haul flights within Europe, BJ would close all of its airline operations and dispose of its fleet of aircraft. All flights for holiday makers and travellers who had already booked seats would be provided by third party airlines. All operations ceased on 31 May 2005.

On 31 July 2005, BJ sold its fleet of aircraft and associated non-current assets for $500 million, the carrying value at that date was $750 million.

At the end of the reporting period, BJ were still in negotiation with some employees regarding severance payments. BJ has estimated that in the financial period October 2005 to September 2006, they will agree a settlement of $20 million compensation.

The closure of the airline operation caused BJ to carry out a major restructuring of the entire entity. The restructuring has been agreed by the directors and active steps have been taken to implement it. The cost of restructuring to be incurred in year 2005/2006 is estimated at $10 million.

Requirement

Explain how BJ should report the events described above and quantify any amounts required to be included in its financial statements for the year ended 30 September 2005. (Detailed disclosure notes are not required.) **(5 marks)**

? Question 10

CB is an entity specialising in importing a wide range of non-food items and selling them to retailers. George is CB's president and founder and owns 40% of CB's equity shares:

- CB's largest customer, XC accounts for 35% of CB's revenue. XC has just completed negotiations with CB for a special 5% discount on all sales.
- During the accounting period, George purchased a property from CB for $500,000. CB had previously declared the property surplus to its requirements and had valued it at $750,000.
- George's son, Arnold is a director in a financial institution, FC. During the accounting period, FC advanced $2 million to CB as an unsecured loan at a favourable rate of interest.

Requirement

Explain, with reasons, the extent to which each of the above transactions should be classified and disclosed in accordance with IAS 24 *Related Party Disclosures* in CB's financial statements for the period. **(5 marks)**

? Question 11

Timber Products is a timber supplies wholesale entity. The end of the reporting period is 31 December. On turnover of $83.5 million, the entity has pre-tax earnings of $31.6 million (last year $40.3 million on sales revenue of $91.2 million).

Timber Products has a small number of customers of which one, Homestead, represents 75 per cent of the sales revenue of Timber Products. Homestead has direct online access to Timber Products' order book and inventory records. Whenever Homestead requires a delivery, it accesses Timber Products' inventory records and order book.

Requirements

Explain whether Homestead is a related party:

(a) if, when there is insufficient quantity of the item it requires in inventory or on order, Homestead asks Timber Products to place an order with its supplier; **(4 marks)**

(b) if, when there is insufficient quantity of the item it requires in inventory or on order, Homestead generates an order from Timber Products to its suppliers. **(4 marks)**

(Total marks = 8)

? Question 12

Holiday Refreshments runs a brewing business. In February 2004, the accounts for the year ended 31 December 2003 are being finalised. The following issues remain outstanding:

1. A customer bought a glass of Holiday Best Beer in his local bar during October 2003 and became ill. He is suing the bar and Holiday Refreshments. The case has not yet come to court and although the entity's solicitors believe they will win the case, the directors offered an out-of-court settlement of $10,000 as a goodwill gesture. Under the terms of the offer, each side would meet their own costs which in the case of Holiday Refreshments are $1,500 up to December 2003. All of this amount had been paid by the year-end. The customer has not yet formally accepted the offer.
2. A consignment of hops costing $95,000 was delivered to the brewery on 20 December 2003. The supplier has not yet issued an invoice.
3. Bottles for the entity's beers are supplied by Bottlebank. Five years ago, in order to secure supplies, Holiday gave a guarantee over a $3,000,000 10-year bank loan taken out by Bottlebank. The guarantee is still in force. Bottlebank's latest accounts indicate net assets of $6.8 million and it has not breached any of the terms and conditions of the loan.
4. Due to a faulty valve, a batch of beer was inadvertently discharged into a river instead of into the bottling plant in March 2003. The entity paid a fine of $20,000 in July 2003 for an illegal discharge. It is also responsible for rectifying any environmental damage. To 31 December 2003, $200,000 had been paid. The extent of further expenditure is uncertain although it is estimated to be between $100,000 and $140,000.

Requirement

Explain how each of the above items should be treated in the accounts of Holiday Refreshments for the year to 31 December 2003. **(10 marks)**

Solutions to Revision Questions

18

Solution 1

The correct answer is (B), see Section 18.2.3.

Further information is now available that throws more light on the prevailing position at the year end.

 (A) is a non-adjusting event occurring after the end of the reporting period.
 (C) is an adjusting event but was discovered at the year-end inventory count. It is therefore an adjusting event but is not after the end of the reporting period.
 (D) if the lack of maintenance cover is material, it could be treated as a non-adjusting event occurring after the end of the reporting period.

Solution 2

The correct answer is (B), see Section 18.6.2.

The directors need to create a provision for $20,000 as the employee's claim is probably going to succeed but the customer's claim is not. Provisions have to be created when it is probable that the organisation will have to transfer economic benefit. Probability is usually taken as more than 50 per cent likely.

Solution 3

The correct answer is (C), see Sections 18.10 and 18.10.1.

IAS 24 presumes directors and shareholders who can exercise significant influence to be related parties. The largest single shareholder is certain to have significant influence.

(A) and (B) are incorrect because IAS 24 does not require parties with whom the reporting entity transacts a significant volume of business to be treated as a related party.

(D) is incorrect because IAS 24 does not require providers of finance in the ordinary course of business to be treated as a related party.

Solution 4

The correct answer is (B), see Section 18.10.1.

Solution 5

The correct answer is (C), see Section 18.6.5.

 Solution 6

The correct answer is (C), see Section 18.6.

 Solution 7

Warranty cost provision = ($3m × 0.14) + ($12m × 0.01) = $540,000, see Section 18.6.5.

 Solution 8

IAS 24 – A party is related to an entity if:

(a) directly, or indirectly the party:
  (i) controls, is controlled by, or is under common control with, the entity;
  (ii) has an interest in the entity that gives it significant influence over the entity; or
  (iii) has joint control over the entity.
(b) the party is an associate;
(c) the party is a joint venture in which the entity is a venturer;
(d) the party is a member of the key management personnel of the entity or its parent,
(e) the party is a close member of the family of any individual referred to in (a) or (d);
(f) the party is an entity that is controlled, jointly controlled or significantly influenced by, or for which significant voting power in such entity resides with, directly or indirectly, any individual referred to in (d) or (e); or
(g) the party is a post-employment benefit plan for the benefit of employees of the entity, or of any entity that is a related party of the entity.

Related party transaction: Transfer of resources, services or obligations between related parties, regardless of whether a price is charged.

The transfer of resources or obligations can include any transaction, including purchases or sales of goods, property or other assets and rendering of receipt of services.

 Solution 9

IFRS 5 defines a discontinued operation as a component of an entity that has been disposed of and that represents a separate major line of business. A component of an entity is defined as operations and cash flows that can be clearly distinguished, operationally and for financial reporting purposes, from the rest of the entity. The disposal of the airline business represents a separate major line of business, which can be clearly distinguished and it was disposed of during the year.

Conclusion

The closure of the airline business should be treated as a discontinued operation and separately disclosed, see Section 18.6.2.

Solution 10

According to IAS 24 *Related Party Disclosures,* a customer with whom an entity transacts a significant volume of business is not a related party merely by virtue of the resulting economic dependence. XC is not a related party and the negotiated discount does not need to be disclosed.

A party is related to an entity if it has an interest in the entity that gives it significant influence over the entity. The party is related to an entity if they are a member of the key management personnel of the entity.

As founder member and major shareholder holding 40% of the equity, George is able to exert significant influence and is a related party of CB.

George is also a related party as he is CB's president. He is a member of the key management personnel of CB.

The sale of the property for $500,000 will need to be disclosed, along with its valuation as a related party transaction.

Providers of finance are not related parties simply because of their normal dealings with the entity. However, if a party is a close member of the family of any individual categorised as a related party, they are also a related party. As Arnold is George's son and George is a related party, Arnold is also a related party. The loan from FC will need to be disclosed along with the details of Arnold and his involvement in the arrangements, see Section 18.10.

 Solution 11

(a) It could be argued that a related party relationship exists because, as a result of Homestead representing 75 per cent of the sales of Timber Products, Homestead has influence over the financial and operating policies of Timber Products to an extent that Timber Products might be inhibited from pursuing at all times its own separate interests. However, paragraph 6(c) of IAS 24 states that no disclosure is required of a relationship that exists simply as a result of a party being a customer of the reporting entity with whom it transacts a significant volume of business.

(b) A related party relationship exists because Homestead has effectively, as a result of its having direct control over the purchase ordering system of Timber Products, influence over the financial and operating policies of Timber Products to an extent that Timber Products might be inhibited from pursuing at all times its own separate interests, see Section 18.10.

 Solution 12

1. *Court case.* An offer has been made but not yet accepted. It is uncertain whether it must be accepted or whether the customer will pursue his case. The offer arose out of a past event (supply of beer in October) and there is a present obligation as an offer has been made. A provision of $10,000 should be made and brief details disclosed, see Section 18.6.2.

2. *Hops.* This is a straightforward accrual. An obligation arises from a past event and there is no significant uncertainty.

3. *Guarantee.* No present obligation exists as Bottlebank has net assets and met the terms of the loan. There is a possibility that the guarantee will be called in during the next

5 years and therefore the granting of the guarantee (a past event) may give rise to a possible obligation. This is a contingent liability which should be disclosed in the notes to the accounts but not provided for in the accounts, see Section 18.7.

4. *Environmental discharge.* The damage occurred as a result of a past event – the discharge of beer. The fine and $200,000 rectification costs will already be included in the accounts. There is an obligation to make good further environmental damage. There is uncertainty concerning the amount. A provision should be made of, say $120,000, with an explanation of the range of possible payments, see Section 18.6.2.

19

Working Capital Ratios

Working Capital Ratios

19

LEARNING OUTCOME

After completing this chapter, you should be able to:

▶ calculate and interpret working capital ratios for business sectors.

Learning aims

The learning aims of this part of the syllabus are that students should be able to:

• assess and control the short term financial requirements of a business entity.

The syllabus topics covered in this chapter are as follows:

• Working capital ratios (e.g. receivable days, inventory days, payable days, current ratio, quick ratio) and the working capital cycle.
• Working capital characteristics of different businesses (e.g. supermarkets being heavily funded by payables) and the importance of industry comparisons.

19.1 Introduction

This final part of the syllabus will examine various aspects of working capital management. This chapter discusses working capital policy and working capital ratios. Chapter 20 discusses various alternatives for short-term investing, various sources of short-term funding and funding for international trade. The following three chapters discuss the elements of working capital in more detail; Chapter 21 covering receivables and payables; Chapter 22 dealing with inventory management; Chapter 23 discusses cash management and cash flow forecasts.

19.2 Working capital management

In CIMA's *Management Accounting: Official Terminology*, working capital is defined as follows:

 The capital available for conducting the day-to-day operations of an organisation; normally the excess of current assets over current liabilities.

In accounting terms, this is a static statement of financial position concept, referring to the excess at a particular moment in time of permanent capital plus non-current liabilities over the non-current assets of the business. As such, it depends on accounting rules, such as what is capital and what is revenue, what constitutes retained earnings, the cut-off between long term and short term (twelve months from the end of the reporting period for published accounts) and when revenue should be recognised.

If working capital, thus defined, exceeds net current operating assets (inventory plus receivables less payables), the entity has a cash surplus (usually represented by bank deposits and investments); otherwise it has a deficit (usually represented by a bank loan and/or overdraft). On this basis the control of working capital can be subdivided into areas dealing with inventory, receivables, payables, and cash.

A business must be able to generate sufficient cash to be able to meet its immediate obligations and therefore continue trading. Unprofitable businesses can survive for quite some time if they have access to sufficient liquid resources, but even the most profitable business will quickly go under if it does not have adequate liquid resources. Working capital is therefore essential to the entity's long-term success and development and the greater the degree to which the current assets cover the current liabilities, the more solvent the entity.

The efficient management of working capital is important from the point of view of both liquidity and profitability. Poor management of working capital means that funds are unnecessarily tied up in idle assets, hence reducing liquidity and also reducing the ability to invest in productive assets such as plant and machinery, so affecting profitability.

An entity's working capital policy is a function of two decisions:

- First, the appropriate level of investment in, and mix of current assets to be decided upon, for a set level of activity. This is the investment decision.
- Second, the methods of financing this investment – the financing decision.

19.2.1   The investment decision

All businesses, to one degree or another, require working capital. The actual amount required will depend on many factors such as the age of the entity, the type of business activity, credit policy, and even the time of year. There is no standard fixed requirement. It is essential that an appropriate amount of working capital is budgeted for to meet anticipated future needs. Failure to budget correctly could result in the business being unable to meet its liabilities as they fall due. If a business finds itself in such a situation, it is said to be *technically insolvent*. In conditions of uncertainty, firms must hold some minimal level of cash and inventories based on expected sales plus additional safety inventory. With an *aggressive working capital policy*, a firm would hold minimal safety inventory. Such a policy would minimise costs, but it could lower sales because the firm may not be able to respond rapidly to increases in demand.

Conversely, a *conservative working capital policy* would call for large safety inventory levels. Generally, the expected return is lower under a conservative than under an aggressive policy, but the risks are greater under the aggressive policy. A *moderate policy* falls somewhere between the two extremes in terms of risk and returns.

19.2.2 The financing decision

Working capital financing decisions involve the determination of the mix of long- versus short-term debt.

There is a basic difference between cash and inventories on the one hand and receivables on the other. In the case of cash and inventories, higher levels mean safety inventory, hence a more conservative position. There is no such thing as a 'safety level of receivables' and a higher level of receivables in relation to sales would generally mean that the firm was extending credit on more liberal terms. If we characterise aggressive as being risky, then lowering inventories and cash would be aggressive but raising receivables would also be aggressive.

The financing of working capital depends upon how current and fixed asset funding is divided between long-term and short-term sources of funding. Three possible policies exist.

1. *Conservative.* A conservative policy is where all of the permanent assets both non-current assets and the permanent part of the current assets (i.e. the core level of investment in inventory and receivables, etc.) are financed by long-term funding, as well as part of the fluctuating current assets. Short-term financing is only used for part of the fluctuating current assets. The conservative policy is the least risky but also results in the lowest expected return.
2. *Aggressive.* An aggressive policy for financing working capital uses short-term financing to fund all the fluctuating current assets as well as some of the permanent part of the current assets. This policy carries the greatest risk of illiquidity, as well as the greatest return (because short-term debt costs are typically less than long-term costs).
3. *Moderate.* A moderate (or maturity matching) policy matches the short-term finance to the fluctuating current assets, and the long-term finance to the permanent part of current assets plus non-current assets. This policy falls between the two extremes.

19.3 Working capital ratios

Working capital management may be analysed using ratio analysis. We shall consider two groups of ratios: liquidity ratios and those concerned with the calculation of the working capital cycle.

19.3.1 Illustration

The financial statements of Alpha are shown below:

Alpha income statement for the year ended 31 December 20X9

	$	$
Sales revenue		500,000
Opening inventory	25,000	
Purchases	305,000	
Closing inventory	(30,000)	
Cost of goods sold		(300,000)
Gross profit		200,000
Other operating expenses	60,000	
Finance cost	24,000	
		(84,000)
Profit		116,000

Alpha statement of financial position as at 31 December 20X9

	$	$
Non-current assets		540,000
Current assets		
Inventory	30,000	
Receivables	62,500	
Bank	7,000	
		99,500
		639,500
Capital and reserves		
Share capital		125,625
Accumulated profit		256,000
		381,625
Non-current liabilities		
Loan notes		200,000
Current liabilities		
Payables		57,875
		639,500

Ignore taxation.

We will use this set of financial statements to illustrate the calculation of the working capital ratios.

19.3.2 Liquidity ratios

Liquidity refers to the amount of cash in hand or readily obtainable to meet payment obligations. Liquidity ratios indicate the ability to meet liabilities from available assets and are calculated from statement of financial position information. The most commonly used are the current ratio and the quick ratio.

19.3.3 The current ratio

The current ratio is the ratio of current assets divided by current liabilities:

$$\text{Current ratio} = \frac{\text{current assets}}{\text{current liabilities}}$$

Alpha's current ratio is:

$$\frac{99,500}{57,875} = 1.7{:}1$$

Notice that this figure is usually expressed as a ratio rather than as a percentage.

The current ratio provides a broad measure of liquidity. A high current ratio would suggest that the business would have little difficulty meeting current liabilities from available assets. However, if a large proportion of current assets is represented by inventory, this may not be the case as inventories are less liquid than other current assets.

19.3.4 The quick ratio

The quick ratio, or *acid test*, indicates the ability to pay payables in the short term. The quick ratio recognises that inventory may take some time to convert into cash and so focuses on those current assets that are relatively liquid.

$$\text{Quick ratio} = \frac{\text{current assets} - \text{inventory}}{\text{current liabilities}}$$

Alpha's quick asset ratio is:

$$\frac{99,500 - 30,000}{57,875} = 1.2{:}1$$

By ignoring inventory, the ratio concentrates on those current assets which are immediately available to meet payables as and when they fall due.

There are no general norms for these ratios and 'ideal' levels vary depending on the type of business being examined. Manufacturers will normally require much higher liquidity ratios than retailers. If a norm is required, the best guide will usually be the industry average if one is available. The industry average should indicate whether the current and quick ratios required in the industry are generally quite high or relatively low. This will be determined by the trading conditions in the sector. For example, a retailer such as a supermarket will be able to purchase on credit and sell for cash. Therefore, there will be virtually no receivables other than credit card entities and very little inventory. The current and quick ratios will be quite low as a result. Whereas a manufacturing organisation will need to hold inventory in various stages of completion, from raw materials to finished products and the majority if not all of the sales will be on credit. As a result both liquidity ratios will be higher.

When analysing liquidity ratios, the absolute figure calculated for a particular year is less important than the trend from one year to the next. It is important to assess whether the organisation's liquidity is improving or declining over time.

19.4 Efficiency ratios

The efficiency ratios are related to the liquidity ratios. They give an insight into the effectiveness of the entity's management of the components of working capital.

19.4.1 Inventory turnover

It is possible to calculate the average number of days taken by the business to sell an item of inventory, if there are several types of inventory each type must be calculated separately:

$$\frac{\text{Inventory}}{\text{Cost of sales}} \times 365$$

Note: Cost of sales should be the cost of inventories sold, it should not include other expenses, such as depreciation.

This is equivalent to taking the amount of inventory held by the business, dividing by the rate at which inventory is consumed in a year and multiplying by the number of days in a year. Alpha's inventory turnover is:

$$\frac{30,000}{300,000} \times 365 = 37 \text{ days}$$

This means that, on average, any given item of inventory will spend 37 days 'on the shelf' before it is sold.

Obviously, it is desirable for this period to be as short as possible. The shorter the inventory turnover period, the more quickly inventory can be converted into cash. The inventory turnover ratio can, however, be too short. It is easy to reduce the figure produced by this ratio: the entity can simply allow its inventory to run down. This could, however, be counter productive if this led to stoppages in production because there were inadequate inventories of materials or components. Similarly, holding inadequate inventories of finished goods could cost the entity both trade and goodwill if it is unable to meet customer demand.

It is difficult to tell whether 37 days is 'good' or 'bad'. It would be helpful if Alpha could be compared to a similar entity or if previous years' figures were available.

Sometimes this ratio is calculated using constants of 52 or 12 to express the turnover in terms of weeks or months. It is also possible to invert the formula and leave out the constant to show how often inventory has 'turned over' during the year:

$$\frac{\text{Cost of sales}}{\text{Closing inventory}} = \frac{300,000}{30,000} = 10 \text{ times}$$

19.4.2 Receivables turnover

This is a measure of the average length of time taken for customers to settle their balance:

$$\frac{\text{Trade Receivables}}{\text{Sales}} \times 365$$

Alpha's ratio is:

$$\frac{62,500}{500,000} \times 365 = 46 \text{ days}$$

Again, it is desirable for this ratio to be as short as possible. It will be better for the entity's cash flow if customers pay as quickly as possible. It can, however, be difficult to press for speedier payment. Doing so could damage the entity's relationship with its customers.

In general, most businesses request payment within 30 days of the delivery of goods. Most customers tend to delay payment for some time beyond this. Alpha's ratio appears reasonable: customers are not taking an unrealistic time to pay and there is nothing to suggest that Alpha is putting undue pressure on its customers.

If the entity sells goods for cash and for credit, then it is important to divide the trade receivables figure by credit sales only. If sales cannot be broken down, then the ratio will be distorted. The classic case of this occurred when a student divided the receivables of a supermarket chain by the sales revenue figure (virtually all of which was cash) and came to the conclusion that the receivables turnover ratio was approximately 0.007 days (about 10 minutes!).

Note: When calculating the receivables turnover, you should only include trade receivables, not total receivables.

19.4.3 Payables turnover

This is the average time taken to pay suppliers:

$$\frac{\text{Trade Payables}}{\text{Purchases}} \times 365$$

Alpha's payables turnover was:

$$\frac{57,875}{305,000} \times 365 = 69 \text{ days}$$

While the entity should collect cash from its customers as quickly as possible, it should try to delay making payments to its suppliers. Effectively, this is equivalent to taking out an interest-free loan, which can be used to help finance working capital. Again, the entity must use some restraint. If it becomes regarded as a slow payer, then it might find it difficult to obtain credit. Indeed, there are credit-rating agencies which compile lists of entities that have poor reputations.

Alpha's ratio of just over 2 months does not seem too unreasonable, although it does seem fairly slow.

Published financial statements do not usually state the purchases figure. It is possible to obtain a crude estimate of the payables turnover by using the cost of sales figure instead, this method will often have to be used in examination questions.

Note: Only trade payables should be included, taxation, interest and other payables should be excluded.

19.5　The working capital cycle

The efficiency ratios are related to those which measure liquidity. The working capital cycle gives an indication of the length of time cash spends tied up in current assets.

The working capital cycle is the length of time between the entity's outlay on raw materials, wages and other expenditures, and the inflow of cash from the sale of the goods.

In a manufacturing entity, this is the average time that raw materials remain in inventory less the period of credit taken from suppliers plus the time taken for producing the goods plus the time the goods remain in finished inventory plus the time taken by customers to pay for the goods. On some occasions, this cycle is referred to as the cash cycle or operating cycle.

This is an important concept for the management of cash or working capital because the longer the working capital cycle, the more financial resource the entity needs. Management needs to ensure that this cycle does not become too long. The working capital cycle can be calculated approximately as shown in the calculation below. Allowances should be made for any significant changes in the level of inventory taking place over the period. If, for example, the entity is deliberately building up its level of inventory, this will lengthen the working capital cycle.

Calculation of the working capital cycle

Raw materials *Days*

Period of turnover of raw materials inventory $= \dfrac{\text{average value of raw material inventory}}{\text{Consumption of raw material per day}}$ x

Less

Period of credit granted by suppliers $= \dfrac{\text{average level of payables}}{\text{purchase of raw materials per day}}$ (x)

Add

Period of production $= \dfrac{\text{average value of work in progress}}{\text{average cost of goods sold per day}}$ x

Period of turnover of finished goods inventory $= \dfrac{\text{average value of inventory of finished goods}}{\text{average cost of goods sold per day}}$ x

Period of credit taken by customers $= \dfrac{\text{average values of receivables}}{\text{average value of sales per day}}$ x

Total working capital cycle x

Some writers advocate computation of an annual working capital cycle and of a cycle for each quarter, since with a seasonal business the cycle would vary over different periods. The numerators in the equations can be found by taking the arithmetic mean of the opening and closing balances for inventories, payables and receivables. If a quarterly statement is being prepared, the opening and closing balances for the quarter would be used.

The calculation of the working capital cycle may alternatively be expressed as:

		Days
Raw materials inventory turnover period $= \dfrac{\text{average raw materials inventory}}{\text{purchases}} \times 365$		x
Less		
Payables payment period $\quad = \dfrac{\text{trade payables}}{\text{purchases}} \times 365$		(x)
Add		
Work in progress turnover period $\quad = \dfrac{\text{average work in progress}}{\text{manufacturing cost}} \times 365$		x
Finished goods turnover period $\quad = \dfrac{\text{average finished goods inventory}}{\text{cost of sales}} \times 365$		x
Receivables collection period $\quad = \dfrac{\text{average } \cancel{\text{finished goods inventory}} \; \textit{receivables}}{\text{credit sales}} \times 365$		$\underline{x}$
		$\underline{x}$

In an examination situation, the information supplied in order to calculate the length of the working capital cycle is often simplified as shown below.

Example 19.A

The table below gives information extracted from the annual accounts of Davis for the past 2 years.

You are required to calculate the length of the working capital cycle for each of the 2 years.

Davis Extracts from annual accounts

	Year 1	Year 2
	$	$
Inventories: Raw materials	108,000	145,800
Work in progress	75,600	97,200
Finished goods	86,400	129,600
Purchases	518,400	702,000
Cost of goods sold	756,000	972,000
Sales	864,000	1,080,000
Receivables	172,800	259,200
Trade payables	86,400	105,300

Solution

	Year 1		Year 2	
	%	Days	%	Days
Raw materials inventory holding (raw materials inventory ÷ purchases)	20.83	76	20.77	76
Less: Finance from suppliers (trade payables ÷ purchases)	16.67	(61)	15.00	(55)
		15		21
Production time (work in progress ÷ cost of sales)	10.00	37	10.00	37
Finished goods inventory holding (finished goods inventory ÷ cost of sales)	11.43	42	13.33	49
Credit given to customers (receivables ÷ sales)	20.00	73	24.00	88
		167		195

Note that, owing to the nature of the simplified information provided, end-of-year values rather than average values have been used for inventory, receivables and payables. The percentages calculated are multiplied by 365 to give figures expressed in numbers of days.

In a non-manufacturing entity, the working capital cycle can be calculated as follows:

Inventory turnover + receivables turnover − payables turnover

The logic behind this is that inventory cannot be converted into cash until it has been sold and then the customer pays for the goods. This must be offset against the fact that no cash is actually invested until the entity has paid the supplier for the goods. Thus, Alpha's working capital cycle is:

37 + 46 − 69 = 14 days

This means that, on average, the entity's money is tied up in any given item of inventory for 14 days before it is recovered (with profit).

19.6 Overtrading

Overtrading is the condition of a business which enters into commitments in excess of its available short-term resources. This can arise even if the entity is trading profitably.

Entities are particularly at risk of overtrading when they are growing rapidly and they do not raise further long-term finance. The additional inventories and trade receivables are funded by increases in payables. Additional non-current assets may be required for the expansion and will be paid for out of current funds, reducing the working capital.

If this continues for too long without raising further long-term funds, the entity may run into problems of cash shortages. The entity may not be able to meet its liabilities as they fall due, and although the entity is trading profitably it may be forced into liquidation.

19.6.1 Symptoms of overtrading

Symptoms that may indicate overtrading include:

- increasing revenue;
- increasing inventory and receivables;
- increasing current and non-current assets;
- increase in assets funded by credit;
- current liabilities exceed current assets and there is a decrease in both current and quick ratios.

The solution is to issue more equity shares or raise more long-term loan funds.

19.7 Shortening the working capital cycle

A number of steps could be taken to shorten the working capital cycle:

- *Reduce raw materials inventory holding.* This may be done by reviewing slow-moving lines and reorder levels. Inventory control models may be considered if not already in use. More efficient links with suppliers could also help. Reducing inventory may involve loss of discounts for bulk purchases, loss of cost savings from price rises, or could lead to production delays due to inventory shortages.

- *Obtain more finance from suppliers by delaying payments.* This could result in a deterioration in commercial relationships or even loss of reliable sources of supply. Discounts may be lost by this policy.
- *Reduce work in progress* by reducing production volume (with resultant loss of business and the need to cut back on labour resources) or improving production techniques and efficiency (with the human and practical problems of achieving such change).
- *Reduce finished goods inventory* perhaps by reorganising the production schedule and distribution methods. This may affect the efficiency with which customer demand can be satisfied and result ultimately in a reduction of sales.
- *Reduce credit given to customers* by invoicing and following up outstanding amounts more quickly, or possibly offering discount incentives. The main disadvantages would be the potential loss of customers as a result of chasing too hard and a loss of revenue as a result of discounts.

The volume of receivable balances could be cut by a quicker collection of debt; finished goods could be turned over more rapidly; the level of raw materials inventory could be reduced or the production period could be shortened.

The working capital cycle is only the *time span* between production costs and cash returns; it says nothing in itself about the amount of working capital that will be needed over this period. In fact, less will be required at the beginning than at the end.

19.8 Summary

In this chapter we have examined working capital ratios and considered a range of techniques that may be used to manage the working capital cycle.

Revision Questions

? Question 1

An entity has a current ratio of 1.75. It has decided in future to pay its trade payables after 40 days, rather than after 30 days as it has in the past. What will be the effect of this change on the entity's current ratio and its cash operating cycle?

	Current ratio	Working capital cycle
(A)	Increase	Increase
(B)	Increase	Decrease
(C)	Decrease	Increase
(D)	Decrease	Decrease

(2 marks)

? Question 2

Which of the following is most likely to reduce a firm's working capital?

(A) Paying payables early
(B) Lengthening the period of credit given to receivables
(C) Repaying an overdraft out of cash
(D) Giving a discount to a customer for immediate cash settlement **(2 marks)**

? Question 3

An entity has a current ratio of 1.5:1. It decides to use surplus cash balances to settle 30% of its total current liabilities. The current ratio will

(A) decrease by more than 30%
(B) decrease by less than 30%
(C) increase by more than 30%
(D) increase by less than 30% **(2 marks)**

Question 4

An entity buys goods on credit and then, before payment is made, it is forced to sell all of these goods on credit for less than the purchase price. What is the consequence of these two transactions immediately after the sale has taken place?

(A) Inventory decreases and cash decreases
(B) Cash decreases and payables increase
(C) Inventory decreases and receivables increase
(D) Receivables increase and payables increase   **(2 marks)**

 Question 5

A retailing entity has an annual turnover of $36 million. The entity earns a constant margin of 20% on sales. All sales and purchases are on credit and are evenly distributed over the year. The following amounts are maintained at a constant level throughout the year:

Inventory $6 million
Receivables $8 million
Payables $3 million

What is the entity's working capital cycle to the nearest day (i.e. the average time from the payment of a supplier to the receipt from a customer)?

(A) 81 days
(B) 111 days
(C) 119 days
(D) 195 days   **(4 marks)**

 Question 6

Working capital is most likely to increase when

(A) payments to trade payables are delayed
(B) the period of credit extended to customers is reduced
(C) fixed assets are sold
(D) inventory levels are increased   **(2 marks)**

 Question 7

An entity's current assets exceed its current liabilities (which include an overdraft). The entity pays a trade payable, taking advantage of a cash discount. What will be the effect of this transaction upon the entity's working capital and on its current ratio?

	Working capital	Current ratio
(A)	Constant	Decrease
(B)	Constant	Increase
(C)	Decrease	Decrease
(D)	Increase	Increase

                                                                 (2 marks)

? Question 8

Which ONE of the following transactions is most likely to affect the overall amount of working capital?

(A) Receipt of full amount of cash from a receivable
(B) Sale of a fixed asset on credit at its net book value
(C) Payment of a trade payable
(D) Purchase of inventory on credit   **(2 marks)**

? Question 9

If the current ratio for an entity is equal to its acid test (that is, the quick ratio), then

(A) the current ratio must be greater than one
(B) the entity does not carry any inventory
(C) trade receivables plus cash is greater than trade payables minus inventory
(D) working capital is positive   **(2 marks)**

? Question 10

An entity's working capital financing policy is to finance working capital using short-term financing to fund all the fluctuating current assets as well as some of the permanent part of the current assets.

   The above policy is an example of

(A) an aggressive policy.
(B) a conservative policy.
(C) a short-term policy.
(D) a moderate policy.   **(2 marks)**

? Question 11

A conservative policy for financing working capital is one where short-term finance is used to fund

(A) all of the fluctuating current assets, but no part of the permanent current assets.
(B) all of the fluctuating current assets and part of the permanent current assets.
(C) part of the fluctuating current assets and part of the permanent current assets.
(D) part of the fluctuating current assets, but no part of the permanent current assets.
                                    (2 marks)

? Question 12

'Although many financial analysts use the current ratio to assess the liquidity position of firms, it is essential that care is taken in reaching any decision.'

   The following information has been obtained from two small entities regarding the working capital that is being used at 30 September 2003.

	Entity A	Entity B
	$	$
Inventories	6,000	20,000
Trade receivables	5,800	10,000
Cash	2,200	–
Trade payables	7,000	7,000
Bank overdraft	–	3,000

Requirements

(a) Calculate the current ratio for each of the two firms. **(2 marks)**

(b) Discuss the implications of the ratios that you have calculated in terms of a request for credit from both of these entities. **(3 marks)**

(Total marks = 5)

? Question 13

DR has the following balances under current assets and current liabilities:

Current assets		$
Inventory	50,000	
Trade receivables	70,000	
Bank		10,000
Current liabilities	$	
Trade payables		88,000
Interest payable	7,000	

DR's quick ratio is

(A) 0.80:1
(B) 0.84:1
(C) 0.91:1
(D) 1.37:1

(2 marks)

? Question 14

Which ONE of the following is most likely to increase an entity's working capital?

(A) Delaying payment to trade payables.
(B) Reducing the credit period given to customers.
(C) Purchasing inventory on credit.
(D) Paying a supplier and taking an early settlement discount. **(2 marks)**

Solutions to Revision Questions

19

☑ Solution 1

The correct answer is (D), see Sections 19.3 and 19.5.

☑ Solution 2

The correct answer is (D), see Section 19.3.

☑ Solution 3

The correct answer is (D), see Section 19.3.

> Original ratio = 1.5/1 = 1.5
> Settlement = 0.3
> New current ratio = 1.2/0.7 = 1.71
> Increase = [(1.71/1.5) − 1] = 14%

☑ Solution 4

The correct answer is (D), see Section 19.3.

☑ Solution 5

The correct answer is (C), see Section 19.5.

> Receivable days = (8/36) × 365 = 81.11
> Inventory days = (6/36 × 0.8) × 365 = 76.04
> Payable days = (3/36 × 0.8) × 365 = (38.02)
> WCC = 81.11 + 76.04 − 38.02 = 119.13

☑ Solution 6

The correct answer is (C), see Section 19.3.

☑ Solution 7

The correct answer is (D), see Section 19.3.3.

Payables fall more than the overdraft increases because of the discount. Current assets are unchanged. Thus working capital and the current ratio increase.

Solution 8

The correct answer is (B), see Section 19.3.

 ## Solution 9

The correct answer is (B), see Section 19.3.3.

 ## Solution 10

The correct answer is (A), see Section 19.2.2.

 ## Solution 11

The correct answer is (D), see Section 19.2.2.

 ## Solution 12

(a) The current ratio is calculated as:
Current assets/Current liabilities

Entity A	$14,000/7,000 = 2
Entity B	$30,000/10,000 = 3

(b) From the ratios, it would appear that the liquidity position of Entity B is superior to that of Entity A. However, this does not reflect the real situation. Entity B owes more than Entity A and has an overdraft already. On the other hand, it also has significantly more inventory and trade receivables than Entity A.

   To form an opinion on the liquidity position of these two entities, it is necessary to judge the likelihood of the inventory being sold and the amounts being collected from the trade receivables. It is necessary to focus on the time that will be needed to turn all these current assets into cash. The position of Entity B is not necessarily better as implied by the current ratio. In assessing the request for credit from both entities, the current ratio is not particularly helpful and should be used with caution, see Section 19.3.3.

 ## Solution 13

(70,000 + 10,000):(88,000 + 7,000)
80,000:95,000
0.84:1

Therefore the answer is (B), see Section 19.3.4.

 ## Solution 14

The correct answer is (D), see Section 19.2.

20

Sources of Short-term Finance and Types of Investment

Sources of Short-term Finance and Types of Investment

20

LEARNING OUTCOMES

After completing this chapter, you should be able to:

▶ identify sources of short-term funding;

▶ identify appropriate methods of finance for trading internationally;

▶ identify alternatives for investment of short-term cash surpluses.

The syllabus topics covered in this chapter are as follows:

- types and features of short-term finance: trade payables, overdrafts, short-term loans and debt factoring;
- use and abuse of trade payables as a source of finance;
- the principles of investing short-term (i.e. maturity, return, security, liquidity and diversification);
- types of investments (e.g. interest-bearing bank accounts, negotiable instruments including certificates of deposit, short-term treasury bills and securities);
- the difference between the coupon on debt and the yield to maturity;
- export finance (e.g. documentary credits, bills of exchange, export factoring, forfaiting).

20.1 Introduction

In the first part of this chapter, we consider a number of potential short-term sources of finance. Some of these sources (e.g. trade credit, overdrafts, factoring and invoice discounting) are introduced here, with a more detailed explanation of their nature and characteristics contained in later chapters. The classification of some sources as short-term is fairly arbitrary given that they may in some cases be used over a number of years. We conclude this chapter with an evaluation of the alternatives for investing short-term cash surpluses.

20.2 Sources of short-term finance

Short-term finance may be obtained from a variety of sources including:

- trade credit from suppliers;
- overdrafts;
- short-term loans;
- using trade receivables as security for a loan, through factoring or invoice discounting.

There are other sources that tend to be specifically associated with financing export sales such as:

- bills of exchange;
- documentary credits.

20.2.1 Trade credit

Trade credit is an important source of finance for most businesses. Trade credit is the money owed to the suppliers of goods and services as a result of purchasing goods or services on one date, but paying for those goods on a later date. Trade credit is often viewed as being a free source of finance as interest is not usually charged by a supplier unless payment is overdue. Trade credit does have a cost, although those costs may be hidden.

As interest is not usually charged on trade credit, the temptation is to maximise the use of trade credit, but it is important that this is not abused. Exceeding the normal credit terms may lead to a number of potential problems:

- difficulty in obtaining credit terms from new suppliers;
- cash-flow problems for key suppliers that could adversely affect the viability of both organisations;
- existing suppliers may be unwilling to extend further credit;
- supplier goodwill will be eroded;
- suppliers may refuse to supply in the future;
- credit rating may be reduced.

The problems of late payment have been a particular concern for smaller entities selling goods on credit to large entities in a number of countries. For example, the difficulties in obtaining payment from large entities prompted the UK government to introduce legislation in 1998 to help smaller entities. In the UK, smaller entities now have a statutory right to charge larger entities interest at a high interest rate (base rate + 8 per cent) on any overdue amounts. Entities that suffer from late payment usually have to resort to additional overdraft finance while waiting for their customers to pay.

20.2.2 Overdrafts

One of the most important external sources of short-term finance, particularly for small firms, is the overdraft. Features that make the overdraft popular are:

- *Flexibility.* The bank will agree to a maximum overdraft limit or facility. The borrower may not require the full facility immediately, but may draw funds up to the limit as and when required.

- *Minimal documentation.* Legal documentation is fairly minimal when arranging an overdraft. Key elements of the documentation will be to state the maximum overdraft limit, the interest payable and the security required.
- Interest is only paid on the amount borrowed, rather than on the full facility.

The drawback of overdraft finance is that it is, strictly speaking, repayable on demand, which means that the facility could be withdrawn at any time. Entities with few assets to offer as security will find it difficult to arrange further overdraft finance. The interest rate charged by the bank will vary depending on the perceived credit risk of the borrower.

20.2.3 Term loans

Term loans are offered by the high street banks and their popularity has increased for a number of reasons, not least their accessibility, which is of importance to smaller businesses. A term loan is for a fixed amount with a fixed repayment schedule. Usually the interest rate applied is slightly less than for a bank overdraft. The lender will require security to cover the amount borrowed and an arrangement fee is payable dependent on the amount borrowed.

Term loans also have the following qualities:

- *They are negotiated easily and quickly.* This is particularly important when a cash-flow problem has not been identified until recently and a quick but significant fix is needed.
- *Banks may offer flexible repayments.* High street banks will often devise new lending methods to suit their customers; for example, no capital repayments for, say 2 years, thus avoiding unnecessary overborrowing to fund capital repayment.
- *Variable interest rates.* This may be important given the uncertainty that exists with interest rates.

20.2.4 Factoring

Entities selling goods on credit may have to wait 30, 60 or more days to receive payment from the customer. In the meantime, they have to finance their day-to-day activities, and purchase more supplies. Factoring organisations may help improve cash flow by speeding up the cash receipt relating to outstanding invoices by:

- advancing, say 80 per cent of invoice value immediately, a balance being settled when the client's customer settles the debt.
- taking over responsibility for the operation of the client's sales ledger, including assessment of creditworthiness and dealing with customers.
- offering non-recourse finance, that is, guarantee settlement even if they are not paid by the customer.

For a full discussion of factoring see 21.6.

20.3 Export finance

Selling goods overseas may involve offering longer credit periods than for similar domestic sales. The credit customer may not be as well known as a domestic customer. There is potentially a greater risk of delay or non-payment for goods. Entities may seek to raise finance in such circumstances to ease cash-flow problems.

20.3.1 Export factoring

Export factoring is essentially the same as for domestic factoring described above, with the factor providing a cash advance, typically of about 80 per cent of invoice value. The credit insurance element of the factor's service will also protect against bad-debt risk.

Whereas factoring and the methods of finance mentioned above are relevant to an entity to finance domestic or export sales, there are methods of finance that are specifically associated with financing export sales.

20.3.2 Bill of exchange

A bill of exchange is defined in CIMA's *Management Accounting: Official Terminology* as follows:

> A negotiable instrument, drawn by one party on another, for example, by a supplier of goods on a customer, who by accepting (signing) the bill, acknowledges the debt, which may be payable immediately (a sight draft) or at some future date (a time draft). The holder of the bill can thereafter use an accepted time draft to pay a debt to a third party, or can discount it to raise cash.

The bill of exchange is essentially a written acknowledgement of a debt. They are more commonly used for export transactions than for domestic transactions.

A bill of exchange is a device that may enable the supplier to receive the benefit of payment well before the customer actually pays. The way it works is like this:

1. The *supplier* draws up a simple document (the bill of exchange) requiring the customer to pay the amount due at some fixed future date. (The supplier is the *drawer* of the bill.)
2. The supplier signs the bill and sends it to the customer, who also signs it to signify that he/she agrees to pay, and returns the bill to the supplier. (The customer is the *acceptor* of the bill.)
3. The supplier now has a piece of paper that is worth money, because it constitutes an agreement on the customer's part to pay the debt on the due date. The supplier can now do one of three things:
   (a) hold the bill until the due date and collect the money;
   (b) arrange to transfer the benefit of the bill to the bank in exchange for immediate cash. The bank will make a charge for what is effectively a loan, so the amount received by the supplier will be less than the face value of the bill. This is called *discounting* the bill of exchange with the bank;
   (c) transfer the bill to his/her own supplier in a settlement of the debt. That supplier may in turn pass the bill to one of his/her own supplier, discount it or hold it to maturity.
4. When the due date of the bill arrives, the person holding it at that time presents it to the original acceptor for payment. If the acceptor pays, that is the end of the matter. If the acceptor does not pay on the due date, the bill is said to be dishonoured. Legal action by the parties concerned may then be initiated to recover the money from the original acceptor. A bank bill is a bill of exchange drawn on a bank and is typically used for arranging payment for imports.

Calculating the amount of discount on a bill

When a financial instrument such as a bill of exchange is sold or issued at a discount and redeemed at face value, we may need to calculate the amount of discount or the selling price.

The amount of discount is the rate of discount or discount yield (R) multiplied by the face value (F) multiplied by the time to redemption expressed as a number of days (T) over the days in the year (Y). The price is the face value less the discount amount. To calculate the price, use the formulae:

$$\text{Price} = F \times [1 - RT/Y]$$

Example 20.A

A bill of exchange with a face value of $1,000 has 91 days to maturity. The discount yield required by the investor is 5%. Assume a 365 day year. What is the price the investor is willing to pay for the bill?

$$\text{Price} = \$1,000 \times [1 - (0.05 \times 91)/365] = \$987.53$$

Advantages of bills of exchange

- provides a convenient method of collecting debts from foreign customers;
- foreign buyer receives full period of credit and the exporter can use the bill to raise immediate finance by discounting the bill;
- if the bill of exchange is dishonoured, it may be used by the drawer to support legal action against the drawee in the drawee's country.

20.3.3 Documentary credits

Documentary credits, or letters of credit as they are also called, provide an exporter with a secure method of obtaining payment for overseas sales. Documentary credits also provide the exporter with a method of raising short-term finance from a bank.

CIMA's *Management Accounting: Official Terminology* defines a letter of credit as follows:

> A document issued by a bank on behalf of a customer authorising a person to draw money to a specified amount from its branches or correspondents, usually in another country, when the conditions set out in the document have been met.

The process of payment using a documentary credit would be as follows. An exporter and a foreign buyer would complete a sales contract with payment agreed to be by documentary credit. The foreign buyer would then advise its bank (the issuing bank) to provide credit in favour of the exporter. The issuing bank would then ask the exporter's bank to advise and/or confirm credit to the exporter. The issuing bank would at this stage be providing a guarantee of payment for the goods. The exporter would then dispatch the goods and present the documents of title for the goods to its bank. Once the exporter's bank has checked the documents, it will be prepared to advance finance to the exporter and will forward the documents to the issuing bank. The issuing bank will check the documents and, if satisfied, will reimburse the exporter's bank. The issuing bank will release the documents to the foreign buyer after payment has been received, which will then enable the foreign buyer to take delivery of the goods.

Documentary credits are time-consuming and expensive to arrange and so will only tend to be used in situations where there is a high risk of non-payment.

20.3.4 Forfaiting

Forfaiting is an arrangement whereby exporters, normally of capital goods or raw materials, can obtain medium-term finance. The forfaiting bank buys at a discount to face value a series of promissory notes (or bills of exchange) usually extending over a period of between 6 months and 5 years. The promissory notes may be in any of the world's major currencies. For promissory notes to be eligible for forfaiting (and to provide the forfaiting bank's security), the notes must be guaranteed or avalised by a highly rated international bank (often in the importer's country). Forfaiting is non-recourse, with no claim on the exporter after the notes have been purchased by the bank; payment of the notes is guaranteed by the avalising bank.

Advantages of forfaiting include the following:

(i) trade receivables are turned into immediate cash;
(ii) as it is non-recourse, no liability appears on the statement of financial position;
(iii) future foreign-exchange and interest-rate risk is eliminated;
(iv) overdraft and other credit limits are not affected;
(v) forfeited notes are negotiable.

Forfaiting was developed for East European trade, where governments sought finance for capital equipment purchases, but the time span of the projects was too long for bank or government export credits financing. Forfaiting enables exporters to offer clients medium-term fixed-rate finance with which to fund the order, while at the same time offering the exporter a means of obtaining immediate cash payment for the order, transferring default risk to the forfaiter.

20.4 Managing cash surpluses

When the cash budget of an organisation indicates a cash surplus, the financial manager needs to consider opportunities for short-term investment. A cash surplus may arise as a result of profitable trading, an uneven trade cycle or from a lack of suitable long-term investment opportunities, or perhaps as a result of a disposal programme. In principle, where there is no foreseeable use for the surpluses, the cash should be returned to shareholders or used to repay debt. Usually, cash will be retained to protect against unexpected losses or to fund unexpected investment opportunities.

Any cash surplus beyond the immediate needs should be put to work, even if only invested overnight. The following considerations should be made in assessing how to invest short-term cash surpluses:

- length of time for which the funds are available;
- amount of funds available;
- return offered on the investment in relation to the amount involved;
- risks associated with calling in the investment early (e.g. the need to give three months' notice to obtain the interest);
- ease of realisation.

The aim would be to maximise the post-tax return from the investment, but also to minimise the risk to the original capital invested.

20.5 Debt yields

The rate of return, or yield, on debentures, loan stocks and bonds is measured in two different ways.

20.5.1 Interest yield

Interest yield is also referred to as running yield or flat yield and is calculated by dividing the gross interest by the current market value of the stock as follows:

$$\text{Interest yield} = \frac{\text{gross interest}}{\text{market value}} \times 100\%$$

Example 20.B

A 6 per cent debenture with a current market value of $90 per $100 nominal would have an interest yield of:

$$\frac{6}{90} \times 100\% = 6.7\% \text{ grass or pre-tax}$$

Compound interest yield

If interest is paid half yearly, quarterly or even monthly, the interest rate will need to be compounded to give the annual yield.

Example 20.C

An investment pays 5% interest quarterly. What is the annual yield?

$$[[1 + 0.05]^4 - 1] \times 100 = 21.55\%$$

20.5.2 Yield to maturity (redemption yield)

The yield to maturity (or redemption) is the effective yield on a redeemable security, taking into account any gain or loss due to the fact that it was purchased at a price different from the redemption value.

 Exercise 20.1

You are asked to put a price on a bond with a coupon rate of 8 per cent. It will repay its face value of $100 at the end of 15 years. Other similar bonds have a yield to maturity (YTM) of 12 per cent.

 Solution

The price of the bond is:

$8 \times$ (annuity factor for $t = 15$, $r = 12$) + $100 \times$ (discount factor $t = 15$, $r = 12$)
        = (8×6.811) + (100×0.1827) = $72.76

Note: The annuity factors and discount factors are obtained from tables at the end of this chapter. These tables will be provided in the examination.

What we are doing here is adding the NPV of 15 years of interest payments to the present value of the sum receivable on redemption.

We can turn this example round to calculate the YTM. If the price of the bond is known to be $78.40, what is the yield to redemption? This is basically an internal rate of return calculation and the answer is approximately 11 per cent.

The calculation is as follows. Assume two discount rates as for an IRR interpolation, between which the required percentage is likely to fall. Let us say, in this case, 10 per cent and 14 per cent. Then the equations are:

$$t = 15, r = 10, \text{ so } \$8 \times 7.606 + \$100 \times 0.239 = \$84.75$$
$$t = 15, r = 14, \text{ so } \$8 \times 6.142 + \$100 \times 0.140 = \$63.14$$

Then, by interpolation, bearing in mind that $r = 10$ is closer to $78.40 than is $r = 14$, so that the required rate must be nearer 10, then:

$$\text{Redemption yield} = 10\% + \left(\frac{84.75 - 78.40}{84.75 - 63.14} \times 4 \right)$$
$$= 10\% + 1.17\% = 11.17\%$$

When selecting the two discount rates, it can sometimes be useful to estimate the likely rate by using simple annual returns. In the above example, it would be the return each year, without compounding, divided by the cost. The return is $100 − $78.40 = $21.60 over 15 years is $1.44 a year. Add the annual interest of $8 on to this and we get $9.44, divide by the cost of $78.40 and we get 12%. We would then select rates either side of this rough estimate, say 10% and 14%. This saves picking two rates to find that the yield is not between them.

20.5.3 Coupon rate

A connected issue that is often misunderstood is the relationship of face value to market value and coupon rate (on debt) to rate of return.

When a bond or debenture or any fixed-interest debt is issued, it carries a 'coupon' rate. This is the interest rate that is payable on the face, or nominal, value of the debt. Unlike shares, which are rarely issued at their nominal value, debt is frequently issued at par, usually $100 payable for $100 nominal of the bond. At the time of issue, the interest rate will be fixed according to interest rates available in the market at that time for bonds of similar maturity. The credit rating of the entity will also have an impact on the rate of interest demanded by the market.

Example 20.D

An entity issues bonds at par (the face or nominal value) with a coupon rate of 12 per cent. This means that for every $100 of debt the buyer will receive $12 per annum in gross interest. Assume that interest is payable annually (it is usually paid bi-annually but this would require more tricky calculations). Mr A bought $1,000 of this debt on 1 January 2002. He will receive $120 in interest every year as long as he owns the bond. This might be until it matures or it might be when he sells it in the market. If the opportunity cost to investors of bonds of similar risk and maturity is 12 per cent, then the coupon rate and the rate of return are the same.

However, assume that inflation increases at a much higher rate than expected by the market when the bond was issued. In January 2004, the opportunity cost to investors of similar bonds has risen to 15 per cent. Mr A continues to receive $120 on his $1,000 nominal value, but no new buyer would now pay $1,000 to get a return of 12 per cent – they now want 15 per cent. The price of the bond therefore falls to the level where the return on the debt is 15 per cent. This is $80 per $100 nominal of the bond.

Mr B buys $1,000 nominal of the bond in January 2004. He will receive $120 per year in interest, just like Mr A, but as Mr B paid only $800, his return is 15 per cent (120/800 × 100). The coupon rate stays at 12 per cent, the nominal value at $1,000, but the rate of return is 15 per cent and the market value $800.

FINANCIAL ACCOUNTING AND TAX PRINCIPLES

SOURCES OF SHORT-TERM FINANCE AND TYPES OF INVESTMENT

20.6 Short-term investments

Examples of short-term investment opportunities that might be considered by an organisation include the following:

20.6.1 Treasury bills

Treasury bills are issued by central banks, they are guaranteed by the government of the country of issue. No interest is paid as such, but they are issued at a discount and redeemed at par after a fixed period, for example, UK Treasury Bills are 91 days. They are negotiable, so the bills can be sold on the discount market at any time before their maturity date. There is an implied rate of interest in the price at which Treasury bills are traded.

20.6.2 Bank deposits

A wide range of interest-earning investment opportunities are available from the banks. A *term deposit* offers a fixed rate of interest for a fixed period, usually from 1 month to 6 years. For shorter periods, typically up to 3 months, the interest may be at a variable rate based on money-market rates.

20.6.3 Certificates of deposit

Certificates of deposit (CDs) are issued by the banks at a fixed interest rate for a fixed term (usually between 3 and 5 years). CDs are negotiable documents for which there is an active secondary market, meaning that the holder of a CD can realise the investment on the discount market at any time.

20.6.4 Money-market accounts

Most major financial institutions offer schemes for investment in the money market at variable rates of interest. There is a large money market in the UK for inter-bank borrowing and lending, with terms ranging from overnight to 12 months or more. Large entities will be able to lend surplus cash directly to a borrowing bank on the inter-bank market.

20.6.5 Local authority deposits

Local authorities have a requirement for short-term cash, with terms ranging from overnight to 12 months or more. Interest would be payable on these deposits.

20.6.6 Commercial paper

Large entities may issue unsecured short-term loan notes, referred to as commercial paper. These loan notes will generally mature within 9 months, typically between a week and 3 months. Commercial paper is negotiable, so the bills can be sold on the discount market at any time before their maturity date. There is an implied rate of interest in the price at which the commercial paper is traded.

20.6.7 Local authority bonds

These bonds are issued by local authorities and may be purchased with their remaining maturity. They are tradable, but have a lower level of marketability than most marketable securities, although this is dependent upon the size of the particular local authority.

20.6.8 Corporate bonds

These are bonds issued by entities to raise debt finance. They are long term, but are tradable and thus can be sold in money markets at any time. The level of liquidity depends on the cumulative volume issued by the entity. The level of risk depends on the individual entity and on the terms of the bond, but a credit score is available from credit rating agencies.

20.6.9 Government bonds

These are bonds issued by a government. They normally have lower default risk than corporate bonds (depending upon the government that issued them). They are tradable in money markets and tend to be more liquid than corporate bonds as they are issued in higher volumes.

20.6.10 Risk and return

When investing surplus cash in short-term investments, consideration must be given to the trade-off between return and risk. The liquidity of the investments must also be considered, how quickly could the investment be realised if it is required.

- *Default risk.* The risk that interest and/or principal will not be paid on schedule on fixed-interest investments. Most short-term investment in marketable securities is confined to investments with negligible risk of default.
- *Price risk.* Where interest rates change and this has not been anticipated, this will have an impact upon the tradable value of a security. Thus, if interest rates rise unexpectedly, then the value of a tradable fixed interest security will tend to fall until its yield is equal to the equivalent market yield for that type of security. If securities are held to redemption, the full nominal value is repaid, but the risk still exists in the opportunity cost of the higher interest lost on alternative investments. Financial managers normally wish to avoid substantial price risk.
- *Foreign exchange risk.* If the funds are invested in an overseas currency, there is the risk that exchange rate movements may reduce the value of the principal in terms of the domestic currency. Given that the entity may purchase an overseas entity, then the investment may represent hedging against this in terms of currency matching. This may actually reduce risk. This, of course, depends upon identifying the particular country in which the entity is to be purchased.
- *Taxation and regulation risk.* Unexpected changes in tax rates or other regulation changes may impact upon the tradable value of a marketable security.
- *Return.* Managers will usually try to achieve the maximum yield possible, consistent with a satisfactory level of risk and marketability. It is unlikely that short-term cash surpluses will be invested in equities owing to the risks associated with achieving that return over a short period.

- *Liquidity*. Managers need to consider the ease with which they can access the invested funds if their forecasts prove inaccurate. For example, treasury bills and certificates of deposit can be traded in the market and realised at any time, whereas a fixed term deposit may not be available until the end of the deposit term.

20.7 Summary

In this chapter, we have identified a number of sources of short-term finance, as well as considering alternatives for investing short-term cash surpluses.

Revision Questions

20

? Question 1

Which ONE of the following most appropriately describes *forfaifing*?

(A) It is a method of providing medium-term export finance
(B) It provides long-term finance to importers
(C) It provides equity finance for the redemption of shares
(D) It is the surrender of a share because of the failure to make a payment on a partly-paid
share **(2 marks)**

? Question 2

Which of the following is NOT a method used for raising finance to fund export sales:

(A) Bills of exchange
(B) Credit insurance
(C) Documentary credits
(D) Countertrade **(2 marks)**

? Question 3

Which of the following would NOT be regarded as a source of short-term finance:

(A) Trade credit from suppliers
(B) Treasury bills
(C) Factoring of trade receivables
(D) Bank overdraft **(2 marks)**

? Question 4

List six sources of short-term investments. **(3 marks)**

? Question 5

In no more than 40 words, define the meaning of 'yield to maturity'. **(2 marks)**

? Question 6

After a bill of exchange has been accepted, there are a number of possible actions that the drawer could take. Which ONE of the following is NOT a possible course of action?

(A) Ask the customer for immediate payment
(B) Discount the bill with a bank
(C) Hold the bill until the due date and then present it for payment
(D) Use the bill to settle a trade payable   **(2 marks)**

? Question 7

CX purchased $10,000 of unquoted bonds when they were issued by Z. CX now wishes to sell the bonds to B. The bonds have a coupon rate of 7% and will repay their face value at the end of five years. Similar bonds have a yield to maturity of 10%. Calculate the current market price for the bonds.   **(3 marks)**

? Question 8

BH purchased a bond with a face value of $1,000 on 1 June 2003 for $850. The bond has a coupon rate of 7%. BH intends holding the bond to its maturity on 31 May 2008 when it will repay its face value.

Requirements
(i) Explain the difference between the coupon rate of a security and its yield to maturity.
                                                                        (2 marks)
(ii) Calculate the bond's yield to maturity.   **(3 marks)**
                                                                        (Total marks = 5)

? Question 9

Explain the main sources of short-term and medium-term funds.   **(5 marks)**

? Question 10

Discuss a situation where it is better to obtain overdraft facilities rather than a term loan.
                                                                        (5 marks)

? Question 11

'Delaying payment to suppliers of goods and services is always a cheap form of borrowing funds.' Discuss this statement.   **(5 marks)**

? Question 12

A bond has a current market price of $83. It will repay its face value of $100 in 7 years' time and has a coupon rate of 4%.

If the bond is purchased at $83 and held, what is its yield to maturity?   **(4 marks)**

Solutions to Revision Questions

✓ Solution 1

The correct answer is (A), see Section 20.3.4.

✓ Solution 2

The correct answer is (B), see Section 20.3.

✓ Solution 3

The correct answer is (B), see Sections 20.2 and 20.6.

✓ Solution 4

Any six from the following list:

- treasury bills,
- bank deposits,
- certificates of deposit,
- bills of exchange,
- money-market accounts,
- local authority deposits,
- commercial paper,
- local authority bonds,
- corporate bonds,
- government bonds.

See Section 20.6.

✓ Solution 5

The yield to maturity is the effective yield on a redeemable security, taking into account any gain or loss due to the fact that it was purchased at a price different from the redemption value, see Section 20.5.2.

Solution 6

The correct answer is (A), see Section 20.3.2.

 Solution 7

$700 × (annuity factor for $t = 5$; $r = 10$) + 10,000 × (discount factor $t = 5$; $r = 10$)
   = ($700 × 3.791) + (10,000 × 0.621) = 2,653.7 + 6,210 = \$8,863.7
Annuity factor and discount factor are from tables, see Section 20.3.2.1.

 Solution 8

(i) The coupon rate is the interest rate payable on the face, or nominal, value of the debt. BH's bond has a coupon rate of 7% on $1,000, which equals $70 interest.

   The yield to maturity, or redemption yield, is the effective yield on a redeemable security. It takes into account the actual interest receivable and any gain or loss due to the fact that it was purchased at a price different from the redemption value. BH's yield to maturity takes into account that the $1,000 bond was purchased for $850.

(ii) The yield to maturity can be calculated as the discounted annual rate of return at which the present value of future interest payments and redemption value of the bond at maturity equals the current market value of the bond.

   Let $t = 5$ and $r = 9$ and
   ($70 × 3.890) + ($1,000 × 0.650) = 272.3 + 650 = 922.3

   Let $t = 5$ and $r = 12$ and
   ($70 × 3.605) + ($1,000 × 0.567) = 252.35 + 567 = 819.35

   See Section 20.5.2.

 Solution 9

An overdraft from a bank is a common form of short-term loan and most businesses would have overdraft facilities arranged with their bank. However, term loans are also used widely to provide medium-term finance.

   By being able to withdraw more than was deposited in a bank account, a business can use an overdraft to fund temporary shortages of cash resources. The problem is that the bank can withdraw the right to use the overdraft at any time and so there is an element of uncertainty. However, banks tend to treat their customers fairly and so will usually try to assist them in difficult times.

   Trade credit is another form of short-term credit that is used by businesses. By delaying payments to suppliers, credit can be obtained without incurring cost unless cash discounts are forgone or suppliers increase prices recognising that payments are delayed unduly by some of their customers, see Section 20.2.

Solution 10

An overdraft provides the management with flexibility. The exact amount of funding required and the timings, especially of repayment, can be adjusted to suit the funding needs of the organisation.

If the overdraft facilities are only used when it is essential, the cost of borrowing can be kept to a minimum. The interest on an overdraft is calculated on the daily balance and so interest will only be incurred when the facilities are used. It is likely, however, that the rate of interest charged will be high.

At any time, the bank can ask for the amount outstanding to be repaid. The bank manager will regularly require cash-flow projections in order to judge the borrower's creditworthiness, and it is not unusual for the owners or the managers responsible for the organisation to be asked to provide collateral security to reduce the default risk of the lender.

It is generally recognised that bank overdrafts are a convenient form of short-term borrowing that is used by most businesses because of the flexibility that it provides at a relatively low cost, see Section 20.2.0 and 20.2.3.

 Solution 11

By delaying payments to suppliers, it is possible for a business to obtain short-term finance. Thus, by taking a relatively long time before settling the amounts owed to trade payables, the funds can be used for other purposes. In the simplest position, inventory will be delivered and sold before a payment is made to the supplier of the inventory. It is possible that the firm's customer has already paid before the amount is paid to the supplier.

Provided that the selling price is not increased or cash discounts lost, trade credit is provided free and is particularly beneficial to small firms, although it is used by all businesses. It is extremely important that opportunities to receive cash discounts are not lost, as the annualised rate of interest forgone can be significant. However, as the annualised cost of offering cash discounts is high, it is relatively unusual to be offered this form of discount and so it is not often necessary to pay trade payables early. The period that is acceptable will be a matter that will be negotiated at the time of placing the order and it is not unusual to delay payments and so enjoy the 'free loan' for a longer period of time, see Section 20.2.1.

 Solution 12

Yield to maturity:

Using $t = 7$ and $r = 6$ and 8, from tables

$$(4 \times 5.582) + (100 \times 0.665) = 22.328 + 66.5 = 88.828$$
$$(4 \times 5.206) + (100 \times 0.583) = 20.824 + 58.3 = 79.124$$
$$6 + \frac{88.828 - 83.00}{88.828 - 79.124} \times 2 = 6 + \frac{5.828}{9.704} \times 2$$
$$= 6 + 1.20 = 7.20\%$$

See Section 20.5.2.

21

Working Capital: Receivables and Payables

Working Capital: Receivables and Payables

21

LEARNING OUTCOMES

After completing this chapter, you should be able to:

▶ analyse trade receivable information;

▶ evaluate receivable and payable policies.

The syllabus topics covered in this chapter are as follows:

- the credit cycle from receipt of customer order to cash receipt;
- evaluation of payment terms and settlement discounts;
- preparation and interpretation of age analyses of receivables and payables;
- establishing collection targets on an appropriate basis (e.g. motivational issues in managing credit control);
- the payment cycle from agreeing the order to making payments.

21.1 Introduction

This chapter will discuss the credit cycle from the receipt of the customer order through to the collection of the debt and the payment cycle from the placing of an order to the payment of the supplier. The chapter will also discuss payment terms and discounts and the preparation and use of an age analysis of receivables and payables.

21.2 Managing receivables

An entity may have a ratio of trade receivables to total assets in the region of 20–25 per cent. This represents a considerable investment of funds and so the management of this asset can have a significant effect on the profit performance of an entity.

By international standards, the UK does not have a good record for the collection of debts. In the UK manufacturing sector, it takes on average about 60 days for an entity

475

to collect the funds due from a receivable. In contrast, in the USA, the average collection period for manufacturing industry is in the region of 40 days.

In order to reduce the trade receivable days to a more respectable figure, entities may offer customers inducements in the form of *cash discounts.* These discounts may well speed up collection but reduce the amount from each sale when collected.

Credit management involves balancing the benefits to be gained from extending credit to customers against the costs of doing so and finding the optimum level of credit and discounts that will maximise the entity's profits. It also involves such things as assessing the credit risk of customers wanting credit, collecting debts which are overdue, assessing what effect changing credit terms will have on the occurrence of bad debts and setting individual credit limits for customers.

21.3 The credit cycle

The credit cycle refers to the events that take place between the receipt of a customer's order, through to the receipt of cash from the customer. The credit cycle can be broken down into two elements: the order cycle, being the period between the receipt of a customer's order and the raising of an invoice; and the collection cycle, which is the period from raising the invoice until cash is received from the customer.

The stages in the credit cycle are as follows:

- receipt of customer order;
- credit screening and agreement of terms;
- goods dispatched with delivery note;
- invoice raised stating credit terms;
- debt collection procedures;
- receipt of cash.

The longer the credit cycle, the more cash there is locked into working capital. Reducing the length of the credit cycle will improve cash flow and thus improve the entity's liquidity position.

21.3.1 Credit control

As stated above, to have good credit management you should assess the credit risk of your customer base. This would involve giving consideration to your credit control procedures. Detailed below are key elements that need to be taken into account in setting a *credit control policy.*

- The terms of trade, notably the period of credit to be granted and any discounts to be allowed for early settlement. This will largely be determined by practice within the industry, but there is usually some scope for differentiation – from competitors and between customers (the riskier prospects being put on a shorter-period, higher-discount arrangement). It is important to record all the terms agreed.
- On a customer-by-customer basis, it is necessary to assess creditworthiness and to establish limits in terms of amount and time. New customers should be checked for creditworthiness before being given a credit account.

Sources of credit information include:

- bank reference from the customers bank;
- trade references from other entities the customer deals with;
- credit reference agency report;
- sales representative visit to customers premises;
- checking legal sources of information for example records of court judgements;
- carry out an analysis of the entity's latest financial statements;
- view the customers website, if one exists, for information;
- ask prospective customers to complete a credit application form and carry out credit scoring;
- check the entity's credit rating if it is large enough to have one.

Late payment is seen as a major problem in UK industry, with large entities accused of pressurising small ones. Various ideas have been put forward to counteract this:

- legislation to give suppliers a statutory right to interest on overdue debts;
- disclosure in published accounts of credit taken;
- a code of practice, including paying according to agreed terms;
- inclusion of payment to agreed terms as a requisite for receiving a quality certificate.

21.3.2 Payment terms

The payment terms will need to consider the period of credit to be granted and how the payment will be made. The terms agreed will need to specify the price, the date of delivery, the payment date or dates, and any discounts to be allowed for early settlement.

Examples of payment terms may be:

- *Payment within a specified period.* For example, customers must pay within 30 days.
- *Payment within a specified period with discount.* For example, a 2 per cent discount would be given to customers who pay within 10 days, and others would be required to pay within 30 days.
- *Weekly credit.* This would require all supplies in a week to be paid by a specified day in the following week.
- *Related to delivery of goods.* For example, cash on delivery (COD).

21.3.3 Cash discounts

Cash discounts are sometimes offered by entities as a means of improving cash flow by encouraging customers to settle their accounts early. The cost of offering a cash discount in order to generate better cash flow is sometimes overlooked. The savings made by the entity from a lower receivable balance and shorter average collecting period should be compared with the cost of the discount to see if the reduced period of credit could be financed by alternative means, for example, a bank overdraft.

 Exercise 21.1

Tandijono normally offers its customers 50-day payment terms, but to improve its cash flow is considering a 2 per cent discount for payment within 10 days.

You are required to advise the entity on the cost of this proposed action.

Assume a 365-day year and an invoice for $100.

Solution

The entity would receive $98 on day 10 instead of $100 on day 50. Tandijono would then be able to invest the $98 for 40 days (50 − 10).

If the prevailing interest rate is r per cent per annum, the entity will benefit as follows:

$$\$98 \times r\% \times \frac{40}{365}$$

However, to achieve this the entity has to grant $2 in discount. To break even on this scheme, we must have:

$$\$98 \times r\% \times \frac{40}{365} \geq \$2$$

Rearranging:

$$r\% \geq \frac{\$2}{\$98} \times \frac{365}{40} = 18.6\%$$

The 18.6 per cent would then be compared with the entity cost of capital to establish if this is an efficient method of financing the shorter credit period.

Note: A more accurate method can be used that deals with the compound interest effect.

The compound interest formula states that the value S attained by a single sum X, after n periods at r per cent, is:

$$S = X(1 + r)^n$$

Using this formula to quantify the cost of offering the cash discount:

$$100 = 98 \ (1 + r)^1$$

where

r = periodic rate (in this case the rate is for a 40-day period)
$1 + r = 1.0204$
$r = 2.04\%$

This periodic rate must then be converted into an annual rate using the formula:

$$(1 + \text{annualised rate}) = (1 + \text{periodic rate})^n$$

where

n = number of compounding periods in the year (in this example $\frac{365}{40} = 9.125$)

$(1 + \text{annualised rate}) = (1.0204)^{9.125} = 1.202$
$$\text{annualised rate} = 20.2\%$$

This compounding process can be short cut as shown below:

$$1 + r = \left(\frac{100}{98}\right)^{9.125}$$
$$1 + r = 1.202$$

The cost of offering the cash discount is then 20.2 per cent.
For the examination, the compound interest approach should be used.

Use the formula:

$$1 + r = [fv/dv]^n$$

where:

fv = face value
dv = discounted value
n = number of compounding periods in the year

21.3.4   Methods of payment

Payments from customers may be accepted in a number of forms, including:

- cash;
- Bankers Automated Clearing Service (BACS);
- cheques;
- banker's draft;
- standing orders;
- direct debit;
- credit cards;
- debit cards;
- Clearing House Automated Payments System (CHAPS).

21.3.5   The stages in debt collection

There is no optimal debt collection policy that will be applicable to all entities. Debt collection policies will differ according to the nature of the business and the level of competition.

An effective solution will require the following:

- dedicated, well-trained credit control personnel;
- well-defined procedures for collection of overdue debts that take account of the potential costs of collecting an outstanding debt, and the need to maintain good relationships with customers;
- monitoring of overdue accounts;
- flexibility to allow for changing circumstances.

The longer a debt is outstanding, the higher the probability of default. There need to be well-defined procedures for following up – allowing in the first instance for the possibility of a genuine query – and keeping notes that can be referred to later. If the worst comes to the worst, there will be a need to understand the law relating to contracts, insolvency, winding up and liquidation. In practical terms, the danger of 'throwing good money after bad' needs to be considered.

One way of encouraging customers to pay within the agreed credit period is to charge interest on any overdue debts. While this would normally have to be agreed by the parties at the time of the sale, small businesses in the UK are provided with some protection against late payment by the Late Payment Act.

Since 1 November 1998, small businesses – those with less than 50 employees – can choose whether to charge large entities interest at 8 per cent above base rate on bills that are paid more than 30 days after they fall due.

21.4 Age analysis of trade receivables

As an aid to effective credit control, an age analysis of outstanding debts may be produced. This is simply a list of the customers who currently owe money, showing the total amount owed and the period of time for which the money has been owed. The actual form of the age analysis report can vary widely, but a typical example is shown below.

Robins

Age analysis of trade receivables as at 30 September 2005

Account number	Customer name	Balance	Up to 30 days	31–60 days	61–90 days	Over 90 days
B002	Brennan	294.35	220.15	65.40	8.80	0.00
G007	Goodridge	949.50	853.00	0.00	96.50	0.00
T005	Taylor	371.26	340.66	30.60	0.00	0.00
T010	Thorpe	1,438.93	0.00	0.00	567.98	870.95
T011	Tinnion	423.48	312.71	110.77	0.00	0.00
Totals		3,477.52	1,726.52	206.77	673.28	870.95
Percentage		100%	49.6%	6%	19.4%	25%

To prepare the analysis, either use a computer programme or manually analyse each customer, account. For each customer, every invoice is allocated to the month it was issued. Then when payment is received, the invoice is cancelled from the analysis, leaving the total of unpaid invoices for each month. Difficulties analysing the balance can occur if the customer pays lump sum on account, rather than specific invoices. Care must be taken to allocate all adjustments other than cash, such as credit notes, discounts given etc.

The age analysis of trade receivables can be used to help decide what action should be taken about debts that have been outstanding for longer than the specified credit period. It can be seen from the table above that 41 per cent of Robins's outstanding trade receivable balance is due by Thorpe. It may be that Thorpe is experiencing financial difficulties. There may already have been some correspondence between the two entities about the outstanding debts.

As well as providing information about individual customer balances, the age analysis of trade receivables provides additional information about the efficiency of cash collection. The table above shows that over 50 per cent of debts at 30 September 2005 have been outstanding for more than 30 days. If the normal credit period is 30 days, there may be a suggestion of weaknesses in credit control. It may also be useful to show the credit limit for each customer on the report, to identify those customers who are close to, or have exceeded, their credit limit.

The age analysis can also provide information to assist in setting and monitoring collection targets for the credit control section. A collection target could be expressed as a percentage of credit sales collected within a specified period or it could be expressed in terms of the average number of trade receivable days outstanding. When trying to achieve a collection target the age analysis can be very useful in identifying large balances that have been outstanding for long periods; these can be targeted for action to encourage payment.

21.5   Credit insurance

To protect against the risk of bad debts, an entity can take out credit insurance. There are a number of entities specialising in this form of insurance, offering a wide variety of services with costs to match.

Policies may be arranged that cover the whole of an entity's turnover. The credit insurer will normally place a limit on value of a single invoice that will be insured without special approval. The insured entity will need to assess each customer's creditworthiness, using approved information sources to ensure it is covered under the terms of the insurance.

Alternatively, an entity may wish to take out insurance on specific invoices. The premium payable will be determined by the perceived risk of non-payment.

21.6   Factoring

In CIMA's *Management Accounting: Official Terminology* factoring is defined as follows:

> The sale of debts to a third party (the factor) at a discount, in return for prompt cash. A factoring service may be *with recourse,* in which case the supplier takes the risk of the debt not being paid, or *without recourse* when the factor takes the risk.

Specialist finance entities (usually subsidiaries of banks) offering factoring arrangements will provide three main services:

1. provide finance by advancing, say 80 per cent of invoice value immediately, the remainder being settled when the client's customer settles the debt (but net of a charge for interest, typically 3 per cent per annum above base rate);
2. take responsibility for the operation of the client's sales ledger, including assessment of creditworthiness and dealing with customers for an additional service charge, typically 2 per cent of turnover;
3. they may, for an additional fee, offer non-recourse finance, that is, guarantee settlement even if they are not paid by the customer.

In order to do this economically, they have developed their expertise in credit control in terms of market intelligence (including credit scoring), information management (sophisticated databases, processing and decision support systems) and the skills required for dealing with customers especially those who are in no hurry to pay!

Alternatively, they may offer a *confidential invoice discounting* facility under which they provide the finance as above, but do not get involved with the operation of the sales ledger or hence become known to the customers. This has, to date, been more popular than the overt factoring arrangement. It is cheaper, of course, and avoids creating a barrier between the business and its customers. It is less attractive to the providers of finance, however, being in the nature of supplying a commodity rather than adding value through expertise.

Though, as mentioned, these financiers are usually subsidiaries of banks, they like to distinguish their approach from that of their parents. They argue that the mainstream banks, when deciding on the extent to which they are prepared to lend, have traditionally looked backwards – to an entity's past profits and tangible assets. This explains why they are reluctant to lend just when the entity needs it, that is, ahead of a growth phase. A sales-based package is a logical, flexible alternative. Having siphoned off the trade receivables in this way, the returns from a business are going to be more uncertain, making it difficult to raise more traditional forms of finance except at high interest rates. It is also worth noting that factoring is associated in many people's minds with financial difficulties ('the banks do not refer their best prospects to their factoring subsidiaries') or at best with small businesses, which may have an impact on the image of the business in the eyes of its suppliers.

Apart from the factors and invoice discounters, it is worth noting some other players in the receivables industry:

- the specialist information providers, covering credit assessments, increasingly available electronically. This means that the sales function can have access, thereby reducing the potential for friction, for example, taking an order only to find that 'finance' reject it on the grounds of credit risk;
- *Credit insurance.* clients typically pay around 1 per cent of sales, depending on the industry into which they are selling and on their perceived credit control skills. It should be seen as complementary to, rather than a substitute for, in-house vigilance;
- debt collectors, often members of the legal profession, who take over responsibility for dealing with unpaid bills – sometimes on commission, otherwise for a fee.

These various services are mutually supportive and there have been signs of convergence, that is, of providers who offer a menu from which businesses can pick.

> Examination questions could ask you to consider whether it is beneficial for an entity to use factoring or to raise the finance by an alternative method, for example, bank overdraft.

Exercise 21.2

(a) *You are required to* summarise the services that may be obtained from various forms of agreement for the factoring of trade debts and from invoice discounting.
(**5 marks**)

(b) B has been set up for the purpose of importing commodities that will be sold to a small number of reliable customers. Sales invoicing is forecast at $300,000 per month. The average credit period for this type of business is 2½ months.

The entity is considering factoring its accounts receivable under a full factoring agreement without recourse. Under the agreement, the factor will charge a fee of 2½ per cent on total invoicing. He will give an advance of 85 per cent of invoiced amounts at an interest rate of 13 per cent per annum.

The agreement should enable B to avoid spending $95,000 on administration costs.

You are required:

(i) to calculate the annual net cost of factoring;
(ii) to discuss the financial benefits of such an agreement, having regard to current interest rate on bank overdrafts of 12½ per cent. (**10 marks**)
(**Total marks = 15**)

Solution

(a) Factoring and invoice discounting are methods of raising finance from trade receivables. In factoring the debts are sold, while invoice discounting is the assignment of debts as security for a loan.

The main services associated with entities offering this finance are:

- Provision of finance of between 80 per cent and 85 per cent of approved debts from the moment the goods or services are invoiced.
- Sales ledger service covering credit-checking, invoicing and collection. In effect, the sales ledger function or part thereof is subcontracted.
- Bad-debt insurance to cover the firm in the event of default on an invoice or invoices.
- Confidentiality to prevent the arrangement being apparent to customers and others.

(b) (i)

Annual sales: $300,000 × 12	$3,600,000
Annual net cost of factoring	$
Fee: 2.5% of $3,600,000	90,000
Annual interest* (85% × 2.5/12 × 3.6 m × 13%)	82,875
Total annual cost	172,875
Less: administration costs	95,000
Net cost	77,875

*Assuming the agreement is based on existing invoices and does not phase in.

(ii) The borrowing of $637,500 (2.5/12 × 3.6 m × 85%) from the bank would cost $79,687.50. Therefore, factoring offers a saving of around $2,000 as well as providing certain advantages:

- *Flexibility.* As sales increase with the corresponding demand for finance, so finance from this source increases.
- *Security.* It allows the firm to pledge other assets as security for the finance.
- *Last resort.* It may be the most cost-effective lender to a firm that has no assets to offer as security.
- *Responsibility.* Relieves management of the responsibility for the sales ledger and can probably perform credit-checking better than the firm. Management must balance the disruption from cutting back its administrative costs with the financial and other advantages of factoring. Before reaching a decision, management should consider the possibility that the financial advantages may change and that re-establishing a sales ledger function may be costly.

21.7 Assessing the effectiveness of credit control

An outsider wishing to assess the effectiveness of a credit control function is generally limited to using static information and ratios, for example:

	Year 1	Year 2
$m		
(a) sales for the year	100.0	120.0
(b) trade receivables at the end of the year	16.0	20.0
Times per annum		
Asset velocity (a)/(b)	6.3	6.0
Days		
Average collection period 365(b)/(a)	58.4	60.8

WORKING CAPITAL: RECEIVABLES AND PAYABLES

WORKING CAPITAL: RECEIVABLES AND PAYABLES

This would be interpreted as an apparent deterioration in performance, but such an approach inevitably ignores a number of possible explanations:

- changes in the pattern of sales across the year, for example, more towards the end;
- changes in the mix of sales as between customers, for example, more to those granted longer credit;
- changes in terms, for example, less attractive discounts to some or all customers;
- different degrees of window dressing, for example, sales pulled forward from subsequent year.

Internally, of course, these problems do not arise, thanks to the availability of management information, including daily sales and receipts. As sales are entered into the ledger, for example, it is possible to identify when they should be paid, thus providing an appropriate yardstick against which to measure performance.

Entities that seek to apply the principles of value assurance to activities characterised as giving rise to 'indirect costs' could do worse than start with credit control. Value in this context is the cost of the next best alternative, for example, handing over the job to the professional factors.

This amounts to regarding the function as a business unit. It is credited with its actual receipts, having been debited with:

- the price at which the factor would buy the debts, for example, 98 per cent of their face value;
- the cost of finance, say 0.03 per cent per day on the aggregate balance;
- the costs of administration, etc.

If the net result is positive, the function is adding value to the entity.

21.8 Evaluating a change in credit policy

> In an examination, you may be required to evaluate whether a proposed change in credit policy is financially justified. The example below illustrates the approach required to carry out this evaluation.

✋ Exercise 21.3

The table below gives information extracted from the annual accounts of Supergeordie.

	$
Raw materials	180,000
Work in progress	93,360
Finished goods	142,875
Purchases	720,000
Cost of goods sold	1,098,360
Sales	1,188,000
Trade receivables	297,000
Trade payables	126,000

The sales director of Supergeordie estimates that if the period of credit allowed to customers was reduced from its current level to 60 days, this would result in a 25 per cent reduction in sales but would probably eliminate about $30,000 per annum bad debts.

It would be necessary to spend an additional $20,000 per annum on credit control. The entity at present relies heavily on overdraft finance costing 9 per cent per annum.

You are required to make calculations showing the effect of these changes, and to advise whether they would be financially justified. Assume that purchases and inventory holdings would be reduced proportionally to the reduction in sales value.

 Solution

The first stage is to identify the reduction in the level of working capital investment as a result of the change in policy. Inventory and trade payables are assumed to fall by 25 per cent in line with sales, but the new level of trade receivables will need to be calculated using the trade receivable collection formula.

Reduction in working capital

	Existing level $		New level $	Change $
Raw materials	180,000	× 75% =	135,000	45,000
Work in progress	93,360	× 75% =	70,020	23,340
Finished goods	142,875	× 75% =	107,156	35,719
Trade receivables	297,000	*	146,466	150,534
Trade payables	(126,000)	× 75% =	(94,500)	(31,500)
Total	587,235		364,142	223,093

$$\text{Receivable collection period} = \frac{\text{trade receivables}}{\text{sales}} \times 365$$

$$60 = \frac{\text{trade receivables}}{1,188,000} \times 75\% \times 365$$

$$*\text{Trade receivables} = \frac{891,000 \times 60}{365}$$

$$= \$146,466$$

The second stage is to consider the annual costs and benefits of changing the credit policy. A key element here is to recognise the saving in finance costs as a result of the reduction in the level of working capital investment recognised above.

Annual costs and benefits

		$
Saving in finance costs	223,093 × 9% =	20,078
Reduction in gross profit (1,188,000 − 1,098,360)	= 89,640 × 25% =	(22,410)
Reduction in bad debts	=	30,000
Credit control costs	=	(20,000)
Net saving per annum before tax		7,668

The change in credit policy appears to be justified financially, but it should be remembered that there are a number of assumptions built in that could invalidate the calculations.

21.9 Trade payables

The term trade payables refers to the money owed to suppliers for goods and services. Taking credit from suppliers is a normal part of business, and is often viewed as being a free source of finance. The policy adopted regarding trade payables often then tends to be to maximise this resource, paying suppliers as late as possible. This policy may lead to a number of potential problems, discussed in the previous chapter, Section 20.2.1.

Trade payable management will broadly reflect trade receivable management, as one entity's receivable will be another entity's payable. Trade payable management will involve trying to maximise the credit period without jeopardising relationships with suppliers, while also seeking to optimise the level of inventory held.

21.10 The payment cycle

The payment cycle refers to the events that take place between agreeing the order, through to making payment.

The stages in the payment cycle are as follows:

- agreeing the order;
- credit control – evaluating whether to accept settlement discounts and deciding which invoices to pay first;
- method of payment;
- making payment to supplier.

Example: Trade payable payment policy at Marks and Spencer plc

The annual report for 2003 of Marks and Spencer plc states that its policy concerning the payment of its trade payables is:

'For all trade payables, it is the company's policy to:

- agree the terms of payment at the start of business with that supplier;
- ensure that suppliers are aware of the terms of payment;
- pay in accordance with its contractual and other legal obligations.'

The main trading company's (Marks and Spencer plc) policy concerning the payment of its trade creditors is as follows:

- General merchandise is automatically paid for 11 working days from the end of the week of delivery
- Foods are paid for 13 working days from the end of the week of delivery (based on the timely receipt of an accurate invoice) and
- Distribution suppliers are paid monthly for costs incurred in that month, based on estimates, and payments are adjusted quarterly to reflect any variations to estimate.

Trade creditor days for Marks and Spencer plc for the year ended 29 March 2003 were 14.3 days (10.3 working days), based on the ratio of company trade creditors at the end of the year to the amounts invoiced during the year by trade creditors.

21.10.1 Cash discounts

An entity may benefit from paying a supplier early in order to take advantage of settlement discounts. However, the benefit of the discount must be evaluated against the finance cost involved.

 Exercise 21.4

Claud has been offered credit terms from a supplier whereby, Claud may claim a cash discount of 2 per cent if payment is made within 10 days of the invoice or pay on normal credit terms within 50 days.

You are required to advise the entity whether it should take advantage of the cash discount.

Assume a 365-day year and an invoice for $100.

 Solution

This is the mirror image of Exercise 21.1 (Tandijono). There we calculated that offering the discount was equivalent to an interest rate of 18.6 per cent per annum.

The implied interest cost of 18.6 per cent would then be compared with the overdraft rate. If Claud Ltd could borrow $98 for 40 days at a rate less than 18.6 per cent, it would be worthwhile taking advantage of the cash discount.

As before, by using the compound interest formula we arrive at a more accurate figure of 20.2 per cent per annum for the interest rate.

21.10.2 Methods of payment

Businesses may use a number of methods of payment for goods and services provided, including:

- cash;
- Bankers Automated Clearing Services (BACS);
- cheques;
- banker's draft;
- standing orders;
- direct debit;
- credit cards;
- debit cards;
- Clearing House Automated Payments System (CHAPS).

21.11 Age analysis of trade payables

As an aid to effective management, an age analysis of trade payables may be produced. This is similar to the age analysis of trade receivables we saw earlier and is simply a list of the suppliers to whom we currently owe money, showing the total amount owed and the period of time for which the money has been owed. The actual form of the age analysis report can vary widely, but a typical example is shown below.

Anglo-Dutch

Age analysis of trade payables as at 30 September 2003

Account number	Customer name	Balance	Up to 30 days	31–60 days	61–90 days	Over 90 days
B004	Van Basten	294.35	220.15	65.40	8.80	0.00
D002	Van Dalen	949.50	853.00	0.00	96.50	0.00
D005	Dunister	371.26	340.66	30.60	0.00	0.00
H001	Van den Hoeven	1,438.93	0.00	0.00	567.98	870.95
K006	Koeman	423.48	312.71	110.77	0.00	0.00
Totals		3,477.52	1,726.52	206.77	673.28	870.95
Percentage		100%	49.6%	6%	19.4%	25%

The age analysis of trade payables will highlight any supplier accounts that are overdue. In the table above, $870.95 owed to Van den Hoeven has been outstanding for more than 3 months. The age profile shows that of the debts outstanding at 30 September 2003, nearly 45 per cent have been outstanding for more than 60 days, with the majority of those being outstanding payments due to Van den Hoeven.

21.12 Summary

In this chapter, we have considered a range of techniques that may be used to manage trade receivables and trade payables.

Factoring and invoice discounting have been considered in this chapter as techniques for the management of receivables, but they can equally have been considered as useful alternative methods of raising short-term finance.

APPLICABLE MATHS TABLES AND FORMULAE

(Provided in the examination)

Present value table

Present value of $1, that is $(1 + r)^{-n}$ where r = interest rate; n = number of periods until payment or receipt.

Periods (n)	Interest rates (r)									
	1%	2%	3%	4%	5%	6%	7%	8%	9%	10%
1	0.990	0.980	0.971	0.962	0.952	0.943	0.935	0.926	0.917	0.909
2	0.980	0.961	0.943	0.925	0.907	0.890	0.873	0.857	0.842	0.826
3	0.971	0.942	0.915	0.889	0.864	0.840	0.816	0.794	0.772	0.751
4	0.961	0.924	0.888	0.855	0.823	0.792	0.763	0.735	0.708	0.683
5	0.951	0.906	0.863	0.822	0.784	0.747	0.713	0.681	0.650	0.621
6	0.942	0.888	0.837	0.790	0.746	0.705	0.666	0.630	0.596	0.564
7	0.933	0.871	0.813	0.760	0.711	0.665	0.623	0.583	0.547	0.513
8	0.923	0.853	0.789	0.731	0.677	0.627	0.582	0.540	0.502	0.467
9	0.914	0.837	0.766	0.703	0.645	0.592	0.544	0.500	0.460	0.424
10	0.905	0.820	0.744	0.676	0.614	0.558	0.508	0.463	0.422	0.386
11	0.896	0.804	0.722	0.650	0.585	0.527	0.475	0.429	0.388	0.350
12	0.887	0.788	0.701	0.625	0.557	0.497	0.444	0.397	0.356	0.319
13	0.879	0.773	0.681	0.601	0.530	0.469	0.415	0.368	0.326	0.290
14	0.870	0.758	0.661	0.577	0.505	0.442	0.388	0.340	0.299	0.263
15	0.861	0.743	0.642	0.555	0.481	0.417	0.362	0.315	0.275	0.239
16	0.853	0.728	0.623	0.534	0.458	0.394	0.339	0.292	0.252	0.218
17	0.844	0.714	0.605	0.513	0.436	0.371	0.317	0.270	0.231	0.198
18	0.836	0.700	0.587	0.494	0.416	0.350	0.296	0.250	0.212	0.180
19	0.828	0.686	0.570	0.475	0.396	0.331	0.277	0.232	0.194	0.164
20	0.820	0.673	0.554	0.456	0.377	0.312	0.258	0.215	0.178	0.149

Periods (n)	Interest rates (r)									
	11%	12%	13%	14%	15%	16%	17%	18%	19%	20%
1	0.901	0.893	0.885	0.877	0.870	0.862	0.855	0.847	0.840	0.833
2	0.812	0.797	0.783	0.769	0.756	0.743	0.731	0.718	0.706	0.694
3	0.731	0.712	0.693	0.675	0.658	0.641	0.624	0.609	0.593	0.579
4	0.659	0.636	0.613	0.592	0.572	0.552	0.534	0.516	0.499	0.482
5	0.593	0.567	0.543	0.519	0.497	0.476	0.456	0.437	0.419	0.402
6	0.535	0.507	0.480	0.456	0.432	0.410	0.390	0.370	0.352	0.335
7	0.482	0.452	0.425	0.400	0.376	0.354	0.333	0.314	0.296	0.279
8	0.434	0.404	0.376	0.351	0.327	0.305	0.285	0.266	0.249	0.233
9	0.391	0.361	0.333	0.308	0.284	0.263	0.243	0.225	0.209	0.194
10	0.352	0.322	0.295	0.270	0.247	0.227	0.208	0.191	0.176	0.162
11	0.317	0.287	0.261	0.237	0.215	0.195	0.178	0.162	0.148	0.135
12	0.286	0.257	0.231	0.208	0.187	0.168	0.152	0.137	0.124	0.112
13	0.258	0.229	0.204	0.182	0.163	0.145	0.130	0.116	0.104	0.093
14	0.232	0.205	0.181	0.160	0.141	0.125	0.111	0.099	0.088	0.078
15	0.209	0.183	0.160	0.140	0.123	0.108	0.095	0.084	0.079	0.065
16	0.188	0.163	0.141	0.123	0.107	0.093	0.081	0.071	0.062	0.054
17	0.170	0.146	0.125	0.108	0.093	0.080	0.069	0.060	0.052	0.045
18	0.153	0.130	0.111	0.095	0.081	0.069	0.059	0.051	0.044	0.038
19	0.138	0.116	0.098	0.083	0.070	0.060	0.051	0.043	0.037	0.031
20	0.124	0.104	0.087	0.073	0.061	0.051	0.043	0.037	0.031	0.026

Cumulative present value of $1 per annum

Receivable or Payable at the end of each year for n years $\dfrac{1-(1+r)^{-n}}{r}$

Periods	Interest rates (r)									
(n)	1%	2%	3%	4%	5%	6%	7%	8%	9%	10%
1	0.990	0.980	0.971	0.962	0.952	0.943	0.935	0.926	0.917	0.909
2	1.970	1.942	1.913	1.886	1.859	1.833	1.808	1.783	1.759	1.736
3	2.941	2.884	2.829	2.775	2.723	2.673	2.624	2.577	2.531	2.487
4	3.902	3.808	3.717	3.630	3.546	3.465	3.387	3.312	3.240	3.170
5	4.853	4.713	4.580	4.452	4.329	4.212	4.100	3.993	3.890	3.791
6	5.795	5.601	5.417	5.242	5.076	4.917	4.767	4.623	4.486	4.355
7	6.728	6.472	6.230	6.002	5.786	5.582	5.389	5.206	5.033	4.868
8	7.652	7.325	7.020	6.733	6.463	6.210	5.971	5.747	5.535	5.335
9	8.566	8.162	7.786	7.435	7.108	6.802	6.515	6.247	5.995	5.759
10	9.471	8.983	8.530	8.111	7.722	7.360	7.024	6.710	6.418	6.145
11	10.368	9.787	9.253	8.760	8.306	7.887	7.499	7.139	6.805	6.495
12	11.255	10.575	9.954	9.385	8.863	8.384	7.943	7.536	7.161	6.814
13	12.134	11.348	10.635	9.986	9.394	8.853	8.358	7.904	7.487	7.103
14	13.004	12.106	11.296	10.563	9.899	9.295	8.745	8.244	7.786	7.367
15	13.865	12.849	11.938	11.118	10.380	9.712	9.108	8.559	8.061	7.606
16	14.718	13.578	12.561	11.652	10.838	10.106	9.447	8.851	8.313	7.824
17	15.562	14.292	13.166	12.166	11.274	10.477	9.763	9.122	8.544	8.022
18	16.398	14.992	13.754	12.659	11.690	10.828	10.059	9.372	8.756	8.201
19	17.226	15.679	14.324	13.134	12.085	11.158	10.336	9.604	8.950	8.365
20	18.046	16.351	14.878	13.590	12.462	11.470	10.594	9.818	9.129	8.514

Periods	Interest rates (r)									
(n)	11%	12%	13%	14%	15%	16%	17%	18%	19%	20%
1	0.901	0.893	0.885	0.877	0.870	0.862	0.855	0.847	0.840	0.833
2	1.713	1.690	1.668	1.647	1.626	1.605	1.585	1.566	1.547	1.528
3	2.444	2.402	2.361	2.322	2.283	2.246	2.210	2.174	2.140	2.106
4	3.102	3.037	2.974	2.914	2.855	2.798	2.743	2.690	2.639	2.589
5	3.696	3.605	3.517	3.433	3.352	3.274	3.199	3.127	3.058	2.991
6	4.231	4.111	3.998	3.889	3.784	3.685	3.589	3.498	3.410	3.326
7	4.712	4.564	4.423	4.288	4.160	4.039	3.922	3.812	3.706	3.605
8	5.146	4.968	4.799	4.639	4.487	4.344	4.207	4.078	3.954	3.837
9	5.537	5.328	5.132	4.946	4.772	4.607	4.451	4.303	4.163	4.031
10	5.889	5.650	5.426	5.216	5.019	4.833	4.659	4.494	4.339	4.192
11	6.207	5.938	5.687	5.453	5.234	5.029	4.836	4.656	4.486	4.327
12	6.492	6.194	5.918	5.660	5.421	5.197	4.988	7.793	4.611	4.439
13	6.750	6.424	6.122	5.842	5.583	5.342	5.118	4.910	4.715	4.533
14	6.982	6.628	6.302	6.002	5.724	5.468	5.229	5.008	4.802	4.611
15	7.191	6.811	6.462	6.142	5.847	5.575	5.324	5.092	4.876	4.675
16	7.379	6.974	6.604	6.265	5.954	5.668	5.405	5.162	4.938	4.730
17	7.549	7.120	6.729	6.373	6.047	5.749	5.475	5.222	4.990	4.775
18	7.702	7.250	6.840	6.467	6.128	5.818	5.534	5.273	5.033	4.812
19	7.839	7.366	6.938	6.550	6.198	5.877	5.584	5.316	5.070	4.843
20	7.963	7.469	7.025	6.623	6.259	5.929	5.628	5.353	5.101	4.870

Revision Questions

21

? Question 1

FGH requires a rate of return of 12.85% each year.

Two of FGH's suppliers, P and Q are offering the following terms for immediate cash settlement:

Entity	Discount period	Normal settlement
P	1%	1 month
Q	2%	2 months

Which of the discounts should be accepted to achieve the required rate of return?

(A) Both P and Q
(B) P only
(C) Q only
(D) Neither of them   **(2 marks)**

? Question 2

A retailing entity had cost of sales of $60,000 in April. In the same month, trade payables increased by $8,000 and inventory decreased by $2,000. What payment was made to suppliers in April?

(A) $50,000
(B) $54,000
(C) $66,000
(D) $70,000   **(2 marks)**

? Question 3

Which ONE of the following services is NOT normally undertaken by a debt factor?

(A) Taking customer orders and invoicing
(B) Attempting to recover doubtful debts
(C) Making payments to entities before the cash is received from trade recievables
(D) Administering a entity's sales ledger   **(2 marks)**

Question 4

If an entity regularly fails to pay its suppliers by the normal due dates, it may lead to a number of problems:

(i) Having insufficient cash to settle trade payables;
(ii) Difficulty in obtaining credit from new suppliers;
(iii) Reduction in credit rating;
(iv) Settlement of trade receivables may be delayed.

Which TWO of the above could arise as a result of exceeding suppliers' trade credit terms?

(A) (i) and (ii)
(B) (i) and (iii)
(C) (ii) and (iii)
(D) (iii) and (iv)   **(2 marks)**

 ## Question 5

BE has been offering 60-day payment terms to its customers, but now wants to improve its cash flow. BE is proposing to offer a 1 × 5% discount for payment within 20 days.

Assume a 365-day year and an invoice value of $1,000.

What is the effective annual interest rate that BE will incur for this action?   **(4 marks)**

 ## Question 6

DN currently has an overdraft on which it pays interest at 10% per year. DN has been offered credit terms from one of its suppliers, whereby it can either claim a cash discount of 2% if payment is made within 10 days of the date of the invoice or pay on normal credit terms, within 40 days of the date of the invoice.

Assume a 365-day year and an invoice value of $100.

Requirement

Explain to DN, with reasons and supporting calculations, whether it should pay the supplier early and take advantage of the discount offered.   **(5 marks)**

 ## Question 7

An entity offers its goods to customers on 30 days' credit, subject to satisfactory trade references. It also offers a 2 per cent discount if payment is made within ten days of the date of invoice.

Requirement

Calculate the cost to the entity of offering the discount, assuming a 365-day year.

                                                                           (4 marks)

❓ Question 8

Compare offering discounts to customers to encourage early settlement of bills with using debt factors. **(5 marks)**

❓ Question 9

Two aspects of working capital policy that require managerial decisions are the level of current assets and the manner in which they are financed.

Discuss aggressive, moderate and conservative policies in these areas. **(10 marks)**

❓ Question 10

AAD is a newly created subsidiary of a large listed entity. It commenced business on 1 October 2004, to provide specialist contract cleaning services to industrial customers. All sales are on credit.

More favourable credit terms are offered to larger customers (class A) than to smaller customers (class B). All sales are invoiced at the end of the month in which the sale occurs. Class A customers will be given credit terms requiring payment within 60 days of invoicing, while class B customers will be required to pay within 30 days of invoicing.

Since it is recognised, however, that not all customers comply with the credit terms they are allowed, receipts from trade receivables have prudently been estimated as follows:

Customer type	Within 30 days	31 to 60 days	61 to 90 days	91 to 120 days	Bad debts
Class A		50%	30%	15%	5%
Class B	60%	25%	10%		5%

The above table shows that trade receivables are expected either to pay within 60 days of the end of the credit period, or not at all. Bad debts will therefore be written off 60 days after the end of the credit period.

Budgeted credit sales for each class of customers in the first 4 months of trading are as follows:

Customer	October	November	December	January
	$'000	$'000	$'000	$'000
Class A	100	150	200	300
Class B	60	80	40	50

Assume all months are of 30 days.

Requirements

(a) Prepare a statement showing the budgeted cash to be received by AAD from trade receivables in each of the 3 months of November 2004, December 2004 and January 2005, based upon the prudently estimated receipts from trade receivables.

(7 marks)

(b) Prepare a budgeted age analysis of trade receivables for AAD at 30 January 2005 for each of the two classes of customer. It should show the total budgeted trade receivables outstanding at that date analysed into each of the following periods:
  (i) within credit period;
  (ii) up to 30 days overdue;
  (iii) 30 to 60 days overdue. **(8 marks)**
(c) Explain the purposes of entities preparing an age analysis of trade receivables analysed by individual customers. **(5 marks)**
(Total marks = 20)

Solutions to Revision Questions

21

☑ Solution 1

The correct answer is (C), see Section 21.10.1.

$P = (100/99)^{12} - 1 = 12.82\%$

$Q = (100/98)^{6} - 1 = 12.89\%$

☑ Solution 2

The correct answer is (A), see Section 21.10.

☑ Solution 3

The correct answer is (A), see Section 21.6.

☑ Solution 4

The correct answer is (C)

☑ Solution 5

$s = x(1 + r)^{n}$

$1,000 = 985 (1 + r)^{365/40}$

$1 + r = (1,000/985)^{9 \times 125}$

$1 + r = 1 \times 148$

$r = 14 \times 8\%$

☑ Solution 6

DN pays $98 on day 10 instead of day 40.

Need to borrow $98 for 30 days

Effective annual interest rate is: $\dfrac{365}{30} = 12.1667$

$$1 + r = \left[\frac{100}{98}\right]^{12.1667}$$

$r = 0.2786$ or 27.86%

DN receives 27.86% interest if it takes the discount. If DN needs to borrow on overdraft to make the payment, it is to its advantage to borrow the money and take the discount as long as the interest rate is less than 27.86%.

If DN has surplus cash in its current account and it is earning less than 27.86% interest, it would be beneficial for DN to use the cash to pay early. If DN has any short-term investments yielding less than 27.86%, it may be worthwhile using these to fund early payment, see Section 21.10.1.

Solution 7

On the policy as described, the entity is offering 2 per cent for 20 days, i.e. 36.5 per cent per annum using simple interest. In accounting terms, the cost to the entity is 2 per cent of the sales in respect of which the discount is taken, but it will show correspondingly lower receivables. Assume sales of $1,000 per day, for simplicity: the discount would cost $7,300 per annum, but receivables would be $20,000 lower, 7,300/20,000 = 36.5 per cent. The cost of offering a cash discount should ideally be calculated using a compounded annual rate. In this example, the compounded annual rate is given by:

$$\left(\frac{100}{98}\right)^{365/20} - 1 = 1.446 - 1 = 44.6\%$$

This can be compared with the entity's cost of capital to arrive at an opportunity cost.

Solution 8

The offering of a discount to customers is normally influenced by practice in the industry/trade in question and may therefore be unavoidable in principle although subject to customisation, firm by firm. The benefits (compared with factoring) are attributable to the maintenance of a direct relationship with the customer. In these days of developing long-term relationships, this can be very important. Also, sales ledger clerks and managers can pick up useful 'intelligence' from their contacts and head off potential problems, including bad debts, and all managers are prompted to think about the time value of money. There is a cost, however, that is not limited to the actual discount: keeping on top of the situation (e.g. reacting quickly to lapses) can be costly, though the latest computer systems have eliminated the need for clerks to go through ledgers.

Factoring, on the other hand, takes the administration of the sales ledger away from the entity and exploits the economies of scale and expertise of the specialists. Different payment terms can be negotiated, for example, some payment immediately on invoicing, thereby releasing further working capital, and/or the guaranteeing of payment. A particular advantage of this approach is that receipts are more predictable: customers may or may not pay in time to earn their discount, but the factor must pay to terms. There is a cost, of course, in respect of the administration and financing, and it must be acknowledged that the factor can be a barrier between the entity and its customers. A 'confidential invoice discounting' service can be an effective compromise.

Experience suggests that, thanks to avoiding double handling, a well-run sales accounting function adds value to a business; factoring is primarily attractive to entities who cannot raise funds from more traditional sources.

 # Solution 9

Some working capital is essential to the process, for example, where different crops are blended or need time to mature or incubate. Some, such as trade credit, is a straight trade-off between cost and investment. The remainder, to which the question addresses itself, is determined by uncertainty and the response thereto. Take, for example, a business that chooses to sell from inventory, rather than to order. Its production plan is going to be based on a forecast of demand, but the latter must be subject to a margin of error. Should the entity plan to carry enough inventory to meet the maximum demand, with all that entails in terms of holding costs? Or should it carry enough to meet the minimum, with all that means in terms of lost business and hence contribution? Put in that way, it is clear that a rational business will seek to optimise, to produce to the point where incremental holding cost equates with incremental contribution. Different degrees of sophistication are applied, for example, some work on three numbers – lowest, highest, and most likely – while others use probability curves. The difficult part in practice is assessing the value of lost contribution: what future orders might be lost, owing to customer dissatisfaction? The terms 'aggressive … conservative … moderate' mean different things to different people but could correspond to preparing to meet maximum demand, minimum demand, or something in between. Alternatively, if we characterise aggressive as being prepared to shoulder a greater risk, it would be associated with lowering cash and inventory, but raising receivables.

Modern financial practice does not think in terms of current assets (an accounting term, after all), being financed separately from fixed assets and revenue investments – rather the focus is on projected cash flows and the margin of error therein. However, there are some empirical relationships, for example, businesses with a high proportion of current (as opposed to fixed or intangible) assets that are likely to be able to attract a higher proportion of their funds in the form of bank overdraft finance. On a different axis, those with wide margins of error in sales forecasts are likely to find it difficult to attract such finance. The scales on these axes have changed considerably over recent years as banks have 'burned their fingers' on loans they thought were safe, but were not.

The link between the investment needs and the funding pattern of a business boils down to the familiar relationship between risk and reward. The more conservative the policy (as defined above) the lower the return, but the lower the risk associated with it.

Solution 10

(a)

Credit sales	Total sales	November	Cash received December	January
Class A				
October	100		50	30
November	150			75
December	200		–	–
Total			50	105
Class B				
October	60	36	15	6
November	80		48	20
December	40	–	–	24
Total		36	63	50
Overall total (A + B)		36	113	155

(b)

Age Analysis of Receivables

	Total	Within credit period	Up to 30 days late	30 to 60 days late
Class A <W1>	595	500	75	20
Class B <W2>	78	50	16	12

Working 1–
Class A

	Total	Cash received (per (a))	Within credit period	Overdue up to 30 days	Overdue 31–60 days	Bad debts
Oct	100	80			20	
Nov	150	75		75		
Dec	200		200			
Jan	300		300			

Working 2 –
Class B

	Total	Cash received (per (a))	Within credit period	Overdue up to 30 days	Overdue 31–60 days	Bad debts
Oct	60	57				3
Nov	80	68			12	
Dec	40	24		16		
Jan	50		50			

(c) An age analysis of receivables is a useful control tool to identify those receivables that are at greatest risk of non-payment or late payment.

It provides an analysis of the total amounts outstanding according to their age. This may be based upon total receivables, a class of receivable or a particular receivable.

Individual receivable data can show accounts that are at risk and appropriate follow-up procedures can be entered into depending upon the period by which normal credit terms have been exceeded.

Progressively this might mean:

- a reminder letter;
- telephone call;
- personal visit;
- withholding supplies;
- debt collection agency;
- legal action.

This progression is likely to be based upon the age of the receivable, but also the nature of the response to initial enquiries. More general age analysis data of classes of business or total or receivables will, when compared over time, enable credit managers to pick up trends in payments giving early warning signals. This might include problems with liquidity in the sector (e.g. through a downturn) or reduced internal efficiency in invoicing and follow-up procedures.

The information about the age of receivables may also help predict cash inflows from the business and decide appropriate action to speed up receipts arising from receivables (e.g. cash discounts, debt factoring, invoice discounting). The age analysis may also indicate when to make a provision for doubtful debts and how much this should be.

22

Working Capital: Inventory

Working Capital: Inventory

22

LEARNING OUTCOME

By the end of this chapter, you should be able to:

▶ evaluate appropriate methods of inventory management.

The syllabus topics covered in this chapter are as follows:

- centralised versus decentralised purchasing.
- the relationship between purchasing and inventory control.
- the economic order quantity (EOQ) model (i.e. reorder levels, reorder quantities, safety inventory and evaluating whether bulk order discounts should be accepted).

22.1   Introduction

This chapter continues with the theme of working capital management and concentrates on inventory management. Valuation of inventory and its accounting treatment was discussed in Chapter 15, we are now going to examine the different types of inventory and its management. The chapter first defines inventory and then looks at the cost of holding inventory and methods that can be used to control it.

22.2   Inventory management

Inventory, like receivables, involve the commitment of a large amount of a firm's resources. Their efficient management is of great concern to the financial manager. Inventory should not be viewed as an idle asset, rather they are an essential part of a firm's investment and operations. The optimum holding of inventory will maximise the benefits less costs involved.

Holding higher levels of finished goods inventory will enable the entity to be more flexible in supplying customers. More customers would receive immediate delivery rather than waiting for new items to be produced, and they might obtain a greater choice of types of product. There would be a smaller chance of sales being disrupted through interruptions in production. These benefits would have to be balanced against the storage costs incurred, the capital costs of financing the inventory and the cost of inventory becoming obsolete.

22.3 The nature of inventory

There are three main categories of inventory: raw materials, work-in-progress and finished goods.

22.3.1 Raw materials

These are used in the manufacturing or production process, for example, components, materials, fuel, etc. Inventory of raw materials are important because they allow *the production* process to be kept separate from the *supply* of raw materials.

22.3.2 Work-in-progress

These are partly finished goods, sub-assemblies, etc., that arise at, or between, various stages of the production process. They allow these various stages of production to be treated independently of each other.

22.3.3 Finished goods

These are completed goods, ready for sale, and held in inventory to meet anticipated customer demand.

The distinction between the categories is somewhat arbitrary (e.g. the finished goods of one entity may be the raw material of another – the 'finished' flour from a mill is a raw material to a bakery).

22.4 The costs of inventory

Three main types of cost are distinguishable.

22.4.1 Holding costs

These include storage costs, insurance, handling, auditing, deterioration, etc. Also, when money is tied up in inventory, it clearly cannot be used for other purposes, so that the opportunity cost of holding inventory (e.g. interest on other capital investments) must be considered.

22.4.2 Order costs

This is the cost of placing a (repeat) order to replenish inventory, for example, administrative costs, computer time, postage, unloading, quality control, etc. – whether the goods are obtained from outside or inside the entity.

22.4.3 The cost of running out of inventory

The costs associated with the consequences of running out of inventory include the obvious loss of contribution to profit arising from lost sales, as well as the loss of goodwill and the effect on future sales of unsatisfied customers going elsewhere. These costs are often difficult to quantify. There is also the cost of interrupted production.

22.4.4 Unit cost

Although not a category of cost in the same sense as the three types above, this is a term widely used to indicate the cost of acquiring one unit of product, taking all costs into account.

22.5 Inventory control policy

Though often undervalued as a management activity, inventory control policy, or a lack of it, can have a critical effect on working capital requirements, on the liquidity of the entity, on the smooth working of the production system and on customer service levels.

Therefore, an inventory control policy should reflect the following four criteria (despite the fact that they usually operate against each other):

1. keep total costs down (ideally to a minimum);
2. provide satisfactory service levels to customers;
3. ensure smooth-running production systems;
4. be able to withstand fluctuations in business conditions, for example, changes in customer demand, prices, availability of raw materials, etc.

Entity policy will dictate which of these will take precedence.

22.5.1 Dependent or independent demand

Products may be loosely considered to be subject to 'dependent' or 'independent' demand. For example, a mountain bike would be considered to have an 'independent' demand, whereas its components – wheels, tyres, frame, pedals, saddle, gears, etc. – have a dependent demand. This chapter will consider only 'independent demand'.

22.6 Inventory control systems

Three main systems are used to monitor and control inventory levels:

1. reorder level system;
2. periodic review system;
3. mixed systems, incorporating elements of both of the above.

22.6.1 Reorder level system

With this system, whenever the current inventory level falls below a pre-set 'reorder level' (ROL), a replenishment (replacement) order is made. Since there is normally a gap (delivery time) between issue and receipt of orders, say T, this 'lead time' (T) has to be allowed for. This is illustrated in Figure 22.1, with the reorder quantity (for the replenishment order) shown as Q. (The actual size of this Q is often the economic order quantity, which is defined in the next section.) Buffer inventory is usually held as insurance against variations in demand and lead time.

This system used to be known as the 'two-bin' system. Inventory is kept in two bins, one with an amount equal to the ROL quantity, and the rest in the other. Inventory is drawn from the latter until it runs out, whence a replenishment order is triggered.

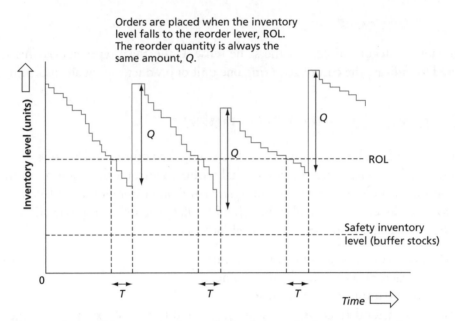

Orders are placed when the inventory level falls to the reorder lever, ROL. The reorder quantity is always the same amount, Q.

Figure 22.1 A simple reorder level system for inventory control

A reorder level system is simple enough to implement if the variables (such as average usage, supplier lead time, etc.) are known with certainty. In practice, this is rarely the case.

22.6.2 Periodic review system

This is also referred to as a 'constant cycle' system. Inventory levels are reviewed after a fixed interval, for example, on the first of the month. Replenishment orders are issued where necessary, to top up inventory levels to pre-set target levels. This means that order sizes are variable (see Figure 22.2, where the Q-values, set by management, do not always ensure that the target is met, owing to variations in demand during the lead time, T).

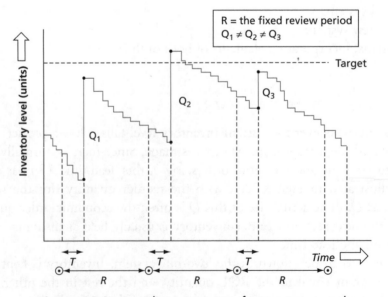

R = the fixed review period
$Q_1 \neq Q_2 \neq Q_3$

Figure 22.2 Periodic review system for inventory control

22.6.3 Mixed systems

In practice, mixtures of both systems are sometimes used, depending on the nature of the problem, the amount of computerisation and so on.

22.7 Economic order quantity (EOQ)

Consider the following simplified situation, in which an entity requires 24,000 boxes a year at a price of $8 per box. The order costs are $200 (delivery, admin, etc.) and the holding costs are 10 per cent per year, i.e. each order costs $200 to place and each box costs $0.80 per year to hold in inventory.

The table below shows a few simple calculations that illustrate how the economic order quantity operates. (These types of calculations are usually carried out using a spreadsheet.)

Order size (000) (1)	Average orders/yr 24,000 ÷ Col 1 (2)	Annual order cost ($) Col 2 × 200 (3)	Mean inventory-holding Col 1 ÷ 2 (4)	Annual holding cost ($) Col 4 × $0.80 (5)	Total variable cost ($) Col 3 + Col 5 (6)	Total annual cost ($) Col 6 + cost of purchase ($192,000)
1	24	4,800	500	400	5,200	197,200
2	12	2,400	1,000	800	3,200	195,200
3	8	1,600	1,500	1,200	2,800	194,800
4	6	1,200	2,000	1,600	2,800	194,800
4.8	5	1,000	2,400	1,920	2,920	194,920
6	4	800	3,000	2,400	3,200	195,200

By inspection of the table (column 6), it appears that total variable cost is least when the order size is between 3,000 and 4,000 boxes, maybe about halfway between them since total variable cost is a curve. This is confirmed by Figure 22.3, which shows cost plotted against order size, using columns 1, 3, 5 and 7. The total annual cost (column 7) = total variable cost (column 6) + the purchase cost of 24,000 boxes at $8 ($192,000). The large differences between column 6 and column 7 should not be taken to imply that the basic purchase cost of inventory is always large in comparison to the variable costs of holding and ordering inventory and, of course, many entities have to hold a considerable range of inventory lines, so that a small saving in column 7, for many inventory lines, can mean big savings overall.

22.7.1 Comments on Figure 22.3

1. The annual total variable cost is minimised at the point where holding costs equal order costs, in this case when the order size is about 3,460 units.
2. The minimum annual total cost associated with a reorder quantity of 3,460 units is about $2,770 plus the purchase cost of $192,000, i.e. $194,770.
3. A reorder quantity of 3,460 units implies 6.93 orders per year, which is obviously impractical. In practice, this would clearly be rounded to 7 orders of 3,430 units. (24,000/7 = 3,430 to the nearest 10).
4. Such a reorder quantity is termed the *economic order quantity.*

WORKING CAPITAL: INVENTORY

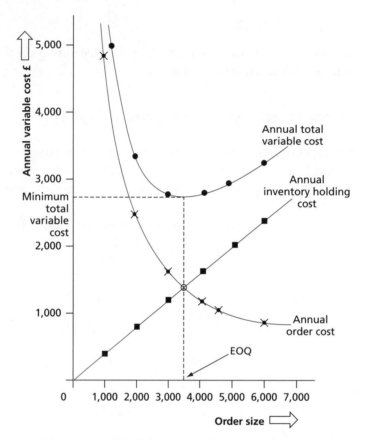

Figure 22.3 Graphical illustration of the economic order quantity

The EOQ model assumes that there is a steady demand for a product, causing its level of inventory to be depleted at a constant rate. It is also assumed that inventory levels are replenished (replaced) by a reorder quantity (ROQ) at regular time intervals, with negligible lead time.

Two types of variable inventory costs have been considered above: order costs, which will be denoted C_o per order, and holding costs, which will be denoted C_h per unit per year. Let the annual demand for the product be D units and the reorder quantity (ROQ) be shortened to Q for simplicity. Then the EOQ is

$$EOQ = \sqrt{\frac{2 \times C_o \times D}{C_h}}$$

Note: The EOQ formula is provided on the formula sheet in the examination.
We shall use the data from the previous example to illustrate how it works.

The requirement is for 24,000 boxes a year; $\therefore D = 24,000$, $C_o = 200$, $C_h = \$8 \times 10\% = \$0.80$. Substituting these numbers into the EOQ formula gives:

$$EOQ = \sqrt{\frac{2 \times \$200 \times 24,000}{\$0.80}} = \sqrt{\$12,000,000} = 3,464 \text{ units}$$

$\therefore$ The number of orders made per year $= 24,000/3,464 = 6.93$. In practical terms this means seven orders a year of about $24,000/7 = 3,430$ units for the reorder quantity.

It could be seen from the costs graph (Figure 22.3) that total variable costs are minimised, theoretically, when total ordering cost $=$ total holding cost, i.e. when the holding costs are $\$0.80 \times 3,464/2$, that is, $\$1,385.60$. Therefore, in theory, total variable costs are $2 \times \$1,385.60 = \$2,771.20$.

In practice, $C_o = 7 \times 200 = \$1,400$, and $C_h = 0.5 \times 3,430 \times \$0.80 = \$1,372$, giving a total variable cost of $\$2,772$, which is extremely close to the theoretical value of $\$2771.20$.

 Exercise 22.1

A retailer has a steady demand for 600 units a year. Each unit costs the retailer $20. The costs of ordering are $100, regardless of the size of the order. The cost of holding a unit in inventory is 40 per cent of its value per year. What order size will minimise total inventory cost, and what is the minimum total annual inventory cost?

 Solution

$$D = 600 \quad C_o = \$100 \quad C_h = \$20 \times 40\% = \$8$$

$$\text{EOQ} = \sqrt{\frac{2 \times C_o \times D}{C_h}}$$

$$\text{EOQ} = \sqrt{\frac{2 \times \$100 \times 600}{\$8}} = \sqrt{\$15,000} = 122.47 \text{ units}$$

In practice, this would be rounded to 120 units, which would be ordered $600/120 = 5$ times a year, i.e. every 10 weeks or so.

The annual order costs would be	$5 \times \$100$	=	$500
The annual holding costs would be	$0.5 \times 120 \times \$8$	=	$480
The purchase cost would be	$\$20 \times 600$	=	$12,000
$\therefore$ The total annual inventory cost would be			$12,980

22.8 Quantity discounts

It is quite common for some suppliers to offer discounts on items that are bought in large quantities. This not only reduces the unit purchase cost, but also the order cost because fewer orders will be made. In contrast, the higher average inventory levels result in increased holding costs. Although it may not be appropriate to use the EOQ formula (because the price per item is not fixed), the calculations shown below, manually, are quite easily done with a spreadsheet.

 Exercise 22.2

Suppose that our manufacturer (with $D = 24,000$, $C_o = \$200$, $C_h = \$0.80$ and with the assumptions of the EOQ model), faced with buying from an external supplier, is offered a discount of 5 per cent on purchases of 5,000 boxes or more, all other factors being the same. What are the implications of this offer?

 Solution

A sketch graph will illustrate the situation (see Figure 22.4).

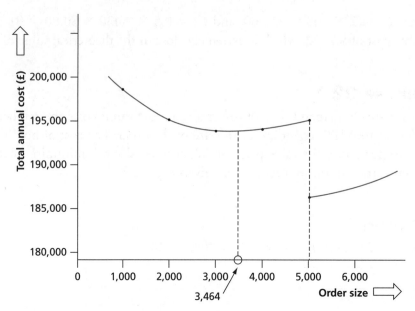

Figure 22.4 Total annual cost and order size: price discount of 5%

The total annual cost in column 7 of the table developed earlier is discontinuous at the point where the discount begins to operate. The EOQ formula can only be used up to the point where $Q = 5,000$.

The graph demonstrates this point clearly, where $Q = 5,000$. Some calculations at this value are now made to see if the discount is worth while and by how much.

At Q = 5,000 units, with the discount
Total order costs = $200 × D/Q = \$200 × 24,000/5,000 = \$960$
With the 5 per cent discount, the price per item falls from \$8 to \$7.60.
∴ Holding cost per item = ($7.60 × 10\%) = \$0.76$
∴ Total holding cost = ($0.5 × 5,000 × \$0.76) = \$1,900$
Total variable cost = ($960 + \$1,900) = \$2,860$
The total annual cost = total variable cost + purchase cost
$$= (\$2,860 + 24,000 × \$7.60)$$
$$= (\$2,860 + \$182,400)$$
$$= \$185,260$$

At Q = 3,464 units (EOQ), without the discount
The total variable cost was \$2,772.
The purchase cost was \$192,000.
The total annual cost was \$194,772.
Therefore, the discount produces a saving of $(194,772 − 185,260)$, that is, \$9,512.

22.9 Lead times

The models considered here assume that lead times (the time lags between the issuing of orders and their receipt) are negligible or at least constant. In practice, time lags occur and vary, so it is crucial to allow for them. We look here at constant lead times so that EOQ values remain the same, but the timings of placing orders have to change.

22.9.1 Lead times with constant demand

Suppose that our supplier requires 1 week to fulfil an order. The annual requirement of the manufacturer was for 24,000 units, so that 24,000/48 = 500 units are needed each week, assuming 48 working weeks to a year. Thus, whenever the inventory level falls to 500, a replenishment order to the EOQ value of 3,430 units should be made.

This leaves no margin for error and assumes constant usage, if 501 units were required in the week there would be a shortfall. If demand is not constant or lead times are variable, the ROL will need to be increased to ensure that inventory does not run out before the order is delivered.

In principle, a new order is placed whilst there is still sufficient inventory to cover the maximum demand over the maximum likely lead time. Setting ROL at this level will create a buffer inventory which is a quantity of inventory that will not usually be needed but could be needed if demand or lead times are above average.

22.10 Just-in-time (JIT) purchasing

JIT was developed in Japan, and it is claimed that the implementation of JIT systems has been one of the major factors contributing to the country's economic progress. It involves a continuous commitment to the pursuit of excellence in all phases of manufacturing. Its aims are to produce the required items of the required quality in the required quantity at the required time.

There are two aspects to JIT: JIT purchasing and JIT production. CIMA's *Management Accounting: Official Terminology* provides the following definitions:

- *Just-in-time.* A system whose objective is to produce or to procure products or components as they are required by a customer or for use, rather than for inventory. A just-in-time system is a 'pull' system, which responds to demand, in contrast to a 'push' system, in which inventory act as buffers between the different elements of the system, such as purchasing, production and sales.
- *Just-in-time production.* A production system which is driven by demand for finished products whereby each component on a production line is produced only when needed for the next stage.
- *Just-in-time purchasing.* A purchasing system in which material purchases are contracted so that the receipt and usage of material, to the maximum extent possible, coincide.

With JIT purchasing it means that materials or components are received from the supplier just in time to use them. They are in effect delivered to the factory floor.

The objectives of JIT purchasing may be stated as:

- raw material inventory reduction;
- frequent deliveries with smaller orders from a smaller number of suppliers;
- long-term contracts with suppliers;
- quality assurance, with the supplier becoming responsible for the inspection of goods supplied.

The objectives of JIT production are to obtain low-cost, high-quality, on-time production, to order, by minimising inventory levels between successive processes and, therefore, minimising idle equipment, facilities and workers.

The introduction of JIT may bring the following benefits:

- reduced inventory;
- savings in storage space required;
- increased customer satisfaction – elimination of waste will lead to a better-quality product;
- weaknesses and problems may be identified – problems such as bottlenecks, supplier reliability and inadequate documentation may be revealed;
- flexibility and the ability to supply small batches.

JIT will not, however, be appropriate in all situations. A full work study will be required to look at the production methods. A large amount of capital is needed to operate a JIT system, and flexibility is lost due to the nature of the contracts with suppliers.

22.11 Summary

Various types of inventory costs have been considered. Brief criteria for an inventory control policy were examined. The simpler characteristics of inventory control systems were described. The simple EOQ model was studied in detail. The effects of quantity discounts and lead times were explained briefly at the end. The need for a scientific approach to the control of inventory should have been evident throughout.

Revision Questions

? Question 1

Which ONE of the following would not normally be considered a cost of holding inventory?

(A) Inventory obsolescence
(B) Insurance cost of inventory
(C) Lost interest on cash invested in inventory
(D) Loss of sales from running out of inventory

(2 marks)

? Question 2

An entity uses the economic order quantity model (EOQ model). Demand for the entity's product is 36,000 units each year and is evenly distributed each day. The cost of placing an order is $10 and the cost of holding a unit of inventory for a year is $2. How many orders should the entity make in a year?

(A) 60
(B) 120
(C) 300
(D) 600

(2 marks)

? Question 3

An entity uses the economic order quantity model (that is, the EOQ model) to manage inventory.

Situation 1 – interest rates rise;
Situation 2 – sales volumes increase.

What would happen to the economic order quantity in each of these two situations?

	Situation 1	*Situation 2*
(A)	Increase	Increase
(B)	Increase	Decrease
(C)	Decrease	Increase
(D)	Decrease	Decrease

(2 marks)

WORKING CAPITAL: INVENTORY

 Question 4

Calculate the economic order quantity (EOQ) for the following item of inventory:

- Quantity required per year 32,000 items;
- Order costs are $15 per order;
- Inventory holding costs are estimated at 3% of inventory value per year;
- Each unit currently costs $40. **(2 marks)**

 Question 5

BF manufactures a range of domestic appliances. Due to past delays in suppliers providing goods, BF has had to hold an inventory of raw materials, in order that the production could continue to operate smoothly. Due to recent improvements in supplier reliability, BF is re-examining its inventory holding policies and recalculating economic order quantities (EOQ).

- Item 'Z' costs BF $10.00 per unit
- Expected annual production usage is 65,000 units
- Procurement costs (cost of placing and processing one order) are $25.00
- The cost of holding one unit for one year has been calculated as $3.00

The supplier of item 'Z' has informed BF that if the order was 2,000 units or more at one time, a 2% discount would be given on the price of the goods.

Requirements

(i) Calculate the EOQ for item 'Z' before the quantity discount. **(2 marks)**
(ii) Advise BF if it should increase the order size of item 'Z' so as to qualify for the 2% discount. **(3 marks)**
(Total marks = 5)

 Question 6

WCM is an entity that sells a wide range of specialist electrical and manual tools to professional builders through a trade catalogue.

The entity is considering the improvement of its working capital management in order to reduce its current overdraft. Most customers are required to pay cash when they place an order and thus there is little that can be done to reduce trade receivables. The focus of the board's attention is therefore on trade payables and inventory.

The working capital position at 30 April 2002 was as follows:

	$	$
Inventory	300,000	
Trade receivables	50,000	350,000
Trade Payables	150,000	
Overdraft	550,000	
		700,000
Net current liabilities		350,000

Trade payables

WCM has two major suppliers, INT and GRN.

INT supplies electrical tools and is one of the largest entities in the industry, with international operations. GRN is a small, local manufacturer of manual tools of good quality. WCM is one of its major customers.

Deliveries from both suppliers are currently made monthly, and are constant throughout the year. Delivery and invoicing both occur in the last week of each month. Details of the credit terms offered by suppliers are as follows:

Supplier	Normal credit period	Cash discount	Average monthly purchases
INT	40 days	2% for settlement in 10 days	$100,000
GRN	30 days	none	$50,000

WCM always takes advantages of the cash discount from INT and pays GRN after 30 days.

Inventory

The entity aims to have the equivalent of 2 months' cost of sales (equal to 2 months' purchases) in inventory immediately after a delivery has been received.

New working capital policy

At a meeting of the board of directors, it was decided that from 1 May 2002, all payments would be based upon taking the full credit period of 40 days from INT, and similarly taking 40 days before paying GRN.

A review of inventory is also to be commissioned to assess the level of safety (that is buffer) inventory held. In particular, it would examine the feasibility of a just-in-time inventory management system. Meanwhile, it was decided to make no purchases in May in order to reduce inventory levels.

While most of the board supported these changes, *the purchasing manager* disagreed, arguing that working capital would be even worse after the changes.

Requirements

(a) Calculate the annual rate of interest implied in the cash discount offered by INT. Assume a 365-day year. **(3 marks)**

(b) Calculate the anticipated current ratio of WCM at 31 May 2002, assuming that the changes in trade payable payment policy take place, and that there are no inventory purchases during May 2002.

Assume for this purpose that, in the absence of any change to trade payable policy, the overdraft would have remained at its 30 April 2002 level.

Clearly state any assumptions made. **(5 marks)**

(c) As a management accountant of WCM, write a memorandum to the directors that evaluates:

(i) the proposed changes to the trade payable payment policy;

(ii) the proposed policy to introduce a just-in-time system for inventory management.

(12 marks)
(Total marks = 20)

Question 7

STK sells bathroom fittings throughout Europe. In order to obtain the best price, it has decided to purchase all its annual demand of 10,000 shower units from a single supplier. After investigation, it has identified two possible manufacturers – SSS and RRR. Each has offered to provide the required number of showers each year under an exclusive long-term contract.

Demand for shower units is at a constant rate all year. The cost to STK of holding one shower unit in inventory for 1 year is $4 plus 3% of the purchase price.

SSS is located only a few miles from the STK main showroom. It has offered to supply each shower unit at $400 with a transport charge of $200 per delivery. It has guaranteed such a regular and prompt delivery service that STK believes it will not be necessary to hold any safety inventory (i.e. buffer inventory) if it uses SSS as its supplier.

RRR is located in the Far East. It has offered to supply each shower unit at $398 but transport charges will be $500 per delivery. There is also a minimum order size of 1,000 shower units. Deliveries will be by ship and will therefore take some time to arrive. There is also significant uncertainty about the lead time which means that STK will need to hold a safety inventory of 600 shower units.

Requirements

(a) Using the EOQ model, calculate the optimal order size, assuming that SSS is chosen as the sole supplier of shower units for STK. **(4 marks)**

(b) (i) Prepare calculations to determine whether SSS or RRR should be chosen as the sole supplier of shower units for STK. **(7 marks)**

(ii) Describe any further factors that STK should consider before making a final choice of supplier. **(4 marks)**

(c) Assume you are a consultant advising the Far East based entity RRR. Write a brief memorandum explaining how RRR could finance the necessary working capital for its proposed contract to supply STK. **(5 marks)**

(Total marks = 20)

Solutions to Revision Questions

✓ Solution 1

The correct answer is (D), see Section 22.4.

✓ Solution 2

The correct answer is (A), see Section 22.8.

$$\text{EOQ} = \sqrt{(2 \times 36{,}000 \times \$10)/2} = 600$$
$$\text{Orders} = 36{,}000/600 = 60$$

✓ Solution 3

The correct answer is (C), see Section 22.8.

✓ Solution 4

Using the EOQ formula from the formulae sheet:

$$\sqrt{\frac{2 \times \$15 \times 32{,}000}{\$1.2}} = \sqrt{800{,}000} = 894.43$$

See Section 22.7.

✓ Solution 5

(i) Using the formula from the formula sheet:

$$\text{EOQ} = \sqrt{2C_o D/C_h}$$
$$= \sqrt{(2 \times 25 \times 65{,}000)/3} = \sqrt{1{,}083{,}333} = 1{,}040.83$$

EOQ for item 'Z' is 1,041 units per order.

(ii)

Total cost using EOQ	$
Unit cost 65,000 × $10 =	650,000
Holding cost $3 × 1,041/2 =	1,562
Ordering cost $25 × 65,000/1,041 =	1,561
Total cost	653,123

Assume order size = 2,000 units

	$
Unit cost 65,000 × $9.8=	637,000
Holding cost $3 × 2,000/2=	3,000
Ordering cost $25 × 65,000/2,000=	813
Revised total cost	640,813

The total cost is $12,310 less, therefore it is worthwhile for BF to increase the order size and claim the discount, see Section 22.8.

 ## Solution 6

(a)

$$(100/98)^{365/30} - 1 = 27.86\%$$

(b)

	$
Payables (April deliveries)	150,000
Overdraft (550,000 − 150,000)	400,000
Inventory (one month's purchases)	150,000
Receivables	50,000

$$\frac{\text{Current assets}}{\text{Current liabilities}} = 20,000 : 550,000 = 0.36 \text{ to } 1$$

(c)

Memorandum

To:	The Board of WCM	**From:**	Management Accountant
Subject:	Working capital Management	**Date:**	21 May 2002

Introduction

If the objective of the review is to reduce the entity's overdraft, then, while working capital can have a role, it must be viewed alongside other methods of reducing the overdraft including the raising of new long-term finance, divestment of assets and improvements in operating results.

The entity currently has negative working capital, but this is not of itself a problem and it is not unusual for cash business. If receivables are low because of mainly cash sales, but credit is taken from suppliers, then essentially cash is being received before the entity pays for the goods.

(i) Payable payment policy

INT

The entity currently pays after 10 days to take advantage of a cash discount. Delaying payment improves short-term liquidity, but loses the discount of 27.86% per year [see requirement (a)]. This is quite a high rate of return to lose, but must be weighed against the saving in overdraft interest.

In addition, while the overdraft will be lower in May than it was in April, this is a one-off benefit in the sense that continuing the policy will not lower the overdraft any further.

GRN

The current terms being offered by GRN are 30 days settlement. Taking 40 days is essentially a breach of this contract, although not uncommon in practice. The potential cost is that if this policy is decided upon unilaterally by WCM, then it may damage the relationship with the supplier.

Given that GRN is only a small entity, it may not wish to alienate WCM as a major customer. On the other hand, much may depend upon whether there are alternative suppliers at equivalent cost for WCM.

Moreover, GRN may seek to recover the cost of lost liquidity by other means: for example, higher prices, charging interest on overdue amounts, delaying deliveries until payment is made, reduced goodwill. More generally, the payment delay, if it becomes more widely known, may damage WCM's credit rating. This may make obtaining credit finance in future more difficult or more costly.

(ii) Just-in-time system (JIT)

Inventory

JIT may be defined as: 'A system whose objective is to produce or to procure products or components as they are required by a customer or for use, rather than for inventory' (from *CIMA Terminology* 2005 edition).

The basic decision for WCM is therefore whether it wishes to supply customers from inventory, or obtain supplies to match customer orders (i.e. obtaining inventory just in time). In the latter case, minimal (or even zero) inventory could be held.

The major disadvantage of supplying to order is that the delay in supplying customers may reduce sales and therefore profitability. Ultimately, this will feed through into reduced liquidity. If, however, demand is predictable, then very low levels of safety inventory could be maintained with orders being made on a JIT basis in anticipation of imminent sales, rather then responding to actual orders.

The advantages of holding lower inventory as a result of JIT include:

- Lower storage costs;
- Less cash tied up in inventory;
- Saved interest costs;
- Lower costs from damage, wastage and obsolescence.

In order to obtain these advantages, certain procedures and relationships must be in place. However, the current policy of monthly deliveries is incompatible with JIT, which requires:

- frequent deliveries (preferably daily);
- small deliveries being economic;
- reliable and quick deliveries in terms of timing (i.e. a short and certain lead time);
- reliable deliveries in terms of product quality;
- good relationship with suppliers;
- supplier flexibility.

The credit policy of delaying may be seen as incompatible with maintaining the good supplier relationships necessary for JIT.

Comparing the current policy to JIT indicates the actions necessary for implementation. Historically, it appears that at the time of a new delivery, there are 1 month's sales in inventory. Immediately after the delivery, there are 2 months' sales in inventory.

The new policy of omitting May's purchases will mean that if the next order is in the last week in June, then inventory would have fallen to zero before the order and one month's sales immediately thereafter. This seems inappropriate as:

- monthly orders cause wide fluctuations in inventory levels;
- many different lines of inventory are held. Unless sales can be predicted a month in advance then rather than zero inventory, some lines of inventory are likely to run out while significant inventory could be held for other goods;
- while zero or near zero inventory is held for part of the month, none of the above conditions for JIT appears to be met.

Conclusion

Overall, the policy changes have worsened the current ratio from 0.5:1 to 0.36:1. Of itself, this does not matter if inventory and payables are being managed efficiently without affecting the service to customers.

This does not, however, appear to be the case at the moment and careful consideration of the conditions necessary for JIT need to be assessed and agreed with suppliers before the costs and benefits can be judged.

The issue of supplier payment management is inter-related to the issue of JIT inventory management and thus should be considered simultaneously.

Signed: Management Accountant

 ## Solution 7

(a)

Holding cost = $4 + (3\% \times \$400) = \$16$

$$\text{EOQ} = \sqrt{(2C_o D / C_h)} = \sqrt{2 \times 10,000 \times \frac{\$200}{\$16}} = 500 \text{ units}$$

(b)

Holding cost = $4 + (3\% \times \$398) = \$15.94$

$$\text{EOQ} = \sqrt{\frac{(2 \times 10,000 \times \$500)}{15.94}} = 792$$

Examiner's note

It is necessary to check the EOQ to ascertain if the minimum delivery volume of 1,000 is a relevant (that is binding) constraint. In this case, it is, thus an order quantity of 1,000 applies.

	SSS	RRR
Order size	500	1,000
Annual demand	10,000	10,000
Number of orders	20	10
	$	$
Order cost	4,000	5,000
Holding cost	4,000	17,534
Purchase cost	4,000,000	3,980,000
	4,008,000	4,002,534

Thus ordering from overseas is $5,466 cheaper than the domestic purchase.

		Ordering cost	
SSS		$200 \times 20=$	$4,000
RRR		$500 \times 10=$	$5,000

Holding costs $(EOQ/2 \times C_h)$

SSS	$\dfrac{500}{2} \times \$16.00 = \$4,000$	
RRR	$\dfrac{1,000}{2} \times \$15.94 =$	$7,970

Plus safety inventorys:	$600 \times \$15.94=$	$9,564
		$17,534

		Purchase cost	
SSS	$10,000 \times \$400=$	$4,000,000	
RRR	$10,000 \times \$398=$	$3,980,000	

Further factors that need to be considered are:

- The uncertainty of supply from RRR may lead to additional costs from running out of inventory, despite the safety inventories.
- Exchange rate movements may mean that the cost may increase if the contract with RRR has been written in the overseas currency. Hedging may lead to additional costs. Given that the two options are very close in terms of overall costs this may make a difference to the decision.
- If deliveries are incorrect or faulty, then re-supply may take a significant amount of time from RRR.
- The length of the lead time with RRR will require additional forward planning of inventory requirements.

(c)
Memorandum

To:	RRR	**From:**	A Consultant
Subject:	Financing STK contract	**Date:**	19 November 2002

Financing needs

In financing exports, there are a number of specific factors to be considered in addition to those present for domestic sales:

- The long lead time in delivering to STK by ship will mean additional working capital is tied up in inventory.
- International settlement may take longer as, for instance, it may be more difficult to put pressure on STK if it is slow in settling its debts.
- Foreign currency exchange may cause additional costs and/or risks depending on which of the two currencies forms the basis of the contract.
- Regulatory and compliance problems may cause additional delays in the transfer of goods or funds.
- There is an increased risk of bad debts where it is more difficult to obtain information due to geographic remoteness.

Methods of export finance

Examiner's note

Explanations by candidates do not require the level of detail supplied below in order to earn the required mark.

Export factoring

Debts may be sold to an export factor in much the same way as domestic factoring. This may include credit insurance to reduce bad debt risk.

Bills of exchange

A bill of exchange is an unconditional order by one person/entity to pay another a given sum at a specified future date. These are tradable, having a short date, normally within 180 days. They are, however, subject to default risk depending upon the creditworthiness of the drawee.

Bills of exchange are commonly used in export finance and will mean they can be sold at a discount to obtain more immediate cash.

Documentary credits (letters of credit)

This is a document issued by a bank on behalf of a customer authorising a person to draw money to a specified amount from its branches or correspondents, usually in another country, when the conditions set out in the document have been met.

It thus provides a secure means of obtaining payment from an overseas sale. These are, however, time consuming and expensive for trade and are thus only normally used where there is a high risk of a bad debt.

Forfaiting

This is normally most appropriate to capital goods where payment is over a number of years, but may also apply to a long-term contract such as that with STK as a means of obtaining medium-term export finance.

The buyer (STK) must undertake to make regular payments. It issues a series of promissory notes maturing on a regular basis (for example, every 6 months). The buyer must also find a bank to guarantee (avalise) the notes.

RRR must find a bank to act as forfeiter. RRR will then receive the notes when STK receives the goods. It can then sell them to the forfeiting bank, at a discount, but without recourse, for immediate payment.

This reduces bad debt risk, reduces foreign exchange risk and provides immediate settlement – at a cost.

Advanced payment

As part of the contract, partial or full advanced payment might be arranged with STK (for example, when the goods are in transit).

Signed: A Consultant

23

Working Capital: Cash

Working Capital: Cash

23

LEARNING OUTCOMES

By the end of this chapter, you should be able to:

▶ prepare and analyse cash flow forecasts over a 12-month period;

▶ compare and contrast the use and limitations of cash management models and identify when each model is most appropriate;

▶ identify measures to improve a cash forecast situation.

The syllabus topics covered in this chapter are as follows:

- cash flow forecasts, use of spreadsheets to assist in this in terms of changing variables (e.g. interest rates or inflation) and in consolidating forecasts;
- variables that are most easily changed, delayed or brought forward in a forecast;
- the link between cash, profit and the statement of financial position;
- the Baumol and Miller–Orr cash management models.

23.1 Introduction

This is the final chapter on elements of working capital, in the previous chapters we covered trade receivables, trade payables and inventory. In this chapter, we are going to discuss cash, cash-forecasting and cash-management models.

23.2 Cash management

The management of cash resources holds a central position in the area of short-term financing decisions. Results of investment decisions are estimated in cash terms and the value of an entity to a shareholder lies in its ability to add to their command over resources over time, which means to add to the shareholder's command over cash.

Cash management is part of the wider task of treasury management, which covers not only the management of the entity's cash in the normal course of business – making sure the entity always has enough cash on hand to meet its bills and expenses, and investing any surplus cash – but also other things too. Examples include foreign exchange dealings when the entity either imports or exports goods, arranging suitable mixes of short-, medium- and long-term borrowing, and dealing on the foreign currency markets and the Eurocurrency market to maximise investment opportunities or to borrow funds on the most advantageous terms.

However, holding cash carries with it a cost – the opportunity cost of the profits that could be made if the cash were either used in the entity or invested elsewhere. Therefore, an entity has to balance the advantages of liquidity against profitability: cash should be held until the marginal value of the liquidity it gives is equal to the value of the interest lost.

Cash management is therefore concerned with optimising the amount of cash available to the entity and maximising the interest on any spare funds not required immediately by the entity.

23.2.1 The time value of money

A recurring theme of financial management is the time value of money – or the money value of time, depending on your point of view. It needs to be remembered, however, that there is not one generally applicable, constant price of money. Interest rates vary, according to the length of time of the investment, as portrayed in the familiar yield curve, and the yield curve itself varies over time. Interest rates are different according to whether you are lending to, or borrowing from, the banking system, and according to the flexibility of the arrangement, for example, how much notice is required to move funds into or out of an account.

Other things being equal, in what amounts to a reflection of their expected costs, the banks:

- pay higher interest on accounts subject to longer notices of withdrawal than they do on current accounts;
- charge higher interest on fluctuating overdrafts than they do on term loans.

A key task for the treasury function in any entity, therefore, is the management of the various accounts. Money is switched between them, so as to minimise aggregate costs (or maximise net income, as the case may be), recognising both transaction costs and interest rate differentials.

23.3 Cash budgets

It is vital for entities to identify their cash requirements, so as to optimise the method of financing. It is equally important, therefore, for entities to budget for future financing needs so that the funding process can be planned and achieved as smoothly and efficiently as possible.

Cash budgets are vital to the management of cash. They show, over periods varying between a single day, a week, a month, a year or even longer, the expected inflows and outflows of cash through the entity. They help to show cash surpluses and cash shortages.

Management can therefore use cash budgets to plan ahead to meet those eventualities – arranging borrowing when a deficit is forecast, or buying short-term securities during times of excess cash.

The accuracy of the budget depends on the forecasts on which it is based, principally the forecast of future sales. This affects not only the amount of cash that will come into the entity but also the timing of the receipts: credit sales will mean that payment for goods is delayed a month or two, while seasonal sales will mean that the entity will have some months of large cash inflows and some of much smaller ones. This causes problems because, generally, cash outflows associated with production and day-to-day operations do not vary as much. The entity may thus face *cash shortages* at times during the budget period and these will have to be made up somehow.

Deviations from budgeted figures are almost inevitable and so some entities will prepare several budgets based on possible future situations:

- an optimistic budget, which assumes that the entity achieves above-forecast growth;
- a pessimistic budget, which assumes below-forecast growth;
- a target budget, which assumes forecast growth is achieved.

Computer spreadsheets are almost essential to modern entities, as they allow managers to change their original specifications to present alternative 'versions of the future'.

23.3.1 Preparation of cash budgets

Four distinct stages are involved:

1. *Forecast the anticipated cash receipts.* The main source of cash is likely to be sales and the sales forecast will therefore be the primary data source. Sales can be divided into cash sales and credit sales, the cash flow arising from the latter depending on the agreed credit terms. Thus, for example, the sales forecast for January would appear in the cash budget in April if all sales were on credit terms of 90 days. Other cash receipts would include income on investments, cash from sales of non-current assets, etc.
2. *Forecast the anticipated cash payments.* The principal payment is generally the payment of trade purchases. Once again, the credit period taken must be allowed for. Other cash payments include wages and salaries, administrative costs, taxation, capital expenditure and dividends.
3. *Compare the anticipated cash payments and receipts* to determine the net cash flow for each period.
4. *Calculate the cumulative cash flow* for each period by adding the opening cash balance to the net cash flow for the period.

Remember that there will be differences between the cash budget for a period and the forecast statement of comprehensive income for that period. This is because the cash budget is concerned with cash payments and cash receipts, while the statement of comprehensive income is concerned with income earned and expenses consumed in a period.

Areas where the two statements may show different amounts are:

- the cash budget will record budgeted cash receipts from customers, while the statement of comprehensive income will show forecast sales for the period;
- the cash budget will record budgeted cash payments to suppliers, while the statement of comprehensive income will show forecast cost of sales, which will reflect opening inventory, plus purchases, less closing inventory;
- the cash budget shows the budgeted cash payments for expenses such as wages, electricity and rates. The statement of comprehensive income will record the expenditure expected to be consumed in the period, which will reflect any accruals or prepayments;

- the cash budget will reflect the cost of purchasing a non-current asset at the expected date of purchase and the proceeds at the date of sale. The statement of comprehensive income will record a depreciation charge for the consumption of the asset and a profit or loss on disposal;
- the cash budget will show the anticipated payment for tax at the time when it is due to be paid. The statement of comprehensive income will show the expected tax charge against profits earned in that period.

Exercise 23.1

The following information relates to Mansel, a publishing entity.

The selling price of a book is $15, and sales are made on credit through a book club and invoiced on the last day of the month.

Variable costs of production per book are materials ($5), labour ($4), and overhead ($2).

The sales manager has forecast the following volumes:

	Nov	Dec	Jan	Feb	Mar	Apr	May	Jun	Jul	Aug
No of books:	1,000	1,000	1,000	1,250	1,500	2,000	1,900	2,200	2,200	2,300

Customers are expected to pay as follows:

One month after the sale	40%
Two months after the sale	60%

The entity produces the books 2 months before they are sold and the trade payables for materials are paid 2 months after production.

Variable overheads are paid in the month following production and are expected to increase by 25 per cent in April; 75 per cent of wages are paid in the month of production and 25 per cent in the following month. A wage increase of 12.5 per cent will take place on 1 March.

The entity is going through a restructuring and will sell one of its freehold properties in May for $25,000, but it is also planning to buy a new printing press in May for $10,000. Depreciation is currently $1,000 per month, and will rise to $1,500 after the purchase of the new machine.

The entity's income tax (of $10,000) is due for payment in March.

The entity presently has a cash balance at bank on 31 December 2003 of $1,500.

Requirement

Produce a cash budget for the 6 months from 1 January 2004 to 30 June 2004.

✓ Solution

Workings

1. Sales receipts

Month	Nov	Dec	Jan	Feb	Mar	Apr	May	Jun
Forecast sales (S)	1,000	1,000	1,000	1,250	1,500	2,000	1,900	2,200
	$	$	$	$	$	$	$	$
S × 15	15,000	15,000	15,000	18,750	22,500	30,000	28,500	33,000
Trade receivables pay:								
1 month 40%	–	6,000	6,000	6,000	7,500	9000	12,000	11,400
2 month 60%	–	–	9,000	9,000	9,000	11,250	13,500	18,000
Total sales receipts	–	6,000	15,000	15,000	16,500	20,250	25,500	29,400

2. Payment for materials – books produced two months before sale

Month	Nov	Dec	Jan	Feb	Mar	Apr	May	Jun
Qty produced (Q)	1,000	1,250	1,500	2,000	1,900	2,200	2,200	2,300
	$	$	$	$	$	$	$	$
Materials (Q × 5)	5,000	6,250	7,500	10,000	9,500	11,000	11,000	11,500
Paid (2 month after)	–	–	5,000	6,250	7,500	10,000	9,500	11,000

3. Variable overheads

Month	Nov	Dec	Jan	Feb	Mar	Apr	May	Jun
Qty produced (Q)	1,000	1,250	1,500	2,000	1,900	2,200	2,200	2,300
	$	$	$	$	$	$	$	$
Var. overhead (Q × 2)	2,000	2,500	3,000	4,000	3,800			
Var. overhead (Q × 2.50)						5,500	5,500	5,750
Paid (one month later)		2,000	2,500	3,000	4,000	3,800	5,500	5,500

4. Wages payments

Month	Dec	Jan	Feb	Mar	Apr	May	Jun
Qty produced (Q)	1,250	1,500	2000	1,900	2,200	2,200	2,300
	$	$	$	$	$	$	$
Wages Q × 4	5,000	6,000	8,000				
Wages Q × 4.50				8,550	9,900	9,900	10,350
75% this month	3,750	4,500	6,000	6,413	7,425	7,425	7,762
25% next month	–	1,250	1,500	2,000	2,137	2,475	2,475
cash paid in wages	3,750	5,750	7,500	8,413	9,562	9,900	10,237

Cash budget – 6 months ended June

	Jan $	Feb $	Mar $	Apr $	May $	Jun $
Receipts:						
Credit sales	15,000	15,000	16,500	20,250	25,500	29,400
Premises disposal	–	–	–	–	25,000	–
	15,000	15,000	16,500	20,250	50,500	29,400
Payments:						
Materials	5,000	6,250	7,500	10,000	9,500	11,000
Var. overheads	2,500	3,000	4,000	3,800	5,500	5,500
Wages	5,750	7,500	8,413	9,562	9,900	10,237
Non-current assets	–	–	–	–	10,000	–
Income tax	–	–	10,000	–	–	–
Net cash flow	1,750	(1,750)	(3,413)	(3,112)	15,600	2,663
Balance b/f	1,500	3,250	11,500	(11,913)	(15,025)	575
Cumulative cash flow	3,250	1,500	(11,913)	(15,025)	575	3,238

23.3.2 Managing cash deficits

Short-term cash deficits are usually financed (by default) by utilising the entity's overdraft facility. In the example above, we are not aware of any *overdraft facility* and as such need to identify a suitable method of financing the deficit that exists in March and April.

Efficiency improvements arising from prompt banking (see below) are unlikely to release sufficient funds to cover a cash requirement of $15,025, so Mansel should consider the following steps:

- *Delay major items of capital expenditure.* The purchase of the new printing press could be delayed and although this would not affect the deficit in March or April, delaying the purchase until, say June or July would ease the cash drain in a very difficult month – particularly if the premises sale did not go through in May.
- *Improve collection period or delay trade payable collection period.* This was referred to above and there are associated problems (such as lost customers). However, if Mansel could increase the trade receivable collection period so that 80 per cent of money was collected 1 month after the sale and only 20 per cent 2 months after the sale, the cash flow would benefit significantly.

Similarly, if payments for materials could be delayed by another month (although this would seem unlikely) this would also have a beneficial effect.

- *Reduce inventory levels.* Mansel is effectively holding 2 months' inventory. Cash flow would improve if this figure was reduced.
- *Delay non-essential payments.* Delaying the income tax could be problematic: would the Revenue authorities consider payment by instalments?

If none of the above is possible, then the entity must consider approaching a bank to obtain an *overdraft facility,* consider some form of *factoring, invoice discounting,* or *sale and leaseback or raise additional long term funding through a bank loan or a share issue.*

23.3.3 Float

Float refers to the money tied up because of the time lag between a customer initiating payment (perhaps posting a cheque), and those funds being available for use by the recipient once the cheque has been cleared by the bank. This time lag will mean that the entity's cash at bank figure will be different in its own books of account from the figure on its bank statement.

There are three elements of time delay that cause float:

1. *Transmission delay.* This is the time delay caused by sending a cheque through the post.
2. *Lodgement delay.* When a cheque is received, there may be a delay in presenting the cheque to the bank for clearance.
3. *Clearance delay.* When a cheque is presented to a bank for clearance, it may take 3 days or more to clear.

Float could be reduced if customers paid by electronic funds transfer. Payment by electronic funds transfer has the advantage over cheque payment of being more secure, and it will reduce administrative time. However, these systems can be expensive to introduce.

23.4 Cash-management models

23.4.1 The Baumol model

Early theories in this area (generally credited to W.J. Baumol in the early 1950s) borrowed from the techniques that had been developed for controlling inventory.

We saw in the last chapter that the economic order quantity for inventory is given by the following:

$$\text{EOQ} = \sqrt{\frac{2C_o D}{C_h}}$$

where C_o is the cost of placing an order, C_h is the inventory-carrying cost, and D is the annual demand.

Baumol argued that cash can be considered in a similar way, assuming that cash is steadily consumed over time. Baumol also assumed that a business would hold an inventory of marketable securities, assumed to be treasury bills, which would be sold in order to replenish the cash balance. The main carrying cost of holding cash is the interest forgone from not investing that cash. The cost of placing an order would be the administration cost incurred for each sale of treasury bills.

The Baumol model identifies the optimum amount of treasury bills to sell, by value, each time the cash balance needs replenishing. This is given by the following:

$$\text{Optimal sale} = \sqrt{\frac{2 \times \text{annual cash disbursements} \times \text{cost per sale of securities}}{\text{interest rate}}}$$

where annual cash disbursements is the annual demand for cash (cash consumed in a year), interest rate is the interest rate on treasury bill, cost per sale of securities is the transaction cost for sale of treasury bills.

Assume, for example, that:

- outgoings are $300,000 per annum, spread evenly throughout the year;
- money on deposit earns 10 per cent per annum more than money in a current account;
- switching costs $20 per transaction.

According to Baumol, the optimum amount to be transferred (in $) each time is stated as:

$$\sqrt{\frac{2 \times \text{annual cash disbursements} \times \text{cost per sale of securities}}{\text{interest rate}}}$$

that is:

$$\sqrt{\frac{2 \times 20 \times 300,000}{0.1}}$$

that is, approximately $11,000. At this point, the number of transactions would be around 27 per annum, the average balance in the short notice account would be $5,500, for an aggregate cost of $540 + $550, that is, $1,090 per annum.

Such a model was a gross oversimplification, of course, but did draw attention to the directional impact of the various factors, for example, if the interest rate differential was increased, then the size of the optimum transfer would be reduced.

One of the most serious weaknesses was seen to be the assumption that the net cash outflow from the short-notice account was steady and therefore predictable. In the real world, there are bound to be fluctuations, the exact timing of which may be difficult to predict.

23.4.2 The Miller–Orr model

In the late 1950s, a more elaborate approach was developed, M.H. Miller and D. Orr being credited with its origination.

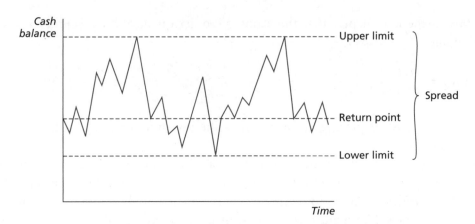

Figure 23.1 Miller–Orr cash management model

Instead of assuming that cash is consumed at a constant rate, Miller and Orr assumed that cash flows are entirely unpredictable. The approach of their model is to set upper and lower cash limits rather than considering how often the cash balance needs replenishing. When the cash balance hits an upper limit, the treasurer will buy short-term investments to bring the cash balance back to a predetermined normal level, called the return point. When the cash balance hits a lower limit, the treasurer will sell short-term investments to bring the cash balance back to the return point. This is illustrated in Figure 23.1.

The lower limit would be set by management, and the upper limit and return points by way of formulae that assume that cash inflows and outflows are random, their dispersion usually being assumed to repeat a pattern exhibited in the past. The Miller–Orr formulae are:

- Spread between upper and lower limits

$$= 3 \times \left(\frac{3/4 \times \text{transaction cost} \times \text{variance of daily cash flow}}{\text{interest rate}} \right)^{1/3}$$

where return point is the lower limit plus one-third of spread.

Assume, for example, that:

- a lower control limit of $1,000 is decided upon;
- the interest rate is 0.025 per cent per day;
- the standard deviation of the daily cash flows has been measured as $500, i.e. a variance of $250,000 (the variance is the standard deviation squared);
- switching costs $20 per transaction.

Then the spread would be

$$3 \times \left(\frac{3/4 \times \$20 \times \$250,000}{0.00025} \right)^{1/3}$$

that is, approximately $7,400. Hence the upper limit would be $8,400 (lower limit of $1,000 plus spread) and the return point $3,467 (lower limit of $1,000 plus one-third of $7,400).

Again, the directional pointers provide useful reminders, for example, if the variability of cash flows increases, so does the spread. Variations on the theme can be developed to take account of seasonality, numerous different accounts, the lead time between breaking the limit and cash actually being transferred, etc., but these are likely to be of only specialist appeal.

More to the point is the recognition that cash flows are not completely random, are not totally unpredictable, and are not independently variable. Treasurers will be forewarned of many of the payments to be made, for example, wages, dividends and tax. Also, they will have some flexibility as regards the timing of many others, for example, to hold a payment to a trade payable until after receipt from a trade receivable. Consequently, as in so many fields, decisions are rarely made on the basis of models that require you to believe that cash flows behave like a game of chance, constrained by a pattern derived from an analysis of the facts of the past.

Rather, they are made on the basis of a synthesis of judgements about the future. Spreadsheets provide a useful form in which to prepare and express these and offer the facility of asking the 'what if?' type of question.

23.5 Efficient-cash management

The amount of cash available to an entity at any given time is largely dependent on the efficiency with which cash flows are managed. Purely from the point of view of efficiency, for a given level of sales, debts should be collected and banked as quickly as possible while payments owed (to suppliers, etc.) should be delayed as long as possible. This approach is something of an oversimplification – it ignores the fact that a reduction in the credit granted to customers may reduce the overall sales level. Also, excessive delay in paying trade payables may reduce the entity's credit standing so that suppliers will only be prepared to deal with the entity on slightly less favourable terms. Cheques normally take three working days to progress through the banking system and be credited to or debited from the entity's account. The delay will, of course, be greater if the cheque is posted! These delays can be both advantageous to the entity (payments that have been made remaining in the entity's account a few days longer, either to earn interest or to keep overdraft interest down) or disadvantageous (cash not becoming available for the entity's use until a few days after debts have been paid by customers).

Part of the efficient management of cash is the practice of prompt banking of cash takings. By banking takings only once or twice a week, the entity misses the opportunity to earn interest on a positive cash balance or to reduce interest payments on an overdraft.

23.6 The link between cash, profit and the statement of financial position

> Examination questions in this area can require you to calculate profit forecasts from cash forecasts or cash flow forecasts from profit and statement of financial position forecasts.

Exercise 23.2

CBA is a manufacturing entity in the furniture trade. Its sales have risen sharply over the past six months as a result of an improvement in the economy and a strong housing market. The entity is now showing signs of 'overtrading' and the financial manager, Ms Smith, is concerned about its liquidity. The entity is 1 month from its year-end. Estimated figures for the full 12 months of the current year and forecasts for next year, on present cash management policies, are shown below.

	Next year $'000	Current year $'000
Income Statement		
Turnover	5,200	4,200
Less		
Cost of sales (Note 1)	3,224	2,520
Operating expenses	650	500
Operating profit	1,326	1,180
Interest paid	54	48
Profit before tax	1,272	1,132
Tax payable	305	283
Profit after tax	967	849
Dividends declared	387	339
Current assets and liabilities as at the end of the year		
Inventory/work in progress	625	350
Trade receivables	750	520
Cash	0	25
Trade payables	(464)	(320)
Other payables (tax and dividends)	(692)	(622)
Overdraft	(11)	0
Net current assets/(liabilities)	208	(47)
Note 1:		
Cost of sales includes depreciation of	225	175

Ms Smith is considering methods of improving the cash position. A number of actions are being discussed:

Trade receivables

Offer a 2 per cent discount to customers who pay within 10 days of despatch of invoices. It is estimated that 50 per cent of customers will take advantage of the new discount scheme. The other 50 per cent will continue to take the current average credit period.

Trade payables and inventory

Reduce the number of suppliers currently being used and negotiate better terms with those that remain by introducing a 'just-in-time' policy. The aim will be to reduce the end-of-year forecast cost of sales (excluding depreciation) by 5 per cent and inventory/work in progress levels by 10 per cent. However, the number of days' credit taken by the entity will have to fall to 30 days to help persuade suppliers to improve their prices.

Other information

- All trade is on credit. Official terms of sale at present require payment within 30 days. Interest is not charged on late payments.
- All purchases are made on credit.
- Operating expenses will be $650,000 under either the existing or proposed policies.
- Interest payments would be $45,000 if the new policies are implemented.
- Capital expenditure of $550,000 is planned for next year.

Requirements

(a) Provide a cash flow forecast for next year, assuming:
  (i) the entity does not change its policies;
  (ii) the entity's proposals for managing trade receivables, trade payables and inventory are implemented.

In both cases, assume a full twelve-month period, i.e. the changes will be effective from day 1 of next year.

(b) As assistant to Ms Smith, write a short report to her evaluating the proposed actions. Include comments on the factors, financial and non-financial, that the entity should take into account before implementing the new policies.

 ## Solution

(a) *All figures in $'000s*

	No change in policy	Changes implemented
Profit from operations	1,326	1,424
Add depreciation	225	225
+/−change in trade receivables	−230	72
+72 +/−change in trade payables	144	−86
Cash flow from operations	1,465	1,635
Interest paid	−54	−45
Tax paid	−283	−283
Dividends paid	−339	−339
Investing activities		
Non-current assets	−550	−550
Inventory	−275	−212
Net cash flow	−36	206
Opening balance	25	25
Closing balance	−11	231

Changes implemented

1. Profit from operations:

Turnover	=	5,200
Less discounts	=	−52
CoS (3,224 − 225) × 95% + 225	=	−3,074
Operating expenses (unchanged)	=	−650
		1,424

2. Decrease in trade receivables:
   $520 − [($2,600/365 × 53*) + ($2,600/365 × 10*)] = 72$
   Decrease in trade payables:
   $[$320 − ($2,849**/365 × 30)] = 86$

3. Inventory:
   $[$350 − (625 × 90%)] = 212$

*Forecast receivables = $750/5,200 × 365 = 53 reduces to 10 for 50% of turnover.

**Payables forecast are $3,224 − 225 = $2,999; these reduce by 5% to $2,849.

(b) Report

To: Ms Smith
From: Assistant
Subject: Proposed working capital policy changes

The answer should be set out in report format and include the following key points:

- Comment that cash flow is improved by almost a quarter of a million pounds if the proposed changes are made.
- Problems appear to have arisen because trade receivables and inventory control have not been adequate for increased levels of turnover.
- Liquidity: current ratio was 0.95:1 (all current assets to trade and other payables), will be around 1.2:1 under both options. Perversely, ratio looks to improve even

if the entity takes no action and causes an overdraft. This is because of high receivables and inventory levels. Moral: high current assets do not mean high cash. Cash ratio perhaps a better measure.

- Receivables' days last year was 45, forecast to rise to 53 on current policies despite 'official' terms being 30. Entity could perhaps look to improve its credit control before offering discounts.
- Trade payables' days were 46, forecast to rise to 52. Are discounts being ignored? Are relationships with suppliers being threatened?*
- Dramatic increase in inventory levels forecast: 50 days last year, 71 days forecast this year. If change implemented, inventory will still be 67 days.*
- Operating profit percentage forecast to fall to 25.5 per cent from 281.1 per cent if no changes made. Percentage will fall to 27.4 per cent if changes implemented; a fall probably acceptable if cash flow improved and overdraft interest saved.
- Non-financial factors include relationships with customers and suppliers.
- Other financial factors, is increase in turnover sustainable?

* Using cost of sales figures including depreciation.

23.7 Summary

Cash budgets are an essential tool for the financial manager. They enable him or her to obtain a vision of the future, facilitating financial decision-making that will utilise the entity's cash/credit resources in the most efficient manner.

The preparation of cash budgets will help to identify periods of cash surplus or cash deficits that will require management action. In this chapter, we have identified some of the factors affecting investment of short-term cash surpluses as well as techniques for managing cash surpluses and cash deficits.

Revision Questions

? Question 1

An entity commenced trading on 1 January and total sales for January were $150,000. Sales are made up of 60% on credit and 40% for cash. Sales grow at a monthly rate of 10%. Bad debts were 3% of credit sales. Half of the remaining trade receivables paid in the month following the sale and the remainder in the month after that.

The cash received during February was:

(A) $103,650
(B) $107,670
(C) $109,650
(D) $153,300   (2 marks)

? Question 2

The following items were extracted from an entity's budget for next month:

	$
Purchases on credit	360,000
Expected decrease in inventory over the month	12,000
Expected increase in trade payables over the month	15,000

What is the budgeted payment to trade payables for the month?

(A) $333,000
(B) $345,000
(C) $357,000
(D) $375,000   (2 marks)

? Question 3

Examine the validity of the following statements with respect to the Miller–Orr cash management model.

Statement 1 The greater the variability in cash flows, the greater is the spread between the upper and lower cash balance limits.

Statement 2 The return point is the lower limit plus one third of the spread.

	Statement 1	Statement 2
(A)	True	False
(B)	True	True
(C)	False	False
(D)	False	True

(2 marks)

Question 4

An entity uses the Baumol cash management model. Cash disbursements are constant at $20,000 each month. Money on deposit earns 5% a year, while money in the current account earns a zero return. Switching costs (that is, for each purchase or sale of securities) are $30 for each transaction. What is the optimal amount (to the nearest $100) to be transferred in each transaction?

(A) $500
(B) $1,700
(C) $4,900
(D) $17,000

(2 marks)

Question 5

Which ONE of the following transactions would NOT affect the amount of a bank overdraft?

(A) A payment by direct debit
(B) A bad debt write off
(C) An investment in treasury bills
(D) Bank charges

(2 marks)

Question 6

An entity commenced business on 1 April 2002. Sales in April 2002 were $20,000, but this is expected to increase at 2% a month. Credit sales amount to 60% of total sales. The credit period allowed is 1 month. Bad debts are 3% of credit sales, but other trade receivables pay on time. Cash sales represent the other 40% of sales. The cash expected to be received in May 2002 is

(A) $19,560
(B) $19,640
(C) $19,800
(D) $20,160

(2 marks)

Question 7

CT uses the Miller–Orr cash management model to help manage cash flows. The management accountant has agreed with the directors that the lower limit for cash will be $2,500.

The current rate of interest that CT pays is $0 \times 025\%$ per day. Each transaction costs CT \$30. CT's daily cash flows have been measured and the variance calculated as \$300,000.

Calculate the Miller–Orr return point and upper limit for CT. **(3 marks)**

? Question 8

BB is a private sector training entity, which provides short courses and various in-house courses for large employers.

BB's forecast financial statements for the year ended 31 December includes the following:

Forecast statement of financial position at 31 December 2005 (extract)

Current assets	
Trade receivables: In-house training courses	\$34,100
Bank	\$12,460

Forecast Income Statement for the year ended 31 December 2005 (extract)

Revenue: In house training courses	\$125,000

BB is preparing its budgets for the year 1 January 2006 to 31 December 2006, but the cash budget has not yet been completed. The Finance Director is concerned about the cash flow forecast for the first 6 months and has asked you, a trainee management accountant, to prepare a cash budget for the 6 months from January to June 2006 from the budgeted information provided.

Budgeted revenue

Short training courses
Short training courses budgeted charge \$100 per person per course.

Short courses are generally one night a week for 4 weeks commencing on the first of each month, except December and January.

	Jan	Feb	Mar	Apr	May	Jun	Jul
Budgeted short course information:							
Number of courses	0	2	3	3	4	4	4
Forecast students per course	0	10	12	12	14	13	15

BB expects to receive payment in advance of each course. Experience shows that, on average, one-third of students pay 1 month in advance and the rest pay on the first day of the course.

In-house training courses
The exact number and type of in-house training courses is unknown at present but, during 2006, BB is expecting to earn \$130,000 spread evenly throughout the year. Based on previous experience, the following receipts are forecast:

	Jan $	Feb $	Mar $	Apr $	May $	Jun $
In-house training course fee receipts (including trade receivables at 31 December 2005)	5,000	8,000	10,000	11,000	12,000	6,000

BB has previously experienced problems of slow payment from some large employers and is monitoring the trade receivables collection period.

Budgeted expenditure

BB employs permanent full-time members of staff to run the entity and provide key lecturing skills. Most of the trainers are part-time tutors at an hourly rate.

Budgeted wages 2006	Jan	Feb	Mar	Apr	May	Jun
	$	$	$	$	$	$
Part-time tutor wages	0	2,500	4,000	4,000	5,000	6,000

Permanent staff salaries are currently $4,000 a month. All full-time staff will receive an increase of 5% from 1 March 2006. BB rents the premises for $2,500 a year, payable in quarterly instalments in January, April, July and October.

Teaching materials, printing and photocopying average $150 per short course (paid in the month of the course). The in-house courses cost, on average, $100 per month.

Budgeted payments in respect of overheads (electricity, telephone and so on) for January and April are $1,500 and for February, March, May and June are $600.

Capital expenditure in the first 6 months of 2006 is planned as follows:

(i) New furniture for the managing director's office $5,000 payable in April.
(ii) BB needs to replace all the IT equipment in one of its computer labs early in 2006. This is currently planned to take place in April, with payment in May 2006. The budgeted cost of the equipment is $40,000 for 20 top-of-the-range PCs and related equipment.

Other information

BB has negotiated an overdraft facility with the bank for an overdraft up to $5,000.

Requirements

(a) Calculate BB's in-house training course trade receivables days outstanding
   (i) according to the forecast at 31 December 2005;
   (ii) according to the projected figures at 30 June 2006, assuming the revenue and cash flow budgets are implemented. **(5 marks)**
(b) Prepare BB's cash budget for the first 6 months of 2006 (January to June).

(10 marks)

(c) Advise BB of any actions it can take to make sufficient funds available to purchase the new technology as budgeted in May 2006. **(5 marks)**

(Total marks = 20)

? Question 9

PRT is a rapidly growing printing entity that uses the latest technology to operate a quick and efficient service to other businesses and to private individuals. Some printing is undertaken to order, while other work, such as posters, is held in inventory until sold. Sales to business customers are on credit, while sales to individuals are for cash.

Expansion has been rapid, as indicated by the number of print shops owned at each financial year ended 31 March:

Year	1998	1999	2000	2001	2002
Number of print shops	8	12	18	27	40

While expansion has been very rapid, concerns have arisen regarding the increasing overdraft, which is now approaching the limit of $1 million set by the bank. The entity has used equity and debt finance to expand in recent years, but is unlikely to be able to raise further finance from the sources in the immediate future.

Extracts from the financial statements for the years ended 31 March are as follows:

	2001 $'000	2002 $'000
Raw materials inventory	55	80
Finished goods inventory	185	185
Purchases of raw materials	600	850
Cost of sales	1,570	1,830
Administrative expenses	45	65
Revenue	1,684	1,996
Trade receivable	114	200
Trade payable	50	70
Overdraft	400	950
Additions to non-current assets	700	900

Cost of sales includes all relevant production costs including manufacturing overheads and labour.

Requirements

(a) Calculate the length in days of PRT's operating cycle, for the year ended 31 March 2002.

(5 marks)

(b) So far as the information permits, calculate the cash generated from operating activities for PRT for the year ended 31 March 2002. State any relevant assumptions.

(4 marks)

(c) As PRT's management accountant, write a memorandum to the board that analyses the entity's cash and working capital position, recommending appropriate actions. Indicate any additional information that would be needed to make a fuller assessment.

(11 marks)
(Total marks = 20)

? Question 10

CK is an entity that sells computer spare parts and peripherals to computer retail stores. The entity's sales and purchases accrue evenly throughout the year and inventory is managed in such a way as to give a constant inventory level throughout the year.

CK had the following figures for the year ended 31 March 2006

	$'000
Revenue from credit sales during the year	6,192
Purchases on credit during the year	4,128
Trade receivables balance at 31 March 2006	1,083
Trade payables balance at 31 March 2006	344
Inventory balance at 31 March 2006	1,020
Cash balance at 31 March 2006	622

The directors wanted working capital management improved and commissioned a consultant to prepare a report on working capital management in CK. The consultant's report indicated that efficiency savings were possible and, if the recommendations were implemented, the following changes in outstanding days would be achieved:

– Trade receivables reduced to 45 days.
– Suppliers would be willing to wait a total of 40 days for payment.
– Inventory could be reduced by 40% (from 31 March 2006 $ value levels) without having an adverse impact on sales.

The budgets for the year to 31 March 2007 have been commenced, but are incomplete. Budgeted revenue from credit sales is based on the year to 31 March 2006 figure, plus a price increase of 10% from 1 April 2006 and a reduction of an estimated 3% in volume caused by the price increase.

Cost of sales is budgeted at the same percentage of credit sales revenue as the year to 31 March 2006

	$'000
Salaries and wages are budgeted at	620 for the year
Other operating expenses budget is	432 for the year
Budgeted capital expenditure is	2,500

The consultant's report recommended that $1,500,000 of the proposed purchase of non-current tangible assets could be leased instead of purchased. The terms of the lease would be five payments of $400,000 each, payable in advance of 1 April each year, commencing on 1 April 2006.

The lease would be classified as a finance lease by IAS 17 *Leases*.

The implicit interest rate is 16 × 875%.

Requirements

(a) Calculate the following for CK at 31 March 2006:

- Trade receivables days outstanding;
- Trade payables days outstanding;
- Inventory days outstanding.

   (*Note:* You should base your calculations on a 365-day year)   **(3 marks)**

(b) Prepare a cash budget for the year to 31 March 2007 based on the budgeted data and assuming CK implements the efficiency changes recommended by the consultant from 1 April 2006.   **(10 marks)**

(c) Explain the effect on CK's cash budget if it decides to lease $1,500,000 of the non-current assets, instead of purchasing them.

   (*Note*: You are not required to recalculate CK's cash budget)   **(2 marks)**

(d) Comment on any possible difficulties that CK may encounter when implementing the efficiency changes.

   (*Note*: All workings should be to the nearest $'000)   **(5 marks)**

   (Total = 20 marks)

Solutions to Revision Questions

23

✅ Solution 1

The correct answer is (C), see Section 23.3.

Jan $(0.6 \times 150{,}000 \times 0.97)/2 = \$43{,}650$
Feb $(0.4 \times 150{,}000 \times 1.1) = \$66{,}000$
Total $= \underline{\$109{,}650}$

✅ Solution 2

The correct answer is (B), see Section 23.3.

$\$360{,}000 - \$15{,}000 = \$345{,}000$

✅ Solution 3

The correct answer is (B), see Section 23.4.2.

✅ Solution 4

The correct answer is (D), see Section 23.4.1.

$$\sqrt{(2 \times 30 \times 240{,}000)/0.05} = \$16{,}970 \text{ (that is approximately } \$17{,}000).$$

✅ Solution 5

The correct answer is (B), see Section 23.6.

✅ Solution 6

The correct answer is (C), see Section 23.3.

$(20{,}000 \times 1.02 \times 40\%) + (20{,}000 \times 60\% \times 0.97) = \$19{,}800$

Solution 7

Formula from formulae sheet in examination:

Spread $= 3 \times [(3/4 \times 30 \times 300{,}000)/0.00025]^{1/3} = 9{,}000$

Return point $= 2{,}500 + (9{,}000 \times \frac{1}{3}) = 5{,}500$

Upper limit $= 2{,}500 + 9{,}000 = 11{,}500$, see Section 23.4.2.

 Solution 8

(a)

	$
Trade receivables – in-house training courses	
Forecast balance at 31 December 2005	34,100
Budgeted revenue for half year to 30 June 2006	65,000
	99,100
Less: Budgeted receipts	52,000
Projected balance at 30 June 2006	47,100

Trade receivable days outstanding:

At 31 December 2005 $= \$34{,}100/\$125{,}000 \times 365 = 100$ days

At 30 June 2006 $= \$47{,}000/\$130{,}000 \times 365 = 132$ days

(b)

Workings

W1 Short course income

	Jan	Feb	Mar	Apr	May	Jun	Jul
No. courses	0	2	3	3	4	4	4
Avg no. persons	0	10	12	12	14	13	15
Total persons	0	20	36	36	56	52	60
	$	$	$	$	$	$	$
Amount due @ $100 pp	0	2,000	3,600	3,600	5,600	5,200	6,000
Receipts							
1/3	667	1,200	1,200	1,867	1,733	2,000	
2/3	0	1,333	2,400	2,400	3,733	3,467	
Total	667	2,533	3,600	4,267	5,466	5,467	

BB Cash Budget for 6 months to June 2006

	Jan	Feb	Mar	Apr	May	Jun
	$	$	$	$	$	$
Cash inflows:						
Short courses	667	2,533	3,600	4,267	5,466	5,467
In-house courses	5,000	8,000	10,000	11,000	12,000	6,000
Total cash inflows	5,667	10,533	13,600	15,267	17,466	11,467
Less cash outflows:						
Salaried staff	4,000	4,000	4,200	4,200	4,200	4,200
Wages	0	2,500	4,000	4,000	5,000	6,000
Rent	625					
Overheads	1,500	600	600	1,500	600	600
Materials – short courses	0	300	450	450	600	600
Materials – in-house courses	100	100	100	100	100	100
Total outflows (excluding capital expenditure)	6,225	7,500	9,350	10,875	10,500	11,500
MD's furniture				5,000		
IT equipment					40,000	
Net cash flow	(558)	3,033	4,250	(608)	(33,034)	(33)
Balance b/fwd	12,460	11,902	14,935	19,185	18,577	(14,457)
Balance c/fwd	11,902	14,935	19,185	18,577	(14,457)	(14,490)

(b) The cash flow forecast currently shows that there is likely to be an overdraft of nearly $15,000 if all the capital expenditure takes place as planned. If the bank overdraft facility is utilised, there is still a shortfall of $10,000.

Actions that could be taken to increase the amount to provide sufficient funds to purchase the new technology as budgeted could involve either raising new cash or re-examining the forecast and implementing actions to improve the current forecast. It must also be borne in mind that sufficient working capital needs to be available to run BB after the new equipment has been purchased.

Actions could include:

   (i) Considering delaying or cancelling the purchase of the MD's furniture, will release $5,000.
  (ii) Arranging a long-term loan with a bank, or other financial institution, for $20,000, to provide additional working capital.
 (iii) Issuing new equity to cover the non-current asset purchase and provide additional working capital, a minimum of $20,000.
 (iv) Negotiating an increase in the overdraft facility from $5,000 to $20,000.
  (v) Considering increasing course fees to generate more income.
 (vi) Investigating the possibility of acquiring the IT equipment and furniture by hire purchase or lease.
 (vii) Examining the in-house training courses debt collection procedures and implement action to speed up revenue collection. If the trade receivable days can be reduced from the projected 132 to say 90 days, an extra one-receipt of $15,000 would accrue in the period.
(viii) Checking the accuracy of the forecast opening bank balance and the likelihood of it being significantly different to forecast.
 (ix) Considering enforcing the requirement for all short course participants to pay in advance of the course instead of allowing payment on the first day of the course, see Section 23.1 and 23.2.

 Solution 9

(a)

	Length in days	
Raw materials cycle	$\dfrac{(55+80)/2}{850} \times 365$	= 29 days
Finished goods cycle	$\dfrac{(185+185)}{1,830} \times 365$	= 37 days
Receivables cycle	$\dfrac{(114+200)/2}{1,996} \times 365$	= 29 days
Payables cycle	$\dfrac{(50+70)/2}{850} \times 365$	= 26 days
Cash operating cycle		= 69 days

(b)

	Receipts/(Payments)
	$'000
Sales (1,996 − 200 + 114)	1,910
Expenses (1,830 − 70 + 50 + 80 − 55 + 65)	(1,900)
Cash generated from operations	10

This calculation assumes that there are no non-cash items in cost of sales. (It thus ignores depreciation on plant and machinery, accruals, prepayments and so on.)

(c)

Memorandum

To: The Board of PRT   **From:** Management Accountant

Subject: Cash Management   **Date:** 21 May 2002

Introduction

The entity appears to be suffering from overtrading as indicated by the number of outlets growing at 50% a year. These appear to be purchased, hence this would be a major drain on cash resources.

To the extent that this expansion could be financed by new equity and new debt, it is not a major problem. It would appear, however, that more recently an overdraft has been used to finance some of the expansion. This appears to be particularly unwise as it is financing a long-term asset with a short-term liability.

In particular, if no new finance can be raised, then the bank could force the entity into liquidation by calling-in the overdraft at any time. This may occur notwithstanding the actual, and potential, profitability of the business.

Cash management

The most important feature of cash management would therefore appear to be maintaining a good relationship with the bank. This could include:
- supplying monthly management accounts;
- informing the bank of any problems in advance, that is before they affect the management accounts;
- provision of additional security if possible – either entity assets or director's personal assets.

Notwithstanding efforts to maintain the banks goodwill, it is necessary to reduce the overdraft or at least prevent it increasing. If this does not occur, the overdraft is almost certain to be called-in. The most obvious remaining sources of finance (given debt and equity capital appear to be exhausted) are:
- capital assets;
- operating activities;
- improved working capital management.

Current ratios

Current ratios provide a summary measure of working capital. These are as follows:

2001

$$\frac{55 + 185 + 114}{50 + 400} = 0.787{:}1$$

2002

$$\frac{80 + 185 + 200}{70 + 950} = 0.456{:}1$$

The deterioration in the current ratio reflects the increase in the overdraft. The ratio is, however, a static representation at a point in time. The primary concern is whether future cash inflows are sufficient to meet the future cash outflows necessary to sustain and expand the business.

Capital assets

The cause of the cash management problems appears to be over-investment in new outlets. No further outlets should therefore be opened. Cash can, however, be raised from existing outlets given that they appear to be owned by the entity.

Outlets could be sold. Unfortunately, sales of property may take some time unless the price is reduced significantly. This is likely to generate a significant loss. This is even more true of plant, machinery and fixtures, which are likely to have a low net realisable value.

Rather than buying the outlets, significant cash savings could have been made by leasing them. While the purchase decision is in the past, cash can still be recovered using a sale and leaseback arrangement – perhaps with the entity's bankers.

Operating cash flows

While the number of outlets has risen by 50% a year, sales have increased by only 18.5% in the last year. There may be a number of reason for this:

- sales have not yet become established at new outlets;
- price cutting has taken place to penetrate new markets so sales volume growth has not been matched by sales value growth;
- the size of later outlets could be smaller than earlier outlets.

Whatever the reason, the cash flow generated from operations is small at $10,000 in the current year [see requirement (b)]. As a result, either substantial growth in operating cash flows is needed or realisation of capital assets by sale or lease.

Working capital management

Improved working capital management may generate extra funds, but it is unlikely to be sufficient on its own.

The *raw materials cycle* appears reasonable at 29 days, but some materials are purchased for immediate use on made-to-order jobs. This means that the holding period on the remaining inventory may be significant. More information is therefore needed on the holding period for individual inventory lines. Similarly, some of the sales are in respect of made-to-order jobs, thus the *finished goods inventory* relating to the remaining sales may be disproportionately high.

The *receivables cycle* appears reasonable at 29 days, but this is an average, and given that sales to private customers are for cash, it means that the credit period extended to business customers is rather longer than 29 days. Improvements to cash flow from receivables management may include:

- factoring of debts may produce increased cash, but may be costly;
- similarly, the credit terms offered by the entity could be managed via an outside finance entity;
- discounts for cash settlement or reduced credit terms may be offered.

The payables cycle at 26 days seems rather short and it might be worth investigating the possibility of suppliers extending further credit. If cash discounts are taken, this may explain the short cycle, but they may be worth forgoing in the short term to help liquidity. As with all ratios, care needs to be taken as the statement of financial position figure may be atypical because of:

- growth;
- seasonality;
- large sales/purchases just before the year end;
- manipulation.

Conclusion

The need for cash is urgent. While operating activities and improved working capital management may provide some help, a more significant immediate injection of cash may be needed to maintain the goodwill and co-operation of the bank. In this context, the sale or the sale and leaseback of fixed assets may be the most appropriate policy. Information in respect of these possibilities is therefore urgently needed.

Signed: Management Accountant.

 Solution 10

(a)

Trade receivables days outstanding =	1,083/6,192 × 365 = 63 × 8 day
Trade payables days outstanding =	344/4,128 × 365 = 30 × 4 day
Inventory days outstanding =	1,020/4,128 × 365 = 90 × 2 days

(b)

CK Cash Budget (revised policies) for the year to 31 March 200

	$'000	$'000
Receipts		
Revenue receipts (W1)		6,875
Payments		
Payments to trade payables (W3)	3,903	
Salaries and wages	620	
Other operating expenses	432	
Non-current asset purchases	2,500	
Total payments		7,455
Net cash outflow		(580)
Cash balance b/fwd		622
Cash balance c/fwd		42

Workings: all figures in $'000

(W1)

$$\frac{Cost\ of\ sales}{Turnover} = \frac{4,128}{6,192} = 66.7\%$$

Budget to 31 March 2007

Revenue	
6,192 × 110% × 97% =	6,607
Cost of sales 6,607 × 66 × 667% =	(4,405)
Gross profit	2,202

Trade receivables revised days outstanding = 45 days
Trade receivables c/fwd = 45/365 × 6,607 = 815
Trade receivable – receipts

Balance b/fwd	1,083
Revenue	6,607
	7,690
Less: Balance c/fwd	(815)
	6,875

(W2)
Inventory

Balance 31 March 2007 = 1,020 × 60% =	612
Balance b/fwd	1,020
Purchased (to balance)	3,997
Cost of sales	(4,405)
Balance c/fwd	612

(W3)
Trade payables

Revised days outstanding =	40 day	
Balance c/fwd = 40/365 × 3,997 =	43	
Balance b/fwd		344
Purchases (from (W2) inventory)		3,997
		4,341
Balance c/fwd		438
Paid		3,903

(c) The effect on the cash budget in the year to 31 March 2007 would be a reduction in cash outflow of $1,100,000.

> However, the lease instalment is due on 1 April 2006, which is probably several months earlier than CK planned to purchase the non-current assets.

> The cash outflow for the four subsequent years would be increased by $400,000 a year.

(d) Difficulties implementing the new policies:

Trade receivables – reduction from 63 × 8 days to 45 days.

Customers will have become accustomed to paying late and to change their attitudes will require tact and possibly some time. If CK suddenly starts vigorously chasing trade receivables, customers may go elsewhere. The sudden change to obtain more rapid payment may also be misinterpreted as CK being in financial difficulties. Customers may also try and obtain further incentives before they place orders as they may feel that their terms of trade have been adversely affected. CK may struggle to get the days outstanding down to 45 days within a reasonable time scale.

Trade payables – increase from 30 × 4 days to 40 days.

The original period of 30 × 4 days is very short, given that trade receivables take 63 × 8 days to pay. The new level of 40 days is still less than the proposed level for trade receivables of 45 days. CK is currently paying quickly and will have built up a reputation for a good payer and for paying promptly. Any slow down in payment may affect its credit rating, although a reduction to 40 days is unlikely to cause it to be labelled a slow payer. CK will still need to be careful that the longer payment time does not lose its suppliers who refuse to supply on the new payment terms.

Inventory – reduction by 40%.

This is a large reduction in inventory. If inventory is simply left to run down, by not ordering more for a period of time, certain products may become unavailable and service to customers will be impaired. CK will need to manage the run down of inventory levels. This will mean reassessing requirements and recalculating reorder levels and reorder quantities. Ordering less and more frequently will reduce inventory levels, but may increase costs. It will not be possible to continue with its current policy of maintaining a constant level of inventory.

Preparing for the
Examination

Preparing for the Examination

This chapter is intended for use when you are ready to start revising for your examination. It contains:

- a summary of useful revision techniques;
- details of the format of the examination;
- a bank of examination-standard revision questions and suggested solutions. These solutions are of a length and level of detail that a competent student might be expected to produce in an examination;
- a complete past examination paper. This should be attempted when you consider yourself to be ready for the examination, and you should emulate examination conditions when you sit for it.

Revision technique

Planning

The first thing to say about revision is that it is an addition to your initial studies, not a substitute for them. In other words, don't coast along early in your course in the hope of catching up during the revision phase. On the contrary, you should be studying and revising concurrently from the outset. At the end of each week, and at the end of each month, get into the habit of summarising the material you have covered to refresh your memory of it.

As with your initial studies, planning is important to maximise the value of your revision work. You need to balance the demands for study, professional work, family life and other commitments. To make this work, you will need to think carefully about how to make best use of your time.

Begin as before by comparing the estimated hours you will need to devote to revision with the hours available to you in the weeks leading up to the examination. Preparing a written schedule setting out the areas you intend to cover during particular weeks, and break that down further into topics for each day's revision. To help focus on the key areas try to establish:

- which areas you are weakest on, so that you can concentrate on the topics where effort is particularly needed,
- which areas are especially significant for the examination – the topics that are tested frequently.

Don't forget the need for relaxation, and for family commitments. Sustained intellectual effort is only possible for limited periods, and must be broken up at intervals by lighter activities. And don't continue your revision timetable right up to the moment when you enter the exam hall: you should aim to stop work a day or even two days before the exam.

Beyond this point the most you should attempt is an occasional brief look at your notes to refresh your memory.

Getting down to work

By the time you begin your revision, you should already have settled into a fixed work pattern: a regular time of day for doing the work, a particular location where you sit, particular equipment that you assemble before you begin and so on. If this is not already a matter of routine for you, think carefully about it now in the last vital weeks before the exam.

You should have notes summarising the main points of each topic you have covered. Begin each session by reading through the relevant notes and trying to commit the important points to memory.

Usually this will be just your starting point. Unless the area is one where you already feel very confident, you will need to track back from your notes to the relevant chapter(s) in the *Learning System*. This will refresh your memory on points not covered by your notes and fill in the detail that inevitably gets lost in the process of summarisation.

When you think you have understood and memorised the main principles and techniques, attempt an exam-standard question. At this stage of your studies, you should normally be expecting to complete such questions in something close to the actual time allocation allowed in the exam. After completing your effort, check the solution provided and add to your notes any extra points it reveals.

Tips for the final revision phase

As the exam approaches, consider the following list of techniques and make use of those that work for you:

- Summarise your notes into more concise form, perhaps on index cards that you can carry with you for revision on the way into work.
- Go through your notes with a highlighter pen, marking key concepts and definitions.
- Summarise the main points in a key area by producing a wordlist, mind map or other mnemonic device.
- On areas that you find difficult, rework questions that you have already attempted, and compare your answers in detail with those provided in the *Study System*.
- Rework questions you attempted earlier in your studies with a view to producing more 'polished' answers (better layout and presentation may earn marks in the exam) and to completing them within the time limits.
- Stay alert for practical examples, incidents, situations and events that illustrate the material you are studying. If you can refer in the exam to real-life topical illustrations, you will impress the examiner and may earn extra marks.

Format of the examination

Structure of the paper

The examination for *Financial Accounting and Tax Principles* is a three-hour written paper which has three sections:

- Section A will be compulsory for 40 per cent of the marks, this section will comprise between 14 and 19 objective test questions with a total of 40 marks. The questions will include a number of multiple choice questions and other objective test question formats.

- Each question will be worth between 2 and 4 marks. Questions worth 3 or 4 marks will allow marks for correct workings where the final answer is incorrect.
- Section B will be a compulsory section worth 30 marks. There will be six questions of 5 marks each.
- Section C will be one compulsory question for 30 marks. This question will be on preparation of financial statements, including statement of comprehensive income statement of financial position statement of changes in equity and statement of cash flows.

The paper will include a formula sheet.

Any changes in the structure of the examination or in the format of questions will be indicated well in advance in the appropriate CIMA journals.

The rest of this chapter is split into two sections, the first is objective test questions and answers; the second is more traditional type of examination questions and answers; the third section is the *Financial Accounting and Tax planning* past examination paper and answers.

Revision Questions I

Objective Test Questions

Each of the questions below, has only **one** correct answer.

Please note that in the examination you will not receive marks for any workings to questions unless they are worth 3 marks or more.

Objective test questions matched to learning outcomes

Learning Outcomes	Question Number
A – Principles of Business Taxation – 20%	
(i) Identify the principal types of taxation likely to be of relevance to an incorporated business in a particular country, including direct tax on the entity's trading profits and capital gains, indirect taxes collected by the entity, employee taxation withholding taxes on international payments	1, 3, 11, 14, 15
(ii) Describe the features of the principal types of taxation likely to be of relevance to an incorporated business in a particular country (e.g. in terms of who ultimately bears the tax cost, withholding responsibilities, principles of calculating the tax base)	2, 4, 5, 6, 7, 8, 9,12,13
(iii) Describe the likely record-keeping, filing and tax payment requirements associated with the principal types of taxation likely to be or relevance to an incorporated business in a particular country	
(iv) Describe the possible enquiry and investigation powers of taxing authorities	
(v) Identify situations in which foreign tax obligations (reporting and liability) could arise and methods for relieving foreign tax	19, 20
(vi) Explain the difference in principle between tax avoidance and tax evasion	16,17
(vii) Describe sources of tax rules and explain the importance of jurisdiction	18, 35
(viii) Explain and apply the accounting rules contained in IAS 12 for current and deferred taxation	21, 22, 23, 26, 27, 28, 47
B – Principles of Regulation of Financial Reporting – 10%	
(i) Explain the need for regulation of published accounts and the concept that regulatory regimes vary from country to country	
(ii) Explain potential elements that might be expected in a regulatory framework for published accounts	
(iii) Describe the role and structure of the International Accounting Standards Board (IASB) and the International Organisation of Securities Commissions (IOSCO)	75
(iv) Explain the IASB's *Framework for the Presentation and Preparation of Financial Statements*	43, 76, 77

(v) Describe the process leading to the promulgation of an international
accounting standard (IAS)

(vi) Describe ways in which IAS's can interact with local regulatory
frameworks

(vii) Explain in general terms, the role of the external auditor, the   78
elements of the audit report and types of qualification of that report

C – Single Entity Financial Accounts – 45%

(i) Prepare financial statements in a form suitable for publication, with   24, 25, 49
appropriate note

(ii) Prepare a cash flow statement in a form suitable for publication

(iii) Explain and apply the accounting rules contained in IAS's dealing with   29, 36, 52
reporting performance, tangible non-current assets and inventories

(iv) Explain the accounting rules contained in IAS's governing share   10, 41, 50
capital transactions

(v) Explain the principles of the accounting rules contained in IAS's   30, 31, 32, 33, 34, 38,
dealing with disclosure of related parties to a business, construction   39, 44, 45, 46, 48, 51
contracts (and related financing costs), research and development
expenditure, intangible non-current assets (other than goodwill
on consolidation), impairment of assets, post-balance sheet events,
contingencies, and leases (lessee only)

D – Managing Short Term Finance – 25%

(i) Calculate and interpret working capital ratios for business sectors   40, 63, 65, 66, 67, 70, 72

(ii) Prepare and analyse cash-flow forecasts over a twelve-month period   55, 62

(iii) Identify measures to improve a cash forecast situation   69

(iv) Compare and contrast the use and limitations of cash management   54, 60, 61, 64
models and identify when each model is most appropriate

(v) Analyse trade receivable information   68

(vi) Evaluate receivable and payable policies   42, 53

(vii) Evaluate appropriate methods of inventory management   58

(viii) Identify alternatives for investment of short-term cash surpluses   57, 59, 73, 37

(ix) Identify sources of short-term funding   56, 71

(x) Identify appropriate methods of finance for trading internationally   74

Question 1

List Adam Smith's characteristics of a good tax.   **(2 marks)**

Question 2

In no more than 25 words, define the meaning of the tax gap.   **(2 marks)**

Question 3

The following are common taxes used in many countries:

(i) Corporate income tax

(ii) Import duty payable on alcoholic drinks

(iii) Value-added tax/sales tax

(iv) Individual income tax deducted at source (such as PAYE)

Which of the above would normally be defined as a direct tax:

(A) (i) and (ii)
(B) (i) and (iv)
(C) (ii) and (iii)
(D) (ii) and (iv)

(2 marks)

Question 4

In no more than 30 words, define 'effective incidence'.   **(2 marks)**

Question 5

What is the meaning of 'Hypothecation':

(A) the tax charge is estimated by the tax authorities
(B) a new tax law has to be passed each year for the tax to be legally collected
(C) the products of certain taxes are devoted to specific types of expenditures
(D) tax is deducted from amounts due before they are paid to the recipient

(2 marks)

Question 6

In a country the tax on entity profits is:

- 0% on the first $30,000,
- 10% on amounts between $30,001 and $50,000,
- 30% on amounts over $50,001.

The above tax regime could be described as:

(A) Proportional
(B) Regressive
(C) Stepped
(D) Progressive

(2 marks)

Question 7

In no more than 15 words, define the meaning of 'tax base'.   **(2 marks)**

Question 8

An entity commenced business on 1 January 2002, making up the first accounts for the year to 31 December 2002.

The entity's purchases and sales of non-current assets were as follows:

Purchases			$
2002	1 January	Industrial building	400,000
	1 January	Plant	60,000
2004	1 January	Plant	80,000
Sales			
2003	31 December	Plant bought on 1 June 2002	20,000

The entity qualifies for accelerated first-year allowance on the plant at the rate of 50% for the first year. The second and subsequent years will be at 25% on the reducing balance method. No additional charge will result if the asset is disposed of early.

The industrial building qualifies for an annual tax depreciation allowance of 5% on the straight-line basis.

What is the entity's tax depreciation for the year ended 31 December 2003?

(4 marks)

? Question 9

The following payments were made by an entity during the year:

 (i) payments to the spouse of a director for living expenses,
 (ii) dividends paid to equity share holders,
(iii) salaries and pensions paid to directors,
(iv) fees and charges paid to solicitors for the purchase of new office buildings,
 (v) interest paid on loan notes.

Which of the above are normally allowable as deductions from revenue for tax purposes:

(A) (i) and (iii)
(B) (ii) and (iv)
(C) (iii) and (v)
(D) (iv) and (v)

(2 marks)

? Question 10

IAS 32 *Financial Instruments – Disclosure and Presentation* classifies issued shares as either equity instruments or financial liabilities. An entity has the following categories of funding on its statement of financial position:

 (i) A preference share that is redeemable for cash at a 10% premium on 30 May 2015.
 (ii) An ordinary share which is not redeemable and has no restrictions on receiving dividends.
(iii) A loan note that is redeemable at par in 2020.
(iv) A cumulative preference share that is entitled to receive a dividend of 7% a year.

Applying IAS 32, how would *each* of the above be categorised on the statement of financial position?

	As an equity instrument	As a financial liability
(A)	(i) and (ii)	(iii) and (iv)
(B)	(ii) and (iii)	(i) and (iv)

(C)	(ii)	(i), (iii) and (iv)
(D)	(i), (ii) and (iii)	(iv)

(2 marks)

? Question 11

An entity makes a taxable profit of $200,000 and pays corporate income tax at 25%, tax paid $50,000.

The entity pays a dividend to shareholders, a shareholder receiving $2,000 dividend then pays personal income tax on the dividend at the standard personal income tax rate of 20% and pays a further $400 tax.

In the country described, the corporate income tax system could be said to be a:

(A) Split rate system
(B) Imputation system
(C) Partial imputation system
(D) Classical system

(2 marks)

? Question 12

A Country has the following tax regulations:

- Taxable profits are subject to tax at 25%.
- Capital gains are added to profits from trading to give taxable profits.
- Trading losses can be carried forward indefinitely but cannot be carried back to previous years.
- Capital gains/losses cannot be offset against trading gains/losses or visa versa.

An entity started trading in 2001 and has the following profits/losses

	Trading profit/(loss) $'000	Capital gain/(loss) $'000
2001	(450)	0
2002	(220)	0
2003	660	(150)
2004	800	120

Calculate the amount of tax due for 2004.

(4 marks)

? Question 13

A Country has a VAT system which allows organisations to reclaim input tax paid. VAT is at 20% of selling price.

X manufactures sports clothing and sells an outfit to Y, a wholesaler. Y resells them to Z, a retailer. Z eventually sells them to C for $180 plus VAT. The prices at which transactions take place (excluding VAT) are as follows:

- X sells to Y for $70;
- Y sells to Z for $110.

Calculate the VAT due from X, Y and Z.

(4 marks)

Question 14

A country has a duty that is levied on all tobacco and tobacco products. This levy is $100 per kilo. This duty could be said to be:

(A) Ad valorem tax
(B) Specific unit tax
(C) General consumption tax
(D) Value added tax   **(2 marks)**

Question 15

An entity provides services which are all classified as exempt for VAT purposes. For VAT this means that the entity can:

	Input tax	*Output tax*
(A)	Reclaim	Charge
(B)	Not reclaim	Charge
(C)	Reclaim	Not charge
(D)	Not reclaim	Not charge

                                                      (2 marks)

Question 16

Which of the following statements is the least likely to be a description of tax evasion:

(A) the illegal manipulation of the tax system to avoid paying taxes
(B) exploiting loopholes in the legislation to legally avoid paying tax
(C) the intentional disregard of legislation in order to escape paying taxes
(D) falsifying tax returns and claiming fictitious expenses   **(2 marks)**

Question 17

Tax authorities attempt to reduce tax avoidance and tax evasion.

 (i) deduct tax at source whenever possible;
 (ii) increase tax rates to compensate for losses due to evasion;
(iii) simplify the tax structure, reduce the number of allowances and exceptions;
(iv) reduce penalties for avoidance.

   Which of the above methods could be used to help reduce tax evasion and tax avoidance:

(A) (i) and (ii)
(B) (i) and (iii)
(C) (ii) and (iv)
(D) (ii) and (iv)   **(2 marks)**

Question 18

The most important criteria for determining corporate residence is:

(A) The country where the entity is registered
(B) The country where the entity has its main office

(C) The country where the effective management of the entity is carried out
(D) The country where the majority of the entity's trade is carried out **(2 marks)**

Question 19

Which of the following would normally be subject to a withholding tax if paid to an entity abroad:

(A) Fees for work done
(B) Payments for materials
(C) Dividends
(D) Payments for the purchase of capital equipment **(2 marks)**

Question 20

An entity receives dividends from an overseas subsidiary. The withholding tax on the dividend is $5,000. The entity deducts the $5,000 tax paid overseas from its 'home' tax bill and pays the net amount. This is called:

(A) Relief by exemption
(B) Relief by tax credit
(C) Relief by deduction
(D) No relief from double taxation **(2 marks)**

Question 21

The corporate income tax estimate for the current year is $330,000. The settlement of income tax due for last year left a credit balance of $7,000 outstanding on the income tax account. Deferred tax was estimated to require an increase of $32,000 in the statement of financial position provision. The income tax charge for the year in the profit or loss and the payables due in less than 1 year – income tax on the statement of financial position should be:

	Profit or loss	*Statement of financial position*
(A)	$323,000	$330,000
(B)	$355,000	$330,000
(C)	$362,000	$323,000
(D)	$369,000	$362,000

(3 marks)

Question 22

An asset cost $320,000 and had an estimated useful life of 8 years, with no residual value at the end. Depreciation was calculated on the straight-line basis. Capital allowances were given at 25 per cent on a reducing balance basis. Assume corporate income tax at 25 per cent. At the end of the second year of operation, the deferred tax provision on the statement of financial position should be:

(A) $15,000
(B) $20,000
(C) $60,000
(D) $80,000 **(3 marks)**

Question 23

Plant and machinery, original cost 1 April 20X0, was $60,000. This was depreciated for 2 years at 25 per cent using the reducing-balance method. On 1 April 20X2 the machinery, original cost $20,000, was sold for $15,000. Replacement machines were acquired on the same date for $40,000. What was the net book value at 1 April 20X3?

(A) $45,000
(B) $33,750
(C) $44,062
(D) $46,875   **(3 marks)**

Data for Questions 24 and 25

Trade receivables as at 31 December 20X1 were $25,000.

The bad debt provision as at 1 January 20X1 was $812.

During the year to 31 December 20X1, bad debts of $2,000 have been written off to administration expenses.

After the year-end, but before the accounts had been completed, the entity discovered that a major trade receivable had gone into liquidation and that their outstanding balance of $3,000 was very unlikely to be paid.

As a result of the recent bad debt experience, the directors have decided to increase the bad debt provision at 31 December 20X1 to 5 per cent of outstanding trade receivables.

 Question 24

What is the correct balance for trade receivables, net of bad debt provision, as at 31 December 20X1?

(A) $19,000
(B) $20,900
(C) $23,750
(D) $21,188   **(2 marks)**

 Question 25

What is the correct charge to the profit or loss for bad debts and bad debt provisions for the years to 31 December 20X1?

(A) $4,100
(B) $6,100
(C) $5,288
(D) $3,288   **(2 marks)**

Data for Questions 26 and 27

The corporation tax estimate for the current year 20X1 is $280,000. The balances on the taxation accounts in the statement of financial position for last year were:

	20X0 $
Current tax liability	240,000
Deferred tax liability	60,000

The settlement of income tax due for last year left a debit balance of $15,000 outstanding on the income tax account. Deferred tax was estimated to require an increase of $11,000 in the statement of financial position provision for 20X1.

? Question 26

The income tax charge for the year in the profit or loss should be:

(A) $284,000
(B) $276,000
(C) $306,000
(D) $254,000   (2 marks)

? Question 27

The taxation paid shown in the statement of cash flows would be:

(A) $280,000
(B) $255,000
(C) $240,000
(D) $251,000   (2 marks)

? Question 28

A non-current asset cost $150,000 and had an estimated useful life of 15 years, with no residual value at the end. Depreciation was calculated on the straight-line basis. Tax depreciation allowances were given at 25 per cent on a reducing-balance basis. Assume income tax at 30 per cent. At the end of the second year of operation, the deferred tax provision on the statement of financial position should be:

(A) $13,687
(B) $16,500
(C) $45,625
(D) $6,187   (2 marks)

? Question 29

Inventory code ABC290 had 1,153 items in inventory at 31 March, the entity year-end. The original cost of the inventory, according to the inventory control system, was $4,612.

Alternative valuations were obtained at 31 March for this inventory item. Which value should be used in the accounts at 31 March?

(A) Original cost $4,612
(B) Replacement cost $2,306
(C) Net realisable value $3,459
(D) Selling price $5,765   **(2 marks)**

Data for Questions 30, 31 and 32

Details of long-term contract number 12234–56 are:

	$'000
Values of work completed	520
Costs incurred to date:	
Attributable to work completed	545
Further costs attributable to partly completed work	60
	605
Progress payments received	550
Expected further loss on completion	55

Using the above data, identify the correct entries required in Questions 30, 31 and 32 for contract 12234–56.

? Question 30

The cost of sales figure should be:

$'000
(A) 545
(B) 550
(C) 600
(D) 605   **(2 marks)**

? Question 31

The 'value of payables, gross amounts due to customers' figure should be:

$'000
(A)   5
(B) 25
(C) 30
(D) 90   **(2 marks)**

? Question 32

The 'value of gross amounts due from customers for long-term contract work' figure should be:

$'000
(A)   0
(B)   5
(C) 60
(D) 545   **(2 marks)**

? Question 33

The finance lease runs for 4 years, with annual payments in arrears of $30,000. The fair value of the asset was $100,000. Using the sum-of-digits method, what would the statement of financial position figure be for the outstanding lease payable at the end of year 2?

(A) $50,000
(B) $54,000
(C) $60,000
(D) $74,000   **(2 marks)**

? Question 34

Z is currently defending two legal actions:

(a) a competitor is suing Z for $500,000, claiming that Z has copied their product infringing their copyright. Z's lawyers are contesting the claim and have advised the directors of Z that there is not really a case to answer and there is very little chance of Z losing.

(b) a customer is suing for $50,000, claiming that Z's sun tan products damaged their skin and gave no protection from the sun. Z's lawyers are contesting this claim, but have advised Z's directors that the claim is almost certain to succeed.

How much should Z provide in its year-end accounts for these legal claims?

(A) $0
(B) $50,000
(C) $500,000
(D) $550,000   **(2 marks)**

? Question 35

In no more than 15 words, define the meaning of 'competent jurisdiction'.   **(2 marks)**

? Question 36

IAS 8 – *Accounting Policies Changes in Accounting Estimates and Errors* specifies the definition and treatment of a number of different items. Which of the following is not specified by IAS 8:

(A) The effect of a change in an accounting estimate
(B) Prior period adjustments
(C) Extraordinary items
(D) Provisions   **(2 marks)**

? Question 37

A bond with a coupon rate of 7% is redeemable in 8 years' time for $100. Its current purchase price is $82. What is the percentage yield to maturity?   **(4 marks)**

Data for Questions 38 and 39

B entered into a three-year construction contract to build a leisure centre for an entity. The contract value was $6 million. B recognises profit on the basis of certified work completed. At the end of the first year, the following figures were extracted from B's accounting records:

	$'000
Certified values of work completed (progress payments billed)	2,000
Cost of work certified as complete	1,650
Cost of work in progress (not included in completed work)	550
Estimated cost of remaining work required to complete the contract	2,750
Progress payments received from entity	1,600
Cash paid to suppliers for work on the contract	1,300

? Question 38

How much profit should B recognise in its profit or loss at the end of the first year?

(A) $200,000 (loss)
(B) $300,000
(C) $350,000
(D) $400,000

(2 marks)

? Question 39

What values should B record as 'current liabilities – trade and other payables' and 'gross amounts due from customers for contract work':

	Current liabilities – trade and other payables	*Gross amounts due from customers for contract work*
(A)	$350,000	$950,000
(B)	$600,000	$1,250,000
(C)	$900,000	$950,000
(D)	$900,000	$2,550,000

(2 marks)

? Question 40

The following balances were extracted from the books of A:

	31 March 03
	$'000
Revenue	300
Cost of Sales	200
Gross profit	100
Closing inventory	15
Trade receivables	36
Trade payables	28

A's average working capital cycle for the year ended 31 March 2003 is:

(A) 11.0 days
(B) 20.1 days
(C) 34.7 days
(D) 37.1 days   **(3 marks)**

? Question 41

R issued 500,000 new $1 equity shares on 1 April 2002. The issue price of the shares was $1.50 per share. Applicants paid $0.20 per share with their applications and a further $0.80 on allotment. All money was received on time.

A final call of $0.50 per share was made on 31 January 2003. One holder of 5,000 shares failed to pay the call by the due date and the shares were forfeited. The forfeited shares were reissued for $1 per share on 31 March 2003. Which of the following is the correct set of accounting entries to record the reissue of the forfeited shares?

	Investment in own shares a/c	Bank a/c	Investment in own shares a/c	Share premium a/c
(A)	$5,000 credit	$5,000 debit	$2,500 debit	$2,500 credit
(B)	$5,000 credit	$5,000 debit	0	0
(C)	$5,000 credit	$5,000 debit	$2,500 credit	$2,500 debit
(D)	$5,000 debit	$5,000 credit	$2,500 credit	$2,500 debit

(2 marks)

? Question 42

AL's customers all pay their accounts at the end of 30 days. To try and improve its cash flow, AL is considering offering all customers a 1.5% discount for payment within 14 days.

Calculate the implied annual (interest) cost to AL of offering the discount, using com pound interest methodology and assuming a 365-day year.   **(3 marks)**

? Question 43

The IASB's *Framework for the Preparation and Presentation of Financial Statements* (Framework) lists the qualitative characteristics of financial statements.

  (i) Comparability,
 (ii) Relevance,
(iii) Prudence,
 (iv) Reliability,
  (v) Understandability,
 (vi) Matching,
(vii) Consistency.

Which THREE of the above are NOT included in the principal qualitative characteristics listed by the Framework?

(A) (i), (iii) and (vii)
(B) (i), (ii) and (v)
(C) (iii), (vi) and (vii)
(D) (iii), (iv) and (vi)   (2 marks)

? Question 44

Which of the following is NOT regarded as a related party of an entity by IAS 24 – *Related Party Disclosures?*

(A) Directors of the entity
(B) A bank providing a loan to the entity
(C) The entity's employee pension fund
(D) A close relative of a director of the entity   (2 marks)

? Question 45

IAS 10 – *Events After the Reporting Period,* distinguishes between adjusting and non-adjusting events.

Which of the following is an adjusting event?

(A) One month after the year-end, a customer lodged a claim for $1,000,000 compensation. The customer claimed to have suffered permanent mental damage as a result of the fright she had when one of the entity's products malfunctioned and exploded. The outcome of the court case cannot be predicted at this stage
(B) There was a dispute with the workers and all production ceased 1 week after the year-end
(C) A fire destroyed all of the entity's inventory in its finished goods warehouse 2 weeks after the year-end
(D) Inventory valued at the year-end at $20,000 was sold 1 month later for $15,000.   (2 marks)

? Question 46

X signed a finance lease agreement on 1 October 2002. The lease provided for five annual payments, in arrears, of $20,000. The fair value of the asset was agreed at $80,000.

Using the sum-of-digits method, how much should be charged to the profit or loss for the finance cost in the year to 30 September 2003?

(A) $4,000
(B) $6,667
(C) $8,000
(D) $20,000   (2 marks)

? Question 47

D purchased a non-current asset on 1 April 2000 for $200,000. The asset attracted tax depreciation allowances at 25% on the reducing balance. Accounting depreciation was 10% on the straight-line basis. Assume income tax is at 30%.

The deferred tax balance for this asset at 31 March 2003 is

(A) $9,000
(B) $16,688
(C) $27,000
(D) $55,625   **(3 marks)**

? Question 48

C started work on a contract to build a dam for a hydroelectric scheme. The work commenced on 24 August 2001 and is scheduled to take 4 years to complete. C recognises profit on the basis of the certified percentage of work completed. The contract price is $10 million.

An analysis of C's records provided the following information:

Year to 30 September	2002	2003
Percentage of work completed and certified in year	30%	25%
	$'000	$'000
Total cost incurred during the year	2,900	1,700
Estimated cost of remaining work to complete contract	6,000	3,900
Total payments made for the cost incurred during the year	2,500	2,000

How much profit should C recognise in its profit or loss for the years ended

	30 September 2002	30 September 2003
	$'000	$'000
(A)	100	375
(B)	330	375
(C)	330	495
(D)	500	825

(4 marks)

? Question 49

F's year end is 30 June. F purchased a non-current asset for $50,000 on 1 July 2000.

Depreciation was provided at the rate of 20% per annum on the straight-line basis. There was no forecast residual value.

On 1 July 2002, the asset was revalued to $60,000 and then depreciated on a straight-line basis over its remaining useful economic life which was unchanged. On 1 July 2003, the asset was sold for $35,000.

(i) Debit profit or loss with a loss on disposal of $5,000.
(ii) Credit profit or loss with a gain on disposal of $25,000.
(iii) Transfer $60,000 from revaluation reserve to retained profits as movement on reserves.
(iv) Transfer $30,000 from revaluation reserve to retained profits as movement on reserves.

(v) Reclassify $30,000 from revaluation reserve to profit or loss as a reclassification adjustment.

(vi) Reclassify $60,000 from revaluation reserve to profit or loss as a reclassification adjustment.

In addition to the entries in the non-current asset account and provision for depreciation account, which TWO of the above statements correctly record the entries required on disposal of the non-current asset?

(A) (i) and (iv)
(B) (ii) and (iii)
(C) (i) and (v)
(D) (ii) and (vi) **(2 marks)**

? Question 50

S announced a rights issue of 1 for every 5 shares currently held, at a price of $2 each.

S currently has 2,000,000 $1 ordinary shares with a quoted market price of $2.50 each. Directly attributable issue costs amounted to $25,000.

Assuming all rights are taken up and all money paid in full, how much will be credited to the share premium account for the rights issue?

(A) $200,000
(B) $308,333
(C) $375,000
(D) $400,000 **(2 marks)**

? Question 51

Which of the following best describes an operating lease?

(A) A contract for a specific time that is usually the expected working life of the asset leased
(B) A short-term lease that can be terminated easily
(C) An agreement that can be cancelled, but the cost is usually prohibitive
(D) A lease agreement in which a firm sells assets to a finance house, which then allows the firm to continue to use the asset in return for regular payments **(2 marks)**

? Question 52

An item of plant and equipment was purchased on 1 April 2001 for $100,000. At the date of acquisition, its expected useful economic life was 10 years. Depreciation was provided on a straight-line basis, with no residual value.

On 1 April 2003, the asset was revalued to $95,000. On 1 April 2004, the useful life of the asset was reviewed and the remaining useful econmic life was reduced to 5 years, a total useful life of 8 years.

Calculate the amounts that would be included in the statement of financial position for the asset cost/ valuation and provision for accumulated depreciation at 31 March 2005.

(4 marks)

Question 53

An entity is considering a proposal to offer a cash discount of 2 per cent to customers if they settle the amounts owing within 10 days. All sales offer 30 days' credit currently. What is the annualised compounded cost of giving this cash discount to a customer?

(A) 24.83%
(B) 36.5%
(C) 37.23%
(D) 44.6% **(2 marks)**

Question 54

The Miller–Orr cash model assumes that short-term cash movements cannot be predicted since they change in a random fashion. This means that the following tactics should be used to manage the cash resources of an entity:

(A) if the daily variation in cash balances is large, then the control limits should be set far apart
(B) if the cost of buying and selling securities is high, then the control limits should be set far apart
(C) if the rate of interest is high, the control limits should be set close together
(D) all these factors should be considered **(2 marks)**

Question 55

Cash-flow forecasts will be affected adversely by which one of the following?

(A) A reduction in the operating profit as a result of increased rates of depreciation being charged on the firm's plant and machinery
(B) A change in purchasing policy so that all cash discounts are now taken and this has reduced the payables in the statement of financial position
(C) Non-current assets have been sold at a substantial loss
(D) The working capital cycle has been reduced **(2 marks)**

Question 56

Which of the following statements about an overdraft facility is incorrect?

(A) The overdraft is repayable on demand
(B) Assets are normally required as security
(C) Interest is paid on the full facility
(D) Legal documentation is minimal compared with other types of loan **(2 marks)**

Question 57

Which one of the following statements about certificates of deposit is NOT true?

(A) Certificates of deposit are negotiable deposits issued by banks
(B) Certificates of deposit will typically have maturity periods of between 1 month and 5 years

(C) Certificates of deposit are non-negotiable

(D) Certificates of deposit are issued in bearer form **(2 marks)**

 **Question 58**

PB uses 2,500 units of component X per year. The entity has calculated that the cost of placing and processing a purchase order for component X is $185, and the cost of holding one unit of component X for a year is $25.

What is the economic order quantity (EOQ) for component X, and assuming a 52-week year, what is the average frequency at which purchase orders should be placed?

	EOQ	Frequency of orders
(A)	136 units	3 weeks
(B)	136 units	6 weeks
(C)	192 units	4 weeks
(D)	192 units	5 weeks

(2 marks)

Question 59

Bankers Automated Clearing Services (BACS) is an example of an electronic funds transfer system. Which of the following best describes the system?

(A) Provides same-day settlement for large sums of money

(B) Is most concerned with processing payrolls and transactions involving standing orders and direct debits

(C) Is a network for rapid transmission of international remittances between participating banks

(D) Requires cheques to be completed to ensure settlement of a transaction **(2 marks)**

Question 60

An entity maintains a minimum cash holding of $1,000. The variance of its daily cash flows has been measured as $250,000. The transaction cost for each sale or purchase of treasury bills is $20. The daily interest rate is 0.025 per cent per day and is not expected to change in the foreseeable future. Using the Miller–Orr cash management model, the maximum cash-holding level would be:

(A) $1,594

(B) $2,594

(C) $7,400

(D) $8,400 **(2 marks)**

Question 61

An entity has cash outgoings of $1,260,000 per annum, spread evenly throughout the year. The interest rate on a Treasury bill is 8 per cent per annum, and every sale of Treasury bills costs $20. According to the Baumol cash-management model, the optimum amount of Treasury bills to be sold each time cash is replenished is:

(A) $7,937

(B) $17,748

(C) $25,100
(D) $88,741 **(2 marks)**

? Question 62

LM is a trading entity. During the year to 31 December 20X8, LM received $850,000 from trade receivables, and paid $325,000 to trade payables. Purchase for the 3 months to the end of December 20X7 were $90,000; sales revenue for that period was $150,000. Purchases for the 3 months ended December 20X8 were $80,000; sales revenue for that period was $120,000. LM typically takes 90 days' to pay for goods supplied, and allows 90 days' credit to customers. Production is scheduled evenly throughout the year. Inventories increased by $75,000 during the year.

The gross profit for the year was:

(A) $505,000
(B) $525,000
(C) $580,000
(D) $600,000 **(4 marks)**

? Question 63

The statement of financial position of KSS includes the following figures:

	$
Current assets	
Inventory	300,000
Trade receivables	200,000
	500,000
Current liabilities: Amounts due within one year	
Trade payables	200,000
Bank overdraft	50,000
	250,000

The quick ratio calculated from these figures is:

(A) 0.8
(B) 1.0
(C) 1.2
(D) 2.0 **(2 marks)**

? Question 64

An entity has cash outgoings of $1,850,000 per annum, spread evenly throughout the year. The interest rate on a Treasury bill is 6 per cent per annum, and every sale of Treasury bills costs $20. According to the Baumol cash-management model, the optimum amount of Treasury bills to be sold each time cash is replenished is:

(A) $1,434
(B) $3,512
(C) $35,119
(D) $143,372 **(2 marks)**

Question 65

Swinson, a retailing entity, has an annual revenue of $40 million. The entity earns a constant margin of 20% on sales. All sales and purchases are on credit and are evenly distributed throughout the year. The following amounts are maintained at a constant level throughout the year:

Inventory	$5 million
Trade receivables	$7 million
Trade payables	$2 million

What is the length of the entity's cash cycle to the nearest day?

(A) 64 days
(B) 92 days
(C) 98 days
(D) 114 days   (2 marks)

Question 66

Working capital is most likely to decrease when

(A) The period of credit extended to customers is increased
(B) Inventory levels are decreased
(C) Non-current assets are purchased
(D) Payables are paid before the balance is due   (2 marks)

Question 67

In October, an entity made credit purchases of $18,000 and credit sales of $24,000. All sales are made on the basis of cost plus 25%. By how much will working capital increase in October as a result of these transactions?

(A) $2,000
(B) $4,000
(C) $4,800
(D) $6,000   (2 marks)

Question 68

The following items have been extracted from an entity's budget for next month:

	$
Sales on credit	240,000
Expected increase in inventory next month	20,000
Expected decrease in trade receivables next month	12,000

What is the budgeted receipt from trade receivables next month?

(A) $228,000
(B) $232,000
(C) $252,000
(D) $272,000   (2 marks)

? Question 69

An entity has a positive level of working capital but has an overdraft. What will be the impact of the following transactions on the current ratio?

Transaction 1:
Cash is received from trade receivables and is then used to reduce the overdraft.

Transaction 2:
A non-current asset is sold for cash thus is used to reduce the overdraft.

	Transaction 1	*Transaction 2*
(A)	Increase	Increase
(B)	Increase	Decrease
(C)	Decrease	Increase
(D)	Decrease	Decrease

(2 marks)

? Question 70

If payments to trade payables are delayed, what is the impact on the total level of working capital (ignore cash discounts)?

(A) Increase
(B) Decrease
(C) No effect
(D) Depends on whether working capital is positive or negative

(2 marks)

? Question 71

Invoice discounting normally involves

(A) Offering a cash discount for early settlement of invoices
(B) Selling an invoice to a discount house at a profit
(C) Selling individual invoice for cash to a factoring entity at a discount
(D) Writing off an invoice, partly or in total, as a bad debt.

(2 marks)

? Question 72

Which of the following is not normally associated with overtrading?

(A) Falling sales
(B) Increase overdraft
(C) Falling current ratio
(D) Rising profit

(2 marks)

? Question 73

The Clearing House Automated Payment System (CHAPS) provides

(A) A system to clear cheques for customers within three working days
(B) Same-day settlements between banks which are members of the clearing system

(C) A system of payment for the purchase of shares within the settlement period

(D) A financial transfer system, normally for the payment of payrolls by entities

(2 marks)

? Question 74

Which of the following most appropriately describes *forfaiting?*

(A) It is a method of providing medium-term export finance

(B) It provides short-term finance for purchasing non-current assets which are denominated in a foreign currency

(C) It provides long-term finance to importers

(D) It is the forced surrender of a share due to the failure to make a payment on a partly paid share **(2 marks)**

? Question 75

The International Accounting Standards Committee (IASC) Trustees have a number of responsibilities, which of the following is a responsibility of the IASC Trustees?

(A) Fundraising

(B) To publish reports on international accounting standards

(C) To enforce international accounting standards

(D) To report to the international organisation of securities commissions on financial reporting matters **(2 marks)**

? Question 76

According to the International Accounting Standards Board's (IASB) *Framework for the Preparation and Presentation of Financial Statements* (Framework) Chapter 4, 'equity' is defined as:

(A) The amount paid into the business by the owner

(B) Accumulated profits less amounts withdrawn

(C) A residual interest in the assets less liabilities

(D) Owners capital investment in the business **(2 marks)**

? Question 77

Chapter 3 of the IASB Framework sets out the characteristics of useful information.

 (i) Confirmatory value,

 (ii) Completeness,

(iii) Prudence,

 (iv) Consistency,

 (v) Neutrality,

 (vi) Predictive value.

According to the IASB Framework Chapter 3, which three of the above are not sub-characteristics of 'reliability'?

(A) (i), (iii) and (vi)
(B) (i), (iv) and (vi)
(C) (ii), (iv) and (v)
(D) (ii), (iii) and (v) **(2 marks)**

? Question 78

When an external auditor is unable to agree the accounting treatment of a material item with the directors of an entity, but the financial statements are not seriously misleading, he will issue

(A) an unqualified audit report
(B) an adverse opinion
(C) a qualified audit report using 'except for'
(D) an unqualified audit report using 'except for' **(2 marks)**

Solutions to Revision Questions I

 Solution 1

- Equity,
- Certainty,
- Convenience,
- Efficiency.

 Solution 2

The tax gap is the difference between the amount of tax owed and the amount of tax collected.

 Solution 3

The correct answer is (B).

The following are direct taxes:

- corporate income tax,
- individual income tax deducted at source (such as PAYE).

 Solution 4

Effective (or actual) incidence, the person or organisation who ends up bearing the cost of the tax as they cannot pass it on to someone else.

 Solution 5

The correct answer is (C).

Hypothecation means the products of certain taxes are devoted to specific types of expenditures.

Solution 6

The correct answer is (D).

This tax is progressive.

 # Solution 7

A tax base is something that is liable to tax.

 # Solution 8

	Industrial building $	Plant $	Total tax depreciation for year $
01/01/2002 Purchase	400,000	60,000	
31/12/2002 First year allowance		(30,000)	}
Tax depreciation for the year	(20,000)		} 50,000
Balance at 31/12/2002	380,000	30,000	
31/12/2003 Disposal		(20,000)	
Balancing allowance		(10,000)	}
Tax depreciation for the year	(20,000)		} 30,000
Balance at 31/12/2003	360,000		
01/01/2004 Purchase		80,000	

The entity's tax depreciation for the year to 31/12/2003 is $30,000.

 # Solution 9

The correct answer is (C).

Payments for domestic expenses are not allowable; dividends paid to equity share holders are usually paid out of taxed profits; fees and charges paid to solicitors for the purchase of new office buildings relate to capital expenditure and should be included as a part of the cost of the asset.

Salaries and pensions paid to directors and interest paid on loan notes are legitimate expenses normally allowed as deductions for tax purposes.

 # Solution 10

The correct answer is (C).

An ordinary share which is not redeemable and has no restrictions on receiving dividends is classified by IAS 32 as equity. All the other options have a restriction and are therefore classified as debt.

 # Solution 11

The correct answer is (D).

The country is using the classical system which causes dividends to be taxed twice.

Solution 12

The correct answer is $197,500

	Trading profit/(loss) $'000	Capital gain/(loss) $'000	Taxable profit $'000	Tax due at 25% $'000
2001	(450)	0	0	0
Loss carried forward	(450)			
2002	(220)	0	0	0
Loss carried forward	(450 + 220) = 670	0		
2003	(660 − 660) = 0	(150)	0	0
Loss carried forward	(670 − 660) = 10	(150)		
2004	(800 − 10) = 790	(120 − 120) = 0	790	197.50
Loss carried forward	0	(30)		

The tax due in 2004 is $197,500.

 Solution 13

The correct answer is X pays $14; Y pays $8 and Z pays $14.

Entity	Input tax $	Output tax $	VAT paid $
X			
Sale to Y		14.00	14.00 paid by X
Y			
Purchase form X	14.00		
Sale to Z		22.00	8.00 paid by Y
Z			
Purchase from Y	22.00		
Sale to C		36.00	<u>14.00</u> paid by Z
Total suffered by C			<u>36.00</u>

 Solution 14

The correct answer is (B).

This is an example of a specific unit tax.

 Solution 15

The correct answer is (D).

The entity cannot charge any VAT and cannot reclaim any VAT suffered on inputs.

 Solution 16

The correct answer is (B).

Exploiting loopholes in the legislation to legally avoid paying tax is tax avoidance rather than tax evasion.

 Solution 17

The correct answer is (B).

Using taxation at source reduces the opportunity for evasion and simplifying the tax system also removes opportunities to falsify claims for non-existent expenses etc.

Solution 18

The correct answer is (C).

The country where the effective management of the entity is carried out is the main criterion used in the OECD model convention.

 Solution 19

The correct answer is (C).

The other items are payments made in the normal course of business and are not normally subject to withholding taxes.

 Solution 20

The correct answer is (B).

This is relief by taking credit for the tax already paid. It is not relief by deduction as that means deducting the tax paid from the taxable income in its 'home' country.

 Solution 21

The correct answer is (B).

The credit balance on the corporate income tax account means that there was an over-provision last year. The overprovision of $7,000 can be deducted from the current year's estimate. The increase in deferred tax needs to be included under the tax charge for the year. The profit or loss would show the income tax expense as $355,000, the note to the profit or loss would show the $355,000 made up as follows:

	$
Estimate of current year's income tax charge	330,000
Over-provision previous year	(7,000)
Increase in deferred tax provision	32,000
	355,000

The statement of financial position payables for income tax would be the estimate for the current years tax charge, $330,000.

 Solution 22

The correct answer is (A).

	$
Cost	320,000
2 years' accounting depreciation at $40,000 per year is	(80,000)
Carrying value in accounts	240,000
Cost	320,000
2 years' tax depreciation at 25% is	(140,000)
Tax written down value	(180,000)
Temporary difference (240,000 − 180,000)	60,000
Tax at 25%	15,000

☑ Solution 23

The correct answer is (D).

		$
Cost		60,000
25% depreciation		15,000
		45,000
25% depreciation		11,250
		33,750
Less disposal, net book value		
Cost	20,000	
Depreciation, 2 years	8,750	
		11,250
		22,500
Add acquisition		40,000
		62,500
Less 25% depreciation		15,625
		46,875

☑ Solution 24

The correct answer is (B).

	$
Trade receivables balance	25,000
Less bad debt	3,000
	22,000
Less 5% provision	1,100
	20,900

☑ Solution 25

The correct answer is (C).

		$
Bad debts already written off in year		2,000
Bad debt at year end		3,000
		5,000
Increase in provision		
Bad debt provision b/f	812	
Bad debt provision c/f	1,100	
Increase		288
Total		5,288

☑ Solution 26

The correct answer is (C).

The debit balance on the income tax account means that there was an underprovision last year. The underprovision of $15,000 needs to be added on to the current year's estimate. The increase in deferred tax needs to be included under the tax charge for the year.

The note to the profit or loss would show the charge for the year as $306,000, made up as follows:

	$
Estimate of current year's corporation tax charge	280,000
Underprovision previous year	15,000
Increase in deferred tax provision	11,000
	306,000

 ## Solution 27

The correct answer is (B).

Last year's outstanding balance plus the underprovision of $15,000.

 ## Solution 28

The correct answer is (A).

	$
Two years' depreciation at 1/15 per year is	20,000
Two years' tax depreciation allowances at 25% is	65,625
Cumulative difference	45,625
Tax at 30%	13,687

 ## Solution 29

The correct answer is (C).

IAS 2 requires inventory to be valued at cost or net realisable value, whichever is the lower.

 ## Solution 30

The correct answer is (C).

The cost of sales must include the full provision for expected future losses: 545 + 55 = 600.

 ## Solution 31

The correct answer is (C).

The excess payment received 550 − 520 = 30.

 ## Solution 32

The correct answer is (B).

The 'gross amounts due from customers for long-term contract work' balance of partly completed work is $60,000. This has been set off against the provision for future losses, leaving a balance of $5,000.

✅ Solution 33

The correct answer is (B).

Payments (4 of $30,000) =		$120,000
Fair value		$100,000
Finance charge		$20,000
Interest charges		
Year 1: 4/10 × 20 = $8,000		
Year 2: 3/10 × 20 = $6,000		
Lease payables		
Initial balance		$100,000
Interest		$8,000
Payment 1		($30,000)
Interest		$6,000
Payment 2		($30,000)
Balance		$54,000

✅ Solution 34

The correct answer is (B).

The directors need to create a provision for $50,000, as the customer's claim is probably going to succeed but the competitor's claim is not. Provisions have to be created when it is probable that the organisation will lose. Probable is usually taken as more than 50 per cent likely.

✅ Solution 35

The competent jurisdiction is the country whose tax laws apply to the enterprise.

✅ Solution 36

The correct answer is (D).

✅ Solution 37

$t = 8$; $r = 10$
$(7 \times 5.335) + (100 \times 0.467) = 37.345 + 46.7 = \$84.045$
$t = 8$; $r = 12$
$(7 \times 4.968) + (100 \times 0.404) = 34.776 + 40.4 = \$75.176$
By interpolation:
$10\% + (((84.045 - 82.0)/(84.045 - 75.176)) \times 2) = 10\% + (2.045/8.869 \times 2) = 10\% + 0.461 = 10.461\% \approx 10.5\%$

✅ Solution 38

The correct answer is (C).

		$'000
	Certified value of work completed	2,000
Less	Cost of work certified as complete	1,650
		350

Solution 39

The correct answer is (C).

		$'000
Current liabilities – trade and other payables are calculated as:		
	Cost of work certified as complete	1,650
	Cost of work in progress (not included in completed work)	550
		2,200
Less	Cash paid to suppliers for work on the contract	1,300
		900
Gross amounts due from customers are calculated as:		
	Certified value of work completed	2,000
Less	Cash received from entity	1,600
		400
Plus	Work in progress	550
		950

 ## Solution 40

The correct answer is (B).

Inventory turnover is inventory divided by cost of goods sold times 365 days:
$(15/200) \times 365 = 27.4$ days
Receivables $(36/300) \times 365 = 43.8$ days
Payables $(28/200) \times 365 = 51.1$ days
Working capital cycle $= 27.4 + 43.8 - 51.1 = 20.1$ days

 ## Solution 41

The correct answer is (A).

		$
Cash received on application and allotment $1.00 $\times$ 5,000		5,000
Balance share capital due		2,500
Cash received on reissue of shares $1 $\times$ 5,000		5,000
Additional share premium		2,500
Investment in own Shares a/c	$2,500 Dr	
Share Premium	$2,500 Cr	
Bank	$5,000 Dr	
Investment in own Shares a/c	$5,000 Cr	

 ## Solution 42

AL offers 1.5% interest for 16 days
$(100/98.5)^{(365/16)} - 1 = (1.015)^{22.813} - 1$
$= 40.4\%$ or 41.2% depending on rounding

 ## Solution 43

The correct answer is (C).

 **Solution 44**

The correct answer is (B).

 **Solution 45**

The correct answer is (D).

 **Solution 46**

The correct answer is (B).

	$
Lease payments 5 × 20,000 =	100,000
Fair value	(80,000)
Finance charge	20,000

Year one using sum of digits is $20,000 \times \dfrac{5}{15} = \$6,667$

 **Solution 47**

The correct answer is (B).

Tax depreciation allowances are:

	$
2001–200,000 × 25% =	50,000
2002–150,000 × 25% =	37,500
2003–112,500 × 25% =	28,125
Total =	115,625

Accounting depreciation is $200,000 × 10% × 3$ years = $60,000

Deferred tax is therefore $115,625 − $60,000 = $55,625 × 30% = $16,688

 **Solution 48**

The correct answer is (C).

	2002	*2003*
	$'000	$'000
Revenue	10,000	10,000
Costs (incurred and estimated)	(8,900)	(8,500)
Total Profit	1,100	1,500
Cumulative profit	30%	55%
	330	825
Less: Already recognised		330
		495

PREPARING FOR THE EXAMINATION

 Solution 49

The correct answer is (A).

		$
Cost	(on 1/7/00)	50,000
Depreciation	(to 30/6/01)	(10,000)
Depreciation	(to 30/6/02)	(10,000)
		30,000
Revaluation	(at 1/7/02)	30,000
		60,000
Depreciation	(to 30/6/03)	(20,000)
		40,000
Disposal	(on 1/7/03)	(35,000)
Loss on disposal recognised in profit or loss		5,000

In addition, the revaluation gain of $30,000 becomes realised on disposal and can be transferred to accumulated profits. This is treated as a movement on reserves and shown in the statement of changes in equity.

 Solution 50

The correct answer is (C).

2,000,000 shares with 1 for 5 rights = 400,000 **new shares**
400,000 shares at a premium of $1 = $400,000
Less: Issue costs ($25,000)
$375,000

 Solution 51

The correct answer is (B).

Operating leases commit the lessee to a short-term contract and it is not expected that the lease will remain in force for the whole life of the asset.

 Solution 52

Cost	100,000
Two years depreciation at 10%	(20,000)
	80,000
Revaluation	15,000
	95,000
Depreciation at 12.5%	(11,875)
	83,125
Depreciation at 20%	(16,625)
Net book value	66,500
Either	
At valuation	95,000
Accumulated depreciation	(28,500)
Net book value	66,500
Or	
Alternative treatment allowed by IAS 16:	
At valuation	115,000
Accumulated depreciation	(48,500)
Net book value	66,500

Solution 53

The correct answer is (D).

$$1 + r = (100/80)^{365/20}$$
$$1 + r = (1.0204)^{18.25}$$
$$1 + r = (1.446)$$
Cost of discount = 44.6%

 Solution 54

The correct answer is (D).

All three propositions are correct.

 Solution 55

The correct answer is (B).

Settling the amounts owed to trade payables earlier will reduce the cash balance sooner and so will affect the cash forecasts.

 Solution 56

The correct answer is (C).

Interest is paid on the amount borrowed, rather than on the whole facility.

 Solution 57

The correct answer is (C).

 Solution 58

The correct answer is (C).

$$EOQ = \sqrt{\frac{2C_o D}{C_h}}$$

$$\text{Economic order quantity} = \sqrt{\frac{2 \times 185 \times 2,500}{25}} = 192 \text{ units}$$

$$\text{Frequency of ordering} = \frac{192}{2,500} \times 52 \text{ weeks} = 4 \text{ weeks}$$

 Solution 59

The correct answer is (B).

Solution 60

The correct answer is (D).

$$\text{Spread} = 3 \left[\frac{3/4 \times \text{transaction cost} \times \text{variance of cash flows}}{\text{interest rate}} \right]^{1/3}$$

$$\text{Spread} = 3 \left(\frac{3/4 \times 20 \times 250,000}{0.00025} \right)^{1/3} = 7,400 \text{ Upper limit} = 7,400 + 1,000$$

$$= 8,400$$

 Solution 61

The correct answer is (C).

$$\text{Optimal sale} = \sqrt{\frac{2 \times \text{annual cash disbursements} \times \text{cost per sale of securities}}{\text{interest rate}}}$$

$$Q = \sqrt{\frac{2 \times 1,260,000 \times 20}{0.08}} = 25,100$$

 Solution 62

The correct answer is (C).

	$
Closing trade receivables	120,000
Cash received	850,000
Opening trade receivables	(150,000)
Sales	820,000
Closing trade payables	80,000
Cash paid	325,000
Opening trade payables	(90,000)
Purchases	315,000
Sales	820,000
Cost of sales ($315,000 − $75,000)	(240,000)
Gross profit	580,000

 Solution 63

The correct answer is (A).

$$\text{Quick ratio} = \frac{\text{current assests} - \text{stock}}{\text{current liabilities}}$$

$$= \frac{200,000}{250,000} = 0.8{:}1$$

 **Solution 64**

The correct answer is (C).

$$\text{Optimal sale} = \sqrt{\frac{2 \times 1,850,000 \times 20}{0.06}} = 35,119$$

 **Solution 65**

The correct answer is (C).

Cost of sales = 40 million × 80% =	32 million
Receivable days = 5/32 × 365 =	57
Inventory days = 7/40 × 365 =	64
Payable days = 2/32 × 365 =	(23)
	98

 **Solution 66**

The correct answer is (C).

 **Solution 67**

The correct answer is (C).

Purchases increase inventory and increase trade payables, leaving working capital unchanged.

$$\text{Profit on sales increase in WC} = \$24,000 \times \frac{0.25}{1.25}$$
$$= \$4,800$$

 **Solution 68**

The correct answer is (C).

$240,000 + $12,000 = $252,000

 **Solution 69**

The correct answer is (A).

 **Solution 70**

The correct answer is (C).

Solution 71

The correct answer is (C).

 Solution 72

The correct answer is (A).

 Solution 73

The correct answer is (B).

 Solution 74

The correct answer is (A).

 Solution 75

The correct answer is (A).

 Solution 76

The correct answer is (C).

 Solution 77

The correct answer is (B).

 Solution 78

The correct answer is (C).

Revision Questions II

Many of the questions in this chapter are prior examination questions.

Questions matched to learning outcomes

Learning Outcomes	Question Numbers
A – Principles of Business Taxation – 20%	
(i) Identify the principal types of taxation likely to be of relevance to an incorporated business in a particular country, including direct tax on the entity's trading profits and capital gains, indirect taxes collected by the entity, employee taxation, withholding taxes on international payments	
(ii) Describe the features of the principal types of taxation likely to be of relevance to an incorporated business in a particular country (e.g. in terms of who ultimately bears the tax cost, withholding responsibilities, principles of calculating the tax base)	2
(iii) Describe the likely record-keeping, filing and tax payment requirements associated with the principal types of taxation likely to be of relevance to an incorporated business in a particular country	
(iv) Describe the possible enquiry and investigation powers of taxing authorities	
(v) Identify situations in which foreign tax obligations (reporting and liability) could arise and methods for relieving foreign tax	
(vi) Explain the difference in principle between tax avoidance and tax evasion	
(vii) Describe sources of tax rules and explain the importance of jurisdiction	
(viii) Explain and apply the accounting rules contained in IAS 12 for current and deferred taxation	1, 3
B – Principles of Regulation of Financial Reporting – 10%	
(i) Explain the need for regulation of published accounts and the concept that regulatory regimes vary from country to country	
(ii) Explain potential elements that might be expected in a regulatory framework for published accounts	
(iii) Describe the role and structure of the International Accounting Standards Board (IASB) and the International Organisation of Securities Commissions (IOSCO)	
(iv) Explain the IASB's *Framework for the Presentation and Preparation of Financial Statements*	5
(v) Describe the process leading to the promulgation of an international accounting standard (IAS)	26
(vi) Describe ways in which IAS's can interact with local regulatory frameworks	

(vii) Explain in general terms, the role of the external auditor, the elements of the audit report and types of qualification of that report — 7, 8

C – Single Entity Financial Accounts – 45%

(i) Prepare financial statements in a form suitable for publication, with appropriate notes — 6, 16, 27, 28, 29, 30, 32

(ii) Prepare a cash flow statement in a form suitable for publication — 9, 10, 31

(iii) Explain and apply the accounting rules contained in IAS's dealing with reporting performance, tangible non-current assets and inventories — 11, 12, 15

(iv) Explain the accounting rules contained in IAS's governing share capital transactions — 14

(v) Explain the principles of the accounting rules contained in IAS's dealing with disclosure of related parties to a business, construction contracts (and related financing costs), research and development expenditure, intangible non-current assets (other than goodwill on consolidation), impairment of assets, post-balance sheet events, contingencies, and leases (lessee only) — 13

D – Managing Short-Term Finance – 25%

(i) Calculate and interpret working capital ratios for business sectors — 18

(ii) Prepare and analyse cash-flow forecasts over a twelve-month period — 19, 21

(iii) Identify measures to improve a cash forecast situation — 22

(iv) Compare and contrast the use and limitations of cash management models and identify when each model is most appropriate — 25

(v) Analyse trade receivable information

(vi) Evaluate receivable and payable policies — 20

(vii) Evaluate appropriate methods of inventory management — 17

(viii) Identify alternatives for investment of short-term cash surpluses

(ix) Identify sources of short-term funding — 23, 24

(x) Identify appropriate methods of finance for trading internationally

? Question 1

On 1 January 2003, TX had an opening debit balance of $12,000 on its income tax account, which represented the balance remaining after settling its tax liability for the previous year. TX had a credit balance on its deferred tax account of $990,000 at the same date.

TX has been advised that the estimated income tax due for the year ended 31 December 2003 will be $600,000. TX has been advised that it should increase its deferred tax account by $100,000.

Requirement

Prepare extracts from the income statement for the year ended 31 December 2003, statement of financial position at that date and notes to the accounts showing the tax entries required. **(5 marks)**

? Question 2

BC commenced business on 1 January 2001, making up the first accounts for the year to 31 December 2001.

The entity's purchases and sales of non-current assets were as follows:

			$
Purchases			
2001	1 January	Industrial building	400,000
	1 January	Plant	60,000
2004	1 January	Plant	75,000
Sales			
2004	31 December	Plant bought on 1 January 2001	10,000

BC qualifies for accelerated first-year allowance on the plant at the rate of 50% for the first year. The second and subsequent years will be at 25% on the reducing balance method.

The industrial building qualifies for an annual tax depreciation allowance of 3% on the straight-line basis.

Calculate BC's tax depreciation for the years ended 31 December 2001, 2002 and 2003.

(5 marks)

Question 3

CD purchases an item of plant and machinery costing $300,000 in 20X1 which qualifies for 33.33% capital allowances (on straight-line basis) in the first 3 years. CD's policy in respect of plant and machinery is to charge depreciation on a straight-line basis over 5 years.

Requirement

Assuming there are no other capital transactions in the period and a tax rate of 25% over the 5 years, calculate the statement of comprehensive income and statement of financial position impact of deferred tax from 20X1 to 20X5.

(5 marks)

Question 4

AF is a furniture manufacturing entity. The trial balance for AF at 31 March 2005 was as follows:

	$'000	$'000
6% loan notes (redeemable 2010)		1,500
Accumulated profits at 31 March 2004		388
Administrative expenses	1,540	
Available for sale investments at market value at 31 March 2004	1,640	
Bank and cash	822	
Cost of sales	3,463	
Distribution costs	1,590	
Dividend paid 1 December 2004	275	
Interest paid on loan notes – half year to 30 September 2004	45	
Inventory at 31 March 2005	1,320	
Investment income received		68
Land and buildings at cost	5,190	
Ordinary shares of $1 each, fully paid		4,500
Plant and equipment at cost	3,400	
Provision for deferred tax		710
Provisions for depreciation at 31 March 2004: Buildings		1,500
Provisions for depreciation at 31 March 2004: Plant and equipment		1,659
Revaluation reserve		330
Sales revenue		8,210
Share premium		1,380
Trade payables		520
Trade receivables	1,480	
	20,765	20,765

Additional information provided:

(i) Available for sale investments are carried in the financial statements at market value. The market value of the available for sale investments at 31 March 2005 was $1,750,000.

(ii) There were no sales or purchases of non-current assets or available for sale investments during the year ended 31 March 2005.

(iii) Income tax due for the year ended 31 March 2005 is estimated at $250,000. There is no balance outstanding in relation to previous years' corporate income tax. The deferred tax provision needs to be increased by $100,000.

(iv) Depreciation is charged on buildings using the straight-line basis at 3% each year. The cost of land included in land and buildings is $2,000,000. Plant and equipment is depreciated using the reducing balance method at 20%. Depreciation is regarded as a cost of sales.

(v) AF entered into a non-cancellable five-year operating lease on 1 April 2004 to acquire machinery to manufacture a new range of kitchen units. Under the terms of the lease, AF will receive the first year rent-free, then $62,500 is payable for 4 years commencing in year two of the lease. The machine is estimated to have a useful economic life of 20 years.

(vi) The 6% loan notes are ten-year loans due for repayment March 2010. AF incurred no other finance costs in the year to 31 March 2005.

Requirement

Prepare the statement of comprehensive income for AF for the year to 31 March 2005 and a statement of financial position at that date, in a form suitable for presentation to the shareholders and in accordance with the requirements of International Financial Reporting Standards.

> Notes to the financial statements are *not* required, but all workings must be clearly shown. Do not prepare a statement of accounting policies or a statement of changes in equity.

(20 marks)

Question 5

Requirement

List the FIVE elements of financial statements defined in the IASB's *Framework* and explain the meaning of each. **(5 marks)**

Question 6

BG provides office cleaning services to a range of organisations in its local area. BG operates through a small network of depots that are rented spaces situated in out-of-town industrial developments. BG has a policy to lease all vehicles on operating leases.

The trial balance for BG at 30 September 2005 was as follows:

	$'000	$'000
10% bonds (redeemable 2010)		150
Administrative expenses	239	
Available for sale investments at market value at 30 September 2004	205	
Bank and cash	147	
Bond interest paid – half year to 31 March 2005	8	
Cost of cleaning materials consumed	101	
Direct operating expenses (including cleaning staff)	548	
Dividend paid	60	
Equipment and fixtures, cost at 30 September 2005	752	
Equity shares $1 each, fully paid		200
Income tax	9	
Inventory of cleaning materials at 30 September 2005	37	
Investment income received		11
Provision for deferred tax		50
Provision for depreciation at 30 September 2004:		
Equipment and fixtures		370
Provision for legal claim balance at 30 September 2004		190
Retained earnings at 30 September 2004		226
Revaluation reserve at 30 September 2004		30
Revenue		1,017
Share premium		40
Trade payables		24
Trade receivables	141	
Vehicle operating lease rentals paid	61	
	2,308	2,308

Additional information:

(i) Available for sale investments are carried in the financial statements at market value. The market value of the available for sale investments at 30 September 2005 was $225,000. There were no purchases or sales of available for sale investments held during the year.

(ii) The income tax balance in the trial balance is a result of the underprovision of tax for the year ended 30 September 2004.

(iii) The taxation due for the year ended 30 September 2005 is estimated at $64,000 and the deferred tax provision needs to be increased by $15,000.

(iv) Equipment and fixtures are depreciated at 20% per annum straight line. Depreciation of equipment and fixtures is considered to be part of direct cost of sales. BG's policy is to charge a full year's depreciation in the year of acquisition and no depreciation in the year of disposal.

(v) The 10% bonds were issued in 2000.

(vi) BG paid an interim dividend during the year, but does not propose to pay a final dividend as profit for the year is well below expectations.

(vii) At 30 September 2004, BG had an outstanding legal claim from a customer alleging that BG had caused a major fire in the customer's premises. BG was advised that it would very probably lose the case, so a provision of $190,000 was set up at 30 September 2004. During 2005, new evidence was discovered and the case against BG was dropped. As there is no further liability, the directors have decided that the provision is no longer required.

Requirement

Prepare the statement of comprehensive income and a statement of changes in equity for BG for the year to 30 September 2005 and a statement of financial position at that date, in a form suitable for presentation to the shareholders and in accordance with the requirements of International Financial Reporting Standards.

Notes to the financial statements are *not* required, but all workings must be clearly shown. All workings should be to the nearest $'000. *Do not* prepare a statement of accounting policies.

(20 marks)

Question 7

The latest annual report of G contained the following audit report:

Auditor's report to the shareholders of GC

Disagreement on accounting treatment – failure to allow for debt – qualified opinion

We have audited the accompanying statement of financial position of GC as of 31 December, 20X1, and the related statements of income and cash flows for the year then ended. These financial statements are the responsibility of the entity's management. Our responsibility is to express an opinion on these financial statements based on our audit.

We conducted our audit in accordance with International Standards on Auditing. Those Standards require that we plan and perform the audit to obtain reasonable assurance about whether the financial statements are free of material misstatement. An audit includes examining, on a test basis, evidence supporting the amounts and disclosures in the financial statements. An audit also includes assessing the accounting principles used and significant estimates made by management, as well as evaluating the overall financial statement presentation. We believe that our audit provides a reasonable basis for our opinion.

Included in the receivables shown on the statement of financial position is an amount of $960,000 due from an entity which has ceased trading. GC has no security for this debt. In our opinion, GC is unlikely to receive any payment and full allowance of $960,000 should have been made, reducing profit before tax and net assets by that amount.

In our opinion, except for the absence of this allowance, the financial statements give a true and fair view of the entity as of 31 December 20X1, and of the results of its operations and its cash flows for the year then ended in accordance with International Accounting Standards and relevant statutes.

AUDITOR

Date

Address

At the annual general meeting following the publication of this annual report, GC's management explained that this audit report was 'qualified' because of a disagreement between the management and the auditor.

Requirements

(a) Explain why this report should be described as qualified and explain the meaning of this qualification to the readers of the financial statements. **(8 marks)**

(b) Describe the circumstances in which the auditor would be forced to qualify the report on the financial statements using the form of qualification as applied above.

(8 marks)

(Total marks = 16)

? Question 8

A friend has asked you for some advice. She owns some shares in S, a large quoted entity. The external auditor of her entity has recently been criticised for failing to detect a staff fraud. The auditor has rejected the criticisms on the grounds that the fraud was not, in itself, material and, in any case, it is not the auditor's responsibility to prevent or detect all fraud.

Requirements

(a) Explain what is meant by 'materiality' and describe the importance of the concept of materiality in the audit process. **(8 marks)**

(b) Describe the auditor's duties with respect to the financial statements, explaining why it is not the auditor's duty to detect all fraud. **(8 marks)**

(Total marks = 16)

? Question 9

The financial statements of AG are given below:

Statement of financial position as at	31 March 2005		31 March 2004	
	$'000	$'000	$'000	$'000
Non-current assets				
Plant, property and equipment	4,500		4,800	
Development expenditure	370	4,870	400	5,200
Current assets				
Inventories	685		575	
Trade receivables	515		420	
Cash and cash equivalents	552	1,752	232	1,227
Total assets		6,622		6,427
Equity and liabilities				
Equity				
Share capital	2,600		1,900	
Share premium account	750		400	
Revaluation reserve	425		300	
Retained earnings	1,430		1,415	
Total equity		5,205		4,015
Non-current liabilities				
10% loan notes	0		1,000	
5% loan notes	500		500	
Deferred tax	250		200	
Total non-current liabilities		750		1,700

Current liabilities

Trade payables	480	350
Income tax	80	190
Accrued expenses	107	172
Total current liabilities	667	712
Total equity and liabilities	6,622	6,427

Income statement for the year ended 31 March 2005

	$'000	$'000
Revenue		7,500
Cost of sales		4,000
Gross profit		3,500
Distribution costs	900	
Administrative expenses	2,300	3,200
Profit from operations		300
Finance costs		45
Profit before tax		255
Income tax expense		140
Profit for the period		115

Additional information:

(i) On 1 April 2004, AG issued 1,400,000 $0.50 ordinary shares at a premium of 50%.

(ii) On 1 May 2004, AG purchased and cancelled all its 10% loan notes at par.

(iii) Non-current tangible assets include properties which were revalued upwards by $125,000 during the year.

(iv) Non-current tangible assets disposed of in the year had a net book value of $75,000; cash received on disposal was $98,000. Any gain or loss on disposal has been included under cost of sales.

(v) Cost of sales includes $80,000 for development expenditure amortised during the year.

(vi) Depreciation charged for the year was $720,000.

(vii) The accrued expenses balance includes interest payable of $87,000 at 31 March 2004 and $12,000 at 31 March 2005.

(viii) The income tax expenses for the year to 31 March 2005 is made up as follows:

	$'000
Corporate income tax	90
Deferred tax	50
	140

(ix) Dividends paid during the year were $100,000.

Requirement

Prepare a statement of cash flows, using the indirect method, for AG for the year ended 31 March 2005, in accordance with IAS 7 Statement of Cash Flows.

(Total for Question Four = 20 marks)

? Question 10

Y's income statement for the year ended 31 December 20X2 and Statement of financial position at 31 December 20X1 and 31 December 20X2 were as follows:

Y – income statement for the year ended 31 December 20X2

	$'000	$'000
Revenue		360
Raw materials consumed	35	
Staff costs	47	
Depreciation	59	
Loss on disposal	9	
		(150)
Profit from operations		210
Interest payable		(14)
Profit before tax		196
Income tax		(62)
		134

Y: Statements of financial position at 31 December

	20X2		20X1	
	$'000	$'000	$'000	$'000
Non-current assets				
Cost		798		780
Depreciation		159		112
		639		668
Current assets				
Inventory	12		10	
Trade receivables	33		25	
Bank	24	69	28	63
		708		731
Equity and liabilities				
Equity				
Share capital		180		170
Share premium		18		12
Retained earnings		343		245
		541		427
Non-current liabilities				
Long-term loans		100		250
Current liabilities				
Trade payables	6		3	
Income Tax	46		39	
Dividend (declared before end of reporting period)	15	67	12	54
		708		731

During the year Y paid:

- $45,000 for a new piece of machinery;
- $21,000 interim dividend.

Requirement

Prepare a statement of cash flows for Y for the year ended 31 December 20X2 in accordance with the requirements of IAS 7 *Statement of Cash Flows*.   **(20 marks)**

Question 11

It can be difficult to determine precisely when a profit has been earned. Even a simple manufacturing process can create the following events, any of which might be deemed to be the critical event:

(i) customer places an order for goods which have not yet been manufactured,*
(ii) raw materials acquired to fill order,*
(iii) goods produced,*
(iv) goods delivered,
(v) customer pays,
(vi) customer makes use of agreed after-sales service or warranties.

(*If the customer places an order for goods that have already been manufactured, then these steps will occur in the order (ii), (iii) then (i).)

Requirements

Explain which of the events (i) to (vi) listed above is the most sensible point at which to recognise a profit according to IAS 18 *Revenue*. **(5 marks)**

 # Question 12

Publisher is an entity that publishes a range of popular fiction. The entity has recently launched a new novel written by one of its established authors. Publisher has entered into the following contracts:

(i) *Bigseller books.* This is a large chain of bookstores. Publisher has supplied Bigseller Books with a large number of copies of the new novel on a 'sale or return basis'. This is a common arrangement in book publishing. From experience, Publisher expects approximately 20 per cent of the books to be returned for a full refund.
(ii) *Newspro.* Newspro publishes a leading Sunday newspaper. It has signed a contract which will allow it to publish three substantial extracts from the new novel in return for a fee of $800,000.

You are required to explain how the principles for recognising income, as defined in IAS 18 *Revenue,* would apply to each of the cases (i) to (iii) above. **(5 marks)**

 # Question 13

V is a large manufacturing entity. During the year, the entity entered into the following transactions:

(a) Q Consultancy undertook a comprehensive study of V's marketing practices and submitted a detailed report. The fee for this work amounted to $67,000. The husband of V's finance director owns Q Consultancy.
(b) Hector own 22 per cent of V's ordinary shares. During the year, the entity ordered a substantial quantity of inventory from H, an entity that is wholly owned by Hector. H charged its normal selling price and required payment under its normal terms and conditions.

Requirements

Explain whether either Q Consultancy or H are related parties, as defined by IAS 24 *Related Party Disclosures*. **(5 marks)**

? Question 14

R's latest statement of financial position is shown below:

R – Statement of financial position as at 31 December 20X0

	$'000	$'000
Non-current assets		4,800
Net current assets (excluding cash)	2,100	
Cash	850	
		2,950
		7,750
Equity and liabilities		
$1 ordinary shares		2,500
8% redeemable preference shares		1,000
Share premium		2,200
Retained earnings		2,050
		7,750

The redeemable preference shares were originally issued at par to an entity which supports new businesses. The terms of the redemption are that R must pay a premium of 10 per cent on redemption.

The directors have decided to redeem the shares. They plan to issue 600,000 $1 ordinary shares at a premium of 20 cents per share. The balance of the redemption will be paid for from the entity's existing cash balances.

The legal requirements in force in this situation in the country in which R is resident are:

(i) An amount equal to the nominal value of shares redeemed must be transferred from retained earnings to a non-distributable capital reserve, unless they are redeemed out of a new issue of shares;

(ii) Any premium on redemption must be charged against retained earnings.

Requirements

(a) Prepare R's statement of financial position, showing how it will appear immediately after the redemption of the redeemable preference shares and the issue of the fresh ordinary shares. **(10 marks)**

(b) Explain the purpose of the required transfer to capital reserve. **(5 marks)**

(Total marks = 15)

? Question 15

T is a manufacturing entity which produces several product ranges at a number of factories spread across the country.

The directors of T have asked for your advice on the following issues relating to tangible non-current assets.

(i) The entity is in the process of building a new factory. T is required to pay for the construction work in instalments throughout the building work. T has arranged a loan to cover the cost of the new factory. The directors are unsure whether they should capitalise the interest costs as a part of the cost of the factory.

(ii) The entity has a production line in an existing factory. This line is used to manufacture a product which has a declining market. The production line has a net book value of $2.3 million. The line could be dismantled and sold for $0.9 million. T's accountants have estimated that if the production line is retained, it will generate net cash flows worth $1.1 million to the entity. The directors are unsure whether an impairment has occurred on this asset and, if so, how the asset should be valued.

(iii) The directors are concerned about the valuation of the entity's delivery vehicle engine division. This division has three factories in different parts of the entity. The capacity of all three factories taken together exceeds demand for the engines that the entity makes. However, there is insufficient slack capacity to enable the entity to close down even one of the factories. The directors are unsure how to identify the income-generating unit for the delivery vehicle engine division.

Requirements

(a) Describe the arguments both for and against the capitalisation of interest charges on the construction of non-current assets. Explain the requirements of IAS 23 *Borrowing Costs*. **(5 marks)**

(b) Calculate the value that should appear in respect of the book value of the production line in (ii) above. Your answer should reflect the requirements of IAS 36 *Impairment of Assets*. **(5 marks)**

(c) Identify the income-generating unit associated with the delivery vehicle engine division and explain why IAS 36 *Impairment of Assets* has created the concept of the income-generating unit. **(5 marks)**

(Total marks = 15)

? Question 16

Hi, listed on its local stock exchange, is a retail organisation operating several retail outlets. A reorganisation of the entity was started in 2002 because of a significant reduction in profits. This reorganisation was completed during the current financial year.

The trial balance for Hi at 30 September 2003 was as follows:

	$'000	$'000
10% loan notes (redeemable 2010)		1,000
Retained earnings at 30 September 2002		1,390
Administrative expenses	615	
Bank and cash	959	
Buildings	11,200	
Cash received on disposal of equipment		11
Cost of goods sold	3,591	
Distribution costs	314	
Equipment and fixtures	2,625	
Interest paid on loan notes – half year to 31 March 2003	50	
Interim dividend paid	800	
Inventory at 30 September 2003	822	
Investment income received		37
Non-current asset investments at market value 30 September 2002	492	
Ordinary shares of $1 each, fully paid		4,000
Provision for deferred tax		256
Provision for reorganisation expenses at 30 September 2002		1,010
Provisions for depreciation at 30 September 2002:		
Buildings		1,404
Equipment and fixtures		1,741

Reorganisation expenses	900	
Revaluation reserve		172
Sales revenue		9,415
Share premium		2,388
Trade payables		396
Trade receivables	852	
	23,220	23,220

Additional information provided

(i) The reorganisation expenses relate to a comprehensive restructuring and reorganisation of the entity that began in 2002. Hi's financial statements for 2002 included a provision for reorganisation expenses of $1,010,000. All costs had been incurred by the year-end, but an invoice for $65,000, received on 2 October 2003, remained unpaid and is not included in the trial balance figures. No further restructuring and reorganisation costs are expected to occur and the provision is no longer required.

(ii) Non-current asset investments are carried in the financial statements at market value. The market value of the non-current asset investments at 30 September 2003 was $522,000. There were no movements in the investments held during the year.

(iii) On 1 November 2003, Hi was informed that one of its customers, X, had ceased trading. The liquidators advised Hi that it was unlikely to receive payment of any of the $45,000 due from X at 30 September 2003.

(iv) Another customer is suing for damages as a consequence of a faulty product. Legal advisers are currently advising that the probability of Hi being found liable is 75 per cent. The amount payable is estimated to be the full amount claimed of $100,000.

(v) The income tax due for the year ended 30 September 2003 is estimated at $1,180,000 and the deferred tax provision needs to be increased to $281,000.

(vi) During the year, Hi disposed of old equipment for $11,000. The original cost of this equipment was $210,000 and accumulated depreciation at 30 September 2002 was $205,000. Hi's accounting policy is to charge no depreciation in the year of the disposal.

(vii) Depreciation is charged using the straight-line basis on non-current assets as follows:

Buildings	3%
Equipment and fixtures	20%

Depreciation is regarded as a cost of sales.

(viii) On 1 April 2003, Hi made a rights issue of 1 new share for 4 existing shares, at a price of $3. The fair value of one share prior to the rights issue was $4.25 per share. All the rights were taken up and all money paid by 30 September 2003.

Requirements

(a) Prepare the statement of comprehensive income for Hi for the year to 30 September 2003 and a statement of financial position at that date, in a form suitable for presentation to the shareholders, in accordance with the requirements of International Accounting Standards.

Notes to the financial statements are NOT required, but all workings must be clearly shown. DO NOT prepare a statement of accounting policies or a statement of recognised gains and losses. **(20 marks)**

(b) Prepare a statement of changes in equity for Hi for the year ended 30 September 2003.
(5 marks)
(Total marks = 25)

PREPARING FOR THE EXAMINATION

Question 17

A firm estimates that it uses 50,000 units of Material B each year to produce its only product. The order costs are $100 per order and holding costs are $0.40 per unit.

(a) Determine the economic order quantity. **(5 marks)**

(b) The supplier has offered a quantity discount of $0.02 per unit if the entity buys batches of 10,000 units. Should the entity take advantage of the quantity discount?
(8 marks)

(c) Discuss the problems that most firms would have in using the EOQ formula.
(7 marks)
(Total marks = 20)

Question 18

CBA is a manufacturing entity in the furniture trade. Its sales have risen sharply over the past 6 months as a result of an improvement in the economy and a strong housing market. The entity is now showing signs of 'overtrading' and the financial manager, Ms Smith, is concerned about its liquidity. The entity is 1 month from its year-end. Estimated figures for the full 12 months of the current year and forecasts for next year, on present cash management policies, are shown below.

	Next year $'000	Current year $'000
Income statement		
Revenue	5,200	4,200
Less		
Cost of sales (Note 1)	(3,224)	(2,520)
Operating expenses	(650)	(500)
Operating profit	1,326	1,180
Interest paid	(54)	(48)
Profit before tax	1,272	1,132
Tax payable	(305)	(283)
Profit after tax	967	849
Dividends declared	387	339
Current assets and liabilities as at the end of the year		
Inventory/work in progress	625	350
Trade receivables	750	520
Cash	0	25
Trade payables	(464)	(320)
Other payables (tax and dividends)	(692)	(622)
Overdraft	(11)	0
Net current assets/(liabilities)	208	(47)
Note 1		
Cost of sales includes depreciation of	225	175

Ms Smith is considering methods of improving the cash position. A number of actions are being discussed:

Trade receivables
Offer a 2 per cent discount to customers who pay within 10 days of despatch of invoices. It is estimated that 50 per cent of customers will take advantage of the new discount scheme. The other 50 per cent will continue to take the current average credit period.

Trade payables and inventory

Reduce the number of suppliers currently being used and negotiate better terms with those that remain by introducing a 'just-in-time' policy. The aim will be to reduce the end-of-year forecast cost of sales (excluding depreciation) by 5 per cent and inventory/WIP levels by 10 per cent. However, the number of days' credit taken by the entity will have to fall to 30 days to help persuade suppliers to improve their prices.

Other information

- All trade is on credit. Official terms of sale at present require payment within 30 days. Interest is not charged on late payments.
- All purchases are made on credit.
- Operating expenses will be $650,000 under either the existing or proposed policies.
- Interest payments would be $45,000 if the new policies are implemented.
- Capital expenditure of $550,000 is planned for next year.

Requirements

(a) Provide a cash-flow forecast for next year, assuming:
  (i) the entity does not change its policies;
  (ii) the entity's proposals for managing trade receivables, payables and inventory are implemented.

   In both cases, assume a full twelve-month period, i.e. the changes will be effective from day 1 of next year. **(14 marks)**

(b) As assistant to Ms Smith, write a short report to her evaluating the proposed actions. Include comments on the factors, financial and non-financial, that the entity should take into account before implementing the new policies. **(6 marks)**

(Total marks = 20)

? Question 19

MP is a manufacturing entity that trades with a large number of suppliers of raw materials, components, etc. The entity's financial manager has asked you, her assistant, to review the terms of trade and their associated costs. As a part of the exercise, you randomly choose three regular suppliers of one particular component. They have the following terms:

Supplier A	Charges a fixed penalty of 2 per cent of invoice value for late payment.
Supplier B	Charges compound interest at 2 per cent per 30-day period after the due date of payment.
Supplier C	Offers a 2 per cent discount if payment is made within ten days of invoice date but charges simple interest at 10 per cent per annum on the invoice value if payment is after the due date.

Assume that the due date for payment in each case is 30 days, but that MP's current credit control policy is to take an average of 90 days to pay these suppliers' invoices.

To simplify your calculations, assume also that MP purchases $1,000 worth of goods from each supplier every month.

Requirements

Write a report to the financial manager that includes:

(i) a calculation of the annualised interest rate (i.e. per cent per annum) for each of the three suppliers. **(8 marks)**

(ii) a discussion of the arguments for and against using trade credit as a source of funds, in general and from MP's point of view, given their current credit policy. **(8 marks)**

(iii) a discussion of the advantages and disadvantages to MP of introducing standard terms of trade with which all suppliers will have to conform. **(4 marks)**

(Total marks = 20)

 ## Question 20

AM is a trading entity operating in a country where there is no sales tax. Purchases are on credit, with 70% paid in the month following the date of purchase and 30% paid in the month after that.

Sales are partly on credit and partly for cash. Customers who receive credit are given 30 days to pay. On average 60% pay within 30 days, 30% pay between 30 and 60 days and 5% pay between 60 and 90 days. The balance is written off as irrecoverable. Other overheads, including salaries, are paid within the month incurred.

AM plans to purchase new equipment at the end of June 2005, the expected cost of which is $250,000. The equipment will be purchased on 30 days' credit, payable at the end of July.

The cash balance on 1 May 2005 is $96,000.

The actual/budgeted balances for the 6 months to July 2005 were:

All figures $'000		Actual			Budgeted	
	Feb	Mar	Apr	May	Jun	Jul
Credit sales	100	100	110	110	120	120
Cash sales	30	30	35	35	40	40
Credit purchases	45	50	50	55	55	60
Other overhead expense	40	40	40	50	50	50

Requirement

Prepare a monthly cash budget for the period May to July 2005 and assess the likelihood of AM being able to pay for the equipment when it falls due. (Round all figures to the nearest $'000.) **(5 marks)**

Question 21

SF is a family-owned private entity with five main shareholders.

SF has just prepared its cash budget for the year ahead, details of which are shown below. The current overdraft facility is $50,000 and the bank has stated that it would not be willing to increase the facility at present, without a substantial increase in the interest rate charged, due to the lack of assets to offer as security.

The shareholders are concerned by the cash projections, and have sought advice from external consultants.

All figures, $'000

						MONTH						
	J	*F*	*M*	*A*	*M*	*J*	*J*	*A*	*S*	*O*	*N*	*D*
Collections from customers	55	60	30	10	15	20	20	25	30	40	55	80
Dividend on investment						10						
Total inflows	55	60	30	10	15	30	20	25	30	40	55	80
Payments to suppliers		20		20		25		28		27		25
Wages and salaries	15	15	15	15	15	20	20	15	15	15	15	15
Payments for non-current assets			2		5	10		15				
Dividend payable				25								
Income tax										30		
Other operating expenses	5	5	5	5	7	7	7	7	7	7	8	8
Total outflows	20	40	22	65	27	62	27	65	52	49	23	48
Net in or (out)	35	20	8	(55)	(12)	(32)	(7)	(40)	(22)	(9)	32	32
Bank balance (overdraft)												
Opening	20	55	75	83	28	16	(16)	(23)	(63)	(85)	(94)	(62)
Closing	55	75	83	28	16	(16)	(23)	(63)	(85)	(94)	(62)	(30)

The following additional information relating to the cash budget has been provided by SF:

- all sales are on credit. Two months' credit on average is granted to customers;
- production is scheduled evenly throughout the year. Year-end inventory of finished good are forecast to be $30,000 higher than at the beginning of the year;
- purchase of raw materials are made at two-monthly intervals. SF typically takes up to 90 days to pay for goods supplied. Other expense are paid in the month in which they arise;
- the capital expenditure budget comprises:

Office furniture	March	$2,000
Progress payment on building extensions	May	$5,000
Car	June	$10,000
New equipment	August	$15,000

Requirement

Assume you are an external consultant employed by SF. Prepare a report for the board advising on the possible actions it might take to improve its budgeted cash flow for the year, and consider the possible impact of these actions on the entity's business. Your report should also identify possible short-term investment opportunities for the cash surpluses identified in the first part of the budget year. **(20 marks)**

❓ Question 22

ABC is a small manufacturing entity that is suffering cash-flow difficulties. The entity already utilises its maximum overdraft facility. ABC sells an average of $400,000 of goods per month at invoice value, and customers are allowed 40 days to pay from the date of invoice. Two possible solutions to the entity's cash-flow problems have been suggested.

- *Option 1.* The entity could factor its trade debts. A factor has been found who would advance ABC 75 per cent of the value of its invoices immediately on receipt of the invoices, at an interest rate of 10 per cent per annum. The factor would also charge a service fee amounting to 2 per cent of the total invoices. As a result of using the factor, ABC would save administration costs estimated at $5,000 per month.

- *Option 2.* The entity could offer a cash discount to customers for prompt payment. It has been suggested that customers could be offered a 2 per cent discount for payments made within 10 days of invoicing.

Requirements

(a) Identify the services that may be provided by factoring entities. **(4 marks)**
(b) Calculate the annual net cost (in $) of the proposed factoring agreement. **(6 marks)**
(c) Calculate the annualised cost (in percentage terms) of offering a cash discount to customers. **(3 marks)**
(d) Discuss the relative merits of the two proposals. **(7 marks)**

(Total marks = 20)

? Question 23

DF is a manufacturer of sports equipment. All of the shares of DF are held by the Wong family.

The entity has recently won a major three-year contract to supply FF with a range of sports equipment. FF is a large entity with over 100 sports shops. The contract may be renewed after 3 years.

The new contract is expected to double DF's existing total annual sales, but demand from FF will vary considerably from month to month.

The contract will, however, mean a significant additional investment in both non-current and current assets. A loan from the bank is to be used to finance the additional non-current assets, as the Wong family is currently unable to supply any further share capital. Also, the Wong family does not wish to raise new capital by issuing shares to non-family members.

The financing of the additional current assets is yet to be decided. In particular, the contract with FF will require orders to be delivered within 2 days. This delivery period gives DF insufficient time to manufacture items, thus significant inventory need to be held at all times. Also, FF requires 90 days' credit from its suppliers. This will result in a significant additional investment in trade receivables by DF.

If the entity borrows from the bank to finance current assets, either using a loan or an overdraft, it expects to be charged annual interest at 12%. Consequently, DF is considering alternative methods of financing current assets. These include debt factoring, invoice discounting and offering a 3% cash discount to FF for settlement within 10 days rather than the normal 90 days.

Requirements

(a) Calculate the annual equivalent rate of interest implicit in offering a 3% cash discount to FF for settlement of debts within 10 days rather than 90 days.

Briefly explain the factors, other than rate of interest, that DF would need to consider before deciding on whether to offer a cash discount. **(6 marks)**

(b) Write a report to the Wong family shareholders explaining the various methods of financing available to DF to finance the additional current assets arising from the new FF contract. The report should include the following headings:

   (i) bank loan;

   (ii) overdraft;

   (iii) debt factoring;

   (iv) invoice discounting.

(14 marks)

(Total marks = 20)

? Question 24

HRD owns a number of small hotels. The room occupancy rate varies significantly from month to month. There are also high fixed costs. As a result, the cash generated each month has been very difficult to estimate.

Christmas is normally a busy period and large cash surpluses are expected in December. There is, however, a possibility that a rival group of hotels will offer large discounts in December and this could damage December trade for HRD to a significant extent.

January is a poor period for the industry and therefore all the entity's hotels will close for the month, resulting in a negative cash flow. The Finance Director has identified the following possible outcomes and their associated probabilities:

	$'000s	Probability
Expected cash balance at 30 November 2002	+175	1.0
Net operating cash flow in December 2002	+700	0.7
	−300	0.3
Net operating cash flow in January 2003	−900	1.0

Assume cash flows arise at month ends.

Money can be put on deposit at the following rates:

Maturity period	Compounded annualised yield
1 month	5% (i.e. 0.4074% per month)
2 months	6% (i.e. 0.9759% for two months)

The entity's overdraft carries a compounded annualised interest rate of 10% (i.e. 0.7974% per month).

After January 2003, trade is expected to improve, but there is still a high degree of uncertainty in relation to the cash surpluses or deficits that will be generated in each month.

Requirements

(a) Calculate the expected cash balance or overdraft of HRD at 31 January 2003. Briefly comment, with reasons, on whether this figure should be used for short-term cash planning. **(5 marks)**

(b) As a member of the treasury team of HRD, write a memorandum to the Directors, with supporting calculations, advising them regarding the investment of short-term cash balance is December 2002 and January 2003. Ignore transaction costs and make all calculations to the nearest $1. **(10 marks)**

(c) Consider whether the use of the Miller–Orr model would be useful for determining HRD's policy for investment of short-term cash balances *beyond* January 2003. Calculations are NOT required. **(5 marks)**

(Total marks = 20)

Question 25

A general manager in your entity has recently enrolled on a management course at the local college. She is studying a module on finance and accounting and is having some difficulty understanding the theory. She has asked you, the trainee management accountant, if you could explain the consultative process used to produce a new International Financial Reporting Standard (IFRS). **(5 marks)**

 Question 26

E, a food retailer, decided to start a home delivery service from 1 November 2002. As E had no vehicles suitable for use by the new service, it purchased three small delivery vehicles to enable them to provide the service.

The invoice for the vehicles included the following details:

	$
Cost price – per vehicle	12,000
Less trade discount	(2,400)
	9,600
Delivery charge	250
One vehicle	9,850
Three vehicles	29,550
1 year's insurance for the three vehicles	2,100
Total cost of three vehicles	31,650

By 31 October 2003, there had been a general price increase in all new delivery vehicles of 25%. The directors of E decided to revalue the three delivery vehicles to 125% of their net book value at 31 October 2003.

During the next year, it became apparent that the delivery service was so successful that the delivery vehicles were now too small. On 1 April 2004, E traded in the three delivery vehicles for three new larger vehicles. The new larger delivery vehicles cost $18,000 each and the vendor allowed a trade-in value of $9,000 for each of the old vehicles. E paid the balance of $9,000 per vehicle on 1 May 2004.

All vehicles are depreciated using the reducing balance method at 25% per annum, charged on a time basis.

E purchased new computer equipment, costing $5,000, to assist in running the delivery service.

The software required to provide the service was also purchased at the same time. The initial cost of the delivery scheduling software was $950 plus the cost of adapting the software to E's detailed specifications $2,600. The computer equipment and the adapted software were delivered on 1 November 2002, and brought into use at once. During December 2002, the software developed reliability problems, often crashing for no apparent reason. E's in-house programmer spent time resolving these problems at an estimated cost of $2,000 in December 2002 and $1,000 in January 2003. E depreciates all computer equipment and software on a straight line basis over 4 years, assuming no residual value.

IAS 16 *Property, Plant and Equipment* describes the asset recognition process as:

- Initial recognition;
- Subsequent remeasurement;
- Derecognition.

Requirements

(i) Apply the IAS 16 asset recognition process to the above situations and explain the relevance of each stage of the process to each of the situations. **(6 marks)**

(ii) Prepare statement of comprehensive income and Statement of financial position extracts for the years ended 31 October 2003 and 31 October 2004 to show how the above transactions would be recorded. Explain your treatment with reference to appropriate International Financial Reporting Standards. **(14 marks)**

(Total marks = 20)

The following questions have been included to give an indication of the type of question that could be set for the new compulsory 30 mark question in Section C of the paper.

[?] Question 27

M is an enterprise which manufactures components for sale to the electronics industry. The following trial balance has been extracted from the enterprise's financial records:

M – Trial balance at 30 September 20X2

	$m	$m
Administrative expenses	64	
Cash and cash equivalents	98	
Cost of sales	1,142	
Deferred tax		291
Disposal of plant and equipment	11	
Distribution costs	148	
Dividend – interim paid	300	
Income tax expense		37
Interest	72	
Interest-bearing borrowings (repayable 20Y8)		1,618
Inventories at 30 September 20X2	45	
Plant and equipment – cost	794	
Plant and equipment – depreciation to date		324
Property – cost	4,456	
Property – depreciation to date		811
Provision for cost of sales		300
Retained profit brought forward		1,132
Revenue		2,970
Issued capital		600
Trade payables		27
Trade receivables	980	
	8,110	8,110

(i) Seller is an enterprise which is one of M's largest suppliers. G, one of M's Directors, owns 98% of Seller. M purchased $43 million of goods from Seller during the year ended 30 September 20X2, all under Seller's normal terms and conditions. M owed Seller $3 million at 30 September 20X2.

(ii) Plant and equipment which had cost $125 million and had been depreciated by $78 million was sold during the year. New plant and equipment was purchased for $160 million. These transactions have been included in the above figures. There were no other transactions involving non-current assets.

(iii) Depreciation for the year has still to be charged as follows:

Property 2% of cost
Plant and equipment 25% reducing balance

A whole year's depreciation is charged in the year of acquisition and none in the year of disposal.

(iv) The trial balance figure for inventories is calculated on the following basis:

	Purchase price	Attributable manufacturing overheads	Attributable nonmanufacturing overheads	Total cost	Net realizable value
	$m	$m	$m	$m	$m
Current inventory	26	7	3	36	51
Obsolete inventory	6	2	1	9	5
Total				45	56

Total cost is lower than total net realisable value and so the directors have valued the inventory at $45 million. The external auditors have refused to accept this valuation, arguing that it is inconsistent with the requirements of IAS 2 *Inventories*. M's directors have agreed to correct the inventory figure to bring it into line with IAS 2.

(v) The directors have estimated the tax charge for the year at $120 million. The balance on the income tax expense account is the amount remaining after settling the liability for the year ended 30 September 20X1.

(vi) The provision for deferred tax has arisen from the timing differences arising from accelerated capital allowances on the enterprise's non-current assets. The tax written down value of non-current assets at 30 September 20X2 was $2,985 million. It is estimated that tax will be paid at a rate of 30% when these timing differences reverse.

(vii) The directors declared a final dividend of $150 million before the end of the reporting period.

(viii) M is a quoted enterprise. Authorised share capital is 800 million shares of $1.00. Issued share capital is 600 million shares of $1.00, fully paid.

The following notes are NOT relevant to requirement (a)

(ix) M's largest customer placed an order during September 20X2 for all of the goods that it is likely to require during the year ending 30 September 20X3. M invoiced this customer for these goods during September 20X2. A total of $800 million was debited to trade receivables and credited to revenue in respect of this invoice. A provision for $300 million was created in respect of the estimated cost of manufacturing the invoiced goods.

(x) M's customer agreed to place the order referred to in note (ix) above only after receiving a number of written assurances from M's directors. The goods themselves will be delivered at times and in quantities decided by the customer. The customer will pay for the goods in accordance with M's normal credit terms after delivery. The customer can cancel the order without penalty at any time and any remaining balance on the invoice will be cancelled immediately.

Requirements

(a) Prepare M's statement of comprehensive income for the year ended 30 September 20X2 and its statement of financial position at that date. These should be in a form suitable for publication and should be accompanied by notes as far as you are able to prepare these from the information provided.

Do NOT adjust any figures in the financial statements in respect of the information provided in notes (ix) and (x) in the scenario.

Do NOT prepare a statement of accounting policies, a statement of recognised gains and losses or a statement of changes in equity. **(25 marks)**

The International Accounting Standards Committee's *Framework for the Preparation and Presentation of Financial Statements* (Framework) effectively defines profits on individual transactions in terms of increase in net assets. This means that profits are normally associated with an increase in the value of assets, where an asset is defined as 'a resource controlled by the enterprise as a result of past events and from which future economic benefits are expected to flow to the enterprise'.

(b) Explain whether M is justified in treating the transaction described in notes (ix) and (x) in the scenario as a sale. **(5 marks)**

(Total marks = 30)

? Question 28

AZ is a quoted manufacturing enterprise. The finished products are stored in a nearby warehouse until ordered by customers. AZ has performed very well in the past, but has been in financial difficulties in recent months and has been reorganising the business to improve performance.

The trial balance for AZ as at 31 March 20X3 was as follows:

	$'000's	$'000's
7% Loan Notes (redeemable 20X7)		18,250
Accumulated profits at 31 March 20X2		11,444
Administrative Expenses	16,020	
Bank & Cash	2,250	
Cost of goods manufactured in the year to		
31 March 20X3 (excluding depreciation)	94,000	
Distribution Costs	9,060	
Dividends paid	1,000	
Dividends received		1,200
Interest Paid	639	
Inventory at 31 March 20X2	4,852	
Investments at market value	24,000	
Ordinary Shares $1 each, fully paid		20,000
Plant & Equipment	30,315	
Provision for Depreciation at 31 March 20X2:		
Plant & Equipment		6,060
Vehicles		1,670
Provision for Deferred Tax		138
Provision for doubtful debts		600
Restructuring Costs	121	
Revaluation Reserve		3,125
Sales revenue		124,900
Share issue expenses	70	
Share Premium		500
Taxation	30	
Trade payables		8,120
Trade receivables	9,930	
Vehicles	3,720	
	196,007	196,007

Additional information provided

(i) Non-current assets are depreciated as follows:

Plant & Equipment   20% p.a. Straight line
Vehicles   25% reducing balance

Depreciation of plant and equipment is considered to be part of cost of sales and depreciation of vehicles should be included under distribution costs.

(ii) The balance on taxation account is the previous year's income taxes underestimated in last year's financial statements by $30,000. Taxation due for the year to 31 March 20X3 is estimated at $150,000.

(iii) A transfer to deferred tax for the year to 31 March 20X3 of $11,000 is to be made.

(iv) The closing inventory at 31 March 20X3 was $5,180,000. An inspection of finished goods inventory found that a production machine had been set up incorrectly and several production batches, which had cost $50,000 to manufacture had the wrong packaging. The goods cannot be sold in this condition, but could be repacked at an additional cost of $20,000. They could then be sold for $55,000. The wrongly packaged goods were included in closing inventory at their cost of $50,000.

(v) A dividend of 5 cents per ordinary share was paid in February 20X3.

(vi) The 7% loan notes are ten-year loans due for repayment by 31 March 2007. AZ incurred no other interest charges in the year to 31 March 20X3.

(vii) The provision for doubtful debts is to be adjusted to 5% of the closing trade receivables balance.

(viii) The restructuring costs in the trial balance represent the cost of a major fundamental restructuring of the enterprise to improve its competitiveness and future profitability.

(ix) As at 31 March 20X3, AZ was engaged in defending a legal action against the enterprise. Legal advisers have indicated that it is reasonably certain that the outcome of the case will be against the enterprise. The amount of compensation is currently estimated at $25,000.

(x) On 1st October 20X2, AZ issued 1,000,000 ordinary shares at $1.50 each. All money had been received and correctly accounted for by the year-end.

Requirement

Prepare AZ's Statement of Comprehensive Income for the year to 31 March 20X3, its Statement of Financial Position at that date, and a Statement of Changes in Equity for the year. These should be in a form suitable for presentation to the shareholders, in accordance with the requirements of International Accounting Standards.

> Notes to the financial statements are not required but all workings must be clearly shown. Do not prepare a statement of accounting policies.

(Total marks = 30)

? **Question 29**

ZZ produces two different groups of products, range A and range B. The range A brand was developed in house but the range B brand name was purchased 7 years ago.

The B product range has been losing popularity and sales have been in sharp decline for the last 2 years. By the end of the third quarter of 20X2, the level of sales had declined to a point where the directors decided it was no longer viable to produce the B product range and a provision of $100,000 for closure expenses was set up in the accounts for the year ended 30 September 20X3. The closure was delayed until 1 January 20X4 when the production lines ceased production and all the assets relating to the B product range were put up for sale.

ZZ's trial balance at 30 September 20X4 is shown below:

	$'000	$'000
10% Loan 20Y0		2,600
Administration expenses-A product range	96	
Administration expenses-B product range	34	
Bank and Cash	3,192	
Brand name – B product range	197	
Buildings at cost	2,500	
Cash received on disposal of factory		2,000
Cash received on disposal of machinery		50
Closure costs	125	
Income tax	20	
Cost of goods sold-A product range	513	
Cost of goods sold-B product range	127	
Trade payables		90
Loan interest paid – half year	130	
Trade receivables	140	
Distribution costs-A product range	92	
Distribution costs-B product range	12	
Land at valuation at 30 September 20X3	1,500	
Machinery and equipment at cost	1,706	
Equity shares $1 each, fully paid		1,500
Retained earnings at 30 September 20X3		436
Provision for amortisation of brand name –		
B product range at 30 September 20X3		138
Provision for closure costs at 30 September 20X3		100
Provision for deferred tax at 30 September 20X3		203
Provision for depreciation at 30 September 20X3:		
Buildings		860
Machinery and equipment		415
Revaluation reserve		900
Turnover – A product range		1,260
Turnover – B product range		42
Inventory at 30 September 20X4 – A product range	210	
	10,594	10,594

Further information

(i) The assets relating to the B product range were disposed of as follows:

- The land and the factory buildings were sold on 1 March 20X4 for $2,000,000.
- The machinery was sold for $50,000 on the same date.

- All the cash received is included in the trial balance.
- The purchased brand name was deemed to have no value and should be written off.

The book values of the assets sold were:

Asset type	Cost	Valuation	Accumulated depreciation
	$'000	$'000	$'000
Land	300	750	0
Buildings	400		220
Machinery and equipment	462		195

(ii) Buildings are depreciated at 5% per annum on the straight-line basis. Machinery is depreciated at 25% per annum using the reducing balance method. Depreciation is treated as a cost of sales.

(iii) There were no purchases of tangible non-current assets during the year.

(iv) ZZ's accounting policy for amortisation and depreciation is to charge a full year in the year of acquisition and make no charge in the year of disposal.

(v) The directors decided to downsize the enterprise and used the cash received to repay a loan rather than invest in new production facilities. The loan was redeemed on 30 September 20X4, a payment equal to the nominal value outstanding plus accrued interest to date was made from the bank account on 30 September 20X4. This transaction has not been recorded in the trial balance. The interest for the year should be allocated to discontinued operations.

(vi) The director's estimate the income tax charge on the year's profits at $113,000, of this $12,000 relates to discontinued operations. The balance on the income tax account is the amount remaining after settling the amount due for the year ended 30 September 20X3.

(vii) The deferred tax provision needs to be reduced to $170,000.

(viii) No interim dividend was paid during the year.

Requirements

(a) Prepare the tangible non-current assets note to the accounts for the year ended 30 September 20X4. **(6 marks)**

(b) Prepare the statement of comprehensive income of ZZ for the year ended 30 September 20X4 and a statement of financial position at that date. These should be in a form suitable for publication and in accordance with all current regulations. **(24 marks)**

Notes to the financial statements are not required (except as specified in requirement (a) of the question) but all workings must be clearly shown. Do not prepare a statement of accounting policies or a statement of Changes in equity.

(Total marks = 30)

? Question 30

The financial statements of C for the year to 31 March 20X4 were as follows:

Statement of financial position at	31 March 20X4		31 March 20X3	
	$'000	$'000	$'000	$'000
Non-current assets				
Intangible assets	111		90	
Tangible assets	7,724	7,835	4,923	5,013
Current assets:				
Inventories	1,337		864	
Trade receivables	743		435	
Investments	0		730	
Bank	489		7	
Cash	27		22	
		2,596		2,058
Total assets		10,431		7,071
Equity and liabilities				
Equity				
Ordinary shares $1 each	2,000		1,500	
Share premium account	1,500		500	
Revaluation reserve	1,080		630	
Accumulated profits	3,311		2,876	
		7,891		5,506
Non-current liabilities:				
Loans	1,006		410	
Deferred tax	254		291	
		1,260		701
Current liabilities:				
Trade payables	626		552	
Tax	234		188	
Interest payable	20		4	
Other provisions	400		120	
Total equity and liabilities		1,280		864
		10,431		7,071

Income Statement for the Year to 31 March 20X4

	$'000	$'000
Revenue		14,780
Cost of Sales		(9,607)
Gross Profit		5,173
Distribution costs	(1,222)	
Administrative expenses (including provisions)	(2,924)	(4,146)
Profit from operations		1,027
Finance cost	(45)	
Income from investments	0	(45)
Profit before tax		982
Income tax expense		(197)
Net profit for the period		785

Additional information

(i) Tangible Non-current assets balances were as follows:

	31 March 20X4	31 March 20X3	
	Cost or valuation	Cost or valuation	Accumulated depreciation/ amortisation
	$'000	$'000	$'000
Land	3,636	3,186	0
Buildings	3,063	1,663	416
Plant, machinery & equipment	2,188	1,108	671
Assets under construction	0	53	0

(ii) Intangible non-current assets comprise development expenditure incurred in previous years and in the current year, and being carried forward to future periods. Development expenditure amortised during the year was $18,000.

(iii) Tangible non-current assets include land which was revalued by $450,000 on 31 March 20X4.

(iv) Machinery disposed of in the year had originally cost $400,000; accumulated depreciation at 31 March 20X3 was $380,000. The agreed selling price of $31,000 had not been received by the year-end and is included in receivables.

(v) Assets under construction refer to a contract, started in February 20X3, to build and supply C with new machinery. The machinery was installed and testing completed by 31 December 20X3. Production began early January 20X4. C had taken out a specific loan to finance the payments under the contract and in accordance with IAS 23 *Borrowing Costs,* has decided to capitalise the interest payments up to 31 December 20X3. The interest paid was $24,000; this amount was transferred from the interest paid account to the assets under construction account. The balance on the assets under construction account was transferred to the plant and machinery account on 31 January 20X4. The amount transferred was:

Balance at 31 March 20X4	526
Interest	24
Total cost	550

In addition to this contract, other new plant and machinery had been purchased during the year.

(vi) Depreciation charged for the year was:

Buildings	2.5% straight line
Plant, machinery & equipment	20% reducing balance

C's accounting policy is to charge a full year's depreciation in the year of acquisition and no depreciation in the year of disposal.

(vii) Receivables consist of:

	31 March 20X4	31 March 20X3
Trade receivables	712	401
Receivable arising from sale of non-current assets	31	0
Interest receivable on current asset investments	0	34

(viii) The current asset investment was a government bond, which matured on 31 March 20X3 and was redeemed in April 20X3 for $750,000.

(ix) C did not purchase any of its shares during the year.

(x) The estimated income tax charge for the year to 31 March 20X4 was $234,000 and the deferred tax balance reduced by $37,000.

(xi) An interim dividend of $350,000 was paid during the year.

Requirements

(a) Prepare the following disclosure notes for the year ended 31 March 20X4, as required by international accounting standards:

   (i) Property, plant and equipment   **(8 marks)**

   (ii) Finance cost   **(2 marks)**

(b) Prepare the following for C for the year ended 31 March 20X4, in the form prescribed by IAS 7 *Cash Flow Statements:*

   (i) A statement of cash flows, using the indirect method   **(18 marks)**

   (ii) An analysis of cash and cash equivalents   **(2 marks)**

        (Total marks = 30)

❓ Question 31

H, a wholesaling entity, employs just over 100 people and purchases food in bulk for sale to small shops and hotels. H buys from a large number of suppliers of various sizes, spread across the country. H's trial balance at 31 March 20X1 is as follows:

	$'000	$'000
Administration costs	90	
Bank	11	
Income tax		20
Distribution costs	60	
Dividend received		600
Non-current asset investment	6,575	
Dividends paid	1,200	
Loan (repayable 20X4)		200
Loan interest	24	
Plant and machinery – cost	900	
Plant and machinery – depreciation		440
Premises – cost	2,400	
Premises – depreciation		720
Accumulated profits		921
Purchases	2,027	
Revenue		5,000
Share capital		7,000
Inventory at 1 April 20X0	165	
Trade payables		168
Trade receivables	417	
Wages – administration	800	
Wages – distribution	400	
	15,069	15,069

(i) Inventory was physically counted at close of business on 31 March 20X1 and was valued at $167,000.

(ii) The premises were revalued at $2.5 million on 1 April 20X0. The directors have decided to incorporate this valuation into the Statement of financial position. There have been no other transactions or adjustments in respect of non-current assets.

(iii) Premises are to be depreciated by 2 per cent of cost or valuation, and plant and machinery by 20 per cent, on the reducing balance method. All depreciation is to be treated as a distribution cost.

(iv) The tax charge for the year has been estimated at $270,000.

(v) The balance on the tax account represents the amount remaining after the settlement of the liability for the year ended 31 March 20X0.

(vi) *Dividends paid and proposed during the year were*:

	$
Final for year ended 31 March 20X0	700,000
Interim for year ended 31 March 20X1	500,000
Directors' proposed final dividend	900,000

Requirement

Prepare H's statement of comprehensive income and a statement of changes in equity for the year ended 31 March 20X1, and its Statement of financial position at that date. These should be in a form suitable for publication, and accompanied by notes as far as you are able to prepare these from the information provided.

You are NOT required to prepare a statement of accounting policies or to calculate earnings per share. **(30 marks)**

? Question 32

DZ is a manufacturing entity and produces one group of products, known as product Y.

DZ's trial balance at 31 March 2007 is shown below:

	$'000	$'000
8% loan 2020 (see note (xiv))		2,000
Administration expenses	891	
Bank and cash	103	
Cash received on disposal of land		1,500
Cash received on disposal of plant		5
Cost of raw materials purchased in year	2,020	
Direct production labour costs	912	
Distribution costs	462	
Equity shares $1 each, fully paid		1,000
Income tax (see note (xi))	25	
Inventory of finished goods at 31 March 2006	240	
Inventory of raw materials at 31 March 2006	132	
Land at valuation at 31 March 2006	1,250	
Loan interest paid – half year	80	
Plant and equipment at cost at 31 March 2006	4,180	
Production overheads (excluding depreciation)	633	
Property at cost at 31 March 2006	11,200	
Provision for deferred tax at 31 March 2006 (see note (xii))		773

Provision for depreciation at 31 March 2006: (see notes (iv) and (v))		
Property		1,900
Plant and equipment		2,840
Research and development (see note (vi))	500	
Retained earnings at 31 March 2006		2,024
Revaluation reserve at 31 March 2006		2,100
Revenue		8,772
Trade payables		773
Trade receivables	1,059	
	23,687	23,687

Further information

(i) The property cost of $11,200,000 consisted of land $3,500,000 and buildings $7,700,000.

(ii) During the year, DZ disposed of non-current assets as follows:

- A piece of surplus land was sold on 1 March 2007 for $1,500,000;
- Obsolete plant was sold for $5,000 scrap value on the same date;
- All the cash received is included in the trial balance;

Details of the assets sold were:

Asset type	Cost	Revalued amount	Accumulated depreciation
Land	$500,000	$1,250,000	$0
Plant and equipment	$620,000		$600,000

(iii) On 31 March 2007, DZ revalued its properties to $9,800,000 (land $4,100,000 and buildings $5,700,000).

(iv) Buildings are depreciated at 5% per annum on the straight line basis. Buildings depreciation is treated as 80% production overhead and 20% administration.

(v) Plant and equipment is depreciated at 25% per annum using the reducing balance method, the depreciation being treated as a production overhead.

(vi) Product Y was developed in-house. Research and development is carried out on a continuous basis to ensure that the product range continues to meet customer demands. The research and development figure in the trial balance is made up as follows:

	$'000
Development costs capitalised in previous years	867
Less: Amortisation to 31 March 2006	534
	333
Research costs incurred in the year to 31 March 2007	119
Development costs (all meet IAS 38 *Intangible Assets* criteria) incurred in the year to 31 March 2007	48
Total	500

(vii) Development costs are amortised on a straight line basis at 20% per annum.

(viii) Research and development costs are treated as cost of sales when charged to the income statement.

(ix) DZ charges a full year's amortisation and depreciation in the year of acquisition and none in the year of disposal.

(x) Inventory of raw materials at 31 March 2007 was $165,000. Inventory of finished goods at 31 March 2007 was $270,000.

(xi) The directors estimate the income tax charge on the year's profits at $811,000. The balance on the income tax account represents the underprovision for the previous year's tax charge.

(xii) The deferred tax provision is to be reduced to $665,000.

(xiii) No interim dividend was paid during the year.

(xiv) The 8% loan is a 20-year loan issued in 2000.

Requirements

(a) Prepare DZ's Property, Plant and Equipment note to the accounts for the year ended 31 March 2007.

(6 marks)

(b) Prepare the income statement and a statement of changes in equity for the year to 31 March 2007 and a balance sheet at that date, in a form suitable for presentation to the shareholders and in accordance with the requirements of International Financial Reporting Standards.
   (All workings should be to the nearest $'000).

(24 marks)

Notes to the financial statements are NOT required (except as specified in part (a) of the question), but ALL workings must be clearly shown. Do NOT prepare a statement of accounting policies.

(Total marks = 30 marks)

Solutions to Revision Questions II

 **Solution 1**

Notes to the accounts

Note 1: Tax expenses

	$
Balance brought forward	(12,000)
Tax for current year	600,000
Deferred tax increase	100,000
Profit or loss	688,000

Note 2: Deferred tax

	$
Deferred tax – balance at 1 January 2003	990,000
Increase in the year	100,000
Balance at 31 December 2003	1,090,000

Income Statement (extract) for the year ended 31 December 2003

Tax expenses (note 1) $688,000

Statement of financial position at 31 December 2003 (extracts)

Current liabilities:	
Tax payable	$600,000
Non-current liabilities:	
Deferred tax (note 2)	$1,090,000

Solution 2

		Industrial building $	Plant $	Total tax depreciation for year $
01/01/2001	Purchase	400,000	60,000	
31/12/2001	First-year allowance		(30,000)	
	Tax depreciation for the year	(12,000)		42,000
	Balance at 31/05/2002	388,000	30,000	
31/12/2002	Tax depreciation for the year	(11,640)	(7,500)	19,140
	Balance at 31/05/2003	376,360	22,500	
31/12/2003	Disposal		(10,000)	
	Balancing allowance		12,500	
	Tax depreciation for the year	11,290		23,790
	Balance at 31/05/2004	365,070	0	
01/01/2004	Purchase		75,000	

 # Solution 3

	20X1 $'000	20X2 $'000	20X3 $'000	20X4 $'000	20X5 $'000
Carrying value	300	240	180	120	60
Accounting depreciation	(60)	(60)	(60)	(60)	(60)
Closing carrying value	240	180	120	60	0
Opening balance for tax purposes	300	200	100	0	
Tax depreciation	(100)	(100)	(100)	0	0
Tax written down value (tax base)	200	100	0	0	0
Temporary difference (carrying value – tax base)	40	80	120	60	0
Deferred tax provision required at 25%	10	20	30	15	0
Charge/(release) to profit or loss	10	10	10	(15)	(15)

 # Solution 4

AF – Statement of comprehensive income for the year ended 31 March 2005

	$'000	$'000	$'000
Revenue			8,210
Cost of sales (W1)			(3,957)
Gross Profit			4,253
Other income			68
Administrative expenses		(1,540)	
Distribution costs		(1,590)	(3,130)
Profit from operations			1,191
Finance cost (W6)			(90)
Profit before tax			1,101
Income tax expense (W7)			(350)
Profit for the period			751
Other comprehensive income:			
Available for sale investments			110
Total comprehensive income for the period			861

AF – Statement of financial position as at 31 March 2005

	$'000	$'000	$'000
Non-current assets			
Property, plant and equipment (W4)			4,987
Available for sale investments			1,750
Current Assets			
Inventory		1,320	
Trade receivables		1,480	
Cash and cash equivalents		822	
			3,622
Total Assets			10,359
Equity and liabilities			
Equity			
Share capital		4,500	
Other reserves (W8)		1,820	
Retained earnings (W9)		864	
Total equity			7,184
Non-current Liabilities			
6% Loan	1,500		
Deferred tax (W7)	810		
Total non-current liabilities		2,310	
Current liabilities			
Trade and other payables (W10)	615		
Tax payable (W7)	250		
Total current liabilities		865	
Total liabilities			3,175
Total equity and liabilities			10,359

Workings

W1 – Cost of sales	$'000
Cost of goods	3,463
Depreciation – buildings (W2)	96
Depreciation equipment (W3)	348
Operating lease (W5)	50
	3,957

W2 – Depreciation Buildings	
Land and buildings at cost	5,190
Less cost of land	(2,000)
	3,190
Depreciation for year @ 3%	96 (IS)
Depreciation b/f	1,500
Depreciation c/f	1,596

W3 – Depreciation Plant and equipment	
Plant and equipment cost	3,400
Depreciation b/f	1,659
	1,741
Depreciation for year at 20%	348
Depreciation c/f	2,007

W4 – Property, plant and equipment

	At cost	Depreciation	Total
	$'000	$'000	$'000
Property	5,190	1,596	3,594
Plant and equipment	3,400	2,007	1,393
			4,987

W5 – Operating lease

Total payments (4 × 62.5)	250	
Allocated evenly over 5 periods (250/5)	50	a year
Profit or loss charge	50	

W6 – Finance cost

Interest = 1,500 × 6% = 90

W7 – Income tax expense

Profit or loss

Income tax accrued for year	250
Deferred tax charge for year	100
Profit or loss	350

Statement of financial position

Income tax – current	250

Deferred tax – non-current liability

Provision for deferred tax, b/f	710
Charge for year	100
Provision for deferred tax c/f	810

W8 – Other Reserves

Share premium		1,380
Revaluation reserve		
Balance b/f	330	
Increase in year investments	110	440
		1,820

W9 – Retained earnings

Balance b/f	388
Profit for the year	751
	1,139
Less dividend paid	(275)
	864

W10 – Trade and other payables

Trade payables	520
Operating lease rental accrued	50
Finance cost	45
	615

✓ Solution 5

According to the ASBs *Framework,* the five elements of financial statements are:

Asset	An asset is a resource controlled by the entity as a result of past events and from which future economic benefits are expected to flow to the entity;
Liability	A liability is a present obligation of the entity arising from past events, the settlement of which is expected to result in an outflow of resources from the entity;
Equity	The residual interest in the assets of the entity after deducting all its liabilities;
Income	Increases in economic benefits during the accounting period in the form of inflows or enhancements of assets or decreases of liabilities that result in increases in equity, other than those relating to combinations from equity participants;
Expenses	Decreases in economic benefits during the accounting period in the form of outflows or depletions of assets that result in decreases in equity, other than those relating to distributions to equity participants.

Solution 6

BG Statement of comprehensive income for the year ended 30 September 2005

	$'000	$'000	$'000
Revenue			1,017
Cost of sales (W1)			(799)
Gross profit			218
Other income			11
			229
Administrative expenses (W4)		(300)	
Release of provision		190	(110)
Profit from operations			119
Finance cost (W3)			(15)
Profit before tax			104
Income tax expense (W5)			(88)
Profit for the period			16
Other comprehensive income:			
Available for sale investments		20	
Total comprehensive income for the period	36		

BG Statement of financial position as at 30 September 2005

	$'000 At cost/valuation	$'000 Depreciation/amortisation	$'000 Total
Assets			
Non-current tangible assets			
Property, plant and equipment	752	520	232
Non-current financial assets			
Available for sale investments (W6)	225	0	225
			457
Current assets			
Inventories	37		
Trade receivables	141		
Cash and cash equivalents	147		
			325
Total assets			782
Equity and liabilities			
Equity			
Equity shares		200	
Reserves			
Share premium	40		
Retained earnings	182		
Revaluation reserve	50	272	
Total equity			472
Non-current liabilities			
10% loan	150		
Deferred tax (W5)	65		
Total non-current liabilities		215	
Current liabilities			
Trade payables	24		
Tax payable	64		
Interest payable	7		
Total current liabilities		95	
Total liabilities			310
Total equity and liabilities			782

BG Statement of changes in equity for the year ended 30 September 2005

	Equity Shares $'000	Share premium $'000	Retained earnings $'000	Revaluation reserve $'000	Total $'000
Balance at 1 October 2004	200	40	226	30	496
Total comprehensive income for period			16	20	36
Interim dividend	—	—	(60)	—	(60)
Balance at 30 September 2005	200	40	182	50	472

Workings

W1 Cost of sales	$'000
Direct cost – TB	548
Add depreciation – equipment & fixtures (W2)	150
Direct materials	101
	799

W2 Depreciation, equipment and fixtures	
Trial balance at cost	752
Depreciation for year 20%	150 to cost of sales
Depreciation b/fwd	370
Depreciation for year	150
Depreciation c/fwd	520 to Statement of financial position

W3 Finance costs	
Interest on loan 10% × 150 =	15

W4 Administrative expenses	
Per trial balance	239
Operating lease	61
	300

W5 Income tax expense	
Profit or loss	
Balance per trial balance	9
Income tax accrued for year	64
Deferred tax charge for year	15
Profit or loss	88
Statement of financial position	
Income tax – current	64
Deferred tax – non-current liability	
Provision for deferred tax, b/fwd	50
Charge for year	15
Provision for deferred tax c/fwd	65

W6 Available for sale investments	
Book value	205
Market value	225
Revaluation gain	20

☑ Solution 7

(a) The report contains a subheading to the effect that it has been qualified. That high-lights the more substantive fact that the report goes on to describe a problem with the accounting treatment of a possible bad debt. The auditor is of the opinion that a pro-vision that should have been made has not been accounted for. The final indicator is that the auditor's opinion states that the accounts give a true and fair view, but that is only 'except for' the absence of a provision. That means that the auditor does not have an unreserved opinion that the statements give a fair presentation.

The qualification suggests that the directors have overstated the profit for the year by $960,000. It also suggests that the current assets have been overstated by the same amount. This would suggest that any ROCE ratios, liquidity ratios and, possibly, receivables turnover ratios could be misleading. It is, however, up to the shareholders to decide for themselves whether they agree with the auditor's opinion on the treatment of the potential bad debt. They may feel that the auditor is an impartial commentator and would not have raised the matter without good reason. Alternatively, they might be of the opinion that the auditor has been overcautious and that the statement of comprehensive income and Statement of financial position prepared by management are fine as they stand.

(b) Auditors use this form of qualification if they are of the opinion that the financial statements contain a material misstatement. In other words, if they disagree with the facts, figures or disclosures prepared by the directors and if the extent of this disagreement is sufficient to affect the behaviour of the users of the financial statements.

Deciding to use this form of qualification is a serious matter. By reporting in this way, the auditor could undermine the shareholders' confidence in the figures prepared by the directors. They could even undermine confidence in the reliability of the directors themselves.

If the auditor disagrees with the directors, the first question to decide is whether that disagreement is material. If the amounts involved are insignificant then there is very little point in raising them in the audit report.

Then the auditor must decide whether the disagreement is a legitimate difference of opinion or whether there is a matter of fact or principle which is definitely unacceptable. For example, if the directors have chosen one of two acceptable treatments for a particular balance, their treatment is consistent over time and the policy is clearly stated, then it would not really matter that the auditor preferred the alternative treatment.

Finally, the auditor should attempt to persuade the directors to change their statements. It would be better for all concerned if the auditor could justify an opinion that the accounts give a fair presentation. It is possible that the directors will be willing to change their proposed treatment to accommodate the auditor.

✅ Solution 8

(a) Materiality is the quality that determines whether a matter is worth reporting or disclosing. A matter is material if knowledge of it would alter the behaviour of the users of the financial statements. Thus, the auditor would not normally be concerned about whether something that was immaterial was disclosed in the financial statements or, indeed, uncovered during the audit.

Normally, materiality is determined by size. A matter might be considered material because it exceeds a particular percentage of profit or sales revenue. Materiality can also be associated with qualitative issues. For example, a small error in the disclosure of directors' remuneration if required might not be material because of its size, but could still be of some significance to the shareholders because they take a keen interest in the amounts paid to directors.

Materiality is important to the auditor because the audit is essentially about detecting and reporting material irregularities. Audit tests will be designed to uncover material misstatements. Thus, deciding on a materiality threshold will influence the amount of audit work carried out. Materiality will also affect the reporting decision. Auditors are required to decide whether the financial statements give a true and fair view. It does not really matter whether the auditor agrees with everything in the accounts provided any disagreement is immaterial.

(b) The auditor's duty is to form an opinion on the fair presentation of the financial statements and to report that opinion to the shareholders. The auditor's responsibilities are, therefore, far narrower than many readers of financial statements realise. For example, the auditor does not prepare the statements, which is the responsibility of the directors.

Forming an opinion on fairness involves a number of subsidiary duties. The auditor must, for example, gather sufficient evidence to support this opinion. The auditor must also consider whether the accounting policies are acceptable, for example, do they comply with international accounting standards?

The auditor has no specific duty to prevent or detect fraud. The auditor must, however, consider the possibility that the statements might have been distorted in order to conceal some fraud. For example, an employee might attempt to conceal the theft of some cash by deliberately understating sales by the amount stolen. The auditor would have no direct interest in the theft itself, but would be concerned if the amount stolen was material because that would lead to a material understatement of the sales figure.

The question of the auditor's duty to report fraud is complicated by the fact that the shareholders might consider any serious fraud to indicate mismanagement on the part of the directors. That could, in turn, lead to the materiality threshold being lower for fraudulent irregularities than for those due to errors. Furthermore, the detection of fraud will normally be complicated by the fact that some attempt will have been made to conceal the theft. That will mean that the auditor will often feel less confident that all significant fraud has been detected.

✔ Solution 9

(i) AG – Statement of cash flows for the year ended 31 March 2005

	$'000	$'000
Cash flows from operating activities		
Profit before taxation	255	
Adjustments for:		
Depreciation	720	
Development expenditure amortisation	80	
Finance cost	45	
Gain on disposal of non-current tangible asset (W1)	(23)	
Operating profit before working capital changes		1,077
Increase in inventory	(110)	
Increase in trade receivables	(95)	
Increase in trade payables	130	
Increase in accrued expenses (W2)	10	
		(65)

Cash generated from operations		1,012
Interest paid (W3)	(120)	
Income taxes paid (W4)	(200)	(320)
		692
Net cash from operating activities		
Cash flows from investing activities		
Purchase of property, plant and equipment (W5)	(370)	
Proceeds from sale of equipment	98	
Development expenditure (W6)	(50)	
Net cash used in investing activities		(322)
Cash flows from financing activities		
Proceeds from issue of share capital (W7)	1,050	
Repayment of loans	(1,000)	
Equity dividends paid*	(100)	
Net cash used in financing activities		(50)
Net increase in cash and cash equivalents		320
Cash and cash equivalents at 1 April 2004		232
Cash and cash equivalents at 31 March 2005		552

*This could also be shown as an operating cash flow

Workings

W1 – Gain on disposal of property, plant and equipment

	$'000	$'000
Net book value	75	
Cash	98	
Gain	23	

W2 – Accrued expenditure

Balance b/f	172	
Interest b/f	(87)	
		85
Balance c/f	107	
Interest c/f	(12)	
		95
		10

W3 – Interest Paid

	$'000
Balance B/F	87
P & L	45
	132
Balance C/F	12
Paid	120

W4 – Income Taxes paid

	$'000	$'000
Balance b/f – corporate income tax	190	
– deferred tax	200	
Profit or loss		390
		140
		530
Balance c/f – corporate income tax	80	
– deferred tax	250	330
Tax paid		200

W5 – Purchase of property, plant and equipment

	$'000
Balance b/f	4,800
Disposals	(75)
	4,725
Revaluation	125
	4,850
Depreciation for year	(720)
	4,130
Balance c/f	4,500
Purchases	370

W6 – Development expenditure

	$'000
Balance b/f	400
Amortised in year	80
	320
Balance c/f	370
New expenditure	50

W7 – Proceeds from issue of share capital

		$'000
Shares	1,400 × 0.5	700
Share premium	1,400 × 0.5 × 0.5	350
Received		1,050

☑ Solution 10

Y: Statement of cash flows for the year ended 31 December 20X2

	$'000	$'000
Cash flows from operating activities		
Net profit before tax	196	
Adjustments for:		
Depreciation	59	
Loss on disposal of non-current assets	9	
Interest expense	14	
Operating profit before working capital changes	278	
Increase in inventory	(2)	
Increase in receivables	(8)	
Increase in payables	3	
Cash generated from operations	271	
Interest paid	(14)	
Income tax paid	(55)	
Net cash from operating activities		202
Cash flows from investing activities		
Purchase of non-current assets	(45)	
Proceeds of sale of non-current assets	6	(39)
Cash flows from financing activities		
Proceeds of issue of shares	16	
Repayment of loans	(150)	
Dividends paid	(33)	(167)
Net decrease in cash and cash equivalents		(4)
Cash and cash equivalents at 31 December 20X1		28
Cash and cash equivalents at end of period at 31 December 20X2		24

Working notes

Dividends paid

	$'000
Declared dividend at 31 December 20X1	12
Add: Interim dividend paid in the year to 31 December 20X2	21
Dividend paid during year	33

Income tax

	$'000
Balance due at 31 December 20X1	39
Add tax charge for the year to 31 December 20X2	62
	101
Less tax due at 31 December 20X2	46
Tax paid during year	55

Non-current assets – cost

	$'000
Balance at 31 December 20X1	780
Add machinery purchased	45
	825
Less balance at 31 December 20X2	(798)
Disposal in the year	27

Non-current assets – depreciation

	$'000
Balance at 31 December 20X1	112
Add: charge for the year	59
	171
Less: balance at 31 December 20X2	(159)
Depreciation on disposal	12

Receipts from sales of tangible non-current assets

	$'000
Cost (calculated above)	27
Depreciation (calculated above)	(12)
Written-down value	15
Loss on sale	(9)
Proceeds from sale	6

 ## Solution 11

IAS 18 *Revenue* requires revenue from the sale of goods to be recognised when the significant risks and rewards of ownership have been transferred, provided that the amount of revenue can be estimated reliably and it is probable that payment will be received.

It would thus seem reasonable to recognise the revenue when the goods were despatched. That would normally be the point at which the entity would lose any real rights over the asset. It would also normally be the point at which the customer would be deemed to be committed to purchasing the goods.

Recognition at an earlier stage would be misleading because the entity could decide not to despatch the goods (e.g. if they were needed for another transaction, or some doubts arose as to the customer's credit rating). Recognition at a later stage would also be misleading because the entity becomes entitled to receive payment in full long before the customer actually pays.

If the likelihood of the customer using any warranty or guarantee at a later date can be predicted and valued with any certainty, then the entity might create a provision for such costs and these could be offset against the profit. If these costs cannot be predicted in any meaningful way, then the entity would be better to recognise the profit as the selling price less the cost price and to recognise all warranty costs as and when they are incurred.

 ## Solution 12

(i) Strictly, the entity should not recognise any profits from this arrangement until the books have been sold by Bigseller Books. It would, however, be acceptable to look at the underlying substance of this transaction and treat the despatch of the books as a sale, but to create a provision for returns against any books in the customer's hands as at the year-end.

(ii) The newspaper appears to be committed to publishing the extracts and so there is nothing to stand in the way of Publisher receiving the $800,000. It would, therefore, be acceptable to treat this as a source of income.

Solution 13

Q Consultancy is a related party because a relative of a member of the board of directors owns the entity. This creates the possibility that the contract may have been awarded to Q Consultancy because of favouritism or that the report's findings could have been influenced by the consultant's wife.

H is a related party because an individual who holds more than 20 per cent of the entity's share capital is in a position to exercise significant influence over the entity. The fact that H is a major supplier has no direct relevance in itself to the entity's status as a related party.

Solution 14

(a) Nominal value of shares purchased = $1,000,000
Nominal value of fresh issue = $600,000
Premium on purchase = $100,000

	$	$
Debit 8% redeemable preference share capital	1,000,000	
Debit premium on purchase	100,000	
Credit bank		1,100,000
Debit retained earnings	500,000	
Credit premium on purchase		100,000
Credit capital redemption reserve		400,000
Debit bank	720,000	
Credit share capital		600,000
Credit share premium		120,000

R: Statement of financial position as at 31 December 20X0

	$'000	$'000
Non-current assets		4,800
Net current assets (excluding cash)	2,100	
Cash	470	
		2,570
		7,370
Ordinary shares		3,100
Share premium		2,320
Capital reserve		400
Retained earning		1,550
		7,370

(b) The capital redemption reserve exists to protect the interests of lenders. In general, share capital is intended to be a permanent investment of capital in the entity. Dividends are effectively restricted to the amount of retained profits. This means that the book value of assets should always exceed the book value of liabilities by the amount of the undistributable capital. This should mean that the entity will always be able to repay its payables in full, even if it has to dispose of its assets under duress.

Entities are permitted to repurchase their own shares. As a part of this process, they are required to transfer a sum equal to the permanent capital that is being repaid out of distributable reserves and into an undistributable capital redemption reserve. This means that the payables are no worse off than they would have been if the entity had made a dividend payment of the same amount. The repurchase may not proceed if there are insufficient distributable profits to make the transfer into capital redemption reserve. This limits the maximum reduction in capital due to share repurchase to the amount that would be permissible from dividend payments.

✅ Solution 15

(a) The arguments in favour of capitalising borrowing costs are largely related to the fact that the construction of a major non-current asset will frequently be financed by a loan which can, therefore, be seen to be directly attributable to the construction project. This means that the entity could view the costs of financing the construction to be just as much a part of the project as the costs of the labour or the building materials.

It might also be argued that those contractors who do not require progress payments will include their financing costs in the final contract price. This means that failure to capitalise finance costs when they arise will lead to inconsistency between assets.

The arguments against capitalisation include the illogical nature of the distinction between interest paid on the loan while the asset is being constructed and that paid on the same loan on the same asset once the construction phase has been completed and the asset is in use.

It can also be argued that interest is a period cost that should be treated as an expense regardless of the reason for the underlying borrowing.

IAS 23 *Borrowing Costs* requires entities to capitalise borrowing costs that are directly attributable to the acquisition, construction or production of a qualifying asset. IAS 23 does, however, require that there is consistency of treatment between assets.

(b) IAS 36 requires that the asset should be written down if its underlying value is less than book value. The underlying value is effectively what the asset is worth to the entity. The production line is worth $1.1 million if it is kept and used for manufacturing purposes or $0.9 million if it is sold. Logically, the asset will be worth more if it is kept and used and so that is the most logical basis on which to value it.

Thus, the asset has suffered an impairment in value because the books attach a value of $2.3 million to it even though it is worth only $1.1 million. It should, therefore, be written down to $1.1 million.

(c) IAS 36 defines a cash-generating unit as the smallest group of assets which generates cash that is largely independent of the entity's other cash streams. In that case, the individual engine factories are not independent cash-generating units in their own right because the output from each will be affected by the entity's production schedules for the other two factories. Presumably, the entity makes these decisions on the basis of efficient use of resources and minimisation of costs.

This means that the division as a whole is the cash-generating unit in this case.

It is necessary to have the concept of the cash-generating unit because otherwise it would be impossible to place a value on the entity's assets. For example, it would be impossible to tell how much income could be generated by a factory's fire alarm. All that the entity could tell is that it would be illegal to operate without an adequate safety system and so the value of the alarm would have to be considered in the context of the value of the factory as a whole.

 Solution 16

(a)

Hi – Statement of comprehensive income for the year ended 30 September 2003

	$'000	$'000	$'000
Revenue			9,415
Cost of sales (W1)			(4,404)
Gross profit			5,011
Other income			37
Administrative expenses (W3)		(760)	
Distribution costs		(314)	(1,074)
			3,974
Reorganisation expenses incurred (W4)		(965)	
Reorganisation provision utilised		1,010	45
			4,019
Finance cost			
Profit before tax			3,919
Income tax expense (W6)			(1,205)
Net profit for the period			2,714
Other comprehensive income:			
Available for sale investments			30
Total comprehensive income for the period			2,744

Hi – Statement of financial position at 30 September 2003

	$'000	$'000	$'000
Non-current assets			
Tangible assets	Cost	Depreciation	Net Book Value
Buildings (W2)	11,200	1,740	9,460
Equipment & fixtures (W2)	2,415	2,019	396
	13,615	3,759	9,856
Available for sale investments			522
			10,378
Current assets			
Inventory		822	
Trade receivables (W5)		807	
Cash at bank & in hand		959	
			2,588
Total assets			12,966
Equity and liabilities			
Equity			
Called up share capital			
Ordinary share capital – $1 shares, fully paid		4,000	
Share premium		2,388	
Revaluation reserve (W7)		202	
Retained earnings		3,304	

Total equity		9,894
Non-current liabilities		
10% loan notes (redeemable in 2010)	1,000	
Deferred tax	281	
Other provisions	100	
		1,381
Current liabilities		
Trade payables	396	
Other trade payables including tax (W8)	1,245	
Accrued loan note interest	50	
		1,691
		12,966

Workings

W1 – Cost of sales	$'000
Cost of goods	3,591
Add depreciation – buildings (W2)	336
– equipment (W2)	483
Gain on disposal of equipment (W2)	(6)
	4,404

W2 – Depreciation	
Buildings – cost	11,200
Depreciation for year @ 3%	366 (IS)
Depreciation b/fwd	1,404
Depreciation c/fwd	1,740 (BS)
Equipment & fixtures – cost	2,625
Less disposal	(210)
	2,415 (BS)

Depreciation for year @ 20%	483 (IS)
Depreciation b/fwd	1,741
Less: Disposal	(205)
Depreciation c/fwd	2,019 (BS)
Disposal of equipment	
Cost	210
Less depreciation	(205)
	5
Cash received	11
Gain	6

W3 – Administrative expenses	
Per trial balance	615
Provision for legal claim	100
Bad debt written off (W5)	45
	760

W4 – Reorganisation expenses	
Per trial balance	900
Accrued	65
	965

W5 – Trade receivables	
Trade receivables	852
Less bad debt written off	(45)
	807

W6 – Tax

Income tax accrued for year	1,180
Deferred tax charge for year	25
profit or loss	1,205
Provision for deferred tax, b/fwd	256
Charge for year	25 (IS)
Provision for deferred tax c/fwd	281 (BS)

W7 – Revaluation reserve

Balance b/fwd	172
Increase in available for sale investments	30
Balance c/fwd	202

W8 – Other trade payables including tax

Tax	1,180
Reorganisation costs	65
	1,245

(b)

Hi – Statement of changes in equity for the year ended 30 September 2003

	Share capital $'000	Share premium $'000	Revaluation reserve $'000	Retained earnings $'000	Total $'000
Balances 30/9/2002	3,200	788	172	1,390	5,550
Share issue	800	1,600			2,400
Total comprehensive income for period			30	2,714	2,744
Dividends				(800)	(800)
Balances 30/9/2003	4,000	2,388	202	3,304	9,894

 ## Solution 17

(a) The formula to determine the economic ordering quantity is as follows:

$$EOQ = \sqrt{\frac{2 \times C_o \times D}{C_h}}$$

C_o = Cost of placing one order
D = Annual demand
C_h = Cost of holding one unit for a year

$$EOQ = \sqrt{\frac{2 \times 100 \times 50,000}{0.40}} = 5,000 \text{ units}$$

This means that the firm will place ten orders each year and the ordering costs will be $1,000. The holding costs will also be $1,000 (0.5 × 5,000 × $0.40).

(b) The annual savings from the discount will be 50,000 units × $0.02 = $1,000

The savings in ordering costs will be (10 − 5 batches) × $100 = $500

However, the holding costs will increase to $2,000 which is calculated as (0.5 × 10,000 × 0.40).

	$
Net savings as a result of the additional discount is:	
Discount	1,000
Ordering cost	500
Holding cost	(1,000)
	500

The offer of a quantity discount should be accepted.

(c) The problems that firms face in using the EOQ formula relate to the problems of forecasting the annual demand for each item of inventory. There is always the possibility that unexpected orders will be received or sales of different products will vary unexpectedly. In order to avoid running out of inventory, many firms carry buffer inventorys as they consider that the additional holding costs are justified by having the inventory available to meet the unexpected orders.

The holding costs and the ordering costs can also be different from plan but these differences are likely to be less significant than the problems of estimating annual demand.

If the discount is taken, then only five purchases of 10,000 units will be required. This means that the average holding will double from 5,000/2 = 2,500 units to 5,000 units. The additional costs will, therefore, be 2,500 × $0.40 = $1,000.

✓ Solution 18

(a) All figures in $'000s

	No change in policy	Changes implemented
Profit from operations	1,326	1,424
Add depreciation	225	225
½ change in trade receivables	−230	+72
½ change in payables	+144	−86
Cash flow from operations	1,465	1,635
Interest paid	−54	−45
Tax paid	−283	−283
Dividends paid	−339	−339
Investing activities		
Non-current assets	−550	−550
Inventory	−275	−212
Net cash flow	−36	206
Opening balance	25	25
Closing balance	−11	231

Changes implemented

1. Profit from operations:

Revenue	=	5,200
Less discounts	=	−52
CoS (3,224 − 225) × 95% + 225	=	−3,074
Operating expenses (unchanged)	=	−650
		1,424

2. Decrease in trade receivables:

$520 − [($2,600/365 × 53) + ($2,600/365 × 10)] = 72

Decrease in trade payables:

[$320 − ($2,849/365 × 30)] = 86

3. Inventory:

[$350 − (625 × 90%)] = 212

(b) **Report**

To: Ms Smith
From: Assistant
Subject: Proposed working capital policy changes

To include:

- Comment that cash flow is improved by almost a quarter of a million pounds if the proposed changes are made.
- Problems appear to have arisen because credit and inventory control have not been adequate for increased levels of revenue.
- Liquidity: current ratio was 0.95:1 (all current assets to trade and other payables), will be around 1.2:1 under both options. Perversely, ratio looks to improve even if the entity takes no action and causes an overdraft. This is because of high trade receivables and inventory levels. Moral: high current assets do not mean high cash. Cash ratio perhaps a better measure.
- Trade receivables' days last year was 45, forecast to rise to 53 on current policies despite 'official' terms being 30. Entity could perhaps look to improve its credit control before offering discounts.
- Payables' days were 46, forecast to rise to 52. Are discounts being ignored? Are relationships with suppliers being threatened?*
- Dramatic increase in inventory levels forecast: 50 days last year, 71 days forecast this year. If change implemented, inventory will still be 67 days.*
- Operating profit percentage forecast to fall to 25.5 per cent from 28.1 per cent if no changes made. Percentage will fall to 27.4 per cent if changes implemented; a fall probably acceptable if cash flow improved and overdraft interest saved.
- Non-financial factors include relationships with customers and suppliers.
- Other financial factors, is increase in revenue sustainable?

* Using cost of sales figures including depreciation.

Solution 19

Report

To:	Financial manager
From:	Assistant financial manager
Subject:	Credit taken from suppliers
Date:	

(i) You asked me to compare the terms of trade imposed by three suppliers. Say, for illustration, that purchases amount to $1,000 per 30 days, that is, $12,200 p.a.

- *Supplier A.* If payment is late every period, this would cost $20 for every $1,000 owed. If the entity delays payment for 60 days beyond the due date, this is $365 \div 60 \times \$20 = \$122$, or 12.2 per cent.
- *Supplier B.* The formula is $(1 + r)^p - 1$, where p is the number of 30-day delayed payment periods. There are 12.2 30-day periods in 365 days, therefore $(1 + 0.02)^{12.2} - 1 = 27.3$ per cent on an annualised basis.

    An alternative approach would use an interest charge of 2 per cent compounded for two 30-day periods = 24.6 per cent.
- *Supplier C.* If the discount is not taken, the cost of the lost discount is $365 \div 20 = 18.25$ times, approximately 36 per cent or 42 per cent if compounded.

    If MP ignores the discount and also pays late, then the annualised cost is 10 per cent as given in the question, plus the opportunity cost of the lost discount.

(ii) Trade credit is often talked of as being 'free' credit. Of course, it is not free, as the financing costs of the supplier are built into the cost of goods and services. Factors to consider are:

- Suppliers' goodwill – essential if the entity operates 'just-in-time' systems.
- Entity image – does the firm want a reputation as a poor payer or, worse, as having financial difficulties that might have the result of suppliers increasing their prices to cover perceived risk of default?
- Effect on credit rating by agencies, which might raise the cost of all borrowing.
- Buying power of the entity and its relative position in the industry.
- Industry norms.
- The cost of lost discounts, which can be substantial.
- Suppliers' bargaining position. Very few entities are sole suppliers of anything, but the fewer suppliers there are, the more strength they have to refuse to supply slow payers.

(iii) An advantage of having a common policy is that the entity can have one payment policy covering all suppliers, which might reduce administrative costs and reduce errors.

Disadvantages are that some suppliers may refuse to supply on MP 's terms, which reduces the number of competitive quotes that the entity may need to obtain. If the terms are more onerous than the supplier is accustomed to, it might also result in increased costs although, clearly, the costs of credit would have to be seen alongside the increased cost of goods and services.

Summary

MP already appears to have a partially common policy, in that we insist on 30 days' credit. The entity should consider whether this is in their best interests, given the evidence of lost discounts. Bank overdraft finance may be cheaper than forgoing discounts. The entity could also approach suppliers who do not give discounts at present, to enquire if they will allow better terms for earlier payment.

I hope that you find the above sufficient for your needs. If I can be of further help, please let me know.

 Solution 20

Cash Budget for the three month period May to July 2005

	May $'000	*June* $'000	*July* $'000
Cash receipts			
Cash sales	35	40	40
Credit sales receipts (working 1)	101	104	111
Total receipts	136	144	151
Credit purchase payments (working 3)	50	54	55
Expenses paid	50	50	50
Equipment purchase paid	0	0	250
Total payments	100	104	355
Net cash movement in month	36	40	(204)
Balance b/f	96	132	172
Balance c/f	132	172	(32)

Workings

W1 – Credit sales – receipts

	Total $'000	May $'000	June $'000	July $'000
Feb. sales	100	5		
Mar. sales	100	30	5	
Apr. sales	110	66	33	6
May sales	110		66	33
June sales	120			72
Totals		101	104	111

W2 – Credit purchases – payments

	Total $'000	May $'000	June $'000	July $'000
Mar	50	15		
Apr	50	35	15	
May	55		39	16
June	55			39
Totals		50	54	55

 # Solution 21

To:　　The Board, SF
From:　Consultant
Re:　　Review of cash budget

I have reviewed the cash budget for the year. The closing balance of cash at the bank is $50,000 lower than at the beginning of the year. Between August and November the deficit is in excess of the overdraft facility that the bank is willing to make available. The following actions might be considered to improve the budgeted cash flow for the year.

(a) *Trade receivables.* SF could attempt to improve the collection period from trade receivables. The normal credit period for the industry is not known, but the existing average credit period of two months does not seem excessive. A selective tightening of credit control (including collection) procedures might be possible. Offering cash discounts might speed up some collections, but could prove an expensive method of improving cash flow. Factoring of debts would be another possibility. The cost of the factoring service will be offset in part by savings from the outsourcing of the credit control and sales ledger departments and potential savings in bad debts.

(b) *Investment.* The amount invested must be significant, given a dividend receivable of $10,000. It might be possible to dispose of part of this investment. Assuming a return on the investment of 5 per cent, the investment itself may be worth as much as $200,000. Such action should be taken only if all other possibilities have failed, as this action would remove the opportunity to benefit from the long-term growth of the investment. The nature of the investment is also important, as it may have strategic business links.

(c) *Payables.* The entity is already taking up to 90 days' credit, so the scope for delaying payments to payables further must be limited. It might be possible to take temporary longer credit from selected suppliers by arrangement. The build-up of inventory should be investigated; it may be in anticipation of a future increase in sales. The business is seasonal, and there may be scope for altering the production pattern. This in turn may lead to changes in the payment pattern for materials, wages and other operating expenses.

(d) *Wages and salaries.* While not suggesting any actions to improve cash flow, it should be recognised that, if wages are paid weekly, the overdraft at the end of the month understates the maximum position. For instance, the overdraft of $94,000 at the end of October will continue to rise by three weekly wage payments before any cash is received from customers at the end of November. This assumes that customer receipts are not spread over the month. In this case, it would help if employees could be persuaded to move to a monthly payment basis.

(e) *Payments for non-current assets.* It may be possible to delay or cancel the purchase of office furniture if it is considered non-essential, although the amount is relatively small and so will have little impact on the cash-flow problems. The progress payment on the building extension is likely to be a commitment that cannot be avoided. The purchase of the car could perhaps be deferred if it is a replacement, as it may not be essential at the time scheduled. The new equipment should be investigated to establish whether it is an essential replacement, or whether it is perhaps in anticipation of an expansion of the business; however, delaying payment by 1 or 2 months would not alter the forecast overdraft position. If the equipment must be replaced, consideration may be given to leasing, which would ease the cash-flow problems.

(f) *Dividend.* The payment of the dividend may be forgone, which will significantly help the cash-flow problems. It is recognised, however, that the dividend may be an important source of income to some of the shareholders. Alternatively, there may be scope to delay payment of the dividend.

(g) *Taxation.* Corporation tax would be payable 9 months after the entity's year end. It would be possible to defer payment, subject to agreement from the revenue authorities. There would be an interest charge, but it might be lower than the bank's interest charge.

(h) *Long-term capital.* It appears that no new equity investment is being made to cover the proposed capital expenditure. Consideration should therefore be given urgently by the directors to increasing the permanent capital of SF. If the existing shareholders are unable, or unwilling, to provide additional finance, the directors could explore the possibility of attracting new shareholders. External equity may be provided by a venture capital provider, or a 'business angel'. This would possibly involve the new equity providers taking a substantial stake in the business. The budgeted profit or loss and statement of financial position have not been provided, but the income tax bill of $30,000 would suggest a reasonably profitable business that should help to attract investors.

Additional points

- It should also be recognised that the cash budget does not allow for the interest charged on the overdraft by the bank, which itself will increase the overdraft balance, and will usually be applied each quarter.
- SF's cash balance could potentially be improved by investing cash surpluses identified in the early part of the year for the short term. The possible opportunities may be restricted by the amount of surplus cash available and the length of time the cash is available, but may include bank deposits, gilts close to redemption and bills of exchange.

Signed: Consultant

Solution 22

Working capital management

(a) Factoring is a method of raising finance from trade receivables, whereby invoices are sold to a factoring entity.

The main services associated with entities offering this finance are:

- provision of finance, often between 75 per cent and 85 per cent of approved debts from the moment the goods or services are invoiced;
- sales ledger administration covering credit checking, invoicing and collection. In effect, the sales ledger function is outsourced;
- bad-debt insurance to cover the firm in the event of default upon an invoice or invoices;
- the provision for a confidentiality agreement to prevent the arrangement being apparent to customers and others.

(b)

Annual sales $400,000 \times 12 = \$4,800,000$

Annual net cost of factoring	$
Service fee: $4,800,000 \times 2\%$	96,000
Interest charge:	
($4,800,000 \times 75\% \times 10\% \times 40/365$)	39,452
Total annual cost	135,452
Less administration savings ($5,000 \times 12$)	60,000
Net cost	75,452

(c) Using compound interest:

$V = X(1 + r)^n$, $400 = 392(1 + r)^1$, $1.0204 = 1 + r$,

$r = 2.04\%$ for a 30 day period (40 days − 10 days)

$(1 + \text{annual rate}) = (1 + \text{periodic rate})^{\text{number of periods in year}}$

$(1 + \text{annual rate}) = (1.0204)^{12.17} = 1.2786$

$\therefore$ True cost of cash discount = 27.9%.

(d) The cost of offering the cash discount is high (27.9 per cent), particularly compared with the cost of a bank overdraft, and may not be the most cost-effective way of improving cash flow from trade receivables. Discounts are customary in some industries, and may have to be offered as part of the entity's overall marketing mix. However, the impact of offering discounts is difficult to access because not all customers will take advantage of the discount. On the other hand, some customers may take the discount *and* the normal credit period, which then creates the problem of having to chase the customer for a relatively small amount.

Factoring of debts should eliminate the need for a sales ledger department, but may lead to a loss of direct contact with the customer. Factoring will improve the certainty of the cash flows from customers. The factor will also be able to assess the credit rating of each customer. Although the image is changing, factoring has traditionally been seen as lending in the last resort.

While both proposals are aimed at improving cash flow, factoring will bring immediate cash on per cent of sales, while discounts will still involve a ten-day delay before cash is received.

Solution 23

(a)

$$\left(\frac{100}{97}\right)^{365/80} - 1 = 14.9\%$$

This is a higher rate of interest than the 12% each year charged by the bank, but there are some benefits of offering a cash discount compared to bank finance:

- Gearing is not increased as with bank finance. Thus, the true cost of bank finance is not just 12% each year, but also the increase in the required rate of return by owners to compensate them for increased financial risk as a result of increased gearing.
- Bank finance may involve additional conditions such as more security in the form of fixed and/or floating charges and perhaps more debt covenants. These are likely to result in reduced financial flexibility for DF.
- Discounts are based upon current sales and future cash flows whereas bank finance may, at least in part, be constrained by historic performance and historic assets.

There are, however, a number of problems with offering a cash discount:

- Other customers may require the same credit terms as those offered to FF;
- The annual equivalent rate of interest is quite high at 14.9%;
- The high cost of offering a discount may be worthwhile in overcoming initial liquidity difficulties arising from setting up this contract. However, once established, the discount may be difficult to withdraw when liquidity improves, without the loss of customer goodwill;
- The fact that a discount is offered does not mean it will be accepted. Thus, this form of finance is dependent upon FF taking up the discount at the terms being offered;
- It builds in the norm of a three-month settlement period, which might otherwise be subject to future negotiation.

(b)
Report

To:	The Wong Family	*From*:	Management Accountant
Subject:	Financing of additional current assets from FF contract	*Date*:	20 November 2001

The financing of current assets
Individual current assets such as inventory or trade receivables are temporary and should be realised into cash in the short term. Current assets as a pool, however, are, at least in part, permanent, as some are always needed. In the context of the FF contract, the total additional current assets needed are likely to have a permanent element, so long as the contract continues. Also, however, given that sales are expected to fluctuate from month to month, part of the current assets are likely to fluctuate from month to month. This will happen automatically with trade receivables and to the extent that such fluctuations are predictable, it will also happen with inventory.

A simple conclusion is, therefore, that the permanent element of current assets could be financed with long-term finance and the fluctuating element with short-term finance. This conclusion of time dependence is, however, subject to a range of other considerations.

In addition, to some extent, the incremental current assets required for the FF contract are self-financing, in that, the additional sales will be partially matched by increased purchases for which credit terms are likely to be available from suppliers. These additional payables will go some way toward off-setting additional trade receivables.

It should also be noted that the financing of incremental inventory needs to be considered in light of the existing inventory policy. Assuming that existing customers are supplied with similar goods to FF, the inventory holding policy needs to be considered as a whole, rather than separately for FF sales and other sales. In particular, if sales volumes double, this does not mean that inventory needs to double. The Economic Order Quantity model would predict that inventory should increase in square root proportion to sales (that is by 41% when sales double). This, of course, depends upon the assumptions of the model holding and in particular the predictability of demand.

Predicting current asset requirements is vital in determining the necessary finance; thus management of working capital is an issue which needs to be considered simultaneously with financing.

Bank loan

The need for financing additional permanent (or hard core) current assets may be most appropriate to a medium-term loan in terms of matching the timing. Such a loan would reduce risk and uncertainty in the short term if the conditions are met. Interest rates may also be fixed giving additional certainty.

Disadvantages of a loan include:

- It is likely to come with additional conditions of further security and covenants;
- It will increase gearing and may increase the required return on equity due to increased financial risk; thus the real cost would be above 12% each year;
- If existing gearing is high, it may place a significant strain on the entity's liquidity to the extent that bankruptcy may become a possibility, particularly as additional equity capital appears to be unavailable in a liquidity crises.

Overdraft

An overdraft must be repaid on demand and thus there are risks if it becomes part of permanent financing, or could not be repaid quickly from other sources of immediately available finance.

An overdraft is, thus, a flexible form of financing which may be most appropriate for financing the fluctuating element of current assets, as interest will only be paid when the account is overdrawn.

It is also likely that the necessary finance will be greater in the early months of the contract, as there will be no cash coming in for the first 3 months, but inventory needs to be established and payables (with terms of less than 90 days) will need to be paid. Thereafter, profitable trading from the contract should reduce the need for financing. As a result, an overdraft may be appropriate for temporary front-end finance needs.

An overdraft does not always come into gearing calculations, but if it is significant and rolls over into the long term, it would have a similar effect to a loan in terms of financial risk. Also, similar security and covenants may be required. The question of the overdraft facility extended by the bank needs to be considered. If DF is close to this facility, it may be appropriate to use other means to finance the increase in current assets (see below) to leave the maximum financing flexibility with the remaining available overdraft.

Debt factoring

Debt factoring may be defined as:

'The sale of debts to a third party (the factor) at a discount, in return for prompt cash.'
The nature of the service is likely to vary, but typically:

- an advance of about 80% of the invoice value is made immediately by the factor;
- the balance, less an interest charge (perhaps 3% over the base rate), is paid when the customer settles the account;
- the factor may take responsibility for managing the sales ledger for an additional fee (perhaps 2% of sales);
- factoring may be offered with or without recourse. With recourse is where the client entity takes the risk of bad debts. Without recourse is where the factor takes the bad debt risk. A further charge would be made for non-recourse debt factoring.

The advantages of debt factoring include:

- cash is received immediately without security, covenants or increased gearing;
- the implied interest rates tend to be similar to other forms of finance as the service is offered in a competitive market;
- debt factors have economies of scale and specialist expertise in collecting debts and they may thus be more efficient than DF in this context;
- costs of maintaining the sales ledger are largely saved although some records are needed as a control over the factoring entity;
- bank finance tends to be based, in part at least, on historic sales and profits. Factoring is based upon current sales and profits. This tends to make more finance available when the business is growing, as is the case with DF.

Problems and other considerations relating to factoring for DF include:

- it needs to be decided whether a factoring service is to be used for all trade receivables, only FF or only non-FF customers;
- FF, and indeed other customers, may lose confidence in DF's continued solvency if they discover that a debt factor is being used;
- non-recourse finance will depend upon an estimate of FF's creditworthiness relative to the charges the factor is likely to make.

Invoice discounting

Invoice discounting is the sale of specific trade debts to a third party (the provider of the discounting service). It shares many of the same advantages and problems as debt factoring. The key distinguishing features are that:

- it tends not to involve the taking over of the administration of the sales ledger;
- it relates to specific invoices selectively sold by the client entity;
- it can be confidential (that is confidential invoice discounting) whereby the customer remains unaware of the sale of the debt and the involvement of a third party.

Solution 24

(a)

	$'000	$'000
Opening balance (1/12/2002)		175
December		
+ 700 × 0.7	490	
− 300 × 0.3	−90	
		400
January		−900
Closing balance (31/1/2003)		−325

The expected balance at 31 January is an overdraft of $325,000. This, however, provides a poor basis for planning, as this particular outcome will not occur.

This is because, based on the probabilities provided, there will either be cash inflow of $700,000 in December or a cash outflow of $300,000. The mean expected value would only be relevant if the event could be repeated a significant number of times. The basis of planning should thus be for each of the two possible outcomes.

Examiner's note

The above calculations exclude interest paid/received. However, these could be included [see calculations to requirement (b)], but the overall conclusions with respect to the use of the mean expected value would be unchanged.

(b)

Memorandum

To:	The Board	*From*:	Treasury assistant
Subject:	Investment of short term cash balances	*Date*:	19 November 2002

Two possibilities arise with respect to trading in December:

- Favourable conditions (70% probability)
- Rival chain discounts (30% probability)

The impact on operating cash flows is as follows:

	Favourable	*Rival discounts*
	$'000	$'000
Opening balance (1/12/2002)	175	175
December	700	−300
January	−900	−900
Closing balance (31/1/2003)	−25	−1,025

In either case there is no surplus cash at the end of January, so there is no point investing beyond 2 months (that is 31 January 2003).

The choices are thus:

Option 1. Invest $175,000 for 1 month. Then $875,000 (plus interest on the $175,000 initial investment) for a further month if conditions are favourable, or borrow $125,000 (less interest on the $175,000 initial investment) in the second month if conditions are unfavourable.

Option 2. Invest $175,000 for 2 months. Then a further $700,000 for a further month if conditions are favourable and borrow $300,000 in the second month if conditions are unfavourable.

Unfortunately, under *Option 2,* if conditions are unfavourable, then the initial investment will need to be financed by overdraft in the second month at an annualised rate of 10% as opposed to the amount earned of 6%.

Specifically, the interest rates are:

One month deposit	$(1.05)^{1/12} - 1 = 0.004074$	
Two month deposit	$(1.06)^{2/12} - 1 = 0.009759$	

One month overdraft $(1.10)^{1/12} - 1 = 0.007974$

Option 1

		$
Invest $175,000 for 1 month	$(0.004074 \times 175,000)$	713

Then either:

(1) invest $875,713 for 1 month $(0.004074 \times 875,713) \times 70\%$	2,497
(2) overdraft of $124,287 1 month $(0.007974 \times 124,287) \times 30\%$	−297
	2,913

Option 2

		$
Invest $175,000 for 2 months	$(0.009759 \times 175,000)$	1,708

Then either:

(1) $700,000 for 1 month $(0.004074 \times 700,000) \times 70\%$	1,996
(2) overdraft of $300,00 for 1 month $(0.007974 \times 300,000) \times 30\%$	−717
	2,987

Before a final decision can be taken, however, a number of other factors should be considered. Expected values ignore risk. Thus, in *Option 2,* there is a significant loss due to overdraft interest if trading is unfavourable in December. While only having a 30% probability, this may be regarded as risking additional financial cost at a time of high operating losses.

Transactions costs would reduce the benefit of both options, as in each case there are two deposits.

The scale of the existing overdraft needs to be considered. This is particularly the case if the entity is nearing its overdraft facility. This would favour *Option 1* where the deposit maturing could be used to reduce the overdraft necessary in January 2003.

(c) The Miller–Orr model assumes that cash flows are entirely unpredictable. This is consistent with the uncertainty that appears to exist for HRD after January 2003.

The model sets lower and upper bounds for the cash balance.

When cash falls to the lower level, investments are sold to return cash to a predetermined level, called the return point.

When cash balances rise to the upper level, the treasurer will buy short-term investments to return cash down to the return point.

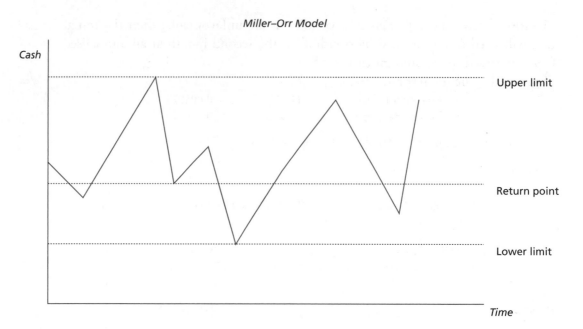

Miller–Orr Model

The lower limit is set by management. The return point and the upper limit are then set by the model based on the formula for the spread between the upper and lower limits.

$$3 \times \left[\frac{3/4 \times \text{transaction costs} \times \text{variance of daily cashflows}}{\text{Interest rate}} \right]^{1/3}$$

Thus, if variability of cash flows increase so does the spread. Variations can, however, take into account seasonality (for example, for HRD's Ltd's Christmas or Holiday trade peaks) different accounts, lead times and so on.

There are, however, a number of problems in applying the Miller–Orr model to HRD:

- The model assumes cash flows are random whereas there appears to be some predictability in HRD's cash movements. Some costs are known. Also, even sales can be estimated, though only with probabilities attached.
- The difficult trading conditions appear to imply that, as with many entities, a hard core overdraft will be maintained for much of the year, leaving no available surplus cash balances to implement the model.

☑ Solution 25

The International Accounting Standards Board (IASB) is responsible for devising and issuing international financial reporting standards (IFRS). To issue an IFRS, the IASB must have eight of the 14 members of the Board voting in favour.

The process for the development of an international standard involves the following:

- During the early stages of a project, IASB may establish an Advisory Committee to advise on the issues arising in the project. Consultation with this committee and the Standards Advisory Council occurs throughout the project.
- IASB may develop and publish a *Discussion Document* for public comment.
- Following the receipt and review of comments on the discussion document, IASB develops and publishes an *Exposure Draft* for public comment.

- Following the receipt and review of comments on the exposure draft, the IASB may hold a public hearing or carry out field tests.
- An *International Financial Reporting Standard* is issued along with any dissenting view expressed by an IASB member and a *Basis of Conclusions* to explain how the IASB reached its conclusions.

 Solution 26

(i) **Initial recognition** – on purchase the attributable costs will be recognised.

Delivery vehicles recognised at $29,550 ($9,850 × 3).

Computers – the attributable cost is the cost of acquiring and getting the system ready for use or enabling it to become functional. This can include the initial adaptations but does not include the in-house programmers as the work was done at a later stage and is regarded as an additional cost incurred. For any additional cost to be capitalised, it must enhance or improve the asset beyond its original specification. The in-house programmers were checking and fixing the software to get it up to its original specification, not enhancing beyond the original specification.

Subsequently remeasured – the vehicles are subsequently remeasured when they are revalued on 31 October 2003.

The computer system has no subsequent remeasurement.

Derecognised – the vehicles are derecognised when they are traded in as E Ltd no longer has access to the risks and rewards of ownership. On derecognition, the value received is deducted from their carrying value to calculate the loss on disposal. The computers are still in use and have not been derecognised.

(ii) *IAS 16 Property, Plant and Equipment requires* the cost of the tangible non-current assets to be recognised. Cost includes delivery charge and is net of any trade discount. Annual running costs such as insurance are revenue expenditure and are charged to the profit or loss.

IAS 16 allows tangible non-current assets to be revalued; any increase in value is credited to revaluation reserve.

Statement of financial position (extract) as at 31 October 2003

	$
Tangible non-current assets	
Delivery vehicles at valuation (W1)	27,703
Computers (W2)	8,550
Provision for depreciation – computers (W2)	2,138
Revaluation reserve (W1)	5,541

(*Note*: VAT would be reclaimed before the year end so does not appear in the year-end balances)

Statement of comprehensive income (extract) for the year ended 31 October 2003

	$
Depreciation – delivery vehicles (W1)	7,388
Depreciation – computers (W2)	2,138
Adjusting software	3,000
Insurance – delivery vehicles	2,100

Statement of financial position (extract) as at 31 October 2004

	$
Tangible non-current assets	
Delivery vehicles at valuation (18,000 × 3)	54,000
Computers	8,550
Provision for depreciation – delivery vehicles	7,875
(7/12 × 54,000 × 25%)	
Depreciation – computers	2,138
(As the revaluation is realised on disposal of the vehicles it can be transferred to the profit or loss)	
Revaluation reserve	5,541

Statement of comprehensive income (extract) for the year ended 31 October 2004

	$
Depreciation – delivery vehicles	7,875
Gain on disposal of small delivery vehicles	(2,183)
Depreciation computers	2,138

Workings	$
W1	
Delivery vehicles – cost	29,550
Depreciation for year – 25%	7,388
	22,162
Gain on revaluation	5,541
31 October 2003 Revalue to 125% of balance	27,703
Less 5 months depreciation	2,886
1 April 2004 Trade in ($9,000 × 3)	27,000
Gain on disposal	2,183

W2	
Computers at cost	$
Hardware	5,000
Software	950
Adaptation	2,600
Total cost	8,550
Depreciation	2,138

✓ **Solution 27**

M – Statement of comprehensive income for the year ended 30 September 20X2

	Notes	$m	$m
Revenue			3,970
Cost of sales			(1,367)
Gross profit			1,603
Distribution costs		(148)	
Administrative expenses		(64)	
			(212)
Profit from operations	1		1,391
Finance cost			(72)
Profit before taxation			1,319
Income tax expense	3		(69)
Profit after taxation			1,250
Other comprehensive income			0
Total comprehensive income for the period			1,250

M – Statement of financial position at 30 September 20X2

	Notes	$m	$m
Assets			
Non-current assets			
Property, plant and equipment	6		3,908
Current assets			
Inventories		38	
Trade receivables		980	
Cash and cash equivalents		98	
			1,116
Total assets			5,024
Equity and liabilities			
Equity			
Share capital	9		600
Retained earnings	5		1,932
Total equity			2,532
Non-current liabilities			
Interest bearing borrowings		1,618	
Deferred tax	7	277	
Cost of sales provision	8	300	
			2,195
Current liabilities			
Trade payables		27	
Taxation		120	
Dividend		150	
			297
Total equity and liabilities			5,024

Notes

1. *Operating profit*

   Operating profit was arrived at after charging:

	$m
Depreciation	207

2. *Related party*

   During the year ended 30 September 20X2, $43 million of goods were purchased from Seller. $3 million was owed to Seller at 30 September 20X2. Seller is owned by G, a member of M's board.

3. *Income tax expense*

	$m
Charge for year	120
Overprovision brought forward	(37)
	83
Decrease in deferred tax	(14)
	69

4. *Dividends*

	$m
Interim paid	300
Final declared	150
	450

5. *Retained earnings*

Retained profit for the financial year	1,250
Less dividends	(450)
Balance brought forward	1,132
Balance carried forward	1,932

6.

Property, plant and equipment	Property $m	Plant and machinery $m	Total $m
Cost or valuation			
At 30 September 20X1	4,456	759	5,215
Additions	0	160	160
Disposals	0	(125)	(125)
At 30 September 20X2	4,456	794	5,250
Depreciation			
At 30 September 20X1	811	402	1,213
Disposals	0	(78)	(78)
Charge for year	89	118	207
At 30 September 20X2	900	442	1,342
Net book value			
At 30 September 20X2	3,556	352	3,908
At 30 September 20X1	3,645	357	4,002

7. *Deferred tax*

	$m
Balance at 30 September 20X1	291
Decrease for year	(14)
Balance at 30 September 20X2	277

8. *Share capital*

	Number	$m
Authorised Ordinary Share of $1	800 million	800
Issued and fully paid Ordinary Share of $1	600 million	600

Workings

W1 – Closing inventory

	Purchase prize $m	Attributable production overheads $m	Total relevant cost $m	Net realizable value $m	Lower of cost and net realizable value $m
Current inventory	26	7	33	51	33
Obsolete inventory	6	2	8	5	5
Total					38
Adjustment (45 – 38)					7

Cost of sales	$m
Trial balance	1,142
Inventory adjustment (45 – 38)	7
Loss on disposal	11
Depreciation – plant	118
Depreciation – premises	89
	1,367

Deferred tax	$m
NBV of assets	3,908
Tax wdv	2,985
Timing difference	923
× 30%	277
Decrease (291 – 277)	14

(b) It is only appropriate to recognise a profit on the transaction if there has been an increase in M's net assets. The enterprise does have an order from the customer, but this is not binding. The fact that the sale can be cancelled at any time means that the enterprise does not have any real 'rights' to economic benefits. It is, therefore, misleading to treat the transaction as a sale.

The transaction cannot be treated as a sale because of the agreement that the order can be cancelled without penalty. Even if it is likely that the customer will buy the goods in question, there has not been a past transaction or event that creates rights or access to economic benefits. Otherwise, this logic would permit the enterprise to recognise all anticipated sales to this customer, not merely those for the forthcoming year and for all customers.

The lack of commercial logic underlying the exchange of documents in this transaction tends to suggest that there was an ulterior motive behind it.

Solution 28

Statement of comprehensive income of AZ for the year ended 31 March 20X3

	$'000	$,000	$'000
Revenue			124,900
Cost of sales (W1)			99,750
Gross Profit			25,150
Distribution costs (W3)		9,573	
Administration expenses (W2)		15,942	
Other operating expenses		121	25,636
Profit from operations			(486)
Finance cost		(1,278)	
Income from other fixed asset investments		1,200	(78)
Profit before tax			(564)
Income tax expense (W4)			(191)
Net loss for the period			(755)
Other comprehensive income			0
Total comprehensive income for the period			(755)

Statement of Changes in Equity of AZ for the year ended 31 March 20X3

	Share Capital	Share Premium	Revaluation Reserve	Accumulated Profits	Total Equity
Balance at 31 March 20X2	19,000	0	3,125	11,444	33,569
Issue of Shares	1,000	500			1,500
Share issue costs		(70)			(70)
Total comprehensive income for the period				(755)	(755)
Dividends				(1,000)	(1,000)
Balance at 31 March 20X3	20,000	430	3,125	9,689	33,244

	$'000	$'000	$'000
Statement of financial position of AZ as at 31 March 20X3			
Non-current Assets	*Cost*	*Depreciation*	*Net Book Value*
Property, plant and equipment	34,035	14,296	19,729
Investments			24,000
Current Assets			
Inventory		5,165	
Trade receivables		9,433	
Cash at bank & in hand		2,250	
			16,848
			60,577
Equity and Liability			
Equity			
Called up share capital		20,000	
Share premium account		430	
Revaluation reserve		3,125	
Accumulated profits		9,689	
			33,244
Non-current liabilities			
7% Loan notes (redeemable 20X7)		18,250	
Deferred tax		149	
Other provisions		25	18,424
			51,668
Current liabilities			
Trade payables		8,120	
Other Trade payables including tax		150	
Accruals and deferred income		639	8,909
			60,577

Workings (all figures in $'000)

W1 – Cost of sale

Opening Inventory		4,852
Cost of goods manufactured in year		94,000
	–	98,852
Less closing Inventory	(5,180)	
Less Inventory write-off (w7)	15	(5,165)
		93,687
Add depreciation – plant and equipment		6,063
		99,750

Depreciation

Plant and equipment, cost	30,315
Depreciation for year @ 20%	6,063 (IS)
Depreciation b/f	6,060
Depreciation c/f	12,123 (BS)

W2 – Administration Expenses

Per trial balance	16,020
Provision for legal claim	25
Reduction in provision for bad debts (W6)	(103)
	15,942

W3 – Distribution expenses

Per trial balance	9,060
Depreciation vehicles	513
	9,573

Depreciation

Vehicles, cost	3,720
Depreciation b/f	1,670
	2,050
Depreciation for year @ 25%	513 (IS)
Depreciation b/f	1,670
Depreciation c/f	2,183 (B/S)

W4 – Tax

Profit & loss account

Corporation tax b/f	30
Accrued for year	150 (B/S)
	180
Deferred tax charge for year	11
	191 (IS)
Deferred tax, b/f	138
Charge for Year	11
Provision for deferred tax c/f	149 (B/S)

W5 – Dividends and interest paid

Dividends paid

Ordinary dividend 0.05 × 20,000,000 shares=	1,000 (SCE)
7% interest on Loan notes	1,278 (IS)
Paid	639
Accrued interest	639 (B/S)

W6 – Trade receivables	9,930
Provision to be 5%	497
Current provision	600
Credit to administration	(103)

Statement of financial position Trade receivables
9,930 − 497 = 9,433

W7 – Inventory Adjustment

Realisable value	55
Less additional cost	20
Net realisable value	35
Cost	50
Inventory write off	15

☑ Solution 29

a) Note – Tangible non-current assets

	Land	Buildings	Machinery & equipment	Total
Cost/valuation	$'000	$'000	$'000	$'000
Cost/valuation balance b/f	1,500	2,500	1,706	5,706
Disposals	(750)	(400)	(462)	1,612
Cost/valuation balance c/f	750	2,100	1,244	4,094

Accumulated depreciation

Balance brought forward		860	415	1,275
Disposals		(220)	(195)	(415)
Charge for the year		105*	256*	361
Balance carried forward		745	476	1,221
Net book value at 30 September 20X4	750	1,355	768	2,873
Net book value at 30 September 20X3	1,500	1,640	1,291	4,431

*Depreciation charge for the year:
Buildings: 2,100 × 5% = 105
Machinery & equipment: 1,244 − (415 − 195) = 1,024 × 25% = 256

Statement of comprehensive income of ZZ for the year ended 30 September 20X4

	$'000 Continuing operations	$'000 Discontinuing operations	$'000 Total
Continuing operations:			
Revenue		1,260	
Cost of sales (W1)		874	
Gross Profit			386
Distribution costs		(92)	
Administraive expenses		(96)	
			198
Finance cost (W3)		0	
Profit on ordinary activities before taxation	198		
Income tax expense (W5)		(88)	
Profit for the year		110	
Discontinued operations:			
Profit for the year after tax (W10)		366	
Profit for the year		476	
Other comprehensive income	0		
Total comprehensive income	476		

Statement of financial position of ZZ as at 30 September 20X4

	$'000	$'000 Net Book Value	$'000
Non-current assets			
Tangible			
Land		750	
Buildings		1,355	
Machinery & equipment		768	
			2,873
Current Assets			
Inventory		210	
Trade receivables		140	
Cash at bank & in hand (W7)		462	
			812
			3,685
Equity and liabilities			
Equity			
Share capital			1,500
Revaluation reserve (W9)			450
Retained earnings (W8)			1,362
Total equity			3,312

Non-current liabilities		
Deferred tax		170
Current liabilities		
Trade payables	(90)	
Income tax	(113)	203
Total liabilities		373
Total equity and liabilities		3,685

Workings

W1 – Cost of sales – A product range

Trial balance	513
Depreciation	361
	874

W2 – Disposal of non-current assets

Brand name	197	
Less amortised	(138)	59
Revalued land		750
Buildings	400	
Less depreciation	(220)	180
Equipment	462	
Less depreciation	(195)	267
Carrying value of assets		1,256
Less proceeds		2,050
Gain on disposal		794

W3 – Finance cost

Interest charge for year:	
Trial balance	130
Accrued	130
	260

W4 – Loan redemption

Trial balance	2,600
Accrued interest	130
	2,730
Cash	2,730

W5 – Taxation

Accrued for year	113
Last years balance	20
Reduced deferred tax provision	(33)
Tax charge for the year	100

W6 – Deferred tax

Balance b/f	203
Balance c/f	170
Reduction	33

W7 – Bank

Trial balance	3,192
Redemption of loan	2,730
Balance	462

W8 – Retained earnings

Balance b/f	436
Revaluation reserve – realised on disposal	450
Profit for the year	476
	1,362

W9 – Revaluation reserve

Balance per trial balance	900
Less realised on disposal	450
	450

W10 – Discontinued operations $'000

Revenue	42	
Cost of sales (W1)	127	
Gross Profit		(85)
Distribution costs	(12)	
Administrative expenses	(34)	
Profit from operations	(131)	
Gain on sale of non-current assets (W2)	794	
Closure costs	(125)	
Less provision brought forward	100	
		638
Finance cost (W3)	(260)	
Profit before taxation	576	
Income tax expense (W5)	(12)	
Profit for the year	366	

✅ Solution 30

(a) C – Notes to the accounts for the year ended 31 March 20X4

(i)

Property, plant and equipment
Cost/Valuation

	Land $'000	Buildings $'000	Plant & machinery $'000	Under constr $'000	Totals $'000
Balance 1 April X3	3,186	1,663	1,108	53	6,010
Revaluation of assets	450				450
Disposal of machinery	(400)				(400)
Interest on loan				24	24
Transfers			550	(550)	0
New Purchases (balance)	.	1,400	930	473	2,803
Balance 31 March X4	3,636	3,063	2,188	0	8,887
Depreciation					
Balance 1 April 20X3		416	671		1,087
Disposal of plant & machinery			(380)		(380)
Depreciation for year		77*	379**		456
Balance 31 March 20X4	0	493	670	0	1,163
Net book value 31/3/X4	3,636	2,570	1,518	0	7,724
Net book value 31/3/X3	3,186	1,247	437	53	4,923

*Depreciation – buildings $3063 \times 2.5\% = 77$
**Depreciation – Plant and machinery $2188 - 671 + 380 = 1897 \times 20\% = 379$
$$2188 - 671 = 1517 \times 20\% = 303$$

(ii)

	$'000
Finance cost	69
Interest due on loans	(24)
Transferred to tangible non-current assets	45

(b) (i)

C – Statement of cash flows for the year ended 31 March 20X4

	$'000
Cash flows from operating activities	
Net Profit before tax	982
Adjustments for:	
Depreciation	456
Amortisation of development expenditure	18
Profit on disposal of non-current assets (W1)	(11)
Finance cost	45
Operating profit before working capital changes	1,490
Less increase in inventory	(473)
Less increase in trade receivables	(311)
Add increase in trade payables	74
Add increase in provisions	280
Cash generated from operations	1,060
Interest paid (W2)	(53)
Income tax paid (W3)	(188)
Net cash from operating activities	819
Cash flows from investing activities	
Purchase tangible non-current assets (from (part a)	(2,803)
Development expenditure paid (W4)	(39)
Interest received	34
(2,808)	
Net cash used in investing activities	(2,808)
Cash flows from financing activities	
Proceeds from issue of ordinary shares (W5)	1,500
Proceeds from new loans raised (W6)	596
Equity Dividends paid	(350)
Net cash from financing activities	1,746
Net increase in cash and cash equivalents	(243)
Cash and cash equivalents at 31 March 20X3	759
Cash and cash equivalents at 31 March 20X4	516

(ii) Analysis of cash and cash equivalents

	Balance 31 March 20X3	Balance 31 March 20X4
	$'000	$'000
Bank	7	489
Cash	22	27
Current asset investments	730	0
Total cash and cash equivalents	759	516

Workings

W1 – Disposal of non-current asset	$'000
Original cost	400
Accumulated depreciation	380
	20
Proceeds from sale	31
Gain on disposal	11

W2 – Interest paid

Balance at 1 April 20X3		4
Profit or loss		<u>45</u>
		49
Balance at 31 March 20X4		<u>20</u>
		29
Add interest capitalized		<u>24</u>
Paid in year		<u>53</u>

W3 – Income tax paid

Balance at 1 April X3		
Tax		188
Deferred tax		<u>291</u>
		479
Profit or loss – income tax expense		<u>197</u>
		676
Balance at 31 March 20X4		
Tax	234	
Deferred tax	<u>254</u>	<u>488</u>
Tax paid in year		<u>188</u>

W4 – Development expenditure

Balance at 1 April X3		90
Profit or loss, amortised		<u>(18)</u>
		72
Balance at 31 March 20X4		<u>111</u>
New expenditure		<u>39</u>

W5 – Share issue

		$'000
Share capital – 1 April 20X3	1,500	
– 31 March 20X4	<u>2,000</u>	500
Share premium – 1 April 20X3	500	
– 31 March 20X4	<u>1,500</u>	<u>1,000</u>
Cash received from share issue		<u>1,500</u>

W6 – New Loans

Balance at 1 April X3		410
Balance at 31 March 20X4		<u>1,006</u>
New loans raised in year		<u>596</u>

☑ Solution 31

H – Statement of comprehensive income for the year ended 31 March 20X1

	Note	$'000
Sales revenue		5,000
Cost of sales		(2,025)
Gross profit		2,975
Distribution costs		(602)
Administrative expenses		<u>(890)</u>
Profit	1	1,483
Income from fixed asset investments		600
Finance cost		<u>(24)</u>
Profit before tax		2,059
Tax expense	2	<u>(250)</u>
Profit after tax		1,809
Other comprehensive income:		
Surplus on revaluation of land		820
Total comprehensive income for the period		<u>2,629</u>

H – Statement of financial position at 31 March 20X1

	Note	$'000	$'000
Assets			
Non-current assets			
Property, plant and equipment	3		2,818
Investments			6,575
			9,393
Current assets			
Inventory		167	
Receivables		417	
Bank		11	695
Total assets			9,988
Equity and Liabilities			
Capital and reserves			
Issued capital		7,000	
Revaluation reserve		820	
Retained earnings		1,530	
			9,350
Non-current liabilities			
Long-term loans			200
Current liabilities	4		438
Total equity and liabilities			9,988

H – statement of changes in equity, year ended 31 March 20X1

	Share capital $'000	Revaluation reserve $'000	Retained earnings $'000	Total $'000
Balance at 31 March 20X0	7,000		921	7,921
Total comprehensive income for the period		820	1,809	2,629
Dividends paid (Note 5)			(1,200)	(1,200)
	7,000	820	1,530	9,350

H – notes to the financial statements

1. *Profit from operations*

   Profit from operations is stated after charging:

	$'000
Depreciation	142
Staff costs	1,200

2. *Taxation*

	$'000
Tax charge for the year	270
Overprovision from previous year	(20)
	250

3. *Tangible non-current assets*

	Buildings $'000	Plant and machinery $'000	Total $'000
Cost or valuation at 1 April 20X0	2,400	900	3,300
Surplus on revaluation	100	–	100
Cost or valuation at 31 March 20X1	2,500	900	3,400
Depreciation at 1 April 20X0	720	440	1160
Adjustment on revaluation	(720)	–	(720)
Provided during the year	50	92	142
Depreciation at 31 March 20X1	50	532	582
Net book value at 31 March 20X1	2,450	368	2,818
Net book value at 1 April 20X0	1,680	460	2,140

   The buildings were revalued at $2.5 m on 1 April 20X0.

4. *Current liabilities*

	$'000
Trade payables	168
Taxation	270
	438

5. *Dividends*

Dividends paid during the year were:

	$'000
Final for year ended 31 March 20X0	700
Interim for year ended 31 March 20X1	500
	1,200

The directors propose a final dividend for the year ended 31 March 20X1 of $900,000.

Workings

	$'000
Cost of sales	
Opening inventory (per TB)	165
Add: Purchases	2,027
Less: Closing inventory	(167)
	2,025
Depreciation	
Premises 2% $\times$ $2.5 m=	50
Plant 20% $\times$ RB of (900 − 440)	92
	142
Distribution costs	
Per trial balance	60
Depreciation charge (50 + 92)	142
Wages	400
	602
Administrative expenses	
Per trial balance	90
Wages	800
	890

☑ Solution 32

DZ – Property, Plant and Equipment

Cost/valuation	Land	Property Land	Buildings	Plant & Equipment	Total
	$'000	$'000	$'000	$'000	$'000
Balance at 31 March 2006	1,250	3,500	7,700	4,180	16,630
Disposals	−1,250	0	0	−620	−1,870
	0	3,500	7,700	3,560	14,760
Revaluation	0	600	(2,000)	0	(1,400)
	0	4,100	5,700	3,560	13,360
Depreciation					
Balance at 31 March 2006	0	0	1,900	2,840	4,740
Disposals	0	0	0	−600	−600
	0	0	1,900	2,240	4,140
Revaluation adjustment	0	0	(1,900)	0	(1,900)
Charge for year	0	0	285	330	615
	0	0	285	2,570	2,855
Net book value at 31 March 2007	0	4,100	5,415	990	10,505
Net book value at 31 March 2006	1,250	3,500	5,800	1,340	11,890

Workings: All figures in $'000

Depreciation

Buildings

5,700 × 5%	=285
Split: Production 80% = 228	
Admin 20%	=57

Machinery and equipment

Reducing balance = 3,560 − 2,240 = 1,320

1,320 @ 25% = 330

Total production depreciation = 228 + 330 = 558

DZ – Statement of comprehensive income for the year ended 31 March 2007

		$'000	$'000
Revenue			8,772
Cost of sales	(W1)		(4,377)
Gross profit			4,395
Gain on disposal of non-current asset	(W2)		250
Administrative expenses	(W3)	(948)	
Distribution costs		(462)	(1,410)
Profit from operations			3,235
Finance cost			(160)
Profit before tax			3,075
Income tax expense	(W4)		(728)
Profit for the period			2,347
Other comprehensive income:			
Surplus on revaluation of property			500
Total comprehensive income for the period			2,847

DZ –Statement of financial position at 31 March 2007

	$'000	$'000	$'000
Non-current assets			
Property, plant and equipment (answer (a))			10,505
Intangible assets – development costs (W5)			198
Current assets			
Inventory (W6)		435	
Trade receivables		1,059	
Cash and cash equivalents		103	
			1,597
Total assets			12,300
Equity and liabilities			
Equity			
Share capital		1,000	
Revaluation reserve		1,850	
Retained earnings		5,121	
Total equity			7,971
Non-current liabilities			
8% loan	2,000		
Deferred tax (W4)	665		
Total non-current liabilities		2,665	
Current liabilities			
Trade and other payables (W7)	853		
Tax payable (W4)	811		
Total current liabilities		1,664	
Total liabilities			4,329
Total equity and liabilities			12,300

DM – Statement of changes in equity for the year ended 31 March 2007

	Equity shares $'000	Revaluation reserve $'000	Retained earnings $'000	Total $'000
Balance at 1 April 2006	1,000	2,100	2,024	5,124
Realised revaluation gain (W8)		−750	+750	0
Total comprehensive income for period		500	2,347	2,847
Balance at 31 March 2007	1,000	1,850	5,121	7,971

Workings

(W1) *Cost of sales*

	$'000
Inventory raw materials at 1 April 2006	132
Purchases	2,020
	2,152
Less inventory raw materials at 31 March 2007	(165)
	1,987
Direct labour	912
Production overheads	633
Depreciation	558
Production cost	4,090
Inventory finished goods at 1 April 2006	240
	4,330
Less inventory finished goods at 31 March 2007	(270)
Loss on disposal of machinery (W2)	15
Research and development cost (W5)	302
Total	4,377

(W2) *Gain on disposal of non-current assets*

Land – book value	1,250	
Less – receipt	1,500	
Gain	250	(This could be deducted from expenses, but as it's a material amount, it can be shown separately on Income statement.)
Machinery – book value	20	
Less – receipt	5	
Loss	(15)	(Treated as an adjustment of previous depreciation and added to Cost of sales)

(W3) *Administration expenses*

Per trial balance	891
Depreciation	57
	948

(W4) *Income tax expense*

Income tax for year		811
Previous year balance		25
		836
Deferred tax		
Balance 1 April 2006	773	
Balance 31 March 2007	665	
		(108)
Income statement		728

(W5) *Intangible assets – Research and development*

Cost balance 1 April 2006		867
Add incurred in year		48
		915
Less amortisation for year at 20%		(183)
Less amortisation b/fwd at 1 April 2006		(534)
Balance 31 March 2007		198
Amortisation for the year	183	
Research cost	119	
Charge to Income statement	302	

(W6) *Inventory*

Raw materials	165
Finished goods	270
	435

(W7) *Trade and other payables*

Trade payables	773
Interest due on loan	80
	853

(W8) *Realised gain on disposal*

Land disposed of	
original cost	500
revalued amount	1,250
Realised gain	750

November 2007
Examinations

November 2007 Examinations

Managerial Level

Paper P7 – Financial Accounting and Tax Principles

The answers published here have been written by the Examiner and should provide a helpful guide for both tutors and students.

Published separately on the CIMA website (www.cimaglobal.com/students) from mid-February 2008 is a Post Examination Guide for this paper, which provides much valuable and complementary material including indicative mark information.

Financial Management Pillar

Managerial Level Paper

P7 – Financial Accounting and Tax Principles

22 November 2007 – Thursday Afternoon Session

Instructions to candidates

You are allowed three hours to answer this question paper.
You are allowed 20 minutes reading time **before the examination begins** during which you should read the question paper and, if you wish, highlight and/or make notes on the question paper. However, you will **not** be allowed, **under any circumstances**, to open the answer book and start writing or use your calculator during this reading time.
You are strongly advised to carefully read ALL the question requirements before attempting the question concerned (that is all parts and/or sub-questions). The requirements for the questions in Sections B and C are highlighted in a dotted box.
ALL answers must be written in the answer book. Answers or notes written on the question paper will **not** be submitted for marking.
Answer the ONE compulsory question in Section A. This has 15 sub-questions on pages 3 to 7.
Answer the SIX compulsory sub-questions in Section B on pages 8 to 11.
Answer the ONE compulsory question in Section C on pages 12 to 14.
Maths Tables and Formulae are provided on pages 15 to 17.
The list of verbs as published in the syllabus is given for reference on the inside back cover of this question paper.
Write your candidate number, the paper number and examination subject title in the spaces provided on the front of the answer book. Also write your contact ID and name in the space provided in the right hand margin and seal to close.
Tick the appropriate boxes on the front of the answer book to indicate which questions you have answered.

SECTION A – 40 MARKS

[the indicative time for answering this Section is 72 minutes]

ANSWER *ALL* FIFTEEN SUB-QUESTIONS

> *Instructions for answering Section A:*
> The answers to the fifteen sub-questions in Section A must ALL be written in your answer book.
>
> Your answers should be clearly numbered with the sub-question number and then ruled off, so that the markers know which sub-question you are answering. **For multiple choice questions, you need only write the sub-question number and the letter of the answer option you have chosen.** You do not need to start a new page for each sub-question.
>
> For sub-questions **1.9, 1.10, 1.11, 1.13, 1.14** and **1.15** you should show your workings as marks are available for the method you use to answer these sub-questions.

? Question One

1.1 The International Accounting Standards Board's (IASB) *Framework for the Preparation and Presentation of Financial Statements* (Framework), sets out four qualitative characteristics of financial information.

Two of the characteristics are relevance and comparability. List the other TWO characteristics. **(2 marks)**

1.2 IAS 16 *Property, Plant and Equipment* requires an asset to be measured at cost on its original recognition in the financial statements.

EW used its own staff, assisted by contractors when required, to construct a new warehouse for its own use.

Which ONE of the following costs would NOT be included in attributable costs of the non-current asset?
(A) Clearance of the site prior to work commencing.
(B) Professional surveyors' fees for managing the construction work.
(C) EW's own staff wages for time spent working on the construction.
(D) An allocation of EW's administration costs, based on EW staff time spent on the construction as a percentage of the total staff time. **(2 marks)**

1.3 An external auditor gives a qualified audit report that is a "disclaimer of opinion".
This means that the auditor
(A) has been unable to agree with an accounting treatment used by the directors in relation to a material item.
(B) has been prevented from obtaining sufficient appropriate audit evidence.
(C) has found extensive errors in the financial statements and concludes that they do not show a true and fair view.
(D) has discovered a few immaterial differences that do not affect the auditor's opinion. **(2 marks)**

1.4 The trial balance of EH at 31 October 2007 showed trade receivables of $82,000 before adjustments.

On 1 November 2007 EH discovered that one of its customers had ceased trading and was very unlikely to pay any of its outstanding balance of $12,250.

On the same date EH carried out an assessment of the collectability of its other trade receivable balances. Using its knowledge of its customers and past experience EH determined that the remaining trade receivables had suffered a 3% impairment at 31 October 2007.

What is EH's balance of trade receivables, as at 31 October 2007?

(A) $66,202
(B) $67,290
(C) $67,657
(D) $79,540   **(2 marks)**

1.5 EX is preparing its cash forecast for the next three months.

Which ONE of the following items should be left out of its calculations?

(A) Expected gain on the disposal of a piece of land.
(B) Tax payment due, that relates to last year's profits.
(C) Rental payment on a leased vehicle.
(D) Receipt of a new bank loan raised for the purpose of purchasing new machinery.

                                                                                             (2 marks)

1.6 The following details relate to EA:

- Incorporated in Country A.
- Carries out its main business activities in Country B.
- Its senior management operate from Country C and effective control is exercised from Country C.

Assume Countries A, B and C have all signed double tax treaties with each other, based on the OECD model tax convention.

Which Country will EA be deemed to be resident in for tax purposes?

(A) Country A
(B) Country B
(C) Country C
(D) Both Countries B and C   **(2 marks)**

1.7 Treasury shares are defined as

(A) equity shares sold by an entity in the period.
(B) equity shares repurchased by the issuing entity, not cancelled before the period end.
(C) non-equity shares sold by an entity in the period.
(D) equity shares repurchased by the issuing entity and cancelled before the period end.

                                                                                             (2 marks)

1.8 EE reported accounting profits of $822,000 for the period ended 30 November 2007. This was after deducting entertaining expenses of $32,000 and a donation to a political party of $50,000, both of which are disallowable for tax purposes.

EE's reported profit also included $103,000 government grant income that was exempt from taxation. EE paid dividends of $240,000 in the period.

Assume EE had no temporary differences between accounting profits and taxable profits.

Assume that a classical tax system applies to EE's profits and that the tax rate is 25%. What would EE's tax payable be on its profits for the year to 30 November 2007?

(2 marks)

1.9 EG purchased a property for $630,000 on 1 September 2000. EG incurred additional costs for the purchase of $3,500 surveyors' fees and $6,500 legal fees. EG then spent $100,000 renovating the property prior to letting it. All of EG's expenditure was classified as capital expenditure according to the local tax regulations.

Indexation of the purchase and renovation costs is allowed on EE's property. The index increased by 50% between September 2000 and October 2007. Assume that acquisition and renovation costs were incurred in September 2000. EG sold the property on 1 October 2007 for $1,250,000, incurring tax allowable costs on disposal of $2,000.

Calculate EG's tax due on disposal assuming a tax rate of 30%. **(3 marks)**

1.10 A government wanted to encourage investment in new non-current assets by entities and decided to change tax allowances for non-current assets to give a 100% first year allowance on all new non-current assets purchased after 1 January 2005.

ED purchased new machinery for $400,000 on 1 October 2005 and claimed the 100% first year allowance. For accounting purposes ED depreciated the machinery on the reducing balance basis at 25% per year. The rate of corporate income tax to be applied to ED's taxable profits was 22%.

Assume ED had no other temporary differences.

Calculate the amount of deferred tax that ED would show in its balance sheet at 30 September 2007. **(3 marks)**

1.11 EP sells refrigerators and freezers and provides a one year warranty against faults occurring after sale.

EP estimates that if all goods with an outstanding warranty at the balance sheet date need minor repairs the total cost would be $3 million. If all the products under warranty needed major repairs the total cost would be $12 million.

Based on previous years' experience, EP estimates that 85% of the products will require no repairs; 14% will require minor repairs and 1% will require major repairs.

Calculate the expected value of the cost of the repair of goods with an outstanding warranty at the balance sheet date. **(3 marks)**

1.12 List FOUR advantages of forfaiting for an exporter. **(4 marks)**

1.13 A bond has a coupon rate of 7%. It will repay its face value of $1,000 at the end of six years. The market expects this type of bond to have a yield to maturity of 10%.

What is the current market value of the bond? **(4 marks)**

1.14 EB has an investment of 25% of the equity shares in XY, an entity resident in a foreign country.

EB receives a dividend of $90,000 from XY, the amount being after the deduction of withholding tax of 10%.

XY had profits before tax for the year of $1,200,000 and paid corporate income tax of $200,000.

How much underlying tax can EB claim for double taxation relief? **(3 marks)**

1.15 EV had inventory days outstanding of 60 days and trade payables outstanding of 50 days at 31 October 2007.

EV's inventory balance at 1 November 2006 was $56,000 and trade payables were $42,000 at that date.

EV's cost of goods sold comprises purchased goods cost only. During the year to 31 October 2007, EV's cost of goods sold was $350,000.

Assume purchases and sales accrue evenly throughout the year and use a 365 day year. Further assume that there were no goods returned to suppliers and EV claimed no discounts.

Calculate how much EV paid to its credit suppliers during the year to 31 October 2007. **(4 marks)**

(Total for Question One = 40 marks)

SECTION B – 30 MARKS

[the indicative time for this Section is 54 minutes]

ANSWER *ALL* SIX SUB-QUESTIONS. EACH SUB-QUESTION IS WORTH 5 MARKS.

? Question Two

(a) On 1 September 2007, the Directors of EK decided to sell EK's retailing division and concentrate activities entirely on its manufacturing division.

The retailing division was available for immediate sale, but EK had not succeeded in disposing of the operation by 31 October 2007. EK identified a potential buyer for the retailing division, but negotiations were at an early stage. The Directors of EK are certain that the sale will be completed by 31 August 2008.

The retailing division's carrying value at 31 August 2007 was:

	$'000
Non-current tangible assets – property, plant and equipment	300
Non-current tangible assets – goodwill	100
Net current assets	43
Total carrying value	443

The retailing division has been valued at $423,000, comprising:

	$'000
Non-current tangible assets – property, plant and equipment	320
Non-current tangible assets – goodwill	60
Net current assets	43
Total carrying value	423

EK's directors have estimated that EK will incur consultancy and legal fees for the disposal of $25,000.

Requirements

(i) Explain whether EK can treat the sale of its retailing division as a "discontinued operation", as defined by IFRS 5 *Non-current Assets held for Sale and Discontinued Operations*, in its financial statements for the year ended 31 October 2007.

(3 marks)

(ii) Explain how EK should treat the retailing division in its financial statements for the year ended 31 October 2007, assuming the sale of its retailing division meets the classification requirements for a disposal group (IFRS 5).

(2 marks)

(Total for sub-question (a) = 5 marks)

(b) EF is an importer and imports perfumes and similar products in bulk. EF repackages the products and sells them to retailers. EF is registered for Value Added Tax (VAT).

   EF imports a consignment of perfume priced at $10,000 (excluding excise duty and VAT) and pays excise duty of 20% and VAT on the total (including duty) at 15%.

   EF pays $6,900 repackaging costs, including VAT at 15% and then sells all the perfume for $40,250 including VAT at 15%.

   EF has not paid or received any VAT payments to/from the VAT authorities for this consignment.

Requirements

   (i) Calculate EF's net profit on the perfume consignment.
   (ii) Calculate the net VAT due to be paid by EF on the perfume consignment
   (Total for sub-question (b) = 5 marks)

(c) The trade receivables ledger account for customer X is as follows:

		Debits	Credits	Balance
01-Jul-07	Balance b/fwd			162
12-Jul-07	Invoice AC34	172		334
14-Jul-07	Invoice AC112	213		547
28-Jul-07	Invoice AC215	196		743
08-Aug-07	Receipt RK 116 (Balance + AC34)		334	409
21-Aug-07	Invoice AC420	330		739
03-Sep-07	Receipt RL162 (AC215)		196	543
12-Sep-07	Credit note CN92 (AC112)		53	490
23-Sep-07	Invoice AC615	116		606
25-Sep-07	Invoice AC690	204		810
05-Oct-07	Receipt RM223 (AC420)		330	480
16-Oct-07	Invoice AC913	233		713
25-Oct-07	Receipt RM360 (AC615)		116	597

Requirements

   (i) Prepare an age analysis showing the outstanding balance on a monthly basis for customer X.

   (3 marks)

   (ii) Explain how an age analysis of receivables can be useful to an entity.
   (2 marks)
   (Total for sub-question (c) = 5 marks)

(d) EJ publishes trade magazines and sells them to retailers. EJ has just concluded negotiations with a large supermarket chain for the supply of a large quantity of several of its trade magazines on a regular basis.

EJ has agreed a substantial discount on the following terms:

- The same quantity of each trade magazine will be supplied each month;
- Quantities can only be changed at the end of each six month period;
- Payment must be made six monthly in advance.

The supermarket paid $150,000 on 1 September 2007 for six months supply of trade magazines to 29 February 2008. At 31 October 2007, EJ had supplied two months of trade magazines. EJ estimates that the cost of supplying the supermarket each month is $20,000.

Requirements

(i) State the criteria in IAS 18 *Revenue Recognition* for income recognition.

(2 marks)

(ii) Explain, with reasons, how EJ should treat the above in its financial statements for the year ended 31 October 2007.

(3 marks)

(Total for sub-question (d) = 5 marks)

(e) The objective of IAS 24 *Related Party Disclosures* is to ensure that financial statements disclose the effect of the existence of related parties.

Requirement

With reference to IAS 24, explain the meaning of the terms "related party" and "related party transaction".

(Total for sub-question (e) = 5 marks)

(f) ES estimates from its cash flow forecast that it will have $120,000 to invest for 12 months.

ES is considering the following investments:

(i) Purchase of fixed term bonds issued by a "blue chip" entity quoted on the local stock exchange. The bonds have a maturity date in 12 months' time and pay 12.5% interest on face value. The bonds will be redeemed at face value in 12 months' time. ES will incur commission costs on purchasing the bonds of 1% of cost. The bonds are currently trading at $102 per $100.

(ii) An internet bank is offering a deposit account that pays interest on a monthly basis at 0.8% per month.

Requirement

Identify which is the most appropriate investment for the year, giving your reasons.

(Total for sub-question (f) = 5 marks)

(Total for Section B = 30 marks)

SECTION C – 30 MARKS

[the indicative time for this Section is 54 minutes]

ANSWER THIS QUESTION

? Question Three

EY is an office and industrial furniture manufacturing entity that specialises in developing and using new materials and manufacturing processes in the production of its furniture.

The balance sheet below relates to the previous year, 31 October 2006, which is followed by a summary of EY's cash book for the year to 31 October 2007.

EY Balance Sheet at 31 October 2006

	$'000	$'000	$'000
Non-current assets			
Development costs – cost	1,000		
– amortisation	200	800	
Property, plant and equipment – cost	7,300		
– depreciation	1,110	6,190	6,990
Current assets			
Inventory	1,200		
Trade receivables	753		
Cash and cash equivalents	82		
			2,035
			9,025
Equity and liabilities			
Equity			
Share capital		3,000	
Revaluation reserve		600	
Retained earnings		1,625	
			5,225
Non-current liabilities			
Loan notes	2,260		
Deferred tax	180		
		2,440	
Current liabilities			
Trade and other payables	573		
Tax payable	670		
Interest payable	117		
		1,360	
			3,800
Total liabilities			9,025

EY's summarised cash book for the year ended 31 October 2007

	Note	Receipts/(Payments) $'000
Cash book balance at 1 November 2006		82
Expenditure incurred on government contract	(i)	(600)
Interest paid during the year	(ii)	(160)
Administration expenses paid		(500)
Research and development costs	(iii)	(1,600)
Income tax	(iv)	(690)
Purchase cost of property, plant and equipment	(v)	(3,460)
Final dividend of 25c per share for year ended 31 October 2006		(750)
Receipt for disposal of land	(vi)	1,200
Cash received from customers		7,500
Payments to suppliers of production materials, wages and other production costs		(3,000)
Distribution and selling costs		(730)
Cash received from increase in loan notes		2,500
Cash book balance at 31 October 2007		(208)

Notes:

(i) The government contract is a long-term project for the supply of a new type of seating for government offices involving the development of new materials. The total contract value is $1,400,000. The expenditure includes all costs incurred during the first year of the contract. The project leader is confident that the remainder of the work will cost no more than $400,000. The contract provides that EY can charge for the proportion of work completed by 31 October each year. The percentage of cost incurred to total cost should be used to apportion profit/losses on the contract.

(ii) Interest outstanding at 31 October 2007 was $130,000.

(iii) During the year EY spent $1,600,000 on research and development. This comprised three projects:

- Cost in the year $300,000 – Funded research projects carried out at the local university;
- Cost in the year $500,000 – Development of a new type of laminate expected to be a very profitable product line. The final development phase has just finished, and production of the laminate is expected from January 2008.
- Cost in the year $800,000 – Development of a new type of artificial wood, to replace real wood in some furniture and help reduce EY's use of wood. The development produced a good substitute for wood, but was five times more expensive and hence not viable.

Capitalised development expenditure is amortised on the straight line basis over five years and treated as a cost of sale.

(iv) Income tax due for the year was estimated by EY at $420,000.

(v) The property, plant and equipment balance at 31 October 2006 was made up as follows:

	Land $'000	Premises $'000	Plant & equipment $'000	Total $'000
Cost/valuation	2,000	1,500	3,800	7,300
Depreciation	0	350	760	1,110
Net book value	2,000	1,150	3,040	6,190

During the year EY purchased new premises at a cost of $1,600,000, and new plant and equipment for $1,860,000. Premises are depreciated on the straight line basis at 6% per year, and plant and machinery are depreciated on the reducing balance at 15% per year and are treated as a cost of sale. EY charges a full year's depreciation in the year of acquisition. No assets were fully depreciated at 31 October 2006.

(vi) Land originally costing $600,000, which had previously been revalued to $1,000,000 was sold during the year for $1,200,000.

(vii) A bonus issue of shares was made on the basis of one new share for every six shares held.

(viii) Deferred tax is to be increased by $42,000.

(ix) Balances at 31 October 2007 included:

trade receivables		$620,000;
outstanding trade payables		$670,000;
inventory		$985,000.

Requirement

Prepare the income statement and a statement of changes in equity for the year to 31 October 2007 and a balance sheet at that date, in a form suitable for presentation to the shareholders and in accordance with the requirements of International Financial Reporting Standards. (All workings should be to the nearest $'000)

Notes to the financial statements are NOT required, but all workings must be clearly shown. Do NOT prepare a statement of accounting policies.

(Total for Question Three = 30 marks)

Maths Tables and Formulae

Present value table

Present value of $1, that is $(1 + r)^{-n}$ where r = interest rate; n = number of periods until payment or receipt.

Periods (n)	Interest rates (r)									
	1%	2%	3%	4%	5%	6%	7%	8%	9%	10%
1	0.990	0.980	0.971	0.962	0.952	0.943	0.935	0.926	0.917	0.909
2	0.980	0.961	0.943	0.925	0.907	0.890	0.873	0.857	0.842	0.826
3	0.971	0.942	0.915	0.889	0.864	0.840	0.816	0.794	0.772	0.751
4	0.961	0.924	0.888	0.855	0.823	0.792	0.763	0.735	0.708	0.683
5	0.951	0.906	0.863	0.822	0.784	0.747	0.713	0.681	0.650	0.621
6	0.942	0.888	0.837	0.790	0.746	0.705	0.666	0.630	0.596	0.564
7	0.933	0.871	0.813	0.760	0.711	0.665	0.623	0.583	0.547	0.513
8	0.923	0.853	0.789	0.731	0.677	0.627	0.582	0.540	0.502	0.467
9	0.914	0.837	0.766	0.703	0.645	0.592	0.544	0.500	0.460	0.424
10	0.905	0.820	0.744	0.676	0.614	0.558	0.508	0.463	0.422	0.386
11	0.896	0.804	0.722	0.650	0.585	0.527	0.475	0.429	0.388	0.350
12	0.887	0.788	0.701	0.625	0.557	0.497	0.444	0.397	0.356	0.319
13	0.879	0.773	0.681	0.601	0.530	0.469	0.415	0.368	0.326	0.290
14	0.870	0.758	0.661	0.577	0.505	0.442	0.388	0.340	0.299	0.263
15	0.861	0.743	0.642	0.555	0.481	0.417	0.362	0.315	0.275	0.239
16	0.853	0.728	0.623	0.534	0.458	0.394	0.339	0.292	0.252	0.218
17	0.844	0.714	0.605	0.513	0.436	0.371	0.317	0.270	0.231	0.198
18	0.836	0.700	0.587	0.494	0.416	0.350	0.296	0.250	0.212	0.180
19	0.828	0.686	0.570	0.475	0.396	0.331	0.277	0.232	0.194	0.164
20	0.820	0.673	0.554	0.456	0.377	0.312	0.258	0.215	0.178	0.149

Periods (n)	Interest rates (r)									
	11%	12%	13%	14%	15%	16%	17%	18%	19%	20%
1	0.901	0.893	0.885	0.877	0.870	0.862	0.855	0.847	0.840	0.833
2	0.812	0.797	0.783	0.769	0.756	0.743	0.731	0.718	0.706	0.694
3	0.731	0.712	0.693	0.675	0.658	0.641	0.624	0.609	0.593	0.579
4	0.659	0.636	0.613	0.592	0.572	0.552	0.534	0.516	0.499	0.482
5	0.593	0.567	0.543	0.519	0.497	0.476	0.456	0.437	0.419	0.402
6	0.535	0.507	0.480	0.456	0.432	0.410	0.390	0.370	0.352	0.335
7	0.482	0.452	0.425	0.400	0.376	0.354	0.333	0.314	0.296	0.279
8	0.434	0.404	0.376	0.351	0.327	0.305	0.285	0.266	0.249	0.233
9	0.391	0.361	0.333	0.308	0.284	0.263	0.243	0.225	0.209	0.194
10	0.352	0.322	0.295	0.270	0.247	0.227	0.208	0.191	0.176	0.162
11	0.317	0.287	0.261	0.237	0.215	0.195	0.178	0.162	0.148	0.135
12	0.286	0.257	0.231	0.208	0.187	0.168	0.152	0.137	0.124	0.112
13	0.258	0.229	0.204	0.182	0.163	0.145	0.130	0.116	0.104	0.093
14	0.232	0.205	0.181	0.160	0.141	0.125	0.111	0.099	0.088	0.078
15	0.209	0.183	0.160	0.140	0.123	0.108	0.095	0.084	0.079	0.065
16	0.188	0.163	0.141	0.123	0.107	0.093	0.081	0.071	0.062	0.054
17	0.170	0.146	0.125	0.108	0.093	0.080	0.069	0.060	0.052	0.045
18	0.153	0.130	0.111	0.095	0.081	0.069	0.059	0.051	0.044	0.038
19	0.138	0.116	0.098	0.083	0.070	0.060	0.051	0.043	0.037	0.031
20	0.124	0.104	0.087	0.073	0.061	0.051	0.043	0.037	0.031	0.026

Cumulative present value of $1 per annum

Receivable or Payable at the end of each year for n years $\dfrac{1-(1+r)^{-n}}{r}$

Periods (n)	Interest rates (r)									
	1%	2%	3%	4%	5%	6%	7%	8%	9%	10%
1	0.990	0.980	0.971	0.962	0.952	0.943	0.935	0.926	0.917	0.909
2	1.970	1.942	1.913	1.886	1.859	1.833	1.808	1.783	1.759	1.736
3	2.941	2.884	2.829	2.775	2.723	2.673	2.624	2.577	2.531	2.487
4	3.902	3.808	3.717	3.630	3.546	3.465	3.387	3.312	3.240	3.170
5	4.853	4.713	4.580	4.452	4.329	4.212	4.100	3.993	3.890	3.791
6	5.795	5.601	5.417	5.242	5.076	4.917	4.767	4.623	4.486	4.355
7	6.728	6.472	6.230	6.002	5.786	5.582	5.389	5.206	5.033	4.868
8	7.652	7.325	7.020	6.733	6.463	6.210	5.971	5.747	5.535	5.335
9	8.566	8.162	7.786	7.435	7.108	6.802	6.515	6.247	5.995	5.759
10	9.471	8.983	8.530	8.111	7.722	7.360	7.024	6.710	6.418	6.145
11	10.368	9.787	9.253	8.760	8.306	7.887	7.499	7.139	6.805	6.495
12	11.255	10.575	9.954	9.385	8.863	8.384	7.943	7.536	7.161	6.814
13	12.134	11.348	10.635	9.986	9.394	8.853	8.358	7.904	7.487	7.103
14	13.004	12.106	11.296	10.563	9.899	9.295	8.745	8.244	7.786	7.367
15	13.865	12.849	11.938	11.118	10.380	9.712	9.108	8.559	8.061	7.606
16	14.718	13.578	12.561	11.652	10.838	10.106	9.447	8.851	8.313	7.824
17	15.562	14.292	13.166	12.166	11.274	10.477	9.763	9.122	8.544	8.022
18	16.398	14.992	13.754	12.659	11.690	10.828	10.059	9.372	8.756	8.201
19	17.226	15.679	14.324	13.134	12.085	11.158	10.336	9.604	8.950	8.365
20	18.046	16.351	14.878	13.590	12.462	11.470	10.594	9.818	9.129	8.514

Periods (n)	Interest rates (r)									
	11%	12%	13%	14%	15%	16%	17%	18%	19%	20%
1	0.901	0.893	0.885	0.877	0.870	0.862	0.855	0.847	0.840	0.833
2	1.713	1.690	1.668	1.647	1.626	1.605	1.585	1.566	1.547	1.528
3	2.444	2.402	2.361	2.322	2.283	2.246	2.210	2.174	2.140	2.106
4	3.102	3.037	2.974	2.914	2.855	2.798	2.743	2.690	2.639	2.589
5	3.696	3.605	3.517	3.433	3.352	3.274	3.199	3.127	3.058	2.991
6	4.231	4.111	3.998	3.889	3.784	3.685	3.589	3.498	3.410	3.326
7	4.712	4.564	4.423	4.288	4.160	4.039	3.922	3.812	3.706	3.605
8	5.146	4.968	4.799	4.639	4.487	4.344	4.207	4.078	3.954	3.837
9	5.537	5.328	5.132	4.946	4.772	4.607	4.451	4.303	4.163	4.031
10	5.889	5.650	5.426	5.216	5.019	4.833	4.659	4.494	4.339	4.192
11	6.207	5.938	5.687	5.453	5.234	5.029	4.836	4.656	4.486	4.327
12	6.492	6.194	5.918	5.660	5.421	5.197	4.988	7.793	4.611	4.439
13	6.750	6.424	6.122	5.842	5.583	5.342	5.118	4.910	4.715	4.533
14	6.982	6.628	6.302	6.002	5.724	5.468	5.229	5.008	4.802	4.611
15	7.191	6.811	6.462	6.142	5.847	5.575	5.324	5.092	4.876	4.675
16	7.379	6.974	6.604	6.265	5.954	5.668	5.405	5.162	4.938	4.730
17	7.549	7.120	6.729	6.373	6.047	5.749	5.475	5.222	4.990	4.775
18	7.702	7.250	6.840	6.467	6.128	5.818	5.534	5.273	5.033	4.812
19	7.839	7.366	6.938	6.550	6.198	5.877	5.584	5.316	5.070	4.843
20	7.963	7.469	7.025	6.623	6.259	5.929	5.628	5.353	5.101	4.870

FORMULAE

Valuation models

(i) Future value of S, of a sum X, invested for n periods, compounded at $r\%$ interest:
$$S = X[1 + r]^n$$

(ii) Present value of $1 payable or receivable in n years, discounted at $r\%$ per annum:

$$PV = \frac{1}{[1+r]^n}$$

(iii) Present value of an annuity of $1 per annum, receivable or payable for n years, commencing in one year, discounted at $r\%$ per annum:

$$PV = \frac{1}{r}\left[1 - \frac{1}{[1+r]^n}\right]$$

(iv) Present value of $1 per annum, payable or receivable in perpetuity, commencing in one year, discounted at $r\%$ per annum:

$$PV = \frac{1}{r}$$

(v) Present value of $1 per annum, receivable or payable, commencing in one year, growing in perpetuity at a constant rate of $g\%$ per annum, discounted at $r\%$ per annum:

$$PV = \frac{1}{r - g}$$

Inventory management

(i) Economic Order Quantity

$$EOQ = \sqrt{\frac{2C_oD}{C_h}}$$

where: C_o = cost of placing an order
C_h = cost of holding one unit in Inventory for one year
D = annual demand

Cash management

(i) Optimal sale of securities, Baumol model:

$$\text{Optimal sale} = \sqrt{\frac{2 \times \text{Annual cash disbursements} \times \text{Cost per sale of securities}}{\text{interest rate}}}$$

(ii) Spread between upper and lower cash balance limits, Miller–Orr model:

$$\text{Spread} = 3\left[\frac{\frac{3}{4} \times \text{transaction cost} \times \text{variance of cash flows}}{\text{interest rate}}\right]^{\frac{1}{3}}$$

LIST OF VERBS USED IN THE QUESTION REQUIREMENTS

A list of the learning objectives and verbs that appear in the syllabus and in the question requirements for each question in this paper.

It is important that you answer the question according to the definition of the verb.

LEARNING OBJECTIVE	VERBS USED	DEFINITION
1 KNOWLEDGE What you are expected to know.	List	Make a list of
	State	Express, fully or clearly, the details of/facts of
	Define	Give the exact meaning of
2 COMPREHENSION What you are expected to understand.	Describe	Communicate the key features
	Distinguish	Highlight the differences between
	Explain	Make clear or intelligible/State the meaning of
	Identify	Recognise, establish or select after consideration
	Illustrate	Use an example to describe or explain something
3 APPLICATION How you are expected to apply your knowledge.	Apply	To put to practical use
	Calculate/compute	To ascertain or reckon mathematically
	Demonstrate	To prove with certainty or to exhibit by practical means
	Prepare	To make or get ready for use
	Reconcile	To make or prove consistent/compatible
	Solve	Find an answer to
	Tabulate	Arrange in a table
4 ANALYSIS How you are expected to analyse the detail of what you have learned.	Analyse	Examine in detail the structure of
	Categorise	Place into a defined class or division
	Compare and contrast	Show the similarities and/or differences between
	Construct	To build up or compile
	Discuss	To examine in detail by argument
	Interpret	To translate into intelligible or familiar terms
	Produce	To create or bring into existence
5 EVALUATION How you are expected to use your learning to evaluate, make decisions or recommendations.	Advise	To counsel, inform or notify
	Evaluate	To appraise or assess the value of
	Recommend	To advise on a course of action

The Examiner for Financial Accounting and Tax Principles offers to future candidates and to tutors using this booklet for study purposes, the following background and guidance on the questions included in this examination paper.

Important Note: This paper is an all-compulsory paper, with Section A for 40 marks, Section B for 30 marks and Section C for 30 marks, which will contain one question covering at least two of three key financial reporting statements.

Section A – Question One – Compulsory

Question One consists of 15 objective test sub-questions, designed to cover a variety of syllabus topics not covered elsewhere in the paper and addressing a selection of learning outcomes in all four sections of the syllabus.

Section B – Question Two – Compulsory

(a) Tests candidates' ability to explain whether the entity concerned can treat the sale of a division as a "discontinued operation", per IFRS 5 *Non-current Assets held for Sale and Discontinued Operations*; and if the sale meets the Standard's classification requirements and how this is then treated in its financial statements. Tests learning outcome B (iv).

(b) Tests candidates' ability to calculate both the net profit on the perfume consignment and the net VAT due to be paid by the entity concerned on it. Tests learning outcome A (ii).

(c) Tests candidates' ability to prepare an age analysis showing the outstanding balance on a monthly basis for a customer of the entity concerned and to explain its usefulness to the entity. Tests learning outcome D (v).

(d) Tests candidates' ability to state the criteria in IAS 18 *Revenue Recognition* and explain their treatment in the financial statements of the entity concerned. Tests learning outcome C (v).

(e) Tests candidates' ability to explain the meaning of the terms "related party" and "related party transaction" with reference to IAS 24 *Related Party Disclosures*. Tests learning outcome C (v).

(f) Tests candidates' ability to identify and justify, for the entity concerned, what would be the most appropriate investment for it to make for the year. Tests learning outcome D (viii).

Section C – Question Three – Compulsory

Question Three tests candidates' ability to prepare (from information provided in the question scenario) an income statement, balance sheet and a statement of changes in equity for the entity concerned. The financial statements required should be in a form suitable for publication and in accordance with current International Financial Reporting Standards. Tests learning outcomes A (viii) and C (i).

Managerial Level Paper

P7 – Financial Accounting and Tax Principles

Examiner's Answers

SECTION A

Answers to Question One

1.1 Reliability and understandability
1.2 D
1.3 B
1.4 C
1.5 A
1.6 C
1.7 B
1.8

	$'000
Profit	822
Add back entertaining expenses	32
Political party donation	50
	904
Less grant	(103)
	801

Tax due = 801 × 25% = 200

1.9

Purchase price:	$'000	$'000
Cost	630	
Fees	10	
	640	
Renovation	100	
		740
Indexation at 50%		370
		1,110
Selling price	1,250	
Less cost of disposal	2	1,248
Taxable amount		138

Tax at 30% = 41.4

1.10

Deferred tax balance:	$'000
Accounting depreciation:	
Cost	400
Depreciation to September 2006	100
	300
Depreciation to September 2007	75
	225
Tax allowances:	
Allowance to September 2006	400

Temporary difference at September 2007 is $400 - 175 = 225$
Deferred tax provision is 225 @ 22% = 49.5

1.11 Warranty cost provision = ($3m × 0.14) + ($12m × 0.01) = $540,000

1.12 Advantages of forfaiting; any FOUR of the following:
- trade receivables are turned into immediate cash;
- as it is non-recourse, no liability appears on the balance sheet;
- future foreign-exchange and interest-rate risk is eliminated;
- overdraft and other credit limits are not affected;
- any other reasonable advantage.

1.13 ($70 × (annuity factor $t = 6$, $r = 10$)) + ($1,000 × (discount factor $t = 6$, $r = 10$))
($70 × 4.355) + ($1,000 × 0.564) = 304.85 + 564 = 868.85

1.14 Gross dividend = 90 × 100/90 = 100
After tax profits 1,000
Underlying tax = 100/1,000 × 200 = 20

1.15 At 31 October 2007:

Cost of goods sold = $350,000
Inventory = $350,000 × 60/365 = $57,534

Inventory b/fwd 1/11/06	56,000
Purchases (balancing figure)	351,534
	407,534
Inventory c/fwd 31/10/07	57,534
	350,000

Closing trade payables = $351,534 × 50/365 = $48,155

Trade payables b/fwd 1/11/06	42,000
Purchases	351,534
	393,534
Trade payables c/fwd 31/10/07	48,155
Paid	345,379

SECTION B

Answers to Question Two

Answer to (a)

(i) EK can treat the disposal of its retailing division as discontinued if it is a component of EK that has been disposed of, or is classified as held for sale. It must also be the disposal of a major line of business or a geographical area of operations. EK's disposal has not been completed by the balance sheet date, so does not meet that requirement. Income and expenses of the disposal group will require to be shown separately on the income statement.

IFRS 5 says that non-current assets or a disposal group can be classified as held for sale, where the carrying value will be recovered through a sale transaction, rather than their continuing use. The assets must be available for immediate sale in their present condition and the sale must be "highly probable". Highly probable means that the directors are committed to the sale and there is an active programme to locate a buyer and the assets are being actively marketed at a reasonable price. The sale must be expected to be completed within a year.

These terms appear to be met in EK's case and the retail division will be designated as held for sale. This means that they will be treated as discontinued operations in the year to 31 October 2007.

(ii) A disposal group is valued at fair value less cost to sell. If this gives rise to a lower value than the current book value, the assets have become impaired and must be written down. The reduction in value is charged to the income statement.

EK has valued the retail division at $423,000 and cost to sell is estimated at $25,000; this will give a net value of $398,000.

The assets in the disposal group will be recognised at the lower of their book value or fair value less cost to sell as follows:

	$'000
Non-current assets, property, plant and equipment	300
Non-current assets, goodwill	55
Net current assets	43
	398

The reduction of $45,000 will be charged to the income statement.

Assets and disposal groups designated as held for sale are shown separately on the balance sheet and are not depreciated.

Answer to (b)

Perfume consignment income, expenditure and VAT are as follows:

	Total cost (incl VAT) $	VAT $	Net of VAT $
Expenditure:			
Cost	10,000		10,000
Excise duty	2,000		2,000
	12,000		12,000
Input VAT @ 15%	1,800	1,800	0
	13,800		12,000
Repackaging costs	6,900	900	6,000
Total costs	20,700		18,000
Sales revenue	(40,250)	(5,250)	(35,000)
Net	19,550	2,550	17,000

(i) Net profit is $17,000

(ii) Net VAT due to be paid is $2,550

Answer to (c)

(i) Age analysis for customer X:

>90 days (July onwards)	>60 days <90 days (Aug)	>30 days <60 days (Sept)	Current (Oct)	Total
160	0	204	233	597

(ii) The age analysis of trade receivables can be useful to an entity in the following ways:

- It can be used to identify customers that are slow paying or have not paid for some time. This allows credit control to give more attention to these customers;
- It can be used to help decide what action should be taken about debts that have been outstanding for longer than the specified credit period;
- It can provide information to assist in setting and monitoring collection targets for the credit control section;
- It can be used to assist management decision making, for example to calculate the effect of a change in credit terms;
- It can be used to assist at the year end when deciding on the size of the bad debt provision.

Answer to (d)

(i) IAS 18 *Revenue Recognition* sets out the following criteria that must be met before revenue can be recognised:

    (a) the significant risks and rewards of ownership of the goods have been transferred to the buyer;

    (b) the entity selling does not retain any continuing influence or control over the goods;

    (c) revenue can be measured reliably;

(d) it is reasonably certain that the buyer will pay for the goods;

(e) the costs to the selling entity can be measured reliably.

Items (c), (d) and (e) have been met, but (a) and (b) have not yet been met for months three to six.

(ii) EJ can recognise $50,000 revenue and related costs of $40,000 for the year. EJ cannot recognise the revenue from the next four months sales of trade magazines and will need to treat the $100,000 received as deferred income and include it under current liabilities in its balance sheet at 31 October 2007.

Answer to (e)

IAS 24 – A party is related to an entity if:

(a) directly, or indirectly the party:
   (i) controls, is controlled by , or is under common control with, the entity;
   (ii) has an interest in the entity that gives it significant influence over the entity; or
   (iii) has joint control over the entity.
(b) the party is an associate;
(c) the party is a joint venture in which the entity is a venturer;
(d) the party is a member of the key management personnel of the entity or its parent;
(e) the party is a close member of the family of any individual referred to in (a) or (d);
(f) the party is an entity that is controlled, jointly controlled or significantly influenced by, or for which significant voting power in such entity resides with, directly or indirectly, any individual referred to in (d) or (e); or
(g) the party is a post-employment benefit plan for the benefit of employees of the entity, or of any entity that is a related party of the entity.

Related party transaction: Transfer of resources, services or obligations between related parties, regardless of whether a price is charged.

The transfer of resources or obligations can include any transaction, including purchases or sales of goods, property or other assets and rendering of receipt of services.

Answer to (f)

(i) Purchasing the bonds on the terms given will mean that after redemption ES will have $131,042.

Workings:
Amount invested = $120,000 less commission at 1% of amount invested
   = 120,000 × 1/101 = $1,188 commission
Investment = 120,000 − 1,188 = 118,812
Nominal value of bonds purchased = 118,812 × 100/102 = 116,482
Annual interest payment = 116,482 × 12.5% = 14,560
Cash received in 12 months will be $116,482 + $14,560 = $131,042

(ii) $120,000 invested in an internet bank account at 0.8% per month will become $132,041 in 12 months.

Workings:

0.8% per month, compounded for 12 months will be $(1 + 0.008)^{12} = 1.100339$

$120,000 invested for 12 months will give $120,000 \times 1.100339 = 132,041$

In addition to considering the option with the highest return, ES should also consider the relative security of each investment, for example is the blue chip company financially sound and be able to repay the bond when due?

The internet bank pays the highest return, how sound is the bank?

Which country is it based in?

How good is the control of banks in that country?

Is there any chance that the bank may default on repayment of the investment?

If the bank is sound and based in a country with a good reputation for financial institutions, then the internet bank would seem to be the best investment. If it turns out that ES needs some of the funds within 12 months, this investment has the added advantage of being easier to access than the bonds.

SECTION C

Question Three

EY Financial Statements for the year ended 31 October 2007

EY – Income Statement for the year ended 31 October 2007

		$'000	$'000
Revenue	(W1)		8,207
Cost of sales	(W2)		(6,233)
Gross profit			1,974
Other income (gain on disposal of non-current asset)	(W8)		200
Administrative expenses		500	
Distribution and selling costs		730	(1,230)
Profit from operations			944
Finance cost	(W5)		(173)
Profit before tax			771
Income tax expense	(W6)		(482)
Profit for the period			289

EY – Balance Sheet at 31 October 2007

		$'000	$'000	$'000
Non-current assets				
Intangible assets – development costs	(W10)			1,000
Property, plant and equipment	(W9)			7,729
				8,729
Current assets				
Inventory			985	
Trade receivables		620		
Government contract	(W3)	840	1,460	2,445
Total assets				11,174
Equity and liabilities				
Equity				
Share capital			3,500	
Revaluation reserve			200	
Retained earnings			1,064	
Total equity				4,764
Non-current liabilities				
Loan notes		4,760		
Deferred tax	(W7)	222		
Total non-current liabilities			4,982	
Current liabilities				
Trade payables		670		
Bank overdraft		208		
Tax payable		420		
Interest payable		130		
Total current liabilities			1,428	
Total liabilities				6,410
Total equity and liabilities				11,174

EY – Statement of changes in equity for the year ended 31 October 2007

		Equity shares	Revaluation reserve	Retained earnings	Total
		$'000	$'000	$'000	$'000
Balance at 1 November 2006		3,000	600	1,625	5,225
Realised revaluation gain	(W8)		(400)	400	0
Bonus issue		500		(500)	0
Dividend				(750)	(750)
Profit for period				289	289
Balance at 31 October 2007		3,500	200	1,064	4,764

Workings (All figures in $'000)

(W1) Revenue

Receivables b/fwd		(753)
Receipts		7,500
		6,747
Receivables c/fwd		620
		7,367
Government contract	(W3)	840
Income statement		8,207

(W2) Cost of sales

Payables b/fwd		(573)
Payments		3,000
		2,427
Payables c/fwd		670
Purchased		3,097
Inventory b/fwd		1,200
		4,297
Less Inventory c/fwd		(985)
		3,312
Government contract cost	(W3)	600
Research and development cost	(W4)	1,100
Depreciation	(W9)	921
Development amortisation	(W10)	300
Income statement		6,233

(W3) Government contract

Value	1,400
Cost incurred	600
Additional cost to complete	400
Total cost	1,000
Profit	400

Contract is profitable, recognise proportion of work
  completed = 600/1,000 = 60%
Revenue   = 60% × 1,400 = 840
Cost of sales = 60% × 1,000 = 600
Receivables 840

(W4) Research and Development
Research

Research and development cost incurred during the year	1,600
Development costs deferred and capitalized	500
Research cost charged to income statement	1,100

(W5) **Finance cost**

Interest b/fwd	(117)
Paid	160
	43
Interest c/fwd	130
Income statement	173

(W6) **Tax expense**

Balance b/fwd	(670)
Tax paid	690
Tax for current year	420
Increase in deferred tax	42
	482

(W7) **Deferred tax**

Balance b/fwd	180
Increase in the year	42
	222

(W8) **Gain on disposal non-current asset**

Carrying value of land	1,000
Sold for	1,200
Gain on disposal	200

Realised revaluation gain, difference between carrying value and original cost.
Transferred from revaluation reserve to retained profits = 1,000 − 600 = 400

(W9) **Property, plant and equipment**

	Land $'000	Premises $'000	Plant & equipment $'000	Total $'000
Balance b/fwd	2,000	1,500	3,800	7,300
Disposal	(1,000)			(1,000)
Additions		1,600	1,860	3,460
	1,000	3,100	5,660	9,760
Depreciation				
Balance b/fwd	0	350	760	1,110
Charge for year	0	186	735	921
	0	536	1,495	2,031
Net book value	1,000	2,564	4,165	7,729

(W10) **Development costs**

Intangible assets – development expenditure	Cost	Amortisation	Net book value
Balance b/fwd	1,000	200	800
Additions in the year	500	0	500
	1,500	200	1,300
		300	(300)
Amortisation to 31 October 2007	1,500	500	1,000

Index

Index

FINANCIAL ACCOUNTING AND TAX PRINCIPLES

FINANCIAL ACCOUNTING AND TAX PRINCIPLES

ELSEVIER

PUBLISHING

May 08 Q&A

To access the May 08 Q&A for the book you have bought
please follow these instructions:

Go to
http://cimapublishing.com/QandA

- Follow the step-by-step instructions on the site

- Fill in the registration form

- Download the PDF for immediate access to Q&As

Get **10% Discount**
off your next order

Quote ATP8 when ordering or
add it to the offer code box online.

Order Form

For CIMA Official Study Materials for 2008 Exams

QTY	PAPER	TITLE	ISBN-13	PRICE	TOTAL
CIMA Official *Learning Systems*					
	P1	Performance Evaluation	978-0-7506-8688-4	£35.00	
	P2	Decision Management	978-0-7506-8958-8	£35.00	
	P3	Risk and Control Strategy	978-0-7506-8713-3	£35.00	
	P4	Organisational Management & Information Systems	978-0-7506-8689-1	£35.00	
	P5	Integrated Management	978-0-7506-8769-0	£35.00	
	P6	Business Strategy	978-0-7506-8906-9	£35.00	
	P7	Financial Accounting and Tax Principles	978-0-7506-8700-3	£35.00	
	P8	Financial Analysis	978-0-7506-8691-4	£35.00	
	P9	Financial Strategy	978-0-7506-8715-7	£35.00	
	P10	TOPCIMA	978-0-7506-8770-6	£35.00	
CIMA Official *Exam Practice Kits*					
	P1	Performance Evaluation	978-0-7506-8669-3	£14.99	
	P2	Decision Management	978-0-7506-8676-1	£14.99	
	P3	Risk and Control Strategy	978-0-7506-8677-8	£14.99	
	P4	Organisational Management & Information Systems	978-0-7506-8681-5	£14.99	
	P5	Integrated Management	978-0-7506-8675-4	£14.99	
	P6	Business Strategy	978-0-7506-8678-5	£14.99	
	P7	Financial Accounting and Tax Principles	978-0-7506-8690-7	£14.99	
	P8	Financial Analysis	978-0-7506-8674-7	£14.99	
	P9	Financial Strategy	978-0-7506-8679-2	£14.99	
	P10	TOPCIMA	978-0-7506-8680-8	£14.99	
CIMA Official *Revision Cards*					
	P1	Performance Evaluation	978-0-7506-8123-0	£8.99	
	P2	Decision Management	978-0-7506-8124-7	£8.99	
	P3	Risk and Control Strategy	978-0-7506-8120-9	£8.99	
	P4	Organisational Management & Information Systems	978-0-7506-8121-6	£8.99	
	P5	Integrated Management	978-0-7506-8122-3	£8.99	
	P6	Business Strategy	978-0-7506-8119-3	£8.99	
	P7	Financial Accounting and Tax Principles	978-0-7506-8126-1	£8.99	
	P8	Financial Analysis	978-0-7506-8125-4	£8.99	
	P9	Financial Strategy	978-0-7506-8118-6	£8.99	
Books					
		Principles of Business Taxation	978-0-7506-8457-6	£49.99	
		CIMA: Pass First Time!	978-0-7506-8396-8	£12.99	
		Better Exam Results	978-0-7506-6357-1	£12.99	
			Postage and packing		£2.95
			TOTAL		

Elsevier Ltd, Science & Technology Books, retains certain personal information about you in hard copy and on computer. It will be used to inform you about goods and services available from Elsevier Ltd and its offices worldwide in which you may be interested.

Please tick the box if you do NOT wish to receive this information. ☐

Post this form to:

**CIMA Publishing Customer Services
Elsevier
FREEPOST (OF 1639)
Linacre House, Jordan Hill
OXFORD, OX2 8DP, UK**

Or **FAX** +44 (0)1865 314 572
Or **PHONE** +44 (0)1865 474 014
Email: cimaorders@elsevier.com
www.cimapublishing.com

Name: _____

Organisation: _____

Invoice Address: _____

_____

_____

_____

Postcode: _____

Phone number: _____

Email: _____

Delivery Address if different:

FAO _____

Address _____

_____

_____

_____

Postcode _____

Please note that all deliveries must be signed for

1. Cheques payable to Elsevier.

2. Please charge my:

☐ Visa/Barclaycard   ☐ Access/Mastercard
☐ American Express   ☐ Diners Card
☐ Switch   Issue No._____

Card No. _____

Expiry Date _____

Cardholder Name: _____

Signature: _____

Date: _____

Get **10% Discount**
off your next order

Quote ATP8 when ordering or
add it to the offer code box online.

ELSEVIER

CIMA PUBLISHING

Order Form

For CIMA Official Study Materials for 2008 Exams

QTY	PAPER	TITLE	ISBN-13	PRICE	TOTAL
	CIMA Official *Learning Systems*				
	C1	Fundamentals of Management Accounting	978-0-7506-8955-7	£35.00	
	C2	Fundamentals of Financial Accounting	978-0-7506-8696-9	£35.00	
	C3	Fundamentals of Business Maths	978-0-7506-8957-1	£35.00	
	C4	Fundamentals of Business Economics	978-0-7506-8698-3	£35.00	
	C5	Fundamentals of Ethics, Corporate Governance and Business Law	978-0-7506-8956-4	£35.00	
	CIMA Official *Exam Practice Kits*				
	C1	Fundamentals of Management Accounting	978-0-7506-8717-1	£14.99	
	C2	Fundamentals of Financial Accounting	978-0-7506-8716-4	£14.99	
	C3	Fundamentals of Business Maths	978-0-7506-8718-8	£14.99	
	C4	Fundamentals of Business Economics	978-0-7506-8749-2	£14.99	
	C5	Fundamentals of Ethics, Corporate Governance and Business Law	978-0-7506-8714-0	£14.99	
	CIMA Official *Revision Cards*				
	C1	Fundamentals of Management Accounting	978-0-7506-8699-0	£8.99	
	C2	Fundamentals of Financial Accounting	978-0-7506-8722-5	£8.99	
	C3	Fundamentals of Business Maths	978-0-7506-8950-2	£8.99	
	C4	Fundamentals of Business Economics	978-0-7506-8697-6	£8.99	
	C5	Fundamentals of Ethics, Corporate Governance and Business Law	978-0-7506-8748-5	£8.99	
	eSuccess CDs				
	C1	CIMA eSuccess Fundamentals of Management Accounting	978-0-7506-8181-0	£24.99	
	C2	CIMA eSuccess Fundamentals of Financial Accounting	978-0-7506-8180-3	£24.99	
	C3	CIMA eSuccess Fundamentals of Business Maths	978-0-7506-8178-0	£24.99	
	C4	CIMA eSuccess Fundamentals of Business Economics	978-0-7506-8182-7	£24.99	
	C5	CIMA eSuccess Fundamentals of Ethics, CG and Law	978-0-7506-8179-7	£24.99	
		Complete eSuccess CD	978-0-7506-8183-4	£99.99	
	Books				
		Principles of Business Taxation	978-0-7506-8457-6	£49.99	
		CIMA: Pass First Time!	978-0-7506-8396-8	£12.99	
		Better Exam Results	978-0-7506-6357-1	£12.99	
			Postage and packing	£2.95	
			TOTAL		

Post this form to:

CIMA Publishing Customer Services
Elsevier
FREEPOST (OF 1639)
Linacre House, Jordan Hill
OXFORD, OX2 8DP, UK

Or **FAX** +44 (0)1865 314 572
Or **PHONE** +44 (0)1865 474 014
Email: cimaorders@elsevier.com
www.cimapublishing.com

Name: _____

Organisation: _____

Invoice Address: _____

_____

_____

_____

Postcode: _____

Phone number: _____

Email: _____

Delivery Address if different:

FAO _____

Address _____

_____

_____

_____

Postcode _____

Please note that all deliveries must be signed for

1. Cheques payable to Elsevier.

2. Please charge my:

☐ Visa/Barclaycard   ☐ Access/Mastercard

☐ American Express   ☐ Diners Card

☐ Switch   Issue No. _____

Card No. _____

Expiry Date _____

Cardholder Name: _____

Signature: _____

Date: _____

CIMA Official *Exam Practice Kits*

Supplement the Learning Systems with a bank of additional questions
focusing purely on applying what has been learnt to passing the exam.
Ideal for independent study or tutored revision courses. Prepare with
confidence for exam day, and pass the new syllabus first time.

- Avoid common pitfalls with fully worked model answers
- Type and weighting of questions match the format of the exam
  by paper, helping you prepare by giving you the closest available
  preview of the exam
- Summaries of key theory

CIMA Official *Revision Cards*

- Pocket-sized books for learning all the key points – especially for
  students on the move
- Relevant, succinct and compact reminders of all the bullet points
  and diagrams needed for the new CIMA exams
- Break down the syllabus into memorable bite-size chunks

Better Exam Results
A Guide for Business and Accounting Students
2nd Edition
Sam Malone

- Shows CIMA students how to make the best use of valuable
  study time to pass exams first time
- Explains how to organise study, make notes, read faster and
  more effectively and improve your memory for maximising
  performance in the exam room
- Leading training consultant provides study and exam tips for
  success, particularly in CIMA exams but also for wider business
  exams and lifelong learning

ISBN-13: 978 07506 63571 : Price:£12.99

CIMA: Pass First Time!
David Harris

- Get the most out of your study time, and
  maximum marks at exam time – this book
  shows you how to work smarter, not harder
- Written by a CIMA Examiner and Tutor, this
  study buddy shows you exactly what the
  examiner is looking for
- Illustrations, mind-maps and cartoons cool your
  nerves and show you how to plan and write
  your answer succinctly and successfully

ISBN-13: 978 07506 83968 : Price:£12.99

Science & Technology Books, Elsevier Ltd.
Registered Office: The Boulevard, Langford Lane, Kidlington, OXON, OX5 1GB
Registered in England: 1982084

Give CIMA Publishing Your Feedback and Win a Prize

Win your choice of 3 further *Learning Systems* or an iPod

Help us to improve our product for next year by telling us of your experience using this product. All feedback forms returned will be entered into a prize draw. The first three forms drawn on 30 November 2008 will receive either three *Learning Systems* of their choice or an 2Gb iPod Nano. The winners will be notified by email.

Feedback form:

CIMA Official *Learning Systems*
2008 Editions

Name: _____

Address: _____

_____

Email: _____

■ **How did you use your CIMA Official *Learning System*?**

☐ Self-study (book only)

☐ On a full course?
How long was the course? _____
Which college did you attend? _____
_____

☐ On a revision course?
Which college did you attend? _____
_____
_____

☐ Other
_____

Additional comments: _____
_____
_____
_____
_____
_____

■ **How did you order your CIMA Official *Learning System*?**

☐ Carrier sheet from CIMA Financial Management magazine

☐ CIMA Publishing catalogue found in Financial Management magazine

☐ Order form from the back of a previous *Learning System*

☐ www.cimapublishing.com website

☐ Bookshop
Name _____
Branch _____

☐ Other
_____

Additional comments: _____
_____
_____
_____
_____
_____

Your ratings and comments would be appreciated on the following aspects. Please circle your response, where one indicates an excellent rating and four a poor rating.

	Excellent			Poor
☐ Topic coverage	1	2	3	4
☐ Accuracy	1	2	3	4
☐ Readings	1	2	3	4
☐ End of chapter				
questions and solutions	1	2	3	4
☐ Revision section	1	2	3	4
☐ Layout/Presentation	1	2	3	4
☐ Overall opinion of this study system	1	2	3	4

Additional comments:

_____

_____

_____

_____

■ Would you recommend CIMA Official *Learning Systems* to other students?

Please circle: Yes   No

Additional comments:

_____

_____

_____

_____

■ Which CIMA Publishing products have you used?
☐ CIMA Official *Learning Systems*
☐ Q&As
☐ CIMA eSuccess CDs
☐ CIMA Revision Cards
☐ CIMA Exam Practice Kits

Additional comments:

_____

_____

_____

_____

■ Are there any related products you would like to see from CIMA Publishing? If so, please elaborate below.

_____

_____

_____

_____

_____

_____

_____

■ Please note any further comments or errors found in the space below.

_____

_____

_____

_____

_____

_____

_____

_____

_____

_____

_____

Thank you for your time in completing this questionnaire. We wish you good luck in your exam.

Please return to:
CIMA Marketing
CIMA Publishing
FREEPOST – SCE 5435
Linacre House
Jordan Hill
Oxford, OX2 8DP, UK

Revision Resource on CD

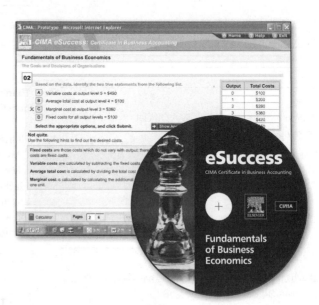

- The only CBA preparation software and question bank endorsed by CIMA
- Questions written by the CIMA Faculty
- Assess your readiness for the CBA
- Identify areas you need to prioritise in your revision
- Increase your mark with the e-tutorials and feedback

C1	CIMA eSuccess Fundamentals of Management Accounting	978 0 7506 8181 0	£24.99
C2	CIMA eSuccess Fundamentals of Financial Accounting	978 0 7506 8180 3	£24.99
C3	CIMA eSuccess Fundamentals of Business Maths	978 0 7506 8178 0	£24.99
C4	CIMA eSuccess Fundamentals of Business Economics	978 0 7506 8182 7	£24.99
C5	CIMA eSuccess Fundamentals of Ethics, CG and Law	978 0 7506 8179 7	£24.99
Complete eSuccess CD		978 0 7506 8183 4	£99.99

1 Self Review Mode
Progress questions to help you test and develop your knowledge. Receive immediate marking on your answer, with full workings to explain the correct one

2 Self Test Mode
A timed test to simulate the CBA. At the end you will receive a report showing your overall mark and areas of strength and weakness

www.cimapublishing.com/esuccess